Communicate!

First Canadian Edition

Communicate!

First Canadian Edition

Patrick Lahey
Acadia University

Mary Trant
Seneca College

Rudolph F. Verderber
Distinguished Teaching
Professor of Communication,
University of Cincinnati

Kathleen S. Verderber
University of Northern Kentucky

THOMSON
NELSON

Australia Canada Mexico Singapore Spain United Kingdom United States

THOMSON
NELSON

Communicate!
First Canadian Edition

by Patrick Lahey, Mary Trant, Rudolph F. Verderber, and Kathleen S. Verderber

Editorial Director and Publisher:
Evelyn Veitch

Executive Editor:
Anne Williams

Senior Marketing Manager:
Murray Moman

Senior Developmental Editor:
Mike Thompson

Permission Coordinator:
Indu Ghuman

Production Editor:
Wendy Yano

Copy Editor/Proofreader:
Kelli Howey

Indexer:
Elizabeth Bell

Production Coordinator:
Ferial Suleman

Creative Director:
Angela Cluer

Interior Design:
Ross Carron Design

Interior Design Modifications:
Erich Falkenberg

Cover Image:
© Jon Feingersh/Masterfile

Compositor:
Courtney Hellam

Printer:
Courier

Adapted from *Communicate!*, 10th ed., by Rudolph F. Verderber and Kathleen S. Verderber, published by Wadsworth, Copyright ©2000 by Wadsworth.

Printed and bound in United States
2 3 4 0 7 06 05

For more information contact Nelson, 1120 Birchmount Road, Toronto, Ontario, M1K 5G4. Or you can visit our Internet site at http://www.nelson.com

National Library of Canada Cataloguing in Publication Data

Lahey, Patrick E. (Patrick Edward), 1952–
Communicate!/Patrick Lahey ... [et al.]. — 1st Canadian ed.

Includes bibliographical references and index.
ISBN 0-17-641590-4

1. Communication. I. Title.

P90.C59 2004 302.2
C2004-902612-7

Brief Contents

Contents

 NEL

Preface

In this first Canadian edition of *Communicate!* we have tried not only to impart conceptual understanding of relevant communication theory and research but also to provide the kind of guidance and features that will help you, the student, to translate what you have learned into genuine communication competence.

The text combines theory, skills, practice, and competency evaluation, allowing you to

1. understand the major concepts of communication theory and research
2. recognize how these concepts provide a basis for developing communication skills
3. develop a range of skills essential to communication competence
4. apply what you learn in class to real-life situations, thereby increasing your communication competence.

Strengths of the Text

Communicate! emphasizes the elements of communication competence in a way that is helpful both to you as a student learning the skills and to the instructor who is guiding your learning. A major challenge is to be responsive to the burgeoning research in communication while still providing a manageable, coherent introduction that makes a real difference to the development of your skills. Thus, the text features what users of ten editions of the U.S. version of *Communicate!* have confirmed as a reliable learning model. This model consists of six integrated steps:

1. **explanation** of communication theories that provide the foundation for specific skills
2. **examples** which enable you to identify effective skill usage
3. **analysis** of the steps involved in the performance of skills
4. **practice** in following the steps to perform the skills
5. **self-assessment** through which you can work toward mastery of key skills
6. **review**

We develop this model through a clear, straightforward, and concise writing style and set examples and practices in contexts that are relevant and meaningful to young people in our modern, multicultural Canadian society.

Organization

Communicate! is divided into five parts, each one focused on a related body of communication theory and skills. In every case, learning is progressive, with concepts learned in earlier parts and chapters being carried forward and applied in various combinations in the later ones.

Part I **Foundations of Communication,** comprising five chapters, begins by introducing you, in Chapter 1, to a basic model of human communication, an overview of communication functions, settings and principles, and the concept of communication competence. Chapters 2 through 5 focus on additional fundamental concepts of communication: perception, verbal communication, nonverbal communication, and the related processes of listening, responding, and remembering.

Part II **Interpersonal Communication** is designed to assist you in developing communication competence in interpersonal contexts. It features chapters on conversation, self-disclosure and feedback, relationships, and intercultural communication. Chapter 9 (Communicating Across Cultures) pays particular attention to the multicultural Canadian context.

Part III **Group Communication,** comprising Chapters 10 and 11, will introduce you to issues in team building, group communication, and leadership.

Part IV **Public Speaking,** Chapters 12 through 14, will show you how to plan a speech, how to organize informative and persuasive speeches, and how to master the art of public speaking.

Part V **Workplace Communication** features two chapters: Chapter 15 will assist you to acquire the communication skills needed to mount an effective job search, and Chapter 16 will introduce you to communication in the modern organization.

Throughout our discussion of this broad range of communication concepts and skills, we will return regularly to four central themes especially relevant to communication in professional and academic contexts in Canada today:

- communication and culture
- communication and gender
- communication ethics
- communication and technology

Features

Throughout *Communicate!* you will encounter recurring features designed to aid your understanding of communication concepts and theory and your mastery of communication skills:

- ***Skill Builders*** boxes visually reinforce learning of many specific skills that are described and exemplified in the text. Each box includes a definition of the skill, a brief description of its use, a step-by-step guide to performing the skill, and an example to illustrate the skill.
- ***In Brief*** boxes, which occur at the end of every major section of each chapter of the text, provide a short summary of the key points in that section. This feature will help you to review what you have read and to prepare for tests and examinations.
- ***Glossary***: Presented at the end of each chapter, this feature allows you to review all of the key communication terms introduced in the chapter—another great study aid.
- ***Thinking About. . .*** exercises, which appear in the margins of every chapter, ask you to reflect on your own motivations, behaviours, and values in order to better understand how you relate to and communicate with others.
- ***Observe & Analyze: Journal Activity*** exercises, which also appear in the margins of all chapters, require you to observe a specific event or series of events that are related to concepts you are learning about and then to analyze what happened, using the theories and concepts from the chapter.
- ***Test Your Competence*** exercises require you to put your understanding of communication skills into practice.
- ***Communicate! Using InfoTrac College Edition***: This margin feature integrates research tasks based on articles available through InfoTrac College Edition, an on-line library, to each chapter of the text. We encourage you to use the free subscription to InfoTrac College Edition that accompanies a new copy of this text to explore chapter topics in detail and to complete research assignments for your course.
- ***Communicate! Using Technology*** margin features provide useful tips for making the most of on-line resources as well as insights into technologies that impact communication. Many segments include questions and exercises that lead you to sites on the World Wide Web, expanding your classroom into an on-line environment.

- *Diverse Voices* features appear throughout the text to give voice to the experiences of people from a wide range of backgrounds and cultural experiences. These excerpts highlight the personal thoughts and experiences of individual Canadians on topics related to the content of the chapters in which they appear. They will help you to understand how culture affects communication and provide an excellent basis for classroom or group discussion.

- *Spotlight on Scholars* boxes feature the work of eminent scholars in communication-related fields. Each one describes a scholar's background, and includes an explanation of his or her motivation for undertaking communication research and a brief summary of his or her research methods and major findings. This feature is designed to help you understand the research and theory-building process.

- *What Would You Do? A Question of Ethics* is a feature that outlines ethical challenges and requires you and your classmates to think critically in sorting through a variety of ethical dilemmas faced by communicators. Material on communication ethics presented in Chapter 1 introduces the criteria on which you may base your judgments and assessments, but in each case the dilemma posed focuses on issues raised in the specific chapter.

- *Self-Review* exercises appear at the end of each of the five parts of *Communicate!* In accord with the findings of noteworthy research, these features allow you to set specific goals for improving your communication skills by writing skills-improvement plans.

Supplementary Materials

This first Canadian edition of *Communicate!* is accompanied by the following resources for students and instructors.

Student Resources

- ***Communicate!*** **Web Site** www.communicate1e.nelson.com

  This Web site contains videos of communication scenarios linked to the text, as well as study questions, activities, sample speeches, and many additional resources for both students and instructors.

- **InfoTrac College Edition** A *free* four-month subscription to this extensive on-line library is enclosed with every new copy of *Communicate!* This easy-to-use database of reliable, full-length articles (not abstracts) from hundreds of top academic journals and popular publications is ideal for expanding text content and for researching essays, speeches, or other assignments.

- **InfoTrac College Edition Student Activities Workbook for Communication 2.0** This workbook features extensive individual and group activities that use the InfoTrac College Edition on-line library. ISBN 0-534-52993-3.

- **A Guide to the Basic Course for ESL Students** This guide assists the non-native speaker and features FAQ's, helpful URLs, and strategies for accent management and overcoming speech apprehension. ISBN 0-534-56779-7.

Instructor Resources

- **Instructor's Resource Manual with Test Bank** This indispensable manual provides instructors with sample syllabi, chapter-by-chapter outlines, summaries, vocabulary lists, suggested lecture and discussion topics, classroom exercises and assignments, and a comprehensive *Test Bank* and answer key. Contact your local Thomson Nelson representative for more information.

- ***Communicate!* Web Site** www.communicate1e.nelson.com
  In addition to the material described under Student Resources, the Web site also contains a downloadable Instructor's Manual and PowerPoint slides. (To obtain an electronic version of the *Test Bank*, contact your local Thomson Nelson representative).

- **CNN Today Videos** Organized by topics covered in a typical course, this multivolume video series is available to qualified adopters. Videos are divided into short segments—perfect for introducing key concepts. Please contact your Thomson Nelson representative for more information.

- **Thomson Communication Video Library** The video library includes a variety of instructional videos as well as the Great Speeches® video series. Available to qualified adopters. Please contact your Thomson Nelson representative for more information.

Acknowledgments

This first Canadian edition of *Communicate!* could not have been completed without the help of many people. Most important are the reviewers: Kathleen Bell, Seneca College; Janice Cook, University of Calgary; Brent Cotton, Georgian College; Geoff Cragg, University of Calgary; Shaniff Esmail, University of Alberta; Sherry Ferguson, University of Ottawa; Jay Haddad, Humber College; Lori Kambeitz, Lethbridge Community College; Janice Magee, Seneca College; Alexandre Sévigny, McMaster University; Elizabeth Skitmore, Algonquin College; Shannon Watson, Seneca College; and James Wong, Wilfrid Laurier University. Their insights, candour, and suggestions for refining the book were invaluable. We are grateful for their support.

We would like to express our gratitude to research assistant Jan Hermiston; to copy editor Kelli Howey; and to Christina Rostek, Thomson Nelson's Atlantic Sales and Editorial Representative, as well as the members of the Thomson Nelson team: Evelyn Veitch, Editorial Director, Higher Education; Anne Williams, Executive Editor; Mike Thompson, Senior Developmental Editor; Murray Moman, Senior Marketing Manager; and Wendy Yano, Production Editor. Thanks also to Fabrizio Macagno of the Catholic University of Milan for providing the photo and biographical information on Douglas Walton featured in Chapter 5.

Patrick Lahey
Acadia University

Mary Trant
Seneca College

February 2004

Communicate!

First Canadian Edition

one

Although we communicate in specific settings, the principles and skills of perception, verbal communication, nonverbal communication, and listening are common to all of them. This five-chapter unit provides a solid foundation on which to develop skills in interpersonal communication, group communication, and public speaking.

I

FOUNDATIONS OF COMMUNICATION

Jonathan Hayward/CP Picture Archive

OBJECTIVES

After you have read this chapter, you should be able to answer these questions:

- What is the definition of communication?
- Why is communication effectiveness so important?
- How does the communication process work?
- What functions does communication serve?
- How do communication settings vary?
- Why should a communicator be concerned about diversity?
- What major ethical issues face communicators?
- What are seven basic principles of communication?
- What are the measures of communication competence?
- How can we improve our communication skills?

CHAPTER 1

Communication Perspective

As the members of the selection committee deliberated, they felt they had four viable candidates for the position. "They all look good on paper," Carson said, "but I was especially impressed with the way Corrie Jackson presented herself to us. Not only did she have a clear vision of where we need to be in five years, but she also explained that vision with precise, concrete statements. I'm really convinced that she's on the right track. She gets my vote."

Your presence in this course may be far more important to you than you imagined when you chose (or were required) to take it, for communication effectiveness is vital to success in nearly every walk of life. For instance, studies done in the last several years conclude that communication skills are one of the most important factors that employers consider in evaluating job applicants (Goleman, 1998, pp. 12–13). Whether you aspire to a career in business, industry, government, education, health services, or almost any other field, communication skills are likely to be a prerequisite to your success.

In this introductory chapter, we will explain the communication process, provide an overview of the role of communication in daily life, discuss seven major communication principles, and consider how to become a competent communicator.

The Communication Process

Communication is the process of creating or sharing meaning through interaction with other human beings. The components of this process are participants, context, messages, channels, noise, and feedback.

Participants

The **participants** are the people who communicate. They assume the roles of senders and receivers of messages during communication. As senders, participants form messages and attempt to communicate them to others through verbal symbols and nonverbal cues. As receivers, they process the messages that they receive from others and react to them.

Context

Context is the physical, social, historical, psychological, and cultural setting in which communication occurs.

Physical context The **physical context** of a communication event includes its location, the environmental conditions (temperature, lighting, noise level), the physical distance between communicators, any seating arrangements, and the time of day. Each of these factors can affect the communication. For instance, a boss talking to members of her staff from behind her desk in her office creates a different context than she would by talking to those same people after joining them at a round table in the conference room.

Social context The **social context** includes the purpose of the event and the relationships that exist between and among the participants. Whether a communication event takes place at a casual gathering of friends, a formal wedding, or a business meeting, and whether it occurs among family members, friends,

© Superstock

In what ways, if any, might the conversation of these people differ if they were at a table in a pizza parlour?

acquaintances, work associates, or strangers, influences what is communicated and how messages are formed, shared, and understood. For instance, most people would interact differently with their family at the dinner table than they would with customers at work.

Historical context The **historical context** refers to the background provided by previous communication episodes involving the participants. These earlier exchanges may influence how people understand one another. For instance, suppose one morning Chad tells Chantal that he will get the draft of the report that they had left for their boss to read. As Chantal enters the office that afternoon, she sees Chad and says, "Did you get it?" Another person listening to the conversation would have no idea what *it* refers to, yet Chad may well reply, "It's on my desk." Chantal and Chad understand each other because of their earlier exchange.

Psychological context The **psychological context** includes the moods and feelings each person brings to the communication. Suppose Corinne is under a great deal of stress as she tries to finish a report due the next morning. If her roommate jokingly suggests that she take a speed-typing course, Corinne, who

Ken Faught/Trstr/CP Picture Archive

Toronto is one of the most multicultural cities in the world, creating a wide range of communication contexts.

is normally good natured, may respond with an angry tirade. Why? Because her stress level provides a psychological context which taints her understanding of the message she hears.

Cultural context The **cultural context** includes the beliefs, values, attitudes, meanings, social hierarchies, religion, notions of time, and roles of a group of people (Samovar & Porter, 2000, p. 7). In Canada, the dominant ethnic cultures are western European. Many members of these dominant groups may not think of themselves as *ethnic,* but as Sonia Nieto (2000) points out, "we are all ethnic, whether we choose to identify ourselves in this way or not" (p. 27). When interacting with others, members of a dominant group may assume that everyone shares the beliefs, values, and norms of the dominant group, but such an assumption would be wrong in many instances and could lead to a breakdown of communication. Because Canada is largely a nation of immigrants, and its indigenous people also comprise a number of distinct nations, the citizens of the country are culturally diverse, and a wide variety of cultural contexts influence communication.

Messages

Communication takes place through sending and receiving **messages.** Messages can be spoken, written, or conveyed nonverbally. In considering messages, it is important to be aware of meanings, symbols, encoding and decoding, and form or organization.

Meaning **Meanings** are the ideas and feelings that exist in a person's mind. You may have ideas about the courses you would like to take this year, your career goal, and the cost of post-secondary education; you also experience feelings such as jealousy, anger, and love. The meanings you have within you, however, cannot be transferred magically into another person's mind.

Symbols To share meanings with someone else, we must form messages comprising verbal and nonverbal symbols. **Symbols** are words, sounds, and actions that represent specific content meaning. As we speak, we choose words to convey the meanings that we want to express. At the same time, facial expressions, eye contact, gestures, and tone of voice—all nonverbal cues—accompany our words and also affect the meaning our listeners receive. As a listener, we make use of both verbal symbols and the nonverbal cues to make sense of what is being said.

Encoding and decoding The cognitive process of transforming ideas and feelings into symbols and organizing them into a message is called **encoding;** the process of transforming another person's messages back into ideas and feelings is called **decoding.** Ordinarily, we do not consciously think about either the encoding or the decoding process, but when we have difficulty communicating, we become more aware of them. For example, if Simon was giving a speech and noticed puzzled expressions on the faces of his listeners, he might go through a second encoding process to select expressions to better convey the meaning of what he just said. Similarly, we may become aware of the decoding process when we must figure out the meaning of an unfamiliar word based on its use in a particular sentence.

The decoding process is made more difficult when verbal and nonverbal cues conflict. For instance, if Joe, a member of a study group, says to his partner Kim, "Yes, I'm very interested in the way you arrived at that decision," the meaning she decodes will be very different depending on whether Joe leans forward and looks interested or yawns and looks away.

Form or organization When meaning is complex, we may need to organize it into sections or into a certain order so that others can understand it. Message form is especially important when one person communicates without interruption for a relatively long time, such as in a public speech or a formal written report.

Channels

A **channel** is both the route travelled by a message and its means of transportation. Messages are transmitted through sensory channels. Face-to-face communication, for example, has two basic channels: auditory (for audible symbols such as spoken words) and visual (for visible cues such as gestures). People can and do communicate by any of the five sensory channels, however, and a fragrant scent or a firm handshake may contribute as much to meaning as what is seen or heard. In general, the more channels used to carry a message, the more likely the communication will succeed.

Noise

Noise is any external, internal, or semantic stimulus that interferes with sharing meaning.

External noises are sights, sounds, and other stimuli in the environment that draw people's attention away from what is being said or done. For instance, while Susan is giving Roberto instructions on how to improve his tennis serve, Roberto's attention may be drawn away by the external noise of a radio playing one of his favourite songs.

Internal noises are thoughts and feelings that interfere with the communication process. If you have ever tuned out the words of a person with whom you were communicating and focused instead on a personal problem or a discomfort you were feeling, then you have experienced internal noise.

Semantic noises are communication barriers that are attributable to language. Such barriers can arise when the sender and receiver speak different languages, when the sender uses words the receiver does not understand, when the sender and receiver assign different meanings to words, or when a sender uses language that the receiver finds offensive. If Paul refers to his administrative assistant as "the girl in the office" and Donald thinks *girl* is a condescending term for a 40-year-old co-worker, Donald might not even hear the rest of what Paul has to say. Use of jargon, foreign words, slang, discriminatory language, and vulgar language can also cause semantic noise.

OBSERVE & ANALYZE
Journal Activity

Conversations

Think of two recent conversations that you participated in, one that you thought went really well and one that you thought went poorly. Compare them. Describe the context in which the conversations occurred, the participants, the rules that seemed to govern your behaviour and that of the other participants, the messages that were created to share meaning, the channels used, any noise that interfered with communication, the feedback that was shared, and the result.

Feedback

Feedback is the response to a message. Feedback indicates to the person sending the message whether and how that message was heard, seen, and understood. If the verbal or nonverbal response indicates to the sender that the meaning decoded by the receiver was not the intended meaning, the originator may try to find a different way of encoding the message to align the meaning being understood with his or her intended meaning. This re-encoded message is also feedback because it gives meaning to the original receiver's response. In all of our communication, we want to stimulate as much feedback as the situation will allow.

A Model of the Process

Figure 1.1 illustrates the communication process between two people (participants). In the minds of these people are meanings (thoughts or feelings) that they intend to share. Those thoughts and feelings are created, shaped, and

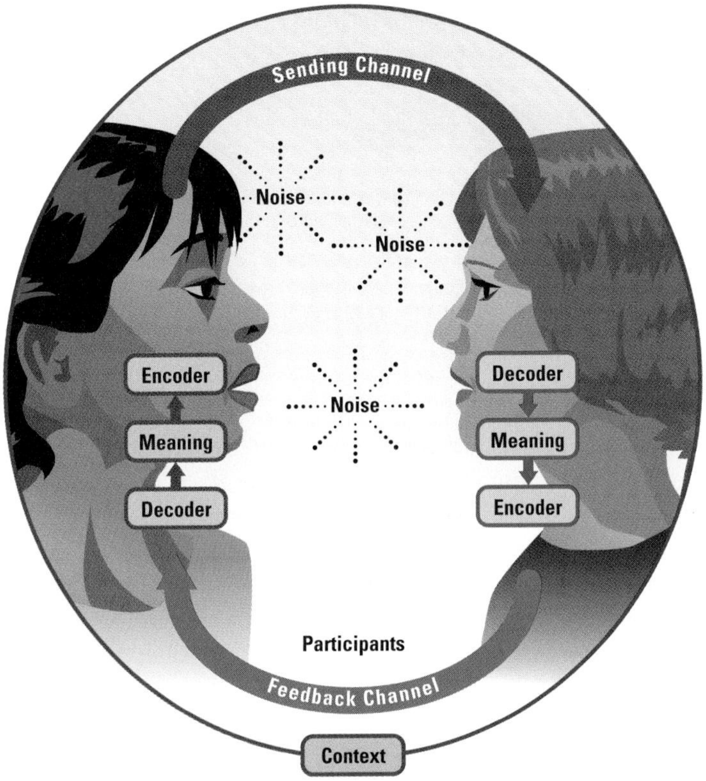

Figure 1.1
A model of communication between two people

affected by their total field of experience, including such specific factors as their values, culture, environment, occupation, sex, sexual orientation, interests, knowledge, and attitudes.

To turn meaning into messages, one participant (the sender) encodes thoughts or feelings into words and actions and sends them via channels—in this case, the auditory channel (speech) and the visual channel (nonverbal behaviour)—to the other participant (the receiver).

Meanings that have been encoded into symbols are turned back into meaning by the receiver through the decoding process. This decoding process is affected by the receiver's total field of experience—that is, by all the same factors that shape the encoding process.

The area around the participants represents the physical, social, psychological, and cultural contexts within which the communication takes place.

During the entire communication process, external, internal, and semantic noise may occur at any point and affect the participants' ability to share meanings.

In a conversation among several people, in a problem-solving group or at a public speech, for example, all these elements of communication operate simultaneously—and differently—for everyone present. As a result, communication among more than two people becomes much more complex. While some people focus on the speaker's message, others may be distracted by noise—whether

TEST YOUR COMPETENCE

Identifying Elements of the Communication Process

In the following interaction, identify the participants, context, message, channel, noise, and feedback.

Maria and Damien are meandering through the park drinking bottled water. As Damien finishes his drink, he tosses the bottle into the bushes at the side of the path. Maria comes to a stop with her hands on her hips, stares angrily at Damien, and says, "I can't believe what you just did!" Damien blushes, averts his gaze, and responds, "Sorry, I'll get it—I just wasn't thinking." As the tension drains from Maria's face, she gives her head a playful toss, smiles, and says, "Well, just see that it doesn't happen again."

IN BRIEF

Six Components of the Communication Process

Participants: A sender, who has a meaning to share, and a receiver, the person or persons with whom he or she wishes to share it.
Context: The physical, social, historical, psychological, and cultural setting in which communication occurs.
Message: The meaning of the sender encoded verbally or nonverbally for the receiver to decode.
Channel: The route travelled by a message and its means of transportation.
Noise: Any internal, external, or semantic stimulus that interferes with the sharing of the sender's meaning.
Feedback: The receiver's verbal or nonverbal response to the message.

external (the hum of the air conditioner), internal (preoccupation with an upcoming party), or semantic (a reaction to the speaker's use of jargon)—and all participants bring a unique perspective to the communication transaction. Less skilful communicators are oblivious to such factors and plunge ahead whether or not they are being understood or even heard. Skilful communicators attend to verbal and nonverbal feedback and adapt their words and nonverbal behaviour to ensure that their listeners receive the meanings they intend to share.

Communication Functions and Settings

Communication serves many functions and takes place in many settings. In addition to the many face-to-face encounters that we have with people every day, consider the written exchanges that we participate in, and the many electronic interactions that have become part of daily life. We are constantly communicating.

Communication Functions

Communication serves several important functions for us.

1. **We communicate to meet needs.** We need food, water, and shelter, but as importantly, because we are by nature social animals, we need other people. At noon, Emily and Zhiran may speak briefly to satisfy Zhiran's need for a sandwich and a glass of milk. But after lunch, they may converse happily for hours, gossiping and chatting about inconsequential matters that neither remembers afterward; though they exchange little information, their communication meets the important need simply to share with another human being.
2. **We communicate to enhance and maintain our sense of self.** Through our communication, we learn who we are, what we are good at, and how people react to our behaviour. We explore this important function of interpersonal communication in detail in Chapter 2, "Perception of Self and Others."

3. **We communicate to fulfill social obligations.** We use expressions such as "How are you doing?" when we meet a person we sat next to in a biology lecture last week, and "What's happening?" or simply "Hi" when we pass friends in the hall. Such expressions allow us to meet social obligations. By saying, "Hi, Josh. How's it going?" we acknowledge a person we recognize. By not speaking, we would risk being perceived as arrogant or insensitive.

4. **We communicate to develop relationships.** Not only do we get to know others through our communication with them, but more importantly, it is through communication that we develop relationships with them—relationships that grow and deepen or stagnate and wither away. We discuss how relationships begin and develop in Chapter 8, "Communicating in Relationships."

5. **We communicate to exchange information.** Some information we get through observation, some through reading, some through television or other electronic media, and a great deal through direct communication with others. Whether we are trying to decide how warmly to dress in the morning or which party to support in the next federal election, all of us participate daily in exchanges that involve sending and receiving information. We discuss communication as information exchange in Chapter 6, "Conversation," Chapter 10, "Participating in Group Communication," and in Chapter 13, "Organization."

6. **We communicate to influence others.** People frequently try to affect or change the thinking or behaviour of others: we try to convince our friends to go to a particular restaurant; urge a co-worker to support our candidate for member of parliament; attempt to persuade a spouse to quit smoking or a professor to change a course grade. We discuss the role of influencing others in Chapter 11, "Member Roles and Leadership in Groups," and in Chapter 13, " Organization."

Communication Settings

In this book, you will be introduced to skills that can help you achieve communication competence in interpersonal settings, problem-solving group setting, public-speaking settings, and electronically mediated settings, whether the exchanges are on a personal or professional level.

Interpersonal communication settings Most of our communication takes place in interpersonal communication settings, typically in informal conversations between two or more people. Talking with a classmate before class, chatting on the phone with a relative, arguing the merits of a movie with friends over dinner in the cafeteria, and comforting a friend who has been jilted by his girlfriend are all examples of interpersonal communication. However, not all interpersonal communication is so informal; meeting with an academic adviser to review course selections for the winter term, being interviewed for a summer job,

OBSERVE & ANALYZE
Journal Activity

Communication Functions

Keep a log of the various communication episodes you engage in today. Tonight, categorize each episode in terms of which of the six functions it served. Any episode may serve more than one function. Were you surprised by the variety of communication you engaged in even in such a relatively short period?

and serving a customer in a shop are examples of interpersonal exchanges which are likely to be more formal, partly because of the settings in which they occur.

In our discussion of interpersonal communication, we will focus on listening actively, holding effective conversations, self-disclosure and feedback, and developing, maintaining, and improving relationships.

Problem-solving group settings Problem-solving group settings are established when participants come together for the specific purpose of solving a problem or arriving at a decision. For many of us, this kind of communication takes place in meetings.

In our discussion of problem-solving group settings, we will focus on group interaction, problem solving and decision making, and leadership.

Public-speaking settings Some of our most important communication occurs in speeches. In a public-speaking setting, a speaker delivers a prepared formal message to an audience in a public setting. All the variables of communication are present in this one-to-many situation, but their use in public speaking differs greatly from their use in other situations.

In our discussion of communication in public-speaking settings, we will focus on determining goals, gathering and evaluating material, organizing and developing informative and persuasive material, adapting material to a specific audience, and presenting the speech. Most students already make conscious or unconscious use of some of these skills, while others are not yet part of their repertoire. Regardless of how accomplished we already are, careful study and practice can enhance our communicative competence and empower us to better achieve our goals.

Electronically mediated communication settings People commonly communicate with others through the use of electronic technology. As we will see, this dependence on technology sets electronically mediated communication settings apart from the others we have looked at because the participants do not share a physical context. As a result, meanings that would normally be transmitted nonverbally may be unavailable to the receiver.

Many people keep in touch with others through the exchange of messages via **e-mail** or **instant messaging** systems. E-mail communication, a form of electronic correspondence, can be conducted between two or more users on a network. Instant messaging (IM) is an Internet-based service that allows subscribers to detect whether other subscribers are connected to the Internet and, if they are, to have real-time, interactive conversations with them. Today, more than 60 percent of Canadians have access to e-mail and instant messaging, and a great number of those people use one or both of these systems to communicate with friends, family members, colleagues, clients, or customers.

Similarly, many Canadians communicate through **newsgroups, message boards,** and on-line **chat rooms** with strangers with whom they share a common interest. A newsgroup is "an electronic gathering place for people with similar interests" (Miller, 1999, p. 187). Think of a newsgroup as a collecting place for

OBSERVE & ANALYZE
Journal Activity

Use of E-mail

Do you use e-mail? Consider the mailing you have done during the last week. Classify the messages you have written (use headings such as letters to friends, inquiries to Web sites, and questions to professors). How many messages do you receive each day? What percentage of those do you reply to? Compare your use of e-mail to your use of regular mail. How many letters (not bills, advertisements, or solicitations) do you send or receive each day?

Steve Dunwell/The Image Bank

E-mail and instant messaging have taken the place of letter writing in most settings.

messages on a common topic. To communicate in a newsgroup, a user posts a message (called an *article*) about a topic appropriate for that group. Other users read the article and, if so disposed, respond to it. The result is an ongoing discussion in which many users (10, 50, or maybe even hundreds) may participate. The Internet offers thousands of newsgroup opportunities (Sherman, 1999, p. 137). Message boards are like newsgroups except that they belong to a particular Web site and are controlled by the owner(s) of that Web site.

A chat room is an electronic gathering place that makes it possible for two or more people with shared interests to communicate in real time. Internet chat is an interactive message exchange similar to instant messaging. In a chat room, typed responses appear instantly on participants' computer screens. As few as two people can hold a conversation; however, some chat rooms are licensed for 25, 50, or hundreds of participants. Like instant messaging, chat approximates face-to-face conversation in that feedback is relatively instantaneous.

If the written communication revolution is taking place on line, the oral communication revolution is taking place on cellular and digital telephones. In the past, a person away from home had to go to a place where a telephone was housed, but many people now carry their telephones with them. They can make and receive telephone calls from wherever they happen to be—in a car, on a bus, in a classroom, or on the street.

As we examine various communication skills throughout this book, we will consider how they can be applied to both electronically mediated and face-to-face communication.

IN BRIEF

Communication Functions and Settings

All communication serves one or more of six functions:

- to meet needs
- to enhance and maintain our sense of self
- to fulfill social obligations
- to develop relationships
- to exchange information
- to influence others.

Four commonly used communication settings are

- interpersonal settings
- problem-solving group settings
- public-speaking settings
- electronically mediated settings.

Communication Principles

Now that we have seen the elements that make up the communication process and considered the nature of communication in our lives, we can turn to the seven principles that guide our communication:

- communication has purpose
- communication is continuous
- communication messages can be spontaneous, scripted, or constructed
- communication is relational
- communication is culturally bound
- communication has ethical implications
- communication is learned.

Communication Has Purpose

When people communicate with one another, they have a purpose for doing so, or as Kathy Kellerman (1992), a leading researcher on interpersonal communication contexts, puts it, "all communication is goal-directed" whether or not the communicator is conscious of his or her purpose (p. 288). The purpose of any particular communication transaction may be serious or trivial, but one way to evaluate the transaction is to ask whether it achieved its purpose. When Beth calls Leah to ask whether she would like to discuss a class project over lunch, her purpose may be to resolve a misunderstanding, to encourage Leah to work more closely with her, or simply to establish a cordial working atmosphere. When Kareem shows other members of the student council the statistics he has found on drug abuse on campus, his purpose may be to contribute information to a group discussion, to demonstrate his own research skills, or to persuade council to confront the problem of drug abuse. In each case, success would be measured in terms of the communicator's goal. A communication transaction may be highly sophisticated, amusing, charming, or bear any number of other positive qualities, but it is a failure if it does not achieve its purpose. Different purposes, of course, call for different communication strategies.

Speakers are not always aware of their purpose. For instance, when Brian passes Tony on the street and says lightly, "Tony, how's it going?" Brian probably does not consciously think, "Tony is an acquaintance, and I want him to understand that I see him and consider him worth recognizing." In this case, the social obligation to recognize Tony is met spontaneously with the first acceptable expression that comes to Brian's mind. Though Brian is not conscious of his purpose, it still motivates his behaviour. In this case, he will have achieved his goal if Tony responds with an equally casual greeting.

Communication Is Continuous

Because communication can be nonverbal as well as verbal, we are always sending behavioural messages from which others draw inferences or meaning. Even silence or absence are communication behaviours if another person infers meaning from them. Why? Because our nonverbal behaviour represents reactions to our environment and to the people around us. If we are cold, we shiver; if we are hot or nervous, we perspire; if we are bored, happy, or confused, our facial expression or body language probably will show it. As skilled communicators, we need to be aware of the messages, whether explicit or implicit, that we are constantly sending to others.

Communication Messages Can Be Spontaneous, Scripted, or Constructed

As we pointed out earlier in this chapter, sharing meaning with another person involves encoding messages using verbal and nonverbal symbols. This encoding process may occur spontaneously; it may be based on a script we have learned or rehearsed; or it may be carefully considered based on our understanding of the situation in which we find ourselves (Reardon, 1987, pp. 11–12).

For each of us, there are times when our communication reflects a **spontaneous expression** of emotion. When this happens, our messages are encoded without much conscious thought. For example, when Natalie's team wins the championship, she is likely to smile and cheer; when she burns her finger, she may blurt, "Ouch!"

At other times, however, our communication is **scripted;** that is, we use conversational phrases we have learned from our past encounters and judge to be appropriate to a present situation. To use scripted expressions effectively, we learn or practise them until they become automatic. Many of these scripts are learned in childhood. For example, when we want the sugar bowl but cannot reach it, we may say, "Pass the sugar, please," followed by, "Thank you," when someone complies with our request. This conversational sequence comes from the table-manners script, which is taught to young children in many families. Scripts enable us to use messages that are appropriate to the situation and are likely to increase the effectiveness of our communication. One goal of this text is to acquaint you with general scripts (or skills) that can be adapted for use in a variety of relationships, situations, and cultures.

Finally, messages also may be carefully constructed to meet the needs of a particular situation. **Constructed messages** are those that we encode in the moment in order to respond to a situation for which our known scripts are inadequate. These messages help us communicate both effectively and appropriately.

Creatively constructed responses are perhaps the ideal communication vehicle, especially in public-speaking settings. When we are able to both recognize the ideas and feelings that we want to express and encode those ideas and feelings using a combination of appropriate verbal and nonverbal symbols, we are likely to form messages that allow us to share our intended meaning with others. Another goal of this text is to help you become familiar with a variety of message-forming skills so that you can use them to construct effective and appropriate messages.

Communication Is Relational

Saying that communication is relational means that in any communication setting people not only share meaning but also negotiate the terms of their relationship. For instance, when Laura says to Jennie, "I've remembered to bring the map," she is reporting some practical information, but her statement can also be understood to say, "You can always depend on me" or "I am the leader here—if it weren't for me, we'd get lost."

Two aspects of relationships can be negotiated during an interaction: affect and control. Negotiation of the affect aspect determines the quality and degree of feeling (from love to hate) present in a relationship. For instance, when José says, "Hal, good to see you," the nonverbal behaviour that accompanies the words may show Hal whether José is genuinely happy to see him (positive affect) or not. If José smiles, uses a warm and sincere tone of voice, looks Hal in the eye, and perhaps pats him on the back or shakes hands firmly, then Hal will recognize the signs of affection. If, however, José speaks quickly with no vocal inflection and with a deadpan facial expression, Hal will perceive that José's comment was intended solely to satisfy social expectations.

Negotiation of the control aspect seeks to determine who is the controlling partner in a relationship (Watzlawick, Beavin, & Jackson, 1967, p. 51). Thus, when Tom says to Sue, "I know you're concerned about the budget, but I'll see to it that we have money to cover everything," he is not merely presenting financial information. Through his choice of words and his tone of voice, he is also asserting that he is in charge of finances, that he is in control. How Sue responds to Tom will determine the true nature of the relationship. The control aspect of relationships can be viewed as complementary or symmetrical.

In a **complementary relationship,** one person is permitted to define who is to have greater power. Thus, the messages of one person may assert dominance while those of the other(s) accept and support that assertion. In some cases, the relationship is clarified in part by the context. For instance, in traditional businesses, most employer–employee relationships are complementary, with the employer in the control position. Likewise, most public-speaking relationships are complementary, for members of the audience have come to hear what the speaker has to say and, in acknowledging his or her authority on the subject of the speech, also acknowledge his or her control in the relationship.

In contrast, a **symmetrical relationship** is one in which the participants do not agree about who is in control. As one partner shows a need to take control, the other(s) challenges that person's right and asserts his or her own power. On the other hand, if one partner abdicates power, the other(s) may refuse to assume it. For example, Tom may say, "I think we need to cut back on credit

Richard Lam/CP Picture Archive

What messages about affect and control do people who are being married send as they place rings on each other's fingers? Power in relationships is influenced by both verbal and nonverbal messages.

card expenses for a couple of months," to which Sue may respond, "No way! I need a new suit for work, the car needs new tires, and we have to replace the couch." Here, both people are asserting control.

Control is not negotiated in a single exchange. Relational control is determined through many message exchanges over time. The interaction of messages, as shown through both language and nonverbal behaviour, defines and clarifies the complementary or symmetrical nature of people's relationships. Conflict is less prevalent in complementary relationships than in symmetrical ones, but in symmetrical relationships power is more likely to be evenly shared.

Communication Is Culturally Bound

What message is formed and how it is interpreted depends on the cultural background of the participants in any particular communication transaction. **Cultural diversity,** the variations that exist among people because of their differing cultural backgrounds, affects every aspect of communication. Even though all of the people participating in a conversation may speak English, their cultural differences will affect their ability to share meaning and influence the meanings they share.

Canada is a multicultural society. The distinct cultures of the mostly European people who first settled the different regions of the country in some measure coloured the culture of those regions, and those regional cultures have been further differentiated by differing local conditions, histories, and ways of life. However, the process of cultural diversification did not stop there. Over the past 50 years, millions of immigrants from all over the world have chosen to relocate to Canada, bringing their cultural background with them.

Canada is becoming more and more ethnically diverse. Data from the 2001 census show that 5.4 million Canadians (18.4% of the population) were born outside the country, and that patterns of immigration have changed drastically (Statistics Canada, 2003). Prior to 1961, the leading source countries for

THINKING ABOUT . . .

Ethnic Diversity

Think about the corner of Canada in which you live. Would you consider it to be ethnically diverse? What ethnic groups are represented? Would you consider one or more groups to be dominant? How has the ethnic mix in your community affected its overall culture? How does the ethnic culture of your community compare to that of other parts of the country, or to what you perceive to be Canada's national culture?

immigrants to Canada were the United Kingdom (24.3%), Italy (16.5%), Germany (10.8%), the Netherlands (8.9%), and Poland (5%). In contrast, of the 1.8 million immigrants who arrived between 1991 and 2001, 58 percent came from Asia including the Middle East; only 20 percent came from all of Europe; 11 percent came from the Caribbean and Central and South America; 8 percent came from Africa; and 3 percent came from the United States.

Of course, the proportion of Canadians of any particular ethnic background will vary from one region of the country to another. For instance, of the roughly 2 million residents of Vancouver who responded to the 2001 census, nearly 347,985 (almost 17.5%) claimed Chinese ancestry. In contrast, in Québec, a city of 673,000, less than half of one percent indicated that they were descendants of Chinese immigrants, but an overwhelming majority claimed French ancestry. In some western cities, a significant majority of the population is made up of descendants of northern, central, and eastern European populations—74 percent of the population of Saskatoon, for example, or 56 percent of the population of Winnipeg. On the other hand, most east coast cities are dominated by descendants of immigrants from the British Isles: St. John's, for example, at 81 percent and Halifax at 82 percent.

In addition, ethnic differences among Canada's indigenous peoples contribute even further to Canada's cultural diversity. Not only do different native groups speak different languages and uphold different traditions, but also significant differences in the degree of their exposure to immigrant cultures and in the cultures to which they have been exposed have further diversified native culture.

Given this degree of cultural diversity, any Canadian is likely to differ from another in some message-formation and interpretation skills, so opportunities for misunderstanding based on cultural difference abound. We often miscommunicate or fail completely to communicate with one another because we unknowingly violate a cultural rule or preference of the person we are communicating with or misinterpret another person's message based on our own cultural rules or preferences.

For example, Ingrid and Shuang, two newly acquainted first-year students, are roommates. Ingrid is a fourth-generation Swedish Canadian from a small town in Saskatchewan. Shuang is a first-generation Chinese Canadian from Toronto. Both women are excited about the opportunity to live with and learn from someone of a different background. Over lunch with several other students, Ingrid suggests to Shuang that they save money on books by sharing the cost of the required text for the Introduction to Psychology class they are both taking. Shuang does not want to share a book, but because other people are present, she observes the Chinese cultural rule requiring that she not say anything that might embarrass Ingrid in front of their friends. She merely lowers her eyes and quietly says, "That might be convenient." Based on this conversation, Ingrid stops by the bookstore and buys the book. When she gets back to their residence room and presents the book to Shuang, she is dumbfounded by Shuang's refusal to pay half the cost. Shuang is equally surprised that Ingrid misinterpreted her face-saving comment as actual agreement.

COMMUNICATE!
Using Technology

Have you ever wondered how people in other parts of the world perceive you as a Canadian? Take a look at the page "Canada: Big Land, Small Talk" on the Web site of the German firm Encompas. Look especially at the checklists of recommended behaviour for German professionals who plan to visit Canada. Do you think that the image of Canadian life and Canadian communication behaviour matches your own experience? Are we really like that?
www.aspetersen.de/canada_e.html

The most widely discussed aspects of cultural diversity are language, ethnicity, and race, but cultural diversity in communication is also occasioned by differences in gender, age, sexual orientation, class, education, occupation, religion, recreational and leisure activities, and other factors. Just as people of different ethnicity may have different rules that guide message construction and interpretation, so too do people who differ in, for example, age or sex or religion. For instance, many older people consider it rude to address someone by his or her first name unless invited by that person to do so. In contrast, many younger people refer to everyone by first name with no disrespect intended.

Within each chapter of this book we will discuss ways in which various cultural groups are different and similar to each other in their communication practices. In addition, Chapter 9 will focus specifically on helping you to develop cross-cultural interpersonal communication skills. Diverse Voices features are also found in a number of chapters; each one focuses on the way cultural diversity in communication has affected one person. Together, they give you an opportunity to empathize with a variety of people who come from different cultural backgrounds.

COMMUNICATE! Using InfoTrac College Edition

Do communication ethics affect your buying choices? Communication ethics is nowhere a more controversial issue than in global business. For example, consumers and consumer groups frequently complain that businesses, especially multinational corporations, and the advertising industry that promotes their interests, are less than ethical in their bid to persuade people to buy particular products. Others complain of public relations and advertising industries that hide or, at least, fail to reveal links between particular consumer products and unethical activities by the companies that produce them. Using InfoTrac College Edition, you can find an interesting article on this subject. After typing in the subject search term *business communication*, subdivision *ethical aspects*, locate the article "Ethics and Social Issues in Business: An Updated Communication Perspective" by Richard Alan Nelson. Consider the author's advice to the business community. Do you think his proposed solution to the problem of unethical business communication would remedy the problem? Do you think it is likely to be put into place? Why or why not?

Communication Has Ethical Implications

In any encounter we choose whether or not we will communicate ethically. **Ethics** is a set of moral values and principles of right conduct that may be held by a society, a group, or a person. Although what is ethical is ultimately a matter of personal judgment, various groups nevertheless expect members to uphold certain prescribed ethical standards. These standards influence the personal decisions we make. When we choose to violate the standards that we are expected to uphold, others are likely to view us as unethical.

When we communicate, we cannot avoid making choices with ethical implications. To understand how our ethical standards influence our communication, we must recognize the ethical principles guiding our behaviour. Five ethical standards influence our communication and guide our behaviour.

1. **Honesty** is a standard that compels us to refrain from lying, cheating, stealing, or deception. "An honest person is widely regarded as a moral person, and honesty is a central concept to ethics as the foundation for a moral life" (Terkel & Duval, 1999, p. 122). Although most people accept honesty as a standard, they still confess to lying on occasion. We are most likely to lie when we are caught in a **moral dilemma,** a situation in which we must choose between alternatives which are both morally proscribed.

   The operating moral rule is to tell the truth if we possibly can. The fundamental requirement of this rule is that we should not intentionally deceive, or try to deceive, others or even ourselves. Only when we are confronted with a true moral dilemma—withholding information from a friend to prevent violence, for example, or misrepresenting a case to protect client confidentiality—should we even consider lying.

2. **Integrity** means maintaining a consistency of belief and action—in other words, adhering to our own moral code. Terkel and Duval (1999) say, "A person who has integrity is someone who has strong moral principles and will successfully resist the temptation to compromise those principles" (p. 135). Integrity is the opposite of hypocrisy. For example, Jane's ethical code includes the principle that it is wrong to talk about another person behind his or her back. She demonstrates integrity by refusing to participate in gossip about Helen, a teammate who is experiencing relationship problems.

3. **Fairness** means achieving the right balance of interests without regard to one's own feelings and without showing favour to any side in a conflict. Fairness implies impartiality or lack of bias. To be fair in making a decision is to gather *all* of the relevant information, to consider *only* information relevant to the decision at hand, and to avoid being swayed by prejudice or bias. For example, a mother who wants to resolve a dispute between her two 10-year-old sons exercises fairness if she discovers all of the facts about the conflict and allows both children to explain their side before she decides who is at fault.

4. **Respect** means showing regard or consideration for a person and for that person's rights. Often we talk of respecting another as a fellow human being. For instance, someone's affluence, job status, or ethnic background should not influence how we communicate with the person. We demonstrate respect through listening to and understanding others' points of view, even when they are vastly different from our own.

5. **Responsibility** means being accountable for one's actions. A responsibility is something that one is bound to carry out either because of a promise or obligation or because of one's role in a group or community. A responsibility may indicate a duty to a moral law or to another human being. Many people would argue that we have a responsibility not to harm or interfere with others. Others would argue that we have a responsibility not only not to harm others but also to help others.

At a number of points in this text we will confront situations where these ethical issues come into play. We often face ethical dilemmas, situations in which we must sort out what is more or less right or wrong. In making these choices we usually reveal the values we hold most dear. At the end of each remaining chapter in this book, you will be asked to think about and discuss various ethical dilemmas that relate to the chapter content.

IN BRIEF

Communication Principles

Seven principles guide our communication:

1. Communication has purpose: We communicate always to satisfy some goal, whether we are aware of it or not.
2. Communication is continuous: We never stop communicating even when we are silent.
3. Communication messages can be spontaneous, scripted, or constructed.
4. Communication is relational: As we communicate with another, we also negotiate the affect and control aspects of our relationship with that person.
5. Communication is culturally bound: Our cultural background affects how we encode the messages we send and how we decode the messages we receive from others.
6. Communication has ethical implications: We choose whether to behave ethically in communicating with others, and others judge us based on whether our behaviour is perceived as ethical.
7. Communication is learned: Through study and practice, we can improve our communication skills.

Communication Is Learned

Because communication appears to be a natural, inborn, unchangeable behaviour, we seldom try to improve our skills, but communication is, in fact, a learned behaviour, and we can get better at it if we make an effort to do so. Throughout this text, we will identify interpersonal, group, and public communication skills that will be valuable to you in all walks of life. In the next section we look at how to go about improving your skills.

Increasing Our Communication Competence

Communication competence is the impression that communicative behaviour is both appropriate and effective in a given situation (Spitzberg, 2000, p. 375). Communication is *effective* when it achieves its goals; it is *appropriate* when it conforms to what is expected in a situation. We create the perception that we are competent communicators through the verbal messages we send and the nonverbal behaviours that accompany them.

Because communication is at the heart of how we relate to one another, one of your goals in this course should be to learn those things that will increase the likelihood that others will view you as competent. Brian Spitzberg believes perceptions of competence depend in part on personal motivation, knowledge, and skills (p. 377).

Motivation is important because we will be able to improve our communication only if we are *motivated*—that is, if we want to. People are likely to be more motivated if they are confident and if they see potential rewards.

Knowledge is important because we must know what is involved in increasing competence. The more *knowledge* people have about how to behave in a given situation, the more likely they are to be able to develop competence.

Spotlight on Scholars

Brian Spitzberg, San Diego State University

Although Brian Spitzberg has made many contributions to our understanding of interpersonal communication, he is best known for his work in interpersonal communication competence. This interest in competence began at the University of Southern California. For an interpersonal communication seminar assignment, he read the research that had been done on interpersonal competence and found that the research conclusions went in different directions. Spitzberg's final paper for the seminar was his first effort to synthesize these perspectives into a comprehensive theory of competence.

Courtesy of Brian Spitzberg

Today, the model of interpersonal communication competence that Spitzberg formulated guides most thinking and research in this area. He views competence neither as a trait nor a set of behaviours. Rather, Spitzberg says that interpersonal communication competence is a perception that people have about themselves or another person. If competence is a perception, it

(continued)

follows that your perception of your interpersonal communication competence or that of another person will affect how you feel about your relationship with that person. So people are more likely to be satisfied in a relationship when they perceive themselves and the other person as competent. According to Spitzberg, we make these competence judgments based on how each of us acts when we talk together, but what determines how we act in a particular conversation?

During the time when Spitzberg was organizing his thinking about competence, he was taking another course that introduced him to the theories of dramatic acting. These theories held that an actor's performance depended on the actor's motivation, knowledge of the script, and acting skills. Spitzberg found that these same variables could be applied to communication competence, and he incorporated them into his theory. How we behave in a conversation depends firstly on how personally motivated we are to have the conversation, secondly on how personally knowledgeable we are about what behaviour is appropriate in such a situation, and thirdly on how personally skilled we are at actually using the appropriate behaviours during the conversation. In addition, Spitzberg suggests that context variables such as the ones discussed in this chapter also affect how we choose to act in a conversation and the perceptions of competence that are created.

Although Spitzberg formed most of these ideas while he was still in graduate school, he and others have spent the last 20 years refining the theory, conducting programs of research based on the theory, and measuring the effectiveness of the theory. Research has fleshed out parts of the theory and provided some evidence of its accuracy. Over the years, Spitzberg has developed about a dozen specific instruments to measure parts of the theory. One of these measures, the Conversational Skills Rating Scale, has been adopted as the standard measure of interpersonal communication skills by the National Communication Association (a leading organization of communication scholars, teachers, and practitioners).

Spitzberg's continuing interest in communication competency has led him to study abusive and dysfunctional relationships from a competence perspective. Recently, he has studied obsessive relational intrusion (ORI) and stalking. In such situations, the intruder's motivation is at odds with the motivation of the victim; the intruder wants to begin, escalate, or continue a relationship, but the victim does not agree with the intruder's definition of the relationship. Their interactions are actually arguments over the very definition of the relationship. The intruders may perceive themselves to be competent within their definitions of competency. As research into these dark side relationships continues, scholars using our understanding of communication competency may be able to determine if certain communication behaviours are more effective than others in discouraging ORI and stalking behaviours. Lately, Spitzberg has expanded his ORI work to examine the new phenomenon of cyber-stalking.

Whether the situation is a first date or a job interview, a conflict with a roommate or an intimate discussion of feelings, Spitzberg believes it is important that others perceive us to be competent.

In addition to the numerous articles that Spitzberg has published based on the results of his work, he has co-authored two books on interpersonal communication competence with William Cupach. For a list of some of Spitzberg's major publications, see the reference list at the end of this book.

Skill is important because we must know how to act in ways that are consistent with our communication knowledge. **Skills** are goal-oriented actions or action sequences that we can master and repeat in appropriate situations. The more skills we have, the more likely we are to be able to structure our messages effectively and appropriately.

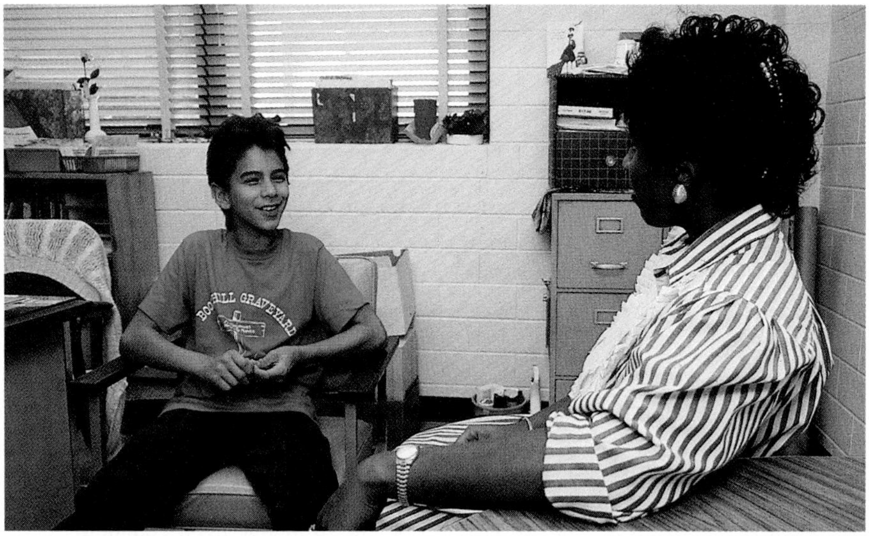

Bob Daemmrich/Stock Boston

As communication motivation, knowledge, and skill increase, communicator competence increases.

The combination of our motivation, knowledge, and skills leads us to perform confidently in our encounters with others. The rest of this book is aimed at helping you increase the likelihood that you will be perceived as competent. In the pages that follow, you will learn about theories of interpersonal, group, and public communication that can increase your knowledge and your motivation. You will also learn how to perform specific skills, and you will be provided with opportunities to practise them. Through this practice, you can increase the likelihood that you will be able to perform these skills when needed.

Writing Goal Statements

To get the most from this course, we suggest that you establish and write out a list of personal goals to improve specific skills in your own interpersonal, group, and public-communication repertoire. Why do you need written goal statements? A familiar saying goes, "The road to hell is paved with good intentions." Regardless of how serious you are about changing some aspect of your communicative behaviour, bringing about changes in behaviour takes time and effort. Writing specific goals makes it more likely that your good intentions to improve will not get lost in the busyness of your life.

Before you can write a goal statement, you must first analyze your existing communication skills repertoire. After you read each chapter and practise the skills described, select one or two skills to work on. Then write down your goal statement in four parts.

1. **State the problem.** Start by identifying a communication problem that you have. For example: "Problem: Even though my boss consistently gives all the interesting tasks to co-workers, I haven't spoken up because I'm not very good at describing my feelings."

2. **State the specific goal.** A goal is *specific* if it is measurable, so you know when you have achieved it. For example, to deal with the problem stated above, you might write, "Goal: To describe my feelings about task assignments to my boss."

3. **Outline a specific procedure for reaching the goal.** To develop a plan for reaching your goal, first consult the chapter that covers the skill you wish to hone. Then apply the general steps recommended in the chapter to your specific situation. This step is critical because successful behavioural change requires that you state your objective in terms of specific behaviours you can adopt or modify. For example: "Procedure: I will practise the steps of describing feelings. (1) I will identify the specific feeling I am experiencing. (2) I will encode the emotion I am feeling accurately. (3) I will include what has triggered the feeling. (4) I will own the feeling as mine. (5) I will then put that procedure into operation when I am talking with my boss."

4. **Devise a method of determining when the goal has been reached.** A good goal is measurable, and the fourth part of your goal-setting effort is to determine your minimum requirements for knowing when you have achieved a given goal. For example: "Test of Achieving Goal: This goal will be considered achieved when I have described my feelings to my boss on the next occasion when his behaviour excludes me."

IN BRIEF

Communication Competence

Communication competence is the impression that communicative behaviour is both effective and appropriate in a given situation. To increase communication competence:

1. develop motivation by recognizing the benefits of becoming competent
2. acquire knowledge through study
3. develop skill through practice.

Once you have completed all four parts of this goal-setting process, you may want to have another person witness your commitment and serve as a consultant, coach, and support person. This gives you someone to talk to about your progress. A good choice would be someone from this class because he or she is in an excellent position to understand and help. Perhaps you can reciprocate by supporting your partner's efforts to achieve his or her communication goals.

At the end of each section you will be challenged to develop a goal statement related to the material presented. Figure 1.2 provides another example of a communication improvement plan, this one relating to a public-speaking problem.

Problem: When I speak in class or in student council meetings, I often find myself burying my head in my notes or looking at the ceiling or walls.

Goal: To look at people more directly when I'm giving a speech.

Procedure: I will take the time to practise oral presentations aloud in my room. (1) I will stand up just as I do in class. (2) I will pretend various objects in the room are people, and I will consciously attempt to look at those objects as I am talking. (3) In giving a speech, I will try to be aware of when I am looking at my audience and when I am not.

Test of Achieving Goal: This goal will be considered achieved when I am maintaining eye contact with my audience most of the time.

Figure 1.2
Communication improvement plan

Summary

We have defined communication as the process of creating or sharing meaning, whatever the context; for example, informal conversation, group interaction, or public speaking.

The elements of the communication process are participants, context, messages, channels, noise, and feedback.

Communication plays a role in all aspects of our lives. Firstly, communication serves many important functions. People communicate to meet needs, to enhance and maintain a sense of self, to fulfill social obligations, to develop relationships, to exchange information, and to influence others. Secondly, communication occurs in interpersonal, group, public-speaking, and electronically mediated settings. In addition to communicating in person and in writing, we now communicate with each other through e-mail, newsgroups, chat rooms, and nearly any place via cellular telephones.

Our communication is guided by seven principles:

- Communication is purposeful.
- Communication is continuous.
- Communication messages can be spontaneous, scripted, or constructed.
- Interpersonal communication is relational, defining the power and affection between people. Relational definitions can be complementary or symmetrical.
- Communication is culturally bound.
- Communication has ethical implications. Ethical standards that influence our communication include honesty, integrity, fairness, respect, and responsibility.
- Communication is learned.

A primary issue in this course is competence—we all strive to become better communicators. Competence is the perception by others that our communication behaviour is appropriate and effective. It involves increasing our knowledge of communication and our understanding of the situations we face, identifying and attaining goals, and being able to use the various behavioural skills necessary to achieve our goals. Skills can be learned, developed, and improved, and you can enhance your learning this term by writing goal statements to systematically improve your own skill repertoire.

Glossary

Review the following key terms:

channel (9) — the route travelled by a message and its means of transportation.

chat room (14) — a Web site that makes it possible for two or more people with shared interests to communicate in real time through interactive message exchange.

communication (6) — the process of creating or sharing meaning through interaction with other human beings.

communication competence (23) — the impression that communicative behaviour is both appropriate and effective in a given situation.

complementary relationship (18) — a relationship in which one person lets the other define who is to have greater power.

constructed messages (17) — messages we encode in the moment when our known scripts are thought to be inadequate.

context (6) — the physical, social, historical, psychological, and cultural settings in which communication occurs.

cultural context (8) — the beliefs, values, attitudes, meanings, social hierarchies, religion, notions of time, and roles of a group of people.

cultural diversity (19) — the variations that exist among people because of their differing cultural backgrounds.

decoding (9) — the process of transforming messages back into ideas and feelings.

e-mail (14) — electronic correspondence conducted by two or more users on a network.

encoding (9) — the process of transforming ideas and feelings into words, sounds, and actions.

ethics (21) — a set of moral values and principles of right conduct that may be held by a society, a group, or a person.

external noise (10) — sights, sounds, and other stimuli that draw people's attention away from what is being said or done.

fairness (22) — achieving the right balance of interests without regard to one's own feelings and without showing favour to any side in a conflict.

feedback (10) — the response to a message.

historical context (7) — the background provided by participants' previous communication episodes which influence understanding of an encounter.

honesty (21) — an ethical standard that compels us to refrain from lying, cheating, stealing, or deception.

instant messaging (IM) (14) — an Internet-based service which allows subscribers to detect whether other subscribers are connected to the Internet and, if they are, to have real-time, interactive conversations with them.

integrity (22) — maintaining consistency of belief and action; adhering to our own moral code.

internal noise (10) — thoughts and feelings that interfere with the communication process.

meaning (9) — the ideas and feelings that exist in a person's mind.

message (8) — encoded verbal or nonverbal symbols organized in such a way that they can be used to convey meaning to others.

message board (14) — an electronic gathering place, similar to a newsgroup, but affiliated with a particular Web site and controlled by the owner(s) of that Web site.

moral dilemma (21) — a situation in which one must choose between alternatives which are both morally proscribed.

newsgroup (14) — an electronic gathering place for people with similar interests.

noise (10) — any stimulus that interferes with sharing meaning.

participants (6) — the people communicating, assuming the roles of sender and receiver, during communication.

physical context (6) — the location, the environmental conditions (temperature, lighting, noise level), the physical distance between communicators, any seating arrangements, and the time of day during a communication event.

psychological context (7) — the moods and feelings each person brings to a communication event.

respect (22) — showing regard or consideration for a person and for that person's rights.

responsibility (22) — being accountable for one's actions.

scripted messages (17) — conversational phrases we have learned from past experience and judge to be appropriate in certain situations.

semantic noise (10) — communication barriers which are attributable to language.

skills (24) — goal-oriented actions or action sequences that we can master and repeat in appropriate situations.

social context (6) — the purpose of a communication event and the relationships existing among the participants.

spontaneous expression (17) — messages encoded without much conscious thought.

symbols (9) — words, sounds, and actions that represent specific content meaning.

symmetrical relationship (18) — a relationship in which the participants do not agree about who is in control.

Peter Code/PhotoDisc Red/Getty Images

OBJECTIVES

After you have read this chapter, you should be able to answer these questions:

- What is perception?
- How does the mind select, organize, and interpret information?
- What is the self-concept, and how is it formed?
- What is self-esteem, and how is it developed?
- How do our self-concept and self-esteem affect our communication with others?
- What affects the accuracy with which we perceive others?
- What are some methods for improving the accuracy of social perception?

CHAPTER 2

Perception of Self and Others

"Allie, I really blew it. I can't believe it."

"What do you mean, Sal?"

"Well, I just forgot everything—I mean it was like I was standing there for five minutes saying nothing!"

"Sal, I saw you pause for a few seconds, really everything fit together well. You really had your speech well organized! It seemed to me that everyone in class thought you were in total control."

"Come on, Allie, you're just trying to make me feel good."

"Trust me, Sal, if you had blown it, I'd let you know. I'd be commiserating with you—not telling you what a good job you'd done."

Whose view is correct? Sal's or Allie's? Of course, we do not know—we did not hear the presentation. However, we do know that Sal and Allie perceived this event very differently. Our perception affects not only how we see things but also how we talk about what we have seen.

In this chapter we consider some basic concepts of perception, how the perceptions we have about ourselves are formed and changed, how we perceive others, and how we can increase the accuracy of both our self-perception and our perceptions of others. As we will see, perception underlies both our own communication and our evaluation of the communication of others.

The Perception Process

Perception is the process of selectively attending to information and assigning meaning to it. Our brains select the information they receive from our sense organs, organize the information selected, and interpret and evaluate it.

Attention and Selection

Although we are subject to a constant barrage of sensory stimuli, we focus attention on relatively little of it. Which stimuli we choose to focus on depends in part on our needs, interests, and expectations.

Needs We are likely to pay attention to information that meets our biological and psychological needs. When we are listening to a presentation, how well we tune in to what is being discussed is likely to depend on whether we believe the information is important to us—that is, does it meet a personal need?

Interests We are likely to pay attention to information that pertains to our interests. For instance, we may not even recognize that music is playing in the background until we suddenly find ourselves humming along to a favourite tune. Similarly, when we are really interested in a person, we are more likely to pay attention to what that person is saying.

Expectations Finally, we are likely to see what we expect to see and to ignore information that violates our expectations. Take a quick look at the phrases in the triangles in Figure 2.1.

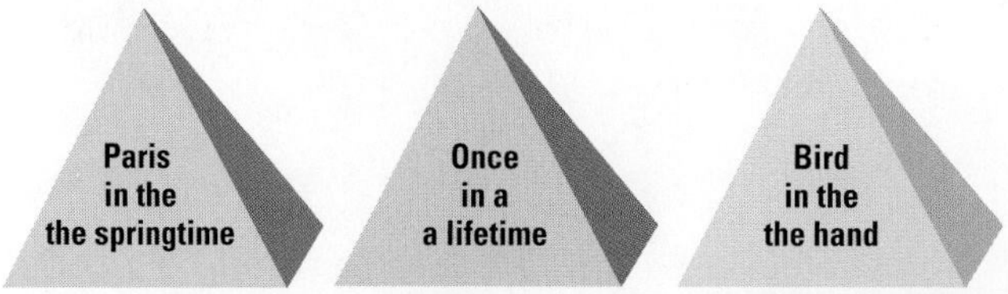

Figure 2.1
A sensory test of expectation

If you have never seen this illustration, you probably read *Paris in the springtime*, *Once in a lifetime*, and *Bird in the hand*. But if you re-examine the words, you will see that what you perceived was not exactly what is written. Do you now see the repeated words? It was easy to miss the repeated word the first time you read the phrases because you did not *expect* to see it.

Organization of Stimuli

Even though our attention and selection process limits the stimuli our brain must process, the absolute number of discrete stimuli we attend to at any one moment is still substantial. Our brains use certain principles to arrange these stimuli in order to make sense out of them. Two of the most common principles we apply are simplicity and pattern.

Simplicity If the stimuli we attend to are very complex, the brain simplifies the stimuli into some commonly recognized form. Based on a quick perusal of what someone is wearing, how she is standing, and the expression on her face, we may perceive her as a businesswoman, a flight attendant, or a soccer mom. Similarly, we simplify the verbal messages we receive. For example, Akram might walk out of the hour-long performance review meeting during which his boss described four of Akram's strengths and three areas for improvement and say to Jerry, his co-worker, "Well, I'd better shape up, or I'm going to get fired!"

Pattern A second principle the brain uses when organizing information is pattern. A **pattern** is a set of characteristics that differentiates some things from others so that items can be grouped according to their shared characteristics. A pattern makes it easy to interpret stimuli. For example, when we see a crowd of people, instead of perceiving each individual human being, we may focus on the characteristic of sex and see males and females, or we may focus on the characteristic of age and see children, teens, adults, and seniors.

In our interactions with others, we try to find patterns that will enable us to interpret and respond to their behaviour. For example, each time Tebogo and Bill encounter Sara, she hurries over to them and begins an animated conversation, yet when Bill is alone and runs into Sara, she merely says, "Hi." After a while Bill may detect a pattern to Sara's behaviour. She is warm and friendly when Tebogo is around and not so friendly when Tebogo is absent.

Interpretation of Stimuli

As the brain selects and organizes the information it receives from the senses, it also **interprets** the information by assigning meaning to it. Look at these three sets of numbers. What do you make of them?

A. 631 7348

B. 110 734 596

C. 4632 7364 2596 2174

IN BRIEF

The Perception Process

Perception is the process of selectively attending to information and assigning meaning to it. People are most likely to

- attend to information that satisfies their needs, interests, or expectations
- organize the information they select for simplicity and to achieve familiar patterns
- interpret or assign meaning to the information as it is selected and organized.

In examining each of these sets of numbers, your mind looked for clues to give them meaning. Because you use similar patterns of numbers every day, you probably interpreted A as a telephone number. How about B? A likely interpretation is a Social Insurance Number. And C? People who use credit cards will likely interpret this set as a credit card number.

In the remainder of this chapter, we will apply this basic information about perception to the study of perceptions of self and others in our communication.

Perceptions of Self: Self-Concept and Self-Esteem

Self-concept and self-esteem are the two self-perceptions that have the greatest impact on how we communicate. **Self-concept** is a person's self-identity (Baron & Byrne, 2000, p. 160). It is the idea or mental image that we have about our skills, abilities, knowledge, competencies, and personality. In other words, it is a detailed description of ourselves, the one that we would make if we set out to make a complete inventory of the qualities that define us. **Self-esteem** is a person's overall evaluation of his or her own competence and personal worthiness (based on Mruk, 1999, p. 26). In this section, we discuss how we come to understand who we are and how we determine whether we approve of who we are. Then we examine what determines how well these self-perceptions match others' perceptions of us and the role self-perceptions play when we communicate with others.

Forming and Maintaining a Self-Concept

How do we learn what our skills, abilities, knowledge, competencies, and personality are? Our self-concept is a composite of the observations we have made about ourselves based on our own experience and others' reactions and responses to us.

Self-perception We form impressions about ourselves based on our own perceptions. Through our experiences, we develop our own sense of our skills, our abilities, our knowledge, our competencies, and our personality. For example, if Hanan perceives that it is easy for her to strike up conversations with strangers and that she enjoys chatting with them, she may conclude that she is outgoing or friendly.

When we have a successful experience, we are likely to believe we possess the personal characteristics that we associate with that experience, and these characteristics become part of our picture of who we are. If Sonya quickly debugs a computer program that Jackie has struggled with, she is likely to incorporate *competent problem solver* into her self-concept. Her experience confirms that she has that skill, so it is reinforced as part of her self-concept.

We place a great deal of emphasis on the first experience we have with a particular phenomenon. For instance, if Roberto is rejected in his first try at dating, he may perceive himself to be unattractive to girls. If additional experiences produce results similar to the first experience, his initial perception will be strengthened. Even if the first experience is not immediately repeated, it is likely to take more than one contradictory additional experience to change the original perception.

Reactions and responses of others Our self-concept is formed and maintained not only by our self-perceptions but also by how others react and respond to us. For example, if during a brainstorming session at work, one of Liang's co-workers tells him, "You're really a creative thinker," he may decide that this comment fits his image of who he is. Such comments are especially powerful in affecting our self-perception if we respect the person making the comment. The power of such comments is increased when the praise is immediate rather than delayed (Hattie, 1992, p. 251). We use other people's comments as a check on our own self-perceptions. They serve to validate, reinforce, or alter our perception of who and what we are.

Some people have very detailed self-concepts; they can describe numerous skills, abilities, knowledge, competencies, and personality characteristics that they possess. Others have underdeveloped self-concepts; they cannot describe the skills, abilities, knowledge, competencies, or personality characteristics that they have. The more highly developed our self-concept, the better we know and understand who we are, and the better able we are to cope with the challenges we face as we interact with others.

OBSERVE & ANALYZE
Journal Activity

Self-Perceptions

How do you see yourself? List the skills, abilities, knowledge, competencies, and personality characteristics that describe how you see yourself. To generate this list, try completing the following sentences: I am skilled at. . . , I have the ability to. . . , I know things about . . . , I am competent at doing. . . , and One aspect of my personality is that I am . . . over and over. List as many characteristics in each category as you can think of. What you have developed is an inventory of your self-concept. Review each item on your list. Recall how you learned that you had each talent or characteristic. How does this review help you to understand the material you are studying?

Skip Nall/PhotoDisc Green/Getty Images

The feedback you get from your parents has an enormous influence on your self-concept and self-esteem.

OBSERVE & ANALYZE
Journal Activity

Others' Perceptions

How do others see you? Repeat the self-perception exercise, but this time use these statements: Other people believe I am skilled at. . . , Other people believe I have the ability to. . . , Other people believe I know things about. . . , Other people believe I am competent at doing. . . , and One aspect of my personality that other people have recognized is. . . . Again review the items on the list. Recall who told you about these talents and characteristics.

Our self-concept begins to form early in life, and it is shaped by the information we receive from our families (Demo, 1987). One of the major responsibilities that family members have is to talk and act in ways that will help develop accurate and complete self-concepts in other family members. For example, the mom who says, "Stephen, your room looks very neat. You are very organized," or the brother who comments, "Kisha, lending Tomika five dollars really helped her out. You are very generous" is helping Stephen or Kisha to recognize important parts of their personalities.

Unfortunately, in many families members hamper children's efforts to develop accurate self-concepts. Blaming, name-calling, and repeatedly pointing out another's shortcomings are particularly damaging. When dad shouts, "Terry, you are so stupid! If you had only stopped to think, this wouldn't have happened," he is damaging Terry's belief in his own intelligence. When big sister teases, "Hey, Dumbo, how many times do I have to tell you, you're too clumsy to be a ballet dancer," she is undermining her younger sister's perception of her gracefulness.

Developing and Maintaining Self-Esteem

We noted earlier that *self-esteem* is our overall evaluation of our competence and personal worthiness—it is our positive or negative evaluation of our self-concept. Notice that self-esteem is not just feeling good about oneself but having reason to do so. Our evaluation of our personal worthiness is rooted in our values and develops over time as a result of our experiences. As Mruk (1999) points out, self-esteem is not just how well or poorly we do things (self-concept) but the importance or value we place on what we do well or poorly (pp. 26–27). For instance, Fred's self-concept tells him he is physically strong, agile, and fast, but if Fred does not believe physical strength, agility, and speed are worthwhile characteristics to have, he will not have high self-esteem. Mruk argues that it is both the perception of having a characteristic and personally believing that the characteristic is of positive value that produce high self-esteem.

When we successfully use our skills, abilities, knowledge, or personality traits in endeavours we believe to be worthwhile, we raise our self-esteem. When we are unsuccessful in using our skills, abilities, knowledge, competencies, or personality traits, or when we use them in unworthy endeavours, we lower our self-esteem.

Accuracy of Self-Concept and Self-Esteem

The accuracy of our self-concept and self-esteem depends on the accuracy of our own perceptions and how we process others' perceptions of us. All of us experience success and failure, and all of us hear praise and criticism. If we are overly attentive to successful experiences and positive responses, our self-concept may become overdeveloped and our self-esteem inflated. If, however, we perceive and dwell on failures and give little value to our successes, or if we remember only the criticism we receive, our self-concept may be underdeveloped and our self-esteem low. In neither case does our self-concept or self-esteem accurately reflect who we are.

Incongruence, the gap between our inaccurate self-perceptions and reality, is a problem because our perceptions of self are more likely to affect our behaviour than are our true abilities (Weiten, 1998, p. 491). For example, Sean may actually possess all the skills, abilities, knowledge, competencies, and personality characteristics for effective leadership, but if he does not perceive that he has these characteristics, he will not step forward when leadership is needed. Unfortunately, people tend to reinforce their self-perceptions by adjusting their behaviour to conform with their perceptions of themselves. That is, people with high self-esteem tend to behave in ways that lead to more affirmation, while people with low self-esteem tend to act in ways that confirm the low esteem in which they hold themselves. The inaccuracy of the distorted picture of oneself is magnified through self-fulfilling prophecies and by filtering messages.

Self-fulfilling prophecies **Self-fulfilling prophecies,** events that happen as the result of being foretold, expected, or talked about, are likely to be either self-created or other-imposed.

Self-created prophecies are those predictions we make about ourselves. We often talk ourselves into success or failure. For example, Stefan sees himself as quite social and able to get to know people easily; he says, "I'm going to have fun at the party tonight." As a result of his self-concept, he looks forward to encountering strangers and, just as he predicted, makes several new acquaintanceships and enjoys himself. In contrast, Arthur sees himself as unskilled in establishing new relationships; he says, "I expect that I'll know hardly anyone—I'm going to have a miserable time." Because he fears encountering strangers, he feels awkward about introducing himself and, just as he predicted, spends much of his time standing around alone thinking about when he can leave.

Self-esteem has an important effect on the prophecies people make. For instance, people with high self-esteem view success positively, and they confidently prophesy that they can repeat the successes that they have already enjoyed. In contrast, people with low self-esteem attribute their successes to luck, and they prophesy that they will not repeat them (Hattie, 1992, p. 253).

The prophecies others make about us also affect our performance. For example, when teachers act as if their students are capable, students are likely to fulfill the teachers' expectations and succeed. In contrast, when teachers act as if students are not capable, students may realize these imposed prophecies and fail. Thus, when we talk to ourselves or when we speak to others, we have the power to affect future behaviour.

Filtering messages A second way that our self-perceptions can become increasingly distorted is through the way we filter what others say to us. Even though we may hear messages (that is, our ears receive the messages and our

OBSERVE & ANALYZE
Journal Activity

Who Am I?

Compare your self-perception list and others' perception list from the earlier Observe & Analyze activities in this chapter. How are the lists similar? Where are they different? Do you understand why they differ? Are your lists long or short? Why do you suppose that is? Reflect on how your own interpretations of your experiences and what others have told you about you have influenced your self-concept. Now, organize the lists you created, perhaps finding a way to group characteristics. Use this information to write an essay entitled Who I Am, and How I Know This.

brain records them), we do not perceive them accurately. For example, suppose Sook prepares an agenda for her study group. Someone comments that she is a good organizer. Though she hears the words, she may, if she has not recognized her own organizational ability or if she places a low value on it, ignore the praise or reply, "Anyone could have done that; it was nothing special." If being a good organizer is part of her self-concept, however, she will pay attention to the compliment and may even reinforce it by responding with something like, "Thanks, I've worked hard to learn to do this, but it was worth it. It comes in handy."

Changing self-concept and self-esteem Self-concept and self-esteem are enduring characteristics, but they can be changed. In his analysis of numerous other research studies, Christopher Mruk (1999) found that self-esteem can be enhanced. He reports, "in the final analysis, then, self-esteem is increased through hard work and practice, practice, practice—there is simply no escaping this basic existential fact" (p. 112).

In this book, we consider many specific communication behaviours that are designed to increase your communication competence. As you begin to practise and to perfect these skills, you may begin to receive positive responses to your behaviour. If you continue to work on these skills, the positive responses you receive will help broaden your self-concept and increase your self-esteem.

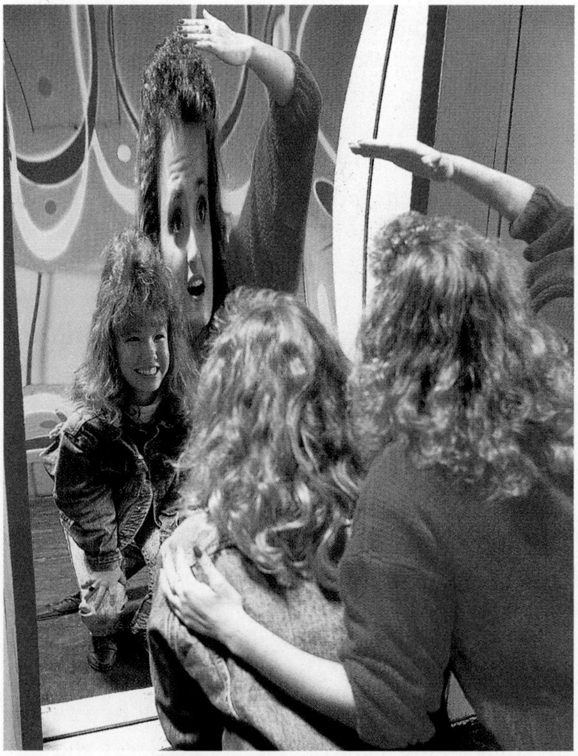

Charles Gupton/Stone/Getty Images

How do you see yourself? A distorted self-concept can become a self-fulfilling prophecy.

Presenting Ourselves

We display our self-concept and self-esteem to others through various roles we play. A **role** is a pattern of learned behaviours that people use to meet the perceived demands of a particular context. For instance, during the run of a day, Yannick may enact the roles of son, brother, student, hockey player, boyfriend, and sales clerk, among others.

The roles that we play may result from our own needs, from the relationships that we form, from the cultural expectations that are held for us, from the groups we choose to be part of, and from our own conscious decisions. For instance, as Farideh is the oldest child in a large family, her parents may have cast her in the role of big sister, a role that can involve functions such as role model, disciplinarian, brothers' and sisters' keeper, babysitter, and housekeeper, depending on how her parents see family relationships. If Bakari's peers look on him as a joker, he may adapt to the role, laughing and telling funny stories even when he really feels hurt or imposed upon. We all play numerous roles each day, and we draw on different skills and attributes as we do. As each new situation arises in our lives, we may test a role we already know how to play, or we may decide to try to play a new role.

OBSERVE & ANALYZE
Journal Activity

Monitor Your Enacted Roles

For three days keep a record of the roles you play in various situations; for example, at lunch with your best friend, in communication class, in a meeting with your coach about your training schedule, or during a consultation with a customer at work. Describe the roles you played and the image you chose to project in each setting. Write an analysis of your self-monitoring. To what extent does your communication behaviour differ and remain the same across situations? What factors in a situation seem to trigger certain behaviours in you? How satisfied are you with the self-concept you displayed in each situation? Where were you most pleased? Least pleased?

Self-Concept, Self-Esteem, and Communication

Just as our self-concept and self-esteem affect how accurately we perceive ourselves, so too do they influence our communication by moderating competing internal messages in our self-talk and influencing our personal communication style.

Self-perceptions moderate competing internal messages When we are faced with a decision, we may be especially conscious of the different and often competing voices in our head. Listen to the voices in Corey's head as he returns from a job interview:

Corey: I think I made a pretty good impression on the personnel director—I mean, she talked with me for a long time. Well, she talked with me, but maybe she was just trying to be nice. After all, it was her job. No, she didn't have to spend that much time with me, and she really lit up when I talked about my internship at Federated. So she *said* she was interested in my internship, but saying that isn't exactly telling me that it would make a difference in her view of me as a prospective employee.

If Corey feels good about himself, he will probably conclude that the interviewer was sincere, and he will feel positive about the interview, but if he believes he is unworthy, that he does not have the relevant skills and abilities to do the job, he is more likely to listen to the negative voices in his head and conclude that he does not have a chance at getting the job.

COMMUNICATE! Using Technology

The Internet has numerous sites and pages devoted to material on self-concept and self-esteem. One particularly provocative opinion is that put forth by Dr. Richard O'Connor in his short article entitled "Self-Esteem: In a Culture Where Winning Is Everything and Losing Is Shameful." He asks whether self-esteem as a general construct is always helpful. What points does O'Connor make? How does his conclusion square with what you have observed? To find his article, go to **www.pioneerthinking.com/esteem.html**.

COMMUNICATE! Using InfoTrac College Edition

Some people believe that it is harder for professional women in our society to develop self-esteem because of traditional beliefs that men are best suited for certain kinds of occupations.

What does research show? Using InfoTrac College Edition, look under the subject *self-perception—research*. See Sylvia Beyer & Edward M. Bowden (1997), "Gender Differences in Self-perceptions: Convergent Evidence from Three Measures of Accuracy and Bias," *Personality & Social Psychology Bulletin*, 23(2), p. 157.

Can you find any additional related studies?

Self-perception influences how we talk about ourselves with others If we feel good about ourselves, we are likely to communicate positively. For instance, people with a well developed self-concept and high self-esteem usually take credit for their successes. Likewise, people with healthy self-perceptions are inclined to defend their views in the face of opposing arguments. In contrast, people who feel bad about themselves are likely to communicate negatively by downplaying their own accomplishments and by giving in to others who challenge their views.

Why do some people put themselves down regardless of what they have done? People who have low self-esteem are likely to be unsure of the value of their contributions and to expect others to view them negatively. As a result, they perhaps find it less painful to put themselves down than to hear the criticism of others. Thus, to prevent others from commenting on their unworthiness, they do so themselves first.

Cultural and Gender Differences

Culture influences perception and affects people's views of self. Most Canadian citizens share what is called the Western view of self, the view that the individual is an independent entity with distinct abilities, traits, motives, and values and that these attributes cause behaviour. Moreover, people who hold this Western view see the individual as the most basic social unit. In Western cultures, self-concept and self-esteem are built on the central values of independence from others and discovery and expression of individual uniqueness.

However, people from other cultures base self-concept and self-esteem on different values. In many Eastern cultures, the family, not the individual, is regarded as the basic social unit. These cultures neither assume nor value independence; rather, *interdependence* among people is valued (Markus & Kitayama, 1991, p. 19). Someone who is a self-reliant individualist would, in a Western culture, regard these characteristics as strengths and develop positive self-esteem. In contrast, a member of an Eastern culture who possessed the same characteristics would view them as shortcomings and develop negative self-esteem.

In Western cultures, children will come to value those personal characteristics that are associated with independence, developing high self-esteem from acquiring them. In Eastern cultures, however, the child is seen as needing to be acculturated toward greater interdependency (Jordan, 1991, p. 137). These children will develop higher self-esteem when they perceive themselves to be co-operative, helpful, and self-effacing.

Similarly, in most cultures, men and women are socialized to view themselves differently and to value themselves based on whether their behaviour corresponds to the behaviour expected of members of their sex in their culture. If, for example, women in a particular culture are expected to be nurturing caregivers who attend to home and family life, then those women who perceive that they have the skills, abilities, knowledge, competencies, and personality needed for these jobs will have enriched self-concepts and high self-esteem, but women who lack these attributes are likely to be less confident of who they are and are likely to have lower self-esteem.

IN BRIEF

Perceptions of Self

- Self-concept and self-esteem are two self-perceptions that affect how we communicate
- Self-concept is the mental image we have of our skills, abilities, knowledge, competencies, and personality. It is formed through experience, based on our perceptions of ourselves and others' reactions and responses to us. Self-esteem is our overall evaluation of our competence and personal worthiness. It is rooted in our values and develops over time as a result of our experiences. Self-concept and self-esteem are also affected by the social roles we adopt.
- The accuracy of our self-concept and self-esteem depends on the accuracy of our own perceptions and how we process others' perceptions of us. It affects how we perceive ourselves and how we communicate with others.
- Culture and gender affect self-perception as different cultures value and promote different personal characteristics, and men and women may be socialized to occupy specific roles in different cultures.

Perception of Others

When two people meet, they form initial impressions of each other to guide their behaviour. As Berger and Bradac (1982) explain, at the beginning of a relationship, we engage in uncertainty reduction, a process of gaining information about the other so that we can predict how he or she will behave. **Uncertainty reduction theory** describes the approaches people use to monitor their social environment and to come to know more about others (Littlejohn, 1999, p. 260). People typically take one or more of three approaches to reducing uncertainty about another: passive strategies (e.g., observing the person in one or more social situations), active strategies (asking others for information about the person), and interactive strategies (actually communicating with the person) (Berger & Bradac, 1982). As people continue to interact, perceptions will be reinforced, intensified, or changed.

Like our self-perceptions, our social perceptions are not always accurate. The factors that are likely to influence our perceptions of others include physical characteristics and social behaviours, stereotyping, and emotional states.

Physical Characteristics and Social Behaviours

Our first impressions are made on the basis of people's physical characteristics, in this order: race, gender, age, appearance, facial expressions, eye contact, movement, personal space, and touch. These characteristics help us to categorize people as friendly, for example, or courageous or intelligent or cool or the opposites of any of these (Gardenswartz & Rowe, 1998, p. 29). Early impressions are also formed on the basis of a person's social behaviours. For instance, a person who is observed interrupting another may be perceived as rude, and a child who addresses adults as Mr. or Ms. may be perceived as well mannered.

Women and men differ in the attributes they perceive in others. Scholar Leslie Zebrowitz (1990) says that men and boys are more likely to see and describe others in terms of their abilities ("She writes well"), while women and girls are more likely to see and describe others in terms of their self-concept ("She thinks she's a good writer"). In addition, Zebrowitz has found that males' descriptions include more nonsocial activities ("He likes to fly model airplanes"), while females' include more interpersonal interactions ("He likes to get together with his friends") (p. 24).

Some judgments of other people are based on what are called implicit personality theories. These are assumptions people have developed about which physical characteristics and personality traits or behaviours are associated with one another (Michener & DeLamater, 1999, p. 106). Because one of our implicit personality theories says that certain traits go together, we are likely to perceive that a person has a whole set of characteristics when we have actually observed only one characteristic, trait, or behaviour. When we make this kind of leap, our perception is exhibiting what is known as the **halo effect.** For instance, Heather sees Martina personally greeting and welcoming every person who arrives at the meeting. Heather's implicit personality theory views this behaviour as a sign of warmth. She further associates warmth with goodness, and goodness with honesty. As a result, she perceives that Martina is good and honest as well as warm. In reality, Martina may be a con artist who uses her warmth to lure people like Heather into a false sense of trust. This example demonstrates a positive halo (Heather assigned Martina positive characteristics), but we also use implicit personality theories to inaccurately impute bad characteristics. In fact, Hollman (1972) found that negative information more strongly influences our impressions of others than does positive information, so we are more likely to negatively halo others than to positively halo them.

THINKING ABOUT ...

Halo Effects

What traits or personal characteristics do you group together? Suppose you discover that a new acquaintance is deeply religious. What attitudes and behavioural characteristics would you now assume this person has? The next time you draw a conclusion about a person, make a mental note to think about whether it was influenced by a halo effect.

Halo effects seem to occur most frequently under one or more of three conditions: (1) when the perceiver is judging traits with which he or she has limited experience, (2) when the traits have strong moral overtones, and (3) when the perception is of a person that the perceiver does not know well.

Given limited amounts of information, then, we fill in details. This tendency to fill in details leads to a second factor that explains social perception, stereotyping.

Stereotyping

Of the factors that influence our perceptions of others, perhaps the most commonly known is stereotyping. **Stereotypes** are simplified and standardized conceptions about the characteristics or expected behaviour of members of an identifiable group. These characteristics, taken as a whole, may be perceived as positive or negative and may be accurate or inaccurate (Jussim, McCauley, & Lee, 1995, p. 6). When we stereotype, we perceive a person as possessing certain characteristics not because we have identified those characteristics in him or her but only because we identify that person as belonging to a certain group. We are likely to develop generalized perceptions about any group with which we come into contact. Subsequently, any number of perceptual cues—skin colour, style of dress, religious medals, hair colour, gender, sexual behaviour, and so on—can lead us to project our generalizations onto a specific person.

THINKING ABOUT ...

Stereotyping

Think of a recent encounter you have had with someone of a different race, ethnic group, gender, sexual orientation, or age. Recall how you felt. To what extent were you comfortable with this person? How did the person's belonging to a group different from yours influence how you acted or reacted? Did it affect the topics you discussed or the care with which you phrased your sentences? To what extent was this conversation effective and satisfying? In what ways would the encounter have been different if you had had it with a member of your own group?

Stereotyping contributes to perceptual inaccuracies by ignoring individual differences. For instance, if part of Dave's stereotype of personal injury lawyers is that they are unethical, then he will use this stereotype when he meets Denise, a highly principled woman who happens to be a successful personal injury lawyer. You may be able to think of instances when you have been the victim of a stereotype based on your gender, age, ethnic heritage, social class, physical characteristics, or other qualities. If so, you know how hurtful the use of stereotypes can be.

If stereotypes lead to inaccurate perceptions and miscommunication, why do they persist? Stereotyping is a shortcut that enables us to confer order on the complex social world in which we interact (McCrae, Milne, & Bodenhausen, 1994, p. 45). In addition, stereotypes are helpful (Deaux, Dane, & Wrightsman, 1993, p. 94). Although people may learn to go beyond a stereotype in forming opinions of individual people, stereotypes provide a working hypothesis. That is, when we encounter a new person from a particular identifiable group, we can reduce our uncertainty about that person by attributing to him or her the characteristics of our stereotype of the group to which he or she belongs. We then relate to this person based on the stereotype until we receive sufficient information to enable us to perceive the person as an individual (Jones, 1990, p. 110).

As these examples suggest, stereotyping can lead to prejudice and discrimination. According to Terkel and Duval (1999), **prejudice** is a preconceived judgment, a belief or opinion that a person holds without sufficient grounds (p. 217). **Discrimination** is treating members of one group differently from members of another in a way that is unfair or harmful (p. 69). Thus, prejudice is evaluative and discrimination is behavioural (Weston, 1999, p. 790). For instance, when Laura discovers that Wasif, a man she has just met, is a Muslim, she stereotypes him as a chauvinist. Because she is a feminist, she uses this stereotype to prejudge him and assume that he will expect women to be subservient. Thus, she holds a prejudice against him. If she acts on her prejudice by being curt and dismissive when talking with Wasif, and perhaps by ending their conversation abruptly,

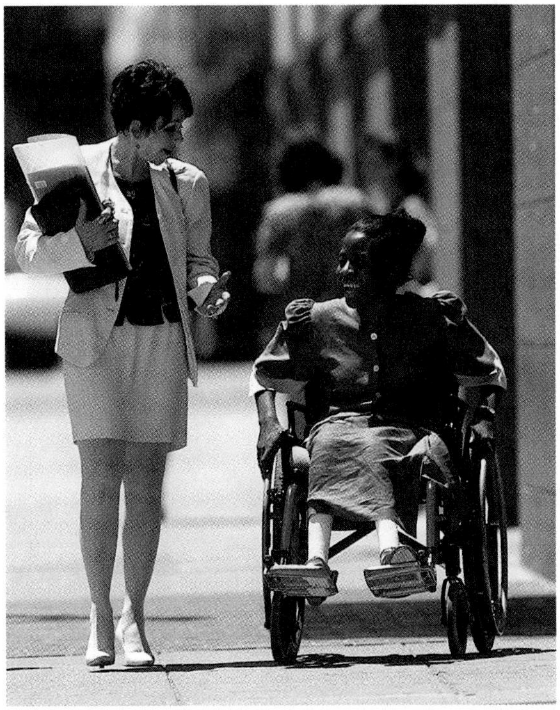

Bob Daemmrich/Stock Boston

What is the relationship between these women? How did stereotyping influence your perception?

then she is discriminating against him. Without really having gotten to know Wasif, Laura may decide that she does not like him. In this case, Wasif may never get the chance to be known for who he really is, and Laura will have lost an opportunity to get to know someone from a different cultural background.

Stereotypes, prejudice, and discrimination, like self-concept and self-esteem, can be difficult to change. People are likely to maintain their stereotypes and prejudices and continue to discriminate against others even in the face of evidence that disproves their biases.

DIVERSE VOICES

Growing Vegetables and Shooting Hoops

by Jutta Mason

Jutta Mason, a resident of Toronto, describes the conflicting perceptions of those who are forced into each other's company in a municipal park in a large multicultural city. Experiencing oneself and being perceived as "other" are powerful determinants of one's self-concept and form filters through which one communicates with others.

I spend a lot of time in my neighbourhood park in downtown Toronto, mostly working in the gardens or baking at the outdoor wood-fired oven there. Over the years, I've met many young people who also spend a lot of time at the park, playing basketball or just "chilling" with their friends. Sometimes those young folks have done odd jobs for the park, baking at the oven or cleaning up the park or helping out with community campfires.

People often ask me: Have the things we do in our park "rehabilitated" any young people who formerly made trouble? The short answer is yes. Certainly we now have very little damage (such as graffiti or vandalism) in the park, and there seems to be a code about fights in the park: "We don't fight here, and we don't let other people come and fight here. We help keep this park safe." That's their theory and, while not strictly adhered to by everyone, it more or less carries the day.

The longer answer is complicated. The young people who come and hang around, particularly in the proximity of the basketball court, have a strong sense of themselves as a separate culture, insiders with everyone else on the outside. In that way, their sense of themselves is parallel with that of many other people who use the park: the middle-class older folks who have a strong sense that we are the insiders, the legitimate people who behave well.

The sharp separations mean that if the older folks in the park come and try to act friendly with the young guys, they are often rebuffed, sometimes very rudely. The young guys tell them to get lost, and the older folks are appalled at their manners. There continues to be a lot of pretty graphic swearing, and if we hadn't disconnected the electrical power outlet near the basketball courts, we would still be hearing a lot of uncensored music that blasts out rape-and-violence songs across the park. There is a fondness for the "ghetto" look—lots of litter and periodic binges of breaking glass. This kind of stuff is cyclical, but seemingly not much under the control of parks staff or other park users.

(continued)

The various social circles that form around the bake ovens or the campfire circle (this includes the outdoor music and theatre rehearsals that are often in our park) are so near the basketball court that the different scenes can't help but overlap. The cooking fires/ovens were added after the young guys had established themselves. The overlap grates continually, because of the forced proximity of unmatched groups. Neither side chooses to be near the other, but the young guys very much want the basketball court and the older people (and their little kids) very much want the cooking fires. Or the older people very much want the fresh air of their evening walk through the park (some of the most beautiful flowerbeds are also near this part of the park) and the young guys very much want their evening campfire, where they can drink and maybe roast hot dogs. So they are constantly forced into each other's grating presence.

This grating is actually rather productive, even if sometimes painfully so. I learned the usefulness of such proximity from a wonderful essay written by the Norwegian criminologist Nils Christie, called "Conflict as Property," and it treats conflict as a precious, practical community resource for summoning up the gifts of the people who live there. Christie wrote about the theft of this resource by lawyers, courts, and others who take conflict out of a community and thereby prevent ordinary people from behaving with courage and generosity and ingenuity—important practical forms of spiritual exercise.

So: not long ago, I was working in the vegetable garden beside the ovens and some of the young people were having a loud, scary discussion relating to sex and prison life, and involving a lot of graphic cursing. Neither of us could move to a different location, so there we were: me with my spade and they with their stories, a very light rain falling on us both. I was forced to listen to things I would never have to listen to inside my house, inside my own social class, and they were forced to get intermittent glares from me. Eventually (after quite a while), the talk modified, toned down a bit, then stopped.

I saw some of them again the day after. I was revolted with them, and they were hostile to me, the middle-aged lady getting mixed up in their business. But I had a pizza-making group to attend to at the outdoor oven, and they had to play basketball, so we were forced to stay near each other. Some of the older children in the pizza-making group went to watch the basketball, and then they got their turn at one of the hoops and began to play too. One of the basketball players came over and played with them because, he told me, kids like to play with a bigger guy; it makes them feel big. The parents at the oven were all busy talking to each other, and there was nothing about the scene to worry them. The usual swearing almost stopped, because of the code of not swearing near young children, but the basketball went on and the drinking went on and the pizza-making went on. Everybody was having a good time.

At some point, well into the evening, one of the young guys walked by and made some friendly remark, and I noticed I wasn't angry anymore. There was such a pleasing, even joyful, normalcy about the scene that I couldn't feel that the end of civilized society had arrived, as I had the day before.

So: who was rehabilitated? Are the shocked older people like me also in need of rehabilitation? Or in need of forgiveness, for all the unfair advantages we routinely gain for ourselves and our group, and which we may try to explain away by pointing to the bad behaviour of others outside our group? What I think I know is this: there have to be standards and, in cities like Toronto, people have to learn to work out the standards across different groups. This work, ideally, is continually in progress and needs proximity. The campfires and bake oven in our park are an interesting, continuous prompt for such proximity. For me, sometimes, such proximity makes me delight in the lively, quirky existence of people quite unlike me. On good days, they do me the honour of delighting in me as well.

Source: Reprinted with permission of the author.

Racism, sexism, ageism, able-ism, heterosexism, religious bigotry and other forms of discrimination occur when the members of a powerful group believe themselves to be superior to those of another group and that this superiority gives them the right to dominate or discriminate against members of the group that they consider inferior. Overt and violent acts of discrimination are condemned by most educated people, but because discrimination can be deeply ingrained and subtle, it is easy to overlook discriminatory behaviours that we engage in ourselves. The behaviour may appear to be inconsequential, such as in not offering to shake hands with an African exchange student when we are introduced, or it may be unconscious, such as in leaving a bit more space than usual between ourselves and a blind person when we sit down on a bus. Telling jokes, laughing at jokes, or encouraging repetition of jokes that demean women, gays and lesbians, disabled persons, or members of particular religious or ethnic groups are common discriminatory behaviours. All people can be prejudiced and can discriminate. However, "prejudices of groups with power are farther reaching in their consequences than others" (Sampson, 1999, p. 131).

Emotional States

A final factor that affects how accurately we perceive others is our emotional state at the time of the interaction. Based on his research findings, Joseph Forgas (1991) has concluded that "there is a broad and pervasive tendency for people to perceive and interpret others in terms of their (own) feelings at the time" (p. 288). If, for example, Jwahir has just been awarded a work-term placement that she applied for, her good mood—brought on by her good fortune—is likely to spill over so that she perceives other things and other people more positively than she might under different circumstances. If, on the other hand, she has just received a low grade on a paper that she had thought was well written, her perceptions of people around her are likely to be coloured by her disappointment or anger resulting from this grade.

Our emotions also cause us to engage in selective perception, ignoring inconsistent information. For instance, if Donna sees Nick as a man with whom she would like to develop a strong relationship, she will focus on the positive side of Nick's personality and tend to overlook or ignore the negative side that is apparent to others.

Finally, our emotions may also affect our attributions (Forgas, 2000, p. 397). **Attributions** are reasons we give for other people's behaviour. In addition to making judgments about people, we attempt to construct reasons for the things that other people do. According to attribution theory, what we determine—rightly or wrongly—to be the causes of others' behaviour has a direct impact on our perceptions of those people. For instance, suppose that Molly had agreed to meet Felix, a classmate, at a restaurant at noon for lunch. At 12:20, Felix has still not arrived. If Molly likes and respects Felix, she is likely to attribute his lateness to something external: an important phone call at the last minute, the need to finish a project before lunch, or some accident that may have

THINKING ABOUT . . .

Prejudiced Speech

Think of a recent situation in which you heard someone tell a racist, sexist, or heterosexist joke or make a racist, sexist, or heterosexist remark. How did you react? How did others present react? Are you pleased with your reaction? If not, think about how you might have reacted differently.

TEST YOUR COMPETENCE

Factors Leading to Misperceptions of Others

For the following situation, use the concepts you have studied to identify the factors influencing Amanda's impression of the dry-cleaning clerk.

Amanda was depressed. Her daughter was having problems in school, she had just been informed that her work hours were being cut back, and her mother was facing possible surgery. On her way home from campus, she stopped at the dry cleaner to pick up her laundry. There was a new man working the counter. From looking at him, Amanda could tell he was quite old. She thought to herself that he could be a problem. When she requested her laundry, he asked to see her claim ticket. Because no one had ever asked her for the tickets before, Amanda had started discarding them, so she responded that she had thrown it away. "Well," the man firmly replied, "I'm not able to give you clothes without a claim ticket. It's store policy." After demanding to see the manager and being informed that she had left for the day, Amanda stormed out of the store. "I'll fix him," she fumed to herself. "It's just like an old man to act so rigidly!"

occurred. If she is not particularly fond of Felix, she is likely to attribute his lateness to something internal: forgetfulness, inconsiderateness, or malicious intent. In either case, her causal attribution further affects her perception of Felix.

Like prejudices, causal attributions may be so strong that they resist contrary evidence. If Molly does not particularly care for Felix, when he does arrive and explain that he had an emergency long-distance phone call, she is likely to disbelieve the reason or discount the urgency of the call. Being aware of the human tendency toward such cognitive biases can help us correct our perceptions and improve our communication.

In the final part of this chapter, we focus on procedures that will enable us to improve our social perceptions of people.

IN BRIEF

Perception of Others

Our perception plays an important role as we form impressions of other people. Our impressions of another are likely to be affected by

- the person's physical characteristics
- the person's social behaviours
- halo effects
- our own stereotypes
- our emotional state at the time that we first encounter the person.

Stereotyping can lead to

- prejudice
- discrimination.

Improving Social Perception

Following these guidelines can aid us in constructing a more realistic impression of others as well as in assessing the validity of our own perceptions.

1. **Question the accuracy of your perceptions.** Questioning accuracy begins by saying, "I know what I think I saw, heard, tasted, smelled, or felt, but I could be wrong. What else could help me sort this out?" By accepting the possibility of error, we may be motivated to seek further verification. In situations where accuracy of perception is important, we should take a few seconds to double-check. It will be worth the effort.

2. **Seek more information to verify perceptions.** If our perception has been based on only one or two pieces of information, we should try to collect additional information before we allow ourselves to form an impression so that we can increase the accuracy of our perceptions. We should at least

note that our perception is tentative—that is, subject to change. We can then make a conscious effort to collect more data to determine whether the original perception was accurate.

The best way to get information about people is to talk with them. Unfortunately, we tend to avoid people we do not know much about. It is okay to be unsure about how to treat someone from another culture or someone who is disabled, but rather than letting this hold us back, we should ask the person for the information we need to be more comfortable.

3. **Realize that perceptions of people may need to be changed over time.** People often saddle themselves with perceptions that are based on old or incomplete information and find it easier to stick with a perception, even if it is wrong, than to change it. Willingness to change means making an effort to observe a person's behaviour at different times without bias and being prepared to modify our perception if the person's behaviour warrants it. It takes strength of character to say to ourselves or to others, "I was wrong." In addition, communication based on outdated or inaccurate perceptions can cost us much more than revising our perceptions.

4. **Use perception checking to verify conclusions you have drawn.** A **perception check** is a verbal statement that reflects our understanding of the meaning of another person's *nonverbal* cues. To do a perception check, we must (1) watch the behaviour of the other person, (2) ask ourselves, "What does that behaviour mean to me?" and (3) put our interpretation of the behaviour into words and ask the other person to verify whether our perception is accurate.

The final sentence in each of these two examples is a perception check:

Ted, the company messenger, delivers a memo to Erin. As Erin reads the note, her eyes brighten and she breaks into a smile. Ted says, "Hey, Erin, you seem really pleased with this news. Am I right?"

SKILL BUILDERS Problem-Solving Policy Questions

Skill	Use	Procedure	Example
Making a verbal statement that reflects your understanding of the meaning of another person's nonverbal cues.	To clarify the meaning of nonverbal behaviour.	1. Watch the behaviour of another. Describe the behaviour to yourself or aloud. 2. Ask yourself: What does that behaviour mean to me? 3. Put your interpretation of the nonverbal behaviour into words and ask the other person to verify your perception.	Vera comes walking into the room with a completely blank expression on her face and neither speaks to Ann nor acknowledges that she is in the room. Ann says, "Vera, I get the feeling that something has happened to put you in a state of shock. Am I right? Is there something I can do?"

Cesar, speaking in short, precise sentences with a sharp tone of voice, gives Bill his day's assignment. Bill says, "From the tone of your voice, Cesar, I can't help but get the impression that you're upset with me. Are you?"

Perception checking brings the meaning that was received through nonverbal cues into the verbal realm where it can be verified or corrected. For instance, when Bill says, "I can't help but get the impression that you're upset with me. Are you?" Cesar may say (1) "No, whatever gave you that impression?" in which case Bill can further describe the cues he received; (2) "Yes, I am," in which case Bill can get Cesar to specify what has caused the feelings; or (3) "No, it's not you; it's just that three of my team members didn't show up for this shift." If Cesar is not upset with him, Bill can deal with what caused him to misinterpret Cesar's feelings. If Cesar is upset with him, Bill has the opportunity to change the behaviour that caused Cesar to be upset. Even though we may be correct most of the time in identifying another person's feelings, if we do not do a verbal perception check, we are still guessing at what the other person is really feeling.

We should check our perceptions whenever the accuracy of our understanding is important (1) to ongoing communication, (2) to the relationship we have with the other person, or (3) to the conclusions we draw about that person. Most of us use this skill far too little, if at all.

Although perception checking may not always eliminate defensive behaviour, it can reduce the likelihood of misinterpreting another's nonverbal cues and thus the likelihood of defensiveness. As with most skills, to become competent we must practise.

IN BRIEF

Improving Social Perception

To improve the accuracy of our perceptions, we should

- question their accuracy
- seek more information for verification
- realize that they may need to change
- do a perception check.

TEST YOUR COMPETENCE

Perception Checking

Write a well-phrased perception check for each of the following situations:

1. Franco comes home from the doctor's office with a pale face and slumped shoulders. Glancing at you with a forlorn look, he shrugs his shoulders.
   You say:
2. As you return the tennis racket you borrowed from Liam, you smile and say, "Here's your racket." Liam stiffens, grabs the racket, and starts to walk away.
   You say:
3. Natalie comes dancing into the room with a huge grin on her face.
   You say:
4. In the past, your academic adviser has told you that almost any time would be all right for working out your schedule for next term. When you tell her that you will be in Wednesday at 4 p.m., she pauses, frowns, sighs, and says "Uh" and nods.
   You say:

Evaluate your written responses in terms of the guidelines for effective perception checking discussed earlier. Edit your responses where necessary to improve them. Now say them aloud. Do they sound like natural conversation? If not, revise them until they do.

WHAT WOULD YOU DO?
A QUESTION OF ETHICS

Neikko, a large out-of-town corporation that had just bought out Rustown's major factory, decided to move its headquarters there and to expand the current plant, creating hundreds of new jobs.

Rustown's inhabitants had mixed reactions to this takeover. They were excited by the increased business that was expected, but they knew that many of the new factory managers as well as some of the new employees were Japanese. There had never been an Asian family in Rustown, and some of the townspeople openly worried about the effect the Japanese would have on their community.

At work on the first day, Sam Nuguki, one of the Neikko managers who had agreed to move to Rustown, noticed that the workers seemed very leery of him, but by the end of the first week the plant was running smoothly, and Mr. Nuguki was feeling the first signs of acceptance. On Monday morning of the next week, Mr. Nuguki accidentally overheard a group of workers talking on their break, trading lies about Japanese people and using vulgarities and racist slurs in exchanging views based on negative stereotypes.

A bit shaken, Mr. Nuguki returned to his office. He had a problem. He recognized his workers' prejudices, but he did not know how to change them. He wanted to establish a good working relationship with his workers for the sake of the company, but he also wanted to create a good working atmosphere for other Japanese employees who would be coming to Rustown. What should Mr. Nuguki do?

Devise a plan for Mr. Nuguki. How could he use his social perceptions of Rustown to address the problem in a way that is within ethical interpersonal communication guidelines?

Summary

Perception is the process of gathering sensory information and assigning meaning to it. Our perceptions are a result of our selection, organization, and interpretation of sensory information. Inaccurate perceptions cause us to see the world not as it is but as we think it is or as we would like it to be.

Self-concept is the mental image we have of our skills, our abilities, our knowledge, our competencies, and our personality. Self-esteem rises or falls depending on our evaluation of that mental image. The inaccuracy of a distorted image of oneself becomes magnified through self-fulfilling prophecies and by filtering messages. Our self-concept and self-esteem moderate competing internal messages in our self-talk, influence our perception of others, influence our personal communication style, and influence how we present ourselves to others in the roles we play.

Perception also plays an important role in forming impressions of others. Factors that are likely to influence our social perceptions are physical characteristics and social behaviours, stereotyping, and emotional states. Because research shows that the accuracy of people's perceptions and judgments varies considerably, our communication will be most successful if we do not rely entirely on our impressions to determine how another person feels or what that person is really like. We will improve (or at least better understand) our perceptions of others if we take into account physical characteristics and social behaviours, stereotyping, and emotional states.

We can learn to improve perception if we actively question the accuracy of our perceptions, seek more information to verify perceptions, talk with the people about whom we are forming perceptions, realize that perceptions of people need to change over time, and check perceptions verbally before we react to them.

Glossary

Review the following key terms:

able-ism (46) — the belief that the behaviours or characteristics of able-bodied people are inherently superior to those of people with disabilities and that this superiority gives able-bodied people the right to dominate or discriminate against the disabled.

ageism (46) — the belief that the behaviours or characteristics of one age group are inherently superior to those of another and that this superiority gives members of the first age group the right to dominate or discriminate against members of the other.

attributions (46) — reasons we give for other people's behaviour.

discrimination (43) — treating members of one group differently from members of another in a way that is unfair or harmful.

halo effect (42) — the perception that a person has a whole set of characteristics when you have actually observed only one characteristic, trait, or behaviour.

heterosexism (46) — the belief that the behaviours or characteristics of heterosexual people are inherently superior to those of homosexual or bisexual people and that this superiority gives heterosexuals the right to dominate or discriminate against homosexuals and bisexuals.

incongruence (37) — the gap between our inaccurate self-perceptions and reality.

interpret (33) — to assign meaning to the information that has been selected and organized.

pattern (33) — a set of characteristics that differentiates some things from others so that items can be grouped according to their shared characteristics.

perception (32) — the process of selectively attending to information and assigning meaning to it.

perception check (48) — a verbal statement that reflects your own understanding of the meaning of another person's *nonverbal* cues.

prejudice (43) — a preconceived judgment; a belief or opinion that a person holds without sufficient grounds.

racism (46) — the belief that the behaviours or characteristics of one race are inherently superior to those of another and that this superiority gives members of the first race the right to dominate or discriminate against members of the other.

religious bigotry (46) — the belief that the behaviours or characteristics of one religious group are inherently superior to those of another and that this superiority gives members of the first religious group the right to dominate or discriminate against members of the other.

role (39) — a pattern of learned behaviours that people use to meet the perceived demands of a particular context.

self-concept (34) — one's self-identity.

self-esteem (34) — one's overall evaluation of his or her own competence and personal worthiness.

self-fulfilling prophecies (37) — events that happen as the result of being foretold, expected, or talked about. They are likely to be either self-created or other-imposed.

sexism (46) — the belief that the behaviours or characteristics of one sex are inherently superior to those of the other and that this superiority gives members of the first sex the right to dominate or discriminate against members of the other.

stereotype (42) — a simplified and standardized conception of the characteristics or expected behaviour of members of an identifiable group.

uncertainty reduction theory (41) — the theory that people beginning a relationship engage in an information-gaining process in order to be able to predict how the other person in the relationship will behave.

Mike Reed/Stock Illustration Source

OBJECTIVES

After you have read this chapter, you should be able to answer these questions:

- What is verbal communication?
- What is the relationship between language and meaning?
- What is the difference between the denotative and the connotative value of words?
- How does specific, concrete, and precise language improve message clarity?
- How can the skills of dating information and indexing generalizations increase the accuracy of a message?
- What happens when people use language that is inappropriate for the situation?
- What types of language are sometimes perceived as inappropriate, and in which situations?

CHAPTER 3

Verbal Communication

"Kyle, why do you keep obfuscating the plan?"

"Now just a minute, Derek. There's no need for you to get obscene with me. I may not have looked at the job the same way you did, but I wouldn't, uh . . . I'm not going to lower myself to repeat your language!"

Obfuscating means confusing. What in the world did Derek mean when he accused Kyle of "obfuscating the plan"? And why did Kyle think Derek was talking obscenely? Many years ago the British rhetorician I. A. Richards (1965) observed that communication is "the study of misunderstanding and its remedy" (p. 3), and in this instance, we have a classic example of misunderstanding. The remedy? Clearer and more appropriate language.

Whether we are trying to agree on weekend plans with a friend, explain our views on the causes of domestic violence in a group discussion, or argue for a decrease in university tuition in a public speech, our effectiveness will depend on our ability to communicate verbally and nonverbally. In this chapter, we discuss **verbal communication**: communication through the use of language. We will discuss how people use language, the relationship between language and meaning, and the skills that help us use language clearly and appropriately.

The Nature of Language

A **language** (e.g., English) comprises the body of words and the systems for their use that are common to the members of a language community (e.g., speakers of English).

Uses of Language

Although language communities differ in the words that they use (e.g., English: *dog*, French: *chien*, German: *hund*) and in their systems of grammar and syntax, all languages serve the same purposes.

1. **We use language to designate, label, define, and limit.** When we identify a dog as a Cocker Spaniel, for example, we are differentiating it from others that might be identified as Labrador Retrievers or Airedale Terriers.
2. **We use language to evaluate.** Through language we show that we feel positively or negatively toward things, persons, or events. For instance, if a professor noticed that Hal was taking much longer than other students to respond to a question, she could describe his behaviour positively as "thoughtful" or negatively as "unprepared."
3. **We use language to discuss things outside our immediate experience.** Language enables us to speak hypothetically, to talk about past and future events, and to communicate about people and things that are not present. For example, we can use language to discuss where we hope to be in five years, to analyze a conversation we had a week ago with an acquaintance, or to learn about the history of ancient Rome.
4. **We use language to talk about language.** We can use language to discuss how someone phrased a statement, to debate or negotiate the meaning of words, and to clarify something we or someone else has said. For instance,

THINKING ABOUT . . .

Labelling and Limiting

Imagine that you are to accompany a friend to a party, where you will meet Terrance, your friend's best friend in high school. Suppose that your friend has told you only that Terrance is a Ph.D. student in anthropology at McGill or that Terrance is a Big Brother who regularly volunteers with Habitat for Humanity. Would you have different expectations of Terrance the McGill Ph.D. student than of Terrance the Big Brother and volunteer? Suppose both descriptions of Terrance were accurate. How would your expectations change?

if a friend says, "I'll see you this afternoon," we might expect her to arrive after lunch. If she does not arrive until five o'clock, we are likely to discuss our understanding of the phrase *this afternoon.*

Language and Meaning

On the surface, the relationship between language and meaning seems perfectly clear: We select the correct word, and people will interpret our meaning accordingly. In fact, the relationship between language and meaning is not nearly so simple, because language must be learned, because the use of language is a creative act, and because words can mean different things to different people.

Firstly, we are not born knowing a language. Rather, each generation within a language community learns the language anew. We learn much of our language early in life from our families; much more we learn in school, but we do not all learn to use the same words in the same way.

A second reason the relationship between language and meaning is complicated is that, even though languages have established systems of syntax and grammar, each utterance is a creative act. When we speak, we use language to create original sentences that represent our exact meaning. Although we occasionally use conventional phrasing or repeat other people's sentence constructions to represent what we are thinking or feeling, much of our expression is unique.

Finally, the relationship between language and meaning is complicated because people interpret the meanings of words differently. Words have two kinds of meanings: denotative and connotative. For example, Melissa has just lost her 12-year-old Collie, a pet which she had raised from a puppy. If she said to her friend Trish, "My dog died yesterday," what Trish understood Melissa to mean would depend on both word denotation and connotation.

Denotation The direct, explicit meaning that a language community formally gives to a word is its **denotation.** The denotative value of a word is the meaning that you would find in a dictionary. So, denotatively, when Melissa said that her "dog died," she meant that her domesticated canine had ceased to live.

OBSERVE & ANALYZE
Journal Activity

Denotative Meanings

Compile a list of 10 popular slang words. Discuss how the meanings you assign to these words differ from the meanings your parents or grandparents might assign to them (for example, "Jen's party was really *sick*!").

TEST YOUR COMPETENCE

Denotative Meanings

Write your own definition of each of the following words; then go to a dictionary and see how closely your definition matches the dictionary definition.

building	justice	peace	honour
love	ring	band	freedom
success	glass	union	health

In some situations, the denotative meaning of a word may not be clear to a receiver. Why? Firstly, because dictionary definitions reflect both current and past usage of a word in the language community and usages that are restricted to certain parts of the language community. Secondly, the dictionary uses words to define words. The result is that words are defined differently in different dictionaries and that dictionary entries for a single word often include multiple meanings, some of which apply only to messages created during certain periods of history or in certain places.

Moreover, denotative meaning may vary depending on the context in which the word is used. For example, the dictionary definition of the word *gay* includes both "displaying a merry, lively mood" and "homosexual." However, **context,** the position of a word in a sentence and the other words around it, assists receivers of the message to correctly interpret which denotation of the word is meant. In addition to the other words in the verbal message and its syntax and grammar, the social context in which words are spoken may also help us to understand the denotative meaning of certain words. Whether the comment "He's really gay" is understood to be a comment on someone's sexual orientation or on his merry mood may depend on the circumstances in which it is said.

Connotation The feelings or evaluations we associate with a word represent its **connotation,** and the connotative value of a word may be even more important than the denotative value to our understanding of its meaning.

C. K. Ogden and I. A. Richards (1923) were among the first scholars to consider the misunderstandings resulting from the failure of communicators to realize that their subjective reactions to words are based on their life experiences. For instance, when Melissa told Trisha, "My dog died yesterday," Trisha's understanding of the message would depend on the extent to which her feelings about pets and death—her connotations of the words—corresponded with Melissa's. Melissa, who regarded her dog as a dear and indispensable

TEST YOUR COMPETENCE

Connotation

Consider the connotation of each of the following words.

1. Classify each one as positive, negative, or neutral in its connotation.
2. Could any of the words have different connotations depending on the context in which they are used? Explain.
3. For each word write another word that has the same denotative value but an opposite connotative value.

gross	innocent	lean	flaccid
devout	clever	bold	arrogant
genius	cheap	carefree	shallow

friend, might have been trying to communicate a sense of profound grief at her loss, but Trish, who had never owned a pet and did not particularly care for dogs, might have missed the sense of Melissa's message.

Understanding denotation and connotation are important to becoming an effective verbal communicator because the only message that counts is the message that our receiver understands, regardless of whether it is the message that we intended to send.

Meaning Varies across Subgroups in the Language Community

Within a larger language community, subgroups with unique cultures sometimes form. These subgroups develop variations on the core language that enable them to share meanings unique to their experience. People from different groups approach the world from different perspectives, so they are likely to experience some difficulty sharing meaning when they talk with each other. As the Diverse Voices feature shows, such cultural variations combined with variations in connotation both within and across cultures can greatly complicate communication about even the simplest things.

DIVERSE VOICES

What's in a Name?

by Martin O'Malley

Martin O'Malley is a well-known Canadian author, columnist, and screenwriter who has served on the editorial board of The Globe and Mail. *In the following excerpt he comments on some of the complexities of language differences among cultures.*

Consider, for a start, the nomenclature. Is it *aboriginal Canadians* or *first peoples* or *natives* or *Indians* or *First Nations People* or *indigenous people*? They're all correct, with some mild fretting over politically correct hemlines, which at least has eliminated such clunkers as the English *redskins* and the French *sauvages*. We still call it the Department of Indian and Northern Affairs. Aboriginals find demeaning the use of possessives such as *Canada's aboriginals* and *Canada's natives*, though *native* is acceptable if used to modify *people* and *leaders* and *communities*.

Consider the languages. The largest aboriginal language group is Algonquian, spoken by some 100,000 people. The Algonquian language group actually contains nine aboriginal languages: Abenaki, Blackfoot, Delaware, Mi'kmaq, Maliseet, Montagnais-Naskapi, Ojibwa, Potawatomi, and Cree. The Crees are spread across Canada in various groupings, each with their own dialects: Plains, Swampy, Northern, Woods, Moose, and East.

On the matter of the Mi'kmaq, the word comes from *nikmaq*, which aboriginals gave to

(continued)

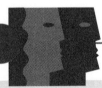

the French and Basque fishermen and explorers in the 17th century. Essentially it means *my kin-friends*. The Mi'kmaq, when referring to themselves, use the term *L'nu'k*, which means *the people* or *humans*. Mi'kmaq is pronounced *Mig-mow* (as in owl).

The complexity cries out for perspective, which I found one afternoon in May 1975 in Inuvik, where the Mackenzie River empties into the Beaufort Sea. I was talking to an Eskimo named Abe Okpik. Abe and I were both on assignment with the Mackenzie Valley Pipeline Inquiry, popularly known as the Berger Inquiry after the chairman, Mr. Justice Thomas Berger.

"Three times this morning I heard someone say Inuit," Okpik told me. Then, with exquisite timing over his mug of coffee, he added, "The anthropologists must be early this summer."

Okpik died early in 1998, by which time he had comfortably embraced the use of *Inuit* to describe *Eskimos*, a southern aboriginal expression for *eaters of raw meat*. And why not? *Inuit* means *the people*, as in "people everywhere." It is also plural; one Inuit is an Inuk. Abe told me an Inuk can denote two Inuit by somehow saying *Inuuk*.

Source: "What's in a Name?" by Martin O'Malley, from http://www.cbc.ca/news/indepth/firstnations/aboriginals.html, January 2002. Reprinted with permission of CBC News Online.

IN BRIEF

The Nature of Language

Language is the body of words and the systems for their use that are shared by members of a language community.

We use language to designate, label, define, and limit; to evaluate; to discuss things outside our immediate experience; and to talk about language.

The relationship between language and meaning is complicated by four factors:

1. Language is learned, and different people learn to use words in different ways.
2. Each utterance is a creative act.
3. Words have two types of meanings: denotative (their direct, explicit meaning) and connotative (the feelings or values associated with them).
4. The meanings of words vary across cultural subgroups in a language community.

In addition to subgroups based on race, religion, ethnic group, age, and sexual orientation, there are also subgroup cultures associated with generation, social class, disability, political position, education, occupation, arts, sport, leisure activity, and many other types of social division. The need for awareness and sensitivity in applying our communication skills is not restricted to situations in which we are communicating with someone who is not a native speaker of English or who is an immigrant or a member of a different ethnic culture. Rather, we should be aware that language differences can be important in every communication transaction. Developing our language skills so that the messages we send are clear and sensitive will increase our communication effectiveness in every situation.

Using Language More Clearly

Regardless of whether we are conversing, communicating in groups, giving speeches, or writing, we can communicate more clearly by reducing linguistic ambiguity and confusion. Compare these two descriptions of a close call:

1. Some nut almost got me with his car a while ago.
2. Yesterday evening, a grey-haired man in a banged-up blue Honda Civic ran a red light at King and Clifton and came within 10 centimetres of hitting me while I was crossing Clifton on the Walk signal.

The differences are in clarity. In the second version, the speaker used language that was specific, concrete, and precise.

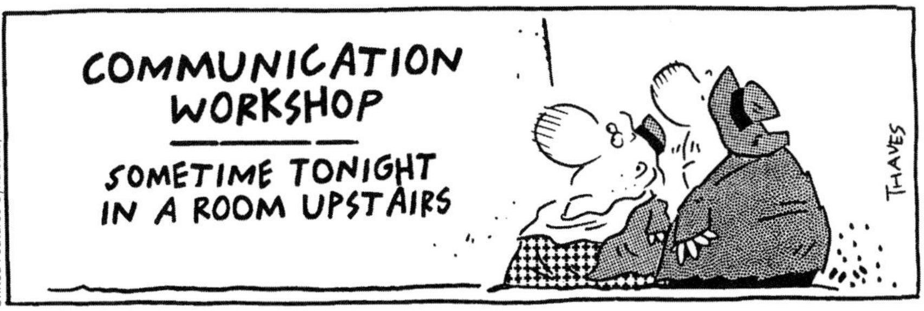

Specificity, Concreteness, and Precision in Language Use

Specific words clarify meaning by narrowing what is being referred to from a general category to a particular item or group within that category. Thus saying *a Honda Civic* is more specific than saying *a car*. **Concrete words** are words that appeal to our senses. They cause us, in our mind, to see, hear, smell, taste, or touch what is being referred to. Thus, we can picture that *banged-up blue* Civic being driven by the *grey-haired* man. Abstract ideas, such as justice, equality, or fairness, can be made concrete through examples or metaphors. **Precise words** are those that express meaning accurately—they capture shades of difference exactly. It is more precise to say that the Civic "came within 10 centimetres of hitting me" than to say "some nut almost got me."

Often, as we try to express our thoughts, the first words that come to mind are general, abstract, and imprecise. The ambiguity of these words forces the receiver of the message to choose from many possible meanings, and the more choices receivers have, the more likely they are to decode meanings different from the ones that we intend. In order to ensure that our verbal messages will be accurately decoded, we want to leave the receiver as few choices as possible. The most effective messages force the receiver to see the single focused image that we have in mind.

For instance, if Nevah says, "Ruben is a blue-collar worker," we might imagine him in one of any number of occupations that fall within this very broad category (e.g., a house painter, a well driller, a truck driver, a janitor). If, instead, she is more specific and says, "Ruben is a construction worker," the number of possible interpretations is reduced. Now, we must select our image from the much smaller subcategory of construction trades, and our meaning is likely to be closer to the one she intended. If she is even more specific and says, "Ruben is a carpenter," we can picture Ruben at work and have a clear understanding of his occupation.

In the preceding example, the continuum of specificity goes from blue-collar worker to construction worker to carpenter. Figure 3.1 provides other examples of this continuum.

As we move from general to specific, we often also move from abstract to concrete because abstract words tend also to be general. Consider the word *speak*. This term is general (it could refer to many ways of voicing words) and

COMMUNICATE! Using Technology

The words you choose to express your ideas can make a great deal of difference in whether people will understand or be influenced by what you say. You can use your word-processing software to help you select the best words. Nearly every word-processing package has a thesaurus (a list of synonyms). For instance, in the Microsoft Word package, you can highlight a specific word, click on Tools, drag down to Thesaurus, and be presented with synonyms for that word. For practice, select any word that you would like to improve upon and look at the synonyms available. Then select the choice you believe would be most accurate and meaningful in your writing or speaking context. For instance, if you highlighted *difficult,* when you clicked on the thesaurus you would be shown *hard, laborious, arduous,* and *strenuous.* If you wanted more choices, you could then highlight one of these words to see additional synonyms. To obtain the precise meaning of each of the listed words, always look them up in a good collegiate dictionary. If you were trying to make the point that studying can be difficult, you might decide to use *arduous* (demanding great effort or labour) as the most precise word.

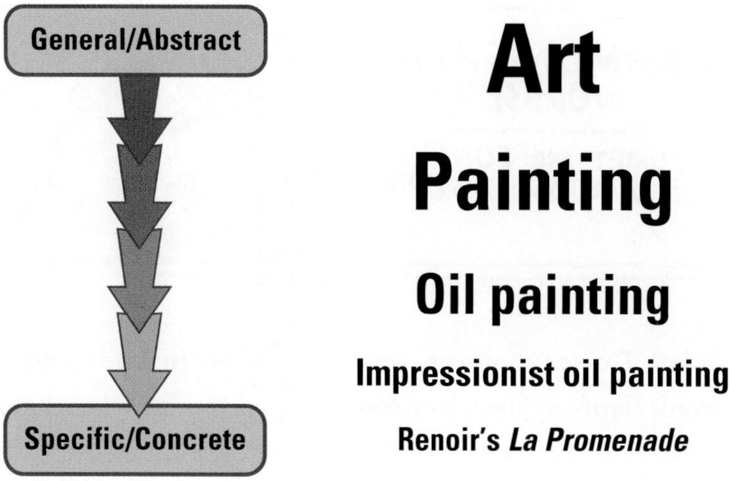

Figure 3.1
Levels of specificity

abstract (it does not appeal strongly to our senses). To be more concrete, we can use words such as *mumble, whisper, bluster, drone, jeer,* or *rant.* These words not only appeal much more directly to our senses (concreteness), but also refer to much more specific manners of speaking. Say these words aloud. Notice how the sound of your voice changes when you say *whisper* as opposed to *bluster, jeer,* or *rant.*

Finally, we seek words that are precise—those that most accurately or correctly capture the sense of what we are saying. In seeking the most precise word to describe Phillip's speech, Sandra might say, "Phillip ranted for an hour about his victory in the election. Well, to be more precise, he blustered." Notice that Sandra is not moving from general to specific; both words are on roughly the same level of abstraction. Nor does she change to a word that is more concrete; both words are concrete. Rather, she is modifying her statement to make her meaning more precise. *Rant* means talking in a way that is noisy or bombastic; *bluster* means talking in a way that is loudly boastful. So, we are considering shades of meaning: depending on how Phillip was talking, either *blustering* or *ranting* would be the more precise word. Consider another example: "Susan laughed at my story, or rather, she chuckled." What is the difference between laughing and chuckling? A laugh is a loud show of mirth; a chuckle is a more gentle sound expressing suppressed mirth. Similar? Yes. But different—showing shades of meaning.

Although the use of specific, concrete, and precise words enables us to reduce ambiguity and sharpen meaning, clarity is sometimes best achieved by adding a detail or an example. For instance, Linda says, "Rashad is a very loyal friend." The meaning of *loyal,* faithful to an idea, person, or group, is abstract, so to avoid ambiguity and confusion, Linda might add, "He never criticizes a friend behind her back." By following her use of the abstract word *loyal* with a concrete example, Linda makes it easier for her listeners to comprehend more clearly the aspect of Rashad's character that she is praising.

OBSERVE & ANALYZE
Journal Activity

Synonyms

One good way to increase specificity, concreteness, and precision is to play Synonyms. Think of a word that you could use to express an idea, and then list words that mean about the same thing. For example, synonyms for the word *happy* are *glad, joyful,* and *pleased.* When you have completed your list, refer to a thesaurus to find additional words. Then, write out what you think is the meaning of each word, focusing on the shades of difference in meaning among them. When you have finished, look up each word in the dictionary, even when you think you are sure of the meaning. The goal of this exercise is to select the most specific, concrete, and precise word to express your idea.

Developing the Ability to Speak More Clearly

Being able to speak clearly requires us to build our working vocabulary and to brainstorm to generate word choices from our active vocabulary.

Vocabulary building As a speaker, the larger your vocabulary, the more choices you have from which to select the word you want. As a listener, the larger your vocabulary, the more likely you are to understand the words used by others. It is important to understand that the goal in increasing your vocabulary is not to be able to impress others by using a great many big or unfamiliar words. Rather, it is to be able to communicate more accurately; a person who commands a large vocabulary is better able to select the best word, the one that most exactly expresses the idea he or she wishes to share.

One way to increase our vocabulary is to study one of the many vocabulary-building books available in almost any bookstore. We can also study magazine features such as "Word Power" in *Reader's Digest*. By completing this monthly quiz and learning the words with which we are unfamiliar, we can increase our vocabulary by as many as 20 words per month.

By far the best way to enlarge a vocabulary, however, is to read books and articles by capable writers and to listen carefully to the speech of articulate speakers, whether we encounter them in person or through the media. We should make note of words that we read or hear that we do not understand, and look them up in a good collegiate dictionary. For instance, suppose Chelsea was watching the CBC news one evening and heard Peter Mansbridge say that "the Prime Minister's office had been inundated with calls and messages" from citizens displeased about a proposed tax increase. If she was unfamiliar with the word *inundated,* she could jot it down and, later, look it up in a dictionary. She would find that *inundated* means overwhelmed or flooded. If she then thought to herself, "the prime minister was inundated—overwhelmed or flooded—with calls and messages today," she would be likely to remember that meaning and apply it the next time she heard the word. By following this practice, a person can quickly enlarge his or her vocabulary.

Mental brainstorming Having a larger vocabulary will not improve our ability to speak or write if we do not have a procedure for using it. One way to practise accessing choices from an increased vocabulary is to brainstorm during practice sessions and later in writing and speaking. **Brainstorming** is an uncritical, non-evaluative process of generating alternatives. Suppose someone asks Todd for his opinion of the university's registration procedures. He might initially say, "Registration was awful." If he does not think that *awful* is the most exact word to express his opinion, he might be able to quickly brainstorm the other words that express his feelings about the process (frustrating, tedious, demeaning, cumbersome, annoying). Then he could add, "What I really mean to say is that I found the whole process cumbersome."

TEST YOUR COMPETENCE

Brainstorming

Set up a tape recorder and talk about a course you are taking, a game you have played or watched, or a movie you saw. When you come to a key word or phrase as you talk, assess whether that word or phrase is specific, concrete, or precise enough for your message to be correctly understood. If you think not, pause momentarily to brainstorm alternative word choices, and then use the more specific, concrete, or precise word.

Clearly wording verbal messages is hard work, but as we build our vocabulary and learn to mentally brainstorm, we will find that we are able to make such adjustments when we need to, even in the middle of sentences. For instance, in describing Mike's behaviour, Florence might say, "Mike was just a jerk yesterday—well, I guess I mean he was extremely inconsiderate." Or when David is analyzing Pauline's talents he might say, "I agree that Pauline is a tough manager, but I think she's a good one because she is fair—she treats everyone exactly alike."

When we are relaxed and confident, our words flow smoothly and we are most likely to be effective at choosing the best words. When we are under pressure, however, our ability to select the best symbols to convey our thoughts is likely to deteriorate. People sometimes think one thing and say something entirely different. For example, a math teacher might say, "We all remember that the numerator is on the bottom and the denominator is on the top of the fraction, so when we divide fractions. . . ." "Ms. Green," a voice from the third row interrupts, "You said the numerator is on the bottom and. . . ." "Is that what I said?" the teacher replies. "Well, you know what I meant!" Did everyone

SKILL BUILDERS **Clarity—Specific, Concrete, Precise Words**

Skill	Use	Procedure	Example
Clarify meaning by narrowing what is understood from a general category to a particular group within that category, by appealing to the senses, or by choosing words that symbolize exact thoughts and feelings.	To help the listener arrive at meanings analogous to the speaker's intended meaning.	1. Assess whether the word or phrase used is less specific, concrete, or precise than it should be. 2. Pause to mentally brainstorm alternatives. 3. Select a more specific, concrete, or precise word.	Instead of saying, "Bring the stuff for the audit," say, "Bring last year's records and receipts for the audit." Or, instead of saying "I was really cold," say "I suffered frostbite on my fingers and toes."

TEST YOUR COMPETENCE

Specific, Concrete, and Precise

1. For each word listed, find three words or phrases that are more specific or more concrete.

tools	building	nice	education
clothes	colours	chair	bad
happy	stuff	things	car

2. Make the following statements clearer by editing words that are not specific, concrete, or precise:
   a. "You know I love snowboarding. Well, I'm practising a lot because I want to get better."
   b. "Paula, I'm really down. Everything is going down the tubes. You know what I mean?"
   c. "Well, she just does these things to tick me off. Like, just a whole lot of stuff—and she knows it!"
   d. "I just bought a beautiful outfit—I mean, it is really cool. You'll love it."
   e. "I've really got to remember to bring my things the next time I visit."

in the class know? Probably not. We will know that we have really made strides in improving the specificity, precision, and concreteness of our words when we find that we can form clear messages even under pressure.

Dating Information

Because many things change with time, it is important that we **date** much of the information we communicate to indicate when it was true. Not dating information can lead to serious and damaging inaccuracies. For instance, Parker says, "I'm being transferred to Scarborough." Laura replies, "Good luck. I hear they've had some real trouble with their schools." On the basis of Laura's statement, Parker may worry about the effect his transfer will have on his children. What he does not know is that Laura's information about this problem in Scarborough is five years old. Scarborough may still be experiencing problems with its schools, but the problems may have been long since corrected. Had Laura replied, "Five years ago, I heard they were having some real trouble with their schools. I'm not sure what the situation is now, but you may want to check," Parker would look at the information differently.

Let's consider two additional examples:

Undated: "Professor Bakshi is a really enthusiastic lecturer."

Dated: "Professor Bakshi is a really enthusiastic lecturer—at least he was *last term in Communication Theory*."

Undated: "You think Mary's depressed? I'm surprised. She seemed her regular high-spirited self when I talked to her."

Dated: "You think Mary's depressed? I'm surprised. She seemed her regular high-spirited self when I talked to her *the day before yesterday*."

To date information, (1) consider or find out when the information was true and (2) verbally label the information to indicate when it was true. We have no power to prevent change, but we can increase the accuracy of our messages by verbally acknowledging the reality of change.

Indexing Generalizations

Generalizing, drawing a conclusion after considering a range of particulars, enables people to apply what they have learned from one experience to another experience. For instance, during her summer job on a vegetable farm, Glenda learns that vegetables grow much better if the soil is properly fertilized before they are planted. She generalizes that fertilizing will help all plants grow better, and she is able to apply that knowledge when she is potting houseplants in her apartment when she returns to school in the fall.

Indexing generalizations is the mental and verbal practice of acknowledging that individual cases can represent exceptions to a general truth. For instance, Bageshwari may have a generalized concept of *men,* but she must recognize that although Fred, Darnell, and William share many characteristics that are common to all men, they are likely to have individual differences. So, how do we index generalizations in ordinary speech? Let's consider two examples:

Generalization: "Men are stronger than women, so Max is stronger than Barbara."	**Indexed Statement:** "Men are generally stronger than women, so *Max is probably stronger* than Barbara."
Generalization: "Your Mazda should go 50,000 km before you need a brake job; Jerry's did."	**Indexed Statement:** "Your Mazda may well go 50,000 km before you need a brake job; Jerry's did, *but of course, not all brakes wear at the same rate.*"

To index a generalization, (1) consider whether what you want to say is about a specific person, place, or thing or whether it is a generalization about a class to which the person, place, or thing belongs. (2) If what you want to say is a generalization about the class, qualify it appropriately so that your assertion does not go beyond the evidence that supports it. We all generalize occasionally, but by indexing generalizations we can avoid the problems that hasty and unsupported generalizations can create.

IN BRIEF

Using Language More Clearly

We are using language clearly when we leave the receiver of our message as few choices as possible about our intended meaning. Five ways to improve the clarity of our language use are

1. To choose words that are specific (particular in meaning), concrete (appealing to the senses), and precise (accurate, capturing shades of meaning).
2. To practise vocabulary building.
3. To mentally brainstorm to find the word which best expresses our meaning.
4. To date information to indicate when it was true.
5. To index generalizations to acknowledge that individual cases can differ from general trends.

Culture, Gender, and Language

Beyond striving for clarity in selecting the words we use and striving to assign appropriate denotative and connotative meanings to the language used by others, we can enhance our ability to communicate verbally by recognizing that different people use language differently.

Cultural Differences in Verbal Communication

Cultures vary in terms of how much meaning is carried by the words of the language itself and how much is interpreted from the context in which the communication occurs.

In **low-context cultures**, such as Northern Europe, Canada, and the United States, meaning (1) is embedded mainly in the messages transmitted, and (2) is presented directly. In other words, in low-context cultures people say what they mean and get right to the point (Gudykunst & Matsumoto, 1996, pp. 29–30), so "Yes" means "Affirmative, I agree to or agree with what you have said."

In **high-context cultures,** such as Asian or Middle Eastern countries, much of the meaning is interpreted based on the physical, social, and relational context of a communication transaction. People from high-context cultures expect others to use context cues to interpret meaning. As a result, they may present meanings indirectly. In a high-context culture, "Yes" may mean "Affirmative, I agree to or agree with what you have said," or it may mean "In this setting it would embarrass you if I said 'No,' so I will say 'Yes' to be polite, but I really don't agree, and you should know this, so in the future don't expect me to act as if I have just agreed with what you said." People from high-context cultures expect others to understand unarticulated feelings and subtle nonverbal gestures that people from low-context cultures do not even process. As a result, misunderstandings often occur when people from the two types of cultures communicate with one another.

Canada has a low-context national culture, but as we observed earlier, Canada is a multicultural country, so individual Canadians differ in terms of whether they are high- or low-context in their approach to language use.

© Superstock

Cultural traditions influence how we learn and interpret language.

Knowing the characteristics of a person's culture of origin may be useful when we are communicating with some Canadians, but we also need to be aware that people, especially those who have been in Canada for a long time, may or may not behave as their ethnic culture would dictate (Adamopoulos, 1999, p. 75). Then why mention these differences at all? Because they can give us a clue as to how and why people of different cultures behave differently. An essential aspect of communication is being sensitive to needs and differences among us, so we must be aware of what the nature of those differences might be.

Gender Differences in Verbal Communication

Over the last two decades, stirred by popular books such as *Men Are from Mars, Women Are from Venus,* people have come to believe that gender differences in verbal communication are genetic. However, research strongly indicates that gender differences in linguistic behaviour are learned rather than biological and that the differences are not nearly as great as some popular writers have suggested (Wood & Dindia, 1998, pp. 34–36).

A number of specific differences between women's and men's message construction patterns have been identified. There is no evidence to suggest that these differences cause problems for either women or men (Canary & Hause, 1993, p. 141); nevertheless, scholars have been intrigued to understand what has caused them. Mulac (1998) notes two such differences (pp. 133–134):

1. **Women tend to use more intensifiers and more hedges than men.** Intensifiers are words that modify other words and strengthen the idea represented by the word being modified. (Words like *very, extremely,* and *quite* are intensifiers.) Hedges are modifying words that soften or weaken the idea represented by the word being modified. (Words like *somewhat, perhaps,* and *maybe* are hedges.) Studies of the speech practices of men and women show that women are more likely to use such words, as shown in the following examples:

   "The ceremony was *quite* lovely." (Intensifier)

   "This contract is *so* important." (Intensifier)

   "The presentation was *somewhat* interesting." (Hedge)

   "It will *perhaps* be better if we do not attend." (Hedge)

2. **Women ask questions more frequently than men.** Women are much more likely to ask questions such as "Do you think so?" and "Are you sure?" In general, women tend to use questions to gain more information, to seek elaboration, and to determine how others feel about information being discussed.

Are these differences really significant? According to Mulac's research, the language used by women and men is "remarkably similar"—so similar, in fact, that native speakers of English cannot distinguish examples produced by

IN BRIEF

Culture, Gender, and Language

Significant differences distinguish the language use of people from high-context and low-context cultures:

- in low-context cultures, speakers express their meaning directly and mostly in words
- in high-context cultures, meaning is derived from the physical, social, and relational context.

Gender has a less significant impact on language use, but two differences have been observed:

- women use more hedges and intensifiers
- women ask questions more frequently.

women from those produced by men (p. 130). However, though the differences are small, Mulac says, they have consequences: "Observers perceive the female and male speakers differently based on their language use" (p. 147). Female speakers are rated higher on *socio-intellectual status* and *aesthetic quality.* Thus, people perceive women as having high social status, being literate, and being pleasant as a result of perceived language differences. Men rated higher on *dynamism.* That is, people perceive men to be stronger and more aggressive as a result of their language differences. These judgments tend to be the same whether observers are male or female, middle-aged or young (p. 148).

Julia Wood (1997) attributes men's and women's differences in language use to the basic psychological orientation each sex acquires in growing up. Women establish gender identity by seeing themselves as *like* or *connected to* mother. They learn to use communication as a primary way of establishing and maintaining relationships with others (p. 167). Men establish their gender identity by understanding how they are *different* or *separate from* mother. Therefore, they use language as a way to "exert control, preserve independence, and enhance status" (p. 173).

Spotlight on Scholars

Kimberly A. Noels, University of Alberta

Kimberly A. Noels' research concerns the social psychology of language and communication processes with a focus on intergroup and intercultural communication.

Her publications include articles on motivation for language learning, the association between language and ethnic identity, and intergenerational communication from a cross-cultural perspective. Because of her long-time interest in languages, she studied linguistics and psychology at the bilingual University of Ottawa. After her third year, she spent a year in Switzerland, where she learned German.

When she returned to Canada to complete her degree, Noels was fortunate to conduct her Honours thesis research under the supervision of Dr. Richard Clément, an expert in the social psychology of intergroup communication, an area of research that was very relevant to her experience of living in a foreign country. In her Honours thesis she examined the reasons why both people of German ancestry and those without German ancestry learned German and how these reasons affected the amount of effort they put into their language studies. Like much of her research, this project was based on the premise that the social context, particularly the group to which one belongs, can profoundly affect language behaviour.

Through her graduate work, Noels sought to understand how situational variations in identity were related to people's comfort in using a second language. In this research, she found support for

(continued)

the idea that contact with other language groups is linked to competence in the language of that group, which in turn influences feelings of ethnic identity. Dr. Noels' current research explores the language–identity link in other language contexts, including first- and second-generation immigrant groups, native–non-native groups in Canada, and Anglo–Latino relations in the United States.

Throughout her graduate studies, Noels continued to be interested in language learning motivation, the topic of her Honours thesis. In her first year of graduate school, she took a course in social motivation where she learned about Deci and Ryan's (1985) self-determination theory, which maintained that learners sustain intrinsic motivation when teachers and other people communicate with them in a manner that supports their sense of autonomy, perceived competence, and feelings of relatedness with relevant others. As a term project for this course, she developed an instrument to assess intrinsic and extrinsic motivation for language learning. Eventually she developed a model of language learning motivation that incorporated aspects of Deci and Ryan's model, and demonstrated how this model could complement other models in the field to explain language learning outcomes. Her current research in this area addresses how contextual factors influence motivational processes. In particular, she is looking at East Asian, Canadian, and European language learners to better understand how cultural values of individualism and collectivism modify the link between autonomy, competence, and relatedness on the one hand, and intrinsic motivation on the other hand.

Noels' interest in intergroup communication took a twist when she went to the Department of Communication at the University of California, Santa Barbara. Under the supervision of Howard Giles, she collaborated on a program of research concerning intergenerational communication. She was part of a 14-nation cross-cultural study of younger and older adults' perceptions of intra- and intergenerational communication. The results indicated that both younger and older adults reported difficulties communicating with members of the other age group, and, curiously, that older adults at times felt that communication with other older adults was problematic. Although it was hypothesized that intergenerational communication would be more positive in Asian nations where there are stronger values of filial piety and respect for elders, the research showed, somewhat surprisingly, that intergenerational communication was viewed much more negatively in some Asian nations than in Western nations. These communication difficulties paralleled negative stereotypes about others, suggesting that negative beliefs about certain groups can contribute to poor communication with members of those groups. Although this research focused on a very different type of group (i.e., age groups instead of language groups), it nonetheless addressed the theme that the intergroup context has important implications for language behaviour.

To learn more about Kimberly Noels' research on the effects of the social context on verbal communication in intergroup settings, you can log on to her homepage at **http://web.psych.ualberta.ca/~knoels/Personal/noels_personal_temp.html.** WWW

Speaking Appropriately

During the last few years, Canadian social leaders have had frequent discussions and disagreements about so-called political correctness. Colleges and universities have been at the forefront of this debate. Although the issues involved in the debate go beyond the scope of this chapter, at the heart of the political correctness controversy is the question of which language behaviours are appropriate and which are inappropriate.

Speaking appropriately means choosing language and nonverbal symbols that are adapted to the needs, interests, knowledge, and attitudes of listeners and avoiding language and nonverbal symbols that would alienate listeners. Through using appropriate language, we communicate our respect and acceptance of those who are different from us. In this section, we discuss specific strategies that are helpful in crafting appropriate verbal messages.

Formality of Language

Language should be appropriately formal for a situation. In interpersonal settings, for example, we are likely to use more informal language when we are talking with our best friends and more formal language when we are talking with our parents. In a group setting, we are likely to use more informal language when the group is made up of our peers and more formal language when the group includes our professors or our work supervisors. In most public-speaking situations, we are likely to use more formal language than in either interpersonal or group settings, but again, the greater the social distance between the speaker and the audience, the more formal the language is likely to be.

One type of formality in language is in the manner in which we address others. In formal settings, we address others by their titles followed by their surnames unless they invite us to do something else. In business settings or at formal parties, it is therefore appropriate to call people Mr. X, Ms. B, Rabbi Z, Dr. S., or Professor P. In addition, we generally view it as appropriate, in all situations, to refer to those older than ourselves, those of higher status, and those whom we respect by title and surname unless otherwise directed.

Jargon and Slang

Appropriate language should be chosen so that **jargon** (specialized technical terminology) and **slang** (informal, nonstandard vocabulary) do not interfere with understanding. We form language communities as a result of the work we do, our hobbies, and the other groups to which we belong, but we can forget that people who are not from our group may not understand language that is a routine part of our daily communication. For instance, when Jenny, who is sophisticated in the use of cyberlanguage, starts talking with her computer-illiterate friend Sarah about "Social MUDs based on fictional universes," Sarah is likely

to be totally lost. If, however, Jenny recognizes Sarah's lack of knowledge about computers, she can make her language appropriate by discussing the concepts in words that her friend will understand. In short, when talking with people outside our language community, we need to carefully explain, if not abandon, the technical jargon or slang associated with that community.

THINKING ABOUT . . .

Profanity and Vulgarity

How much do you use profanity and vulgarity? Has your usage increased, decreased, or remained the same since you started college? Does your use of profanity and vulgarity change depending on whom you are speaking with? If so, list the rules that seem to guide your behaviour. Overall, how comfortable are you with how frequently you use profanity and vulgarity in your verbal messages?

Profanity and Vulgarity

Appropriate language frequently does not include **profanity** (language indicating irreverence for persons or things which may be considered sacred) or **vulgarity** (crude or indecent language). At one time in Canadian society, uttering *hell* or *damn* would have resulted in severe punishment for children and social isolation for adults. Today, many people tolerate these and much stronger expressions, and in some groups the use of profane and vulgar language is commonplace. However, it is important to recognize that in many situations, especially formal situations, such language is likely to cause offence, and its use is likely to be sanctioned. In public speaking, this type of expression is especially unwelcome, but even in informal personal conversations speakers who swear risk offending their listeners.

Why do people use coarse language? DeKlerk (1991, p. 165) suggests that swearing is one way of asserting independence by breaking adult taboos. In a society that prizes adulthood and independence, the trend toward the use of vulgar and profane language at younger and younger ages is not surprising. Today, we commonly hear young schoolchildren utter strings of four-letter words.

Being profane and vulgar are habits that are easy to acquire but hard to break. In fact, an alarming number of people use such language just as filler, which adds little or no meaning to the content of the message. Thus, for some, the ubiquitous *f—k* has come to serve the same purpose as *like* and *you know*.

What does the use of profanity and vulgarity communicate? When used infrequently, profane and vulgar expressions can communicate strong emotion. In this usage, the profanity or vulgarity is meant to shock and to communicate the speaker's deep disgust, contempt, or other strong emotion. When profanity and vulgarity are used more frequently, listeners often assume that the person using such language intends to threaten or intimidate. Unfortunately, for far too many people, profanity and vulgarity have lost all meaning and have become nothing more than symbols indicating that the speaker is unable to express his or her thoughts or feelings at any but the basest and most ignorant level. Competent communicators avoid using profanity and vulgarity because their use is more likely to damage than to strengthen relationships.

Sensitivity

Language is **insensitive** if it includes usages that others perceive as offensive because they suggest bias against members of an identifiable group. Some of the linguistic mistakes that we make result from using expressions that are perceived to be sexist, racist, or otherwise biased—that is, any language that is perceived as belittling any person or group of people because of their race, ethnic background, sex, sexual orientation, age, disability, religion, or other identifying characteristic. Two of the most prevalent types of insensitive language are generic language and nonparallel language.

Generic language **Generic language** uses words that apply only to some members of a group as though they represented all. Such language use is a problem because it linguistically excludes part of the group of people who are ostensibly being discussed. Let's consider some examples.

Traditionally, the rules of English grammar called for the use of the masculine personal pronouns *he, him,* and *his* to stand for persons when the gender of the persons was not specified, so sentences such as this one were common:

When a person shops, *he* should have a clear idea of what *he* wants to buy.

Even though such statements are grammatically correct, they are now considered sexist because they inherently exclude women and girls from the class *persons*. Despite traditional usage, it would be hard to maintain that we picture people of both sexes when we hear the word *he*.

One way to avoid this problem is to recast the problem sentence using plurals. This sentence suggests that all doctors are men:

Because a doctor has high status, *his* views may be given more weight.

To avoid appearing sexist, we could express the same idea this way, with plurals:

Because doctors have high status, their views may be given more weight.

Alternatively, we can use both male and female pronouns:

Because a doctor has high status, his or her views may be given more weight.

These changes seem small, but they may mean the difference between alienating and not alienating the people with whom we are speaking. Stewart, Cooper, Stewart, and Friedley (1998) cite research to show that using *he and she,* and to a lesser extent *they,* causes listeners to include women in their mental images, thus increasing gender balance in their perceptions (p. 63).

A second problem results from the traditional reliance on the use of the generic *man*. Many inherently sexist words, words that apply to only one gender, are in common use in our language. Consider the term *manmade*. What this word really means is that a product was produced by human beings, but its connotation is that a male human being made the item. Some people argue that a word that has *man* within it does not necessarily affect people's understanding of meaning, but research has demonstrated that people usually visualize men (not women) when they read or hear these words. Moreover, when job titles end in *man,* their occupants are assumed to have stereotypically masculine personality traits (Gmelch, 1998, p. 51).

COMMUNICATE! Using InfoTrac College Edition

Although it is easy to spot sexist language when someone uses a negative slang term to describe a person of the opposite sex, there are other ways language can be sexist.

Using the InfoTrac College Edition subject guide, enter the search term *sexism in language.* Click on *periodical references.* See "Gender Issues in Advertising Language," Nancy Artz, Jeanne Munger, and Warren Purdy (1999). Focus on one of the issues discussed in the article. What is the significance of the examples presented? Why should people be concerned about this issue?

TEST YOUR COMPETENCE

Sexist Language

Develop nonsexist alternatives for these words:

firemen	foreman	serviceman	brakeman
airman	stewardess	craftsman	repairman
councilman	doorman	night watchman	co-ed
waitress	bellman	actress	freshman

When considering words such as *policeman*, *postman*, and *chairman*, we can substitute *police officer*, *letter carrier*, and *chairperson*. When considering words such as *mankind* and *manmade*, we can substitute *humankind* and *handmade*, *machine-made*, or *artificial*.

Nonparallel language **Nonparallel language** occurs when terms are changed because of the race, sex, or another characteristic of the person being referred to. Because it treats groups of people differently, nonparallel language is belittling. Two common forms of nonparallel language are marking and unnecessary association.

Marking is the practice of unnecessarily adding indicators of race, sex, age, or another characteristic to a general word. For instance, terms such as *female doctor* or *black lawyer* are marked for gender and race, respectively. Marking is offensive to many people because the speaker or writer appears to be trivializing the person's role by emphasizing an irrelevant characteristic. For instance, this usage seems to imply that Jones is a good enough doctor for a woman or that Smith is a good enough lawyer for a black person. Because we would be very unlikely ever to say or write "Jones is a good male doctor" and "Smith is a good white lawyer," we should leave sex, race, age, and other markers out of labelling altogether.

Another form of nonparallel language is to emphasize one person's association with another when we are not talking about the other person. Very often we hear or read something like this: "Gladys Thompson, whose husband is CEO of Acme Inc., is the chairperson of this year's United Way campaign." The **unnecessary association** of Ms. Thompson with her husband and his position implies that she is important not because of her own accomplishments but because of his. If a person has done or said something noteworthy, we should recognize it without making unnecessary associations.

Causes and Effects of Insensitive Language

We have all heard children chant, "Sticks and stones will break my bones, but names will never hurt me." This nursery rhyme may be popular among children because it gives them a defence against the cruelty of name-calling, but they know it is a lie. Whether we admit it or not, words do hurt, and sometimes they cause permanent harm. Insensitive language is often a sign of prejudice that results in efforts to discriminate. As a result, it can be considered unethical as well. Think of the great personal damage done to people throughout history as a result of being called *hick, nigger, frog, fag,* or *yid*. Think of the fights started by one person calling another's sister or girlfriend a *whore*. Of course, we all know that it is not the words alone that are so powerful; it is the context of the words—the situation, the feelings of the participants, the time, the place, or the tone of voice. You may recall circumstances in which a friend called you a name or used a four-letter word to describe you and you did not even flinch; you may also recall other circumstances in which someone else made you furious by calling you something far less offensive.

Where does racist language come from? According to Molefi Asante (1998), an internationally known scholar, racist language has its roots in our personal beliefs and attitudes. To a great extent, these have been conditioned by the knowledge system to which we have been exposed. Until recently, this knowledge system has had a Eurocentric bias (pp. 95–96). Thus, contributions to the development of humankind by cultures other than European ones have been ignored or minimized.

We should always be aware that our language choices have repercussions. When we do not understand or are not sensitive to our listeners' frame of reference, we may state our ideas in language that distorts the intended communication. Many times, a single inappropriate word, phrase, or sentence has been enough to ruin an entire interaction. For instance, if you say, "And we all know the problem originates downtown," you may be alluding to the city government. However, if your listeners associate "downtown" not with the seat of government but with the residential area of an ethnic or social group, the sentence will have an entirely different meaning to them. Being specific will help you avoid such problems; recognizing that some words communicate far more than their dictionary meanings will help even more.

Avoiding Inappropriate Language

Very few people can escape all unfair language. However, by monitoring our usage, we can guard against frustrating our attempts to communicate by assuming incorrectly that others will react to our language the same way we do, and we can guard against saying or doing things that offend others and perpetuate outdated stereotypes.

How can we speak more appropriately? (1) Assess whether the word or phrase that we are thinking of using (or have used without thinking) is inappropriate; (2) pause to mentally brainstorm alternatives; and (3) select a more appropriate word.

OBSERVE & ANALYZE
Journal Activity

Monitoring Your Use of Language

Tape-record at least 10 minutes of your conversation with a friend or a family member. Talk about a subject that you hold strong views about: for example, abortion, affirmative action, welfare, tuition fees, or political parties. Be sure to get permission from the other person before you tape. At first, you may feel self-conscious about having a recorder going, but as you get into the discussion, it is quite likely that you will be able to converse normally.

Play back the tape and take notes of sections where your language might have been clearer. Using these notes, write better expressions of your ideas for each section you noted by using more specific, concrete, and precise language and by dating and indexing generalizations.

Replay the tape. This time take notes on any racist, sexist, or other biased expressions that you used. Using these notes, replace such expressions with more appropriate ones.

Write a paragraph or two to describe what this experience has taught you about your use of language.

IN BRIEF

Speaking Appropriately

Appropriate language is language that is adapted to the needs, interests, knowledge, and attitudes of the listener. To speak appropriately,

- consider the degree of formality required by the situation in which you are speaking.
- consider whether the listener is familiar with jargon or slang relative to your subject.
- avoid profane and vulgar language in most contexts.
- avoid language that belittles others because of their sex, race, age, disability, sexual orientation, or other identifying characteristic.

Summary

Language is a system of symbols used for communicating. Through language, we designate, label, define, and limit; evaluate; talk about things outside our immediate experience; and talk about language itself.

An effective communicator recognizes that language symbols are arbitrary, that language is learned and is creative, and that language and perception are interrelated.

The denotation of a word is its dictionary meaning. Despite the ease with which we can check a dictionary meaning, word denotation can still present problems. Most words have more than one dictionary meaning because changes in meanings occur faster than dictionaries are revised, because words take on different meanings as they are used in different contexts, and because meanings can become obscured as words become more abstract.

The connotation of a word is its emotional or suggestive value. Regardless of how a dictionary defines a word, we carry with us meanings that stem from our experience with the word and with the object, thought, or action the word represents.

What Would You Do?
A Question of Ethics

One day after class, Heather, Terry, Paul, and Martha stopped at the student centre café. After they had talked about the class for a few minutes, the conversation shifted to students who were taking the class.

"By the way," Paul said, "do any of you know Porky?"

"Who?" the group responded in unison.

"The really fat guy who was sitting a couple of seats from me. We've been in a couple of classes together. He's a pretty nice guy."

"What's his name?" Heather asked.

"Carl, but he'll always be Porky to me."

"Do you call him that to his face?" Terry asked.

"Aw, I'd never say anything like that to him. Man, I wouldn't want to insult him."

"Well," Martha chimed in, "I'd sure hate to think that you'd call me 'Skinny' or 'The Bitch' when I wasn't around."

"Come on, what's with you guys," Paul retorted. "You're trying to tell me that you never talk that way about another person when they're not around?"

"Well," said Terry, "maybe a couple of times, but I've never talked like that about someone I really liked."

"Someone you liked?" queried Heather. "Why does that make a difference? Do you mean it's okay to trash talk someone so long as you don't like the person?"

1. Sort out the ethical issues in this case. How ethical is it to call a person you supposedly like by an unflattering name that you would never use if that person were present?
2. From an ethical standpoint, is whether you like a person or not what determines when such name calling is okay?

We can improve the clarity of our language by selecting the most specific, concrete, and precise word possible and by dating information and indexing generalizations.

Cultural differences in language use result from similarities and differences of behaviour between low-context and high-context cultures. Gender differences in language use are less significant than has previously been suggested, although women tend to use more intensifiers and hedges than men do, and women tend to add tag questions to sentences more than men do.

Speaking appropriately means using language that adapts to the needs, interests, knowledge, and attitudes of the listener and avoiding language that alienates. Inappropriate language can be minimized by avoiding such exclusionary usages as generic *he* and generic *man*, and by eliminating such nonparallel usages as marking and unnecessary association.

Glossary

Review the following key terms:

brainstorming (63) — an uncritical, non-evaluative process of generating alternatives.

concrete words (61) — words which appeal to our senses.

connotation (58) — the feelings or evaluations we associate with a word.

context (58) — the position of a word in a sentence and the other words around it.

dating information (65) — indicating when the information that you are presenting was true.

denotation (57) — the direct, explicit meaning that a language community formally gives to a word.

generalizing (66) — drawing a conclusion after considering a range of particulars.

generic language (73) — language in which words that apply only to one race, gender, or other group are used as though they represented all.

high-context culture (67) — cultures in which messages are presented indirectly, and people must infer meaning from the physical, social, and relational context in which the communication occurs.

indexing generalizations (66) — the mental and verbal practice of acknowledging that individual cases can represent exceptions to a general truth.

insensitive language (72) — language that includes usages that others perceive as offensive because they suggest bias against members of an identifiable group.

jargon (71) — technical terminology associated with a specific activity or group.

language (56) — the body of words and the systems for their use that are common to the members of a language community.

low-context culture (67) — cultures in which information is presented directly and is embedded mainly in the messages transmitted.

marking (74) — the practice of unnecessarily adding indicators of race, sex, age, or another characteristic to a general word.

nonparallel language (74) — language in which terms are changed because of the race, sex, or another characteristic of the person being referred to.

precise words (61) — words that express meaning accurately, capturing shades of difference exactly.

profanity (72) — language indicating irreverence for persons or things which may be considered sacred.

slang (71) — informal, nonstandard vocabulary.

speaking appropriately (71) — choosing language and nonverbal symbols that are adapted to the needs, interests, knowledge, and attitudes of listeners.

specific words (61) — words that clarify meaning by narrowing what is being referred to from a general category to a particular item or group within that category.

unnecessary association (74) — emphasizing one person's association with another when we are not talking about the other person.

verbal communication (56) — communication through the use of language.

vulgarity (72) — crude or indecent language.

Jeff McIntosh/CP Picture Archive

OBJECTIVES

After you have read this chapter, you should be able to answer these questions:

- What is nonverbal communication?
- What types of body motions have communication functions?
- What is paralanguage?
- What are the elements of paralanguage, and how does each affect message meaning?
- How do clothing, touching behaviour, and use of time affect self-presentation?
- How is communication affected by the use of physical space?
- How do temperature, lighting, and colour affect communication?
- What are three ways to improve the communication of nonverbal messages?

CHAPTER 4

Nonverbal Communication

Marsha MacDonald steps into Sean O'Reilly's office and says, "I'm not going to be able to meet with you today to talk about your report because I'm swamped with work."

In a speech to members of her local, union leader Stephanie Jansen says, "I want you to know that I am committed to serving the needs of the members of this union."

How acceptable is Ms. MacDonald's excuse? How much faith will Ms. Jansen's electors have in her commitment? In both cases, the answer will depend to some extent on how credible the words of the speaker are to the audience, but it will depend just as much on how the listeners interpret the speakers' vocal inflections, facial expressions, and gestures. The meaning of any communication is based on interpretations of both the verbal message and the nonverbal behaviour that accompanies and surrounds the verbal message.

In this chapter, we provide a framework for analyzing and improving nonverbal communication behaviour in all contexts. We begin by studying the nature of nonverbal behaviour and the way verbal and nonverbal communication messages interrelate. We then look at the major types of nonverbal communication: body motions, paralanguage, self-presentation, and management of the environment. In each case we then continue our discussion of that type of nonverbal behaviour by examining variations attributable to cultural or gender differences.

The Nature of Nonverbal Communication Behaviour

Nonverbal communication behaviours are those bodily actions and vocal qualities that typically accompany a verbal message, that are usually interpreted as intentional, and that have agreed-upon interpretations within a culture or speech community (Burgoon, 1994, p. 231). People place a great deal of confidence in nonverbal messages. In fact, when verbal and nonverbal cues conflict the nonverbal messages are more likely to be trusted.

© Sidney Harris

When we say that a nonverbal sign is interpreted as intentional, we mean that people act as if the sender intended it to carry meaning, even if the person making the sign is doing so unconsciously or unintentionally (p. 231). When Anita shouts, "I've had it!" as she slams a book down on the table, Sophie interprets the loudness of Anita's voice and the action of slamming the book down as intentionally emphasizing the meaning of her words.

When we refer to agreed-upon interpretations in a culture or speech community, we recognize that people of different cultures use many of the same nonverbal cues, but that they may use and interpret them differently. For instance, a smile is a universally used nonverbal sign, but what a certain type of smile means and when it is permissible or appropriate varies from one culture to another. Depending on the cultural context, a certain smile may, for example, indicate satisfaction with a positive experience, pleasure at personal contact, or an attempt to save face in an awkward situation.

In addition to bodily actions and vocal qualities that accompany verbal messages, nonverbal communication includes the messages sent by our use of time and physical space and our choices of artifacts (clothing, furniture, decorations, etc.), lighting, temperature, and colour.

Because much of what is considered appropriate nonverbal behaviour depends on culture, we begin by discussing each type of behaviour from a Canadian cultural perspective. Then we describe some of the most important ways nonverbal communication behaviour is interpreted differently in other cultures and communities.

Body Motions

Of all the approaches to nonverbal behaviour, the most familiar is probably **kinesics,** the study of body motions, including the use of eye contact, facial expression, gesture, and posture, as a means of communication.

Eye Contact

Eye contact, or **gaze,** refers to the degree to which and the manner in which we look at the people with whom we are communicating. Eye contact serves many functions in our communication. Its *presence* can show that we are paying attention to or that we have an interest in what the other person is saying. We also use the presence or absence of eye contact as a gauge of the other person's honesty, sincerity, and trustworthiness. *How* we look at a person can reveal a range of emotions such as affection, anger, or fear, and we increase the intensity of our eye contact to exercise dominance (Pearson, West, & Turner, 1995, p. 121). Almost everyone has some awareness of variations in eye contact; for instance, we describe people in love as looking "doe eyed," we comment on "looks that could kill," and we speak of someone "staring another person down."

Moreover, through eye contact we monitor the effect that our communication is having on others. By maintaining eye contact, we can tell when or whether people are paying attention to us, when people are in agreement with what we are saying, and whether what we are saying is eliciting feelings.

The amount of eye contact differs from person to person and from situation to situation. Although both parties to a conversation look at each other, studies show that the amount of eye contact is likely to vary depending on a person's role: talkers hold eye contact about 40 percent of the time and listeners nearly 70 percent of the time (Knapp & Hall, 1992, p. 298). We generally maintain better eye contact when we are discussing topics with which we are comfortable, when we are genuinely interested in a person's comments or reactions, or when we are trying to influence another person. Conversely, we tend to avoid eye contact when we are discussing topics that make us uncomfortable, when we lack interest in the topic or person, or when we are embarrassed, ashamed, or trying to hide something.

Because of its importance in public speaking, we will talk more about eye contact in Chapter 14, "Adaptation and Delivery."

Facial Expression

Facial expression is the manipulation of facial muscles to communicate emotional states or reactions to messages. Our facial expressions are especially important in conveying the six basic human emotions: happiness, sadness, surprise, fear, anger, and disgust. These basic facial expressions are recognized across cultures (Ekman & Friesen, 1975, pp. 137–138). Facial expressions can support, add to, or contradict a person's verbal message.

Gesture

Gestures are the movements of body parts, particularly the hands, arms, and fingers, to describe or to emphasize. For example, when a person says, "about this high" or "about this big around," we expect a gesture to accompany the verbal description. Likewise, when a person shouts, "Put that down!" or "Listen to me!" a pointing finger, a pounding fist, or some other gesture often reinforces the point.

People vary in the amount of gesturing that accompanies their speech and in the particular gestures that they use, but most people are well versed at interpreting many gestures that are standard to their culture. The success of many stand-up comedians, for example, depends on the audience's ability to correctly decode their gestures.

Posture

Posture is the position of the body or the orientation of the body parts. Particular postures or changes in posture can communicate. For instance, suddenly sitting upright and leaning forward shows increased attention, whereas standing up may signal, "I'm done now," and turning one's back to another can mean "I don't wish to talk to you anymore."

Christy Gavitt/Nonstock

Although the V for victory sign is recognized by people in most cultures, other gestures, such as the A-Okay sign shown here, have different meanings in different cultures.

How Body Motions Are Used

Body motions in general and gestures in particular help us considerably in conveying meaning (Ekman & Friesen, 1969, pp. 49–98):

1. **Body motions may be used to take the place of a word or phrase.** These motions are called **emblems.** We could make a considerable list of nonverbal symbols that take the place of exact words or phrases that we use frequently. For instance, thumbs up means *everything is a go;* first and second fingers held in a V shape means *peace* or *victory;* shaking the head from side to side means *no,* and up and down means *yes;* shrugging the shoulders means *maybe, I don't care,* or *I don't know.* Some emblems are universal in their meaning, but many are specific to particular cultures.

   In many contexts, emblems are used as a complete language. A **sign language** is a system of body motions used to communicate. Examples of sign languages include those used by the deaf, such as American Sign Language; a sign language used by Trappist monks, who take a vow of silence; and a sign language used by some Australian aboriginal women (Leathers, 1997, p. 70). More restricted sign languages are used in a number of contexts, such as in officiating sports, directing traffic, fighting fires, and buying and selling stock, where the aural channel is unavailable because of external noise.

2. **Body motions may be used to illustrate what a speaker is saying.** We use these gestures, called **illustrators,** to accompany verbal messages. We use illustrators in at least five ways:
   - To *emphasize* speech: Joe may pound the table as he exclaims, "I won't give up!"
   - To show the *path* or *direction* of thought: Professor Darris may move her hands along an imaginary continuum as she says, "The papers ranged from very strong to very weak."
   - To show *position:* A waiter may point as he asks, "Will this table be all right?"
   - To *describe:* In giving a presentation on modern lacrosse, Paul holds his hands about 6 cm apart and says, "The ball is about this big."
   - To *mimic:* Avril causes her hands to quiver as she asks, "Did you see how his hands shook?"
3. **Body motions can display feelings that have not been expressed verbally.** These emotional displays, called **affect displays,** are often unintentional but are likely to be quite noticeable. For instance, if Nicholas stubs his toe as he is getting out of bed in the morning, he is likely to grimace and hop about in pain. If he just failed a major exam or said goodbye to a close friend, his sadness is likely to show in his posture and facial expression (rounded shoulders, hanging head, down-turned mouth, etc). Occasionally, we are fooled by these displays when people purposely de-intensify or overreact to exaggerate their true feelings. For example, a baseball player may remain stone-faced when he is hit by a wild pitch and refuse to rub the spot where he has been struck, or a youngster may howl in feigned pain when her older sister bumps her by accident. Posture, gesture, facial expression, and eye contact may all play a role in affect displays.
4. **Body motions may be used to control or regulate the flow of a conversation or other communication transaction.** We use shifts in eye contact, slight head and hand movements, shifts in posture, raised eyebrows, and nodding head to tell a person when to continue, to repeat, to elaborate, to hurry up, or to finish, or to indicate that we want to have a turn, end a turn, or give up a turn at speaking. These cues are called **regulators.** Effective communicators learn to adjust what they are saying and how they are saying it on the basis of such cues.
5. **Body motions may be used to relieve tension.** As we observe public speakers, we notice that they may scratch their head, tap or shuffle their feet, wring their hands, toy with their hair, or indulge in any number of other seemingly random movements. These movements, called adaptors, help the speakers to feel better by easing their nervousness. **Adaptors** are unconscious movements that help people cope with a physical or emotional stress that they are experiencing. They are usually responses to emotional discomfort.

THINKING ABOUT . . .

Body Motions

Describe the five body motions you most frequently use when you speak. If you are unsure which motions you use, ask others to tell you. Are the motions emblems, illustrators, affect displays, regulators, or adaptors? Are they effective in helping you convey messages? Do they distract from your messages?

Cultural Variations

Several cultural differences in body motions are well documented.

Eye contact As we have said, in Western cultures, eye contact is viewed positively. A majority of Canadians expect those with whom they are communicating to "look them in the eye." However, not all cultures encourage the same sort of behaviour.

In some cultures, avoiding eye contact communicates respect and deference (Martin & Nakayama, 1997, p. 149). For instance, in Japan, people direct their gaze to a position about the Adam's apple and avoid direct eye contact. Chinese, Indonesians, and rural Mexicans lower their eyes as a sign of deference. To them, too much direct eye contact is a sign of bad manners.

Arabs, in contrast, look intently into the eyes of the person with whom they are talking. To them, direct eye contact demonstrates keen interest.

Differences in the use of eye contact have also been observed among groups that are part of larger cultures. For instance, research carried out in the United States has shown that African Americans use more continuous eye contact than whites when they are speaking but less than whites when they are listening (Samovar, Porter, & Stefani, 1998, p. 159).

Gestures, posture, and facial expression People of different cultures also show considerable differences in their use of gestures, posture, and facial expressions. Gestures in particular can assume completely different meanings. For instance, people who are content often communicate by forming a circle with the thumb and forefinger. In Canada, this emblem, the A-Okay sign, means that everything is going well. However the same sign means zero or worthless in France and is a vulgar gesture in Germany, Brazil, and Australia (Axtell, 1999, pp. 44, 143, 212). Displays of emotion also vary. For instance, in some Eastern cultures, people have been socialized to de-intensify affect displays, whereas members of other cultures have been socialized to amplify them. These cultural differences are often reflected in the interpretation that is given to facial expressions (Samovar, Porter, & Stefani, 1998, p. 157).

THINKING ABOUT . . .

Cultural Variations in Nonverbal Behaviour

What is your cultural heritage? What nonverbal behaviours are typically associated with that heritage? Which of these behaviours do you display most frequently? How might knowing the cultural heritage of the person with whom you are interacting help you understand what the other is trying to communicate?

Gender Variations

Men and women differ not only in their use of nonverbal communication behaviour (Canary & Hause, 1993, p. 141), but also in how they interpret the nonverbal communication behaviours of others. Major difficulties in male–female relationships are often created by inaccurately encoding and decoding nonverbal messages. A number of studies have shown that women are better than men at decoding nonverbal, vocal, and facial cues (Stewart, Cooper, Stewart, & Friedley, 1998, p. 74).

IN BRIEF

Body Motions

Kinesics is the study of communication through body movements: eye contact, facial expression, gesture, and posture. Body movements can be used to

1. replace a word or phrase (emblems).
2. illustrate what we are saying (illustrators).
3. display feelings (affect displays).
4. control or regulate the flow of a conversation or other communication transaction (regulators).
5. relieve tension (adaptors).

Research has revealed several significant cultural and gender variations in the use of body motions.

Eye contact In Western cultures, women tend to make more frequent eye contact during conversations than men do (Cegala & Sillars, 1989). Women tend to hold eye contact more than men do regardless of the sex of the person they are interacting with (Wood, 1997, p. 198).

Facial expression Women tend to smile more than men do, but their smiles are harder to interpret. Men's smiles generally mean positive feelings, whereas women's smiles tend to be responses to affiliation and friendliness (Hall, 1998, p. 169).

Gesture and posture Gender differences in the use of gestures and posture are profound. People have been found to attribute masculinity or femininity on the basis of one's manner of gesture alone (Pearson, West, & Turner, 1995, p. 126). For instance, women are more likely to keep their arms close to their body, are less likely to lean forward with their body, play more often with their hair or clothing, and tap their hands more often than men do.

Paralanguage

Paralanguage is the sound of what we hear when someone speaks—it is *how* something is said. We begin our discussion of paralanguage by describing its four component vocal characteristics. Then we discuss how vocal interference can disrupt message flow.

OBSERVE & ANALYZE
Journal Activity

Gender Variations in Body Motions

Find a place in your campus cafeteria or another public spot where you can observe the conversations of others. You are to observe the nonverbal behaviours of three dyads for at least five minutes each. First, observe the interaction of two men, then the interaction of two women, and finally the interaction of a man and a woman. Using the Observation Tally Sheet provided here, record each participant's behaviour and any other behavioural cues you note. Using these observation notes, review the material on men's and women's use of body motions. Did your observations confirm these trends? If they did not, develop an explanation about why they did not.

Nonverbal Behaviour Observation Form: Body Motions

Behaviour (frequency)	**Participant 1 (sex:__)**			**Participant 2 (sex:__)**		
Eye contact	High	Med	Low	High	Med	Low
Smiling	High	Med	Low	High	Med	Low
Forward lean of body	High	Med	Low	High	Med	Low
Touches or plays with hair	High	Med	Low	High	Med	Low
Touches or plays with clothes	High	Med	Low	High	Med	Low
Taps hand or fingers on surface	High	Med	Low	High	Med	Low
Arm position relative to body	High	Med	Low	High	Med	Low

Vocal Characteristics

By controlling the pitch, volume, rate, and quality of the voice—the four major vocal characteristics—we can complement, supplement, or contradict the meaning conveyed by the language of our message.

Pitch is the highness or lowness of tone in a person's voice. People tend to raise and lower vocal pitch to accompany changes in volume. They may also raise the pitch when they are nervous or excited and lower the pitch when they are trying to be forceful.

Volume is loudness or softness of tone in a person's voice. Some people have booming voices that carry long distances, and others are normally soft spoken. Regardless of their normal volume level, people vary their volume depending on the situation in which they are speaking and the topic of discussion.

Rate is the speed at which a person speaks. People tend to talk more rapidly when they are happy, frightened, nervous, or excited and more slowly when they are problem solving aloud or are trying to emphasize a point.

Quality is the overall sound of a person's speaking voice. Each human voice has distinct characteristics. Some voices are raspy, some smoky, some have bell-like qualities, and others are throaty. Moreover, each of us uses a slightly different type of voice to communicate a particular state of mind. For example, we may associate complaints with a whiny, nasal quality; seductive invitations with a soft, breathy quality; and anger with a strident, harsh quality.

Some of us have developed vocal habits that cause others to consistently misinterpret what we say. For instance, Brian has cultivated a tone of voice that causes others to believe that he is being sarcastic when he does not intend to be. Such misunderstandings have the potential to seriously damage Brian's relationships with others. If you have concerns about your vocal characteristics, talk them over with your professor. Your professor can evaluate your voice quality and make recommendations for additional help should you need it.

THINKING ABOUT . . .

Vocal Characteristics

What happens to your voice in stressful situations? When does your pitch go up? Down? When do you talk loudly? Softly? Fast? Slowly? How aware are you of these changes?

Vocal Interferences

Vocal interferences are extraneous sounds or words that interrupt fluent speech. Although most of us are occasionally guilty of including some such interruptions in our speech, these interferences become a problem when others perceive them to be excessive and when they call attention to themselves to the extent that they prevent listeners from concentrating on meaning. The most common interferences that creep into our speech include *eh, uh, er, well, okay, you know,* and *like.*

Vocal interferences may initially be used as place markers, filling momentary gaps in speech that would otherwise stand as silence. In this way, we indicate that we have not finished speaking and that it is still our turn to speak. We may use an *um* when we need to momentarily pause to search for the right word or idea. Although the chance of being interrupted may be real (some people will seek to interrupt at any pause), the intrusion of an excessive number of fillers can lead to the impression that we are unsure of ourselves or confused in what we are attempting to say.

OBSERVE & ANALYZE
Journal Activity

Vocal Interference

Record yourself speaking for several minutes on any subject. Before playing back the recording, estimate the number of vocal interferences you have used. Play the recording and count the actual number. Compare the number with your estimate. How close was your estimate? Wait a day or two and try it again. Keep a record of your improvement. Identify the vocal interference you use most frequently and work to reduce its use.

IN BRIEF

Paralanguage

Paralanguage is the non-speech use of our voice to complement, supplement, or contradict the meaning of our verbal messages. The main vocal characteristics that we manipulate are pitch (high to low), volume (soft to loud), rate (slow to fast), and quality (sound or tone of voice).

Vocal interferences are unwanted non-speech sounds (e.g., *um* or *eh*) which interrupt the flow of our speech.

Equally prevalent, and perhaps even more disruptive, is the overuse of words or phrases such as *like* and *you know*. The *you know* habit may begin as a genuine effort to find out whether what is being said is already known by others. Similarly, the use of *like* may start from making comparisons such as "Nava is really hot! She looks like Shania Twain." Soon the comparisons become shortcuts, however, as in "She's like really hot!" Finally, the use of these words becomes pure filler: "Like, she's really cool, you know. I can't really explain it, but I'll tell you, she's like wow!"

Curiously, no matter how irritating the use of vocal interferences may be to listeners, they are unlikely to verbalize their irritation. However, the habitual use of vocal interferences can prove to be a handicap in many settings. For example, excessive use of vocal interferences during a job interview, a workplace meeting, or a class will adversely affect the impression we make.

Self-Presentation

People learn a great deal about us from how we choose to present ourselves. For example, we reveal information through our choices in clothing and personal grooming, our manner, our use of touch, and the way we manage our time.

Artifactual Communication

Artifacts are possessions and adornments that communicate information about us to others. They include articles of clothing, jewellery, accessories, hairstyles, perfumes or colognes, make-up, body art, furnishings, decorations, vehicles (e.g., cars, bicycles, skateboards), and many other belongings. The artifacts which we choose for our use can tell others many things about us; for example, they can reveal the cultures or groups to which we belong, our social and economic status and the roles we play in life, our age and gender, our interests, our personality, and our attitudes.

Choice of clothing and personal grooming can be a particularly effective way of communicating a message. We determine what message we want to send, and then dress and groom ourselves accordingly. Lawyers and business managers understand the power of dress and grooming quite well. For instance, a barrister knows that a person charged with drug peddling would be foolish to appear in court wearing the local gang colours, oversized pants, and a backward-facing baseball cap. Business managers periodically adjust their dress codes to make sure they reflect the image they want their business to project. For instance, in the 1990s many offices, following the lead of successful major computer companies, adopted so-called *business casual* as their style of dress. When the dot-com bubble burst, however, many of these computer companies were found to have been less than honest with their shareholders, and the casual style of dress was quickly dropped by many companies that wanted to project

Darryl Dyck/CP Picture Archive

What messages are communicated by the artifacts being worn by this dancer?

an image of reliability and integrity (Tomlinson, 2002). As one Bay Street lawyer put it, "With more formality, there is a sense of turning to more integrity and solid values. When you think of the integrity problems of the dotcom industry, we don't want that" (p. 2).

Many people, especially teenagers and young adults, consciously choose clothing styles and personal-grooming behaviours that stretch Western norms of acceptability. From retro fashions to hip-hop styles, from unnatural hair and nail colours to dreadlocks and spiked or uncombed hair, from tattooing to body piercing, more and more people are choosing to use their clothing and appearance to differentiate themselves from some groups and to identify closely with others.

Each of us has the right to express our individuality and to communicate our ideas, beliefs, and feelings in our dress and personal grooming, but we must recognize that doing so sends messages that can create barriers as well as bonds. Part of being a skilled communicator is realizing that the meaning of clothing and grooming depends as much on receivers' perceptions as on our own intentions.

Poise

Poise refers to assurance of manner. As much as 20 percent of the population experiences a high degree of nervousness when encountering strangers, speaking in groups, and in public speaking (Richmond & McCroskey, 1995, p. 35). This

OBSERVE & ANALYZE
Journal Activity

Clothing Choices

Take an inventory of your wardrobe. Divide your clothes into three groups: those you wear for dress-up occasions, those you wear for everyday activities, and those you wear for leisure. Count the number of pairs of pants, shirts, blouses, skirts, dresses, belts, and so on that are in each category. Is your wardrobe balanced, or do you have an overabundance of one type of clothing? If someone were to peruse your closet and drawers, what would that person's impression of you be? Would it be accurate?

nervousness is often communicated through nonverbal behaviour and is perceived by others as a lack of poise. Exhibiting a lack of poise is a problem, especially in professional communication contexts, because many people interpret the deficiency as a lack of confidence or a lack of competence. For most people, nervousness decreases as they gain confidence in their ability to function well in a particular setting. Mastery of the skills discussed in this text should help you cope with the nervousness you might face in a variety of communication situations.

THINKING ABOUT . . .

Touch Orientation

Are you a touchy-feely type of person? Where does your touch orientation come from? Are others in your family similar in their reaction to touch? What kinds of touching behaviour do you associate with power plays? With expressions of concern? With love? How often do you use touching behaviour? How do you respond to the touching behaviours of others? What do you do when someone is touching you more than you are comfortable with?

Touch

One of the most basic forms of human communication is touch. The study of this type of nonverbal communication is known as **haptics.** By using hands, arms, or other body parts to make physical contact with another, we can communicate a variety of meanings. People may pat, hug, kiss, pinch, stroke, hold, embrace, tickle, slap, and punch each other, depending on the feeling they want to share. In Western culture, we shake hands to be sociable and polite, we pat a person on the back for encouragement, we hug a person to show love, and we clasp raised hands to demonstrate solidarity. Our touching can be gentle or firm, perfunctory or passionate, brief or lingering, and how we touch can communicate power, empathy, or understanding, among many other feelings.

People differ in their touching behaviour and in their reactions to touching, particularly unsolicited touching, from others. Some people like to touch and be touched; other people do not. Women tend to touch others less than men do, but they value touching more than men. Women view touching as an expressive behaviour that demonstrates warmth and affiliation. Men view it as an instrumental behaviour; for example, touching a woman is often considered a prelude to sexual activity (Pearson, West, & Turner, 1995, p. 142).

COMMUNICATE! Using InfoTrac College Edition

Touching behaviour, particularly between people who are attracted to one another, can be perceived as a sign of affection or harassment. How can one member of a couple know whether and when it is okay to touch and what kind of touch is okay? Using the InfoTrac College Edition subject guide, enter the term *touch—research.* Then open Frank N. Willis, Jr., & Rebecca A. Dodds, (1998) "Age, Relationship, and Touch Initiation," *The Journal of Social Psychology, 138* (1), p. 115. Do the findings of this research confirm your expectations? Are they consistent with your own practice? How would you explain any differences?

Although Canadian culture is relatively non–contact oriented, the kinds and amounts of touching behaviour that are practised and accepted within our society vary widely. Touching behaviour that seems innocuous to one person may be perceived as overly intimate or threatening by another. Touch that is acceptable to someone in private may embarrass the same person if it is used in public. What we communicate by touching may be perceived positively or negatively. Therefore, if we want to be perceived as sensitive and caring, it is a good idea to ask another person before touching him or her.

Time

A less obvious aspect of our self-presentation is how we manage and react to others' use and management of what Edward T. Hall (1959) calls "informal time" (p. 135). The study of the use of time as a means of communication is called **chronemics,** and it includes considerations of duration, activity, and punctuality.

In examining time as duration, we consider the amount of time that we regard as appropriate for certain events or activities. For instance, we may think a speech should last 15 minutes and a typical class 50 minutes. When the duration of an event or activity differs significantly from our expectations, we begin to attribute meaning to that difference. For example, if we are told that a job interview will take an hour, and it is over in 20 minutes, we may conclude that we did not get the job. On the other hand, if the interview stretches to two hours, we may believe that we are in strong contention for the job. Because our use of time creates its own meanings, we need to be sensitive to polite conventions about the appropriate duration of events and activities.

In considering time with respect to activity, we refer to what people perceive should be done in a given period. Many people work during the day, sleep at night, eat a light meal around midday, and so on. When someone behaves in a way that we deem inappropriate for the time, we are likely to react negatively. For instance, Susan Jones, who operates a consulting firm, prides herself on being available to her employees, yet she is put off when one of her employees, Sung Lei Chan, calls her at home during the dinner hour to discuss a presentation that is she is to deliver on behalf of the company the next week. Sung Lei may think she is presenting herself as a hardworking and organized employee who is dedicated to doing a good job, but her employer may view the call as a rude and insensitive invasion of her private time.

In assessing use of time in terms of punctuality, we are determining the extent to which one strictly adheres to the appointed or regular time. It is the dimension of time that is most closely related to self-presentation. If you make an appointment to meet your professor in her office at 10 a.m., her opinion of you may differ depending on whether you arrive at 9:50, at 10:00, at 10:10, or at 10:30. Similarly, your opinion of her will differ depending on whether or not she is there at the appointed time. In Canada, strict punctuality is a dominant cultural imperative. When a date is made or an appointment set, one is normally expected to be prompt. Early or late arrival is very likely to be interpreted as meaningful.

THINKING ABOUT . . .

Time Orientation

How do you use time? Recall an incident when the duration of an event or appointment violated your expectation for appropriate length. How did this violation affect what you thought of the other person involved or what the other person thought of you? How important is it to you that you be punctual? Do you expect others to be punctual? How does your opinion of others change when they are frequently unpunctual?

Cultural Variations in Self-Presentation

Just as the meaning of body motions and paralanguage are culturally determined, so too are self-presentation behaviours.

Touch According to Gudykunst and Kim (1997), differences in touching behaviour are highly correlated with culture. In some cultures, lots of contact and touching is normal behaviour, while in others, individual space is respected and frequent touching is not encouraged. "People in high contact cultures evaluate *close* as positive and good, and evaluate *far* as negative and bad. People in low contact cultures evaluate *close* as negative and bad, and *far* as positive and good" (p. 235). Latin American and Mediterranean cultures are high-contact cultures; Northern European cultures are medium to low in contact; and Asian cultures are for the most part low-contact cultures. As you can imagine then, Canada, which is largely a country of immigrants, is generally perceived to be medium contact, although there are wide differences in the practice of individual Canadians due to family cultural heritage.

OBSERVE & ANALYZE
Journal Activity

Cultural Differences in Self-Presentation

Develop a list of questions related to the self-presentation behaviours discussed here. Using these questions, interview or converse with two international students from different countries. Try to select students whose cultures differ from the dominant Canadian culture or the culture with which you are most familiar. Try to understand how people in the international student's country differ from you in their use of nonverbal self-presentation behaviours. Prepare to share what you have learned with your classmates.

Time A particularly important area of differences concerns perceptions of time. Some cultures, such of those of Northern Europe and North America, view time monochronically. **Monochronism** is a perception of time as compartmentalized, linear, and one-dimensional. Time is regarded as a scarce resource to be spent, saved, and budgeted, and monochronic people are likely to schedule and do only one thing at a time, completing one task properly before moving on to the next. Because schedules are considered very important, being even a few minutes tardy may require a person to acknowledge his or her lateness. Being 10 to 15 minutes late usually requires an apology, and being more than 30 minutes late is likely to be perceived as an insult requiring a great deal of explanation to earn the other person's forgiveness.

People from other cultural backgrounds, such as those of Latin America, the Middle East, the Mediterranean, and some parts of Asia, tend to view time polychronically. **Polychronism** is the perception that time is continuous and capable of encompassing several activities simultaneously. To those with a polychronic view of time, schedules are less significant, carrying out several activities at once is considered normal, and punctuality is much less valued. One arrives when one has completed what came before. In Latin American or Arab cultures, for instance, it is not unusual for either person to be more than 30 minutes late, and neither is likely to expect or offer an apology (Gudykunst & Kim, p. 160). Although the dominant Canadian culture is monochronic, for some Canadians a polychronic view of time influences behaviour.

IN BRIEF

Self-Presentation

We reveal a great deal about ourselves to others through our self-presentation. Important aspects of self-presentation are

- clothing and personal grooming
- poise
- our use and response to touch
- our use and management of time.

The understanding and use of touch and time as means of communication are strongly influenced by culture.

Communication through Management of Your Environment

In addition to our use of body motions, paralanguage, and self-presentation cues, we communicate nonverbally through manipulation of our physical environment, including the space we occupy, the temperature of our surroundings, the lighting levels, and the colours we use in interior decorations.

Space

The study of the communicative use of space is called **proxemics.** It includes consideration of the communicative use of permanent structures, of movable objects within space, and of informal space.

Management of permanent structures Permanent structures are the buildings in which we live and work and the parts of those buildings that cannot be moved. Although we do not always have much control over their creation, we do exercise control in our selection of them. For instance, if we were choosing a room or apartment to rent or a condominium or a house to buy, we would consider whether or not each available housing option was reflective of our lifestyle. People who select a fourth-floor loft may view themselves differently from those who choose a basement efficiency apartment. Professional people usually search with care to find office space that fits the professional image they want to communicate.

In addition, specific features of our environment affect our communication within that environment. For instance, people who live in rooming houses or apartment buildings are likely to become better acquainted with neighbours who live across the hall and next door than with those who live on other floors. Similarly, people who share common space such as laundry facilities or garages are more likely to become acquainted than those who do not.

THINKING ABOUT . . .

Permanent Structures and Communication

Consider where you live. Which of your neighbours do you know well? How did you happen to meet him or her? Does your experience confirm what you have just read? If not, what other factors seem to account for what you have experienced?

Management of movable objects within space Whether the space is a residence room, a living room, a classroom, or an office, we have the opportunity to arrange and rearrange movable objects to achieve the effect we want. For example, a manager's office arranged so that the manager sits behind the desk and the employee chair is on the other side of that desk says, "Let's talk business—I'm the boss and you're the employee." In contrast, if the manager's desk is pushed against the wall and the manager and employee sit face to face in the middle of the room with no barrier between them, the arrangement says, "Don't be nervous—let's just chat."

Management of informal space The term *informal space* refers to the space around us at any particular moment. In Western cultures, such as the dominant Canadian culture, four distinct distances represent what most people consider appropriate or comfortable in various situations (Hall, 1969):

- *Intimate distance,* up to 45 cm, is appropriate for private conversations between close friends.
- *Personal distance,* from 45 cm to 1.2 m, is the space in which casual conversation occurs.
- *Social distance,* from 1.2 m to 3.5 m, is where impersonal business such as a job interview is conducted.
- *Public distance* is anything more than 3.5 m.

Of greatest concern to us is the intimate distance, that which we regard as appropriate for conversation with close friends, parents, and younger children. People typically become uncomfortable, often reacting with defensiveness or hostility, when outsiders intrude upon this space.

Intrusions into our intimate space are acceptable only in certain settings and then only when all involved follow certain unwritten rules. For instance, people will tolerate being packed into a crowded elevator or subway car, and even touching others they do not know, provided the others follow conventional rules such as standing rigidly, looking at the floor or the indicator above the door, and not making eye contact with others. Only occasionally will people who are forced to invade each other's intimate space acknowledge the other as

Differing concepts of informal space: Although you might find it rude for non-intimates to get this close to you in conversation, these men would find it rude if you backed away.

Robert Azzi/Woodfin Camp & Associates

a person. They are then likely to exchange sheepish smiles or otherwise acknowledge the mutual invasion of intimate distance.

Interpersonal problems occur when one person's use of space violates the behavioural expectations of another. Unfortunately, people sometimes intentionally violate the space expectations of another. When such a violation involves members of the opposite sex, it can be considered sexual harassment. Don may, through violations of informal space, posture, movements, or gestures, appear to be coming on to Mary. If Mary does not welcome the attention, she may feel threatened. In this case, Don's nonverbal behaviour can be construed as sexual harassment. To avoid perceptions of harassment, people need to be especially sensitive to others' definitions of intimate space.

Our intimate or personal space moves when we move, but we seek to claim other space whether we currently are occupying it or not. That is, we are likely to look at certain space as our **territory,** as space over which we may claim ownership. If Marcia decides to eat lunch at the university cafeteria, the space she selects at the table becomes her territory. Suppose that during lunch Marcia leaves her territory to get butter for her roll. The chair she left, the food on the table, and the space around that food are *hers,* and she will expect others to stay away. If, when she returns, Marcia finds that someone at the table has moved some dirty dishes into the area that she regards as her territory, she is likely to feel resentful.

Many people stake out their territory with markers. For example, Ramon arrives early for the first day of class, finds an empty desk, puts his backpack on the seat, and hangs his coat on the seat back. He then makes a quick trip to the washroom. If someone comes along while Ramon is gone, moves his

OBSERVE & ANALYZE
Journal Activity

Intruding on Personal Space

Find a crowded elevator. Get on it and face the back. Make direct eye contact with the person you are standing in front of. Note his or her reaction. On the return trip, introduce yourself to the person who is standing next to you and begin an animated conversation. Note the reaction of others around you. Get on an empty elevator and stand in the exact centre. Do not move when others board. Note their reactions. Record the reactions you have observed and be prepared to share them with your classmates.

backpack and coat, and sits at the desk, that person is violating territory that Ramon has marked as his.

As students of nonverbal communication, we must understand, however, that other people may not look at either the space around us or our territory in quite the same way that we do. Even though the majority of Canadians have learned the same basic rules governing the management of space, not everyone has the same respect for the rules or concern about the consequences of breaking the rules.

Temperature, Lighting, and Colour

Three other elements of the environment can be controlled to affect communication. These are temperature, lighting, and the colours used in the environment.

Temperature can stimulate or inhibit effective communication by altering people's moods and changing their level of attentiveness. Can you recall ever having had difficulty listening to a teacher or professor in a hot, stuffy classroom? Do you find that you become edgy when you are cold?

Lighting levels can add meaning to communication messages. In lecture halls and reading rooms, bright light is expected—it encourages good listening and comfortable reading. In contrast, in a chic restaurant, a music listening room, or a television lounge, we expect the lighting to be soft and rather dim, conditions which make for a cozy atmosphere that invites silence or intimate conversation (Knapp & Hall, 1992, p. 72). We often change the lighting level in a room to change the mood and indicate the type of interaction that is expected. Bright lights encourage activity and boisterous conversations, whereas softer light levels calm and soothe, encouraging quiet and more serious conversations.

Colour may stimulate both emotional and physical reactions. For instance, red excites, blue comforts and soothes, and yellow cheers and elevates mood. Professional interior designers who understand how people react to colours may choose blues when they are trying to create a peaceful, serene atmosphere for a living room, but they will decorate a child's playroom in reds and yellows.

In addition, specific colours also convey information about people and events. For instance, each season, many people choose to wear certain colours dictated by the fashion industry because they want to be considered in style; wearing coloured ribbons has become a popular way of indicating support for a cause; and members of youth gangs often wear bandannas or other articles of clothing in a specific colour to signal their membership.

Cultural Variations in Management of the Environment

As you would expect, the environments in which people feel comfortable depend on their cultural background. In Canada, where we have ample land, many people live in individual homes or in large apartments. In other countries, where land is scarce, people are used to living in more confined spaces and can feel lonely or isolated in larger spaces. In Asia, most people live in spaces that,

THINKING ABOUT . . .

Personal Territory

Do you have your own place at the family dinner table? What happens if you find someone else sitting in your place? Make a mental list of the other territories that you claim.

IN BRIEF

Communication through Management of Your Environment

We communicate nonverbally through the environment in which our conversations occur. The main communicative elements of our environment are

- space (permanent structures, movable objects, and informal space)
- temperature
- lighting
- colour.

The understanding and use of these environmental means of communication are strongly influenced by culture.

by our standards, would feel quite cramped. People from different cultures also have different ideas about what constitutes appropriate distances for various interactions. Recall that in the dominant Canadian culture personal space is in the 45 cm to 1.2 m range. In Middle Eastern cultures, however, men move much closer than this when they are talking to other men (Samovar, Porter, & Stefani, 1998, p. 165). Thus, when a man from an Arab country talks with a man from Canada, one of the two is likely to be uncomfortable. Either the Canadian will feel that his intimate space is being invaded or the Arab will feel isolated and too distant for serious conversation.

People of different cultures also differ in the temperature ranges that they find comfortable and in their use of colour. People who were raised in countries with warm climates can tolerate heat more easily than people who were raised in cooler climates. The meanings we assign to colours vary by national culture and religion. For example, in India white, not black, is the colour of mourning, and Hindu brides wear red.

WHAT WOULD YOU DO?
A QUESTION OF ETHICS

After the intramural mixed-doubles matches on Tuesday evening, most of the players adjourned to the campus pub for a drink and a chat. Marquez and Lisa sat down with Barry and Elana, whom they had lost to that night, largely because of Elana's improved play. Although Marquez and Lisa were only tennis friends, Barry and Elana had been going out together for much of the season.

After some general conversation about the tournament, Marquez said, "Elana, your serve today was the best I've seen it this year."

"Yeah, I was really impressed. And as you saw, I had trouble handling it," Lisa added.

"And you're getting to the net a lot better too," Marquez added.

"Thanks, guys," Elana said gratefully, "I've really been working on it."

"Well, aren't we getting the compliments today," sneered Barry in a sarcastic tone. Then after a pause, he said, "Oh, Elana, would you get my sweater. I left it on that chair by the other table."

"Come on, Barry, you're closer than I am," Elana replied.

Barry looked coldly at Elana, moved slightly closer to her, and said emphatically, "Get my sweater for me, Elana—now."

Elana quickly backed away from Barry as she said, "Okay, Barry, it's cool," and she then got the sweater for him.

"Gee, isn't she sweet," Barry said to Marquez and Lisa as he grabbed the sweater from Elana.

Lisa and Marquez both looked down at the floor. Then Lisa glanced at Marquez and said, "Well, I'm out of here. I've got a lot to do this evening."

"Let me walk you to your car," Marquez said as he stood up.

"See you next week," they both said in unison as they hurried out the door, leaving Barry and Elana alone at the table.

1. Analyze Barry's nonverbal behaviour. What was he attempting to achieve?
2. How do you interpret Lisa's and Marquez's nonverbal reactions to Barry?
3. Was Barry's behaviour ethically acceptable? Explain.

Summary

Nonverbal communication refers to how people communicate through the use of body motions, paralanguage, self-presentation cues, and the physical environment.

Perhaps the most familiar methods of nonverbal communication are the use of body motions and paralanguage. Eye contact, facial expression, gesture, and posture are four major types of body motions. Body motions act as emblems, illustrators, affect displays, regulators, and adaptors. Likewise, a person's vocal characteristics (volume, rate, pitch, and quality) as well as vocal interferences (e.g., *ehs, ahs, ums, you knows,* and *likes*) affect our ability to interpret the meaning of the verbal message.

Although verbal and nonverbal communication work together best when they are complementary, nonverbal cues may replace or even contradict verbal symbols. Generally, nonverbal communication is more likely to be trusted when verbal and nonverbal cues are in conflict.

Through self-presentation cues such as clothing, touching behaviour, and use of time, people communicate about themselves and their relationships to others. The physical environment is often overlooked even though we use it to set the tone for conversations and nonverbally communicate through it. The choices people make in their permanent spaces, the way they arrange the objects in those spaces, and the way they control or react to temperature, lighting, and colour contribute to the quality and meaning of the communication episodes that occur.

Glossary

Review the following key terms:

adaptors (86) — unconscious movements that help people cope with a physical or emotional stress that they are experiencing.

affect display (86) — an often unintentional nonverbal display of emotions that have not been verbalized.

artifacts (90) — possessions and adornments that communicate information about us to others.

chronemics (92) — the study of the use of time as a means of communication.

emblems (85) — body motions used to take the place of a word or phrase.

eye contact or **gaze** (83) — the degree to which and the manner in which we look at the people with whom we are communicating.

facial expression (84) — the manipulation of facial muscles to communicate emotional states or reactions to messages.

WWW

COMMUNICATE!
Using Technology

Watch a DVD or videotape of a movie or a television program. Select a segment where two people are talking. The first time you watch, turn off the sound. Based on body motions alone, determine the climate of the conversation (Are the people flirting? In conflict? Discussing an issue?). What eye movements, facial expressions, gestures, or postures led to your conclusion? Watch the scene a second time, observing body motions again but also listening to variations in volume, pitch, and rate of speech and vocal quality. Do any of these vocal cues add information? Watch a third time, focusing on what the characters are saying. Now analyze the segment. What percentage of meaning came from nonverbal elements? What did you learn from this exercise?

Go to the Web site "Exploring Nonverbal Communication" to expand your research: **http://nonverbal.ucsc.edu.**

gestures (84) — movements of the body parts, particularly the hands, arms, and fingers, to describe or to emphasize.

haptics (92) — the study of the use of touch as a means of communication.

illustrators (86) — body motions which accompany verbal messages and clarify what the speaker is saying.

kinesics (83) — the study of body motions, including eye contact, facial expression, gesture, and posture, as a means of communication.

monochronism (94) — a perception of time, particularly associated with Western cultures, that views time as compartmentalized, linear, and one-dimensional.

nonverbal communication behaviours (82) — bodily actions and vocal qualities that typically accompany a verbal message, that are usually interpreted as intentional, and that have agreed-upon interpretations within a culture or speech community.

paralanguage (88) — the sound of what we hear when someone speaks—*how* something is said.

pitch (89) — the highness or lowness of tone in a person's voice.

poise (91) — assurance of manner.

polychronism (94) — a perception of time that views time as continuous and capable of encompassing several activities at the same time.

posture (84) — the position of the body or the orientation of the body parts.

proxemics (94) — the study of the communicative use of space.

quality (89) — the overall sound of a person's speaking voice.

rate (89) — the speed at which a person speaks.

regulators (86) — body motions used to control or regulate the flow of a conversation or other communication transaction.

sign language (85) — a system of body motions used to communicate.

territory (96) — space over which we may claim ownership.

vocal interference (89) — an extraneous sound or word that interrupts fluent speech.

volume (89) — the loudness or softness of tone in a person's voice.

© Canstock Images Inc/Index Stock Imagery

OBJECTIVES

After you have read this chapter, you should be able to answer these questions:

- What skills are associated with effective listening?
- How can we focus our attention?
- What is empathy?
- How can we ask questions to increase understanding?
- How can we paraphrase both the content of and the feelings associated with another's message?
- How can we evaluate inferences?
- How can we make appropriate supporting statements?
- How can we offer reasonable alternative interpretations of events?
- What are three techniques for remembering information?

CHAPTER 5

Listening, Responding, Remembering

"Garson, do you have an extra key to the document cabinet? I misplaced mine, and I have to get into it right away."

"No, I don't have a key, but it doesn't matter because . . ."

"I can't believe it. When I left home this morning, I was sure I had it."

"Bart, it's okay . . ."

"I pulled out my keys, but of course I just had my car key and main door key. I always carry two sets of keys."

"Bart, I've been trying to tell you, just try the . . ."

"It's just like me. I think I've got everything, but just before I check the last time, Sue will say something to me and I get sidetracked. Then I just take off."

"Bart, calm down. The door's . . ."

"Calm down! If I can't get those documents to the meeting, there's going to be hell to pay. We've got six people coming from all over the city just to look at the documents. What am I supposed to say to them?"

"Bart, you don't have to say anything. I've been trying to . . ."

"Oh, sure, I just go in there and say, 'By the way, the documents are locked up in the cabinet and I left my key at home.' Come on, Garson, who's got the other key?"

"Bart, listen! I've been trying to tell you, Miller was in the cabinet and, knowing you'd be along in a minute, he left the door open."

"Well, why didn't you just tell me that?"

Are you a good listener? Even when you are under pressure like Bart? Or do you sometimes find that your mind wanders when others are talking to you? As we will see in the later sections of this book, **listening,** "the process of receiving, attending to, and assigning meaning to aural and visual stimuli" (Wolvin & Coakley, 1996, p. 69) and the associated skills of responding and remembering are fundamental skills that we must draw upon to be effective in interpersonal, group, and public communication. Having or lacking these skills greatly affects the quality of our performance in social, academic, and professional settings. Despite the importance of these skills, however, most people receive little or no training in using them and, as a result, encounter difficulties in their personal relationships, their education, and their career.

Listening, as Wolvin and Coakley's definition makes clear, is not an isolated event but a complex sensory and intellectual process. In particular, it is not to be confused with hearing, which is merely a physiological response to aural stimuli. Many people do not listen well, and because of this deficiency, they are unable to respond or remember effectively. In this chapter, we will consider the concepts of attending, understanding, evaluating, responding, and remembering.

COMMUNICATE! Using InfoTrac College Edition

Listening skills are perceived to be important in many professions, not only to function as part of an organization, but also to secure opportunities for advancement. Employees of professional organizations are certainly evaluated on their ability to listen. Using InfoTrac College Edition, under the subject of *listening,* click on *periodical references.* Open John W. Haas & Christa L. Arnold, (1995), "An Examination of the Role of Listening in Judgments of Communication Competence in Co-workers," *The Journal of Business Communication, 32*(2) p. 123. How important are effective listening skills to creating the impression of communication competence?

Attending

Attending is the perceptual process of selecting and focusing on specific stimuli from the countless stimuli reaching the senses. Recall from Chapter 2 that we attend to information that interests us and meets our physical and psychological needs, but to be a good listener, we have to train ourselves to attend to what people are saying regardless of our interest or needs.

We will consider three techniques for consciously focusing attention:

1. **Get physically and mentally ready to listen.** Physically, good listeners adopt a listening posture. For instance, when students who are good listeners are told that the next bit of information is likely to be on the test, they are likely to sit upright in their chairs, lean slightly forward, cease any extraneous physical movement, and look directly at the professor. Similarly, they will prepare mentally by blocking out irrelevant thoughts that may pass through their minds and focusing their attention on the professor's words. Although private thoughts may be more interesting or pleasant than what someone is saying, we must compel ourselves to attend to what is being said.

One Big Happy by Rick Detorie. By permission of Rick Detorie and Creators Syndicate.

Of course, sometimes we can afford to listen without much intensity. People often speak of "vegging out in front of the tube," which usually means *listening* to comedy or light drama as a means of passing time pleasurably. Unfortunately, many people approach all situations as if they were listening to pass time.

2. **Make the shift from speaker to listener a complete one.** Unlike a lecture, which requires us to listen for long periods, most conversations require us to switch back and forth between speaking and listening so frequently that we may find it difficult at times to make these shifts complete. If, instead of attending to the words and nonverbal behaviours of the persons we are talking to, we spend the time between our turns to speak rehearsing what we are going to say next, our listening effectiveness will take a nosedive. When we are in a conversation, especially a heated one, we must take a second to ask ourselves whether we are preparing speeches instead of listening. Shifting from the role of speaker to that of listener requires constant effort.

3. **Hear a person out before you react.** Far too often, we stop listening before a person has finished speaking because we think we *know* what the person is going to say, yet our *knowing* is really only a guess. Accordingly, we should cultivate the habit of always letting a person complete his or her thought before we stop attending.

   In addition to prematurely ceasing to listen, we often allow a person's mannerisms and words to distract us. For instance, we may become annoyed when a speaker mutters, stammers, or talks in a monotone, or take offence at a speaker's language or ideas. For instance, some people react negatively or tune out when people speak of *gay rights, family values, distinct societies, welfare bums, workfare, political correctness, big government,* or *rednecks*. Are there words or ideas that create bursts of semantic noise for you, causing you to stop listening attentively? To counteract this effect, we must try to let a warning light go on in our mind when a speaker trips the switch to our emotional reactions. Instead of tuning out or getting ready to fight, we must become aware of this semantic noise and work that much harder to listen objectively. If we can, we will be more likely to receive the whole message accurately before we respond.

OBSERVE & ANALYZE
Journal Activity

Attending

Select an information-oriented television program (such as *Disclosure, The Fifth Estate, W5, Foreign Assignment,* or *The Nature of Things*). Watch at least 15 minutes of the show while lounging in a comfortable chair or while stretched out on the floor with music playing in the background. Then, for the next 15 minutes, make a conscious effort to use the guidelines for increasing attentiveness. Contrast your listening behaviour while lounging with your listening behaviour while attending. What differences did you note?

IN BRIEF

Attending

Attending is the perceptual process of selecting and focusing on specific stimuli from the countless stimuli reaching the senses. To attend effectively,

1. get physically and mentally ready to listen.
2. make the shift from speaker to listener a complete one.
3. hear a person out before you react.

Understanding

Understanding is decoding a message accurately by assigning appropriate meaning to it. Sometimes we do not understand because people use words that are outside our vocabulary, or they use them in a way that we do not recognize. Fully understanding what a person means requires **active listening,** an approach to listening that involves the use of specific techniques, including empathizing, questioning, and paraphrasing.

Empathizing

THINKING ABOUT . . .

Approaches to Empathy

Which of the three approaches to empathy do you rely on most? Under what circumstances would it be difficult for you to use each of these three approaches to empathy?

Empathy is intellectual identification with or vicarious experience of the feelings, thoughts, or attitudes of another. When we empathize, we attempt to understand or experience what another understands or experiences. In order to do so, we generally try to put aside our own feelings, thoughts, and attitudes; to adopt the feelings, thoughts, and attitudes of the person we are empathizing with; and to respond appropriately. Three approaches people use when empathizing are empathic responsiveness, perspective taking, and sympathetic responsiveness (Weaver & Kirtley, 1995, p. 131).

Empathic responsiveness is the ability to experience an emotional response parallel to, and as a result of observing, another person's actual or anticipated display of emotion (Stiff et al., 1988, p. 199). For instance, when Monique tells Mireille that Bertrand broke off their engagement, Mireille will show an empathic response if she senses the sadness that Monique is feeling at her loss and experiences a similar sense of loss.

Perspective taking, imagining yourself in the place of another, is the most common form of empathizing (Zillman, 1991). For example, if Mireille were to personalize Monique's message by picturing herself being told that her engagement is off, anticipate and experience the emotions that she would feel were this to occur, and then assume that Monique must be feeling the same way, she would be exemplifying perspective taking.

Sympathetic responsiveness is the ability to feel concern, compassion, or sorrow for another because of his or her situation or plight. This approach differs from the other two approaches to empathy in that people showing sympathetic responsiveness do not attempt to experience the feelings of the other. Instead, they translate their intellectual understanding of what the other has experienced into their own feelings of concern, compassion, or sorrow for that person. For instance, imagine that Mireille understands that Monique is sad and disappointed, but instead of trying to feel Monique's emotions or experience how she herself would feel in a similar situation, she simply feels concern and compassion for her friend. This reaction would be a sympathetic response. Because of this difference in perspective, many scholars differentiate sympathy from empathy.

Although people vary in their capacity to empathize with others, through practice, nearly everyone can increase their ability. Those who are overly *I*-oriented find it especially difficult to see the world from another's point of view. As a result, their ability to empathize is often underdeveloped. Such people may need to exert extra effort to develop empathizing skills in order to increase their interpersonal effectiveness.

Though it may seem trite, the first step in improving our ability to empathize is to take the time and make the effort to respect the person who is speaking. We do not need to have a deep, personal relationship with others to respect them. **Respecting** others simply requires that we pay serious attention to what they are saying and what they feel about what they are saying. Respect begins by treating a person as a person with value and not as an object. It focuses our time and energy on others, not on ourselves.

How well we empathize also depends on how observant we are of others' behaviour and how clearly we read the nonverbal messages they are sending. To improve our observational skills, we can ask ourselves the following two questions whenever we are conversing with someone: (1) What emotions do I believe this person is experiencing right now? and (2) What are the cues that he or she is giving that I am using to draw this conclusion? Consciously asking these questions helps us focus our attention on the nonverbal aspects of messages, which is where most of the information about the person's emotional state is likely to be conveyed.

OBSERVE & ANALYZE
Journal Activity

Empathizing Effectively

Describe a time when you effectively empathized with another person. Write an analysis of the incident. What was the person's emotional state? How did you recognize it? What were the nonverbal cues? Verbal cues? What type of relationship did you have with this person? How similar was he or she to you? Had you ever had a real or vicarious experience similar to the one the person was reporting?

SKILL BUILDERS Empathy

Skill	Use	Procedure	Example
Intellectually identifying with or vicariously experiencing the feelings, thoughts, or attitudes of another.	To create or to promote a supportive climate.	1. Adopt an attitude of respect by actively attending to what the person says. 2. Concentrate on understanding both verbal and nonverbal messages. 3. Use the person's behavioural cues to ascertain his or her emotional state. 4. Try to feel with the person, or try to recall or imagine how you would feel in similar circumstances, or allow yourself to experience your own feelings of concern, compassion, or sorrow for the person. 5. Respond in a way that reflects those feelings.	When Jerry says, "I really feel embarrassed about wearing braces in college," Mary smiles ruefully and replies, "Yeah, it makes you feel like a little kid, doesn't it? I remember the things I had to put up with when I wore braces."

To further increase our accuracy at reading emotions, we can use the skill of perception checking which we introduced in Chapter 2. Remember that a perception check allows us to verify verbally that we have understood a message sent nonverbally. You will recall from Chapter 4 that cultures vary in terms of how much emotion is expressed nonverbally, so this skill may be especially valuable when the culture of the person with whom we are conversing is different from our own. Once we have understood the emotions the other person is feeling, we can choose the type of empathic response we wish to use.

To become more effective at empathizing with another, (1) adopt an attitude of respect toward the person, (2) concentrate on understanding the nonverbal as well as the verbal messages, (3) use behavioural cues to ascertain his or her emotional state, (4) try to feel with the person, OR try to recall or imagine how you would feel in similar circumstances, OR try to understand what the person is feeling to help yourself experience your own feelings of concern, compassion, or sorrow for that person. Finally, (5) respond in a way that reflects those feelings.

Questioning

Active listeners are willing to question to help them get the information they need to understand. A **question** is, of course, a response designed to get further information or to clarify information already received. Although you may have asked questions for as long as you can remember, you may notice that at times your questions either do not get the information you want or irritate, fluster, or cause defensiveness in the person you are talking to. We can increase the chances that our questions will get us the information we want and reduce negative reactions if we observe these guidelines:

1. **Note the kind of information you need to increase your understanding.** Suppose that Carla is helping Maria decorate a room for a friend's birthday party. Maria says, "I'm so frustrated with this garland for the buffet table. Would you go to the store and buy me some more paper?" At this point, Carla may feel confused and need more information in order to understand Maria's wishes. However, if she responds, "What do you mean?" she is likely to add to the confusion because Maria, who is already anxious, will probably not know precisely what Carla does not understand. To increase her understanding, Carla might ask Maria one of the following three types of questions:
   - *Questions to get more information on important details*: for example, "What kind of paper would you like me to get for you, and how much do you need?"
   - *Questions to clarify the use of a term*: for example, "What exactly is a garland?"
   - *Questions to clarify the cause of the feelings the person is expressing*: for example, "What is frustrating you?"

Nicola Sutton/Life File/PhotoDisc Green/Getty Images

Increasing empathy includes reading nonverbal messages and asking questions to clarify.

Before asking these questions, we must determine whether the information we need is more detail, clarification of a word or idea, or information on the cause of feelings or events; then phrase our question accordingly.

2. **Phrase questions as complete sentences.** Under pressure, people tend to use one- or two-word questions that may be perceived as curt or abrupt. For instance, when Miles says, "Molly just told me that I always behave in ways that are totally insensitive to her needs," instead of asking, "How?" you might ask, "Did she give you any examples of behaviours or incidents to clarify what she meant?" Curt, abrupt questions often seem to challenge the speaker instead of simply identifying the kind of information the respondent needs to improve his or her understanding. By phrasing questions as complete sentences, the questioner shows the respondent that he or she has been heard.

3. **Monitor your nonverbal cues so that they convey genuine interest and concern.** When we ask questions we should use a sincere tone of voice, not one that could be interpreted as bored, sarcastic, cutting, superior, dogmatic, or evaluative. We need to constantly remind ourselves that the way we speak may be even more important than the words we use.

4. **Put the burden of ignorance on your own shoulders.** To minimize defensive reactions, especially when the person we are questioning is under stress, we should preface our question with a short statement that suggests that any problem of misunderstanding may be attributable to *our* listening skills. For instance, when Drew says, "I've really had it with Malone screwing up all the time," Biff might say, "I'm sorry, Drew, but I'm missing some details that would help me understand you better. What kinds of things has Malone been doing?"

Here are two more examples that contrast inappropriate with more appropriate questioning responses.

Example 1

Tamara: "They've turned down my proposal again!"

Art: [Inappropriate] "Well, did you explain your intentions the way you should have?" *(This question can be interpreted as a veiled attack on Tamara in question form.)*

[Appropriate] "Do they say why they've refused you?" *(This question is a sincere request for additional information.)*

Example 2

Emilia: "With all those professors at the party last night, I felt really strange."

Javier: [Inappropriate] "Why?" *(By asking such an abrupt question, Javier is making no effort to be sensitive to Emilia's feelings or to understand them.)*

[Appropriate] "Gee, what was it about the profs being there that made you feel strange?" *(This question is phrased to elicit information that will help Javier understand, and answering it may also help Emilia to better understand her feelings.)*

In summary, to increase your effectiveness at asking questions, (1) note the kind of information you need to increase your understanding of the message, (2) phrase your question as a specific, complete sentence that focuses on getting the needed information, (3) deliver the question in a sincere tone of voice, and (4) in stressful situations, put the burden of ignorance on your own shoulders.

Paraphrasing

In addition to being skilled questioners, active listeners are also adept at **paraphrasing,** restating in their own words their understanding of another person's message. For example, during a meeting with his professor to discuss his performance on a midterm exam, Cale drops his eyes, sighs, and slowly shakes his head as he says, "Well, it looks like I really blew this test. I had a lot of other things on my mind that week." If Professor Jensen responds, "If I understand you correctly, other things were happening to you that diverted your attention from studying for the exam," he would be paraphrasing.

Paraphrases may focus on the content of the original message, on the feelings underlying the content, or on both. In the previous example, Professor Jensen's paraphrase is a **content paraphrase.** It focuses on the denotative meaning of Cale's message. If, as Cale began to speak, Professor Jensen noticed his dropped eyes, his sigh, and his shaking head and said, "So you are pretty upset about your grade on the midterm," his response would be a **feelings paraphrase,** a paraphrase that focuses on the emotions attached to the content of the message.

In real-life settings, we often do not distinguish clearly between content and feelings paraphrases, and our responses might well be a combination of both. All three types of paraphrases of the same statement are shown in this example:

Statement: "Three weeks ago, I gave a revised draft of my honours thesis to my thesis adviser. I felt really good about it because, after a lot of work, I thought I had managed to focus my argument much more clearly and provide much more convincing support for my thesis. Well, yesterday, I stopped by my adviser's office to pick up the manuscript, and she said that she couldn't really see much difference between this draft and the first."

Content paraphrase: "Let me see if I'm understanding this right. Your adviser thought that you hadn't really done much to rework your paper, but you'd put a lot of effort into it and thought this draft was a lot better than the first."

Feelings paraphrase: "You seem to be really disappointed by your adviser's reaction to your paper."

Combination: "Your adviser could see no real difference in the paper even though you think it was much improved. You seem to be really disappointed."

In addition to paraphrasing when we need a better understanding of a message, we should also consider paraphrasing when the message is long and contains several complex ideas, when it seems to have been said under emotional strain, or when we are talking with people whose first language is not English.

In summary, to paraphrase effectively, (1) listen carefully to the message, (2) identify the verbal and nonverbal elements of the message, including the feelings associated with it, (3) determine what the message means to you, and (4) create a restatement of the message that conveys this meaning.

IN BRIEF

Understanding

Understanding is decoding a message accurately by assigning appropriate meaning to it, a process that requires active listening. Three components of active listening are

1. empathizing: using empathic responsiveness, perspective taking, or sympathetic responsiveness
2. questioning: to get needed information
3. paraphrasing: using content, feelings, or combination paraphrases to ensure understanding of a message or the feelings associated with it.

SKILL BUILDERS Paraphrasing

Skill	Use	Procedure	Example
Formulating a response that conveys your understanding of another person's message.	To increase listening efficiency; to avoid message confusion; to discover the speaker's motivation.	1. Listen carefully to the message. 2. Identify the verbal and nonverbal elements of the message, including the feelings associated with it. 3. Determine what the message means to you. 4. Create a restatement of the message that conveys this meaning.	Grace says, "At 10 minutes to five, the boss gave me three letters that had to be in the mail that evening!" Bonita replies, "I hear you. You were really resentful that your boss dumped a lot work on you right before quitting time when she knew you had to pick up your baby at the day-care centre."

TEST YOUR COMPETENCE

Writing Questions and Paraphrases

Provide an appropriate question and paraphrase for each of these statements. To get you started, the first conversation has been completed for you.

1. **Luis:** "It's Diana's birthday, and I've planned a *big* evening. Sometimes I think Diana believes I take her for granted. Well, after tonight she'll know I think she's something special!"
   Question: "What specific things do you have planned?"
   Content paraphrase: "So you've planned a night that's going to be a lot more special than what Diana expects for her birthday."
   Feelings paraphrase: "I get the feeling you're really proud of yourself for making special plans like these for Diana."
2. **Angie:** "Brother! Another dull class. I keep thinking one of these days he'll get excited about something. Professor Romero is such a bore!"
   Question:
   Content paraphrase:
   Feelings paraphrase:
3. **Guy:** "Everyone seems to be talking about that movie on Channel 5 last night, but I didn't see it. You know, I don't watch much that's on the idiot box."
   Question:
   Content paraphrase:
   Feelings paraphrase:
4. **Kaelin:** "I don't know if it's something to do with me or with Mom, but lately she and I just aren't getting along."
   Question:
   Content paraphrase:
   Feelings paraphrase:
5. **Eileen:** "I've got a seminar report to present in my soc class and a paper due in my management class. On top of that, it's my sister's birthday, and so far, I haven't even had time to get her a card. Tomorrow's going to be a disaster."
   Question:
   Content paraphrase:
   Feelings paraphrase:

Critical Analysis

Critical analysis is the process of determining how truthful, authentic, or believable we judge information to be. For instance, when a person tries to convince us to vote for a particular party's candidate for member of parliament or to support efforts to legalize marijuana, we will want to listen critically to these messages to determine the extent to which we agree with the speaker and how we might wish to respond. If we fail to listen critically to the messages we receive, we risk inadvertently concurring in ideas or plans that may violate our own values or principles, be counterproductive to achieving our own goals, or be misleading to others (including the speakers) who value our judgment.

Critical analysis requires that we evaluate the quality of the **inferences** we hear. Inferences are claims or assertions based on observation or fact, but they are not necessarily true. Critical listeners evaluate inferences by examining the context in which they occur. An inference is usually presented as part of an argument; that is, a person makes a claim (an inference) and then presents other statements in support of the claim. Here is an example of a simple argument. Joyce says, "This year is going to be a lot easier than last year. I have been approved for a larger student loan, and my science requirements are all completed." The statements "I have been approved for a larger student loan," and "my science requirements are all completed" are both factual statements that can be documented. However, Joyce's claim, "This year is going to be a lot easier than last year" is an inference, a statement that requires support to validate it. Notice that Joyce's inference suggests that she believes there is a relationship between her claim and the facts she presents. Her argument is based on the assumption that having more money to spend and not having to take science courses will make her year easier.

The critical listener tests any inference by asking at least three questions:

1. **Is there factual information to support the inference?** Perhaps there is no supporting information; perhaps there is not enough; or perhaps the supporting information is inaccurate. Joyce does have factual statements for support: she was approved for a larger loan, and she has completed all of her science requirements.

2. **Is the factual support relevant to the inference?** Perhaps the actual or implied statement of relevance is logically weak. In the example, having more money is one kind of information that is relevant to having an easier year. At this stage, it would appear that Joyce does have the makings of a sound argument; however, we need to ask a third question.

3. **Is there known information that would prevent the inference from logically following the factual statements?** Perhaps there is information that is not accounted for that affects the likelihood of the inference. If we learn that Joyce faces a substantial tuition or rent increase or that she must complete a demanding independent-study project, we might question whether the upcoming year is likely to be "a lot easier" than the last one.

For many people, the most difficult of the three questions to answer is the second one: Is the factual support relevant to the inference? This question is difficult to answer because it requires the listener to create a statement that shows the relevance. The listener must create the statement because, in most informal reasoning, the link between the factual support and the inference is only implied, not stated, by the person presenting the argument. Recall that Joyce never said anything like, "Increased income and elimination of a science requirement are two criteria for predicting that next year will be a lot easier." Because the link is more often implied than stated, we must learn to state it for ourselves.

TEST YOUR COMPETENCE

Evaluating Inferences

For each of these statements, answer three questions: (1) Is the inference supported by factual statements? (2) Is the stated or implied factual support relevant to the inference? (3) Is there any other known information that lessens the quality of the inference? Remember, to evaluate inferences properly, you must phrase a statement to link the supporting information to the inference.

1. "The women's rugby club held a raffle, and they made a lot of money. I think we should hold a raffle too."
2. "Chad is aggressive, personable, and highly motivated. He ought to make a good salesman."
3. "Three of my students got A's on this test last year, five the year before, and three the year before that. There certainly will be some A's this year."
4. "I saw Kali in a maternity outfit. She must be pregnant."
5. "Listen, Darren is here on a full scholarship, Samantha won the mathematics prize in first year, and Marco and Ellen are honours students. All four live in Pearson Hall. It's clear that all the top students are placed in Pearson."
6. "If Greg hadn't come barging in, I never would have spilled my iced tea."
7. "Maybe that's the way you see it, but to me, when high city officials are caught with their hands in the till and when police close their eyes to the actions of people with money, that's corruption."
8. "Krista wears her hair that way and guys fall all over her. I'm getting my hair cut like that."

The key to stating the relationship between factual support and an inference is to ask ourselves: What can I say that would allow this inference to follow logically from these facts? For instance, suppose Hal says to Matilda, "I see frost on the grass. I think our flowers are goners." What can Matilda say that would establish the relevance of the supporting fact "frost on the grass" to the claim "our flowers are goners"? She could think, "The presence of frost means that the temperature is low enough to freeze the moisture on the grass. If it's cold enough to freeze the moisture on the grass, it's too cold for our flowers to survive." Hal's inference seems to make sense because there is a logical relationship between frost and the death of unprotected flowers.

Here is another example. Gina says, "I studied all night and got only a D on the first test, so I'm not going to do any better on this one." This statement suggests that Gina thinks the amount of study time before a test is relevant to the grade received on the test. We could phrase the implied relationship between the factual support and the inference by saying, "Because the amount of study time before the test determines the grade, and Gina could not increase the amount of time that she devoted to study, she cannot improve her grade." In this case, the inference seems questionable. Though the relationship between study time and test scores is unquestionably strong, Gina's reasoning suggests that study time is the only factor that determines a grade. Experience would suggest that many other factors, such as previous time studying, method of study, aptitude for the subject, and state of mind during the writing of the test, are equally important. This inference, then, fails to meet the third test: there is known information that would prevent the inference from logically following from the factual statements.

IN BRIEF

Critical Analysis

Critical analysis is the process of determining the truthfulness, authenticity, or believability of information. Critical analysis requires that you evaluate the quality of inferences used by the speaker. Ask the following three questions:

1. Is there factual information to support the inference?
2. Is the factual support relevant to the inference?
3. Is there known information that would prevent the inference from logically following the factual statements?

In short, we are listening critically when (1) we question whether the inference is supported with factual statements, (2) we question whether the stated or implied factual support is relevant to the inference, and (3) we question whether there is any other known information that lessens the quality of the inference.

Spotlight on Scholars

Douglas Walton, University of Winnipeg

Douglas Walton is a leading scholar in the area of argumentation. Having published 33 books and about 150 journal articles, he is best known for his work in the field of fallacies. He has worked on research projects and workshops in Holland, Scotland, Germany, New Zealand, and Australia; he has been visiting professor at several universities, including Northwestern University and the University of Arizona; he has been a fellow of the NIAS (Netherlands Institute for Advanced Study in the Humanities and Social Sciences); and he has won several prizes for his contributions to the field of argumentation.

In order to explain the importance of his studies, it is necessary to relate argumentation and fallacy to what in ancient times was called dialectic, or the art of reasoned conversation. Dialectic is based on kinds of reasoning used to defend a position, to prove a thesis, to persuade a listener—or a jury, as one might do in a trial—to conduct an inquiry, or to negotiate. The term *dialectic* as used in ancient times revealed a common element in the disciplines of logic and rhetoric, showing their common basis in argumentation.

Now the use of the term is coming back. *Computational dialectic,* for example, has recently emerged as a field of research in multi-agent computing. Until recently, however, there was no systematic theory of dialectical argumentation. Through his research, Douglas Walton developed an original—some would even say revolutionary—dialectical theory applied to the study of reasonable arguments as well as fallacies. Studying the reasons for the strength of common arguments, as well as for their weaknesses and their potential for misleading, he defines fallacies both as errors and as deceptive strategies used to try to unfairly get the best of a speech partner in a discussion.

The first step in the description of Walton's theory is the multiple view of the New Dialectic that postulates different types of dialogues. Persuasion, negotiation, or quarrelling, for example, can have different goals. Walton offered a typology of dialogues in which participants' arguments are used for different conversational purposes and can be judged as fallacious or valid according to their use in a dialogue. The personal verbal attack, or the threat, for example, can be a valid move in a quarrel, but when people are having a discussion for the purpose of resolving a conflict of opinions by rational argumentation, such an attack can be rightly judged irrelevant and conversationally inappropriate.

In all these dialogues, participants use logical and quasi-logical reasoning. The conclusion put forward may be based on an argument that is valid, probable, or simply plausible in terms of

(continued)

commonly accepted opinions and ways of doing things. For this reason, Walton evaluates the process of argumentation by introducing the concept of an *argumentation scheme,* a schematic set of common ways of reasoning. Argumentation schemes are based on the ancient *topoi,* or common fields. Fallacies can be analyzed in many instances as arguments that fail to fulfil the requirements of an argumentation scheme. Other instances of fallacies are analyzed in relation to patterns of deception in a game of dialogue. Dialogues are in fact described in a normative way as regulated by strategic rules, based not only on their goals, but also on the concepts of commitment and burden of proof.

The originality of Walton's work lies in the way he studied the process of argumentation. He utilized not only argumentation schemes but also models of dialogical reasoning, and analyzed fallacies as both misuse of schemes and incorrect strategies to unfairly win a game of dialogue.

This theory has been applied to several fields of human communication, including law, especially evidence law, and computing, especially artificial intelligence and multi-agent computing. It has proven to be a tool that enables one to read behind the words in evaluating real arguments and discovering the tactics used in propaganda. It has become a means of interpreting and studying legal debates, trials, and statutes. Walton analyzed trials from a dialectical perspective, studying their rules and how they can be violated. The goal of artificial intelligence is to make a machine able to duplicate human intelligence. For this reason, Walton's recent research has focused on questioning and argumentation software as well as Wigmore diagrams.

Walton's research contributions extend from logic to law, linguistics, and computer science. He has opened up argumentation theory to a wide range of possible applications, making this new applied science a research field of national and international importance.

A complete outline of Walton's articles, books, and projects can be found on his home page at **http://io.uwinnipeg.ca/~walton/**.

Responding Empathically to Give Comfort

Once we have understood a speaker's message, we may recognize that the speaker is in need of emotional comfort. To **comfort** people means to help them feel better about themselves and their behaviour. Comfort is drawn from feeling respected, understood, and confirmed.

Research on comforting shows that people who use a relatively high percentage of comforting strategies are perceived as more sensitive, concerned, and involved (Samter, Burleson, & Murphy, 1987; Burleson & Samter, 1990; Kunkel & Burleson, 1999). Obviously, we cannot comfort unless we have first empathized.

In the section on understanding, we discussed two important empathic responses: questioning and paraphrasing. In this section, we consider supporting and interpreting.

Supporting

Supporting responses are comforting statements that aim to approve, bolster, encourage, soothe, console, or cheer up. They show that we care about people and what happens to them and demonstrate that we empathize with people's feelings whatever their direction or intensity (Burleson, 1994, p. 5).

Brian Bailey/Stone/Getty Images

We all treasure our good feelings; when we share them, we don't want them dashed by inappropriate or insensitive responses.

Supporting (approving) positive feelings We all treasure our good feelings. When we share them, we do not want them dashed by an inappropriate or insensitive response. Supporting positive feelings is generally easy but still requires some care. Consider this exchange between Kendra and Selena:

Kendra *(hangs up the telephone, does a little dance step, and turns to Selena):* That was my boss. He said that he'd put my name in for promotion. I didn't believe he would really choose me!

Kendra's statement requires an appropriate verbal response. In order to make one, Selena must appreciate the feelings people experience when they receive good news, or she must imagine how she would feel under the same circumstances.

Selena: Kendra, way to go, girl! That's terrific! I am so happy for you. You really seem excited.

Selena's response approves Kendra's excitement. It also shows that she is happy because Kendra seems happy.

Supporting responses like Selena's are very valuable. Think of a time when you have experienced an event that made you feel happy, proud, pleased, relieved, or amused, and when you needed to express that feeling. Did it not further your good feelings when others recognized them and affirmed your right to have them?

THINKING ABOUT . . .

Sharing Good Feelings

Recall an occasion when you were feeling especially happy, proud, or pleased and chose to share your feelings with someone else. Whom did you choose? Why did you choose this person? How did the person react? What effect did the person's reaction have on your immediate feelings? On your relationship with the person? If you had a similar situation, would you again choose to tell this person?

Supporting (giving comfort) when a person experiences negative feelings When a person has had an unfortunate experience and is in the midst of (or is recalling) unpleasant emotional reactions, an effective supporting statement provides much-needed comfort. By acknowledging these feelings and supporting the person's right to them, we can help the person work through them.

For some people, making appropriate responses to painful or angry feelings is very awkward and difficult, but when people are in pain or when they are feeling justifiably angry, they need to be comforted by appropriate supporting statements. Because it can be difficult to provide comfort when we are ill at ease, we need to practise and develop skill at making appropriate supporting statements.

An appropriate comforting statement shows empathy, sensitivity, and may show a willingness to be actively involved if need be. Consider this example:

Bill: My sister called today to tell me that Mom's biopsy came back positive. She's got cancer, and it's untreatable.

Dwight: Bill, you must be in shock. I'm so sorry that this is happening. Do you want to talk about it? Is there anything I can do to help you right now?

Notice how Dwight begins by empathizing: "Bill, you must be in shock." He continues with statements that show his sensitivity to the seriousness of the situation: "I'm so sorry that this is happening." Finally, he shows that he really cares, that he is willing to take time to talk about it, and he asks whether he can do anything for Bill.

We have suggested that supportive responses may reassure, bolster, encourage, soothe, console, or cheer up. Given this range of possible outcomes, different situations will certainly call for different approaches, and on some occasions we may want to use more than one approach. For instance, instead of just recognizing that the person is feeling pain ("That must have been a particularly painful experience for you"), we may also want to extend our willingness to help ("Is there anything I can do for you?") or provide an optimistic note ("Dawn felt really down too when she was in your situation, but she was able to get the kind of help that allowed her to get through the ordeal"). In fact, combination approaches are often perceived as most comforting (Clark et al., 1998, p. 237).

The following example shows a response that seems to be supportive but is really inappropriate:

Jim *(comes out of his boss's office clutching a report that he had been sure he would receive praise for)*: Jacobs tore my report apart. I worked my tail off, tried to do everything he asked, and he just threw it back in my face and told me to redo it.

Aaron *(who has not read the report)*: Jim, I can see why you're angry. You deserved praise for what you did!

Such a response certainly has supporting qualities, and Jim might feel soothed, but support that uncritically sides with the person needing comfort can have unintended side effects, especially in a case like this one, where Aaron is in no position to judge whether the report did in fact deserve praise. Instead, Aaron would do better to focus his supporting response on how hard Jim worked and his resulting feelings of anger:

Aaron: He rejected it? After you worked all that overtime, I can see why you're so upset.

Empathic support is not uncritical praise, and it does not involve making false statements or telling people only what they want to hear. When supportive statements are out of touch with the facts, they can encourage behaviour that is actually destructive. When offering comfort through supporting statements, we must be sure that we do not inadvertently set the other person up to cause himself or herself further trouble or pain by engaging in such behaviour.

Making an appropriate supporting response is most difficult in situations of high emotion and stress. Sometimes the best supporting response is a nonverbal one. Imagine this scenario: In the final few seconds of a basketball game, with her team trailing by one point, Jameela misses an uncontested lay-up. She walks off the floor, looks at the coach, and shouts, "I blew it! I lost us the game!" How should the coach react? A first impulse might be to say, "Don't feel bad, Jameela," but Jameela obviously does feel bad, and she has a right to those feelings. Another response might be, "Hey, Jameela, you didn't lose us the game, the whole team shares the loss," but Jameela's miss did affect the outcome, and in the heat of the moment she is unlikely to comforted by this kind of logic. Perhaps the best thing the coach could do at that moment would be to put an arm around Jameela and give a comforting squeeze that says, "It's okay, I understand." Later, the coach might say, "Jameela, I know you feel bad, but without your steal we wouldn't even have had a chance to win." Still, for the moment, Jameela is going to be difficult to console.

Some people think that comforting, supportive statements come easier to women, or even that they are a female skill. In fact, some people go so far as to say that men and women are totally different in their understanding of comfort. However, in a detailed analysis of views on comforting, Kunkel and Burleson (1999) found that "Men and women tend to use, if not identical, at least very similar rulers in evaluating the sensitivity and effectiveness of emotional support" (p. 334). So it is not that men and women see comforting differently; rather, men and women perform differently. Men focus more on behaviours, and women focus more on feelings. In their laboratory study, Derlega, Barbee, and Winstead (1994) found that men were perceived to be somewhat better than women in providing achievement-related support (such as in supporting a colleague who has been passed over for a promotion).

If men recognize the importance of more personal, feelings-oriented types of comforting statements as much as women do, why do they not do better at providing them? Kunkel and Burleson (1999) conclude that "men lack the competence to perform comforting behaviours as sensitively and effectively as women" (p. 335). In other words, men seem to need more practice than women do in applying the information presented in this section. Whether you are a man or a woman, you can learn to give effective supportive responses.

In summary, to make effective supporting statements, (1) listen closely to what the person is saying, (2) try to empathize with the dominant feelings, (3) phrase a reply that is in harmony with the feelings you have identified, (4) supplement your verbal response with appropriate nonverbal responses, and (5) if it seems appropriate, indicate your willingness to help.

Interpreting

Interpreting responses are those that offer a reasonable alternative explanation for an event or circumstance with the goal of helping another to understand the situation from a different perspective. Especially when people's emotions are running high, they are likely to see only one of a number of possible explanations. Consider the following situation.

Travis returns from his first date with Natasha, a woman he has been interested in for some time. He plops down on the couch, shakes his head, and says, "Well, that was a disaster! We had a great dinner and saw a really good show, but when we got to her door, she gives me a quick little kiss on the cheek, says, 'Thanks a lot,' and rushes into the house. We didn't even have much time to talk about the play. I guess I can forget about her. It's clear she's not interested in me."

Travis is interpreting Natasha's behaviour negatively, as a rejection of him. Martin, Travis's roommate, has been listening to him. Although he does not know what Natasha thinks, he perceives that Travis is seeing only one explanation for these events and that he might be comforted by seeing other possible explanations. So Martin says, "You're right, her behaviour seems to have been a bit abrupt, but maybe she's had bad experiences with other guys—you know, ones who tried to go too far too fast. Maybe she wasn't really trying to reject you; she was just trying to protect herself."

Whose interpretation is correct? Only time will tell. Remember, Martin (like anyone who tries to offer comfort to another) is not a mind reader. No one in this position can know for sure why something was done or said. The primary goal when interpreting is to help a person look at an event from a different point of view.

Like supporting statements, interpretive responses can do more harm than good if they mislead the person we are trying to comfort. We should restrict ourselves, therefore, to offering alternative explanations that seem plausible and

THINKING ABOUT . . .

Comforting Responses

Think of the last time you told someone about an event or circumstance during which you felt scared, hurt, disappointed, or angry. Did the person try to comfort you? If so, report what was said. Did the person try to offer alternative interpretations for what had happened? Did this help you? If so, how? If not, why not? What can you learn from this experience that will help you improve your response skills?

Michael Newman/PhotoEdit, Inc.

People often misinterpret the events that affect them. We can support one another by offering alternatives to negative interpretations.

worth considering. The point is not merely to soothe the person's feelings but to help the person see a possibility that he or she has overlooked. Most events can be interpreted in more than one way, and we can be supportive by helping people see alternative explanations for things that happen to them. When we do this, we both comfort them and help them to more accurately understand what has happened.

Here are two additional examples of appropriate interpreting responses:

Karla: I just don't understand Nikolay. I say we've got to start saving money if we want to get married next year, and he just gets angry with me.

Shelley: I can understand why his behaviour would concern you *(a supportive statement prefacing an interpretation)*. Perhaps he feels guilty about not being able to save money or resentful that you seem to be putting all the blame on him.

Micah: My boss is so unfair. He says I'm the best worker in the department, but I haven't had a pay raise in more than a year.

Khalif: I can see why you'd be frustrated, but maybe it has nothing to do with the quality of your work. Maybe the company just doesn't have the money to pay you more.

Both of these examples follow the guidelines for providing appropriate interpreting responses: (1) Listen carefully to what that person is saying. (2) Think of other reasonable explanations for the event or circumstance and decide which alternative seems to best fit the situation as you understand it. (3) Phrase an alternative to the person's own interpretation, one that is intended to help the person see that other interpretations are available. (4) When appropriate, try to preface the interpretive statement with a supporting response.

IN BRIEF

Responding Empathically to Give Comfort

To provide comfort is to help others feel better about themselves and their behaviour. We can provide comfort in three ways:

- by supporting (approving) a person's positive feelings
- by supporting (with empathy, sensitivity, and willingness to help) when a person is experiencing negative feelings
- by making interpreting responses that offer a reasonable alternative explanation for a troubling event or circumstance.

TEST YOUR COMPETENCE

Supporting and Interpreting

For each of these situations, supply one supporting and one interpreting response.

1. **Statement:** "The milk is all gone! I know there was at least half a carton last night. I'll bet Jeff guzzled it all before he left for work. What did he expect me to put on my cereal, root beer? All my brother ever thinks about is himself!"
   Supporting response:
   Interpreting response:
2. **Statement:** "My manager must be trying to fire me or get me to quit. He told me that it's been a while since I completed my training, and he wants me to take 10 hours of upgrading on my own time."
   Supporting response:
   Interpreting response:
3. **Statement:** "I just got a call from my folks. My sister was in a car accident and ended up in hospital. They say she's okay, but the car was a write off. I don't know whether she's really all right or they just don't want me to worry."
   Supporting response:
   Interpreting response:

COMMUNICATE!
Using Technology

Speaker phones, wireless phones, and cellular phones have brought a new level of convenience to communication. These days, you can work on your computer, drive, or even cook dinner while you are on the phone. But what effects have these devices had on your listening effectiveness? Next time you are using one of these devices, be conscious of your listening. How well are you doing at attending, understanding, evaluating, responding empathically, and remembering? Which of the guidelines provided in this chapter should you apply to improve your listening under these conditions?

OBSERVE & ANALYZE
Journal Activity

Creating Mnemonics

Mnemonics are useful memory aids. Construct a mnemonic to help you remember the following techniques and procedures explained in this chapter: the three techniques for improving attending, the three elements of active listening, the five-step procedure for empathizing, the four guidelines for effective questioning, the four-step procedure for paraphrasing, and the three tests for evaluating inferences.

Tomorrow, while you are getting dressed, see whether you can recall the mnemonics you created. Then see whether you can recall the techniques and procedures from the cues in your mnemonic. How well did you do?

Remembering: Retaining Information

Remembering is being able to retain information and recall it when it is needed. Too often, we forget almost immediately what we have heard. For instance, you can probably think of many times when you were unable to recall the name of a person to whom you were introduced just moments earlier. Three techniques that are likely to work in improving our ability to remember information are repeating, constructing mnemonics, and taking notes.

Repeat Information

Repetition—saying something two, three, or even four times—helps listeners to store information in long-term memory by providing necessary reinforcement (Estes, 1989, p. 7). If information is not reinforced, it will be held in short-term memory for as little as 20 seconds and then forgotten. So, when Hilda is introduced to a stranger named Jack McNeil, if she mentally says, "Jack McNeil, Jack McNeil, Jack McNeil, Jack McNeil," she increases the chances that she will remember his name. Likewise, when a person gives her the directions, "Go two blocks east, turn left, turn right at the next light, and it's in the next block," she should immediately repeat to herself, "two blocks east, turn left, turn right at light, next block—that's two blocks east, turn left, turn right at light, next block."

Construct Mnemonics

Constructing mnemonics helps listeners put information in forms that are more easily recalled. A **mnemonic device** is any artificial technique used as a memory aid. One of the most common ways of forming a mnemonic is to take the first letters of a list of items we are trying to remember and form a word. For example, an easy mnemonic for remembering the names of the five Great Lakes is HOMES (Huron, Ontario, Michigan, Erie, Superior).

When we want to remember items in a sequence, we can try to form a sentence with the words themselves or other words having the same first letters, arranged in the right order to form an easy-to-remember statement. For example, when people study music for the first time, they may remember the lines of the treble clef (EGBDF) by recalling the saying *every good boy deserves favour,* and for the spaces of the treble clef (FACE), they may recall the word *face.*

Take Notes

Although note taking would be inappropriate in most casual interpersonal encounters, it represents a powerful tool for increasing our recall of information when we are participating in telephone conversations, briefing sessions, interviews, meetings, lectures, and workshops, or when we are listening to speeches. Note taking provides us with a written record we can go back to, and it also enables us to take a more active role in the listening process (Wolvin & Coakley, 1996, p. 239). Particularly when we are listening to complex information, it is beneficial to take notes.

What constitutes good notes will vary depending on the situation. Useful notes may consist of a brief list of main points or key ideas plus a few of the most significant details, or they may be a short summary of an entire presentation (a type of paraphrase) written after it is completed. For long or detailed presentations, however, good notes will likely consist of an outline of the points that the speaker has covered, including the central idea (the thesis) of the presentation, the main points offered in support of that idea, and key developmental material. Good notes are not necessarily long, but like a good outline, they should reveal the sequence of the points made in the presentation and the hierarchy of ideas. In other words, they should remind the note-taker which supporting material supports which point and how the points taken together support the thesis.

Many students confuse note taking with stenography, attempting to take down much too much information when they are taking notes. The problem with this approach is that most people cannot write fast enough to get everything down, so they end up with fragmentary and incomplete notes: notes with large gaps, unfinished segments, and incoherent segments. Such notes are likely to be more misleading than helpful when the student refers to them later. Even if this student could write fast enough to get everything down, paying so much attention to note taking is going to prevent him or her from participating in any meaningful way in the class. Most classroom lectures can be reduced to a short outline of major points that will be useful in guiding the review of the material at a later date.

IN BRIEF

Remembering: Retaining Information

Remembering is being able to retain information and recall it when it is needed. Three techniques for improving our ability to remember are:

- repeating information to help store it in long-term memory
- constructing mnemonics
- taking notes.

TEST YOUR COMPETENCE

Listening Test

Have a friend assume the role of a fellow worker on your first day in an office job and read the following information to you once, at a normal rate of speech. As the friend reads the instructions, take notes. Then test yourself by answering the numbered questions without referring to your notes. Then repeat the quiz, this time using your notes. How much did your score improve? Although it may be tempting to read this item to yourself, try not to. You will miss both the enjoyment and the value of the exercise if you do. After you have completed the exercise compare your notes with those shown in Figure 5.1. Did you miss any important points? How much unnecessary information did you include?

Since you are new to the job, I'd like to fill you in on a few details. The boss probably told you that word processing and distributing mail were your most important duties. Well, they may be, but let me tell you, answering the phone is going to take most of your time. Now about the word processing. Goodwin will give the most, but much of what he gives you may have nothing to do with the department. I'd be careful about spending all my time doing his private work. Mason doesn't give much, but you'd better get it right—she's really picky. I've always asked to have tests at least two days in advance. Paulson is always dropping stuff on the desk at the last minute.

The mail situation sounds complicated, but you'll get used to it. Incoming mail comes to the campus post office in Harper Hall twice a day: at 10 a.m. and at 2 p.m. It is delivered here at McDaniel about an hour later. You've got to take all the outgoing mail that's been left on the desk to Charles Hall for pick-up. If you have rush stuff, take it right to the campus post office in Harper Hall. It's a little longer walk, but for rush stuff, it's faster. When you receive the McDaniel Hall mail, sort it. You'll have to make sure that only mail for the people up here gets delivered here. If there is any that doesn't belong here, bundle it back up and mark it for return to the campus post office.

(continued)

Now, about your breaks. You get 15 minutes in the morning, 40 minutes at noon, and 15 minutes in the afternoon. If you're smart, you'll leave for your morning break before the 10:30 classes let out. That's usually a very busy time. Three of the professors are supposed to have office hours then, and if they don't keep them, the students will be on your back. If you take your lunch at 11:45, you'll be back before the main crew goes.

Oh, one more thing. You are supposed to call Jeno at 8:15 every morning to wake him. If you forget, he gets very upset. Well, good luck.

	Without Notes	With Notes
1. Where are you to take the mail that does not belong here?	______	______
2. How often does mail come?	______	______
3. When should you be back from lunch?	______	______
4. What is Paulson's problem with requests for work?	______	______
5. Who gives the most work?	______	______
6. What's the problem with Goodwin's request to do work?	______	______
7. What are your main jobs, according to the boss?	______	______
8. Where are you to take outgoing mail?	______	______
9. Where is the post office?	______	______
10. How many minutes do you get for your morning break?	______	______
11. What is the preferred time to take your lunch?	______	______
12. Who are you supposed to give a wake-up call to?	______	______

Answers

1. Campus post office (or Harper Hall) 2. Twice a day 3. 12:25 4. Last minute 5. Goodwin 6. Not work-related 7. Word processing/distributing mail 8. Charles Hall 9. Harper Hall 10. 10 11. 11:45 12. Jeno

Duties
Typing, distribution of mail important
Answering phone takes most time

Typing
Goodwin gives most—question doing private work
Mason does not give much, but get it right—she's picky.
Ask for tests 2 days in advance (watch out for Paulson's last minute)

Mail
Incoming at 11 and 3
Take outgoing to Charles Hall
Rush stuff goes to campus PO in Harper
Sort mail for McDaniel Hall—bundle what doesn't belong and mark for return to the campus PO

Breaks
15 min. morning—take before 10:30
40 min. lunch—take at 11:45
15 min. afternoon

Extra
Call Jeno 8:15 (93 words)

Figure 5.1
Sample notes

WHAT WOULD YOU DO?
A QUESTION OF ETHICS

Janeen always disliked talking on the telephone. She thought it was an impersonal form of communication. Thus, university was a wonderful respite. When friends would call her, instead of staying on the phone, she could quickly run over to their residence or meet them at a coffeehouse.

One day during the reading period before exams, Janeen received a phone call from Barbara, an out-of-town friend. Before she was able to dismiss the call with her stock excuses, she found herself bombarded with information about old high-school friends and their whereabouts. Not wanting to disappoint Barbara, who seemed eager to talk, Janeen tucked her phone under her chin and began straightening her room, answering Barbara with the occasional "uh-huh," "hmm," or "wow, that's cool!"

As the "conversation" progressed, Janeen began reading through her mail and then her notes from class. After a few minutes, she realized there was silence on the other end of the line. Suddenly very ashamed, she said, "I'm sorry, what did you say? The phone . . . uh there was just a lot of static."

Barbara replied with obvious hurt in her voice, "I'm sorry I bothered you, you must be terribly busy."

Embarrassed, Janeen muttered, "I'm just really stressed, you know, with exams coming up and everything. I guess I wasn't listening very well; you didn't seem to be saying anything really important. I'm sorry. What were you saying?"

"Nothing *important,*" Barbara answered. "I was just trying to figure out a way to tell you. I know that you were friends with my brother Billy, and you see, we just found out yesterday that he's terminal with a rare form of leukemia. But you're right, it obviously isn't really important." With that, she hung up.

1. How ethical was Janeen's means of dealing with her dilemma of not wanting to talk on the phone but not wanting to hurt Barbara's feelings?
2. Identify ways in which both Janeen and Barbara could have used better and perhaps more ethical interpersonal communication skills.

Summary

Listening is an active process that involves attending, understanding, and evaluating. Success at the related skills of responding and remembering depends very much on a person's ability to listen. Effective listening is essential to competent communication.

Attending is the process of selecting the sound waves we consciously process. We can increase the effectiveness of our attention by (1) getting ready to listen, (2) making the shift from speaker to listener a complete one, (3) hearing a person out before reacting, and (4) adjusting our attention to the listening goals of the situation.

Understanding is the process of decoding a message by assigning meaning to it. A key to understanding is to practise active listening: empathizing, asking questions, and paraphrasing. Empathizing is intellectually identifying with or

	Good Listeners	Bad Listeners
ATTENDING	Attend to important information	May not hear what a person is saying
	Ready themselves physically and mentally	Fidget in their chairs, look out the window, and let their minds wander
	Listen objectively regardless of emotional involvement	Visibly react to emotional language
	Listen differently depending on the situation	Listen the same way regardless of the situation
UNDERSTANDING	Assign appropriate meaning to what is said	Hear what is said but are either unable to understand or assign different meaning to the words
	Seek out apparent purpose, main points, and supporting information	Ignore the way information is organized
	Ask mental questions to anticipate information	Fail to anticipate coming information
	Silently paraphrase to solidify understanding	Seldom or never mentally review information
	Seek out subtle meanings based on nonverbal cues	Ignore nonverbal cues
EVALUATING	Listen critically	Hear and understand what is said but are unable to weigh and consider it
	Separate facts from inferences	Don't differentiate between facts and inferences
	Evaluate inferences	Accept information at face value
RESPONDING EMPATHICALLY	Provide supportive, comforting statements	Pass off joy or hurt; change the subject
	Give alternative interpretations	Pass off hurt; change the subject
REMEMBERING	Retain information	Interpret message accurately but forget it
	Repeat key information	Assume they will remember
	Mentally create mnemonics for lists of words and ideas	Seldom single out any information as especially important
	Take notes	Rely on memory alone

Figure 5.2
A comparison of the behaviours of good and bad listeners

vicariously experiencing the feelings, thoughts, or attitudes of another. We can increase our ability to empathize through caring and concentrating.

Evaluating, or critical listening, is the process of separating fact from inference and judging the validity of the inferences made. A fact is a verifiable statement; an inference is a conclusion drawn from facts. To listen critically, a person should (1) question whether an inference is supported with factual statements, (2) question whether the factual support is relevant to the inference, and (3) question whether there is any other known information that lessens the quality of the inference.

Responding empathically gives comfort. Comforting responses give people information about themselves or their behaviour. Comforting can be accomplished through supporting and interpreting responses. In being supportive, a person can soothe, approve, reduce tension, or pacify another by showing understanding of what the other is feeling and supporting that person's right to those feelings. To offer an interpreting response, a person offers a reasonable or alternative explanation for an event or circumstance with the goal of helping another to understand the situation from a different perspective.

Remembering is the process of storing meanings that have been received so they may be recalled later. Remembering is increased by repeating information, by constructing mnemonics, which organize information to make it easier to remember, and, when feasible, by taking notes.

Figure 5.2 summarizes how good listeners and poor listeners deal with attending, understanding, evaluating, responding empathically, and remembering.

Glossary

Review the following key terms:

active listening (106) — using specific listening techniques, including empathizing, questioning, and paraphrasing, to ensure understanding.

attending (104) — the perceptual process of selecting and focusing on specific stimuli from among the countless stimuli reaching the senses.

comforting (116) — helping people feel better about themselves and their behaviour.

content paraphrase (110) — a paraphrase that focuses on the denotative meaning of a verbal message.

critical analysis (112) — the process of determining the truthfulness, authenticity, or believability of the information received from another.

empathic responsiveness (106) — experiencing an emotional response parallel to another person's actual or anticipated display of emotion.

empathy (106) — intellectual identification with or vicarious experience of the feelings, thoughts, or attitudes of another, followed by an appropriate response.

feelings paraphrase (110) — a paraphrase that focuses on the emotions associated with a verbal message.

inferences (113) — claims or assertions which are based on observations or facts but which may or may not be true.

interpreting responses (120) — statements that offer a reasonable alternative explanation for an event or circumstance with the goal of helping another to understand the situation from a different perspective.

listening (104) — the process of receiving, attending to, and assigning meaning to aural and visual stimuli.

mnemonic device (122) — any artificial technique used as a memory aid.

paraphrase (110) — a restatement, in your own words, of your understanding of a speaker's message *(see content paraphrase and feelings paraphrase).*

perspective taking (106) — imagining yourself in the place of another.

question (108) — a response designed to get further information or to clarify information already received.

remembering (122) — being able to retain information and recall it when it is needed.

respecting (107) — paying serious attention to what others are saying and what they feel about what they are saying.

supporting responses (116) — comforting statements which aim to approve, bolster, encourage, soothe, console, or cheer up.

sympathetic responsiveness (106) — feeling concern, compassion, or sorrow for another because of the other's situation or plight.

understanding (106) — decoding a message accurately by assigning appropriate meaning to it.

SELF-REVIEW

Establishing a Communication Foundation from Chapters 2 to 5

What kind of a communicator are you? This review looks at 15 specific behaviours that are basic to effective communicators. On the line provided for each statement, indicate the response that best captures your behaviour:

1 = almost always 2 = often 3 = occasionally 4 = rarely 5 = never

1. When I speak, I tend to present a positive image of myself. (Ch. 2) _____
2. In my behaviour toward others, I look for more information to confirm or negate my first impressions. (Ch. 2) _____
3. Before I act on perceptions drawn from people's nonverbal cues, I seek verbal verification of their accuracy. (Ch. 2) _____
4. My conversation is assisted by a well developed vocabulary. (Ch. 3) _____
5. I speak clearly, using specific, concrete, and precise words that people readily understand. (Ch. 3) _____
6. When I am speaking with people of different cultures, I am careful to monitor my word choices. (Ch. 3) _____
7. I strive always to use language that is appropriate to my listeners. (Ch. 3) _____
8. I tend to look at people when I talk with them. (Ch. 4) _____
9. Most of my sentences are free from interferences such as *uh, well, like,* and *you know.* (Ch. 4) _____
10. When I am making decisions about my clothes and grooming, I consider how others are likely to interpret the choices I make. (Ch. 4) _____
11. I try to control my environment in ways that help my communication. (Ch. 4) _____
12. When I'm not sure whether I understand, I seek clarification. (Ch. 5) _____
13. When a person describes an unfortunate experience, I am able to provide appropriate comfort. (Ch. 5) _____
14. I listen attentively, regardless of my interest in the speaker or the ideas. (Ch. 5) _____
15. I adopt strategies to help me to remember important information. (Ch. 5) _____
16. I critically evaluate the statements I hear. (Ch. 5) _____

Based on your responses, select the communication behaviour you would most like to change. Write a communication improvement plan similar to the one shown in Chapter 1 (page 26). If you would like verification of your self-analysis before you write an improvement plan, have a friend or classmate complete this same analysis for you.

two

Interpersonal communication is informal interaction with others that occurs one on one or in small groups. Talking to a friend in the cafeteria, chatting on the phone or exchanging electronic messages with a classmate about an upcoming test, arguing the merits of a movie with friends, getting news from home in an e-mail message, consoling a close friend who has lost a girlfriend, planning the future with a loved one, being interviewed for a job, and discussing strategies for accomplishing tasks at work are all forms of interpersonal communication.

Through interpersonal communication, we converse, share ideas and feelings, and form relationships. Because much interpersonal communication takes place in informal settings, we are often unaware of the importance of interpersonal skills. Too often, people think, "I am who I am—how I talk is natural to me—I can't change it," but people who hold this attitude are ignorant of the fact that we can control how we communicate even in the most spontaneous situations. In this section, we look at a number of aspects of interpersonal communication to understand the kinds of improvements we can achieve and what we can do to achieve them.

How we communicate affects how others think of us and treat us. Improving our interpersonal communication skills can empower us. People who clearly express their ideas, beliefs, and opinions become influential and exert control over what happens to them and to others whom they care about. When we accurately and precisely encode our thoughts, others gain a better appreciation of our position. This understanding and appreciation increases the likelihood that they will respond in ways that are consistent with our needs.

In this section, we discuss conversation, self-disclosure and feedback, building and maintaining relationships, and the special challenges of interpersonal communication with people from other cultures. With an increased repertoire of interpersonal communication skills, we can select the ones that are most appropriately used in any particular communication context.

II

INTERPERSONAL COMMUNICATION

Rob Melnychuk/PhotoDisc Green/Getty Images

OBJECTIVES

After you have read this chapter, you should be able to answer these questions:

- What is a conversation?
- How does a casual social conversation differ from a pragmatic problem-consideration conversation?
- What are conversational rules, and what are their distinguishing features?
- What is the co-operative principle of conversation?
- What are the maxims underlying the co-operative principle, and how does each apply to conversation?
- What skills are used by effective conversationalists?
- What guidelines regulate turn-taking behaviour?
- What is conversational coherence, and how can it be achieved?
- Why is politeness important in conversation?
- What additional skills are important for electronically mediated conversation?

CHAPTER 6

Conversation

As Claude got into the car, he casually asked Meaghan, "How'd things go today?"

"Oh," Meaghan said, as she shrugged her shoulders, "Alicia lost her ball, but Travis found it."

"That was nice of him."

"Well, I guess saying Travis found it isn't quite accurate—actually his foot found it. Luckily the fall didn't hurt him too badly."

"What do you mean, the fall didn't hurt him too badly?" Claude asked, surprised.

"Well, Dr. Scott says a break like that is often less troublesome than a sprain."

"Travis broke a bone, and you say he's not hurt too badly?" Claude replied incredulously.

"In comparison to the picture window," Meaghan said indignantly. "The floor lamp shattered it."

"What does this have to do with Travis falling?"

"Everything! When Travis fell he landed on Buddy, who was sound asleep. Buddy leapt up barking and charged into the lamp . . ."

"Which fell into the picture window," Claude finished. "Is that all?"

"Yes . . . unless Eleanor decides to sue."

"Our neighbour? Sue about what?" Claude shouted.

"Calm down, Claude. I just knew you'd get all excited about this. See, the crack of the metal post of the floor lamp striking the plate glass window sounded so like a gunshot that poor Eleanor dove to the ground. Unfortunately, she landed on a lawn sprinkler head, which fractured one of her ribs. I doubt she'll sue us, though. Anyway, enough about this. How'd your day go, Claude?"

Conversation is the medium of interpersonal communication, and each successful conversation is a building block in the good interpersonal relationship that exists between the participants in that conversation. In fact, as Steven Duck, a leading researcher on relationships, points out, "If you were to sit and list the things that you do with friends, one of the top items on the list would surely have to be 'talking' " (1998, p. 7). When conversations go well, they are informative, stimulating, and often just good fun. Yet, like Claude and Meaghan's, some conversations can be quite frustrating. By understanding how a conversation works and by taking advantage of its dynamics, we all can become more skilful in the everyday conversations we have with others.

In this chapter, we define conversation and discuss its primary characteristics, discuss the types of conversation and their structures, consider the rules that conversations follow, look at the co-operative principle that helps to explain how conversation works, and consider the skills of effective conversationalists. Finally, we offer a competence test for conversation and supply a sample conversation and analysis.

Characteristics of Conversation

Conversation is a locally managed, interactive, informal, extemporaneous, and sequential interchange of thoughts and feelings between two or more people. This definition highlights several key features mentioned by Jan Svennevig (1999) that distinguish conversations from other forms of communication such as public address and debate (p. 8). Firstly, conversations are *locally managed.* This means that only those involved in the conversation determine the topic, who will speak, the order of speaking, and the length of time that each participant will speak in a turn. Secondly, conversations are *interactive*; that is, they involve at least two people speaking and listening. Thirdly, conversations are *extemporaneous,* which means the participants have not prepared or memorized the words that they will be speaking. Fourthly, conversations are *sequentially organized*; that is, they have openings, middles, and closings. Within each part of the conversation, what one participant says usually relates to what was said by previous speakers, unless the utterance is designed to change the topic on which the participants are conversing.

IN BRIEF

Characteristics of Conversation

Conversations are

- locally managed
- interactive
- extemporaneous
- sequentially organized.

When people find a conversation satisfying, they tend to seek out the other person or people who participated in it for additional conversations. If, for instance, Dan meets Carl at a party and both of them found the talk they had about politics stimulating, they are likely to look forward to and welcome opportunities for later conversations.

In contrast, if the results of a conversation are unsatisfactory, the participants will tend to avoid each other. They are not likely to invest additional time or energy in further attempts to develop a relationship.

Types and Structures of Conversation

In this section, we will consider two common but differently structured types of conversation: casual social conversations and pragmatic problem-consideration conversations. **Casual social conversations** are marked by discussion of topics that arise spontaneously. The discussion of these topics enables participants to share information, ideas, and opinions and to hear the ideas and opinions of others. Casual social conversations help us to meet our interpersonal needs and to build and maintain our relationships. **Pragmatic problem-consideration conversations** are marked by agreement among the participants to discuss and to resolve specific problems or to plot courses of action.

The Structure of Casual Social Conversations

In a casual social conversation, a topic will be introduced by one participant and will be accepted or rejected by the other(s). If it is accepted, it will be discussed until such time as someone introduces another topic that other participant(s) accept. A topic is rejected when other participant(s) choose not to respond or when someone introduces a different topic that then becomes the focus of the discussion. This topic-change process occurs throughout the conversation.

Suppose Donna and Juanita attend a play together. As they find their seats about 15 minutes before the play is set to begin, their conversation might proceed as follows:

Donna: *(looking around)* They really did an Art Deco thing with this place, didn't they?

Juanita: *(surveying the audience)* Yeah. Hey, it looks as if this is going to be a full house.

Donna: It certainly does. I see people in the last row of the balcony.

Juanita: I thought this would be a popular show. It was a hit when it ran in Edmonton, and I hear the attendance has been good here all week.

Donna: Yes, lots of people I've talked with were trying to get tickets.

Juanita: Well it's good for the downtown.

Donna: Yeah. *(She pauses to glance at the notes on the cast.)* I didn't know Geoff Trubiak was from Winnipeg!

Notice how the topic of the conversation is changed. Donna introduces the topic of theatre decor. Juanita acknowledges the observation, but chooses not to discuss it. Instead, she introduces a different topic, the popularity of the show. Donna accepts the topic with a parallel comment. Juanita introduces information about what has happened in Edmonton. The topic is maintained for two more turns, and then Donna introduces a new topic.

For the remainder of the time before the show starts, Juanita and Donna could converse on one or more topics, sit and read their programs, or engage in some combination of conversing and reading.

The Structure of Pragmatic Problem-Consideration Conversations

In pragmatic problem-consideration conversations, the topic, often agreed upon in advance of the conversation, requires the participants to deliberate and reach a conclusion. These conversations may be more orderly than social conversations and may have as many as five parts:

1. **Greeting and small talk.** Problem-consideration conversations usually open with some kind of greeting followed by a very brief conversation on social topics, just to establish a rapport between or among the participants.
2. **Topic introduction and statement of need for discussion.** In the second stage, one participant introduces the problem or issue that is the purpose of the conversation. How this topic is presented or framed affects how the discussion will proceed.
3. **Information exchange and processing.** The conversation then progresses through a series of speaking turns, and participants share information and opinions, generate alternative solutions, discuss the advantages and disadvantages of different options, and so on. Although a number of issues are likely to be addressed, the conversation will probably not be organized like a textbook problem-solving session. The conversationalists may move from subtopic to subtopic and circle back again.
4. **Summarizing decisions and clarifying next steps.** As the participants approach the end of the conversation, they may try to obtain closure on the topic by summarizing their positions and what has been accomplished.
5. **Formal closing.** Once the conversationalists have discussed the issue and clarified the next steps that will be taken, they are ready to end the problem-consideration conversation. Endings enable the conversationalists either to move to a social conversation, begin a new problem consideration, or simply disengage from one another. The formal closing often includes showing appreciation for the conversation.

OBSERVE & ANALYZE
Journal Activity

Problem-Consideration Conversations

Identify two recent problem-consideration conversations you have had: one that was satisfying and one that was not. Try to recall exactly what was said. Write a script for each of these conversations. Then try to identify each of the five parts of a problem-consideration conversation. Were any parts missing? Why was one conversation more successful than the other?

Such problem-consideration conversations will vary in length, depending on the nature of the topic and its complexity. The five steps can be seen in this brief dialogue:

April: Hi, Yolanda. How are you doing?

Yolanda: Oh, I can't complain too much.

April: I'm glad I ran into you—I need to check something with you.

© Jiang Jin/SuperStock

Skills in problem-consideration conversations enable us to resolve difficulties with others while enhancing our relationships.

Yolanda: Can we do this quickly? I've really got to get cracking on this speech I'm doing for class.

April: Oh, it will just take a minute. If I remember rightly, you said that you'd been to L'Auberge de Trois Chênes for dinner with Scott. I'd like to take Rob there to celebrate his birthday, but I wanted to know whether we'd really feel comfortable there.

Yolanda: Sure. It's pretty elegant, but the prices aren't bad and the atmosphere is really nice.

April: So do you think we can have a nice dinner on fifty or sixty dollars?

Yolanda: Oh, yeah. We had a salad, dinner, and a dessert and our bill was under sixty even with the tip.

April: Thanks, Yolanda. I wanted to ask you 'cause I know you like to eat out when you can.

Yolanda: No problem. Gotta run. Talk with you later. Have a great party, and let me know how Rob liked it.

IN BRIEF

Types and Structures of Conversation

Casual social conversations follow this sequence:

1. A topic is introduced
2. The topic is accepted and discussed or rejected
3. If the topic is accepted, discussion continues until a new topic is introduced and accepted.

Pragmatic problem-consideration conversations can have up to five parts:

1. Greeting and small talk
2. Topic introduction
3. Information exchange and processing
4. Summarizing and clarifying next steps
5. Formal closing.

Rules of Conversation

Although our conversations can seem like random activities with little form or structure, they are actually based on **conversational rules,** "unwritten prescriptions that indicate what behaviour is obligated, preferred, or prohibited in certain

John Coletti/Index Stock Imagery

Unwritten rules for conversations determine the kind of messages and behaviours that are appropriate in different physical and social contexts.

contexts" (Shimanoff, 1980, p. 57). These unwritten rules guide our understanding of what kinds of messages and behaviours are proper in a particular physical or social context or with a particular person or group of people, and they also provide us with a framework within which to interpret the behaviour of others.

Characteristics of Rules

Let's begin our discussion by considering what makes a rule a rule and how rules are phrased. To do this, we will use a common conversational rule as an example: If one person is talking, another person should not interrupt.

1. **Rules must allow for choice.** This means that we can choose whether to follow them or not. When someone else is speaking, Phil can hear the person out, or he can break the rule and interrupt the speaker—he has a choice.

2. **Rules are prescriptive.** A rule specifies appropriate human behaviour; that is, it tells us what to do to be successful or effective. If we choose to break the rule, we risk being criticized or punished. If Phil chooses to interrupt, he will be viewed as rude, and the speaker might glare at him or verbally upbraid him.

3. **Rules are proscriptive.** A rule also tells us what not to do. If we choose to indulge in proscribed behaviour, we are likewise likely to risk censure by other participants in the conversation.

4. **Rules are contextual.** Rules that apply in some situations may not apply in others. For example, most of the time we do not interrupt, but if there is an emergency, like a fire, it is permissible to do so. When we communicate with people of a different race, sex, nationality, religion, political affiliation, class, organization, or group, effective communication is likely to be more

difficult than when we communicate with people from our own culture because the communication rules that apply in their culture may be different from those with which we are familiar.

Phrasing Rules

Although we phrase rules in many ways, Shimanoff (1980) suggests that we are best able to understand a communication rule if it is stated as a conditional (*if-then*) sentence (p. 76). She goes on to state that the context within which the rule is operable should be stated in the *if* clause of the sentence, while the *then* clause should specify the nature of the prescription or proscription and the behaviour that is prescribed or proscribed. Hence, rules follow this model: *if* X is the situation or context, *then* Y is preferred or prohibited.

Here are some conversational rules that are common in Western cultures. Notice that in some cases the word *then* is only implied.

- If your mouth is full of food, then you must not talk.
- If you are spoken to, you must reply.
- If another does not hear a question you ask, then you must repeat it.
- If you are being spoken to, you should look at the speaker.
- If you are conversing with others, you should ensure each participant in the conversation has equal opportunity to speak.
- If your conversational partners are significantly older than you, then you should address them in a respectful manner.
- If you are not certain that the other participants in the conversation do not object to profanity and vulgarity, you should avoid using them.
- If you are going to say something that you do not want overheard, then lower the volume of your voice.

THINKING ABOUT . . .

Communication Rules

Identify three communication rules that do not appear in the text list, but that you believe guide your communication behaviour. Be sure to phrase each of the three as a conditional sentence: *if . . . then . . ..*

IN BRIEF

Rules of Conversation

Conversations are based on unwritten rules that vary from one culture to another. Conversational rules

- must allow for choice
- say what you should and should not do
- vary depending on the context
- are phrased as conditional (*if-then*) sentences.

Effective Conversations Follow the Co-operative Principle

Conversations are not only structured by the rules that participants follow but also depend on how well conversational partners co-operate. The **co-operative principle,** developed by the English philosopher H. Paul Grice, states that conversations will be satisfying when the contributions made by conversationalists are in line with the purpose of the conversation (1975, pp. 44–46). Based on this principle, Grice described the following four **conversational maxims** (requirements of successful conversation):

1. The **quality maxim** requires participants to provide information that is truthful. When we purposely lie, distort, or misrepresent, we are not acting co-operatively in the conversation. Being truthful means not only avoiding deliberate lies and distortions but also taking care to avoid any kind of

misrepresentation. Thus, if Gunter asks Trang what the prerequisites for COMM 2013 are, Trang shares them if he knows them, but he does not speculate or offer his best guess as though it were fact. If Trang does not know the correct answer to Gunter's question, he says so.

2. The **quantity maxim** requires participants to provide an amount of information that is sufficient to satisfy the information needs of the other participant(s) and to keep the conversation going, but not so much as to undermine the informal give-and-take that is characteristic of good conversation. Thus, if Sam asks Randy how he enjoyed his visit to Labrador, Randy's answering "fine" would be too brief; his answering with a 30-minute monologue on all the activities of his trip would be far too long. Both answers would violate the quantity maxim.

3. The **relevancy maxim** requires participants to provide information that is related to the topic being discussed. Making comments tangential to the topic or outright attempts at topic change when partners in the conversation are still actively engaged with the topic are unco-operative. For example, imagine that Hal, Corey, and Li-sung are chatting about how much the Terry Fox Run has benefited cancer research in Canada since its inception in 1981. If Corey suddenly asks whether either Hal or Li-sung is taking Introduction to Logic, he will be violating the relevancy maxim. His question does not relate to the subject being discussed.

4. The **manner maxim** requires that participants be specific and organized when communicating their thoughts. We co-operate by organizing our thoughts and using specific language that clarifies our meanings. When we give information that listeners find obscure, ambiguous, or disorganized, we are not co-operating in sharing meaning. Thus, if Julien asked Matt for directions to the post office, Matt would give Julien an orderly set of directions, beginning from the point at which they were standing, that would allow him to reach his destination. Rambling on about how confusing the route is, presenting vague directions, or listing the steps in the wrong sequence would be violations of the manner maxim.

Bach and Harnish (1979, p. 64) have proposed two additions to Grice's maxims, the morality maxim and the politeness maxim.

5. The **morality maxim** requires participants to speak in ways that meet whatever moral/ethical guidelines are in effect in the conversational context. For example, in most Canadian contexts, violations of the morality maxim would include repeating information that had been received in confidence or asking someone else to do so, or persuading someone to break the law or act in a way that is likely to be detrimental to his or her own best interests.

6. The **politeness maxim** requires that participants be courteous to one another. In our conversations, we should attempt to observe whatever

OBSERVE & ANALYZE
Journal Activity

Conversational Maxims

Look again at the two conversation scripts you prepared in the exercise on problem-consideration conversations earlier in this chapter. Which of the conversational maxims were followed? If there were violations, what were they and how did they affect the conversation? Can you identify specific conversational rules that were used? Which of them were respected, and which were violated? How does this analysis help you understand your satisfaction with the conversation?

IN BRIEF

The Co-operative Principle of Conversation

According to the co-operative principle, conversations are satisfying when the contributions of the participants are consistent with the purpose of the conversation. It is supported by six maxims:

- the quality maxim
- the quantity maxim
- the relevancy maxim
- the manner maxim
- the morality maxim
- the politeness maxim.

norms of politeness may apply in the particular cultural or social context and not purposefully embarrass ourselves or others during the interaction. In the next section, we will discuss means of practising politeness.

DIVERSE VOICES

Canadian Rude Is Brazilian Normal

by Ian Colman

Ian Colman is an epidemiologist living in Edmonton. In this article, he illustrates how differences in conversational rules can complicate conversations between people with different cultural backgrounds.

The first time it happened, Helene and I were a bit surprised, but we just assumed it was some sort of mistake.

After all, why would somebody who had been so kind to us leave us sitting in a hotel lobby waiting for hours? Sure, our Portuguese was far from perfect at that point, but Jose had very clearly said, "Let's go to the soccer game on Sunday." We had enthusiastically agreed to go to the game. He and I even made plans for him to pick us up at the hotel. And when Sunday came, Helene and I sat in that hotel lobby for hours. But Jose wasn't late. He just never showed up. And that was only the first time.

We knew that moving to Brazil would bring some unexpected challenges as we adapted to the culture. These challenges were to be exaggerated by this: although we were living in a city of more than one million people, we were never to meet another English-speaking person in one year in that city.

At first, everything seemed so easy. The Brazilians, as per their reputations, were incredibly friendly. Everybody was very keen to meet the Canadians, practise a few words of English, and ask what we thought of the weather, or the soccer, in Brazil. In fact almost every time we met somebody, they would immediately invite us over to their house to lunch. It took us a long time to realize that none of these people ever set a time for this lunch date or gave us directions to their house.

Two months after our arrival it was Christmas time. We had made a few friends by this point, and Jose was still one of our favourites. He invited us to his farm for Christmas celebrations, which we couldn't attend, but we agreed to get together for New Year's Eve. It was our first major holiday in Brazil, and we were pretty excited about celebrating it with a Brazilian friend. The Brazilians, of course, are also known for their wild parties. But come New Year's Eve, history repeated itself. We sat waiting for Jose, and he never showed up. We had been stood up before, but on New Year's Eve it really hurt. And to make matters worse, when we saw Jose a few days later at the office, he gave us a big smile and said, "Hey, how was your holiday?" It was as though we had never made plans to celebrate the New Year together.

We were so frustrated, we finally decided that we had to speak to a Brazilian about this and find out what was going on. We decided that our Portuguese teacher seemed like a pretty understanding guy, so we approached him about it. We were stunned by his reaction. I told him that in Canada, when somebody says, "Let's go out together for dinner on Saturday," it means that the people will actually go out for dinner on Saturday, and if not, somebody would call and

(continued)

cancel. The reaction I got to this statement was uncontrollable laughter. Finally, the Portuguese teacher composed himself and then, when he saw the look on my face, said "Are you serious?" It took me quite a while to persuade him that, in Canada, when people make plans to do something together, they actually intend to do it.

It began to dawn on us that maybe the Brazilians that we knew weren't as rude as we originally thought. Maybe, just maybe, there was a little more to it than just plain rudeness. Maybe it was all part of this intangible thing we call culture. And if it was, who were we to judge another culture? One of the reasons we moved to Brazil was to embrace a different culture.

Ironically enough, maybe things work this way in Brazil because they are trying to avoid the rudeness of having to decline somebody's well-intentioned invitation, so they just say "yes" when everybody knows it really means "maybe." Or perhaps there is another explanation entirely. Either way, it seems to work for about 160 million people in Brazil. So it would have to work for us.

And I'm quite sure there were plenty of Brazilians who thought we were rude. After all, if somebody invited us to do something and we had other plans, or weren't feeling up to it, we would just say "No, thank you." I'm sure the Brazilians were appalled by this, and found our behaviour as strange as we found theirs.

As frustrating as it was at the time for us, we eventually agreed that all we could do was go with the flow. So we slowly got used to it. We slowly adapted. We did embrace a new culture, and it became part of us. Finally, it became fun. If somebody asked us to do something, and we weren't interested at all, I would put on a big smile and give the person an enthusiastic "Yeah, that would be great!" Everybody would walk away happy. We even occasionally double- or triple-booked Saturday nights, knowing that the chance of more than one event actually happening was remarkably slim. It always seemed to work out okay.

The last few months of our sojourn were a lot easier than the first few months. We never quite fit in completely, but we had a great time and got a better understanding of how our different cultures worked.

I'm happy to report that the culture shock of returning to Canada wasn't as severe as leaving. But if Helene or I don't show up for something we've planned with you, forgive us. It's just a little bit of Brazil in us.

Source: Reprinted by permission of Ian Colman.

Skills of Effective Face-to-Face Conversationalists

Regardless of how well we think we converse, almost all of us can learn to be more effective. In this section, we discuss several skills that are basic to effective conversationalists.

Have Quality Information to Present

The more we know about a range of subjects, the greater the chance that we will be an interesting conversationalists. Here are some suggestions for building a high-quality information base:

- Read a newspaper every day (not just the comics or the sports section).
- Read at least one weekly news or special-interest magazine.

- Watch television documentaries and news specials as well as entertainment and sports programs. (Of course, sports and entertainment are favourite topics of conversation too, but not with everyone.)
- Attend the theatre and concerts as well as going to movies.
- Visit museums and historical sites.

Following these suggestions will provide us with an abundant supply of quality information to share in social conversations.

OBSERVE & ANALYZE
Journal Activity

Conversational Variety

During the next three days, deliberately try to introduce greater variety of content into your conversations with others. How well are you able to develop and maintain such conversations? Are they more or less satisfying than conversations on weather, sports, and daily happenings? Why? Record your observations.

As an Initiator, Ask Meaningful Questions

What happens in the first few minutes of a social conversation will have a profound effect on how well it develops. Although asking questions comes easy to some people, many seem at a loss about how to get a conversation started. Four lines of questioning will usually help to get a conversation started. Notice that none of them invites a yes or no response; each requires the responder to share some specific information.

1. **Refer to family:** How is Susan getting along this year at Simon Fraser University? How has your dad been feeling since his surgery?
2. **Refer to work:** How has the environment in your department changed since your new manager took charge? What projects have you been working on lately?
3. **Refer to a sporting activity:** How was your fishing trip last week? How do you think the Blue Jays' pitching staff is shaping up this year?
4. **Refer to a current event:** What do you think of the government's plan to decriminalize possession of marijuana? How do you think the popularity of file sharing is likely to affect the Canadian music industry in the long run?

Reviewing the sample questions listed here will undoubtedly bring to mind other ideas based on your own special interests. You can use such questions to start conversations with acquaintances whom you think are likely to share those interests.

As a Responder, Provide Free Information

Effective conversationalists assist others to continue a conversation by providing free information with their responses. **Free information** is extra information related to the subject of a message.

Many people have difficulty building conversations because of a tendency to reply to questions with one-word responses. If, for instance, Paul asks Jack, "Do you like to play tennis?" and Jack just answers "Yes," Paul has nowhere to go. To keep the conversation going (or to get it started again), Paul has to think of a new line to pursue. Suppose, however, that Jack answers, "Yes, I've been playing for only about a year, but I really enjoy it." Now, Paul has a direction to follow. He might turn the conversation to his own experience: "I haven't been playing long either, but I'm starting to get more confidence, especially with my forehand." Or he might use the information to ask another question, such as: "Are you able to play very often?" or "Where do you play?" or "How is your game progressing?"

As a respondent, it is important to give free information. As an initiator, it is important to listen for free information. The better the quality of the free information, the more likely it is that the conversation will develop and prove rewarding for both participants.

Credit Sources

Crediting sources means acknowledging the borrowing of information, ideas, or words from published sources (e.g., books, magazines, electronic media) or from people. In a research paper, we give credit to the authors whose works we have quoted or paraphrased by including quotation marks and citations and a reference list. Similarly, when we use other people's information, ideas, or words in oral communication, we should credit the source.

By crediting sources we enable other participants in a conversation to evaluate the quality of the information we are sharing. In addition, if the people we are giving credit to are associates or acquaintances, we make them feel that they are being given the recognition they deserve for their contribution, and we avoid hard feelings. Whenever we repeat ideas that we have taken from others, we should be sure to give proper credit.

Giving credit is easy enough, just by mentioning the name of the person or the author and title of the published source that we took an idea from. For example, in responding to a fellow student's argument in a classroom discussion of the effects of the mass media on society, Timothea says, "I agree, Michael, that the electronic media have greatly increased our ability to disseminate information, but they have a down side too. As Harold Innis pointed out in *The Bias of Communication,* the electronic media also encourage centralization and cultural and political imperialism." By acknowledging the source of the idea she is expressing, Timothea accomplishes several goals: she gives due credit to the source of the idea; she acquaints fellow students with an important authority on the subject of their discussion; and she shields herself from any accusation of intellectual dishonesty.

If, in a meeting to organize a fundraising event for the debating society, Thomas says, "Of all the ideas we've considered, sponsoring a comedy night at the student pub, as Kristen suggested last week, offers the best possible return with the least possible risk," Kristen is going to feel that she is receiving the recognition she deserves for her suggestion, and Thomas will not appear to be taking credit for someone else's idea. If Thomas had failed to identify Kristen as the source of the idea, thereby implying that it was his own, Kristen would be likely to feel hurt or angry, and other members of the committee who recalled Kristen making the suggestion earlier would likely lose respect for Thomas.

Balance Speaking and Listening

Conversations are most satisfying when all participants feel that they have had their fair share of speaking time. We balance speaking and listening in a conversation by practising turn-taking techniques.

1. **Effective conversationalists take the appropriate number of turns.** In any conversation, the ideal is for all to have approximately the same number of turns. If we discover that we are speaking more than our fair share, we should try to restrain ourselves by mentally checking whether everyone else has had a chance to talk once before we speak again. Similarly, if we find ourselves being inactive in a conversation, we should try to increase our participation level. Remember, if we have information to contribute, we are cheating ourselves and our conversational partners when we do not share it.

2. **Effective conversationalists speak for an appropriate length of time on each turn.** People are likely to tune out or become annoyed with conversational partners who make speeches, filibuster, or perform monologues rather than engage in the ordinary give-and-take of conversation. Similarly, it is difficult to carry on a conversation with someone who gives one- or two-word replies to questions that are designed to elicit meaningful information. Turns do, of course, vary in length depending on what is being said. If our average statements are much longer or shorter than those of our conversational partners, however, we need to adjust.

3. **Effective conversationalists recognize and heed turn-changing cues.** Paralinguistic cues, such as a decrease in volume or a lowering of pitch, and gestures that signal completion of a point or invite a response to it are the most obvious turn-changing cues. When we are trying to get into a conversation, we should look for them.

   At the same time, however, we should be careful to avoid inadvertent turn-changing cues. For instance, if Hector tends to lower his voice when he has not really finished speaking or to take long pauses for emphasis, he is likely to be interrupted because others will interpret these cues to mean that he is relinquishing his turn. If you find yourself getting interrupted frequently, you might ask others whether you tend to give false cues. On the other hand, when we recognize that another person has a habit of inadvertently giving these kinds of cues, we should try not to interrupt when speaking with that person.

4. **Effective conversationalists use conversation-directing behaviour and comply with the conversation-directing behaviour of others.** In general, a person who relinquishes his or her turn may define who speaks next. For instance, when Ke concludes his turn by saying, "Susan, do you have anything to add to what I've said?" Susan has the right to the floor. Skilful turn takers use conversation-directing behaviour to balance turns between those

who freely speak and those who may be reluctant to speak. Similarly, effective turn takers remain silent and listen politely when the conversation is directed to someone else.

Of course, if the person who has just finished speaking does not verbally or nonverbally direct the conversation to a preferred next speaker, then the turn is up for grabs and goes to the first person to speak.

5. **Effective conversationalists rarely interrupt.** Although interruptions are generally considered inappropriate, interrupting for clarification and for agreement (confirming) are acceptable (Kennedy & Camden, 1983, p. 55). For instance, if Carl is saying, "It is unbearably presumptuous of Stevens to think that he can just barge in here at the last minute to change arrangements and alter commitments that we confirmed six months ago," interruptions that are likely to be accepted include relevant questions or paraphrases intended to clarify, such as "What do you mean by *presumptuous*?" or "I get the sense that you think this presumptuous behaviour is especially bad," and reinforcing statements such as "Good point, Carl" or "I agree, Carl." The interruptions that are likely to be viewed as disruptive and unwelcome include those that seek to change the subject or that seem to minimize the contribution of the interrupted person.

Practise Politeness

Politeness, relating to others in ways that meet their need to be appreciated and protected, is universal to all cultures (Brown & Levinson, 1987). Although levels of politeness and ways of being polite vary, according to Brown and Levinson's politeness theory, all people have **positive face needs,** the desire to be appreciated and approved, liked and honoured, and **negative face needs,** the desire to be free from imposition or intrusion.

To meet people's positive face needs, we

1. make statements that show concern; for example, "Hi, Bob, I'm glad to see you up and about again. I was very sorry to hear about your accident."
2. offer compliments; for example, "Thanks for the tip on how to increase the accuracy of my wrist shot; it really helped."
3. use respectful forms of address; for example, if Ernie met one of his instructors on the street, saying, "Good morning, Professor Reynolds," as he passed would show appropriate respect; offering a high-five and shouting, "Hey, Marilyn!" would not.

To meet people's negative face needs, we make statements that recognize that we are imposing or intruding on their time. For instance, if Camille stopped by her instructor's office outside of office hours and interrupted his work, to acknowledge that she was imposing, she might say, "I can see that you're busy, Dr. Tan, but I wonder whether you could take a minute to answer a question

COMMUNICATE! Using InfoTrac College Edition

Certainly one important aspect of politeness is courtesy. Using InfoTrac College Edition, under the subject *courtesy*, click on *periodical references*. Several of the articles listed lament a decline in civility. See, for instance "What's the Message of Your Manners? (Message Received and Understood)" by Helen Wilkie (2002) and "Managing in the New Millennium; Workplace Civility: Has It Fallen by the Wayside?" by Patricia M. Buhler (2003). Try to get a perspective on such questions as, Does courtesy (politeness) really matter? and To what extent?

about tomorrow's test," or "I don't expect that you will have time to talk with me now, Dr. Tan, but I wanted to ask whether there might be a time that we could meet later today or tomorrow."

Although politeness is always important, it is especially so whenever we say or do something that might cause another person to lose face, statements or actions that Brown and Levinson call **face-threatening acts (FTA's).** We are committing FTA's when our behaviour *fails* to meet the positive or negative face needs of another person. The goal of politeness theory is not to eliminate face threatening, because some degree of face threatening is normal. Rather, the goal is to lessen or eliminate potential conversational or relationship problems that could result from FTA's.

Suppose a professor returns an essay that Tihana submitted last week, and she believes that the grade she has received is not reflective of the quality of the work. She could, of course, say, "I don't think you graded my essay fairly, and I want you to do it again, correctly this time," a statement that is an FTA without consideration for politeness. Making such a comment would suggest that the professor is unjust or incompetent and would cause him or her to lose face. What might Tihana say to her professor that would be more appropriate? She has three choices:

1. **Accompany the FTA with positive politeness:** "I would very much appreciate it if you could look at my essay again. My roommate took your course last year and said that you were usually willing to reconsider a grade if there seemed to be good reason for doing so. Judging from some of your comments on the essay, I think that you may have misunderstood part of the argument I was making. I've marked the places that I'd like you to reconsider." The request still represents an imposition on the professor, but "I would very much appreciate it" appears much less demanding than "I want you to." In addition, the positive politeness statement suggesting the professor has a reputation for being fair and reasonable reduces the degree of face threatening, and makes it much more likely that the professor and student could continue to discuss the problem in a cordial manner.

2. **Accompany the FTA with negative politeness:** "I'm sure you're very busy, Professor, and I understand that you don't have time to reread every essay you grade, but I would be very grateful if you would be willing to look again at this one. I think you may have misunderstood my argument in some parts of the essay. To take as little of your time as possible, I've marked the places that I'd like you to reconsider and written comments to explain why I argued those sections as I did." Although the request is still a direct imposition, the negative politeness statement shows that Tihana recognizes that she is imposing. It also suggests that she would not do so without good reason. Moreover, she has taken time not only to limit how much of the essay the professor needs to review but also to show why she thinks the sections were sound.

OBSERVE & ANALYZE
Journal Activity

Using Politeness

Think about a time you committed a face-threatening act (FTA). What did you say? Try to recall as specifically as possible the exact words you used.

Analyze your FTA in terms of status, power, and risk. Did you have greater or lesser status? Did you have greater or lesser social power? Was the risk of hurting the person large or small? Write three different messages that you could have used to express your meaning: one that uses positive face statements, one that uses negative face statements, and one that combines positive and negative face statements.

3. **Make the FTA indirectly:** "Please don't take this the wrong way, but I was surprised by a few of the comments you made on my essay." By making this remark in a casual way, Tihana hopes her professor might be curious enough to ask what caused her to be surprised. After this opening, she can move to one of the more direct but face-saving approaches.

So, the question is, how do we choose whether to be polite and, if so, which of the three strategies do we use? Brown and Levinson (1987) believe this decision is affected by a combination of three factors:

1. **How well people know each other and their relative status:** The less familiar we are with someone and the higher that person's social status with respect to our own, the more effort we will make to be polite.
2. **The power the listener has over the speaker:** Most of us will strive harder to be polite to those who are powerful than to those who are powerless.
3. **The risk of hurting the other person:** Most of us do not like to intentionally hurt others.

To show how we might apply this theory, we will consider two examples. First, suppose Mio wants to impose on his roommate by asking him to take a look at a term paper before he submits it to his professor. Mio's roommate is his friend, and the two get along quite well. The imposition is relatively minor and only mildly threatening; in the past, each of them has checked work that the other has done. Moreover, Mio's roommate has no special power over him. In light of these considerations, he might not put much effort into being polite. He might make the request without much regard to his roommate's face needs by saying simply, "Danny, take a look at this paper. I need to hand it in tomorrow."

On the other hand, suppose Mio wishes to ask his professor to pre-read this term paper before he submits it for grading. Because his professor is not his friend (they are socially more distant) and because his professor has considerable power over him (she controls his grade), Mio will probably want to approach her much more politely than he did his friend. As a result, he is likely to make a statement that includes a form of positive politeness or a statement that includes a form of negative politeness: "Professor Chung, I wonder if I might trouble you to have a look at this paper before I submit it for grading. I think I have responded appropriately to the assignment, but I wasn't entirely clear about a couple of the instructions. I would very much appreciate any guidance you could offer."

As we come to better understand face needs, we become better able to accurately diagnose situations in which we should take particular care to engage in polite behaviour. In addition, each of us can make the world a bit more humane by working at being polite regardless of situational imperatives.

IN BRIEF

Conversational Skills

We can become more competent conversationalists by consciously practising the following skills:

- having high-quality information to contribute to conversations
- asking meaningful questions to start conversations
- providing free information to continue conversations
- crediting our sources of information
- balancing the amount of time we spend speaking and listening
- practising politeness.

SKILL BUILDERS Politeness

Skill	Use	Procedure	Example
Relating to others in ways that meet their need to be appreciated and protected.	To determine the degree of politeness necessary to achieve your objective.	1. Recognize when what you are planning to say is likely to be recognized as a face-threatening act. 2. Consider how well you know the other person, whether either of you holds power over the other, and the risk of hurting the other person. 3. Construct a positive or negative politeness statement based on the issues of familiarity, power relationship, and risk of hurt.	Chris thinks her boss did not consider all that he should have in determining her year-end bonus. She might construct the following negative politeness statement: "Mr. Seward, I know you put considerable time and consideration into making decisions about the year-end bonuses, but I've heard that you have been willing to discuss your payroll decisions in the past. I was hoping you'd be willing to take a few minutes to discuss your decision on my bonus for this year."

Skills for Effective Electronically Mediated Conversation

Although all of the concepts we have discussed in this chapter are relevant to electronically mediated (EM) communication, communicating on line also introduces some additional considerations. Whether we are conversing via e-mail or exchanging information via instant messaging or using a newsgroup, message board, or chat room, we will want to consider how the medium affects our communication.

Conversing via E-mail and Instant Messaging

In Chapter 1, we defined e-mail as electronic correspondence conducted between two or more users on a network and instant messaging as an Internet-based service that allows subscribers to detect whether other subscribers are connected to the Internet and, if they are, to have real-time, interactive conversations with them. Although using e-mail might seem to be more like letter writing than conversation, e-mail messages can be responded to shortly after they are sent, so the exchange of e-mail messages approaches a kind of conversation. Instant messaging is much more interactive than e-mail, duplicating the give and take of a face-to-face conversation much more exactly. However, like e-mail, it is primarily a written medium. There are several ways that we can improve our e-mail and instant messaging conversations:

1. **Take advantage of delayed feedback.** Many people treat exchanges of electronic messages as conversation. As a result, they have a tendency to respond with the first thought that comes to mind and to pay little attention to how they are phrasing that thought. A first step toward improving our use of e-mail or instant messaging is to remember that we can and should edit what we write. Editing involves critiquing the content and organization of a text, so our edit should consist of much more than just correcting typos. We should never send a message before rereading what we have written and analyzing it in terms of both our intended meaning and how we have expressed that meaning. The wording of many people's instant messages tends to be particularly fragmentary, in the manner of an actual conversation, but there is no reason for it to be unclear.

2. **Include the wording that you are responding to in the return message.** Even though a response to an e-mail message may be sent within hours or even minutes of the original message, the originator may not remember *exactly* what he or she wrote. When we are responding to specific points that senders have made in their messages, it is advantageous to copy, repeat, or paraphrase what they said before presenting our response. By doing so, we can be sure that both we and our readers are clear about the context for our responses. Most instant messaging systems allow participants to easily review ongoing conversations in their entirety, but it will still help our readers to better understand our responses if we place them in context.

3. **Take into account the absence of nonverbal cues to meaning.** Whether we are writing an electronic message or responding to one, we should keep in mind that the person who will read it cannot hear the sound of our voice or see the look on our face or the gestures we are using. Nonverbal communication may provide as much 66 percent of the social meaning of a message, so we must determine what we can do in writing that will fill in the gaps of meaning that are created when it is taken away.

   Most specialists advise that, for written communication, we should choose our words carefully and strive to use specific and concrete words. We are also likely to have to express our ideas at greater length, the extra words compensating to some degree for the absence of nonverbal expression. For instance, instead of writing, "You may be right, but what you said really bugged me," Gary might write, "Your analysis of our problem may be correct, but you expressed your opinion in a very curt manner, and you were very dismissive of my contribution. Your message really hurt my feelings." Now the reader will have a much better idea of Gary's feelings when he reads the original message.

Barbara Alper/Stock Boston

In their hurry to respond quickly to e-mail messages, people tend to go with the first thought that comes to mind.

Many electronic correspondents add icons that express emotion to their personal messages. These icons are called *emoticons*. A detailed list of emoticons is available at www.chatlist.com/faces.html. Others object to the use of emoticons, considering those who use them to be lazy or immature. As in face-to-face conversations, then, it is important to know and observe the rules that apply in any given conversational context.

4. **Use abbreviations and acronyms sparingly, if at all.** Abbreviations and acronyms, especially those that writers invent themselves, may make a message shorter, but they do not necessarily make it more meaningful. Although some frequent users of e-mail and instant messaging can easily decode some of these cryptic notations, many who receive them are at a loss to make sense of them. Some commonly used examples are BTW (by the way), FWIW (for what it's worth), and IMHO (in my humble opinion). We do not sprinkle our face-to-face conversations with such confusing symbols, so why should we sprinkle our electronic messages with them? Some receivers will be offended by a writer who drops acronyms instead of clearly saying what he or she means.

   An especially dangerous shortcut is the use of capital letters to show emphasis. Rather than making a statement sound important, placing it entirely in capital letters merely makes it more difficult to read and often is interpreted as threatening. Using all capitals in electronic messages is the equivalent of shouting in face-to-face conversation. When we want to show emphasis, we should select emphatic language, not relying on typography to express our meaning.

5. **Keep in mind that electronic messages are not secure.** Because electronic communication is so widely used and because it appears to be private, people frequently include very confidential information—information that

COMMUNICATE!
Using Technology

Think of times that you have communicated through instant messaging. How do these conversations differ from face-to-face or telephone conversations you have had? Are they longer? Shorter? More focused on pragmatic problem considerations than on casual social exchanges? Why do you think this is true? Does the etiquette of such conversations differ from that of face-to-face conversations? Go to **http://reviews-zdnet.com.com/4520-6033_16-4207329.html** and read the article "Your Top Instant-Messaging Etiquette Tips." Do you agree with the experts' advice?

they would ordinarily guard carefully—in e-mail or instant messages. We should bear in mind that any e-mail message we write is copied and stored (at least temporarily) on many computers between ours and the recipient's. As Christian Crumlish (1997) has observed, "In some ways, e-mail messages are like postcards. Anyone 'carrying' the message can read it, even if most would never do so" (p. 132). Most of the major instant messaging systems share these same security weaknesses, and many of the so-called peer-to-peer systems are even less secure. When we have something to say that is confidential, that could be used against us in some way, or that could be misinterpreted by third parties, it is better to convey that message by way of a more secure medium such as a written letter or a face-to-face conversation.

For additional guidelines on the effective use of e-mail and on e-mail etiquette, consult this site: www.iwillfollow.com/email.htm.

Conversing via Newsgroups, Message Boards, and Internet Chat

Recall from Chapter 1 that a *newsgroup* is an electronic gathering place for people with similar interests, a *message board* functions like a newsgroup except that it is attached to a specific Web site and is controlled by the owner(s) of that site, and a *chat room* is an electronic gathering place that makes it possible for two or more people with shared interests to communicate in real time. Newsgroups and message boards allow users to post messages but do not have the capacity for interactive messaging. In newsgroups one user posts articles and others post responses. In contrast, in a chat room typed responses appear instantly on participants' computer screens. Thus Internet chat, like instant messaging, approximates face-to-face conversation in that feedback is relatively instantaneous.

Several of the recommendations for improving e-mail and instant messaging conversations are equally applicable to newsgroups, message boards, and chat rooms. Still, newsgroups and message boards are significantly different from chat rooms. For instance, once we have subscribed to a newsgroup or signed on to a message board, we can spend our time listening, posting articles, and responding to articles.

Listening, called *lurking*, allows a subscriber a pseudo-interaction with others. For instance, if we join a newsgroup or message board on golf, we will find that other subscribers will have posted newsgroup articles on issues relating to the sport. These may range from articles discussing a favourite golfer (such as Annika Sorenstam, Mike Weir, Tiger Woods, or Jennifer Wyatt) to those talking about ways for subscribers to improve their game (driving, putting, chipping), to those about golf issues (etiquette, rules), and so forth. We would be lurking if we read an article and the various responses generated by the article but did not respond ourselves. In this way, we get to learn a little about the personalities of those posting articles and those replying.

THINKING ABOUT . . .

Internet Conversation

Consider your experience with electronically mediated conversation. Compared to face-to-face conversation, what is its greatest shortcoming? What can you do to compensate for that shortcoming?

Posting gives us a chance to see whether other subscribers want to comment on our thoughts or ideas. We may post an article and receive little if any response, but, in a newsgroup, if what we write touches a nerve we may receive many replies, some of which may take the form of *flaming,* hostile or negative feedback on what we have written. Sometimes flaming is offered for the specific purpose of engaging the original poster in a *flame war*. Some people may enjoy such anonymous verbal combat, but those who do not are wise to avoid taking the bait. In this way, newsgroups are essentially self-policing; contributions are limited only by what members of the group will collectively tolerate. On message boards, in contrast, the owner of the Web site that controls the board may edit, delete, or otherwise limit submissions. Most importantly, posting opens the door to responses that are designed to get us engaged in interaction. That is, if a number of people respond, we may respond to a responder and thus begin a kind of electronic relationship.

A third way to participate in a newsgroup or message board, of course, is to respond. A thoughtful, favourable response may well motivate the poster to respond to our response.

In newsgroups, on message boards, and in some chat rooms, we may be asked to observe certain rules of etiquette. "Not observing etiquette in a newsgroup will result in almost instant criticism and reprimand, usually by more than one participant" (Banks, 1997, p. 106). Many newsgroups post lists of FAQ's (frequently asked questions) and their answers that include information about the rules observed by the newsgroup. On message boards, the owner may simply choose not to allow contributions that violate the rules. In addition to information about standards of netiquette (Internet etiquette), a newsgroup's

Ralph A. Reinhold/Index Stock Agency

How might cultural differences affect the conversation between these two people?

IN BRIEF

Electronically Mediated Conversations

When conversing electronically

- take advantage of time to consider and edit your responses before sending them
- include the wording that you are responding to
- try to compensate for the absence of nonverbal cues
- avoid abbreviations and acronyms
- remember that electronic messages are never secure.

FAQ's may include information about the history of the group and the kind of jargon that is acceptable. To find a newsgroup's list of FAQ's, look for postings with FAQ in the header or post a polite note asking for the location of the FAQ.

When using a chat room, we will want to consider two items in addition to the advice given for using newsgroups. In most chat rooms, the conversation is focused on subject areas. Therefore, we should look for a chat room that is discussing the kinds of things we want to discuss (Snell, 1998, p. 258). Secondly, in a chat room everything that is typed appears on the screen. Most people try to preserve their anonymity by using nicknames rather than their real names. We can be whomever we want, and so can everyone else. As a result, we really have no idea whether a person we are talking with is male or female, young or old, rich or poor.

Cultural Variations in Effective Conversation

Throughout this chapter, we have been considering behaviours that improve conversation for people in Canada, a low-context culture. Just as verbal and nonverbal rules differ in low- and high-context cultures, so do guidelines for conversation. Gudykunst and Matsumoto (1996, pp. 30–32) explain differences in conversational patterns that distinguish people of low-context cultures from those of high-context cultures.

Firstly, we are likely to see differences in word choice. In conversations between members of low-context cultures, we are likely to hear greater use of categorical words such as *certainly, absolutely,* and *positively.* In contrast, conversationalists in high-context cultures are more likely to use qualifiers such as *maybe, perhaps,* and *probably.*

Secondly, members of low-context cultures strictly adhere to the relevancy maxim by valuing comments that are perceived to be directly to the point. In high-context cultures, the conversationalists' responses are likely to be more indirect, ambiguous, and apparently less relevant because listeners rely more on nonverbal cues to help them understand a speaker's intentions and meaning.

TEST YOUR COMPETENCE

Conversation

Working with another student, prepare to hold either a five-minute social conversation or a problem-consideration conversation before the class. To prepare for the in-class conversation, meet with the other person to select a topic and to practise holding the conversation to get ideas in mind. Criteria for evaluation will include how well you followed conversational rules and maxims and other skills of effective face-to-face conversation.

Thirdly, in low-context cultures, the quality maxim is actualized through truth telling. People are expected to verbally communicate their actual feelings about things regardless of how they might affect others. In contrast, conversationalists in high-context cultures actualize the quality maxim differently. They recognize quality in maintaining harmony, and conversationalists may send messages that verbally mask their true feelings.

Finally, in low-context cultures, periods of silence are considered uncomfortable because, when no one is speaking, little information is being shared. In high-context cultures, periods of silence during conversations are often meaningful. When three or four people sit together and no one talks, the silence may indicate truthfulness, disapproval, embarrassment, or disagreement, depending on the context.

IN BRIEF

Conversation and Culture

Conversation rules in high-context cultures are likely to differ from those observed in Canada, a low-context culture, in the following ways:

- more frequent use of qualifiers such as *maybe* or *perhaps*
- more reliance on nonverbal cues to help understand meaning
- more emphasis on maintaining harmony than on truth telling
- more meaning derived from periods of silence.

Conversation for Analysis

Damien and Chris, two colleagues in their early twenties, work in a shop selling shirts and gifts. Usually they get along well, but lately Chris has seemed standoffish. Damien decides to talk with Chris to see if anything is wrong. He approaches Chris in the staff room. As you read their conversation about Chris's problems, notice what each man says and how they together create this conversation.

Jason Harris

1. What type of conversation is this?
2. Identify the conversational maxims that you observe each man following.
3. Where do you see each man using specific skills of effective conversation?
4. How would you evaluate Damien's listening skills? Why?

In the right-hand column there is space for you to record your analysis. This conversation also appears as a video clip on the *Communicate!* Web site at www.communicate1e.nelson.com. After you have written your analysis of the conversation, you can compare your responses to those appearing on the Web site.

WWW

Conversation	**Analysis**
Damien: Chris, you've been kind of quiet lately, man. What's been going on?	
Chris: Nothing.	

Conversation **Analysis**

Damien: Come on, man. What's going on?

Chris: Just life. (shrugs) I'm just kind of down right now.

Damien: Well, what am I here for? I thought we were friends.

Chris thinks about it and decides to talk about it.

Chris: Well, Carl's been on my case the last few weeks.

Damien: Why? Did you do something?

Chris: Oh, he says that I'm sloppy when I restock and that I'm not always "polite" to our customers. You know, just 'cause I don't smile all the time. I mean, what does he want—little Mary Sunshine?

Jason Harris

Damien: So you're angry with the boss.

Chris: Yeah, I guess . . . no, no, not really angry, I'm just frustrated. I come in to work every day, and I try to do my job, and I don't complain. You know, I'm sick and tired of getting stuck back there in the stock room reorganizing everything. It's not like they're paying us big bucks here. And Carl shouldn't expect us to be charming with everybody who walks through that door. I mean, half of the people who come in here are totally rude and act like jerks.

Damien: Yeah, I feel you on that. Some of those people shouldn't be allowed out in public. What is Carl saying about how you're dealing with the customers?

Conversation | **Analysis**

Chris: Oh, he just says that I've changed and that I'm not being "nice." I mean, he used to call me his top guy.

Damien: Well, you know how Carl is, Chris. He's a fanatic about customer service. You know how, when we first started, he drilled us about being polite and smiling and being courteous all the time. So maybe when he says "you're not being nice," he just means that you're not doing it all the way you used to. I mean, I've noticed a change. I mean, you're just not yourself lately. Is anything going on outside of work?

Chris: You could say that. Sarah and I just bought that house, so money's been a bit tight. Now, she wants to quit her job and start a family, and I'm not sure we can afford it. On top of all that, my kid sister shows up on our doorstep a few weeks ago, pregnant, and now she's living with us, so yeah, it is a bit overwhelming. And I'm a bit worried that Carl's going to fire me!

Damien: Wow, that is a lot of stuff! I can understand why you're down, but did Carl really threaten to fire you?

Chris: No, but I'm not perfect, and he could use my "attitude" as an excuse to fire me.

Damien: Well, did you think about telling him what's been going on? Maybe, you know, he'll understand and cut you some slack.

Chris: Or he could see that I really have changed and can me.

Jason Harris

Conversation	Analysis
Damien: Okay, well, just tell me this. Do you like working here?	
Chris: Yeah, of course I do.	
Damien: Okay, well then, you've just got to tough it out. I mean, you've just got to use the game face on these people. You used to be the best at doing that. So you're just gonna have to get back to being a salesman, and leave everything else behind.	
Chris: I guess I never realized how much my problems were affecting my work. I thought Carl was just out to get me, but if you've been noticing something too, then maybe I have changed. Thanks, thanks for talking this out.	

WHAT WOULD YOU DO?
A QUESTION OF ETHICS

Sarah, John, Louisa, Naima, and Richard all met at a party that the university sponsored during First Year Orientation Week. During a break, they began sharing information about where they were from, where they had been working during the summer, what classes they were taking, and their possible majors. John was having fun talking with Louisa. He thought she was cute, and he wanted to impress her. When she mentioned that she had been involved in theatre during high school and was considering majoring in drama, he began to share his own theatre experiences. Everyone was politely listening, and interested at first, but he kept talking and talking. Finally, Naima interrupted John and changed the subject, for which the rest of the group was quite grateful.

Throughout their 20-minute conversation, whenever someone would bring up a new subject, John would immediately take centre stage and expound on some wild story that remotely applied. Not only was he long-winded, but his stories also seemed to be fabricated. He was the hero in every one—either through his intellect or his strength. In addition, as he talked, he made completely inappropriate side comments that were offensive to all of his listeners. One by one, each person found a reason to excuse himself or herself. Soon John was standing alone. Several minutes later, John heard the other four around the corner talking. Before he could round the corner and come into their sight, he heard one of them say, "Do you guys want to go down to the coffee house so we can talk in peace? That John

(continued)

was really too much, but I think we can avoid seeing him if we zip out the side door. That way the rest of us can have a chance to talk."

1. Have you ever talked with someone like John? Where did John go wrong in his approach to the conversation? What should he have done differently?

2. What are the ethical implications of Louisa and the rest of the group's sneaking out the side door without saying anything to John? Defend your position.

Summary

Conversations are informal interchanges of thoughts and feelings that usually occur in face-to-face settings. There are two types of conversations, social conversations and problem-consideration conversations, each of which has a general structure.

Conversations are guided by unwritten rules that indicate what behaviour is required, preferred, or prohibited. Four characteristics of conversational rules shape the behaviour of the participants: rules allow for choice and are prescriptive, proscriptive, and contextual.

Effective conversations are governed by the co-operative principle, which suggests that conversations work when participants join together to accomplish conversational goals and make the conversation pleasant for each participant. The co-operative principle is governed by six maxims: the quality maxim, the quantity maxim, the relevancy maxim, the manner maxim, the morality maxim, and the politeness maxim.

Effective conversationalists demonstrate conversational skill by honestly presenting information (and crediting their sources), by balancing speaking and listening (through effective turn-taking behaviour), by maintaining conversational coherence, by practising politeness (through engaging in positive and negative face-saving strategies), and by engaging in ethical dialogue.

Glossary

Review the following key terms:

casual social conversations (135) — discussions of topics that arise spontaneously.

conversation (134) — a locally managed, interactive, informal, extemporaneous, and sequential interchange of thoughts and feelings between two or more people.

conversational maxims (139) — the conversational requirements associated with Grice's co-operative principle.

conversational rules (137) — unwritten guidelines that indicate what behaviour is obligatory, preferred, or prohibited in certain conversational contexts.

co-operative principle (139) — the theory that conversations will be satisfying when the contributions made by conversationalists are in line with the purpose of the conversation.

crediting sources (144) — acknowledging the borrowing of information, ideas, or words from published sources (e.g., books, magazines, electronic media) or from people.

face-threatening acts (FTA's) (147) — behaviour that fails to meet the positive or negative face needs of another person.

free information (143) — extra information related to the subject of a message and included in the message to assist others to continue a conversation.

manner maxim (140) — the requirement that information contributed to a conversation be specific and organized.

morality maxim (140) — the requirement that participants in conversations speak in ways that meet moral/ethical guidelines.

negative face needs (146) — the desire to be free from imposition or intrusion.

politeness (146) — relating to others in ways that meet their need to be appreciated and protected.

politeness maxim (140) — the requirement that participants in a conversation be courteous to one another.

positive face needs (146) — the desire to be appreciated and approved, liked and honoured.

pragmatic problem-consideration conversations (135) — conversations in which participants discuss and resolve specific problems or plot courses of action.

quality maxim (139) — the requirement that information contributed to a conversation be truthful.

quantity maxim (140) — the requirement that a participant in a conversation provide the amount of information that is sufficient or necessary—not too much and not too little.

relevancy maxim (140) — the requirement that information contributed to a conversation be related to the topic being discussed.

Jeffry W. Myers

OBJECTIVES

After you have read this chapter, you should be able to answer these questions:

- What is self-disclosure?
- What are guidelines for appropriate self-disclosure?
- When and how does one describe feelings?
- What is the difference between displaying feelings and describing feelings?
- How do passive, aggressive, and assertive responses differ?
- How can you assert yourself appropriately?
- How can you improve your ability to give praise and constructive criticism?

CHAPTER 7

Self-Disclosure and Feedback

"Colin, when that interviewer at the grocery store asked you whether you'd rather have rice than potatoes, you said 'Yes'! We've been married more than twenty years, and I'm just now learning that you like rice more than potatoes."

"Well, I'm sorry, Kathryn," Colin said sheepishly.

"Colin," Kathryn asked, "are there other things that you like or don't like that you haven't told me about during these more than twenty years?"

"Well, probably."

"Colin, why aren't you telling me about these things?"

"Well, I don't know, Kathryn. I guess I didn't think they were all that important."

"Not important? Colin, almost every night that I cook we have potatoes, and frankly, I hate potatoes. I wouldn't care if I never saw a potato again. Now, I find out you like rice better!"

"Kate, why didn't you ever tell me that you don't like potatoes?"

"Well I, uh-uh . . ."

Poor Colin—poor Kathryn—all those years! But is their experience all that unusual? Do we always take the time to tell others what we are really thinking and feeling? For a lot of people, the answer is a resounding *no*.

Because the processes of self-disclosure and feedback are fundamental to interpersonal communication, in this chapter, we will take a closer look at them and elaborate on the skills associated with each. We will discuss self-disclosure, disclosing feelings, owning feelings and opinions, giving personal feedback, and assertiveness.

Self-Disclosure

Almost all effective interpersonal communication requires some degree of self-disclosure. The very process of making friends requires that the people involved learn more about each other. In the broadest sense, **self-disclosure** means sharing biographical information, personal opinions, and feelings. Statements such as "I was already 180 cm tall by the time I entered Grade 7" reveal biographical information, facts about the speaker as an individual. Statements such as "I don't think prisons ever really rehabilitate criminals" disclose personal opinions, revealing what and how the speaker thinks. Statements such as "I get scared whenever I have to make a speech" disclose feelings. Biographical disclosures are the easiest to make, for they are, in a manner of speaking, a matter of public record. It is statements about personal ideas and feelings that most people think of as self-disclosure (Rosenfeld, 2000, p. 6).

Guidelines for Appropriate Self-Disclosure

We know that self-disclosure is important, yet as Affifi and Guerrero (2000) point out, we also know that "individuals often choose to avoid disclosure rather than risk the perceived personal or relational consequences" (p. 179). In other words, disclosure is important, but risky. We can minimize the risk by following guidelines that help us determine appropriate levels of self-disclosure for different interpersonal encounters.

1. **Self-disclose the kind of information you want others to disclose to you.** When people are getting to know others, they begin by sharing information that is usually shared freely among people with that type of relationship in that culture. At early stages in a relationship, this might include information about hobbies, sports, school, and views of current events. One way to determine what information is appropriate to disclose is to ask ourselves whether we would feel comfortable having the other person disclose that kind of information to us.

2. **Move self-disclosure to deeper levels gradually.** Because receiving self-disclosure can be as threatening as giving it, most people become uncomfortable when the level of disclosure exceeds their expectations. As a

relationship develops, the depth of disclosure increases as well. Thus, we are wise to disclose biographical and demographic information early in a relationship and more personal information in a more developed relationship (Dindia, Fitzpatrick, & Kenny, 1997, p. 408).

3. **Continue intimate self-disclosure only if it is reciprocated.** Research shows that people expect a kind of equity in self-disclosure (Derlega, Metts, Petronio, & Margulis, 1993, p. 33). When it is apparent that a disclosure will not be reciprocated, we should seriously limit further self-disclosure. Lack of reciprocation generally suggests that the other person does not feel the relationship is one in which that degree of self-disclosure is appropriate. When the response to our self-disclosure tells us that the disclosure was inappropriate, we should ask ourselves what caused us to make it. We can learn from such mistakes and avoid making the same kind of mistake in the future.

4. **Self-disclose more intimate information only when the disclosure represents an acceptable risk.** There is always some risk involved in disclosing, but as we gain trust in another person, we perceive that the disclosure of more personal information is less likely to have negative consequences. Incidentally, this guideline explains why people sometimes engage in intimate self-disclosure with bartenders or with strangers they meet in travel. They perceive the disclosures as safe (representing reasonable risk) because the other person is in no position to use the information against them or is someone that they probably will never encounter again. Unfortunately, many of the people making such self-disclosures to strangers apparently lack the kinds of relationships with family and friends that would enable them to make self-disclosures to them.

5. **Reserve intimate or very personal self-disclosure for ongoing relationships.** Disclosures about fears, loves, and other deep or intimate matters are most appropriately made to partners in close, well-established relationships. When people disclose deep secrets to acquaintances, they are engaging in potentially threatening behaviour. Making such disclosures before a bond of trust is established risks alienating the other person. Moreover, people are often embarrassed by and hostile toward others who try to saddle them with personal information in an effort to establish a relationship where none exists.

Cultural and Gender Differences

As we might expect, levels of self-disclosure and what is viewed as appropriate self-disclosure differ from culture to culture. People from formal cultures tend to disclose less information and different information about themselves than people from more informal cultures (Samovar, Porter, & Stefani, 1998). Though differences exist among individual Canadians, overall, Canada is considered to be a relatively informal culture. As a result, Canadians tend to disclose more about themselves than do people from many other cultures. Levels of formality can be inferred by how formally people dress, how formally they address each other, and how much they self-disclose. In Germany, for instance, a country that seems to be very much like Canada in many ways, interpersonal interactions involve a much higher degree of formality. Germans are likely to dress well even if they are just visiting friends or going to school. They use formal titles in their interactions with one another and tend to have fewer close friends. Germans are also more private and disclose less than Canadians do in similar relationships.

COMMUNICATE!
Using Technology

Sign on to an Internet chat room. Spend at least five minutes just lurking (listening). Then begin to participate in the chat. Is there really very much self-disclosure occurring? If so, how does it compare to the degree of self-disclosure you would expect in a face-to-face conversation on the same topic? Can you tell whether the disclosures are truthful? If you need an introduction to chat rooms and how to get started, visit the Yahoo! Canada Web site at **http://ca.yahoo.com** and click on *Chat* in the *Connect* menu. Then select Sign Up For Yahoo! Chat!

Particularly in the beginning stages of a relationship, such cultural differences can easily lead to misperceptions and discomfort if the people involved are unaware of them. For instance, a Canadian may perceive an acquaintance from a more formal culture as reserved or less interested in pursuing a genuine friendship, whereas the acquaintance may see the Canadian as discourteously assertive or embarrassingly expressive about personal feelings and other private matters.

Given the differences in culture, can we assume that disclosure always deepens relationships? Gudykunst and Kim (1997) have discovered that, in all cultures, when relationships become more intimate self-disclosure increases. In addition, they found that the more partners self-disclose to each other, the more they are attracted to each other, and the more uncertainty about each other is reduced (p. 325).

Zigy Kaluzny/Stone/Getty Images

In general, men tend to disclose their feelings less than women, but this behaviour varies by individual and by cultural tradition.

Women tend to disclose more than men, are disclosed to more than men, and are more aware than men of cues that affect their self-disclosure (Dindia, 2000b, p. 24; Reis, 1998, p. 213). Of course, this generalization is not true in all cases. Deborah Tannen (1990) argues that one way to capture the differences between men's and women's verbal styles is by paying attention to **"report-talk"** and **"rapport-talk"** (p. 77). Her point is that men in our society are more likely to view conversation as a way to share information, to display knowledge, to negotiate, and to preserve independence. In contrast, women are more likely to regard conversation as a means of sharing experiences and establishing bonds with others. When men and women fail to recognize these differences in the way they have learned to use conversation, the stage is set for misunderstandings about whether or not they are being truly open and intimate with one another. "Learning about style differences won't make them go away," Tannen remarks, "but it can banish mutual mystification and blame" (pp. 47–48).

IN BRIEF

Self-Disclosure

Self-disclosure is sharing biographical information, ideas, and feelings with others.

- To minimize personal risk, we should observe guidelines for appropriate self-disclosure:
  - Disclose what we would want disclosed to us.
  - Move gradually to deeper levels of disclosure.
  - Continue only if disclosure is reciprocated.
  - Disclose intimate information only after assessing the risk.
  - Reserve intimate disclosures for established relationships.
- To prevent misunderstandings, we should recognize that attitudes toward self-disclosure are affected by gender and culture.

Disclosing Feelings

Sharing feelings with someone else is at the heart of intimate self-disclosure, and sharing feelings is a risky business. Why is this so? When we share our feelings about something important, we are generally giving someone else potent knowledge about us that they might use to harm us. All of us experience feelings, and we have to decide whether and how we disclose them. One option we have is to withhold or mask our feelings. If we decide to disclose our feelings, however, we have the choice of displaying them or of describing them.

Withholding or Masking Feelings

To **withhold or mask feelings** is to deny the feelings that we have by keeping them inside and not giving any verbal or nonverbal cues to their existence. In our culture, masking is considered unhealthy and generally regarded as an inappropriate means of dealing with feelings. The practice of withholding feelings is best exemplified by the good poker player who develops a *poker face,* a neutral look that is impossible to decipher. The look is the same whether the player's cards are good or bad. Being able to maintain such an inexpressive face is an advantage in card games. Unfortunately, however, many people also employ such neutral expressions in all of their relationships with others, preventing their partners from knowing whether they are hurt, excited, saddened, or overjoyed, and such masking of feelings is a definitely disadvantageous to maintaining good personal health and healthy relationships.

Psychologists believe habitually withholding feelings can lead to physical problems such as ulcers and heart disease as well as to psychological problems such as stress and depression. Moreover, people who withhold feelings are often perceived as cold, undemonstrative, and not much fun to be around.

Is withholding ever appropriate? When a situation is inconsequential, we may well choose to withhold our feelings rather than to invest time and energy in expressing them. For instance, a stranger's inconsiderate behaviour at a party may bother us, but we may think that there is little to be gained by disclosing our feelings about it. We do not have an ongoing relationship with the person, and we can more easily deal with the situation simply by moving to another part of the room.

Displaying Feelings

To **display feelings** is to act out the emotions we are experiencing. Displays of feelings always include nonverbal behaviour such as body movements or non-speech sounds, but these may be accompanied by verbal messages. Cheering and jumping about excitedly when your team scores the winning goal, howling and clutching your foot after stubbing your toe against the leg of a bed in the dark, and giving a co-worker a high-five after the two of you have solved a longstanding problem are all displays of feelings.

Displays are usually considered appropriate when the feelings being expressed are positive. For instance, if Veronica gives her friend Gloria a hug after Gloria has presented her with an unexpected gift, the display is an appropriate expression of Veronica's feeling of joy. When Timothy's supervisor gives him an important and difficult assignment that he has been hoping to receive, his smiling broadly, shaking his supervisor's hand, and saying, "Thank you for the vote of confidence, Mr. McKay," is an appropriate display of his feelings of satisfaction and appreciation. In fact, many people need to be more demonstrative in expressing good feelings than they typically are. The popular bumper sticker which poses the question "Have you hugged your kid today?" reinforces the point that the people we care about need open displays of love and affection.

Displays become detrimental to communication, however, when the feelings expressed are negative, especially when the display of a negative feeling appears to be an overreaction. If Peter strikes the top of his desk or overturns a chair and kicks the wastebasket after learning that he has lost a contract, the display of negative feelings may make him feel better for a few minutes, but his lack of self-control is likely to diminish his standing with his co-workers and to cause him to feel embarrassed or ashamed after he calms down.

Because displays of feeling can serve as an escape valve for very strong emotions, they may be a healthier approach to dealing with them than withholding feelings, but displays of negative emotions can often damage our relationships (as Peter's uncontrolled outburst did), or they can cause stress in our relational partners. In many families, children learn to "stay out of Dad's way if he's in a bad mood." These children's fears grow out of their experience of the power of Dad's earlier emotional displays. Rather than just display our negative emotions, we can use the self-disclosure skill of describing feelings to help us share our feelings with others in a manner that does not damage our relationships or cause stress.

Describing Feelings

To **describe feelings** is to name the emotions we are feeling without judging them. Describing feelings increases the chances of positive interaction with others and decreases the chances of short-circuiting the lines of communication. Moreover, describing feelings teaches others how to treat us by explaining the effect of their behaviour. This knowledge gives them the information they need to determine the appropriateness of that behaviour. Thus, if Shelagh tells Saul that she feels happy when he visits her, her description of how she feels should encourage him to visit her again. Likewise, when Akonni tells Tony that he feels very angry that Tony borrowed his car without asking, Tony is more likely to ask the next time. Describing our feelings enables us to exercise a measure of control over others' behaviour simply by making them aware of the effects their actions have on us.

Many people think they are describing their feelings when they are in fact displaying feelings or evaluating another person's behaviour. The Test Your Competence exercise at the end of this section focuses on developing your awareness of the differences between describing feelings and displaying feelings or evaluating behaviour.

If describing feelings is so important to effective communication, why do people not do it regularly? There seem to be at least five reasons:

1. **Many people do not have a very good vocabulary for describing the various feelings they experience.** People can sense that they are angry; however, they may not be able to distinguish between feeling annoyed, indignant, cheated, offended, disturbed, furious, outraged, or shocked. Each of these words describes a slightly different aspect of what many people lump together as

THINKING ABOUT . . .

Communicating Your Feelings

Think back over the events of the day. At any time during the day did you feel particularly happy, angry, disappointed, excited, or sad? How did you communicate your feelings to others? Under what circumstances, if any, did you describe your feelings? What appear to be your most common ways of expressing your feelings? Think of ways you might make sharing your feelings more interpersonally effective.

© Image Source/SuperStock

Describing and sharing feelings can be difficult for many people.

THINKING ABOUT . . .

The Vocabulary of Emotions

Looking at each word in Figure 7.1, say "I feel . . . ," and try to identify the feeling this word would describe. Which of these words are meaningful enough to you that you could use them to help communicate your feelings?

anger. As Figure 7.1 shows, a number of related words can be used to distinguish shades of meaning relative to the same general feelings. To become more effective in describing our feelings, we may first need to work to develop a better vocabulary of emotions.

2. **Many people believe that describing their true feelings will make them too vulnerable.** If we tell people what hurts us, we risk their using the information against us when they purposely want to do us harm. It is therefore safer to act angry than to be honest and describe the hurt we feel. Similarly, it is

Words Related to *Angry*

agitated	annoyed	bitter	cranky
enraged	exasperated	furious	hostile
incensed	indignant	infuriated	irked
irritated	mad	offended	outraged
peeved	resentful	riled	steamed

Words Related to *Helpful*

agreeable	amiable	beneficial	caring
collegial	compassionate	constructive	co-operative
cordial	gentle	kindly	neighbourly
obliging	supportive	useful	warm

Words Related to *Loving*

adoring	affectionate	amorous	aroused
caring	charming	fervent	gentle
heavenly	passionate	sensitive	tender

Words Related to *Embarrassed*

abashed	anxious	chagrined	confused
conspicuous	disconcerted	disgraced	distressed
flustered	humbled	humiliated	jittery
overwhelmed	rattled	ridiculous	shamefaced
sheepish	silly	troubled	uncomfortable

Words Related to *Surprised*

astonished	astounded	baffled	bewildered
confused	distracted	flustered	jarred
jolted	mystified	perplexed	puzzled
rattled	shocked	startled	stunned

Words Related to *Fearful*

afraid	agitated	alarmed	anxious
apprehensive	bullied	cornered	frightened
horrified	jittery	jumpy	nervous
petrified	scared	shaken	terrified
threatened	troubled	uneasy	worried

Words Related to *Disgusted*

afflicted	annoyed	nauseated	outraged
repelled	repulsed	revolted	sickened

safer to appear indifferent than to share our happiness and risk being made fun of for being happy. Nevertheless, as the old saying goes, "Nothing ventured, nothing gained." If we do not take reasonable risks in our interactions with others, we are not likely to form lasting and satisfying relationships. For instance, if Simon is embarrassed when his roommate Pete calls him "Newf," a nickname that he considers derogatory, he can tell Pete that calling him by that nickname embarrasses him. Pete does then have the option of calling Simon "Newf" whenever he wants to embarrass him, but

Words Related to *Hurt*

abused	awful	cheated	deprived
deserted	desperate	dismal	dreadful
forsaken	hassled	ignored	isolated
mistreated	offended	oppressed	pained
piqued	rejected	resentful	rotten
scorned	slighted	snubbed	wounded

Words Related to *Belittled*

betrayed	defeated	deflated	demeaned
diminished	disparaged	downgraded	foolish
helpless	inadequate	incapable	inferior
insulted	persecuted	powerless	underestimated
undervalued	unfit	unworthy	useless

Words Related to *Happy*

blissful	charmed	cheerful	contented
delighted	ecstatic	elated	exultant
fantastic	giddy	glad	gratified
high	joyous	jubilant	merry
pleased	satisfied	thrilled	tickled

Words Related to *Lonely*

abandoned	alone	bored	deserted
desolate	discarded	empty	excluded
forlorn	forsaken	ignored	isolated
jilted	lonesome	lost	rejected
renounced	scorned	slighted	snubbed

Words Related to *Sad*

blue	crestfallen	dejected	depressed
dismal	dour	downcast	gloomy
heavyhearted	joyless	low	melancholy
mirthless	miserable	moody	morose
pained	sorrowful	troubled	weary

Words Related to *Energetic*

animated	bold	brisk	dynamic
eager	forceful	frisky	hardy
inspired	kinetic	lively	peppy
potent	robust	spirited	sprightly
spry	vibrant	vigorous	vivacious

Figure 7.1
A list of more than 200 words that can describe feelings

if Pete is ethical and cares about Simon and their friendship, he is more likely to stop calling him by that name. If, on the other hand, Simon does not describe his feelings to Pete, Pete will probably continue to call him by that name simply because he does not realize that Simon considers it to be derogatory or that he is embarrassed by it. By saying nothing, Simon would reinforce the behaviour that he would like to change. The level of risk varies with each situation, but if we have healthy relationships, we will more often improve a relationship by describing feelings than hurt it by doing so.

3. **Many people believe that if they describe their feelings, others will make them feel guilty about having such feelings.** At a tender age, we all learned about tactful behaviour. Under the premise that the truth sometimes hurts, we learn to avoid the truth by not saying anything or by telling little white lies. When Cynthia was five and her grandmother was coming for a visit, her mother said, "Don't forget to give Grandma a great big kiss when she arrives." "Ugh!" Cynthia blurted, "It's yucky to kiss Grandma. She's all wrinkly and she's got a moustache." If Cynthia's mother then responded, "What a terrible thing to say! Your grandma loves you. Now you give her a kiss and never let me hear you talk like that again!" Cynthia would probably have felt guilty for having this *wrong* feeling. Yet the thought of kissing her grandmother did make her feel "yucky," whether it should have or not. In this case, the issue was not Cynthia's having the feelings, but the way she talked about them.
4. **Many people believe that describing feelings causes harm to others or to a relationship.** It really bothers Fyodor when his girlfriend, Lana, bites her fingernails, but Fyodor believes that describing his feelings may hurt her feelings so much that it will drive a wedge between them. So is it better for Fyodor to say nothing? No. If Fyodor says nothing, he is still going to be irritated by Lana's behaviour. In fact, as time goes on, Fyodor's irritation probably will cause him to lash out at Lana for other things because he cannot bring himself to talk about the behaviour that really bothers him. Lana will be hurt by Fyodor's behaviour, but she will not understand its cause. By not describing his true feelings, Fyodor may well drive a wedge into their relationship anyway. If, on the other hand, Fyodor does describe his feelings to Lana in a nonjudgmental way, she might try to quit biting her nails. They might have a conversation through which he learns that she does not want to bite her nails but that she is unable to stop. Perhaps Fyodor can help her in her efforts to stop, or he might come to see that it really is a small thing, and it may not continue to bother him as much. In short, describing feelings yields a better chance of a successful outcome than does not describing them.
5. **Some people belong to cultural groups in which masking or withholding feelings is culturally appropriate behaviour.** In some cultures, for example, harmony among the group or in the relationship is felt to be more important than individuals' personal feelings. People from such cultures may not describe their feelings out of concern for the health of the group.

To describe our feelings, we should (1) indicate what has triggered the feeling. The feeling results from some behaviour, so identify the behaviour. (2) Mentally identify what we are feeling—be specific. This sounds easier than it sometimes is. When people experience a feeling, they will sometimes display it without thinking about it. To describe a feeling, we must be aware of exactly what we are feeling. Studying the vocabulary of emotions provided in Figure 7.1 can help us develop our ability to select specific words to describe our feelings. (3) Verbally own the feeling. Begin the statement with "I feel . . ." and then verbally name the specific feeling (e.g., happy, sad, irritated, vibrant).

Here are two examples of describing feelings:

1. **Zelda:** Thank you for your complimenting my report *[naming trigger]*; I *[owning the feeling]* am really gratified *[naming the feeling]* that you noticed the effort I made.
2. **Darrell:** When you criticize my cooking on days when I've worked as many hours as you have *[naming trigger]*, I *[owning the feeling]* feel very resentful *[naming the feeling]*.

To begin with, we may find it easier to describe positive feelings: "You know, your taking me to that movie really cheered me up," or "When you offered to help me clean the apartment, I felt really relieved." As we gain success with positive descriptions, we can try describing negative feelings attributable to environmental factors: "It's so cloudy; I feel gloomy" or "When the wind howls through the crack like that, I get really jumpy." Finally, we can move to negative descriptions resulting from what people have said or done: "When you cut me off like that when I'm talking, I really get annoyed" or "When you use that negative tone while you are praising my work, I feel really confused."

IN BRIEF

Disclosing Feelings

The ability to disclose feelings is at the heart of intimate self-disclosure. We can deal with our feelings in three ways:

- To mask or withhold feelings is the generally unhealthy practice of keeping them inside.
- To display feelings is to express them through nonverbal signs and emotional language. Displays of positive feelings are good, but displays of negative feelings can harm relationships.
- To describe feelings is to name the emotion one is experiencing without judging it.

SKILL BUILDERS Describing Feelings

Skill	Use	Procedure	Example
Expressing emotions in words.	For self-disclosure; to teach people how to treat you.	1. Indicate what has triggered the feeling. 2. Mentally identify the specific feeling that you are experiencing. 3. Verbally own the feeling. Begin your statement with "I feel . . ." and then verbally name the specific feeling that you have identified.	"Since I found out that I'm not getting the job, I have been feeling depressed and discouraged," or "Because of the way you stood up for me when Leah was putting me down, I'm feeling very grateful and loving toward you."

Owning Feelings and Opinions

THINKING ABOUT . . .

Owning Ideas and Feelings

Under what circumstances are you likely to take credit for your own ideas and feelings? When are you likely to attribute them to some generalized source?

Owning feelings or opinions means taking credit for the ideas or feelings that we express by making *I-statements* to identify ourselves as the source. An *I-statement* can be any statement that includes a first-person pronoun such as *I, my, me,* or *mine. I-statements* help the listener understand fully and accurately the nature of the message. For example, instead of saying, "The defence is the weakest part of the team," a generalized and uncredited assertion, Juan might say, "*I think* the defence is the weakest part of the team." Likewise, instead of saying, "Everybody thinks Collins is unfair in his criticism of junior staff," Madison could say, "*It seems to me* that Collins is unfair in his criticism of junior staff."

Why do people use vague referents to others rather than owning their ideas and feelings? There are two basic reasons.

1. **To strengthen the power of their statements:** If listeners doubt the statement that "Everybody thinks Collins is unfair in his criticism of junior staff," they are bucking the collective evaluation of countless people. Of course, not everybody knows and agrees that Collins is unfair. In this instance, the statement really means that one person holds the belief, but people often think that their feelings or beliefs will not carry much power, so they feel the need to cite unknown or universal sources for those feelings or beliefs.

2. **To escape responsibility:** People use constructions such as *everybody agrees* and *anyone with any sense would know* to escape responsibility for their own feelings and thoughts. It seems far more difficult for a person to say, "I don't like Nik," than it is to say, "No one likes Nik."

TEST YOUR COMPETENCE

Statements That Describe Feelings

In each set of statements, place a D next to the statement or statements that describe feelings:

1. a. That was a great movie!
   b. I was really cheered up by the story.
   c. I feel this is worth an Oscar.
   d. Terrific!
2. a. I feel you're a good writer.
   b. Your writing brings me to tears.
   c. [You pat the writer on the back] Good job.
   d. Everyone likes your work.
3. a. Yuck!
   b. If things don't get better, I'm going to move.
   c. Did you ever see such a hole?
   d. I feel depressed by the dark halls.
4. a. I'm not adequate as a leader of this group.
   b. Damn—I goofed!
   c. I feel inadequate in my efforts to lead the group.
   d. I'm depressed by the effects of my leadership.
5. a. I'm a winner.
   b. I feel I won because I'm most qualified.
   c. I did it! I won!
   d. I'm ecstatic about winning that award.

The problem with such generalized statements is that, at best, they are exaggerations, and, at worst, they are deceitful and unethical. Being both accurate and honest with others requires taking responsibility for our own feelings and opinions. We all have a right to our reactions. If what we are saying is truly our opinion or an expression of how we really feel, we should let others know and be willing to take responsibility for it. Otherwise, we may alienate people who would have respected our opinions or feelings even if they did not agree with them.

IN BRIEF

Owning Feelings and Opinions

Owning feelings and opinions means making I-statements to identify ourselves as the source of our ideas and emotions.

Giving Personal Feedback

There are times in our interactions and relationships with others when it is appropriate to present our views of another's message, behaviour, or accomplishment. Responses that perform this function are generally referred to as **personal feedback.** When we highlight positive behaviour and accomplishments, we give positive feedback through praise. When we identify negative or harmful behaviour or actions, we provide negative feedback through constructive criticism.

Praise

To offer **praise** is to recognize the specific positive behaviours or accomplishments of another. Too often, we fail to acknowledge the positive things people say and do. Yet, as you will recall from our earlier discussion of self-concept, our view of who we are and our behaviour are shaped by how others respond to us. Praise can be used to reinforce positive behaviour and to help another develop a positive self-image.

Praise is not the same as flattery. When we flatter someone, we offer insincere and unjustified compliments in order to ingratiate ourselves with that person. When we praise, our compliments are in proportion with the behaviour or accomplishment we are recognizing, and we express only the admiration that we genuinely feel.

For praise to achieve its goal and not be perceived merely as flattery, it is essential to focus the praise on the specific action that we wish to recognize and make sure that the message is worded so that the praise is in keeping with the significance or value of the accomplishment or behaviour. If Mike's friend Roger, who tends to be forgetful, remembers to return a pair of pliers he borrowed that same day, the behaviour should be praised so that it is reinforced, but if Mike says, "You're such a wonderful guy, Roger, you're on top of everything," the statement will reinforce nothing because it is a general statement that does not identify a particular behaviour or accomplishment. Similarly, if Mike gushes, "Oh, you remembered to return the pliers! I'm so grateful. That was just unbelievably thoughtful of you," the statement is overkill that will be perceived as insincere flattery. Simply saying something like "Thanks for returning the pliers so promptly; I really appreciate having my tools on hand when I need them," would be appropriate. A response like this acknowledges the accomplishment by describing the specific behaviour that is being recognized and the positive outcome and feeling of gratitude that the behaviour has caused. Here are two more examples of appropriate praise.

1. **Behaviour:** Sonya takes responsibility for selecting and buying a group wedding present for a co-worker. The gift is a big hit.

   Selena, one of Sonya's colleagues, says: "Sonya, the present you chose for Stevie was a really thoughtful and appropriate choice. Not only did it fit our price range, but Stevie really liked it."

2. **Accomplishment:** Cole has just received a letter inviting him to a reception at which he is to receive a scholarship for outstanding academic performance and community service.

   Cole's father says: "Congratulations, son, I'm very proud of you. It's really great to see that the effort you've put into your school work and the time and energy you've devoted to the food bank and Big Brothers are being recognized."

Praise does not cost much, but it is valuable and generally appreciated. Not only does offering praise provide information and acknowledge the worth of another person, but it can also deepen the relationship with that person because it increases the openness in the relationship. To increase our effectiveness at praising another, we can try to follow these steps: (1) Make note of the specific behaviour or accomplishment that we want to reinforce. (2) Describe the specific behaviour or accomplishment. (3) Describe the positive feelings or outcomes that we or others have experienced as a result of the behaviour or accomplishment. (4) Phrase the response so that the level of praise appropriately reflects the significance of the behaviour or accomplishment.

Giving Constructive Criticism

Research in reinforcement theory has found that people learn faster and better in response to positive rewards such as praise than they do in response to negative stimuli. Nevertheless, there are still times when personal feedback needs to address negative behaviours or actions. **Constructive criticism** is identifying and describing the specific negative behaviours or actions of another and the effects that these behaviours or actions are having on others. We are more effective in giving constructive criticism if we proceed in the following way:

1. **Ask the person's permission before giving criticism.** Clearly, it is best to give this type of feedback when a person specifically asks for it, but even when people do not ask, we sometimes need to provide constructive criticism. In some situations, where one person's role is to supervise or improve the performance of another (e.g., a coach training an athlete, a teacher instructing a pupil, or a manager overseeing a worker), the permission can be assumed as long as the criticism refers to the activity in which the supervisor has

authority over the other. However, in cases where no such authority has been agreed upon, such as between friends, co-workers, or classmates, we should ask for permission to comment on another's behaviour before we do. Questions, such as, "Bob, may I offer you a piece of advice?" or "Alanna, may I suggest a way for you to improve your results?" will do the job. A person who has agreed to hear the constructive criticism will likely be more receptive to it than someone who has not been accorded the respect of being asked first.

2. **Whenever possible, preface a negative statement with a positive one.** When we are offering criticism, it is a good practice to start with some praise. Of course, general, superficial, or obviously contrived praise will be seen for what it is, so we should omit this step if there is no genuine and relevant praise to offer. Prefacing constructive criticism with empty praise will not help the person accept our feedback. For example, DeShawn asks Harry, "What did you think of the slides I used when I delivered my oral report?" Harry has some constructive criticism to offer DeShawn to help him improve his visuals in future reports, but rather than beginning with that criticism, he could start by saying, "I thought the charts and graphs were useful, and your use of colour really helped us to see the problems you were referring to." This praise is relevant and significant and helps to lead into the constructive criticism that will follow.

3. **Describe the behaviour or action that you wish to criticize by accurately recounting precisely what was said or done without labelling it good or bad, right or wrong.** By describing the behaviour, we lay an informative base for the feedback we are about to give and increase the chances that the person will listen receptively. Feedback that is preceded by an objective description is less likely to be met defensively. Our description shows that we are criticizing the behaviour rather than attacking the person, and it points the way to a solution. To carry on with our example, Harry could follow up his praise with, "The slides weren't very well done, though." However, it would be better for him to say something like, "The type on the first two slides was rather small, though, which made the words hard to read." This objective description does not attack DeShawn personally (You are an ineffective presenter), but focuses on a specific problem with his work (The font size on the visual aids was too small), paving the way for suggestions on what he should do to remedy that problem.

4. **Be as specific as possible.** The more specifically we describe the behaviour or the action we are criticizing, the easier it will be for the other person to understand what needs to be changed. It would not have been helpful for Harry to say, "Some of the slides were kind of hard to read," because such a vague comment would give DeShawn little idea of what to change. He could, in fact, infer that every slide should be redone.

OBSERVE & ANALYZE
Journal Activity

Expressing Criticism

Think about the last time you criticized someone's behaviour. Which of the guidelines for constructive criticism did you follow? Which did you violate? If you were to offer the same criticism again, what would you do differently?

IN BRIEF

Giving Personal Feedback

By giving personal feedback we let others know whether their behaviour is affecting us positively (praise) or negatively (constructive criticism).

- Praise should be specific to and in proportion to the significance of the behaviour or accomplishment we want to reinforce.
- Constructive criticism should be specific, accurate, preceded by praise if possible, and directed to helping the person correct the problem behaviour.

5. **When appropriate, suggest how the person can change the behaviour.** Because the focus of constructive criticism is helping, it is appropriate to provide the person with suggestions that might lead to positive change. Harry might round out his constructive criticism by adding, "When I make slides for oral presentations, I generally try to use 18-point or larger type. You might want to give that a try." By including a positive suggestion, we not only help the person by providing information, we also show that our intentions are positive.

Assertiveness

Assertiveness is standing up for ourselves in interpersonally effective ways by exercising our personal rights while respecting the rights of others. Failure to be assertive may keep people from achieving their goals and may also lower their self-esteem. We can understand the specific characteristics of assertive communication best if we contrast it with other ways of interacting with others when we believe our rights, feelings, or needs are in danger of being violated or ignored.

Contrasting Methods of Expressing Our Needs and Rights

When we believe our rights, feelings, or needs are being ignored or violated by others, we can choose to behave in one of three ways: passively, aggressively, or assertively.

Passive behaviour People behave passively when they do not state their opinions, share their feelings, or assume responsibility for their actions. They may behave passively because they fear reprisal, because they are insecure in their knowledge, or for some other reason. Whatever their motivation, they make no attempt to influence the behaviour of others. Instead, they submit to other people's demands, even when doing so causes them inconvenience, works against their best interests, or violates their rights. In other words, they allow other people to victimize them. For example, while Bill is unpacking a new television set that he has purchased at a local electronics store, he notices a scratch on the left side of the cabinet. If Bill is upset about the scratch but keeps the defective set without making any attempt to have the store replace it with an undamaged model or refund some portion of the money he paid for it, he is behaving passively.

Aggressive behaviour People behave aggressively when they forcefully lash out to achieve their goals or defend their rights with little or no regard for the feelings, needs, or rights of others. Aggressors tend to view every interaction with another person as a contest, and they are determined to always win. In fact, they frequently do, but because their victories often come at the expense of

We often have to assert ourselves. The key is not to fall into aggressive behaviour. He seems to be crowding her (aggressive), but she is setting limits (assertive).

others, their behaviour is unethical, and it is very damaging to relationships. The people who receive aggressive messages or are the targets of aggressive behaviour are likely to feel hurt, regardless of their relationship with the aggressor (Martin, Anderson, & Horvath, 1996, p. 24).

Suppose, after discovering the scratch on the cabinet of his new television set, Bill storms back to the store, corners the first salesclerk he encounters, and loudly demands his money back while accusing the owners and employees of the store of being racists and thieves for having intentionally sold him damaged merchandise in the first place. Such aggressive behaviour might or might not be successful in getting a refund or a replacement television set, but it would certainly not be ethical, and it would undoubtedly sour the relationship between Bill and the staff and management of the store.

Assertive behaviour As we have noted, behaving assertively means standing up for ourselves in an interpersonally effective way. The difference between assertive behaviour and passive or aggressive behaviour is not the feeling behind the response but the way in which we choose to react as a result of what has happened to us. If Bill chooses an assertive response, he will still be angry about

OBSERVE & ANALYZE
Journal Activity

Passive, Aggressive, and Assertive Behaviour

For the next day or two, observe people and their behaviour. Make note of situations in which you believe people behaved in passive, aggressive, or assertive ways. Then, answer the following questions: Which type of behaviour seemed to help people achieve what they wanted? Which type of behaviour seemed to maintain or improve their interpersonal relationships with the people with whom they were interacting?

bringing home a damaged television set, but instead of either doing nothing or verbally assaulting an innocent bystander, he will try to assert his right to receive quality merchandise for his money while still respecting the rights of the store's employees. For example, he may call the store and ask to speak to the salesclerk from whom he had actually purchased the set. When the clerk answers, Bill will describe the condition of the set and his feelings on discovering that the merchandise that he has paid for is defective. He will then ask what steps he should take to return the damaged set and exchange it for a new one. Aggressive behaviour might also achieve Bill's purpose of getting a new television set, but assertive behaviour would achieve the same result at lower emotional cost to everyone involved, and at minimal cost to the business relationship that exists between Bill and the staff of the electronics store.

Paulette Dale (1999), a consultant on assertive behaviour, contrasts these behaviours as follows: Where a submissive or passive response conveys the message "*I'm* not important, *you're* important," and an aggressive response conveys the message "*I'm* important, *you're* nothing," an assertive response conveys the message "*I'm* important, *you're* important, we're *both* important" (pp. 5–6).

Distinguishing among Passive, Aggressive, and Assertive Responses

Because our interpersonal relations often involve responding to the messages, behaviours, or actions of others, it is important to learn to distinguish among passive, aggressive, and assertive responses. To highlight the contrasts among the three response styles, we will examine two situations in which the issue is the quality of interpersonal relations.

At work: Tanisha works in an office. Whenever her boss, Mr. Ward, has an especially interesting and challenging job to be done, he assigns it to Garnett, whose desk is next to Tanisha's. The boss has never said anything to Tanisha or to Garnett that would indicate he thinks less of Tanisha or her ability. Nevertheless, Tanisha is hurt by Mr. Ward's behaviour.

Passive response: Tanisha says nothing to Mr. Ward. She is very hurt by what she feels is a slight, but she swallows her pride.

Aggressive: Tanisha marches into Mr. Ward's office and says, "Why the hell do you always give Garnett the plums and leave me the garbage? I'm every bit as good a worker, and I'd like a little recognition!"

Assertive: Tanisha schedules a meeting with Mr. Ward. At the meeting, she says, "I don't know whether you are aware of it, but during the last three months, every time you had a really interesting task to assign, you gave it to Garnett. To the best of my knowledge, you believe that Garnett and I are equally competent—you've never given either of us any indication that you thought less of my work—but when you reward Garnett with assignments that we perceive as plums and continue to offer me routine tasks, it makes me look like a second-string employee and embarrasses me in front of my co-workers. Do you understand my feelings about this?" In this statement, she has both described her perception of the boss's behaviour and its outcomes and her feelings about both.

If you were Mr. Ward, which of Tanisha's responses would most likely cause you to respond by giving her better work assignments? Probably the assertive behaviour. Which of her responses would most likely cause you to dismiss her? Probably the aggressive behaviour. And which of her responses would most likely cause you to do nothing? Undoubtedly the passive behaviour; you would not even be aware of her feelings, and she would continue to get the boring assignments.

With a friend: Aaron is a doctor doing his residency at a major Toronto hospital. He shares an apartment with two other residents, Shekhar and Felix. Felix is the social butterfly of the group: whenever he has time off, he has a date. Like Aaron and Shekhar, Felix is a bit short of cash, but he does not feel a bit bashful about borrowing clothes or money from his roommates. One evening, Felix asks Aaron if he can borrow his watch, a new, expensive watch that Aaron received as a present from his father only a few days before. Aaron is aware that Felix does not always take the best care of what he borrows, and he is very concerned about the possibility of his damaging or losing the watch. Which of these responses would be most effective?

Passive: "Sure, you can wear my watch."

Aggressive: "Forget it! You've got a lot of nerve asking to borrow a brand-new watch. You know I'd be damned lucky to get it back in one piece."

Assertive: "Felix, I know I've lent you several of my things before, but this watch is important to me because it was a very special gift from my Dad. I just don't feel comfortable lending it. I hope you can understand how I feel."

What are likely to be the consequences of each of these behaviours? If Aaron behaves passively, he is likely to worry the entire evening and harbour some resentment toward Felix even if he does get the watch back undamaged. Moreover, Felix will continue to think that his roommates are willing to lend him anything he wants. If Aaron behaves aggressively, Felix is likely to be completely taken aback by his explosive outburst. Neither Aaron nor Shekhar has ever complained about his borrowing before, so he has no reason to believe that they object to his behaviour. In addition, the relationship between Aaron and Felix would likely become strained. However, if Aaron behaves assertively, he puts the focus on his own feelings about one particular object, the watch his father gave him. His response is not a denial of Felix's right to borrow, nor is it a personal attack on Felix. It is an explanation of why Aaron does not want to lend this item at this time.

COMMUNICATE! Using InfoTrac College Edition

Aggressive behaviour is commonly associated with men, but are males necessarily more agressive than females? Using the InfoTrac College Edition subject guide, enter the term *aggressiveness (psychology)* and then select the subdivision *demographic aspects.* Find the article "Why Are Girls Less Physically Aggressive Than Boys? Personality and Parenting Mediators of Physical Aggression" by Gustavo Carlo, Marcela Raffaelli, Deborah J. Laible, and Kathryn A. Meyer. What does this study reveal about aggressiveness and gender? Does it support the stereotype of the agressive male?

Own your feelings	Assertive people acknowledge that the thoughts and feelings they express are theirs.
Avoid confrontational language	Assertive people do not use threats, evaluations, or dogmatic language.
Use specific statements relevant to the behaviours at hand	Instead of focusing on extraneous issues, assertive people use descriptive statements that focus on the issue that is most relevant.
Maintain eye contact and firm body position	Assertive people look others in the eye rather than shifting their gaze or looking at the floor. They also avoid swaying back and forth, hunching over, or using other signs that may suggest that they are indecisive or lacking in confidence or conviction.
Maintain a firm but pleasant tone	Assertive people speak firmly but at a normal pitch, volume, and rate.
Avoid non-speech sounds	Assertive people avoid vocalized pauses, hemming and hawing, and other signs of indecisiveness.

Figure 7.2
Characteristics of assertive behaviour

For a review of the characteristics of assertive behaviour, see Figure 7.2.

It is important to recognize that being assertive will not always guarantee that we will achieve our goals. The skills discussed in this book are designed to increase the *probability* of achieving interpersonal effectiveness. Just as with self-disclosure and describing feelings, however, there are risks involved in being assertive. For instance, some people will label any assertive behaviour as aggressive. However, people who have difficulty asserting themselves often do not appreciate the fact that the potential benefits far outweigh the risks. Remember, our behaviour teaches people how to treat us. When we are passive, we teach people that they can ignore our feelings, and they will. When we are aggressive, we teach people to respond in kind, and they usually will. Similarly, when we are assertive, we show others how to treat us as we would prefer to be treated.

Here are some useful guidelines for practising assertive behaviour: (1) identify what you are thinking or feeling; (2) analyze the cause of these feelings; (3) choose the most appropriate way to communicate these feelings and the outcome you desire, if any; and (4) communicate these feelings to the appropriate person. If you are having trouble taking the first step to being more assertive, begin with situations in which you are likely to have a high potential for success (Alberti & Emmons, 1995). In addition, try to incorporate the characteristics of assertive behaviour outlined in Figure 7.2.

OBSERVE & ANALYZE
Journal Activity

Learning to Respond Assertively

Identify a situation in which you were passive and another in which you were aggressive. Write a dialogue to illustrate how each situation unfolded. Then, write a substitute dialogue to show how an assertive response would have improved the outcome in each case.

Cultural Variations

Although assertiveness can be thought of as a basic human need, assertive behaviour is practised primarily in Western cultures. In Asian cultures, how one is seen is often considered to be more important than asserting one's beliefs or rights, and a premium is often placed on maintaining a formally correct standard of social interaction. For people from these cultures, maintaining face and politeness may be more important than achieving personal satisfaction. In contrast, in Latin and Hispanic societies, men especially are frequently taught to exercise a form of self-expression that goes far beyond the guidelines presented here for assertive behaviour. In these societies, the concept of *machismo* guides male behaviour. Thus, the standard of assertiveness appropriate in Western culture can seem inappropriate to people whose cultural frame of reference leads them to perceive it as either aggressive or weak.

For this reason, with assertiveness—as with any other skill—we need to be aware that no single standard of behaviour ensures that we will achieve our goals. Although what is labelled appropriate behaviour varies across cultures, the results of passive and aggressive behaviour seem to be universal: passive behaviour can cause resentment, and aggressive behaviour leads to fear and misunderstanding. When talking with people whose culture, background, or lifestyle differs from our own, we may need to observe their behaviour and their responses to our statements before we can be sure of the kinds of behaviour that are likely to communicate our intentions effectively.

IN BRIEF

Assertiveness

Assertive behaviour is the most effective of three ways of interacting with others:

- Passive people submit to others' demands and refuse to state their opinions, share their feelings, or take responsibility for their actions.
- Aggressive people lash out, striving to achieve their goals without any regard for the rights, feelings, or needs of others.
- Assertive people stand up for themselves in interpersonally effective ways, exercising their personal rights while respecting the rights of others.

TEST YOUR COMPETENCE

Developing Assertive Responses

For each of these situations, write a passive response, an aggressive response, and then a more appropriate assertive response.

1. You come back to your dorm, apartment, or house to do an assignment that is due the next day, only to find that someone else is using your computer.
   Passive or aggressive response:
   Assertive response:
2. You have a part-time job in a fast-food restaurant. Your shift is coming to an end and you want to rush home because you have a special evening planned to celebrate your second anniversary with your boyfriend or girlfriend. Just as you are about to leave, your boss says, "I'd like you to work overtime, if you wouldn't mind. Martin is supposed to relieve you, but he just called to say that he can't get here for at least an hour."
   Passive or aggressive response:
   Assertive response:
3. You move to another province to attend university. When you leave home at the end of August, you and your parents agree that you will fly home for the Thanksgiving long weekend. By the beginning of October, you are eager to get home, not only to see your family and to enjoy good food and the other comforts of home, but also to see your high-school friends, some of whom you miss very much. At the beginning of October, your mother phones and says, "Your father and I have decided that we would enjoy a little holiday, so we thought that we would take a trip to see you. We have a day's drive each way, but we could spend one day and two nights in town, and we could celebrate Thanksgiving together on the Sunday."
   Passive or aggressive response:
   Assertive response:

(continued)

4. You and your friend made a date to go dancing, an activity you really enjoy. When you meet, your friend says, "If it's all the same to you, I thought we'd go to a movie instead."
Passive or aggressive response:
Assertive response:

SKILL BUILDERS Assertiveness

Skill	Use	Procedure	Example
Standing up for yourself in interpersonally effective ways by describing your feelings honestly and exercising your personal rights while respecting the rights of others.	To show clearly what you think or feel.	1. Identify what you are thinking or feeling. 2. Analyze the cause of these feelings. 3. Choose the most appropriate way to communicate these feelings, and the outcome you desire, if any. 4. Communicate these feelings to the appropriate person. Remember to own your feelings.	When Gavin believes he is being unjustly charged to refill his drink in the cafeteria, he says, "I understood that beverage refills were free to meal plan card holders. I have never been charged before. Has there been a change in policy?"

Conversation for Analysis

Trevor and Meg have been going together for the last several months of their final year at university. Now that graduation is approaching, they are trying to figure out what to do about their relationship. They sit and talk. As you read Trevor and Meg's discussion of the future of their relationship, focus on how effectively they are communicating.

Jason Harris

1. How well do Trevor and Meg disclose their feelings?

2. How effective is each of the two at owning feelings and opinions?

3. How well do they use praise and constructive criticism?

4. Does either demonstrate assertive behaviour? Where? How effectively?

5. What really is Meg's fear?

In the right-hand column there is space for you to record your analysis. This conversation also appears as a video clip on the *Communicate!* Web site at www.communicate1e.nelson.com. After you have written your analysis of the conversation, you can compare your responses to those appearing on the Web site.

Conversation	**Analysis**
Trevor: Meg, I think it's time we talk about making plans for the future. After all, we'll be graduating next month.	
Meg: Trevor, you know how uncomfortable I feel about making any long-range plans at this time. We still need to know a lot more about each other before we even think about getting engaged.	
Trevor: Why? We've both said we love each other, haven't we?	
Meg nods.	
Trevor: So why, why's this too soon? What else do we need to know?	
Meg: For starters, I'll be going to law school this fall, and this year is going to be difficult. And, you haven't got a job yet.	
Trevor: Come on, Meg. You're going to law school in Halifax, so I'll take a job there. I'll have a degree in business, so I can get a job just about anywhere.	

Jason Harris

Conversation	**Analysis**
Meg: But Trevor, that's just my point. I know I'll be starting law school—I've always wanted to be a lawyer—but you don't really have any idea what you want to do. And that bothers me. I can't be worrying about you and your career when I'm going to need to be focusing on my classes.	
Trevor: But I told you, I can get a job anywhere.	
Meg: Yes, Trevor, but you need more than a job. You need to figure out what kind of job really turns you on. Or else, you risk waking up one day and regretting your life. And, I don't want to be there when that happens. I watched my dad go through a mid-life crisis, and he ended up walking out on us.	
Trevor: I'm not your dad, Meg. I won't leave you. And don't worry about me, I'll find a job.	
Meg: Really? You've known I was going to law school in Halifax for over a month now, but you still haven't even begun a job search. Trevor, right now is the time when people are hiring, and you haven't even made a résumé. The longer you wait, the more difficult your search is going to be.	
Trevor: Come on Meg, you've already said I'm irresistible. What company wouldn't want me?	
Meg: I'm serious, Trevor. Look, I've got a scholarship to pay for my tuition, but it's not going to pay for my living expenses. I'll be taking a student loan to cover those. I won't have the money or the time to be very supportive of you if you haven't found work. I need the security of knowing that you've got a job and that you are saving money.	

Conversation	Analysis
Trevor: Well, they say that two can live as cheaply as one. I was thinking that once you got settled, I'd move in and that will save us a lot of money.	
Meg: Whoa, Trevor. You know how I feel about that. I do love you, and I hope that we have a future together, but living together this year is not an option. I think we need at least a year of living on our own to get ourselves settled and to make sure that we really are compatible. After all, we come from totally different backgrounds. I practically raised myself, and I've paid my own bills since I was 18, while you've been lucky enough to have parents who footed your bills. There have been several times when we've talked about important issues and the differences between us have been obvious, and they worry me.	
Trevor: You mean when I was joking around about our different tastes in cars?	
Meg: No, Trevor, not cars, that's minor, but we also have greatly different feelings about money and family. You've told me that once you get married you want to start a family immediately. As I see it, I've got a three-year commitment to law school, then seven to ten years of hard work in order to make partner in a good firm, so I'm not sure when I want to start a family, but I know it won't be for a number of years at least.	
Trevor: So, what are you saying, Meg? Is it over? "Thanks for the good time, Trevor, but you're not in my plans?"	

Conversation	**Analysis**
Meg: Please don't be sarcastic. I'm not trying to hurt you. It makes me happy to think that we'll spend the rest of our lives together, but I'm worried about several things, so I'm just not ready to commit to that now. Let's just take a year, get settled, and see what happens. I'll love it if you do get a job near Halifax. That way we can have time to sort through some of the issues between us.	
Trevor: You mean if you can fit me into your schedule? Meg, if we love each other now, aren't we still going to love each other next year? If we wait until we have everything settled, we might never get married: there'll always be something. After all, we are two different people. We're never going to agree on everything!	
Meg: Are you saying that, as unsettled as our lives are right now, we can shoulder the additional stress of planning a marriage?	
Trevor: No, what I'm saying is that we live together this year, see how it goes, and if it isn't working, we don't have to get married.	

Jason Harris

WHAT WOULD YOU DO?
A QUESTION OF ETHICS

Farida Mohammed, a graduate of University of Toronto Law School, was excited to be assigned to the Local Employee Fraud Team (LEFT). The group's job was to design a system for uncovering theft on the job for the Comptel Corporation. Farida enjoyed the company of her five associates, but not that of group leader Theresa Waterson, whose social skills were as bad as those of the stereotypical queen bee. Farida wondered why Theresa, of all people, had been appointed to head the project and found herself increasingly angered by Theresa's views on issues such as affirmative action and abortion. Several times Farida wanted to confront Theresa on these issues, but she felt that the harmonious relationship of the group was at stake, and she did not want to risk damaging the group's cohesiveness.

Although Farida was able to control herself in most settings, she began to be critical of Theresa's views during group meetings, forcefully pointing out what she considered to be illogical thinking and openly upbraiding Theresa for her mistakes. When one of the men on the task force confronted her privately, Farida considered trusting him with her problem, yet she unconsciously feared that self-disclosure, particularly to a white man, would make her seem weak. Several days later, when the two other women in the group confronted her about her behavior toward Theresa, Farida broke down and told them her problem.

1. What are the ethical issues in this case?
2. Did Farida behave ethically in this situation?
3. If you were one of the women advising Farida, what would you recommend that she do?

Summary

Self-disclosure statements reveal information about ourselves that is unknown to others. Several guidelines can help us decide when self-disclosure is appropriate.

Three ways to deal with our feelings are to withhold them, display them, or skilfully describe them.

Instead of owning our own feelings and ideas, we often avoid disclosure by making generalized statements. The skill of making *I-statements* can help us to more honestly assume ownership of our ideas and feelings.

Assertiveness is the skill of stating ideas and feelings openly in interpersonally effective ways. Passive people are often unhappy as a result of not stating what they think and feel, and aggressive people get their ideas and feelings heard but create problems for themselves and others through their aggressiveness. What is considered an appropriate degree of assertiveness varies across cultures.

Some of the characteristics of assertive behaviour are owning feelings, avoiding confrontational language, using specific statements relevant to the behaviours at hand, maintaining eye contact and firm body position, maintaining a firm but pleasant tone of voice, and avoiding hemming and hawing.

Glossary

Review the following key terms:

aggressive behaviour (178) — behaviour characterized by a readiness to lash out to achieve one's goals or defend one's rights with little or no regard for the feelings, needs, or rights of others.

assertiveness (178) — standing up for ourselves in interpersonally effective ways by exercising our personal rights while respecting the rights of others.

constructive criticism (176) — identifying and describing the specific negative behaviours or actions of another and the effects that these behaviours or actions have on others.

describing feelings (169) — naming the emotions we are feeling without judging them.

displaying feelings (168) — acting out the emotions we are experiencing.

masking feelings (167) — withholding feelings (See below).

owning feelings or opinions (174) — taking credit for the ideas or feelings that we express by making *I-statements* to identify ourselves as the source.

passive behaviour (178) — behaviour characterized by a reluctance to state opinions, share feelings, or assume responsibility for actions.

personal feedback (175) — responses in which we present our views of another's message, behaviour, or accomplishment.

praise (175) — recognition of the specific positive behaviours or accomplishments of another.

rapport-talk (167) — a style of conversation, associated with women in Western cultures, which focuses on sharing experiences and establishing bonds with others.

report-talk (167) — a style of conversation, associated with men in Western cultures, which focuses on sharing information, displaying knowledge, negotiating, and preserving independence.

self-disclosure (164) — sharing biographical information, personal opinions, and feelings.

withholding feelings (167) — denying feelings by keeping them inside and not giving any verbal or nonverbal cues to their existence.

stockimage/firstlight.ca

OBJECTIVES

After you have read this chapter, you should be able to answer these questions:

- What are the major types of relationships?
- What are effective ways of starting a relationship?
- How are descriptiveness, openness, tentativeness, and equality used in maintaining relationships?
- What does interpersonal needs theory tell us about relationships?
- What does exchange theory tell us about relationships?
- What is conflict, and why does it occur in relationships?
- What are five approaches to managing conflict, and when is each one appropriate?
- What skills are used to initiate conflict effectively?
- What skills are used in responding to a conflict initiated by another?

CHAPTER 8

Communicating in Relationships

"Akasma, you're spending a lot of time with Angie. What is Liam going to think about that?"

"Come on, Mom, I know you're just teasing me. Yeah, Liam's my boyfriend, and we get along really well, but there are things I just can't talk about with him."

"And you can with Angie?"

"Right. I can tell her what's going on with my writing, for example, and she really understands. And I do the same for her. We enjoy a lot of the same activities, so Angie is good company for me."

Akasma is lucky because she has two close relationships. Interpersonal skills are instrumental in starting, building, and maintaining relationships, and in this chapter we discuss relationships and their dynamics. A good relationship is based upon mutually satisfying interactions between two people.

We will identify three types of relationships, explain the stages or cycle that typical relationships flow through, look at on-line relationships, and examine two theories which seek to explain why relationships develop. Then, we examine conflict and explain how to use conflict-management processes to strengthen relationships.

Types of Relationships

We behave differently depending on whether our relationships are personal or impersonal (LaFollette, 1996, p. 4). Moving on a continuum from impersonal to personal, we generally classify the people with whom we have relationships as acquaintances, friends, and close friends or intimates.

Acquaintances

Acquaintances are people whom we may know by name and whom we may talk with when the opportunity arises, but with whom our interactions are largely impersonal. Among others, we become acquainted with those who live near us, those with whom we work or study, and those who perform services for us. Many acquaintanceships grow out of a particular context. For example, Jim, an accountant, has been preparing Sung Lee's taxes for three years, but they have never met outside of Jim's office, and when they do meet they exchange only polite pleasantries or talk about Sung Lee's taxes.

Friends

Friends are people with whom we have voluntarily negotiated more personal relationships (Patterson, Bettini, & Nussbaum, 1993, p. 145). In the early stages of friendships, people move toward interactions that are less role-bound. For example, after discovering that they share an interest in sailing, Jim and Sung Lee may decide to get together for lunch. If they find that they enjoy each other's company, they may eventually become friends.

What we look for in our friends As we seek out people as friends, we are drawn toward people we find attractive, who have good social skills, who are responsive to us, and who have similar interests, attitudes, values, and personalities (Fehr, 1996, pp. 52–68). However, relationships may also develop between people whose personalities are dissimilar: the saying "opposites attract" is as accurate as "birds of a feather flock together." Stated theoretically, relationships depend on mutual need fulfillment, so people can be attracted to those who are different from themselves but who fulfill their needs. Thus, opposites attract when the differences between the people are seen as complementary (Winstead, Derlega, & Rose, 1997, p. 26).

What we expect from our friends Although people may be drawn to each other for many reasons, a variety of research shows that maintaining a real friendship is marked by a high degree of positiveness, assurance, openness, networking, and task sharing (Dindia, 2000a, p. 291; Guerrero & Andersen, 2000, p. 178; Stafford & Canary, 1991).

- *Positiveness*: Friends spend time with each other because they reap positive benefits from doing so. They enjoy each other's company, they enjoy talking with each other, and they enjoy sharing experiences.
- *Assurance*: Friends **trust** each other. They risk putting their well-being in each other's hands because each trusts the other not to intentionally harm his or her interests.
- *Openness*: Friends share personal feelings with each other.
- *Networking*: Friends show a high level of commitment not only to each other but also to each other's friends and family. They are likely to sacrifice their time and energy to engage in activities with family and friends of friends.
- *Task sharing*: Friends help each other with work.

PhotoDisc Collection/PhotoDisc Blue/Getty Images

Friendships are marked by positiveness, assurance, openness, networking, and task sharing.

Close Friends or Intimates

Close friends or **intimates** are those with whom we share our deepest feelings. People may have many acquaintances and a number of friends, but most are likely to have only a few truly intimate friends.

Close friends or intimates differ from other friends mostly in terms of the degree of commitment, trust, disclosure, and enjoyment in their relationship. For instance, although friends engage in some self-disclosure, they are not likely to share the most important secrets of their lives; intimate friends often gain knowledge of the innermost being of their partner.

IN BRIEF

Types of Relationships

The people with whom we have relationships fall into one of three categories:

- *Acquaintances*: those with whom our interactions are largely impersonal
- *Friends*: those with whom we have voluntarily negotiated personal relationships
- *Close friends or intimates*: those with whom we share our deepest feelings.

Communication in the Stages of Relationships

Even though no two relationships develop in exactly the same manner, most relationships move through identifiable stages following a life cycle that includes a starting or building phase, a period of stability, and a deterioration stage (Duck, 1987; Taylor & Altman, 1987). Whether a relationship moves to the next stage depends on how partners interact.

Starting or Building Relationships

Fundamental to starting or building a relationship is **uncertainty reduction,** the process of communicating to gather information about someone else in order to be better able to explain and predict that person's behaviour toward us (Berger & Bradac, 1982; Littlejohn, 1999, p. 260). We collect such information about others passively by observing their behaviour, actively by asking others for information, and interactively by conversing with them directly.

The three communication activities we engage in to start or build relationships are striking up conversations, keeping conversations going, and moving toward intimacy.

COMMUNICATE!
Using Technology

Record a portion of a movie or TV program in which friends are having a conversation. Analyze it on the basis of the expectations of friendship: positiveness, assurance, openness, networking, and task sharing. Which of these factors seem evident in the conversation? What other elements were shown in the conversation? Did these seem to contribute to or detract from the relationship? In what ways is this conversation typical or atypical of those you have had with your friends? Explain.

Striking up a conversation What happens in the first few minutes of a conversation will have a profound effect on the nature of the relationship that develops. As the old saying suggests, you seldom get a second chance to create a first impression. Although thinking up getting-to-know-you lines is easy for some, many people become nearly tongue-tied when they first meet someone and, as a result, make a bad first impression. There are several practical approaches to starting conversations. Most involve asking questions. A cheerful answer to a question suggests that the respondent is interested in continuing the conversation. Refusal to answer or a curt reply may mean that the person is not really interested in talking at this time.

1. **Formally or informally introduce yourself.** "Hi, my name is Gordon. What's yours?"

2. **Refer to the physical context.** "This is awful weather for a game, isn't it?" "I wonder how they are able to keep such a beautiful garden in this climate?" or "Isn't it stuffy in here?"

3. **Refer to your own thoughts or feelings.** "I really enjoy parties, don't you?" "I live on this floor too. Do these steps bother you as much as they do me?" or "The candidates' positions on tax increases are clear at least, wouldn't you agree?"

4. **Refer to the other person.** "Miguel seems to be an excellent pianist. Have you known him for long?" or "I don't believe I've had the pleasure of meeting you before. Do you work in the marketing department?"

Keeping the conversation going Once two people have begun an interaction, they are likely to engage in *small talk* such as information exchange and gossip, conversation that meets social needs with relatively low amounts of risk.

In **idea-exchange communication,** people share information such as facts, opinions, and beliefs, and some of this information may reflect values. At the office, Stan may ask Blaine about last night's hockey scores, or on a more serious level, the two may talk about the important issues in an ongoing election campaign. Although the discussion of election issues may be deeper than the conversation about sports, both conversations represent idea-exchanges. This type of communication is especially important in the early stages of a relationship because, through it, the participants each learn what the other is thinking, reassess their level of attraction, and decide whether they want the relationship to grow.

Gossip, the exchange of information of uncertain accuracy about people known to both (or all) participants in a conversation, is one of the most common forms of interpersonal communication. Eggins and Slade (1997) observe, "Every day a considerable amount of time for millions of people is consumed by gossip, and as such, it is a powerful socializing force" (p. 270).

On one hand, gossip provides an easy approach to conversation that does not require us to share much information about ourselves. Questions such as "Do you know Walter well? I hear he is a really great actor" and "Would you believe that Tarra Manuel and Gord Campbell are going together? They never seemed to hit it off too well in the past," are invitations to gossip. Most gossip is largely benign because the information exchanged is public knowledge. People do break up, lose their jobs, have accidents, win prizes, and so forth. In these circumstances, no secrets are being violated, and the person being talked about probably would, if he or she were present, tell exactly what happened.

This kind of small talk occurs during all phases of a relationship but is most common in the early phase because it is considered safe. We can gossip for a long time with another person without really saying anything about ourselves or learning anything about the other person. Gossip may be a pleasant way to pass time with people we know but have no desire or need to enter into a deeper relationship with.

OBSERVE & ANALYZE
Journal Activity

Friends and Acquaintances

1. Identify five people you consider to be your friends. In what kind of context did you first meet? What attracted you to them? What aspects of attraction have proved to be most important as the relationships developed?
2. Identify five people you consider to be acquaintances. List the ways in which communication with your acquaintances differs from communication with your friends.
3. What would need to happen in order for those people you listed as acquaintances to become friends?

It also provides a safe way to explore the growth potential of a relationship because it enables each person to see whether the other reacts similarly to the views expressed about the subject of the gossip. Not surprisingly, conversations at parties are comprised largely of gossip.

On the other hand, gossip can be unethical and malicious. If the information exchanged is inaccurate, the gossip may damage both the relationship within which it is exchanged and other relationships as well. Perhaps the most malicious kind of gossip is the kind that aims to hurt or embarrass the person who is being talked about. For instance, saying "Lonnie had a car accident. He ran a red light and hit another car" is gossip, but it may be acceptable if the person telling the tale is certain that it is factual. However, if the person goes on, "You know, he was probably drunk. I hear that Lonnie has really been bingeing lately," this speculation goes far beyond reporting what happened, and because the teller has no factual basis for the statements, they are unethical. Such gossip quickly turns into rumour, and rumours can destroy a person's life.

Moving to deep friendship and intimacy levels In addition to engaging in small talk, people who seek a more intimate relationship will also begin to talk about more serious ideas and to share their feelings about important matters. By sharing feelings and through the process of self-disclosure, people really come to know and to understand each other. When people find that they get satisfaction out of being together and that they are able to share ideas and feelings, their friendship grows.

Using affectionate communication is particularly important to the development of more intimate relationships (Floyd & Morman, 1998, p. 157). Affectionate communication includes such nonverbal behaviours as holding hands, putting an arm around a shoulder, sitting close together, looking into each other's eyes, hugging, and kissing. It also includes exchanging verbal messages such as "Our relationship is really important to me," "I like you," or "You're a really good friend."

Stabilizing Relationships

When two people have a satisfactory relationship, whether as acquaintances, as friends, or as intimates, they look for **stabilization,** a means of maintaining the relationship at that level for some time. Stabilization occurs when two people agree on what they want from each other and are satisfied that they are achieving it. Unfortunately, as time goes by, people sometimes fall into communication habits that can undermine the stability of the relationship. To maintain stability in our relationships, we should consciously strive to ensure that, when we and our relational partners speak to each other, we speak descriptively, openly, and tentatively and that we address each other as equals.

Speak descriptively Using descriptive speech simply requires us to state what we see or hear in neutral or objective language, to name our feelings and use *I-statements* when expressing them, and to avoid using evaluative language. In Chapter 7, we presented guidelines for describing feelings and describing behaviour, both of which are necessities in maintaining a stable relationship.

> *Evaluative language:* "You are so careless and so sneaky! Did you think I wouldn't notice what you've done to my car?
>
> *Descriptive language:* "My car has a large dent in the driver's side front fender. I am disappointed that you didn't mention that you had an accident."

Speak openly To remain open with each other, relational partners must continue to share true thoughts and feelings without resorting to manipulation or maintaining hidden agendas. In a good relationship, one person should never be afraid to share a thought with the other. If we find ourselves unwilling to share openly, we must ask ourselves why. What is happening in the relationship that is keeping us from sharing our thoughts and feelings? If we discover a problem in the relationship (e.g., my partner does not listen to me anymore; my partner constantly changes the subject), then we need to discuss that problem *openly* with our partner.

Speak tentatively When we speak tentatively, we state information in a way that allows for the possibility of error or inaccuracy. As time goes by, and relational partners fall into established and comfortable roles, one partner may find himself or herself saying everything as if he or she were a supreme authority on all subjects. Consider the wording and the *sound* of the following pairs of statements:

a. "If I remember correctly, Dalton was the leading scorer last month."
"No, you're wrong, Dalton had the most goals last month."

b. "I think you should consider talking with Glenna before proceeding with this plan."
"You'd be an idiot not to talk with Glenna before doing anything on this."

In each case, the first sentence of the pair is likely to go over better with the receiver, not only because the tentativeness of the phrasing is less antagonistic and dogmatic than that of the second statement, but also because the tentative statement acknowledges that the words come from the speaker, who may have it wrong. "No, you're wrong" leaves no room for possible error; "If I remember correctly" not only leaves room for error but also shows that the statement reflects the speaker's recollection, not certainty.

Speak to others as equals The tendency to sound superior often accompanies the tendency to sound certain. Just as tentativeness leads to more convivial conversation, so does addressing the receiver of a message as an equal. We can demonstrate that we recognize our relational partners as equals by avoiding any words or nonverbal signs that might indicate superiority. Even when we have or think we have greater knowledge on a subject than our partner, we can still state our views in ways that do not allude to our different levels of expertise.

OBSERVE & ANALYZE
Journal Activity

Positive and Negative Climates

Think of two recent interactions you have had, one that was characterized by a positive communication climate and one that was characterized by a negative climate. Recall as best you can specific examples of some of the conversation from each interaction. Write a script of each conversation. Then, analyze each script. Count specific instances of descriptive and evaluative language, of openness and manipulativeness, of tentative wordings and dogmatic wordings. Look for examples of you and your conversational partner treating each other equally and examples of one person speaking in a way that conveyed an attitude of superiority. Discuss your results. How much did using or failing to use the four skills presented in this section contribute to the climate of each interaction?

Successful managers know that treating their subordinates as inferiors will damage the relationship between themselves and their staff. Treating a partner as inferior is asking for trouble.

In addition to choosing language carefully, we must also be conscious of the effects of our tone of voice and facial expressions. As we learned earlier, our nonverbal communication can totally negate the meaning of the words we use.

Frequently, we say things that hurt our relationships because we are just not thinking. It is a good idea to follow the old advice to "engage your brain before putting your mouth into gear." A single thoughtless sentence can inflict on a relationship a wound that could take minutes, hours, or days to heal—if it can be healed at all. Taking a few seconds to consider the likely effects of what we are going to say before we say it can prevent many of the difficulties that arise in relationships.

IN BRIEF

Communication in the Stages of Relationships

Each stage of a relationship presents communication challenges:

- At the starting or building stage, employ conversational skills to develop the relationship.
- During the stability stage, nurture a relationship by speaking descriptively, openly, and tentatively, and by addressing partners as equals.
- During the disintegration stage, use skills of describing feelings, owning feelings and disclosing to make the parting as amicable as possible.

Relationship Disintegration

Regardless of how much one partner would like a relationship to remain stable or grow deeper, there are times when a relationship is destined to disintegrate. Partners may discover that they just do not have enough in common to make a go of it. Sometimes when a relationship ends, we are sad; at other times, we are relieved. Regardless of our feelings, it is helpful to end a relationship in an interpersonally competent manner. Even the painful effects of a wrenching break-up can be lessened through a conscious effort to use good interpersonal communication skills.

Unfortunately, when people decide to end relationships, they often purposely use strategies that are hurtful. Even when relationships have fallen apart, people should still try to use the constructive skills of describing feelings, owning feelings, and disclosing feelings to make the parting as amicable as possible.

Douglas Kirkland/Corbis Sygma/Magma

Mutual respect and equality create a solid foundation for enduring relationships.

DIVERSE VOICES

Queer Fix

by Shawn Mooney

Shawn Mooney, now of Vancouver, lived in Edmonton when he wrote this commentary for Times .10 Magazine. *In it, he reflects not only on the complex rituals of beginning relationships, but also on the significance of our perceptions of ourselves and others in determining whether we enter into them.*

A few weekends ago I went out to a gay bar all by myself. The club wasn't that busy, but I didn't care. I sat down alone at a booth, smoked, sipped my tonic water, and watched people.

I saw a sexy older guy, probably sixty. He was in black dress pants and a trendy short-sleeved black shirt. Nearly bald, what was left of his hair was shaved close. He looked sexy. I didn't want to sleep with him, but it was fascinating to watch him shimmy on the dance floor. There was nothing put-on, no trying-to-be-younger-than-he-was shtick. He was just sexy. I so needed to witness that.

And I watched a yummy young lad in skin-tight plastic pants. Those trousers left little to the imagination, let me tell you.

As I got cruised by another guy whom I was not attracted to, I played with the muscles in my mouth, trying not to freeze the smile off my face. It didn't quite work; that will take practice.

I would love it if we gay men came up with radically new social behaviours. How about if we all smiled and acknowledged each other as a matter of course, devising other ways of indicating sexual interest or disinterest? Like, speaking our desires aloud, or something. I wonder what the energy of a gay bar would be like then?

I sat there with my half-frozen smile, remembering an anecdote in Greg Flood's *I'm Looking For Mr. Right, But I'll Settle For Mr. Right Away*: Frustrated with the superficial, cruisy dynamics of a gay bar, some men organized an ice cream social at a park as an alternative to the scene. And what happened? Dozens of guys showed up, stood around and licked their ice cream cones and cruised one another.

I watched luscious young men dance. I thought about the young gay men I've befriended here and, via the Internet, the world over; how those connections educate my heart. I thought about the fact that I met none of them at a gay bar.

I watched the nubile hotties dancing before my eyes, all strangers to me. I imagined that each and every one had as interesting and meaningful an inner life as the young men I know and adore.

"Eye candy" doesn't begin to cover it.

As the energies of sex, coldness, romance, and friendship swirled around and in me, my eyes welled up. The unknown men surrounding me had probably struggled at least somewhat like me, struggled to love themselves enough to actually arrive on this side of the door. And here we all were. "Now what?" I asked myself, scrunch-faced against happy-sad tears. "Now what might be possible?"

"It depends," came an answer. "How much beauty—and what flavours of joy—shall you allow to pass through you like breath?"

Source: Queer Fix by Shawn Mooney. Reprinted with permission of Times .10 Magazine.

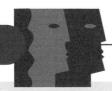

Examining Disclosure and Feedback Ratios in Relationships

As we saw in Chapter 7, self-disclosure is sharing biographical data, ideas, and feelings, and feedback is providing verbal and physical responses to people and their messages. A healthy interpersonal relationship, especially at the level of friendship or close friendship, is marked by a balance of self-disclosure and feedback.

How can we tell whether we and our relational partners are sharing enough to keep our relationships growing? The best method is to discuss communication in our relationships with our partners. As the basis for a worthwhile discussion, we suggest the use of a **Johari window,** named after its two originators, Joe Luft (1970) and Harry Ingham. Each Johari window can represent one side of one relationship between two people. If Esther and Columb wanted to assess their relationship through the use of Johari windows, they would need to create two Johari windows, one showing Esther's side of the relationship and another showing Columb's side.

A Johari window is divided into four sections or panes, as shown in Figure 8.1. The top left quadrant is called the *open pane.* If Esther were preparing a Johari window that represented her side of her relationship with Columb, she would include in the open pane all of the information that both of them know about her: that is, everything about herself that Esther has disclosed to Columb and all of the observations about her that Columb has made and shared with her.

The lower left quadrant is called the *secret pane.* It represents all those things that the person whose side of the relationship is being assessed knows about himself or herself but that the other person in the relationship does not know. In the Johari window that represented her side of her relationship with

THINKING ABOUT . . .

Personal Guidelines for Self-Disclosure

Think about one of your secrets. How many people know it? How have you decided whom to tell? What consequences (good and bad) have resulted from sharing that secret? Determine a set of guidelines appropriate for you in sharing such secrets.

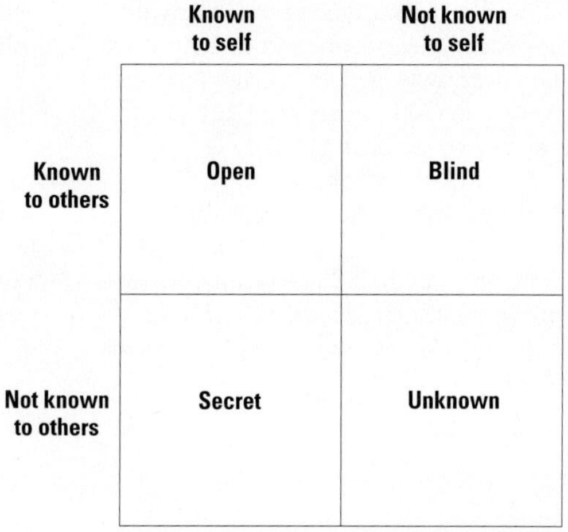

Figure 8.1
The Johari window

Columb, Esther would include in the secret pane all of the information that she has about herself that she has not shared with him. This information could be trivial or profound, anything from where she keeps her pencils, to why she does not eat meat, to deep secrets whose revelation would represent a threat to her. For example, if Esther had once been engaged to be married, but on the day of the wedding her fiancé had backed out, an experience which she found embarrassing and painful to recall, this information would remain in the secret pane of her window until her relationship with Columb had grown to the point that she felt comfortable disclosing it to him; it would then move into the open pane. Through disclosure, the secret pane of a window becomes smaller and the open pane is enlarged.

The top right quadrant is called the *blind pane*. This is the place for information that the person whose side of the relationship is being assessed does not know about himself or herself but which the other person does know. Most people have blind spots—aspects of their behaviour about which they are unaware. For example, Esther may not know that she talks in her sleep or that she frowns when she is concentrating especially hard. Both of these behaviours are known to Columb, who has slept in the same room with her and has observed her at work. Information moves from the blind area of the window to the open area through feedback. If Columb tells Esther about these behaviours, and she believes him, they will move to the open pane. Thus, like disclosure, feedback enlarges the open pane of the Johari window, but in this case it is the blind pane that becomes smaller.

Finally, the lower right quadrant is called the *unknown pane*. It contains information that neither partner in the relationship knows about the person whose side of the relationship is being assessed. Obviously, a person cannot develop a list of this information. So how can he or she know that it even exists? Well, periodically people discover it. If, for instance, Esther has never tried hang gliding, then neither she nor Columb can really know whether she would back out at the last minute or follow through, do it well or crash, love every minute of it or be paralyzed by fear.

Thus, when we disclose and receive feedback in a relationship, the sizes of the various panes in the Johari window change (Figure 8.2). As a relationship becomes more intimate, the open pane of both partners' windows becomes larger, and the secret and hidden parts become smaller.

Figure 8.2a shows a relationship in which little disclosure or feedback is occurring. This person has not shared much information with the other and has received little feedback from this partner as well. We would expect to see this pattern in new relationships or in ones between casual acquaintances.

Figure 8.2b shows a relationship in which a person is disclosing to a partner but the partner is providing little feedback. As you can see, the secret pane is small, but the blind pane is large. A window like this indicates that the person is able to disclose information but that the partner is unable or unwilling to give feedback (or perhaps the person refuses to accept the feedback that is being

THINKING ABOUT . . .

Johari Windows

Draw three Johari windows to depict your relationship with one of your parents or a guardian at three points in your life: one for when you were five years old, one for when you were 14 years old, and one for today. What does comparing the windows reveal about how your relationship with the parent or guardian has changed over time? Why do you think it has changed in this way?

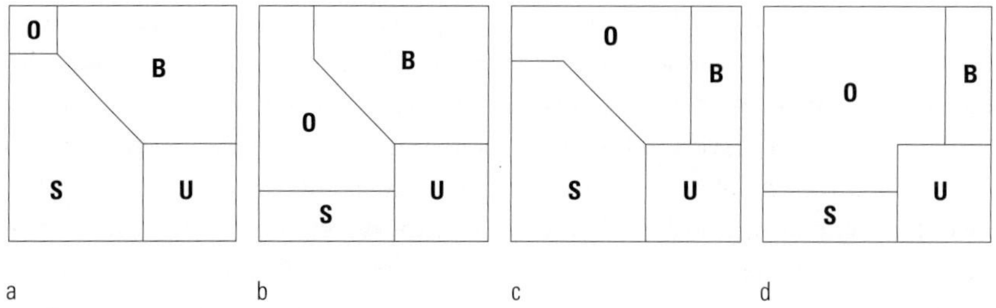

Figure 8.2
Sample Johari windows
(a) low disclosure, low feedback;
(b) high disclosure, low feedback;
(c) low disclosure, high feedback;
(d) high disclosure, high feedback.

given). Part of the way that we learn about who we are comes from the feedback we receive from others, and relationships in which one partner does not provide feedback can become very unsatisfying to the other partner.

Figure 8.2c shows a relationship in which one partner is good at providing feedback but the other is not disclosing. Most of us disclose only when we trust our partners, so this pattern may be an indication that the person does not have confidence in the relational partner.

Figure 8.2d shows a relationship in which the person has disclosed information and received feedback, and the open pane of the window has enlarged as a result of both processes. Windows that look like this indicate that there is sufficient trust and interest in the relationship that both partners are willing to risk disclosing and giving feedback.

Clearly, to get a complete picture of a relationship, each partner's Johari window would have to be examined. As stated at the beginning of this discussion, the window is a useful tool for helping partners examine and discuss the levels of intimacy and trust in their relationship.

IN BRIEF

Self-Disclosure and Feedback Ratios in Relationships

Healthy relationships are marked by a balance of self-disclosure and feedback, and this balance can be assessed through the use of Johari windows:

- Self-disclosure causes the secret pane of the Johari window to shrink and the open pane to grow.
- Feedback causes the blind pane of the Johari window to shrink and the open pane to grow.

Theoretical Perspectives on Relationships

What determines whether or not someone will try to build a relationship with another person? Why do some relationships never move beyond a certain level? Why do some longstanding relationships suddenly begin to deteriorate? Two theories, interpersonal needs theory and exchange theory, provide answers to these questions.

Interpersonal Needs Theory

Interpersonal needs theory proposes that whether or not a relationship is started, built, or maintained depends on how well the people involved meet each other's interpersonal needs for affection, inclusion, and control (Schutz, 1966, pp. 18–20).

The **affection need** reflects a person's desire to express and to receive love. People vary considerably, both verbally and nonverbally, in terms of how much they show and express affection. At one end of the spectrum are those who avoid close ties, seldom show strong feelings for others, and shy away from people who show or want to show affection. At the other end of the spectrum are those who thrive on establishing close relationships with everyone. They think of all others as intimates, immediately confide in persons they have just met, and want everyone to consider them close friends. Somewhere in between these two extremes are those who can express and receive affection easily and who derive pleasure from many kinds of relationships with others.

The **inclusion need** reflects a desire to be in the company of other people, and everyone has some need to be social. At one end of the continuum are those who prefer to be left alone. Occasionally, they seek company or enjoy being included with others, but they do not require a great deal of social interaction to feel satisfied. At the other end of the continuum are those who need constant companionship and feel tense when they must be alone. Their doors are always open: everyone is welcome, and they expect others to welcome them. Of course, most of us do not belong to either of these extreme types. Rather, we are sometimes comfortable being alone and, at other times, need and enjoy interaction with others.

The **control need** reflects a desire to influence the events and people around us. As with the other two interpersonal needs, people vary in how much control they require. At one extreme are persons who seem to shun responsibility and do not want to be in charge of anything. At the other extreme are persons who need to dominate others at all times and become anxious if they cannot. Again, most people fall somewhere between these two extremes, needing to lead at certain times but content to follow the lead of others at other times.

How can this analysis help us understand communication in relationships? Relationships develop and deteriorate in part because of the compatibility or incompatibility of relational partners' interpersonal needs. As we interact with others, we can detect whether their needs for affection, inclusion, and control seem compatible with our own. Suppose that Emily and Roger have been seeing each other regularly, and both see their relationship as close. If, in response to Roger's attempt to put his arm around Emily while they were watching television, Emily stiffened slightly, it might suggest that she does not have quite the same need for affection as Roger. People's needs differ and they change over time. If, at a particular time, a partner's needs differ significantly from our own, and we fail to understand that they do, we can misunderstand what is going wrong in our communication.

Schutz's theory of interpersonal needs is useful because it helps explain a great deal of interpersonal behaviour (Trenholm, 1991, p. 191). In addition, research on this model has been generally supportive of its major themes (Shaw, 1981, pp. 228–231). Interpersonal needs theory does not, however, explain *how* people adjust to one another in their ongoing relationships. The next theory we discuss will help us develop this understanding.

Exchange Theory

Another way of understanding our relationships is on the basis of **exchange theory**, a theory developed by John W. Thibaut and Harold H. Kelley (1986). They believe that relationships can be understood in terms of the exchange of rewards and costs that take place during people's interactions (pp. 9–30). **Rewards** are positively valued outcomes such as good feelings, prestige, useful information, and fulfillment of emotional needs. **Costs** are negatively valued outcomes such as time, energy, anxiety, and emotional pain. For instance, Sharon and Jan are in the same calculus class. Sharon is struggling in the course but Jan, a math whiz, is having no trouble. Tomorrow they must submit their solutions to a series of tough problems. Sharon may wish to spend some time with Jan if she anticipates that she will learn how to solve the problems, but she may be reluctant to do so if she expects to be annoyed by Jan's air of superiority during the interaction.

According to Thibaut and Kelley, people seek interactions in which their rewards/costs ratio is best. Whether Sharon asks Jan to explain the calculus problems to her, therefore, depends on (1) whether Sharon believes the positive value she receives from the information is greater than the cost to her self-esteem of enduring Jan's snide comments, and (2) whether getting this information from Jan will result in a better rewards/costs ratio than if Sharon gets the information elsewhere, perhaps from a paid tutor.

This analysis can be extended from single interactions to relationships. If the rewards/costs ratio of a relationship is higher than that of alternative relationships, then the person will experience the relationship as pleasant and satisfying. If, however, over an extended period, the net rewards (rewards minus costs) of a relationship fall below what is available elsewhere, the person will come to view the relationship as unsatisfactory or unpleasant.

If people have a number of relationships that they perceive as giving them a good rewards/costs ratio, they will establish a high satisfaction level and will probably not be satisfied with low-outcome relationships. In contrast, people who have few positive interactions will be satisfied with relationships and interactions that people who enjoy high-outcome relationships would find unattractive. For instance, Devon may continue to date Eric even though Eric treats him very poorly because, compared to other relationships he has had, the net rewards he gets from this relationship are on par. In fact, some people will stay in a relationship that others view as abusive because they do not see themselves as having better alternatives. Joan may stay with Charley even though he periodically beats her because she believes he is a good provider who is loving when he is sober, and besides, she may think, "Who else would marry a 45-year-old woman with three children?"

Thibaut and Kelley's exchange theory is based on the assumption that people consciously and deliberately weigh the rewards and costs associated with any relationship or interaction and make comparisons with alternative choices; that is, that people seek out relationships that benefit them and avoid those that

THINKING ABOUT . . .

Needs Theory and Exchange Theory

Think of a specific intimate relationship that you have. Explain the development and maintenance of this relationship. How can needs theory or exchange theory be used to explain why this relationship developed as it did?

are costly (Trenholm, 1991, p. 72). It can be useful to examine our relationships from a rewards/costs perspective, especially if a relationship is stagnating. We may recognize areas where costs are greater than rewards either for ourselves or for the other person. If so, we may be able to change some aspects of the relationship before it deteriorates completely.

IN BRIEF

Theoretical Perspectives on Relationships

Two theories can help us to understand why people build and maintain some relationships and why others deteriorate:

- *Interpersonal needs theory* measures relationships in terms of how well the partners satisfy each other's needs for affection, inclusion, and control.
- *Exchange theory* evaluates relationships in terms of the costs and rewards that the partners experience from being in them.

Electronically Mediated Relationships

Modern communication technologies are changing the way we build and maintain relationships. People once became acquainted mostly with those with whom they had physical contact, but today, people are able to easily establish acquaintanceships with people around the world.

Development of Electronically Mediated Relationships

Thanks to technological innovation, people can now be introduced to others they have never seen through such means as newsgroups and message boards, Internet chat rooms, and Internet dating services, and as Parks and Floyd (1996) found, people frequently develop these electronic encounters into personal relationships (p. 93). For example, Andrea and Matt first encounter each other each other when they contribute to an environmental issues newsgroup. They already know that they have at least one thing, an interest in environmental issues, in common. As the postings continue, they notice that they are the only ones who hold a particular view on one specific issue. As time goes on, they discover that they share other views as well. At this point, they decide to meet in a private chat room where they can talk directly with each other. Here, they are able to explore whether they have other common interests. Before long, they have exchanged e-mail addresses and begun a direct correspondence. If their interest in each other continues to grow, they may arrange to chat on the telephone, and if that conversation proves satisfying, to meet in person. At some point during this process, they have begun to have a personal relationship: maybe a friendship, maybe a close friendship.

Of course, many people in electronically mediated (EM) relationships are perfectly content with just having acquaintances and the opportunity to talk with them. Nearly a quarter (23.7%) of the people in Parks and Floyd's newsgroup study reported that they communicated with their partners at least three or four times a week, and more than half (55.4%) communicated with their partners weekly (p. 85). EM relationships are attractive to some busy people largely because they do not have time to socialize in a more conventional way. Other people who begin relationships in face-to-face settings use EM communication to sustain these relationships when work, school, or other commitments require them and their partners to live at a distance from each other. E-mail, which was developed to be a tool for conducting business, and instant messaging are now widely used by families, friends, and lovers.

THINKING ABOUT . . .

Maintenance of Internet Relationships

Have you developed either a same-sex or an opposite-sex relationship on line? What are some of the elements that make such a relationship satisfying? If you are involved in an ongoing on-line relationship, how do you manage to maintain it? If you have ended an on-line relationship, were the reasons for ending it any different from the reasons for ending a similar face-to-face relationship?

Can EM relationships endure? Partners in such relationships seem to lack many of the elements discussed in assessing the development of traditional relationship: physical proximity, information about physical appearance, information about group membership, and information about the broader social context in which each partner operates. However, people in EM relationships can overcome some of these shortcomings by exchanging e-mail or instant messages, by exchanging photographs either electronically or by mail, by talking on the telephone, and ultimately, by arranging meetings. Think about it. What are some of the benefits and drawbacks to a relationship that is carried on at a distance?

Some critics of EM relationships argue that face-to-face interaction has more social presence than electronic exchanges, that the possibility of immediate feedback in face-to-face interaction conveys greater personal closeness (Flaherty, Pearce, & Rubin, 1998, p. 264). In addition, in most EM communication, much of the nonverbal message is lost. Despite such criticisms, however, more and more people are turning to EM communication to develop and maintain relationships. Such relationships are attractive to those who have for one reason or another experienced difficulty making strong interpersonal relationships in person. They are also attractive to highly literate people and to those who are sensitive about physical appearance. Because EM communication is planned, people are able to show qualities such as verbal skilfulness and humour in their writing, and they do not have to deal with issues of physical attraction.

In fact, some people report that their EM relationships are better than face-to-face relationships. For instance, a person who had been active in a computer network for church workers said, "I know some of these people better than some of my oldest and best friends" (Parks & Floyd, 1996, pp. 82–83). A variety of studies report instances of EM relationships blossoming into romance and marriage (Markham, 1998).

There are, however, important differences between in-person and EM communication that can create difficulties for relational development. Bigelow (1999) focuses on three such problems (pp. 636–637):

1. **EM communication is less rich than face-to-face, primarily because text messages are primarily verbal.** As a result of not being able to see or hear the way people present their messages, EM communicators may misinterpret the messages they receive. Only with the addition of videoconferencing is the full range of nonverbal messages available.

2. **EM communication, conducted via keyboard entries, is slower paced than face-to-face conversation.** Although this slower rate may provide a person with more time for thought, the slower transmission reduces the spontaneity that is an important characteristic of face-to-face interaction.

3. **EM communicators are invisible.** EM communicators often preserve their privacy by using on-line identities and perhaps by representing themselves differently than they actually are.

Bruce Ayers/Stone/Getty Images

Many people in electronically mediated (EM) relationships are perfectly content with just having acquaintances and the opportunity to talk.

Building Trust in Electronically Mediated Relationships

In face-to-face relationships, trust is built over time. We meet a person and begin interacting. As a result of the behaviour we encounter, we make decisions about trust. For instance, we lend a book and consider when and if it is returned; we make dates and consider whether and how often the person is on time; we tell the person something that is personal and consider whether or not the person keeps the information to himself or herself. Through such experiences, we determine whether or not we can trust the person and whether or not we want to move toward a more intimate relationship (Goldberg, 1999, p. 113).

In EM relationships, making a trust evaluation is more difficult. Some of the media through which relationships are developed are very opaque. We lose most of the spontaneity and most of the information normally available through nonverbal channels that we would use to evaluate trustworthiness. In addition, because the relationship is being carried on at a distance and without a social context, we frequently are not in a position to know about many aspects of the other person's conduct—we must rely much more heavily on the person's word alone. As a result, our capacity to judge the trustworthiness of the other person is limited.

The Dark Side of Electronically Mediated Relationships

Despite its appeal to many people, using EM communication to form relationships has given rise to several unethical practices.

Abuse of anonymity One unethical practice common in Internet-based relationships is adopting a fictitious on-line persona. A serious question about such Internet relationships is "What kind of a relationship can be forged when users are not honest about who they are?" This practice removes both accountability and responsibility, and without these, it is not possible to develop a sound relationship. Kramer and Kramarae (1997) assert that women have the most to lose from the use of fictitious identities (p. 236).

Dishonesty The ease with which one can deceive while communicating on line leads many people to be dishonest. For example, people lie about their sex and physical attributes, create fictitious careers and social lives, and misrepresent their wealth and social status. Because we do not *know* our EM partners personally, we are severely limited in our ability to independently confirm what we are told. Those in EM relationships need to proceed with caution. It is wise to be skeptical of what people tell you about themselves, especially at the beginning of such a relationship. As Jenny Preece points out, "On-line romances of any sort may fail when real-life meetings result in dashed fantasies. For example, on line, no one is overweight, but in reality a person's extra 25 pounds can make a difference. And dishonesty works only as long as the relationship remains on line only" (2000, p. 156).

In the early stages of a relationship, it is also wise to limit the personal information we divulge. Remember, in any communication situation, self-disclosure should occur only if it is reciprocated. However, unlike a partner in a face-to-face relationship, an EM communicator has no basis for judging whether the reciprocation is truthful. We should therefore begin self-disclosure slowly and stick to less personal issues.

Abuse of anonymity and dishonesty are of special concern in EM relationships formed by children. A 2001 survey conducted by Environics Research Group for the Media Awareness Network and the Government of Canada showed that 99 percent of Canadian children aged 9 to 17 have used the Internet, and 79 percent had Internet access at home. It is especially important for parents to monitor children's EM relationships; however, the survey showed that many Canadian parents do not and that there is a direct correlation between the lack of such supervision and children's involvement in risky behaviour. For example, of those children aged 13 to 17 who have visited private or adult-only chat rooms, 85 percent are at home but unsupervised when they do. The survey also showed that children are easily duped by unethical Internet correspondents: for example, 21 percent would give out both their name and address to win a prize. Most alarmingly, 15 percent of the children and youth surveyed had gone to meet in person someone whom they had previously met only on line (15% of that number went alone to the meeting). In every age group, boys are much more likely than girls to indulge in such high-risk behaviours.

Some parents who decline to monitor their children's on-line chatting liken it to violating their privacy by eavesdropping on their phone calls. However, as

Okrent cautions, "There's a difference: when your child's on the phone; she knows for certain who's on the other end of the line" (1999, p. 41). Parents need to learn how to monitor their children's Internet usage and how to use software capable of blocking access to objectionable and dangerous sites.

Addiction A third potential problem for children and adults alike is **technological addiction,** defined as a non-chemical (behavioural) addiction that involves human–machine interaction (Griffiths, 1998, p. 62). The seductiveness of communicating electronically can result in the disruption of ongoing interpersonal relationships. An episode of the CBC program *Marketplace* (Gruzuk, 2002) reported on serious addiction problems associated with interactive on-line video games. According to the program, addicts have been known to spend dozens of hours per week playing, to withdraw from real-life family, school, work, and social networks, and even to commit suicide when relationships in the on-line universe failed. Addictions counsellor Jay Parker, one of the experts interviewed on the program, offered the following list of signs and symptoms of addiction:

1. Inability to estimate the amount of time spent on the computer.
2. Failed attempts to control computer use for an extended period of time.
3. Having a sense of euphoria while on the computer.
4. Craving more computer time.
5. Neglecting family and friends.
6. Feeling restless, irritable, and discontent when not on the computer.
7. Lying to employers and family about computer activity.
8. Problems with school or job performance as a result of time spent on the computer.
9. Feelings of guilt, shame, anxiety, or depression as a result of time spent on the computer.
10. Changes in sleep pattern.
11. Health issues such as carpal tunnel syndrome, eye strain, weight change, and backache.
12. Denial, rationalization, and downplaying of adverse effects of computer use.
13. Withdrawal from real-life hobbies and social interactions.
14. Obsessing about sexual acting out through the use of the Internet.
15. Creation of enhanced persona to find cyber love or cyber sex.

IN BRIEF

Electronically Mediated Relationships

Electronically mediated communication can be used to develop new relationships or to maintain existing ones, and such relationships can be as or more attractive than face-to-face relationships for some people, but they also are characterized by disadvantages and risks, such as:

- loss of nonverbal communication
- slow pace
- abuse of anonymity
- dishonesty
- risk of addiction.

Conflict

When two people have an honest relationship, it is inevitable that one person's attempt to satisfy his or her own needs will occasionally be at odds with the other person's interests or desires. When this situation arises, the partners experience conflict. **Interpersonal conflict** is the result of a situation in which the needs or ideas of one person are at odds or in opposition to the needs or ideas of another. In such conflict situations, participants have choices about how they act and how they communicate with each other.

Although many people view conflict as bad (and, to be sure, conflict situations are likely to make us anxious and uneasy), it is often useful in confronting and resolving honest differences. In this section, we will look at five styles of managing conflict and then suggest specific communication strategies that can be used to initiate and respond to conflict effectively.

Styles of Managing Conflict

When faced with conflict, people can withdraw, accommodate, force, compromise, or collaborate (Cahn, 1990; Cupach & Canary, 1997; Filley, 1975).

Withdrawal When people **withdraw,** they physically or psychologically remove themselves from the conflict situation. People may physically withdraw by leaving the site. For instance, when Justina says, "Eduardo, I thought we agreed that you'd pay my parents back the $600 you owe them this week," Eduardo may withdraw physically by walking downstairs. Eduardo would be withdrawing psychologically if he ignored Justina and continued to read the paper.

Considered from an individual satisfaction standpoint, withdrawal creates a lose–lose situation because neither party to the conflict really accomplishes what he or she wants. Although Eduardo temporarily escapes from the conflict, he knows it will come up again.

Estate of Cybil Shelton/Peter Arnold, Inc.

Withdrawal during conflict usually just postpones and worsens the confrontation.

Considered from a relational satisfaction standpoint, both kinds of withdrawal usually have negative consequences. When used repeatedly, withdrawal leads to relationship decline. Why? Because neither party eliminates nor attempts to manage the causes of the conflict. Moreover, withdrawal results in what Cloven and Roloff (1991) call "mulling behaviour" (p. 136). **Mulling** occurs when one or both parties to the conflict start thinking about or stewing over an actual or perceived problem to the point that the conflict is perceived as being more severe than it actually is. At this point, blaming behaviour is likely to occur as one or both parties reproach the other for causing the conflict or the problem that led to it.

Withdrawal may be effective as a temporary measure to create time to think. For instance, Eduardo might say, "Hold it a minute; let me think about this while I get a cup of coffee, and then we'll talk about it some more." A few minutes later, having calmed down, Eduardo may return, ready to approach and deal with the conflict.

In certain circumstances, withdrawal may actually be appropriate. When neither the relationship nor the issue is really important, withdrawing is a good strategy. For example, at a party at which Josh and Jerrod have just met, the subject turns to the National Gun Registry. Josh may politely excuse himself to go talk with other people when he realizes that he strongly disagrees with the position Jerrod is advocating. In this case, Josh judges that it simply is not worth the effort to attempt to resolve the disagreement with Jerrod because his relationship with Jerrod is just not that important.

Accommodation An **accommodation** occurs when one participant in a conflict situation gives in to the other's needs while ignoring his or her own. For instance, Cenek would like to spend his vacation alone with his girlfriend, Aloisie, but when she says, "I think it would be fun to have Sarah and Frederick come with us on our camping trip, don't you?" Cenek replies, "Okay, whatever you want."

Considered from an individual satisfaction standpoint, accommodation is a win–lose situation. The person who accommodates loses and allows the other person to win.

From a relational satisfaction standpoint, habitual accommodation has two problems. Firstly, conflicts resolved through accommodation may lead to poor decision making because important facts, arguments, and positions are not voiced. Secondly, from an exchange theory perspective, habitual accommodation causes the accommodator to consistently receive less of whatever good things are available through the relationship. Eventually, being always on the losing end is likely to motivate the accommodator to seek more balanced relationships.

Habitually accommodating is a problem, but in situations where the issue is not really important but the relationship is, it is appropriate and effective to accommodate. For instance, Madison may prefer Italian food to French, but if she has invited important clients to discuss a business proposition over dinner, and they prefer French, she would want to accommodate them.

SPOTLIGHT ON SCHOLARS

Daniel J. Canary, Arizona State University

Dan Canary, citing the personal benefit in studying conflict, stated, "I learned how to control my own behaviour and become more effective in my personal relationships."

Canary's initial curiosity about effective conflict-management behaviours was piqued when he was in graduate school at the University of Southern California. At the time, he was a classmate of Brian Spitzberg, who formulated the theory that relational competence is a product of behaviours that are both appropriate and effective, and Bill Cupach, who was studying conflict in relationships. Although Canary saw the connection between their work, it was several years later, after he experienced successful and unsuccessful resolutions of significant conflict episodes in his personal life, that he began in earnest to study how the way people behave during conflict episodes affects their relationships.

Scholars can become well known by developing a new theory that more clearly describes what really happens when we interact, by carrying out a series of research studies that test and elaborate on the theories developed by others, or by organizing, integrating, and synthesizing the theories and research work that has been done in an area so that people who are not specialists in the particular area can better understand what is known. Dan Canary's reputation has been made in both of the latter types of scholarship.

Canary's research studies are helping to identify the behaviours that lead to perceiving a person as a competent conflict manager. Although people will view some of the communication behaviours used to manage conflict as appropriate and some behaviours as effective, Canary argues that both are necessary to be perceived as competent. Drawing on Spitzberg's competence theory, Canary's research studies are designed to identify conflict behaviours that accomplish both of the goals of appropriateness and effectiveness. The results of his studies consistently show that integrative conflict strategies—problem-solving, collaborating, and compromising—approaches that display a desire to work with the other person, are perceived to be both appropriate and effective (i.e., competent). Furthermore, his studies have shown that when one partner in a relationship is thought to be a competent conflict manager, the other one trusts him or her more, is more satisfied with the relationship, and perceives the relationship to be more intimate.

Canary's research has identified specific conflict-management behaviours that are viewed as appropriate or effective. He has found that when a person acknowledges the arguments of others (e.g., "Uh huh, I can see how you would think that") and when a person agrees with the arguments that others make to support their points (e.g., "Gee that's a good point that I hadn't really thought about") the person was viewed as having appropriately handled the conflict. To be viewed as effective, however, required a different set of behaviours. According to Canary's findings, conflict-handling behaviours that are viewed to be effective included stating complete arguments, elaborating and justifying one's point of view, and clearly developing one's ideas. In a conflict situation, Canary noticed that what was viewed as appropriate alone had the potential to be ineffective because appropriate behaviours seemed to involve some sort of agreement with the other person.

(continued)

Canary reasoned that there must be ways to be both appropriate and effective in conflict situations. This led him to consider methods of sequencing, or ordering, messages in a conflict episode. His preliminary results have revealed that competent communicators (those perceived to be both appropriate and effective) will begin by acknowledging the other's viewpoint or agreeing with part of the other's argument, *before* explaining, justifying, and arguing for their own viewpoint. In using this sequence, Canary believes competent communicators help frame the interaction as one of co-operative problem solving rather than as one of competing interests which only one party can win.

Many of Canary's major contributions to the study of conflict in personal relationships are included in two books: *Relationship Conflict* (co-authored with William Cupach and Susan Messman) is a synthesis of the diverse conflict literature that was written for graduate students and other scholars; *Competence in Interpersonal Conflict* (co-authored with Cupach) focuses on how readers can increase their competence at managing interpersonal conflict in a variety of settings. For complete citations of these and other Canary publications, see the reference list at the end of this book.

Canary teaches courses in interpersonal communication, conflict management, and research methods. His research involves a quickly applied conflict rating system that people can use to observe conflict in an efficient yet valid way.

Finally, it should be noted that accommodating is a preferred style of dealing with conflict in some cultures. In Japanese culture, for instance, it is thought to be more humble and face-saving to accommodate than to risk losing respect through conflict (Lulofs & Cahn, 2000, p. 114).

Force People who attempt to manage conflict through the use of **force** demand, through the use of physical threats, verbal attacks, coercion, or manipulation, that their needs be satisfied or that their ideas be accepted. The cliché *might makes right* captures this conflict-management style.

Considered from an individual satisfaction standpoint, force is a win–lose behaviour. Forceful people get their way with little regard to the cost borne by others.

From a relational satisfaction standpoint, forcing rarely improves and usually harms a relationship. Because of this high likelihood of relational damage, therefore, force is appropriate only when the issue is very important and the relationship is not, and in emergencies when quick and decisive action must be taken to ensure personal safety or to minimize some other potential for harm.

Compromise A **compromise** occurs when both parties to a conflict make sacrifices to find common ground, attempting to resolve the conflict by providing at least some satisfaction for each party. Using this approach, both people give up some part of what they really want or believe, or they trade one thing they want to get for something else.

From a personal satisfaction standpoint, compromising creates a lose–lose situation because both parties in one sense *lose* even as they *win*. Although compromising is a popular style of conflict management, there are significant

THINKING ABOUT . . .

Conflict-Management Style

What is your preferred conflict-management style? Which style is most difficult for you to use?

Approach	Characteristics	Goal	Outlook
Withdrawal	Unco-operative, unassertive	To keep from dealing with conflict	I don't want to talk about it
Accommodation	Co-operative, unassertive	To keep from upsetting the other person	Getting my way isn't as important as keeping the peace
Force	Unco-operative, assertive	To get my way	I'll get my way regardless of what I have to do
Compromise	Partially co-operative, partially assertive	To get partial satisfaction	I'll get partial satisfaction by letting the other person get partial satisfaction as well
Collaboration	Co-operative, assertive	To solve the problem together	Let's talk this out and find the best solution possible for both of us

COMMUNICATE! Using InfoTrac College Edition

How do college and university students deal with conflict? Using the InfoTrac College Edition subject guide, enter the term *interpersonal conflict.* Check the *periodical references.* You'll find articles that look at conflict in a variety of settings such as marriage, family structure, children's adjustment, and so on. See Marianne Bell and David Forde's article, "A Factorial Survey of Interpersonal Conflict Resolution" in the *Journal of Social Psychology* (1999). Does the behaviour described in this article match your own? Do any of the research findings surprise you? Why?

problems associated with it. One of special concern is that the quality of a decision is affected if one of the parties trades away a better solution to effect the compromise. Compromising is appropriate when the relationship is important, the issues have no simple solution, and both people have a strong interest in some parts of the issue.

From a relational satisfaction standpoint, compromise does not damage long-term relationships because both parties gain some satisfaction.

Collaboration **Collaboration** is a conflict-management approach that aims to address the needs and issues of each party to arrive at a solution that is mutually satisfying. The focus of collaboration is problem solving. During collaboration, people discuss the issues and their feelings about the issues and identify what are to them the important characteristics of a solution.

From an individual satisfaction standpoint, collaboration is a win–win situation because the conflict is resolved to the satisfaction of all.

From a relational satisfaction standpoint, collaboration is positive because both sides feel that they have been heard. They get to share ideas and weigh and consider information. Whatever the solution, arriving at it is a truly collaborative

Individual Satisfaction	Relational Satisfaction	Relational Effects	When Appropriate
Lose/lose: neither party gets satisfaction	Negative: no resolution	Drives wedge into relationship: results in mulling and blaming	Either as temporary disengagement or when issue is unimportant
Lose/win: the other party gets satisfaction	Negative: neither party feels good about the process	Hurts relationship because one person takes advantage	To build social credits or when the issue is unimportant
Win/lose: one party, the forcer, gets satisfaction	Negative: physical and psychological pain for the loser	Hurts relationship because one person feels intimidated	In emergencies; when it is critical to one's or others' welfare; if someone is taking advantage of you
Lose/lose: neither party is fully satisfied	Neutral to positive: at least partial satisfaction for both	May help or hurt because satisfaction is compromised	When issue is moderately important, when time is short, or when other attempts don't work
Win/win: both parties feel satisfied with the process	Positive: relationship strengthened because of mutual benefits	Helps the relationship because both sides are heard	Anytime

Figure 8.3
Styles of conflict management

effort. In effect, collaboration proves to be the most appropriate and the most effective means of managing conflict.

As we have said, resolving conflict through collaboration focuses on problem-solving. We will return to Justina and Eduardo's conflict over the $600 loan that Eduardo was supposed to have repaid to Justina's parents. Justina is upset that Eduardo is not respecting the promise that he made to her family, and Eduardo is angry with Justina for failing to recognize his problems. So, how do they collaborate?

In general, the collaborative approach includes five parts: (1) defining the problem, (2) analyzing the problem (what are its causes and symptoms), (3) developing mutually acceptable criteria for judging solutions (what goals do we want to achieve), (4) suggesting possible solutions (what could we do), and (5) selecting the best solution. Sometimes not all of the steps are needed.

For instance, after Justina points out her parents' need for the money, Eduardo quietly explains that he also owes some money on his credit card bill, so he cannot pay her parents immediately. As they discuss this dilemma, Justina sees that because the credit card interest is so high, Eduardo needs to pay off the credit card debt as quickly as possible so that he has money to pay her parents.

IN BRIEF

Interpersonal Conflict

Interpersonal conflict occurs when the needs or ideas of one person in a relationship are at odds or in opposition to the needs or ideas of another. Conflict can be managed in five ways:

- *Withdrawal:* removing oneself from the situation
- *Accommodation:* giving in to the other person
- *Force:* satisfying your needs through threats, attacks, coercion, or manipulation
- *Compromise:* making sacrifices to find common ground
- *Collaboration:* addressing the needs of each party to find a mutually satisfying solution.

After more discussion, Eduardo suggests that while he is paying the credit card debt he could come up with some money each month for Justina's parents. Justina suggests $50 a month until the debt is paid, and Eduardo agrees that he could handle a payment of that amount.

The five different styles of conflict management, with their characteristics, outcomes, and appropriate usage, are summarized in Figure 8.3. Much of the remainder of this chapter focuses on guidelines for accomplishing good collaborative discussion, including a look at the collaborative approach from the point of view of both someone initiating conflict and someone responding to it.

Communication Skills for Resolving Conflicts through Collaboration

When conflict arises between two people, one person usually initiates the conflict, and the other person responds to it. Whether we are initiating conflict or responding to it, we can practise collaboration by using specific communication skills and verbal strategies. In this section, we will consider how to initiate conflict and how to respond to conflicts initiated by others.

Initiating Conflict Appropriately

Many people avoid conflict because they do not know how to initiate a conflict conversation effectively. The following guidelines (as well as those for responding to conflict in the next section) are based on work from several fields of study (Adler, 1977; Gordon, 1970; Whetten & Cameron, 1998) and will help a person to initiate conflict in a way that reduces defensiveness and invites collaboration.

1. **Think through what you will say before you confront the other person, so that your request will be brief and precise.** Perhaps the greatest problem most of us have with initiating conflict is that, despite our good intentions to keep on track, our emotions get the best of us and we either say things we should not or go on and on about the problem to the point that we annoy the other person. Planning is therefore key. We should know exactly what we want to say and exactly how we want to say it. We are not suggesting that people initiating conflict should memorize a speech, but they should review the points they want to make and the order in which they want to make them and consider which approach to the problem is most likely to elicit a favourable response from the other person. Then, they should practise a few statements until they think they are ready to present their case effectively. Thinking through the following four steps in advance of facing the other person will assist in planning a presentation.

2. **State ownership of the apparent problem.** If Tara is in her room trying to study for a test in her most difficult course, and Camilla, her next-door neighbour in the dorm, is playing her stereo so loud that the walls are vibrating and Tara cannot concentrate, it is important for Tara to acknowledge that *she* is the one who has a problem. It is *she* who is annoyed and frustrated. Thus to resolve *her* problem, she decides to confront her neighbour. She shows ownership of the problem by saying something like, "Hi, Camilla, I have a problem that I need your help with. I'm trying to study for my physics midterm . . .."

3. **Describe the conflict in terms of the behaviour you have observed, the consequences, and your feelings about both.** When someone behaves in a certain manner, consequences result, and we feel a certain way (Gordon, 1971). It is important to include all three of these steps for the other person to fully understand the issue. This framework requires us to *describe* for the other person what we have seen or heard, what happened to us as a result, and what feelings we experienced. This behaviour-consequences-feelings approach uses the skills of owning feelings, describing behaviour, and describing feelings—all skills that we discussed earlier.

    To return to the example of Tara's problem with Camilla's loud stereo, Camilla's turning up the volume of the stereo is the *behaviour* that Tara observes. The *consequences* that result from this behaviour are that Tara gets distracted and cannot concentrate on her work. The *feelings* that Tara experiences are frustration and annoyance. Tara therefore might follow up her opening by saying: "When I hear your stereo, I get distracted and can't concentrate on the material I'm trying to study, and that makes me feel frustrated and annoyed."

4. **Avoid letting the other person change the subject.** Suppose that when Tara approaches Camilla about the loud music, Camilla says, "Oh come on, everyone plays their stereo loud on this floor." Tara should not let herself get sidetracked into talking about "everybody" and the general noise level in the dorm. She could get the conversation back on point by saying, "Yes, I understand that it's a noisy dorm, and overhearing other people's music normally doesn't bother me, but I'm still having a problem right now, and I was hoping you could help me." Notice how this statement returns the focus of the conversation to the problem that Tara is having.

5. **Phrase your proposed solution in a way that focuses on common ground.** Once our description of the situation has been understood, we should suggest a solution. Our proposed solution is more likely to be accepted if we can tie it to a shared value, common interest, or shared constraint. In our example, Tara might say, "I think we both have had times when even little things get in the way of our being able to study, so even though I realize I'm asking you for a special favour, I hope you can help me out by turning down your stereo this evening while I'm grinding through this material for my physics midterm."

OBSERVE & ANALYZE
Journal Activity

Conflict Episodes

Describe a conflict episode you have recently experienced. How did you and the other person behave? What was the outcome of the conflict? How did you feel about it then? How do you feel about it now? Could the conflict have had a better outcome if it had been handled in a different way?

By following these five steps in initiating conflict, we can avoid seeming to attack the person we are dealing with and focus instead on solving the problem that has arisen between us. The better we are at initiating conflict appropriately, the more likely we will be to arrive at a satisfactory resolution of that problem.

Responding to Conflict Effectively

It is often more difficult to respond effectively to conflict than it is to initiate it because it is easy to become defensive if the initiator does not initiate the conflict effectively. If Tara initiates the problem of Camilla's loud stereo appropriately as we have suggested, most likely Camilla will say something like, "I'm sorry, I know what you mean. I didn't even think that my stereo might be bothering anyone. Here, I'll turn it down." With this response, the conflict is immediately resolved. However, not all initiators will understand the problem-behaviour-consequences-feelings-solution approach to initiating conflict, so we may often face situations that require great skill.

1. **Disengage emotionally.** When someone is aggressive in initiating a conflict, it is important to prevent ourselves from being caught up in his or her emotion and responding in kind. Some people will immediately become defensive in such a situation, automatically rejecting every assertion made by the initiator and refusing to consider his or her proposed solutions. Others, following the maxim that the best defence is a good offence, will become aggressive in return. In either case, the interaction is likely to spiral out of control as emotions become more and more heated.

   We need to learn to disengage emotionally so we can retain our problem-solving ability. Whether we count to ten, or take a few deep breaths, or just adopt the role of a dispassionate observer, we must resist the impulse to become emotionally involved and give ourselves time to think of how to turn this interaction into a problem-solving session.

2. **Listen to both verbal and nonverbal cues.** Just as in every other kind of interpersonal communication, effective listening is fundamental to resolving conflict. As Allan Barsky (2000, p. 77) points out, "you must not only listen, but ensure that the other parties know that you are listening and understanding them." We must attend carefully to both verbal and nonverbal cues, for as Berger argues (1994), failure to account for the nonverbal communication is to "doom oneself to study the tip of a very large iceberg" (p. 493). Remember that nonverbal signs, in particular, are most likely to reveal the speaker's true feelings.

   Infante, Rancer, and Jordan (1996) found that the people they studied recognized that nonverbal cues such as smiles, pleasant facial expressions, relaxed body postures, and warm and sincere voices are more likely to keep conflict from occurring or from escalating than tense or frowning faces, grinding teeth, stern and staring eyes, clenched fists, and loud voices (p. 322).

SKILL BUILDERS Describing Behaviour, Consequences, and Feelings

Skill	Use	Procedure	Example
Describing the basis of a conflict in terms of behaviour, consequences, and feelings.	To help another person understand a problem completely.	1. State ownership of the problem. 2. Describe the behaviour that you see or hear. 3. Describe the consequences that result. 4. Describe your feelings.	Jason says, "I have a problem that I need your help with. When I tell you what I'm thinking and you don't respond, I start to think you don't care about me or what I think, and this causes me to get very angry with you."

Imagine that before Tara decides to deal with the problem of the loud stereo, Camilla is challenged by another of her neighbours, Heidi, who initiates conflict by saying, "Turn down that damn stereo. Any idiot would realize that playing it so loud is likely to bother people who are trying to study." In addition to the harsh words, Camilla is likely to see and hear nonverbal cues that reveal Heidi's emotions.

3. **Respond empathically with genuine interest and concern.** Whether the initiator of the conflict initiates it appropriately or inappropriately, that person is still watching us closely to see how *we* react. Even if we disagree with the complaint, we should demonstrate empathy for the person's feelings. Sometimes we can do this by allowing the initiator to vent his or her emotions while we listen. Only when he or she has calmed down can we begin to problem solve. In this case, for example, Camilla might well start by saying to Heidi, "I'm sorry to see that you are angry with me."

4. **Paraphrase your understanding of the problem and ask questions to clarify issues.** Most people are unaware of the behaviour-consequences-feelings framework, so we may need to paraphrase their statements to make sure that we are understanding them. Suppose, for instance, that Heidi says, "What in the world are you thinking playing music like that when people are studying?" If information is missing (as with this initiating statement), Camilla can ask questions: "Is it the volume of the music or the type of music that is distracting you?" "So, you were studying all right before I turned on my music?" "Are you angry with me about this music or is something else bothering you?" Sometimes people will initiate a conflict episode on minor issues when what really needs to be considered has not been mentioned.

5. **Seek common ground by finding some aspect of the complaint to agree with.** This guideline does not mean that we should automatically give in to the other person. Nor does it mean that we should feign agreement on a point that we do not agree with. However, by using our supportiveness skills, we can look for points with which we can agree (Adler, 1977).

Consider again our ongoing example: "Turn down that damn stereo. Any idiot would realize that playing it so loud is likely to bother people who are trying to study." In response, Camilla could agree in part: "I understand how frustrating it can be when you can't concentrate." She could agree in principle: "Yes, I agree it's best to study in a quiet place." She could agree with the initiator's perception: "I can see that you are finding it difficult to study with music in the background." Or she could agree with the person's feelings: "It's obvious that you're frustrated and annoyed."

We do not need to agree with the initiator's conclusions or evaluations, but by agreeing with some aspect of the complaint, we create a common ground on which a problem-solving discussion can take place.

6. **Ask the person to suggest a solution.** As soon as we are sure that we and the initiator have agreed on a definition of the problem, we should ask the person what he or she thinks will best solve it. The initiator has probably spent time thinking about what needs to be done, and asking for a suggested solution signals our willingness to listen and co-operate. We may be surprised to find that what is suggested seems reasonable. If not, we may be able to craft an alternative that builds on one of the ideas presented. In either case, by asking for suggestions, we communicate our trust in the other person, thus strengthening the problem-solving climate.

Learning from Conflict-Management Failures

Ideally, we want to resolve conflicts as they occur. However, there will be times when no matter how hard both persons try, they will not be able to resolve the conflict. Especially when a relationship is important to us, it is worthwhile to take time to analyze our inability to resolve a conflict. We can ask ourselves these questions:

1. Where did things go wrong?
2. Did one or more of us become evaluative?
3. Did one of us use a style that was inappropriate in this situation?
4. Did we fail to implement the problem-solving method adequately?

OBSERVE & ANALYZE
Journal Activity

Conflict-Management Failures

Think of a recent conflict situation you experienced in which the conflict was not successfully resolved. Analyze what happened using the concepts from this chapter. What type of conflict was it? What style did you adopt? What was the other person's style? How did styles contribute to what happened? How well did your behaviour match the guidelines recommended for initiating and responding to conflict? How might you change what you did if you could replay this conflict episode?

5. Were the vested interests in the outcome too great?
6. Did we fail to use such basic communication skills as paraphrasing, describing feelings, and perception checking?
7. Did we automatically fall back on what Turk and Monahan (1999, p. 232) label "repetitive non-optimal behaviours": verbal abuse, dishonest replies, or sarcasm?

By taking time to analyze our behaviour, we put ourselves in a better position to perform more effectively in the next conflict episode we experience. Conflict is inevitable, so we can count on having opportunities to apply the knowledge we gain from such analysis.

IN BRIEF

Resolving Conflicts through Collaboration

Whether we are initiating conflict or responding to it, we can increase our effectiveness by employing specific communication skills:

- As an initiator, we should own the problem, describe the basis of the conflict in terms of behaviour, consequences, and feelings, and phrase our proposed solution so that it focuses on common ground.
- As a respondent, we should disengage emotionally, attend to verbal and nonverbal cues, respond empathically, paraphrase and ask questions, seek common ground, and ask the other person to suggest solutions.
- In all cases, we should learn from conflict-management failures.

Conversation for Analysis

Jason Harris

Janice and Ken are in their early twenties. They have been good friends for most of their lives, but because of something that he found out last week, Ken believes that Janice has betrayed their friendship. They meet at Janice's apartment.

As you read Janice and Ken's conversation, focus on how the nature of their relationship influences their interaction.

1. What does each person do to help maintain the relationship?
2. How does each person handle this conflict?
3. How well does each person listen to the other?
4. Are Janice and Ken appropriately assertive?
5. Notice how well each provides feedback and describes feelings.

In the right-hand column there is space for you to record your analysis. This conversation also appears as a video clip on the *Communicate!* Web site at www.communicate1e.nelson.com. After you have written your analysis of the conversation, you can compare your responses to those appearing on the Web site.

Conversation	Analysis
Ken: Janice, we need to talk. Why'd you tell Shannon about what happened between Katie and me? Now Shannon doesn't want to talk to me.	

Conversation | **Analysis**

Jason Harris

Janice: *(silence for a moment as she realizes he knows)* Ken, I'm sorry, I didn't mean to tell her. It just kind of slipped out when we were talking.

Ken: Sorry? Sorry's not good enough. I told you that in confidence and you promised to keep it just between you and me.

Janice: Ken, I told her that long before the two of you started dating. You know, Shannon and I, we've been friends for a long time. We were just talking about guys and cheating and stuff. It wasn't about you specifically.

Ken: It wasn't about me? It was totally about me. You had no right to tell *anyone* that, under any circumstances. Now Shannon doesn't trust me. She thinks I'm a lowlife that sleeps around.

Janice: Well, I'm sorry, but the two of you weren't even dating when I told her.

Ken: Oh, that's irrelevant. You know, it would be irrelevant even if Shannon and I still weren't dating. The point is I thought I could trust you and tell you anything and that it would go no further.

Janice: Yeah, like the time I told you I was thinking about dropping out of school for a semester, and you just happened to tell my dad?

Ken: Ah, that's not the same thing.

Janice: You know what? It's *exactly* the same. I trusted you, and you squealed. My dad lit into me big-time. He should never have known I was thinking about that. I trusted you, and you betrayed me!

Conversation	**Analysis**
Ken: Well look, I was just trying to look out for you. I knew you were making a big mistake, and I was just trying to stop you. And besides, you know I was right! *(gets discouraged)* Don't change the subject, here. Are you saying that your telling Shannon is some sort of payback for my telling your dad?	
Janice: No, I'm just trying to point out that you've got no right to throw stones!	
Ken: Maybe neither of us can trust the other. Maybe we just shouldn't tell each other anything that we don't want broadcast to the whole world, huh?	
Janice: Don't be such a jerk. I'm sorry, okay?	
Ken: Well, that's not good enough. You ruined any chance I had with Shannon.	
Janice: Are you saying that something I said about what you did a long time ago is ruining your chances?	
Ken: Yeah, it might.	
Janice: Ken, if Shannon truly valued your friendship, something that you did a long time ago shouldn't matter.	
Ken: Well, maybe you're right.	
Janice: Look, I said I'm sorry, and I meant it. I'm also sorry about, you know, throwing in what you told my dad. I know that wasn't fair, but you know, you really hurt my feelings when you blew up at me like that.	
Ken: Listen, listen, I shouldn't have, I shouldn't have told your dad. I should probably have encouraged you to talk to him. Are we still friends?	

Jason Harris

What Would You Do?
A QUESTION OF ETHICS

Sally and Ed had been seeing each other for more than three years when Ed moved 300 kilometres away to another city to attend college. When he left, they promised to continue to see each other and agreed that, if either of them should want to start seeing someone else, he or she would tell the other person before doing so.

During the first five months that Ed was away, Sally became friendly with Jacob, a co-worker at the childcare centre in the college at which she worked and attended classes. Jacob had a great sense of humour, and during working hours, he and Sally would often tease each other to the point that other co-workers accused them of flirting. On several occasions, they had dinner together before their night class, usually at Jacob's request, and on a couple of the weekends that Ed had not come home, they had seen a movie together. As time went on, it became apparent to Sally that Jacob's interest in her was going beyond the point of just being friends, but because she did not want to risk losing his companionship, she never mentioned her relationship with Ed.

On Friday of one week, just as Sally and Jacob were about to leave the childcare centre and head for a movie, the door swung open and in walked Ed. Sally had not been expecting him, but she took one look at him, broke into a big smile and ran over and gave him a warm embrace. Too absorbed with her own excitement, Sally did not even notice Jacob's look of shock and disappointment. She quickly introduced Ed to Jacob and then casually said to Jacob, "See you Monday," and left with Ed.

That weekend, Ed confessed to Sally that he wanted to end their relationship. He had gone out with a woman who lived down the hall from him in his dorm a couple of times and saw the relationship blossoming. Sally was outraged. She accused Ed of acting dishonestly by violating their agreement about seeing other people and told him that he had used her until he was secure at college. Their conversation continued to go downhill, and eventually Ed left.

On Monday, when Sally saw Jacob at work, he was very aloof and curt. She asked him if he wanted to get a bite to eat before class and was genuinely surprised when he answered with an abrupt "No." As she ate alone, she pondered her behaviour and wondered how she could ever restore her relationship with Jacob.

1. Sort out the ethical issues in this case. Under which ethical guidelines would Sally's, Ed's, and Jacob's actions be considered ethical or unethical?
2. Using guidelines from this chapter, role-play different key moments in this scenario, changing them to improve the communication ethics and outcome of the situation.

Summary

Interpersonal communication helps develop and maintain relationships. A good relationship is any mutually satisfying interaction with another person.

We have three types of relationships. Acquaintances are people whom we may know by name and talk with, but with whom our interactions are limited in quality and quantity. Friendships are marked by degrees of warmth, affection, trust, self-disclosure, and commitment and the expectation that the relationship will endure. Close or intimate friends are those with whom we share our deepest feelings, spend a lot of time, or mark the relationship in some special way.

The life cycle of a relationship includes starting or building, stabilizing, and disintegration stages. In the starting or building stage, people strike up a conversation, keep conversations going, and move to more intimate levels. People nurture relationships through speaking descriptively, openly, and tentatively and by addressing others as equals. Many relationships end. We may terminate them in interpersonally sound ways or in ways that are hurtful. The Johari window is a tool for assessing the degree of openness in a relationship.

Two theories are especially useful in explaining the dynamics of relationships. Schutz sees relationships in terms of the relational partners' ability to meet each other's interpersonal needs for affection, inclusion, and control. Thibaut and Kelley see relationships as exchanges: people evaluate relationships in terms of their rewards and costs, weighing energy, time, and money invested against satisfaction gained.

Many people develop relationships through electronically mediated communication on the Internet. Electronically mediated relationships may be affected by abuse of anonymity and dishonesty. Addiction to the Internet can disrupt real-world relationships.

A primary factor leading to termination of a relationship is failure to manage conflict successfully. We cope with conflicts in a variety of ways: withdrawing, accommodating, forcing, compromising, and collaborating. When we are concerned about maintaining the relationship in the long term, collaboration is often the most appropriate method of resolving conflicts.

When we have a problem with a person, we should plan what we will say to him or her ahead of time and initiate the conflict using good basic communication skills: owning the problem; describing the basis of the conflict in terms of behaviour, consequences, and feelings; and phrasing our proposed solution so that it focuses on common ground.

When responding to another person who is initiating conflict, we should disengage emotionally, attend to verbal and nonverbal cues, respond empathically with genuine interest and concern, paraphrase and ask questions to ensure that we understand the problem, seek common ground, and ask the person to suggest solutions.

Finally, we should learn from conflict-management failures.

Glossary

Review the following key terms:

accommodation (213) — an approach to conflict management through which one party attempts to satisfy another's needs while ignoring his or her own.

acquaintances (194) — people whom we may know by name and whom we may talk with when the opportunity arises but with whom our interactions are largely impersonal.

affection need (204) — in interpersonal needs theory, people's desire to express and to receive love.

close friends or **intimates** (196) — people with whom we share our deepest feelings.

collaboration (216) — an approach to conflict management which focuses on addressing the needs and issues of each party to arrive at a solution that is mutually satisfying.

compromise (215) — an approach to conflict management characterized by both parties making sacrifices to find common ground.

control need (205) — in interpersonal needs theory, people's desire to influence events and people around them.

costs (206) — in exchange theory, outcomes that a person does not wish to incur.

exchange theory (206) — the proposition that relationships can be understood in terms of the exchange of rewards and costs that take place during the relational partners' interactions.

force (215) — a form of conflict management characterized by the use of physical threats, verbal attacks, coercion, or manipulation in order to have one's needs satisfied or ideas accepted.

friends (194) — people with whom we have voluntarily negotiated personal relationships.

gossip (197) — the exchange of information of uncertain accuracy about people known to both (or all) participants in a conversation.

idea-exchange communication (197) — sharing information such as facts, opinions, and beliefs, some of which may reflect values.

inclusion need (205) — in interpersonal needs theory, people's desire to be in the company of other people.

interpersonal conflict (212) — the result of a situation in which the needs or ideas of one person are at odds or in opposition to the needs or ideas of another.

interpersonal needs theory (204) — the proposition that whether a relationship is started, built, or maintained depends on how well the people involved meet each other's needs for affection, inclusion, and control.

Johari window (202) — a tool for assessing the level of disclosure and feedback in a relationship.

mulling (213) — thinking about or stewing over an actual or perceived problem until the conflict is perceived as more severe than it is and blaming behaviour occurs.

rewards (206) — in exchange theory, outcomes that are valued by a person.

speaking descriptively (198) — stating what you see or hear in neutral or objective language, naming your feelings and using I-statements to express them, and avoiding evaluative language

speaking openly (199) — sharing true thoughts and feelings without resorting to manipulation or hidden agendas.

speaking tentatively (199) — stating information in a way that allows for the possibility of error or inaccuracy.

speaking to others as equals (199) — excluding any words or nonverbal signs that might indicate feelings of superiority.

stabilization (198) — a means of maintaining a relationship at a certain level for some time.

technological addictions (211) — non-chemical (behavioural) addictions that involve human–machine interactions.

trust (195) — a willingness to risk putting your well-being in the hands of another.

uncertainty reduction (196) — the process of communicating to gather information about someone else in order to be better able to explain and predict that person's behaviour toward us.

withdrawal (212) — an approach to conflict management through which one party physically or psychologically removes himself or herself from the conflict situation.

Paul Henry/CP Picture Archive

OBJECTIVES

After you have read this chapter, you should be able to answer these questions:

- What is a culture?
- What is intracultural communication?
- What is intercultural communication?
- How do we form our cultural identities?
- What is a dominant culture?
- What are co-cultures?
- What cultural norms and values affect intercultural communication?
- What barriers commonly prevent intercultural communication from succeeding?
- How can barriers to intercultural communication be overcome?

CHAPTER

9

Communicating Across Cultures

"Jack, I don't think we'd better take this flight," Alicia said. "Why don't we wait and take the next one?"

"What are you talking about, Alicia," Jack replied. "Our reservations are confirmed, our bags are probably on board by now, and why would we want to sit around here for hours anyway? Cuba awaits."

"But Jack, over there," Alicia muttered behind her hand while nodding inconspicuously to her far right.

Jacked turned his head. There on the end of the long bench sat a large bearded man in a turban.

"Jack, I'm afraid," Alicia whispered urgently. "He could be a terrorist!"

"Relax, Alicia," Jack said. "He's a Sikh, not a Muslim. There's nothing to worry about."

"Tell that to the people who were on that Air India plane," Alicia snapped. "I don't think they'd appreciate the difference."

How should we evaluate Alicia's assumptions in this situation? Are the inferences underlying Jack's response more accurate or well founded? In both cases, their judgments are based on their perceptions of people who are culturally different from themselves.

As we have observed repeatedly in the preceding chapters of this book, culture has a profound impact on our communication behaviour. We have seen, for example, that our self-perceptions, our perceptions of others, our use of verbal and nonverbal signs to encode messages or to decode the messages of others, our approaches to conversation, our willingness to self-disclose, and our readiness to assert ourselves are communication variables that can be influenced by our cultural background and conditioning. In this chapter, we will take a closer look at some basic concepts of culture, identify important values and norms which set cultural groups apart, assess communication barriers that arise from such cultural differences, and suggest measures that we can take to overcome those barriers and achieve intercultural communication competence.

© Frank Siteman/Index Stock Agency

Are these two people culturally different? What evidence supports your answer?

Culture and Communication

How often have we heard people observe that the world is getting smaller and smaller and the people in it increasingly similar; that we now live, to use Marshall McLuhan's famous phrase, in a "global village" (1962, p. 31). Some people celebrate this trend as a step toward world unity while others mourn the loss of local cultures, traditions, and controls. Regardless of how we feel about it, however, we must accept that the trend appears to be irreversible. McLuhan coined the phrase "global village" more than 40 years ago to describe how radio had changed the world of the 1920's (McLuhan, E., 1996); he could not have imagined the degree to which more recent developments such as the globalization of trade and the development of the Internet and the World Wide Web would shrink the planet even further. Today, our lives are affected by the decisions and actions of people in other parts of the world, and we can make instant personal contact with people around the globe with the click of a mouse.

Many Canadians enjoy travel, both real and virtual, but as we have already observed, we do not have to journey to other countries to discover people of different cultures. As we noted in Chapter 1, Canada is a multicultural society, including immigrants from all parts of the world, the descendants of earlier immigrants, and people of many culturally distinct indigenous groups. Table 9.1 gives a sense of just how culturally diverse the Canadian population has become.

So what, exactly, is a culture? Over the past half century, scholars have created and debated hundreds of different definitions. Barnett and Lee (2001) summarize the main features of several widely accepted definitions when they define **culture** as "a group's shared collective meaning system through which the group's collective values, attitudes, beliefs, customs, and thoughts are understood" (p. 277).

Intracultural Communication

As Barnett and Lee's definition makes clear, communication and culture are closely related. It is because of our shared meaning system that we are able to understand the verbal and nonverbal messages sent by members of our own culture. For instance, nearly all Canadians know that the boast "We're going to win *the cup* for sure this year!" refers to hockey supremacy and the Stanley Cup, or that the complaint "*Ottawa* is not paying its fair share of the health care budget" is directed to the federal government. The meanings of these verbal symbols are agreed to by the society as a whole and therefore facilitate **intracultural communication,** the exchange of meaningful messages between members of the same cultural group.

Table 9.1 Population by Selected Ethnic Origins, Canada, 2001

	Total responses	Single responses	Multiple responses
Total population	**29,639,035**	**18,307,545**	**11,331,490**
Ethnic origin			
Canadian	11,682,680	6,748,135	4,934,545
English	5,978,875	1,479,525	4,499,355
French	4,668,410	1,060,760	3,607,655
Scottish	4,157,210	607,235	3,549,975
Irish	3,822,660	496,865	3,325,795
German	2,742,765	705,600	2,037,170
Italian	1,270,370	726,275	544,090
Chinese	1,094,700	936,210	158,490
Ukrainian	1,071,060	326,195	744,860
North American Indian	1,000,890	455,805	545,085
Dutch (Netherlands)	923,310	316,220	607,090
Polish	817,085	260,415	556,665
East Indian	713,330	581,665	131,665
Norwegian	363,760	47,230	316,530
Portuguese	357,690	252,835	104,855
Welsh	350,365	28,445	321,920
Jewish	348,605	186,475	162,130
Russian	337,960	70,895	267,070
Filipino	327,550	266,140	61,405
Métis	307,845	72,210	235,635
Swedish	282,760	30,440	252,325
Hungarian (Magyar)	267,255	91,800	175,455
American (USA)	250,005	25,205	224,805
Greek	215,105	143,785	71,325
Spanish	213,105	66,545	146,555
Jamaican	211,720	138,180	73,545
Danish	170,780	33,795	136,985
Vietnamese	151,410	119,120	32,290

Source: Adapted from the Statistics Canada Web site <http://www.statcan.ca/english/Pgdb/demo28a.htm>.

Intercultural Communication

Not all Canadians can easily exchange messages about all subjects, however. Some are restricted by cultural rules from discussing certain topics; some lack necessary vocabulary; some lack experience; some lack knowledge; some lack interest. In other words, with regard to these subjects, the people do not share "a collective meaning system." Glenn, a Calgary tourist visiting Montréal, might be confused, annoyed, even angered when the concierge at his hotel casually asks him whether he plans to be in town for the *Fête nationale du Québec*. Likewise, Rida, a Muslim student, might feel embarrassed, offended, even threatened when her high-school physical education teacher directs her to join a group of male and female students to work on a presentation on safe sex. In both of these examples, the discomfort experienced by the respondent, an experience known as **culture shock,** is caused by an absence of shared meaning between him or her and the other person involved in the interaction. Their values, attitudes, beliefs, customs, and thoughts are not the same. In other words, they are culturally distinct—they are communicating across cultural boundaries. **Intercultural communication,** then, can be simply defined as "the exchange of cultural information" between people "with significantly different cultures" (Barnett & Lee, 2001, p. 276).

It is important to recognize that not every exchange between persons of different cultures exemplifies intercultural communication. If the concierge had asked Glenn whether he planned to visit the *Musée des beaux-arts* while he was in town, or if the physical education teacher had asked Rida to work on a presentation on the circulatory system, no differences in values, attitudes, beliefs, customs, or thoughts would have arisen. The messages sent would easily have been decoded and accommodated by the respondents' meaning systems because no "cultural information" was being exchanged. In other words, these interactions would pose no threat to Glenn or Rida's cultural identity.

OBSERVE & ANALYZE
Journal Activity

Culture Shock

Think of a time when an absence of shared meaning between you and someone with whom you were communicating caused you to experience culture shock. What conflict of values, attitudes, beliefs, customs, or thoughts caused you to feel the discomfort that you experienced? How did you handle the situation at the time? Can you think of a way in which you might have handled it better?

Cultural Identity

As we saw in Chapter 2, our self-concept is the mental image that we have of ourselves, and that image is negotiated and reinforced through our communication with others. According to social identity theory, our self-concept includes both social and personal identities (Tajfel & Turner, 1986). Our **personal identity** is based on the characteristics that we perceive to be unique to us as individuals, while our **social identity** is determined by the groups to which we belong and the meanings we associate with those groups.

Membership in a particular cultural group can contribute to our **cultural identity,** but it need not do so. Research has shown that cultural identity is determined by the importance which we assign to our membership in those cultural groups (Ting-Toomey et al., 2000). Angus, a tenth-generation Scottish Canadian, attends the International Gathering of the Clans every summer, wears his clan tartan on formal occasions, and celebrates Robbie Burns Day with haggis, piping, highland dancing, and fine scotch whisky. He clearly considers his ancestry to be important, and it would play a major role in determining his cultural identity. On the other hand, James, whose ancestors immigrated to Canada at about the same time, is only vaguely aware that his surname is Scottish and takes no interest in the culture of his forebears. His membership in the group Scottish Canadians would not be a significant factor in forming his cultural identity.

COMMUNICATE! Using InfoTrac College Edition

You have probably heard Hugh MacLennan's famous phrase "two solitudes" used to describe the different cultural identities of English Canada and Québec. Using InfoTrac College Edition enter the subject *culture—portrayals.* Click on the article "Guess Who's Here: A Cultural Shift Is Under Way in Québec that Puts French and English in a New Perspective" by Robert Lepage (1999). Do you agree that the degree of difference between French- and English-Canadian cultures is shrinking? Can you identify any evidence of a similar shift taking place in English Canada?

Dominant Cultures and Co-cultures

For more than 30 years, recognition of Canada as a multicultural society and support for the maintenance and promotion of minority cultures through arts and community groups have been official policies of the Government of Canada. As a result, many Canadians think immediately of visible minority groups whenever the word *culture* is mentioned. However, despite our cultural diversity, there are many values, attitudes, beliefs, customs, and thoughts that a majority of citizens hold in common. This shared collective meaning system comprises our **dominant culture,** and like the dominant culture of any country, ours has evolved over time. Until the middle of the twentieth century, the dominant Canadian culture would have reflected the values of white, western European, English-speaking, Protestant, heterosexual men, but as the country has become more culturally diverse, the dominant culture has slowly evolved to reflect those changes.

At all times in our history, of course, some groups within Canadian society did not share some or all of the values, attitudes, beliefs, customs, and thoughts of the dominant culture, and this condition continues today. These groups, called **co-cultures,** live within the dominant culture, but draw some or all of their cultural identity from their membership in other cultural groups that are not dominant. Again, it is important to stress that a person's being a member of an identifiable group does not mean that he or she necessarily participates in the co-culture usually associated with that group: it is only when membership in the group is judged by the person to be important that it contributes to his or her cultural identity.

The following are some of the major contributors to co-cultures in Canadian society today:

Gender Men and women have different cultural identities because they are biologically different and because they are differently socialized throughout their lives (through clothes, games, toys, education, roles, etc.) As we have seen in earlier chapters, women and men communicate differently in a number of ways because of these cultural differences.

Language Naming and classifying are language-based social activities that allow us to exert social control over the things and people around us (Schippers, 2001). As an officially bilingual country, Canada has had more experience than most countries with this struggle for control.

As the language of the majority, English has always been regarded as a threat by the French-speaking minority. In Québec, linguistic control is strongly associated with economic control (Lenden, 1995) because for many decades, members of that province's French-speaking majority were barred from social and professional advancement because of their inability to function in the English-speaking commercial milieu of, first, the British Empire and, later, the modern North American market. In other parts of Canada, cultural survival is a constant preoccupation of francophone minorities which, because of their small numbers, face the constant threat of assimilation.

Though French and English are Canada's official languages, they are by no means the only languages spoken here. Many indigenous groups and many immigrants and descendants of immigrants contribute to their cultural identity through the daily use of the language of their ancestors and involvement in language-based social groups. Table 9.2 shows Canada's major unofficial language groups.

Colour (or race) Traditionally, the term *race* has been used to classify members of the human race in terms of biological characteristics, such as skin and eye colour, hair texture, and body shape. However, scientific justification for such divisions has proved elusive, and the classification system has itself changed drastically over time (Hotz, 1995). For instance, the Irish and Mexican *races*, among others, have disappeared altogether, and many groups have been differently categorized at different times: Indians, for example, have over the years been classified as Hindu, Caucasian, nonwhite, and Asian Indian. Such changes more often reflect the prevailing prejudices of a particular time in history than any actual advancement in our understanding of humankind or its origins.

Nevertheless, racial characteristics, particularly colour, can be an important cultural signifier for many people. Though people of colour are not a homogenous group, research (Vanaja, 2000) shows that, in Canada, they have a shared

Table 9.2 Population by Mother Tongue, Other than French or English

Chinese	853,745	Dutch	128,670
Italian	469,485	Tagalog (Filipino)	174,060
German	438,080	Greek	120,360
Polish	208,375	Vietnamese	122,055
Spanish	245,495	Cree	72,885
Portuguese	213,815	Inuktitut (Eskimo)	29,010
Punjabi	271,220	Other non-official languages	1,506,965
Ukrainian	148,085		
Arabic	199,940	**Total**	**5,202,245**

Source: Adapted from the Statistics Canada publication "Detailed Mother Tongue (160), Sex (3) and Age Groups (15) for Population, for Canada, Provinces, Territories, Census Metropolitan Areas and Census Agglomerations, 1996 and 2001 Censuses—20%, Sample Data (Language Composition of Canada, 2001 Census)" Catalogue 97F0007, December 10, 2002.

experience: "they are racialised on the basis of skin colour, devalued as persons, and their histories and cultures are distorted and stigmatised" (p. 166). The shared experience of such discrimination has itself become a powerful cultural value for many people of colour.

THINKING ABOUT . . .

Race and Ethnicity

What is the difference between *race* and *ethnicity*? Can you think of examples of people who are ethnically different but racially the same? Racially different but ethnically the same? Can you think of anyone for whom both designations might be identical? For whom the two designations might be contradictory? What does this analysis suggest about the accuracy and legitimacy of such classification systems?

Ethnicity Like *race, ethnicity* is an inexact designation. **Ethnicity** refers to a classification of people based on combinations of shared characteristics such as nationality, geographic origin, language, religion, and ancestral customs and traditions. People vary greatly in terms of the importance they attach to their ethnic heritage and, therefore, the degree to which it determines their cultural identity. In Canada, however, ethnicity appears to be a more important determinant of cultural identity for recent immigrants than for descendants of long-ago immigrants. Census data show, for example, that members of the former group are more likely to classify themselves as ethnic, while members of the latter group are more likely to classify themselves more generally as *Canadian*. Some people will classify themselves both ways, suggesting that both their ethnic and Canadian identities are important to them.

THINKING ABOUT . . .

Same-Sex Marriage

Statistics show that older Canadians are most likely to oppose marriage between same-sex partners, often on the basis of religious beliefs or simply out of regard for tradition. Imagine that two of your friends, who are gay, plan to be married in a month but are saddened by the refusal of one of the partner's parents, a couple that you have known all your life, to participate in the ceremony. Think of an argument that you could use to persuade your friend's parents to participate.

Sexual orientation Though heterosexual people tend to think little about their sexual orientation, for gay, lesbian, bisexual, and transgender people, it can be an important component of their cultural identity. Until very recently, many people, including even some educated people, regarded homosexual and bisexual people as immoral or mentally ill. A homosexual or bisexual person would have paid a heavy price, including loss of employment, loss of family connections, and social isolation, for publicly revealing his or her sexual orientation. Gays and lesbians faced both persecution and prosecution for sexually expressing feelings for their loved ones in ways that heterosexual people took for granted.

Since 1992, discrimination based on sexual orientation has been illegal in Canada (Hurley, 2003), but that legal protection has not shielded gays and lesbians from violence at the hands of ignorant and bigoted people. Research shows that hate crimes against gays and lesbians, including 85 homicides, continued through the 1990's (Meadahl, 2000). The popular belief that gay bashing is limited to small rural centres with conservative values is wrong. The evidence shows that discrimination on the basis of sexual orientation occurs throughout the country in communities of all sizes. As it may for people of colour, the shared experience of this discrimination may form a cultural bond among members of the gay, lesbian, bisexual, and transgender community.

Religion A **religion** is a system of beliefs that is shared by a group and that supplies the group with an object (or objects) of devotion, a ritual of worship, and a code of ethics. Table 9.3 gives an overview of Canadians' religious affiliations today. Religious faith and religious observance have declined steadily in Canada since the middle of the twentieth century (Clark, 1998): Statistics Canada data show that weekly attendance at worship services dropped from

Table 9.3 Religion in Canada, 2001

Total population	**29,639,035**		
Catholic	12,936,905	Buddhist	300,345
Protestant	8,654,850	Hindu	297,200
Christian Orthodox	479,620	Sikh	278,410
Christian not included elsewhere	780,450	Eastern religions	37,550
Muslim	579,640	Other religions	63,975
Jewish	329,995	No religious affiliation	4,900,090

Source: Adapted from the Statistics Canada publication "Religion (13) and Age Groups (8) for Population, for Canada, Provinces, Territories, Census Metropolitan Areas and Census Agglomerations, 2001 Censuses—20%, Sample Data," Catalogue 95F050, May 13, 2003.

67 percent in 1946 to 20 percent in 1996, and the number of Canadians who claim to have no religion climbed sharply, from less than 1 percent in 1961 to 16.5 percent in 2001. Not surprisingly, older Canadians are most devoted to their religious faith. In 1996, 34 percent of those aged 65 or older attended church regularly, while only 12 percent of 15- to 24-year-olds did, and 42 percent of adults attended once or twice a year or less.

Despite this decline, however, religion remains an important element in the cultural identity of many Canadians, and for those who actively practise their faith, it can be influential in determining their behaviour. For example, people who attend church regularly tend to be more forgiving in marital conflicts, to hold more traditional family values, to place a greater importance on children in the family and the nurturing role of women, and to live happier, less stressful lives (Clark, 1998).

OBSERVE & ANALYZE
Journal Activity

Cultural Identity

How closely do you identify with the dominant Canadian culture? Of which co-cultures do you feel a part? How influential are those memberships in forming your world-view? Respond to these questions in a short personal essay entitled My Cultural Identity.

Social class **Social class** is an indicator of a person's position in a social hierarchy, as determined by income, education, occupation, and social habits. Though class structures are much less rigid in Canada than in many other countries, and mobility between classes is less restricted, a person's class status still can be a significant cultural determinant. Social class often determines where people live and in what kind of housing, how they dress, what methods of transportation they use, what they eat, and what kinds of entertainment and leisure activities they have access to.

Social class can be particularly influential in determining opportunities for children. For example, research by Human Resources Development Canada (2002) suggests that a number of developmental problems occur more frequently in children raised in economically disadvantaged families: low birth weight, emotional and behavioural problems, physically aggressive behaviour, and lower vocabulary and math skills. However the same research reveals that good parenting can compensate for the disadvantages experienced by these children.

A 2003 survey commissioned by the Association for Canadian Studies (Jedwab, 2003) revealed that social class is the least influential of six major factors in determining Canadians' cultural identity. Thirty-three percent of respondents

IN BRIEF

Culture and Communication

A *culture* is a group's shared collective meaning system, through which its collective values, attitudes, beliefs, customs, and thoughts are understood.

- A *dominant culture* reflects the values, attitudes, beliefs, customs, and thoughts that a majority of a country's citizens hold in common.
- *Co-cultures* are groups which live within the dominant culture, but draw some or all of their cultural identity from their membership in other cultural groups that are not dominant.

Because of the shared meaning system developed through our culture, our culture affects our ability to communicate:

- *Intracultural communication* is the exchange of meaningful messages between members of the same cultural group.
- *Intercultural communication* is the exchange of cultural information between people with significantly different cultures.

(including 61 percent of francophones) rated language most important; 25 percent, ethnic origin and ancestry; 11 percent, religion; 11 percent, political ideology; 9 percent, gender; and only 7 percent social class.

Age None of us gets to choose our age, but the time in which we are born and raised can have a very definite formative influence on us. Generations of people who grew up during the Great Depression, World War II, the 1960's Counterculture, or the Information Age were each formed by different events, and as a result learned to react to different stimuli, to live according to different norms, and to value different things. In the 1940's, for example, a young couple who kissed on a first date would have been considered highly immoral. During the sexual revolution of the 1960's, in contrast, nearly all rules governing sexual behaviour were cast aside, and young people lived by the creed "If it feels good, do it." That freedom was sharply curtailed by the outbreak of the AIDS epidemic in the early 1980's, however, after which sexual behaviour became and has remained much more restrained.

It is not unusual for people of the same age to share a special affinity for the cultural markers of their time, particularly those which they associate with their adolescence. Adolescence and early adulthood is the time during which most of us assert ourselves, form our personal identities, and develop our social networks. It is therefore not surprising that, in forming our cultural identities, we would draw heavily from that period of our lives.

Other factors such as mental or physical ability, political affiliation or ideology, educational background, occupation, leisure activities, style of dress, and even artistic and culinary tastes, to name just a few, can also be significant factors in setting co-cultural boundaries.

Cultural Norms and Values

Some characteristics of a culture may be easy to identify. We can easily deduce that certain people may belong to a specific cultural group by the language that they speak, the clothing that they wear, the way they style their hair, or the artifacts which they wear on their bodies or place in their personal space. For example, when people meet Shimon, they are apt to judge from his sidecurls, his yarmulke, and his black clothes that he is a Hassidic Jew. Other more important cultural differences, however, are less apparent. Geert Hofstede (1980) identifies four major dimensions of culture which affect communication: individualism-collectivism, uncertainty avoidance, power distance, and masculinity-femininity. Each of these dimensions operate on the cultural level to influence communication through the formation of norms and rules. They operate on the individual level to form individual values. Hofstede defines a **value** as "a broad tendency to prefer certain states of affairs over others" (p. 19).

DIVERSE VOICES

Canadian First or First-Canadian?

by Jose A. Kusugak

For members of co-cultures, questions of cultural identity can be difficult to sort out, as this reflection by Jose A. Kusugak reveals. Mr. Kusugak is President of the Inuit Tapirisat Kanatami, Canada's national Inuit association.

Do you consider yourself Inuit or Canadians first? For many Inuit, this is an easy question to answer. Of course they are Inuit first, after all, their ancestors were Inuit before there was a Canada. Canada is only 134 years old, whereas the Inuit homeland is perhaps 20,000 years old. But is that the right answer today? Is the answer as simple as that? Is that the only answer?

As President of Inuit Tapirisat of Canada, I am frequently asked to speak at universities and management cross-cultural courses, along with my fellow Aboriginal leaders. When asked this apparently important question, the audience usually asks the Indians first; knowing the answer they will get, and they are never disappointed—"We are Indians first and foremost" and sometimes "Canadianism" doesn't even come into the picture. Then the questioner gives me a look that says "Okay, Mr. Inuit, are you really that different?" and asks politely, "and you Mr. Kusugak, do Inuit see themselves as Inuit first or as Canadians first?" Well, I answer, I know I have always thought those two sentiments were one and the same. After all, during our many meetings with other Inuit from countries such as Denmark, the United States or Russia, we have always been Canadian Inuit.

The difference asked of course is culturally relevant to Qablunaaq (non-Inuit). Just this morning I received an e-mail asking "Were the Inuit matrilineal or patrilineal, matriarchal or patriarchal?" As I read this question, I realize that there appears to be a need to identify differences, to see if Inuit are "them" or "us." Are you like us or not?

If I answer like my Indian friends, they will leave me alone. But life is not so simple, so I hesitate to answer likewise. This hesitancy makes me think that I should answer that Inuit are Canadians first; but that answer will solicit a further question—"why do Inuit think that?" and to answer "because" simply won't do.

To answer this question I had to draw from my culture and family traditions. My first-born daughter Aliisa just got married to a fine young fellow named Cedric. Traditionally, and tradition continues today, Cedric is my *ningauk*, not my *son-in-law*, as the word *son-in-law* suggests "losing a daughter and gaining a son." *Ningauk* means that, now that she is married, I will never love my Aliisa any less and in no way am I losing her. *Ningauk* reinforces the fact that we are adding Cedric to our family, and that we are also adding Cedric's family to our family. Inuit traditional society law also dictates that I must put my *ningauk* on a pedestal above my Aliisa. Cedric's parents must do the same for Aliisa. This is to ensure that respective in-laws accept and love the one marrying into the family. The point being I will love my daughter always and I want her to be accepted with all her goodness and faults by her new family. My wife and I want her to be accepted by Cedric and his family, so we put Cedric first as Cedric's family puts Aliisa first.

I tell you this story to say that it has everything to do with how I finally answered the question "are Inuit, Inuit first or Canadians first?" As Italian Canadians, Chinese Canadians and Jewish Canadians are proud of their ethnic background, so are Inuit. From our first contacts with settlers,

(continued)

Inuit have participated actively as partners in the fur economy, and we want our partnership with Canada to continue to grow. Since Inuit have been *married* to Canada, we do not need to worry about losing our identity or loving ourselves less. We will always be Inuit and Canada is now our *ningauk*. If Inuit are to be fully accepted as Canadians, Inuit must put Canada first.

Out of necessity, Inuit have focused on land claim issues over the past 30 years. With the signing of agreements in the Inuvialuit Settlement Region, as well as in Nunavik and Nunavut, we expect to see an end to the claims era when the Labrador land claim is signed next year. Inuit can now plan for the next 30 years. Like a marriage that requires constant work and attention in order to be successful, there is much work to be done to get Inuit to an equal starting point with the rest of Canada.

But now, I can proudly say "I am Canadian—first," and I am also a "first-Canadian."

Source: Reprinted from Inuktitut Magazine, *Issue 90, 2001. Copyright 2001 by the Inuit Tapirisat Kanatami. Reprinted with permission.*

Andre Pichette/CP Picture Archive

Québec's different cultural makeup contributes to social values that are sometimes at odds with those of other parts of Canada.

Individualism and Collectivism

Both individualism and collectivism are found in all cultures, but one dimension or the other tends to predominate in each culture. Individualistic cultures value the individual, while collectivist cultures value the group.

In an **individualistic society,** the individual's goals are considered most important (Hofstede & Bond, 1984), and people do not consider the interests of others, except perhaps those of their family, when they set goals: "people are supposed to look after themselves and their immediate family only" (p. 419). Ties between individual people and others outside their family are apt to be numerous but weak in such a culture, and people are apt to be competitive.

In contrast, group goals are the priority in a **collectivist society,** and one group is likely to carefully consider the interests of another in setting its own goals: "people belong to ingroups or collectivities which are supposed to look after them in exchange for loyalty" (p. 419). Collectivist societies are highly integrated, and maintaining co-operation and harmony are valued over competitiveness and personal achievement. Members of collectivist societies are likely to have many fewer relationships (Triandis, 1988), but the bonds within the groups to which they do belong (e.g., family, company, community) are likely to be much stronger, lasting sometimes through generations.

According to Hofstede (1997), the world's most individualistic cultures are, in order, the United States, Australia, Great Britain, Canada, and the Netherlands, followed by other northern and western European countries. The most collectivist cultures are found in South and Central America, followed by those of East and Southeast Asia and Africa.

Whether a person comes from an individualist or collectivist culture affects communication in a number of ways (Kim & Wilson, 1994). Because individualist cultures tend to place a high value on clarity, directness, and assertiveness and to tolerate a high degree of conflict, members of such cultures are inclined to speak their mind and to expect others to do the same. If two people disagree, they will manage the conflict between them, using one of the conflict-management methods we discussed in Chapter 8. Collectivist cultures, in contrast, place a high value on not imposing on others and not hurting others' feelings, and they value reticence over assertive behaviour. Members of such cultures are therefore more likely to express their meanings indirectly and tentatively and to go out of their way to prevent conflicts from arising. In Chapter 6, we distinguished high-context from low-context conversations. Low-context communication is the norm in individualistic cultures while members of collectivist cultures normally prefer high-context communication.

Wakiuru, Yuan, Phil, and Emily are students in a first-year business communication course. Wakiuru is an international student from Kenya, Yuan is a first-generation Chinese immigrant to Canada, and Phil and Emily are Canadians of English ancestry. The four are assigned to work collaboratively to develop a problem-solving report for a fictional music store that is experiencing an upsurge in shoplifting. For two years, Yuan worked part-time in a Vancouver bookstore that had to contend with a high incidence of shoplifting, so he suggests that the group might research the use of an electromagnetic security system, the method that his former employer found most effective in solving the problem. Without doing any research, Emily rejects the suggestion as being too technical and too expensive, suggesting that the group focus instead on video surveillance systems. Phil agrees. Though Yuan knows that video surveillance systems are ineffective in small shops where staff members are too busy to closely monitor customer behaviour, and Wakiuru, who knows of Yuan's business experience, is more inclined to accept his judgment than Emily's, both agree to focus on Emily's approach to the problem. As products of collectivist cultures,

OBSERVE & ANALYZE
Journal Activity

Individualist–Collectivist

Are you primarily an individualist or a collectivist? Why do you classify yourself as you do? Can you identify cultural influences that might account for your values? Under what conditions might your behaviour reflect the opposite cultural value?

Wakiuru and Yuan place a higher value on maintaining group harmony than on promoting their solution. Phil and Emily, on the other hand, both products of individualist cultures, are likely to interpret Yuan's *failure* to assert himself as a lack of confidence in his own idea.

Uncertainty Avoidance

Uncertainty avoidance, Hofstede's second dimension of culture, measures the extent to which members of a society feel threatened by unpredictable situations and the lengths to which they will go to avoid them.

People who come from high uncertainty avoidance cultures have a low tolerance for uncertainty and ambiguity "which expresses itself in higher levels of anxiety and energy release, greater need for formal rules and absolute truth, and less tolerance for people or groups with deviant ideas or behaviour" (Hofstede, 1979, p. 395). High uncertainty avoidance cultures tend to have clear norms and rules to govern every situation and to believe that there is danger in what is different (Hofstede, 1997). People in such cultures seek order and clear structure in relationships and organizations and place a high value on consensus.

In contrast, people from low uncertainty avoidance cultures are better able to cope with uncertain situations. They tend to be less anxious and more prepared to take risks. They welcome dissent and are inclined to be intrigued by people or situations that are different. Low uncertainty avoidance cultures are likely to have norms and rules that are less explicit and more flexible.

Uncertainty avoidance is highest in Japan, Greece, France, Chile, Guatemala, and other Mediterranean and Latin American countries (Hofstede, 1997). People in Scandinavian, northern European, and North American societies as well as in some Asian countries such as India and the Philippines tolerate a higher degree of uncertainty. As with the collectivist–individualist dimension, high uncertainty avoidance people and low uncertainty avoidance people exist in all cultures, but one type or the other tends to dominate in each culture.

High levels of uncertainty avoidance affect communication in two important ways. Firstly, because high uncertainty avoidance people are likely to experience a much higher degree of stress when faced with uncertain situations, their ability to interact with others is likely to be impaired by the feelings which they experience during such interactions. More importantly, however, as Sorrentino and Short observe (1986), high uncertainty avoidance people are likely to simply avoid thinking about, asking questions about, or researching topics that are unfamiliar to them because by doing so, they would expose themselves to uncertainty. In contrast, people with a high tolerance for uncertainty are frequently interested in reducing uncertainty by delving into such searches.

Motoki, an electronics vendor from Osaka, and Alexander, an import buyer from Scarborough, meet at an international trade show in Sydney, Australia. Through the course of conducting business, the men discover that they have several shared interests, including chess and opera, and they agree to go together

COMMUNICATE!
Using Technology

A culture-fair test is a test designed to be free of cultural bias, as far as possible, so that people of no one culture have an advantage over people of another in taking it. Culture-fair tests are designed to be beyond the influence of verbal ability, cultural climate, or educational level. Take the culture-fair memory test at **www.puzz.com/memory.html.** Do you think it is really free of cultural influences? Why or why not?

to dinner and a performance of *La Traviata* at the Sydney Opera House that evening. During dinner, Alexander starts a conversation about his father's military service in the Pacific during World War II and begins questioning Motoki about his family's experience of the bombing and occupation of Japan at the end of the war. Uncomfortable with the subject to begin with, and unsure of Alexander's feelings about it and where he might be going with the discussion, Motoki becomes increasingly anxious, makes several attempts to change the subject, and reduces his responses to mere nods. Finally, to avoid the possibility of a disagreeable confrontation on the subject, he excuses himself to make a phone call and leaves the table in the hope that Alexander will move on to another subject when he returns.

Power Distance

The power distance dimension focuses on how people of different status relate to one another in a culture. Hofstede and Bond (1984) define **power distance** as "the extent to which the less powerful members of institutions and organizations within a country accept that power is distributed unequally" (p. 419). Both high and low power distances exist in all cultures, but once again, one or the other tends to be dominant.

Cultures with a high power distance are hierarchical and authoritarian, with power and wealth concentrated in a small number of elite members of the society. In contrast, countries with low power distance tend to be egalitarian and democratic, with power and wealth distributed more widely among members of the population. High or low power distance in the upper ranks of a society is likely to be reflected in all other ranks. Thus, in a country with an authoritarian style of government, authoritarian control is likely to be displayed also in business and industry, in religion, in schools, and in the family. Members of high power distance cultures regard power and inequality as facts of life and regard their superiors or inferiors as being different from themselves. Members of low power distance cultures consider all citizens to be equal, regard power as something that is vested in the authorities by the public, and accept the exercise of power only when it is legitimate and justified according to whatever rules may apply.

High power distance is found, not surprisingly, in countries with authoritarian governments such as Malaysia, Guatemala, Venezuela, Singapore, and the Arab countries of the Middle East (Hofstede, 1997). Countries where the lowest power distances are found are Austria, Israel, Denmark, New Zealand, and Ireland, and most other northern hemisphere democracies, but countries where Romance languages are spoken tend to show higher power distances than those where Germanic languages predominate.

Differences in the power distance dimension can have a profound effect on communication. Whether it be at home, at school, in the workplace, or in a public forum, members of low power distance cultures feel free to challenge authority and to offer their input for modifying or improving whatever decision

THINKING ABOUT . . .

Power Distance

How much power should unelected authority figures such as parents, teachers, managers, and religious leaders be allowed to exercise in a democratic society? Do you think that the power of such authority figures is adequately controlled in Canada? If not, what additional controls should be put in place?

an authority figure has made. Authorities in low power distance cultures likewise generally expect to be challenged and do not consider it insubordinate of someone under their direction to offer opinions or suggestions. In contrast, a student, worker, or citizen in a high power distance culture would not likely challenge authority, because he or she would expect to be punished for doing so. Likewise, an authority figure in such a society would feel compelled to punish any challenge to his or her authority, both to save face and to maintain control.

Djavan, an exchange student from Brazil, was enjoying his studies in computer science at the University of New Brunswick, but he was becoming increasingly frustrated by an elective course in ethics that he was taking in the Department of Philosophy. The ethical problems that his professor assigned were important and thought-provoking, and the classroom discussions lively, but at the end of each session the professor simply summarized a variety of positions that could be taken in response to the case under consideration and the justification that could be offered for each. Djavan would not think of complaining to his professor, but he was certain that despite hours of extra work in the library, he was going to fail his philosophy exam. "Why oh why doesn't he just tell us the *right* answers?" he wondered to himself.

Masculinity and Femininity

Hofstede's analysis of cultural variables concludes with the masculine-feminine dimension, which attempts to measure how gender roles are distributed in a culture. A **masculine culture** is one in which gender roles are clearly distinct, and a **feminine culture** is one in which men and women may share the same roles. Masculinity and femininity exist in all cultures, but as with the other dimensions, one tends to be predominant in each culture.

Members of cultures high in masculinity (both women and men) place a high value on traditionally masculine traits such as performance, ambition, assertiveness, competitiveness, and power, and they are primarily concerned with material success. Members of cultures high in femininity (both women and men) place a high value on traditionally feminine traits such as service, nurturing, maintaining interpersonal relationships, and helping the disadvantaged, and they are primarily concerned with the quality of life (Hofstede, 1998). In masculine cultures, women are assigned the traditionally feminine roles, while in feminine cultures, both men and women are allowed to perform both traditionally masculine and feminine roles. In masculine cultures people value their jobs above all, and managers are expected to be decisive. In feminine cultures, people work only as a means of personal support, and managers are expected to be consensus builders.

Countries scoring the highest for masculinity include Japan, Austria, Italy, Mexico, and Ireland. Those scoring highest for femininity include Sweden, Norway, Denmark, and the Netherlands. Canada is near the centre of the scale, being slightly more masculine than feminine (see Figure 9.1).

OBSERVE & ANALYZE
Journal Activity

Masculinity-Femininity

Think about a group of people in your own social circle—your friends, your family and relatives, the friends of your family—any people that you have had an opportunity to observe closely for some time. Consider their behaviour in terms of the masculinity-femininity dimension of culture. Do the men display only traditionally masculine behaviour and the women only traditionally feminine behaviour, or are their behaviours mixed? Which of these people would you say is most masculine and which is most feminine? Overall, would you say that the group is more masculine or feminine? Are you satisfied with the group's position on the masculine-feminine scale?

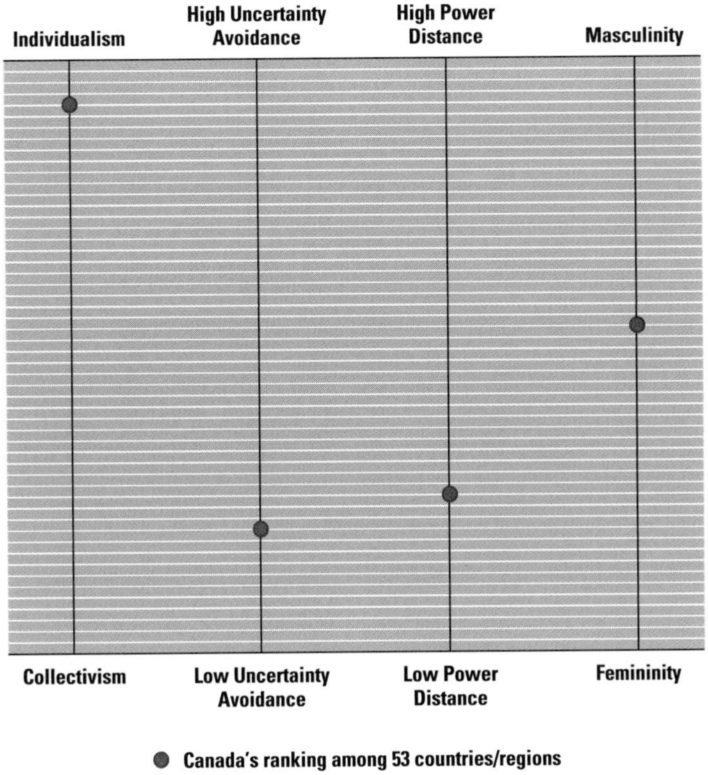

Figure 9.1
Four dimensions of Canadian culture, as compared to other countries/regions

Source: Adapted from Hofstede, G. (1997). *Cultures and organizations: Software of the mind* (rev. ed.). New York: McGraw-Hill.

IN BRIEF

Cultural Norms and Values

Four dimensions of culture affect intercultural communication through the formation of norms, rules, and values:

- *Individualism-collectivism:* individualistic cultures value the individual while collectivist cultures value the group.
- *Uncertainty avoidance:* some cultures feel threatened by uncertainty; others do not
- *Power distance:* some cultures are authoritarian, others egalitarian
- *Masculinity–femininity:* in masculine cultures, gender roles are clearly distinct; in feminine cultures, they are not.

Differences in the masculinity-femininity cultural dimension can have a significant effect on communication. People coming from a highly masculine culture tend to follow traditional cultural definitions of appropriate behaviour (Bern, 1993), while people from highly feminine cultures have a much wider variety of behaviours to choose from. People from a feminine culture are likely to perceive those from a masculine culture as old-fashioned or sexist, while those from a masculine culture are likely to harshly judge both men and women from a feminine culture for failing to play appropriate roles.

Suzie's company, a Montréal marketer of international holiday packages, sends her to Vienna to negotiate a major ski vacation package contract with an Austrian hotel and resort chain. She is to meet the company's sales director, Lukas Schechter, at his office. In the elevator of the Austrian company's office building in Vienna, she is joined by a distinguished looking man in his fifties. As the elevator slowly ascends, the man makes several flattering comments about Suzie's appearance and speaks to her condescendingly, suggesting that such "a pretty girl" must be on her way to meet one of the company's executives for lunch. Offended by the man's condescension, Suzie dismisses his advances

The roles of men and women can vary greatly from one culture to another. Research shows that in terms of the masculinity-femininity dimension of culture, Canada is slightly more "masculine" than "feminine."

© Randy Santos/SuperStock

brusquely. When the elevator stops at the twenty-fifth floor, she exits into a bright reception area, and to her annoyance, the man steps out behind her. "Guter morgen, Herr Schechter," the receptionist says to her companion.

Barriers to Intercultural Communication

Now that we have developed an understanding of culture and the significant differences that can exist among different cultures, it is perhaps easier to understand how communication across cultures can be particularly difficult. In any communication context, we are likely to be faced with someone who differs from us with respect to some cultural norm or value, if not all. In encounters involving several participants, of course, the situation becomes immeasurably more complex, the likelihood of cultural conflicts among the various participants increasing geometrically.

Anxiety

François, an Acadian student from Shippagan, New Brunswick, was nervous. It was the first day of the fall term, and he was beginning to wonder whether his decision to attend an English university had been a good one. Sure, the other students in his residence had all been friendly during orientation week, but he had to admit that a lot of their jokes and banter had gone right over his head. "If I can't understand tavern humour," he asked himself, "how can I expect to understand calculus or chemistry or oceanography?" His palms were sweating by the time the professor strode into the lecture theatre.

François's feelings are typical, and they represent one of the major barriers to intercultural communication: anxiety. Recognizing that we are different from everybody else or entering into a cultural milieu that is foreign to us causes most people to feel nervous: "What if I don't understand?" "What if I say the wrong thing?" "What if everybody laughs at me?" François, of course, is facing two cultural hurdles at once. Not only is he entering university, a foreign cultural milieu to a first-year student, but he is also immersing himself in what is, to him, a foreign language and society. When we are uncertain about whether we are going to be able to perform as we would like, it is natural to feel anxious, but that anxiety is likely to reduce our chances of communicating effectively.

Assuming Similarity or Difference

Iiro and Hanna strolled into the sauna of their Vancouver Hotel and began to chat casually about the sights that they had taken in that day. They did not really notice that the other guests quickly left as they sat down and were completely shocked a few minutes later when a police officer appeared at the door of the sauna and informed them that they were under arrest for public indecency.

Iiro and Hanna made a mistake that many people make when they cross into an unfamiliar cultural environment: they assumed that the norms that applied in their familiar situation matched those that applied in their new one. In Finland, their native country, it is common and unremarkable for men and women to be naked together in a sauna or swimming pool, but of course, different social conventions apply in downtown Vancouver.

It can be just as great a mistake to assume that everything about an unfamiliar culture will be different. For example, many men and women assume, following the lead of a few famous pop psychologists, that people of the opposite sex are different in every respect. As a result, when they are placed in a context dominated by people of the opposite sex, they plan not to understand anything.

In fact, some different norms will apply in almost any new cultural situation, but many others will likely be the same as those that we are familiar with. The wisest course is not to assume anything, but to be prepared to learn from any interaction we have with people of a different culture.

THINKING ABOUT . . .

Similarities and Differences

Recall a time when you visited a place that was different from your usual social milieu: a different country, a different city, a different kind of club or market. Did you assume any similarities or differences? Were your assumptions correct? How did they affect your perception of the place? How did they affect your appreciation for or enjoyment of the place?

Ethnocentrism

Ethnocentrism is the belief that one's own culture is superior to others. The stereotype of the American tourist, going about from place to place loudly commenting on how much better everything is "in America," is the classic example of ethnocentric behaviour; however, Canadians' we-would-never-behave-like-that attitude toward American tourists is also an example of ethnocentrism. Probably all people are guilty of some degree of ethnocentrism, but it is an attitude we should strive to overcome as it can easily lead to prejudice and discrimination. Rooting it out requires a constant and conscious review of our own assessments of others.

TEST YOUR COMPETENCE

Ethnocentrism

Working in a group of four or five students, label four sheets of paper as follows:

In This Community
In This Country
In the World Today
In History

How many examples of ethnocentrism of each type can you identify? What are (or were) the consequences of ethnocentrism in each case? How can (or could) each case be overcome? Be prepared to share your answers with the class.

Members of powerful cultures often seek to devalue less powerful cultures that they wish to manipulate or harm. For example, early European immigrants to Canada regarded the native people of the country as "savages"; German Nazis tried hard to convince themselves that Jews were "vermin"; gay-bashers excuse their crimes with the plea that "he was just a dirty fag"; and misogynists seek to denigrate women by referring to them as "bitches" or "hos." Bosmajian (1983) refers to this practice of objectification as "the language of oppression."

Stereotypes and Prejudice

Ethnocentric attitudes lead readily to stereotypes and prejudices. As we saw in Chapter 2, a stereotype is a simplified and standardized conception of the characteristics or expected behaviour of members of an identifiable group, and a prejudice is a preconceived judgment, belief, or opinion that a person holds without sufficient grounds. Recall that all stereotypes and prejudices (whether we like to think that they are complimentary to the subject or not) are inaccurate. Viewing people through such a distorted lens eliminates any possibility of getting to know them or forming real or meaningful relationships with them.

Incompatible Communication Codes

Zeke could not understand why those Chinese guys always sat together in the cafeteria. They were always fighting: screaming at each other and waving their arms. He had no idea what they were saying because he did not understand Mandarin, but he could tell that they were plenty steamed. He was always expecting a fight to break out.

Zeke was judging the conversation of the Chinese students based on their use of paralanguage and body movement. He could not understand the words they used, but he could imagine the types of angry tirades English speakers would be releasing if they raised their voices in the same way. Zeke did not understand that Mandarin is a tonal language: how the words are voiced affects their meaning, and that the great changes of pitch and volume that he overheard did not represent the expression of strong emotion, but only the expression of different meanings.

As we saw in Chapters 3 and 4, human beings communicate with one another through the use of two great codes: one verbal, the other nonverbal. People who speak different languages quickly comprehend their inability to communicate verbally, and almost invariably turn to some type of nonverbal signing in an effort to overcome the language barrier. As we have seen, however, there are significant differences in the use and meaning of nonverbal signs too. Some basic facial expressions and body movements are universal or nearly universal in their meaning, but to express ideas that are abstract or complex such simple signs are not enough. Differing verbal and nonverbal codes, then, can be a great impediment to intercultural communication. Anyone who has ever attempted to learn another language as an adult can attest to the frustration of having witty, intelligent, or beautiful things to say, but only the vocabulary of a young child with which to try to express them.

Incompatible Norms and Values

As we saw earlier in this chapter, people of all cultures base their communication behaviours on cultural norms and rules and on personal values based on those cultural norms and rules. Sometimes the norms and values of two people of different cultures conflict.

Kevin Frayer/CP Picture Archive

Many Muslims in Canada and other western countries have been the victims of stereotyping and prejudice in the aftermath of the September 11, 2001 terrorist attacks on the U.S.

Jeff and Tabito have been buddies since elementary school. They've shared everything: school work, holidays, sports, camping trips. As they reach Grade 10, their interests are changing: they become interested in girls, and start going out in the evenings. One day Jeff tells Tabito that one of their classmates has offered to supply him with some pot, and that he wants Tabito to smoke it with him. Tabito simply refuses and will offer no explanation. Jeff is confused by Tabito's behaviour; smoking a little bit of pot is no big deal, he reasons, everybody does it. What Jeff does not understand is that Tabito, coming from a Japanese family, has inherited the collectivist values of his parents. Being caught with drugs would bring great disgrace upon his whole family, and to him, the collectivist goal of maintaining the reputation of his family is more important than the personal goal of having fun with his friend.

Sylvana's parents came from Italy, but she was born and educated in Canada. While a student at the University of British Columbia she meets Sergio, who only recently emigrated from Italy with his family. After they have dated for a year, Sergio asks Sylvana to marry him. His parents have offered to support them, he says, while he completes his engineering degree, and Sylvana can drop out of school and help his mother around the house because, as a housewife and mother, she will not need a degree anyway. Sylvana is outraged that Sergio has so little respect for her and breaks off their relationship. Sergio is confused. Coming from a strongly masculine culture, he can think of no greater display of respect for Sylvana than to offer to make her his wife and the mother of his children.

IN BRIEF

Barriers to Intercultural Communication

Six common barriers to effective intercultural communication are

- anxiety
- assuming similarity or difference
- ethnocentrism
- stereotypes and prejudice
- incompatible communication codes
- incompatible norms and values.

Intercultural Communication Competence

To achieve intercultural communication competence, we must learn to overcome the barriers that we have identified. Competent intercultural communicators are likely to have followed three steps: adopting the correct attitude, acquiring the correct knowledge, and developing specific skills.

Adopting the Correct Attitude

The right attitudes for intercultural communication are, according to Samovar and Porter (2003), "cultural-general," because they allow a person to communicate with any other person regardless of his or her culture.

1. **Tolerate ambiguity.** Communicating with strangers creates uncertainty. As we saw in Chapter 8, one of the first things we do in beginning any relationship, even one with someone from our own culture, is to exchange information and indulge in benign self-disclosures in order to become better acquainted with the other person. People beginning intercultural relationships must be prepared to tolerate a much higher degree of uncertainty about the other person and to tolerate it for a much longer time. When interacting with someone of another culture, we are almost certain to be

unable to understand some messages, particularly if the other person speaks a different language, and some of our messages are likely to be misunderstood. If we go into the interaction with the knowledge that this difficulty is likely to occur and with the expectation that we will have to work much harder to make the conversation successful, we are much less apt to become frustrated or discouraged by the high level of uncertainty.

Canadians, coming from a highly individualistic (low-context) culture, are likely to find it particularly difficult to tolerate ambiguity. We are inclined to want everything spelled out in plain English and are not highly skilled at extracting meaning from the communication context. Patient practice is the best means of improving our ability to tolerate ambiguity.

2. **Be open-minded.** An open-minded person is someone who is willing to dispassionately receive the ideas and opinions of others. Open-minded people are aware of their own cultural values and recognize that other people's values are different. They throw off ethnocentric attitudes, resisting the impulse to judge the values of other cultures in terms of those of their own. Open-minded people have also worked to free themselves from the bonds of prejudice and are vigilant in attempting to recognize any tendency on their part to apply halo effects or stereotypes when meeting people of other cultures.

3. **Be altruistic. Altruism** is a display of genuine and unselfish concern for the welfare of others. The opposite of altruism is **egocentricity,** a selfish interest in one's own needs or affairs to the exclusion of everything else. Egocentric people are self-centred, while altruistic people are other-centred. Altruistic communicators do not neglect their own information needs, but they recognize that for a conversation to be successful, both parties must be able to contribute what they want and take what they need from the exchange. If one party's understanding of the conversation is faulty, neither party can benefit from that exchange.

OBSERVE & ANALYZE
Journal Activity

Tolerating Ambiguity

Go out of your way to increase your opportunities for intercultural encounters. You might, for example, participate in activities where you are likely to meet more people of the opposite sex or the opposite sexual orientation, participate in activities sponsored by your campus international student association, or volunteer with a community group that works with seniors or physically or mentally challenged people. Practise tolerating ambiguity. When you feel yourself becoming uncomfortable or frustrated, disengage and analyze the situation to understand what specific factors or combination of factors caused you to feel that way. Next time, see if you can prevent these feelings from arising by anticipating those same factors and making a plan to deal with them. Report on your progress.

Acquiring the Correct Knowledge

In addition to these "culture-general" attitudes, intercultural communicators develop competence by acquiring "culture-specific" knowledge (Samovar & Porter, 2003)—that is, they must develop an understanding of the specific culture or cultures of the person or people that they wish to communicate with. Berger (1979) recommends three means of acquiring this culture-specific knowledge:

1. **Observe passively.** Passive observers study the communication behaviours that are used by members of the subject culture.

2. **Employ active information-gathering strategies.** Active strategies might include research into or individual study of the subject culture, taking courses to better understand the subject culture or language, or interviewing people with expertise in the subject culture.

THINKING ABOUT . . .

Intercultural Communication Skills

Think back to the last time you communicated with someone of a different culture. Did the person use any specific conversational behaviours that were different from those recommended in this text? Do you think the difference was culture-wide or restricted to the person or persons with whom you were conversing? How might the person's behaviour be interpreted by someone from the dominant Canadian culture?

IN BRIEF

Intercultural Communication Competence

To achieve intercultural communication competence, we must

- *Adopt the right attitude:* tolerant of ambiguity, open-minded, and altruistic
- *Acquire the correct knowledge:* through observing passively, gathering information, and practising self-disclosure
- *Develop skills:* for showing respect, directing conversation, listening actively, and practising relational behaviours.

3. **Practise self-disclosure.** By revealing personal information about ourselves to people from another culture, we create an opportunity for them to reciprocate. We could, for example, reveal the difficulties that we are having communicating with them and ask them for their views on how communication between us can be improved. A person thinking of using this approach to information gathering would have to consider, however, whether people from the subject cultural group are likely to react positively to such self-disclosure. As we saw in Chapter 7, self-disclosure is not always welcome in the early stages of a relationship, and the rules of appropriate self-disclosure vary greatly from one culture to another. If the self-disclosure embarrassed or offended the other person, it would be counterproductive.

Developing the Specific Skills

The skills required to communicate in intercultural contexts also tend to be culture-specific:

1. **Learn how and to whom to show respect.** Everyone we communicate with deserves the respect owing to another human being. However, many cultures have rules which specify who is entitled to receive displays of respect and how the respect should be displayed. In most Asian countries, for example, elderly people are respected. In the Mi'kmaq First Nation, on the other hand, elders—not just elderly people, but those who are wise and have gained recognition for the things that they have done—are entitled to respect. In German business culture, elaborate rules of etiquette determine who should be addressed first, who should be introduced first, who should initiate a handshake, and the title that should be used in addressing different types of people, depending on their social rank. Even in the dominant Canadian culture, despite our low power distance, certain signs of respect are due to people in positions of authority. Knowing whom to acknowledge and how to acknowledge him or her is essential when entering any unfamiliar cultural context.
2. **Know and use appropriate conversation-directing behaviour.** In Chapter 6, we reviewed the importance of using and recognizing conversation-directing behaviour in our day-to-day conversations. The same necessity occurs in intercultural contexts, of course, but the rules are very likely to differ. Familiarizing ourselves with the conversational norms of a different culture before interacting with people of that culture is essential if we want to communicate effectively.
3. **Know and use appropriate (active) listening skills.** As we saw in Chapter 5, empathizing, questioning, and paraphrasing are effective means of achieving understanding. Clarifying a speaker's meaning through paraphrase or questioning is an effective strategy for reducing uncertainty in any context. The accepted attending behaviour is not the same in all cultures,

however. As you recall, maintaining eye contact with a speaker is in our culture a sign of receptiveness and respect. Many Asian cultures, however, consider eye contact, especially with an elderly person, to be rude and disrespectful.

4. **Know and practise appropriate relational behaviours.** In Chapters 6, 7, and 8, we reviewed rules and skills of conversation, and guidelines for disclosing feelings and opinions, giving positive and negative feedback, starting and developing relationships, and managing conflict. All of those guidelines are culture-specific. What is considered appropriate and effective in our culture may be regarded as boorish and incompetent in another. If we plan to communicate with people from another culture, we should find out what norms of communication behaviour apply in that culture, identify the specific skills that we need and lack, and practise them until we are sure that we have mastered them.

What Would You Do?
A Question of Ethics

Tyler, Young-Ja, Margeaux, and Madhukar were sitting around Margeaux's dining-room table working on a group marketing project. It was 2:00 a.m. They had been working since 6:00 p.m. and still had several hours' work remaining.

"Oh, the misery," groaned Tyler, pretending to slit his own throat with an Exacto knife. "If I never see another photo of a Highliner fish burger it will be too soon. Why didn't we choose a more interesting product?"

"I think it had something to do with *someone* wanting to promote a healthy alternative to greasy hamburgers," Young-Ja replied sarcastically.

"Right," said Tyler, "I don't know what I could have been thinking. Speaking of greasy hamburgers, is anyone else starving? Anybody want to order a pizza or something?"

"No one will deliver up here this late," Margeaux replied, "but I have a quiche that I could heat up."

"Fancy," Tyler quipped.

"You wish," Margeaux said. "It came out of a box."

"Sure, that sounds great, thanks," Young-Ja said. "I'm hungry too."

"It doesn't have any meat in it, does it?" asked Madhukar. "I don't eat meat."

"Nope, it's a cheese and spinach quiche," Margeaux said.

Tyler and Margeaux went off to the kitchen to prepare the food. Tyler took the quiche, still in its box, from the fridge. "Oh, oh," he said. "My roommate is a vegetarian, and he won't buy this brand because they have lard in the crust. Better warn Madhukar. He's a Hindu, so I imagine it's pretty important to him."

"Shhh!" said Margeaux, "I don't have anything else to offer him, and he'll never know the difference anyway. Just pretend you didn't notice that."

"Okay," Tyler said. "It's your kitchen."

1. What exactly are Margeaux's ethical obligations to Madhukar in this situation? Why?
2. Does the fact that Tyler is not the host relieve him of all ethical responsibility in this case?

Summary

A culture is a group's shared collective meaning system through which the group's collective values, attitudes, beliefs, customs, and thoughts are understood. Culture and communication are closely connected, the former having a profound effect on the latter. Our cultural identity is the part of our self-concept that is based on our membership in a cultural group that we consider important. Intracultural communication is the exchange of meaningful messages among members of the same cultural group. Intercultural communication is the exchange of cultural information between people with significantly different cultures. When such an exchange causes discomfort in a person, he or she is said to have experienced culture shock.

A dominant culture is the shared collective meaning system that reflects the collective values, attitudes, beliefs, customs, and thoughts of the dominant group in a society. Co-cultures are groups that live within the dominant culture, but draw some or all of their cultural identity from membership in other groups. Major contributors to co-cultures in Canada are gender, language, colour or race, ethnicity, sexual orientation, religion, social class, and age.

Four cultural dimensions affect intercultural communication: individualism-collectivism, uncertainty avoidance, power distance, and masculinity-femininity. Barriers to effective intercultural communication include anxiety, assuming similarity or difference, ethnocentrism, stereotypes and prejudice, incompatible communication codes, and incompatible norms and values. To develop intercultural communication competence, we should learn to tolerate ambiguity, be open-minded, and be altruistic. We can acquire knowledge of other cultures' approach to communication by observing passively, employing information-gathering strategies, or practising self-disclosure. Useful skills for interpersonal communication that are specific to a culture are knowing how and to whom to show respect, knowing the appropriate use of conversation-directing behaviour, knowing how to listen, and knowing and practising appropriate relational behaviours.

Glossary

Review the following key terms:

altruism (253) — genuine and unselfish concern for the welfare of others.

co-cultures (236) — groups which live within the dominant culture, but draw some or all of their cultural identity from their membership in other cultural groups that are not dominant.

collectivist society (243) — a culture which places highest value on group satisfaction and achieving group goals. In collectivist cultures, people belong to ingroups which look after them in exchange for loyalty.

cultural identity (235) — the part of our self-concept that is based on our membership in a cultural group that we consider important.

culture (233) — a group's shared collective meaning system through which the group's collective values, attitudes, beliefs, customs, and thoughts are understood.

culture shock (235) — the discomfort that a person involved in an intercultural encounter experiences when faced by an absence of shared meaning between him or her and the other person involved in the interaction.

dominant culture (236) — the shared collective meaning system which reflects the collective values, attitudes, beliefs, customs, and thoughts of the dominant group in a society.

egocentricity (253) — a selfish interest in one's own needs or affairs to the exclusion of everything else.

ethnicity (238) — a classification of people based on combinations of shared characteristics such as nationality, geographic origin, physical appearance, language, religion, and ancestral customs and traditions.

ethnocentrism (249) — the belief that one's own culture is superior to others.

feminine culture (246) — a culture in which men and women may share the same roles.

individualistic society (242) — a culture which places highest value on individual satisfaction and achieving the goals of the individual.

intercultural communication (235) — the exchange of cultural information between people with significantly different cultures.

intracultural communication (233) — the exchange of meaningful messages between members of the same cultural group.

masculine culture (246) — a culture in which gender roles are clearly distinct.

personal identity (235) — the part of our self-concept that is based on the characteristics that we perceive to be unique to us as individuals.

power distance (245) — the extent to which the less powerful members of institutions and organizations within a society accept that power is distributed unequally.

religion (238) — a system of beliefs that is shared by a group and that supplies the group with an object (or objects) of devotion, a ritual of worship, and a code of ethics.

social class (239) — an indicator of a person's position in a social hierarchy, as determined by income, education, occupation, and social habits.

social identity (235) — the part of our self-concept that is determined by the groups to which we belong and the meanings we associate with those groups.

uncertainty avoidance dimension of culture (244) — the extent to which members of a society feel threatened by unpredictable situations and the lengths to which they will go to avoid them.

value (240) — a broad tendency to prefer certain states of affairs over others.

SELF-REVIEW

Interpersonal Communication from Chapters 6 to 9

What kind of an interpersonal communicator are you? This analysis looks at specific behaviours that are characteristic of effective interpersonal communicators. On the line provided for each statement, indicate the response that best captures your behaviour:

1 = almost always 2 = often 3 = occasionally 4 = rarely 5 = never

1. In conversation, I am able to make relevant contributions without interrupting others. (Ch. 6) ____
2. When I talk, I try to provide information that satisfies others' needs and keeps the conversation going. (Ch. 6) ____
3. I describe objectively to others my negative feelings about their behaviour toward me without withholding or blowing up. (Ch. 7) ____
4. I am quick to praise people for doing things well. (Ch. 7) ____
5. I criticize people for their mistakes only when they ask for criticism. (Ch. 7) ____
6. I am able to initiate conflict effectively. (Ch 8) ____
7. I am able to respond to conflict effectively. (Ch 8) ____
8. I am able to maintain a correct attitude for effective intercultural communication. (Ch 9) ____
9. I use effective strategies to understand the communication behaviour of people of other cultures. (Ch 9) ____
10. I attempt to develop specific skills to aid in communication with people of other cultures. (Ch 9) ____

Based on your responses, select the interpersonal communication behaviour that you would most like to change. Write a communication improvement plan similar to the sample in Chapter 1 (page 26 If you would like verification of your self-review before you write a contract, have a friend or a co-worker complete this same analysis for you.

three

We live in a society in which problem solving, in personal, academic, professional, and governmental contexts, is increasingly entrusted to committees, task forces, or teams: small groups of people working together to reach decisions. We rely on these group processes, and the decisions and actions that result from them, in nearly every facet of our lives, but when we work with others in a small group for the purpose of solving problems or creating opportunities, we involve ourselves in a communication process that is much more complex than those that we have so far examined. Our group communication skills can enhance or detract from our ability to develop and maintain relationships with group partners while we together arrive at decisions and solutions that meet personal and group goals. In this two-chapter unit, we begin by discussing the characteristics of group settings which add to the complexity of the communication process and which must be skilfully managed for groups to work effectively. We conclude with a discussion of how roles and leadership can be used to manage the communication process in groups.

III

GROUP COMMUNICATION

© James Kay/Index Stock Imagery

OBJECTIVES

After you have read this chapter, you should be able to answer these questions:

- What is a work group?
- How can group discussion lead to improving group goal statements?
- What is the optimum size for a work group?
- What factors affect cohesiveness in groups?
- How can a work group improve its cohesiveness?
- How do groups form, maintain, and change their norms?
- How does the physical setting affect group interaction?
- What are the stages of group development?
- What is an effective method for problem-solving in work groups?
- What constraints cause work groups to be ineffective at problem solving, and how can they be managed?

CHAPTER 10

Participating in Group Communication

Members of the Alpha Production Team at Meyer Foods were gathered to review the team's hiring policies. At the beginning of the meeting, Kareem, the team facilitator, began, "You know why I called you together. Each production team has been asked to review its hiring practices. So, let's get started." After a few seconds of silence, Kareem said, "Drew, what have you been thinking?"

"Well, I don't know," Drew replied, "I haven't really given it much thought." (There were nods of agreement all around the table.)

"I'm not sure that I even remember what our hiring policies are," Jeremy said.

"But when I e-mailed you the notice of this meeting, I attached a preliminary analysis of our practices and some questions for each of us to think about before the meeting," Kareem replied.

"Oh, is that what that was?" Byron said. "I read the part about the meeting, but I guess I didn't get back to look at the attachment."

"Look," answered Kareem, "I think the CEO is looking for some specific recommendations from our team."

"Kareem, anything you think would be appropriate would be okay with me," Dawn said.

"Well, how about if we each try to come up with some ideas for next time," Kareem suggested. "Meeting adjourned."

As the group dispersed, Kareem overheard Drew whisper to Dawn, "These meetings sure are a waste of time, aren't they?"

Perhaps you have been part of a work group at school, at work, or in an organization of which you are a member. If you have, the opening dialogue probably sounds familiar. When group meetings are ineffective, it is easy to point fingers at the leader, but often, as is the case with this group, responsibility for the wasted time or poor performance lies not with one person but with the group as a whole. Frequently, group members simply do not understand the complex nature of communicating in group settings. Because most of us will spend much of our working lives interacting in group settings, however, we must learn how the group process works and how to participate in that process in ways that maximize the group's effectiveness.

In this chapter, we examine how members of work groups solve problems and make decisions through their interactions with one another. We begin by examining the characteristics of groups that affect how members communicate to solve problems effectively and make decisions. Next, we discuss how groups develop and the kinds of communication that occur during each stage of group development. Then, we identify and consider the strategies that effective groups use to solve problems and make decisions. Finally, we describe three types of constraints that limit the effectiveness of groups and suggest communication tactics for overcoming each type.

Characteristics of Effective Work Groups

A **work group** is a collection of three or more people who must interact and influence one another to accomplish a common purpose. A group is more than an aggregation of individuals. Six people riding in an elevator are not a work group. Should the elevator become stuck between floors, however, and the people begin to exchange ideas on how to solve the problem of their confinement, they would become a work group.

Effective work groups have clearly defined goals to which members are committed and an optimum number of members, representing diverse personalities, knowledge bases, skills, and viewpoints. They develop appropriate levels of cohesiveness, conform to rules and norms that facilitate the open exchange of information, ideas, and opinions, and conduct their work in a physical setting that encourages interaction.

Clearly Defined Goals

A **group goal** is a future state of affairs desired by enough members of the group to motivate the group to work toward its achievement (Johnson & Johnson, 2000, p. 78). Goals become clearer to members, and members become more committed to goals, when the goals are discussed. Through these discussions, members are able to make sure that goal statements are specific, consistent, challenging, and acceptable.

First, goal statements must be specific. A **specific goal** is precisely stated, measurable, and behavioural. For example, the crew at Pizzeria Perfetto, a 24-hour fast-food restaurant, began with the goal statement: "We want to increase profits." They made the goal more specific and meaningful by revising the goal statement to read: "During the next quarter, the night crew will increase the profitability of the restaurant by reducing food costs on their shift by 5 percent by decreasing the amount of food thrown away due to precooking."

Secondly, goal statements must be consistent. **Consistent goals** are complementary; that is, achieving one goal does not prevent the achievement of another. To meet the consistency test, for example, the team at Pizzeria Perfetto will have to believe that reducing the amount of precooking will not prevent them from providing a satisfactory level of customer service. If they do not believe that these two goals can be accomplished simultaneously, they will need to reformulate the goals so that they are compatible.

Thirdly, goal statements must be challenging. **Challenging goals** require hard work and team effort; they motivate group members to do things beyond what they might normally accomplish. The crew at Pizzeria Perfetto determined that the goal of cutting 5 percent from their food costs was a significant challenge for them.

Finally, goals must be acceptable. **Acceptable goals** are those which team members regard as meaningful and those to which they feel personally committed. Because people tend to support things that they help to create, group members who participate in setting their own goals are likely to exert more effort to see that they are achieved. Likewise, group members who do not believe a goal is just or reasonable are likely to be unmotivated to accomplish it or even to resist working toward accomplishing it. Because the members of the Pizzeria Perfetto crew helped to formulate the profitability goal, they are more likely to work to achieve it.

THINKING ABOUT . . .

Group Goals

Have you ever participated in a study group? Did the group discuss its goals? What effect did discussing or not discussing group goals have on the outcome of the group's work?

Optimum Number of Diverse Members

Effective groups are composed of enough members to ensure good interaction but not so many as to make discussion difficult. In general, as the size of a group grows, so does the complexity of its interactions. For example, Bostrom (1970) reminds us that the addition of one member to a group affects the number of inter-group relationships geometrically. When only Jeremiah and Shazia are working together, there is only one relationship to manage, but when a third person, Bryan, joins them the group now has four relationships to manage (Jeremiah-Shazia, Jeremiah-Bryan, Shazia-Bryan, Jeremiah-Shazia-Bryan). As groups grow in size and complexity, the opportunities for each member to participate drop, leading to member dissatisfaction (Gentry, 1980). When many people cannot or will not contribute, the resulting decision is seldom a product of the group's collective thought (Beebe et al., 1994, p. 125).

So what is the *right* size for a group? It depends. In general, research shows that the best size for a group is the smallest number of people capable of effectively achieving the group's goal (Sundstrom, 1990); for many situations, this might mean as few as three to five people. As the size of the group increases, the time spent discussing and deciding increases as well. This fact supports the argument for keeping groups small, because small groups will be able to make decisions more quickly. However, as the goals, problems, and issues become complex, it is unlikely that very small groups will have the diversity of information, knowledge, and skill needed to make high-quality decisions. For many situations, then, a group of five to seven or more might be desirable.

More important than having a certain number of people in a group is having the right combination of people. Notice that the heading of this section is "Optimum Number of *Diverse* Members." To meet this test, it is usually better to have a heterogeneous group than a homogeneous one. A **homogeneous group** is one in which members have a great deal in common. In contrast, a **heterogeneous group** is one in which various demographic characteristics, levels of knowledge, attitudes, and interests are represented. For example, a group composed of seven female accounting students would be considered homogeneous; a group composed of men and women from five different academic departments would be considered heterogeneous.

Effective groups are likely to be composed of people who bring different but relevant knowledge and skills into the group discussion (Valacich et al., 1994). In homogeneous groups, members are likely to know the same things, to approach problems from the same perspective, and consequently, to overlook some important information or take shortcuts in the problem-solving process. In contrast, the members of heterogeneous groups are likely to have different information, perspectives, and values, and consequently, to discuss issues more thoroughly before reaching a decision.

OBSERVE & ANALYZE
Journal Activity

Board Member Skills

Visit the Web site of a large company, such as Scotiabank, Nortel Networks, or CanWest Global Communications. Search the site and find the names and brief background sketches of the members of the Board of Directors. Analyze the ways in which the members are similar or different. Write answers to the following questions: What relevant knowledge and skills might each director bring to the group's decision-making process? What viewpoints are not represented by the board members? How might an absence of these viewpoints affect the board's discussions?

Cohesiveness

Cohesiveness is the degree of attraction that group members have to one another and to the group's goal. In a highly cohesive group, members genuinely like and respect one another and work co-operatively to reach the group's goals (Evans & Dion, 1991). In contrast, in a group that is not cohesive, members may be indifferent toward or dislike one another, have little interest in what the group is trying to accomplish, and even work in ways that prevent the group from being successful.

Research (Balgopal, Ephross, & Vassil, 1986; Widmer & Williams, 1991) has shown that several factors lead to developing cohesiveness in groups:

1. **Attractiveness of the group's purpose:** Social or fraternal groups, for example, build cohesiveness out of devotion to service or brotherhood. In a decision-making group, attractiveness is likely to be related to how important the task is to members. If Daniel is part of a group of students who must develop a computer program using a language they are learning in a computer science course, the cohesiveness of the group will depend in part on how interested the members are in developing such a program and how devoted they are to achieving a high grade on the assignment.
2. **Voluntary membership:** When we are forming groups, we should give people some control over joining. This factor is so important to fostering cohesiveness that each recruit to the Canadian Armed Forces is permitted to choose his or her own specialty. Likewise, Daniel's student work group is likely to develop cohesiveness more easily if its members are able to volunteer to work on developing the computer program.

© Leland Bobbe Studio/CORBIS/MAGMA

As groups become more diverse, achieving cohesiveness becomes more difficult.

If group members are appointed, or if group members are having difficulty getting comfortable with working together, the group may benefit from **team-building activities** designed to help the members work better together (Clark, 1994). This approach to team building often requires the group to meet outside of its normal setting where it can engage in activities designed to help the members recognize each other's strengths, share in group successes, and develop rituals. As they learn to be more comfortable with each other socially, group members are likely to become more comfortable working together as well.

3. **Freedom to share opinions:** Feeling comfortable in disagreeing with the ideas and positions of others is an important aspect of group cohesion. If the members of Daniel's computer science group are comfortable sharing contrasting ideas without fear of being chastised, they are likely to develop more cohesiveness.

   Group members should feel free to converse about their goals very soon after the group is formed. During this discussion, individual members should be encouraged to express their ideas about the goals of the group and to hear the ideas of others. Through this discussion process, the group can clarify goals and build group commitment.

4. **Celebration of accomplishments.** Groups should be encouraged to set sub-goals that can be achieved early. Groups that feel good about the work they are accomplishing develop a sense of unity. When early sub-goals are accomplished, the group can celebrate these achievements, and such celebrations cause members to more closely identify with the group and to see it as a *winner* (Renz & Greg, 2000, p. 54).

We should always keep in mind that the more heterogeneous the group, the more difficult it is to build cohesiveness. We know that heterogeneous groups generally arrive at better decisions, so we need to structure group conversations that can develop cohesiveness in such groups. Team-building activities, developing an environment in which members feel free to express controversial ideas, and celebrating achievements are therefore especially important to heterogeneous groups.

In addition, we should learn to communicate in ways that foster supportive patterns of co-operative interaction. Groups become cohesive when individual members feel valued and respected. By using the skills of active listening, empathizing, describing feelings, and collaborative conflict management, we can help heterogeneous groups become cohesive.

Finally, when we are working in groups, we should allocate time for the group to stop working on its task and focus instead on team relationships. Such off-task sessions enable members to discuss and resolve personal differences before they start to hurt team cohesiveness and team performance.

THINKING ABOUT . . .

Cohesiveness

Can a high level of group cohesiveness ever become counterproductive? Have you ever been part of a group in which this situation arose? If so, consider how high cohesiveness hurt the group's decision-making ability.

DIVERSE VOICES

Not Just "Little Ladies" in Hockey Gear

by Bonnie Slade

Allegiance to a shared goal can generate cohesiveness among diverse group members, creating group loyalty in the face of pressures from outside the group. Bonnie Slade is a graduate student in adult education, community development, and counselling psychology at the ***Ontario Institute for Studies in Education at the University of Toronto.***

As I watched the 2002 Olympic gold medal women's hockey in a crowded bar of cheering, hopeful fans of both genders, I felt a certain amount of disbelief. It is hard to believe how much the profile of women's hockey has changed in 19 years.

I played hockey from 1979 to 1983 in a county league in Ontario. Initially, my experience on the ice fell into the more traditional outlet of figure skating. My dad often reminds me of my unsuitability for this sport: "You sure weren't Barbara Ann Scott." It wasn't until I was 12, when we moved from Scarborough to a small, almost exclusively white town, that my interest in hockey began. Two of my new friends were on a girls' hockey team. It took me two years of advocacy to get my mother to agree to let me play. She was worried about the roughness of the game and the potential for injury, especially since I was barely five feet tall and the other girls were much bigger.

I remember how excited I was when we went to buy my equipment. How I loved my second-hand pair of SuperTacks. The focus of my first season was relearning how to skate and learning how to stay on my feet dressed in the hockey gear. My survival strategy was to pass the puck as quickly as I could to one of the more experienced players, usually to those who had played on a boys' team when they were younger because there were no teams for young girls. They had an intense drive to play hockey as well as parents who supported their unconventional dreams. I played right wing (the only time in my life that I have identified by this term) and didn't provide much in the way of offence until my second season. There was something particularly rewarding about hockey. The short intense shifts on the ice provided opportunities each game to try and improve my skill and confidence.

Our coach for the first two years was the father of the goalie. Later, two women took over the role. As I look back, it is evident that they were lovers. It is difficult for me now, as an out lesbian who enjoys the freedom of a progressive urban centre, to comprehend what it must have been like for them to live, closeted, in a small town. They lived in the same house, coached the hockey team together, and played on the same baseball team. In the late 1970's and early 1980's it was not safe for a lesbian couple to be out in a small town. I doubt that it is safe now. I look back with great sadness at the stories one of the women used to tell about her "boyfriend in Toronto." We all believed her and used to tease her about her visits to see him. The homophobia was so pervasive that it was completely invisible; it never occurred to anyone that they were a couple. As coaches of a girls' hockey team, they would have encountered terrible repercussions from the community if the truth were known. For the players too, heterosexism was a strong force. However powerful we were on the ice, we were expected to wear dresses and look like young ladies at the annual banquet.

Did we have a feminist consciousness about playing a non-traditional sport? Did we recognize the discrimination we faced? I would argue that

(continued)

the discrimination against women was as pervasive, and therefore as *normal* as the homophobia that kept our coaches silent. Uniting together as a team to defeat our rival, another girls' team from a neighbouring small town, was something that gave us a great deal of purpose and satisfaction. But identifying the real barriers was something we never did. We didn't question the fact that we had the worst ice time for practices and games or that we had to drive up to 75 kilometres to play against another team. Nor did we question the lack of infrastructure that could have provided a place for young girls to develop their skills and a future for talented players.

Were we "little ladies" dressed up in big hockey equipment? How did donning the gear affect our gender identities, and how did our behaviour on the ice challenge stereotypical notions of femininity? In my opinion, our games were as competitive and aggressive as boys' games; fighting and penalties for roughing were frequent occurrences. Though we played in a non–body contact league, body checking was a part of every game. While playing the game, we were also breaking out of our restrictive gender roles. I was acutely aware of this; I felt powerful and strong on the ice, a feeling that was rare for a young woman in a patriarchal world. This experience was to be fleeting but intense and satisfying.

The Canadian women's hockey team has been recognized as the best in the world. They have captured the nation's attention and pride. The opportunities that exist today for girls and young women interested in hockey have changed considerably since 1983. How great that a girl can dream of playing in the Women's National Hockey League or on Team Canada at the next Olympic games. Women's hockey has a future that is more than fleeting. It is my hope that for the next generation of female hockey players, barriers such as sexism, homophobia and racism will be named and addressed, making it possible for a more diverse group of women to participate.

Source: "Not Just 'Little Ladies' in Hockey Gear" by Bonnie Slade. Reprinted with permission.

Norms

Norms are expectations of the way group members will behave while in the group. Effective groups develop norms that support goal achievement (Shimanoff, 1992) and cohesiveness (Shaw, 1981). Norms begin to be developed early in the life of the group, and they grow, change, and solidify as the members get to know one another better. Group members usually comply with norms and are sanctioned by the group when they do not.

Norms can be developed through formal discussions or informal group processes (Johnson & Johnson, 2000, p. 28). Some groups choose to formulate explicit **ground rules**, prescribed behaviours intended to help the group conduct its meetings and meet its goals. These may include behaviours such as sticking to the agenda, refraining from interrupting others, actively listening to others, requiring full participation, focusing argument on issues rather than personalities, and sharing decision making.

In most groups, however, norms evolve informally. When we become part of a new group, we try to act in ways that would have been considered appropriate in other groups that we have been part of. If the other members of our new group behave in ways that are consistent with our interpretation of appropriate rules of behaviour, an informal norm is established. For example, suppose Belinda and Oleg arrive late for the first meeting of the student council's newly formed entertainment committee. If the group has already begun discussion and the latecomers are greeted with cold looks, showing that other members of this group do not accept such inconsiderate behaviour, then this group will develop a punctuality norm. A group may never discuss such informal norms as they develop, but all veteran group members will know what they are and adjust their behaviour to conform with them.

When a group member violates a group norm, he or she is usually sanctioned. The severity of the sanction depends on the importance of the norm that has been violated, the extent of the violation, and the status of the person who has committed the violation. Violating a norm that is central to a group's performance or cohesiveness will generally receive a harsher sanction than will violating a norm that is less important. Minor violations of norms, violation of a norm by a newcomer, or violations of norms that are frequently violated will generally receive more lenient sanctions. Group members who have achieved higher status in the group (for example, those that have unique skills and abilities needed by the group) are likely to receive more lenient sanctions or to escape sanctions altogether.

Some norms turn out to be counterproductive. For example, at the beginning of the first meeting of a work group, a few members start clowning around, telling jokes and stories, and generally ignoring attempts by others to begin more serious discussion. If the group seems to encourage or does not effectively sanction this behaviour, then it will become a group norm. As a result, the group may become so involved in clowning that work toward the group's goals gets delayed, set aside, or perhaps even forgotten. If counterproductive behaviour such as this continues for several meetings and becomes a norm, it will be very difficult to change.

What can a group member do to try to change a norm? Renz and Greg (2000) suggest that we can help a group of which we are a part to change a counterproductive norm by (1) observing the norm and its outcome, (2) describing the effect of the norm to the group, and (3) soliciting opinions of other members of the group (p. 52). For instance, Samantha has observed that her physics study group begins every meeting late. She might note that the last two meetings began 25 and 30 minutes late, determine that the discussion carried on during these periods was unproductive, and judge that extra meetings are likely to be necessary because the group is falling behind schedule. Then, she could start the next meeting by reporting the results of her observations and asking for reaction from other group members.

THINKING ABOUT . . .

Group Norms

Think of three work groups that you have been part of. Did each group formulate explicit ground rules or did the norms of behaviour for the group evolve informally? List the norms, including counterproductive norms, that characterized each group. How did each group's norms influence the outcome of the group's work?

The Physical Setting

The **working environment,** the physical setting in which a group works, is important to its effectiveness. The workplace should be conveniently located for most members. It should be at a comfortable temperature, and the space should match the size and the work of the group. The space should be comfortably furnished and contain all of the resources the group needs to perform its tasks. Seating should be arranged to facilitate group interaction.

When a group meets regularly, it will want to choose a convenient location. By choosing a location that is easily accessible, the group makes it easier for all members to attend. When impractical locations are chosen, a norm of tardiness or absenteeism may develop.

The temperature of the room in which a group meets affects the way in which the group interacts. If the room is too warm, group members will not only be uncomfortable but also may feel crowded, a sensation that results in negative behaviours. On the other hand, when the temperature of a meeting place is too cold, group members tend to become distracted.

The space in which a group meets should be appropriate for the size and composition of the group and the nature of work it is trying to accomplish during its time together. When a space is too big for a group, its members will feel overwhelmed and distant from one other and may have trouble hearing one another. When a space is too small, the group members will feel crowded. We have all found ourselves in situations in which room size contributed to negative experiences. Men and women seem to differ in their space preferences. Women generally find smaller rooms more comfortable, while men prefer larger spaces (Freedman, Klevansky, & Ehrich, 1971).

The physical setting can affect both group interaction and decision making (Figure 10.1). Seating can be too formal. When seating approximates a board of directors seating style, as illustrated in Figure 10.1a, where people sit suggests their status in the group. In this style, a dominant-submissive pattern emerges that can inhibit group interaction. People who sit at the head of the table are likely to be looked to for leadership and are seen as having more influence than those members who sit on the sides. People who sit across the table from one another interact with one another more frequently but also find themselves disagreeing with one another more often than they disagree with others at the table.

Seating that is excessively informal can also inhibit interaction. For instance, in Figure 10.1b, the three people sitting on the couch form their own little group; the two people seated next to each other form another group; and two members have placed themselves out of the main flow. In arrangements such as these, people are more likely to communicate with the people adjacent to them than with others. In such settings, it is more difficult to make eye contact with every group member. Johnson and Johnson (2000) maintain that "easy eye contact among members enhances the frequency of interaction, friendliness, co-operation, and liking for the group" (p. 174).

The circle, generally considered the ideal arrangement for group discussions and problem solving, is depicted in Figure 10.1c. Circle configurations increase participant motivation to speak because sight lines are better for everyone, and everyone appears to have equal status. When the location of the group meeting does not have a round table, the group may be better off without a table or with an arrangement of tables that makes a square, which approximates the circle arrangement, as shown in Figure 10.1d.

OBSERVE & ANALYZE
Journal Activity

Physical Settings

During the next week, keep a record of all the group settings you work in. Note the physical setting (location, temperature, size of space, seating configuration), the interaction patterns (who talks, who listens, who agrees, who disagrees), and your satisfaction with the group discussion (high to low). At the end of the week, analyze the data to see how the physical settings might have influenced group interaction and your satisfaction with the process. What conclusions can you draw from this analysis?

IN BRIEF

Characteristics of Effective Work Groups

A work group is a collection of three or more people who must interact and influence one another to accomplish a common purpose. Effective work groups

- have clearly defined goals to which all members are committed
- have an optimum number of diverse members
- develop an appropriate level of cohesiveness
- conform to norms that facilitate the open exchange of ideas
- work in a physical setting that encourages interaction.

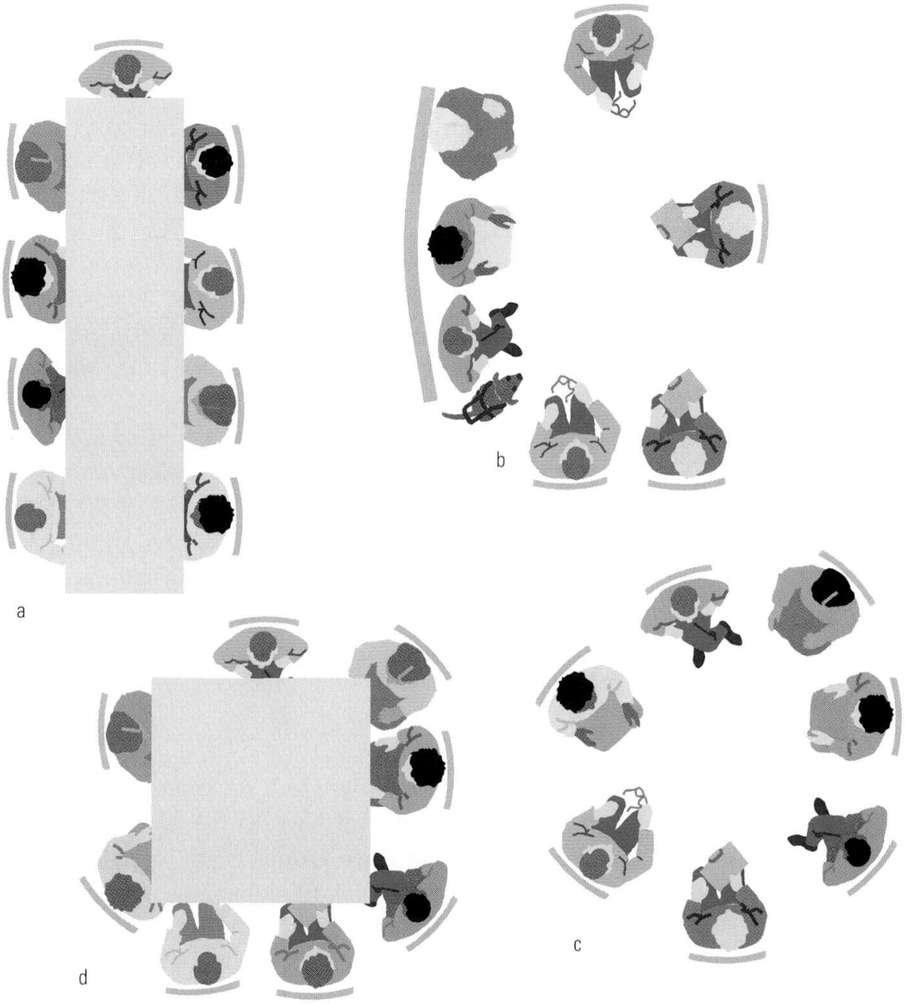

Figure 10.1
Which groups do you think will be able to arrive at a decision easily? Why?

Stages of Group Development

Once assembled, groups tend to move through a series of developmental stages. Although numerous models have been proposed to describe these stages, Tuckman's (1965) model has been widely accepted because it identifies the central issues facing a group at each stage of its development. Tuckman named the five developmental stages in his model forming, storming, norming, performing, and adjourning. Research by Wheelen and Hochberger (1996) has confirmed that groups can be observed moving through each of these stages. In this section, we describe each of the stages of group development and discuss the nature of communication during each phase.

Forming

Forming is the initial stage of group development during which members come to feel valued and accepted and to identify with the group. When the members of any group first come together, they are likely to experience feelings of discomfort caused by the uncertainty they are facing in a new social situation. Politeness and tentativeness may characterize group interactions at this stage as members try to become acquainted with one another, understand how the group will work, and find their place in the group. During forming, any real disagreements between people are likely to remain unacknowledged as members strive to be seen as flexible. If a group has formally appointed leaders, members are likely to depend on them during this stage for clues as to how they should behave. Members will work to fit in and to be seen as likable.

Anderson (1988) suggests that, during forming, we should express positive attitudes and feelings while refraining from abrasive or disagreeable comments; we should make appropriately benign self-disclosures and wait to see if they are reciprocated; and we should try to be friendly, open, and interested in others. Accomplishing these goals will require us to use active listening and empathizing skills to become better acquainted with other members of the group and to use effective nonverbal communication skills to invite conversation and cause it to seem a bit more relaxed.

Storming

Storming is the stage of group development during which the group clarifies its goals and determines the roles each member will have in the group's power structure. The stresses and strains that arise when groups begin to make decisions are a natural result of the conflicting ideas, opinions, and personalities that begin to emerge during decision making. In the forming stage, as we saw above, members are concerned about fitting in. In the storming stage, however, members are concerned about expressing their ideas and opinions and finding their place. If the group has a formally appointed leader, one or more members may begin to question or challenge his or her position on issues. In groups that do not have formally appointed leaders, two or more members may vie for informal leadership of the group. During this phase, the over-politeness exhibited during forming may be replaced by snide comments, sarcastic remarks, or pointedly aggressive exchanges between some members. While storming, members may take sides, forming cliques and coalitions.

Storming, if controlled, is an important stage in a group's development. During periods of storming, the group is confronted with alternative ideas, opinions, and ways of viewing issues. Although storming will occur in all groups, some will manage it better than others. When storming is severe, it can threaten a group's survival. To avoid such an extreme outcome, we should self-monitor what we say to avoid name-calling and using inflammatory language, and use effective listening skills to demonstrate our interest in other group members' points of view.

On the other hand, when a group does not storm, it may experience **groupthink**, a deterioration of mental efficiency, reality testing, and moral judgment that results from in-group pressure (Janis, 1982, p. 9). When groupthink overtakes a group, members will become more concerned with maintaining harmony than with effective decision making and will discourage the open expression of real conflict during discussions. To avoid groupthink, we should encourage constructive disagreement, and we should again rely on active listening skills with emphasis on paraphrasing and honest questioning (Anderson, 1988).

COMMUNICATE! Using InfoTrac College Edition

Using the subject guide, enter the term *groupthink,* and then select the article "Groupthink: Deciding with the Leader and the Devil" (1996) by Zenglo Chen, Robert B. Lawson, Lawrence R. Gordon, and Barbara McIntosh. Under what conditions does this study show that groupthink is most and least likely to occur? How should groups be designed to minimize the likelihood of groupthink?

Norming

Norming is the developmental stage during which a group solidifies its rules of behaviour, especially those that determine how conflict will be managed. As a group successfully completes the storming phase, it moves into this phase during which the norms or standards of the group become clear and members begin to apply pressure on each other to conform. Members for the most part comply with the newly established norms, although those who have achieved higher status or power may continue to occasionally deviate from them. Members who do not comply with the norms are sanctioned.

During norming, competent communicators pay attention to the norms that are developing and adapt their communication style to conform to them. When communicators who are monitoring norm development believe that a norm is too rigid, too elastic, or in other ways counterproductive, they initiate a group discussion about their observations. These conversations are best received when the person initiating them exercises the skill of describing behaviour through specific and concrete language.

Performing

Performing is the stage of group development during which the skills, knowledge, and abilities of all members are combined to overcome obstacles and to achieve goals. Through each of the developmental stages, groups are working toward accomplishing their goals. Once members have formed social bonds, settled power issues, and developed their norms, however, they become more task-oriented and more effective at creative problem solving and task performance. During this stage, conversations are focused on problem solving and sharing task-related information, and little energy is directed to relationship building. Members who spend the group's time in chitchat not only detract from the effectiveness of the group but also risk being perceived as unprepared or lazy. Performing is the most important stage of group development. This is the stage during which members freely share information, solicit ideas from others, and work to solve problems.

Adjourning

Adjourning is the stage of group development during which members assign meaning to what they have done and determine how to maintain or end the interpersonal relations they have developed. Some groups are brought together for a short time, but for others, work is continuous. Regardless of whether a group is short term or ongoing, however, it will experience endings. A short-term project team will face adjourning when it has completed its work and is set to dissolve. An ongoing group will experience endings when it has reached a particular goal, finished a specific project, or lost members through reassignments or resignations.

Keyton's (1993) study of the adjourning phase of group development points to two challenges that groups face. Firstly, they must construct meaning from their shared experience by evaluating and reflecting on it. They may discuss what led to their successes or failures, recall events and share memories of stressful times, and celebrate accomplishments. Secondly, members must find ways to sever or maintain interpersonal relationships that have developed during the group's life. During this phase, people in the group may explore ways

SPOTLIGHT ON SCHOLARS

Judith A. Rolls, University College of Cape Breton

When Judith graduated with a B.Ed., she hoped to work as a creative dramatics teacher. However, that was not to be, and her life took a different turn when she was invited to serve as the first full-time co-ordinator of a communication lab at the University College of Cape Breton, then known as Little X, the Sydney Campus of St. Francis Xavier University. All students enrolled in public speaking and interpersonal communication courses were required to spend an additional hour per week working in small groups in this new lab, and throughout each term, the same small group of 5 to 7 students participated in videotaped experiential learning exercises or practised for upcoming classroom speeches.

Although this work was not what Rolls was looking for at the time, she was able to put her speech and drama background to good use by developing and facilitating a series of imaginative and original exercises. In a short time, she realized that she not only enjoyed working with students at the university level but also was growing increasingly interested in speech communication. After three years in the lab, she knew she had to learn more about the discipline and went on to complete an M.A. at the University of Maine and a Ph.D. at Indiana University, both in speech communication. Dr. Rolls has been a faculty member in the Department of Communication at UCCB since 1980.

As a result of her early interest in experiential learning and communication labs, Rolls maintains a line of research in this area. Her work has demonstrated that not only do students enjoy learning in communication labs, but they also learn at the cognitive, affective, and behavioural levels. That is, communication theory is reinforced, students are provided an opportunity to examine

(continued)

to maintain contact with those they have particularly enjoyed working with. They may continue the relationship on a purely social level or plan to undertake additional work together.

Keyton thinks that it is especially important for groups to have a termination ritual, an event which can range from an informal debriefing session to a formal celebration, including group members and their friends, families, and colleagues. Whatever form the ritual takes, Keyton believes that it "affects how they [members] will interpret what they have experienced and what expectations they will take with them to similar situations" (p. 98).

Understanding the phases of group development assists group members to recognize what they must do to aid the socio-emotional development of the group. How a group develops through these phases has a significant impact on how effectively it works. However, achieving group goals also results from effective use of the problem-solving process. We now turn our attention to understanding that process and the communication skills that drive the performing stage of group development.

IN BRIEF

Stages of Group Development

Small work groups typically develop in five stages:

1. *forming:* during which group members develop a shared identity
2. *storming:* during which goals are clarified and roles determined
3. *norming:* during which rules of behaviour are confirmed
4. *performing:* during which members combine their skills to meet goals
5. *adjourning:* during which members assign meaning to their work.

their emotional responses to communication in interpersonal and public-speaking contexts, and students' communication skills are enhanced, all by virtue of participation in communication labs. Further, her research shows that men and women learn equally well in this environment.

Rolls and Professor Tanya Brann-Barrett recently published the results of a study that examined how peer facilitators who led communication labs benefited from the process. They found that facilitators experienced increased self-confidence and self-esteem, a greater sense of belonging, and more respect for themselves and others. Peer facilitators also honed their public-speaking and interpersonal skills. Interestingly, they gained increased confidence when speaking to those in authority. Peer facilitators also reaped external rewards through increased employment opportunities and feeling better prepared for graduate school.

Rolls has published and presented numerous papers on various aspects of communication labs. In 1997, she and Brann-Barrett and Celeste Sulliman designed and taught a short course which was presented in Chicago at a meeting of the National Communication Association. As a result, several universities across the United States have developed communication labs based on the UCCB model.

Although Rolls is also interested in gender, women and recovery, and health communication, it was her initial experience with communication labs that shaped her continued interest in communication pedagogy. As a result, she is active as a communication trainer. She designs and facilitates communication training packages for a variety of organizations and government agencies and writes training manuals. In the past few years, Rolls has published *Public Speaking Made Easy* (2003) and *Introduction to Public Communication* (2000). She co-edited *The Centre of the World at the Edge of the Continent: Cultural Studies of Cape Breton Island* (1996) with Dr. Carol Corbin, and adapted Ron Adler and Neil Towne's *Looking Out: Looking In* (2001, 2004) for Canadian students.

Rolls and another colleague, Professor Sheila Profit, are now examining the use of communication labs as a vehicle for teaching communication skills to student nurses, and Rolls is writing a book on the communication strategies used by women to deal with the decline and termination of and recovery from romantic relationships.

Problem Solving in Groups

Research shows that groups follow many different approaches to problem solving. Some move linearly through a series of steps to reach consensus, and some move in a spiral pattern, refining, accepting, rejecting, modifying, and combining ideas as they go. Whether they move forward in an orderly pattern or in fits and starts, those groups that arrive at high-quality decisions are likely to accomplish certain tasks during their deliberations. One commonly used method of problem solving in groups is based on John Dewey's (1922) six-step Reflective Thinking Process: defining and analyzing the problem, establishing criteria for a solution, identifying possible solutions, evaluating the possible solutions in terms of the criteria, selecting the best solution or combination of solutions, and planning a course of action.

Defining and Analyzing the Problem

Much wheel-spinning takes place during the early stages of group discussion as a result of members' not understanding their specific goal. It is the duty of the person, agency, or parent group that forms a particular work group to give the group a charge, such as Establish a set of guidelines for apportioning the varsity athletics budget. However, rarely will the charge be stated in such a way that the group does not need to do some clarification of its own. Even when the charge seems clear, effective groups will want to make sure they are focusing on the real problem and not just on symptoms of the problem.

Even when a group is given a well-defined charge, it will need to gather information before it can accurately define the specific problem. Accurately defining the problem requires the group to understand the background, history, and status of the problem, and to do so, it must collect and analyze a variety of information.

As early as possible, the group should formally state the problem in writing. Unless the members can agree on a formal definition of the problem, there is little likelihood of their being able to work together toward a solution. Effective problem definitions have these four characteristics:

1. **They can be phrased as a question.** Problem-solving groups begin from the assumption that solutions are not yet known, so problems should be phrased as questions to be answered. For example, the varsity athletics budget committee might define its problem as We must determine how much money each of the university's varsity athletic teams should receive. This problem statement can be converted to a question as follows: How much money should each of the university's varsity athletic teams receive? Phrasing the group's problem as a question furthers the spirit of inquiry.

2. **They contain only one central idea.** If the charge includes two questions, for example, Should the college abolish its foreign language and social studies requirements? the group should break it down into two separate questions: Should the college abolish its foreign language requirement? Should the college abolish its social studies requirement?

3. **They use specific and precise language to describe the problem.** For instance, the question What should the department do about unpopular courses? may be well intentioned, and may give group participants at least some idea about their goal, but such vague wording as *unpopular courses* could lead to problems later. Notice how this revision makes the intent much clearer: What should the department do about courses that fail to meet the minimum enrolment requirements of 15 students per term?

4. **They can be identified as a question of fact, value, or policy.** How a group organizes its problem-solving discussion will depend on the kind of question it is addressing: a question of fact, of value, or of policy.

Questions of fact are concerned with discovering what is true or to what extent something is true. Such questions anticipate the goal of determining truth through a process of examining facts by way of directly observed, spoken, or recorded evidence. For instance, Did Smith steal equipment from the warehouse? Did Mary's report follow the written guidelines for the assignment? and Do the data from our experiment support our hypothesis? are all questions of fact. In each case a group would analyze and discuss the evidence it has to determine what is true.

Questions of value concern subjective judgments of what is right, moral, good, or just. They often contain evaluative words such as *good, reliable, effective,* or *worthy.* For instance, the program development team for a TV sitcom aimed at young teens may consider, Is the level of violence in the scripts we have developed appropriate for programs designed to appeal to children? or Are the third and fifth episodes too sexually provocative? Although the group can establish criteria for judging *appropriate levels of violence* and *too sexually provocative* and then measure the material in the sitcom against those criteria, the criteria themselves and the evidence the group members choose to examine and accept depends on their judgment. A different group of people using different values might arrive at different conclusions and make a different decision.

Questions of policy concern what courses of action should be taken or what rules should be adopted to solve a problem. Should the university invest in companies that violate the human rights of workers in underdeveloped countries? and Where should the new landfill be built? are questions of policy. The inclusion of the word *should* in problem statements makes them easiest to recognize and easiest to phrase as questions of policy.

TEST YOUR COMPETENCE

Identifying Types of Questions

Indicate whether each of the following is a question of fact (F), a question of value (V), or a question of policy (P).

1. What should we do to increase the quality of our dining room service? ____
2. Are African Canadian drivers stopped by police more frequently than other drivers? ____
3. Should news organizations be permitted to publish poll results shortly before elections? ____
4. Is Hector Smith guilty of public incitement of hatred? ____
5. Is seniority the best method of determining employee promotions? ____
6. What is the best vacation destination for our family this summer? ____

Analysis of a problem entails finding out as much as possible about it. Three types of information can be helpful in analyzing problems.

1. Most groups begin by sharing any information that individual members have acquired through their experience. This is a good starting place, but groups that limit their information gathering to the existing knowledge of members often make decisions based on incomplete or faulty information.
2. Research in secondary sources is a second valuable source of information. Secondary sources are published materials available through libraries, electronic databases, and the Internet. From these sources, a group can access relevant information that has been collected, analyzed, and interpreted by others. Just because information is published, however, does not mean that it is accurate or valid, so the group will also have to evaluate the accuracy and validity of such information.
3. A third source of information about a problem is primary research. For example, the group may want to consult experts for their ideas about a problem or conduct a survey to gather information from people who are affected by it.

The processes of both primary and secondary research are discussed in greater detail in Chapter 12, "Topic and Research."

Once group members have gathered information, it must be shared with all other members. It is important for group members to share new information to fulfill the ethical responsibility that comes with group discussion. A study by Dennis (1996) shows that groups tend to spend more time discussing information common to all group members if those with specialized information do not work to get that information heard. The tendency to discuss common information while ignoring specialized information leads to less effective decisions. To overcome this tendency, groups need to ask each member to present the information he or she has uncovered. When addressing a complex issue, information sharing should be distinguished from decision making by holding separate meetings spaced far enough apart to enable members to think through all of the information presented.

Establishing Evaluation Criteria for a Solution

Once a group understands the nature of the problem it must address, it is in a position to determine what tests a possible solution must pass in order to be acceptable. These criteria become the decisive factors in determining whether a particular solution will solve the problem. The criteria that are selected should be ones that the information gathered in analyzing the problem has suggested are critical to a solution. The criteria that the group decides on will be used to screen alternative solutions. Solutions that do not meet the test of all criteria are eliminated from further consideration.

For example, a citizens' committee is charged with selecting a site for a new municipal swimming pool. The group arrives at the following phrasing for the problem: Where should the new municipal swimming pool be located? After the group agrees on this wording, it can carry out its analysis of the problem. In doing so, suppose members contribute information related to the municipality's budget, the distribution of recreational facilities in the municipality, space requirements for swimming pools (including parking), safety issues, transportation issues, and environmental concerns. After considering this kind of information, the group might then ask the question, What criteria must a good swimming pool site satisfy? In response to that question it might establish a list similar to the following:

- The site must cost no more than $500,000, including the cost of any demolition and site preparation.
- The site must be in the west end of the city.
- The site must be a minimum of 2 hectares with at least 300 metres of street frontage.
- The site must not be on a major thoroughfare or near industrial or commercial operations
- The site must be on a regular (20-minute service) bus route.
- The site must test negative for any hazardous waste or chemicals.

The group would then use these criteria in evaluating any proposed sites. Sites that fail to satisfy the criteria would be rejected.

Once the list of evaluation criteria is established, the group must also decide whether each criterion on the list is equally important or whether certain criteria should be given more weight in evaluating possible solutions. In situations where some criteria are more important than others, the group may assign weights to each criterion on the list. Using weighted criteria is a common practice, for

THINKING ABOUT . . .

Evaluation Criteria for a Solution

Many groups find that establishing evaluation criteria for a solution is one of the most difficult steps in the decision-making process, and it is a step that many groups skip altogether. Have you ever worked in a group where it was skipped or poorly carried out? What effect did the omission have on the quality of the group's decision? On the group's ability to agree on a solution?

example, in evaluating candidates for employment. The selection committee considering applicants for a university teaching position might weight the criteria as follows:

■ appropriate education	50
■ teaching experience	20
■ research experience	20
■ recent publications	10
Total	100

Kathryn Young and her colleagues (2000) suggest that when groups discuss and decide on criteria before they think about specific solutions, they increase the likelihood that they will be able to avoid becoming polarized and will be more likely to come to a decision that all members can accept.

Identifying Possible Solutions

For most policy questions, many possible solutions are possible. The trick is to tap the creative thinking of group members so that many ideas are generated. At this stage of discussion, the goal is not to worry about whether a particular solution satisfies all the criteria but to come up with a large list of possibilities.

One way to identify potential solutions is to brainstorm. **Brainstorming** is a free-association procedure intended to generate as many ideas as possible by being creative, suspending judgment, and combining or adapting the ideas of others. It involves group members verbalizing ideas as they come to mind

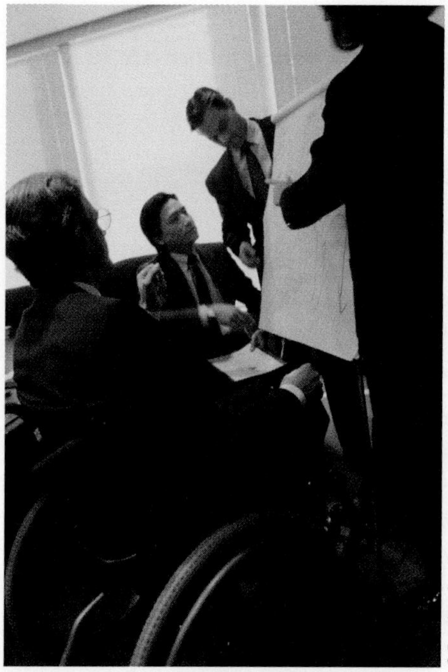
© Francisco Cruz/SuperStock

Brainstorming can be an effective method of identifying possible solutions. Each person is encouraged to state ideas as they come to mind.

SKILL BUILDERS Brainstorming

Skill	Use	Procedure	Example
An uncritical, non-evaluative process of generating associated ideas.	To generate a list of potential solutions to a problem.	1. Verbalize ideas as they come to mind. 2. Refrain from evaluating the merits of ideas. 3. Encourage outrageous and unique ideas. 4. Build on or modify the ideas of others. 5. Use extended effort to generate more ideas. 6. Record the ideas as they are verbalized.	Problem: What should we do to raise money for the senior prom? Ideas: sell cookies, sell candy, sell wrapping paper, wrap packages at the mall for donations, find corporate sponsors, have a corporate golf outing, a youth golf outing, a tennis tournament, a bowling tournament, a paintball tournament, auction donated paintings, do odd jobs for money.

without stopping to evaluate their merits. Members are encouraged, however, to build on the ideas presented by others. In a 10- or 15-minute brainstorming session, a group may come up with 20 or more possible solutions depending on the nature of the problem. For instance, the group working on the swimming pool site question might mention 10 or more possible sites in just a few minutes of brainstorming. These would include sites that individual members have thought of or those they have heard others mention.

Evaluating Solutions

Once the group has identified a list of possible solutions, it needs to evaluate each possible solution in terms of the evaluation criteria that it previously established, including assigning appropriate value for each criterion if the criteria have been weighted. Whether a group weighs certain criteria more heavily or not, it should use a process that ensures that each possible solution is thoroughly and equally assessed in terms of all of the criteria; otherwise, the evaluation will be unbalanced and the decision subsequently made by the group is very likely not to be the best one.

Research by Randy Hirokawa (1987) confirmed that high-quality decisions are made by groups that are "careful, thoughtful, and systematic" in evaluating their options (p. 10). In another study, Hirokawa (1988) noted that it is common for groups to begin by eliminating solutions that clearly do not meet important criteria and then to compare the positive features of solutions that remain.

COMMUNICATE! Using Technology

Visit the Health Canada Web site *Family Group Decision Making: Communities Stopping Family Violence: Questions and Answers* at **www.hc-sc.gc.ca/hppb/familyviolence/html/fvgroupdecision_e.html**. Study the guidelines for family group decision making presented in this online brochure. How do they compare with the guidelines for group decision making presented here? Can you think of reasons to justify the differences that you observe?

Selecting a Solution

A group brought together for problem solving may or may not be responsible for making the actual decision, but it is responsible for presenting its recommendation. **Decision making** is the process of choosing among alternatives. The following five methods differ in the extent to which they require that all members agree with the decision and the amount of time it takes to reach a decision.

1. **The expert opinion method:** Once the group has eliminated those alternatives that do not meet the criteria, the member who has the most expertise is asked to choose among the remaining alternatives. This method is quick, and it is useful when one member is much more knowledgeable about the issues or has a greater stake in implementation of the decision.
2. **The average group opinion method:** When using this approach, each member of the group ranks the alternatives that meet all the criteria. These rankings are then averaged, and the alternative receiving the highest average ranking becomes the choice. This method is useful for routine decisions or when a decision needs to be made quickly. It can also be used as an intermediate straw poll to enable the group to eliminate low-scoring alternatives before moving to a different process for making a final decision.
3. **The majority-rule method:** When using this method, the group votes on each alternative, and the one that receives the majority of votes (50 percent + 1) is selected. Although this method is considered democratic, it can create problems for implementation. If the majority voting for an alternative is slight, nearly as many members oppose the decision as support it. If

OBSERVE & ANALYZE
Journal Activity

Decision Methods

Remember an instance when a group you were part of made a poor decision using a majority-rule method. Analyze why the decision was a poor one. Would a different decision method have helped the group arrive at a better solution? If so, what method might have been more effective? Why?

SKILL BUILDERS Problem-Solving Fact/Value Questions

Skill	Use	Procedure	Example
Arriving at a conclusion about a fact or value question.	A guide for groups to follow in arriving at conclusions to fact or value questions.	1. Identify and analyze the specific fact or value question. 2. Determine the criteria that must be met to establish the fact or value. 3. Identify possible solutions. 4. Examine the available data to determine which possible solution satisfies the criteria determined in 2. 5. Select the correct solution.	The question is whether Branson is an effective leader. The key criteria for determining effective leadership are having a vision and being able to motivate employees. Branson either has these qualities or he does not. Evidence shows that Branson is successful in meeting both criteria, so he is an effective leader.

SKILL BUILDERS Problem-Solving Policy Questions

Skill	Use	Procedure	Example
Arriving at a solution to a policy question by following six steps.	A guide for groups to follow in finding solutions to policy questions.	1. Define and analyze the specific policy problem. 2. Establish evaluation criteria for a solution. 3. Identify as many possible solutions as possible (brainstorm). 4. Apply the evaluation criteria to each possible solution. 5. Select the best solution. 6. Plan a course of action	Question: What should we do to increase alumni donations to the Department Scholarship Fund? The group begins by discussing why alumni are not donating to the fund and identifying criteria an acceptable solution must meet. After brainstorming potential solutions, the group evaluates each one, selects the one that best meets the criteria, and makes a plan for putting it into effect.

these minority members object strongly to the choice, they may intentionally or unintentionally sabotage implementation of the solution through active or passive means.

4. **The unanimous decision method:** When using this method, the group must continue deliberation until every member of the group believes the same solution is best. As we would expect, it is very difficult to arrive at truly unanimous decisions, and to do so takes a lot of time. When a group reaches unanimity, however, it can expect that each member of the group will be fully committed to promoting the decision to others and to helping with its implementation.

5. **The consensus method:** This method is an alternative to the unanimous decision method. When using the consensus method, the group continues deliberation until all members of the group find an acceptable solution, one they can support and are committed to helping implement. Members of a consensus group may believe there is a better solution than the one that has been chosen, but they feel they can support and help implement the one they have agreed to. Although easier to achieve than reaching unanimity, arriving at a consensus is still difficult.

   Although the majority-rule method is widely used, selecting the consensus method is a wise investment if the group needs everyone's support to implement the decision successfully.

Planning a Course of Action

As with decision making, problem-solving groups are not always required to put their solutions into effect, but even those that are not will frequently be required to present to the decision makers to whom they are reporting a detailed plan for putting into effect the solution they are recommending. Groups that are responsible for executing the solution must decide not only what must be done, but also who must do it and when.

If the fundraising committee of the Parent Teacher Association at Lester Pearson Junior High School has decided to raffle a gift basket to raise money for a school band trip to Ottawa, the members might make the following plan:

- John: (by March 3) solicit donations for the prize from local businesses
- Henry: (by March 3) book hallway tables at three local malls for the weekend of March 10–12
- Mary: (by March 6) have 15,000 tickets printed at Speedy Print Ltd.
- Camsok: (by March 7) recruit and register 115 volunteers (including all band members) to sell tickets for a two-hour shift at one of the three malls
- Eliza: (by March 7) organize a team of six volunteers to collect money three times a day at each of the three malls
- Fatima: (March 10–12) receive and count all money and deliver it to the treasurer of the PTA for deposit in the bank.

In planning the implementation of the group's decision, group members must try to anticipate and allow for any problems that could arise.

IN BRIEF

Problem Solving in Groups

Groups can enhance their ability to arrive at high-quality decisions by following a six-step problem-solving process:

1. define and analyze the problem
2. establish evaluation criteria for possible solutions
3. identify possible solutions
4. evaluate possible solutions in terms of the evaluation criteria
5. select a solution
6. plan a course of action.

Constraints on Effective Decision Making

Following a structured problem-solving process should help groups be more effective, but groups may still face cognitive, affiliative, and egocentric constraints that can interfere with constructive decision making (Gouran & Hirokawa, 1996; Janis, 1989).

Cognitive Constraints

Cognitive constraints occur when a group feels under pressure because the task is difficult, information is lacking, or time is limited. Signs of cognitive constraints are comments like "How do they expect us to get this done in a week?" or "We've got a library of material to sift through."

Overcoming such constraints requires a group to assure itself that the task is important enough to justify investing the necessary time and effort. For instance, a group of students has been working together for several months on a team research project that will account for 50 percent of the final course grade. Two days before the group's report is due, the members meet with their professor to clarify some points about presentation. During the course of the consultation, they discover that their approach to the project was seriously flawed and that their report requires substantial revision. Revising the report may take more time than some members of the group would like to spend at the end of term, but if the revision is necessary to ensure the group a satisfactory grade on the term project, then the time is well spent.

Affiliative Constraints

Affiliative constraints occur when some or all members of a group are more concerned about maintaining harmonious relationships with others than they are about making high-quality decisions. Signs of affiliative constraints are members' reluctance to talk, reluctance to disagree with one another, and abandoning their positions for no apparent reason. As we have seen earlier in this chapter, such behaviours, if unchecked, can lead to groupthink.

Working through affiliative constraints is often a matter of practising the interpersonal skills we covered in the early part of this book. If group members are aware of the problem, they may want to try assigning someone to serve as a **devil's advocate,** taking the opposite side of arguments just to test the apparent consensus. Once group members become comfortable with testing each other's positions and recognize that constructive argument is healthy, the group is likely to become more productive.

Egocentric Constraints

Egocentric constraints occur when members of a group have high needs for control or are driven by other personal needs. These people see debating issues in terms of a win–lose paradigm. They feel that by getting the group to accept their positions they win. If the group chooses another alternative, they feel that they have suffered a personal loss. What drives egocentric individuals is not necessarily a strong preference for one alternative but the need to be right. Statements like "Well, I know that most of you are new to the committee and have lots of ideas, but I have served on it for the past two years, so I know what won't work" are sure signs of egocentrism. Egocentric constraints are difficult to overcome, but egocentric people are not incapable of rational thinking and often can be highly talented and resourceful group members. Inviting them to verbalize the information upon which they are basing their conclusions can sometimes help them to modify their positions and move into effective problem solving.

IN BRIEF

Constraints on Decision Making

In making decisions, groups can be constrained by

- *cognitive constraints:* when the group feels unable to meet the challenge
- *affiliative constraints:* when members are more concerned to maintain harmony than to make effective decisions
- *egocentric constraints:* when some members are driven by high control needs or other personal needs.

What Would You Do?
A Question of Ethics

The Community Service Committee of the Students' Union was meeting to determine which charity should benefit from the annual fundraising talent contest that the committee sponsors each spring.

"So," said Krist, "does anyone have any ideas about which cause we should support this year?"

"Well," replied Glenna, "I think we should support a group that's doing literacy work."

"Sounds good to me," replied Krist.

"My aunt is the literacy co-ordinator at the Newman Centre," said Glenna, "so why don't we support them?"

"Gee, I don't know much about the group," said Reed.

"Come on, you know, they help people learn how to read," replied Glenna sarcastically.

"Well, I was kind of hoping we'd take a look at supporting the Maecenas Society," offered Angelo. "They provide help to teens in trouble."

"Listen, if your aunt works at the Newman Centre," Laticia said, "let's go with it."

"Right," said Chi Wai, "that's good enough for me."

"Yeah," replied Hafsa, "let's do it and get out of here."

"I hear what you're saying, Hafsa," Krist responded, "I've got plenty of other stuff to do."

"No disrespect meant to Glenna, but wasn't the Newman Centre in the news because of the fraudalent use of funds?" countered Angelo. "Do we really know enough about it?"

"Okay," said Krist, "enough discussion. I've got to get to class. All in favour of the literacy program at the Newman Centre raise your hands. I think we've got a majority. Sorry, Angelo, you can't win 'em all."

"I wish all meetings went this smoothly," Hafsa said to Glenna as they left the room. "I mean, this was really a good meeting."

1. What did the group really know about the Newman Centre? Is it good group decision making practice to rely on Glenna as a source of information?
2. Regardless of whether the meeting went smoothly, are there any ethical problems with this decision-making process? Explain.

Summary

Effective groups meet several criteria: they develop clearly defined goals, have an optimum number of diverse members, work to develop cohesiveness, establish norms, and establish a good working environment.

Once groups are created, they tend to move through five stages of development: forming, getting people to come to feel valued and accepted so that they identify with the group; storming, clarifying goals while determining the roles each member will have in the group power structure; norming, establishing rules of behaviour; performing, overcoming obstacles and meeting goals; and adjourning, assigning meaning to what they have done and determining how to maintain or end interpersonal relations they have developed.

Once an effective group has reached the performing stage, it begins to move through a series of problem-solving steps, including defining and analyzing the problem, establishing evaluation criteria for possible solutions, identifying possible solutions, evaluating possible solutions, selecting a solution, and planning a course of action.

During the decision-making process, group members may have to deal with cognitive, affiliative, or egocentric constraints.

Glossary

Review the following key terms:

acceptable goals (265) — goals which team members regard as meaningful and to which they feel a personal commitment.

adjourning (275) — the stage of group development during which members assign meaning to what they have done and determine how to maintain or end the interpersonal relations they have developed.

affiliative constraints (287) — constraints on effective decision making that occur when some or all members of the group are more concerned about maintaining harmonious relationships with one another than they are about making high-quality decisions.

brainstorming (282) — a free-association procedure intended to generate as many ideas as possible by being creative, suspending judgment, and combining or adapting the ideas of others.

challenging goals (265) — goals that are difficult to achieve and that require hard work and team effort.

cognitive constraints (286) — constraints on effective decision making that occur when a group feels under pressure because a task is difficult, information is lacking, or time is limited.

cohesiveness (267) — the degree of attraction members of a group have to one another and to the group's goal.

consistent goals (265) — goals that are complementary; that is, achieving one goal does not prevent the achievement of another.

decision making (284) — the process of choosing among alternatives.

devil's advocate (287) — a person who takes the opposite side of the argument during group discussion to test the correctness of the consensus position.

egocentric constraints (287) — constraints on effective decision making that occur when members of the group have high needs for control or are driven by other personal needs.

forming (274) — the initial stage of group development during which members come to feel valued and accepted and to identify with the group.

ground rules (270) — prescribed behaviours intended to help a work group conduct its meetings and meet its goals.

group goal (265) — a future state of affairs desired by enough members of a group to motivate the group to work toward its achievement.

groupthink (275) — a dysfunction in group behaviour which arises when group members become more concerned about maintaining harmony than about effective decision making and discourage the open expression of real conflict during discussions.

heterogeneous group (266) — a group in which various demographic characteristics, levels of knowledge, attitudes, and interests are represented.

homogeneous group (266) — a group whose members have a great deal in common.

norming (275) — the developmental stage during which a group solidifies its rules of behaviour, especially those that determine how conflict will be managed.

norms (270) — expectations of the way group members will behave while in the group.

performing (275) — the stage of group development during which the skills, knowledge, and abilities of all members are combined to overcome obstacles and achieve goals.

questions of fact (279) — questions concerned with discovering what is true or to what extent something is true.

questions of policy (279) — questions that concern what courses of action should be taken or what rules should be adopted to solve a problem.

questions of value (279) — questions that concern subjective judgments of what is right, moral, good, or just.

specific goal (265) — a goal that is precisely stated, measurable, and behavioural.

storming (274) — the stage of group development during which the group clarifies its goals and determines the roles each member will have in the group's power structure.

team-building activities (268) — activities designed to help the members of a group work better together.

work group (264) — a collection of three or more people who must interact and influence one another to accomplish a common purpose.

working environment (271) — the physical setting in which a group works.

Marcio Jose Sanchez/AP/CP Picture Archive

OBJECTIVES

After you have read this chapter, you should be able to answer these questions:

- What are roles, and why are they important in groups?
- How do group members choose their roles?
- What types of roles do group members play?
- What behaviours are required of group members to make meetings effective?
- What is leadership, and why is it important to a group?
- What are the tasks of leadership?
- What characterizes the communication behaviour of a leader?
- How does leadership develop in a group?
- What behaviours can help a person to become a leader?
- What should the leader of a meeting do to make the meeting successful?

CHAPTER 11

Member Roles and Leadership in Groups

"Well, since we're all here, let's get started. The agenda calls for us to begin by reviewing the three bids we received for snow removal services. Dontonio, will you be the secretary again?"

"Sure, Nubia, no problem."

"Okay. Frederick, we know we can depend on you to have studied the bids. So why don't you start us off by summarizing what you found?"

"Well, only three of the six companies submitted detailed bids in line with our request. After reviewing each, I concluded that they all will provide the same basic services and on similar schedules. Two of the bids came in at about the same amount, but the other one is much higher. The two lower bids were from Blizzard and from Conroy and Sons."

"Well, I've never heard of Blizzard, but my brother-in-law's company used Conroy and Sons for a while and dropped them because they damaged his lawns, walkways, and hedges with their machinery. I don't think we want them here."

"Hey, Mikko, be careful, my cousin works for Conroy and Sons, and I don't think his crews are that reckless."

"Judith, I don't think Mikko meant his comment as a personal attack on your cousin. I think he was just trying to share some relevant information he'd heard."

"Yeah, you're right, Shawn, thanks. Sorry, Mikko. It's a good thing we have Shawn here to referee for us."

Our beginning conversation is typical of interactions in groups. If we listen closely, we can hear that the members of this group are not only discussing a snow removal contract but also acting in ways expected of them by their fellow group members.

Our goal in this chapter is to explain how members of groups take on specific roles that help or detract from the effectiveness of the group. A **role** is a specific pattern of behaviour that one group member performs based on the expectations of other members. We will learn about the types of roles that members assume and how these roles are developed. Then, we will look more closely at leadership roles. Most groups can identify one or more persons who serve as their leader(s), and we will examine the characteristics that distinguish leaders from other group members. We will also discuss two types of leaders and how groups develop leaders. Then, we will present behavioural guidelines that will help increase a person's chances of becoming a leader and discuss some common leadership roles. Finally we will present a method of evaluating group effectiveness, including the quality of role performance and leadership.

Member Roles

The roles group members play depend on their personalities and what is required or needed by the group. Four common types of roles are task-related roles, maintenance roles, procedural roles, and self-centred roles.

Task-Related Roles

Task-related roles require specific patterns of behaviour that directly help the group accomplish its goals. Members who play task roles are likely to be information or opinion givers, information or opinion seekers, or analyzers.

Information or opinion givers provide content for a group's discussion. People who perform these roles are expected to have developed expertise in a task or to be well informed about it and to share what they know with the group. The more knowledgeable a person is in a field or the more extensive his or her research, the more valuable his or her contributions relevant to a problem in that field will be. "Well, the articles I've read seem to agree that . . .," "Based on my years of experience . . .," and "Given the results of our recent citizens' poll, I think we should . . ." are statements typical of information and opinion givers.

Information or opinion seekers are expected to probe others for their ideas and opinions on issues relevant to the group's discussion. Typical comments by those performing these roles include, "Before we go any further, what information do we have about how raising fees is likely to affect membership?" or "How do other members of the group feel about this idea?" or "How have we handled problems like this in the past?"

Analyzers are expected to probe the content of other group members' contributions and the soundness of their reasoning during discussion. Their role is to question what is being said and to help other members understand the hidden assumptions or faulty logic that may underlie some statements. Analyzers make statements such as "Stefanos, you're generalizing from only one instance. Can you give us some other examples?" or "These two accounts seem to be contradictory; perhaps we should investigate further" or "That's a very interesting theory Byron, but do we have any data to support it?"

Maintenance Roles

Maintenance roles require specific patterns of behaviour that help a group to develop and maintain good member relationships and group cohesiveness and to control conflict. Members who play maintenance roles are likely to be supporters, tension relievers, harmonizers, or interpreters.

Supporters are expected to encourage others in the group. When another member contributes information or an opinion, a supporter shows appreciation through a nonverbal or verbal response. Nonverbally, supporters may smile, nod, or give a thumbs-up. Verbally, they may demonstrate support through making observations such as "Good point, Ming," "I really like that idea, Nikki," or "It's obvious you've really done your homework, Sam."

Tension relievers are expected to recognize when group members are stressed or tiring and to intervene in some way to relieve the stress or re-energize the group. People who are effective in this role are able to tell jokes, kid around, and tell light-hearted stories so that the group is refreshed when it returns to its task. In some situations, a single well-placed one-liner will get a laugh, break the tension or the monotony, and jolt the group out of its lethargy. Although the tension reliever momentarily diverts the group from its task, this distraction helps the group remain cohesive.

Harmonizers are expected to intervene in a group discussion when conflict is threatening to harm group cohesiveness or the relationship between particular group members. Where tension relievers distract group members, harmonizers mediate and reconcile differences between group members. Harmonizers are likely to make statements such as "Tom, Noriko, hold it a second. I know you're on opposite sides of this, but let's see where you might have some common ground," or "Cool it, everybody, we're really coming up with some excellent ideas; let's not lose our momentum by getting into name-calling."

Interpreters are expected to be familiar with the differences in the social, cultural, and gender orientations of the members of a group and to use this knowledge to help group members understand each other. Interpreters are especially important in groups whose members are culturally diverse (Jensen & Chilberg, 1991). For example, an interpreter might say, "Jim, I know you like to get right to work, but most of us are Latino, and in our culture it is considered impolite to begin business before we socialize and catch up with one another's news," or

"We all share your interest in saving money, Marco, but I'm sure you can appreciate that, for the women in the group, having adequate lighting on the campus footpaths at night is not 'an extravagance.' "

Procedural Roles

Procedural roles require specific patterns of behaviour that help a group manage its problem-solving process. Members who play procedural roles are likely to be expediters, recorders, or gatekeepers.

Expediters are expected to be mindful of what the group is trying to accomplish and to help move the group through the agenda for its meeting. When the group loses its focus or strays from the agenda, expediters will make statements like "I'm enjoying this discussion, but I don't see that it has anything to do with solving our problem," or "Let's see, aren't we still trying to decide whether these are the only evaluation criteria that we should be considering?"

Recorders are expected to take careful notes of what a group has decided and the evidence upon which its decisions are based. Recorders usually distribute edited copies of their notes to group members prior to the next meeting. Sometimes these notes are published as **minutes,** a formal and official record of the group's deliberations and decisions.

Gatekeepers are expected to manage the flow of conversation so that all group members have an opportunity to participate. If one or two members begin to dominate the conversation, the gatekeeper is expected to invite other members of the group to participate. Gatekeepers also notice nonverbal signals that indicate that a member wishes to speak. The gatekeeper is the one who sees

THINKING ABOUT . . .

Roles

Which of the roles discussed in this section on member roles do you perform most frequently when you are in a group? Which role is easiest for you to perform? Which role is most difficult for you? Why?

Ryan McVey/PhotoDisc Red/Getty Images

Some members help the group by performing procedural roles such as expediter or recorder.

that Frantiska is on the edge of her seat, eager to comment, and says, "Let me interrupt you there, Doug. We haven't heard from Frantiska on this point yet, and she seems to have something she wants to say."

Self-Centred Roles

Self-centred roles reflect specific patterns of behaviour that focus attention on members' personal needs and goals at the expense of those of the group. Task-related, maintenance, and procedural roles must be played for a group to be effective, but self-centred roles detract from a group's effectiveness. Members who play self-centred roles are likely to be aggressors, jokers, withdrawers, or monopolizers.

Aggressors seek to enhance their own status by criticizing other group members' contributions, by blaming others for problems, and by deflating the ego or lessening the status of others. Aggressors should be confronted and helped to assume a more positive role. They should be asked whether they are aware of what they are doing and of the effect their behaviour is having on the group.

Jokers attempt to draw attention to themselves by joking, clowning, and being generally disruptive. Unlike a tension reliever, a joker is not attempting to help the group to relieve stress or tension. Rather, a joker disrupts work when the group is trying to focus on the task. Jokers should also be confronted and encouraged to use their abilities when the group needs a break but to refrain from disrupting the group when it is being productive.

Withdrawers can be expected to meet their own goals at the expense of those of the group by not participating in the discussion or the work of the group. Sometimes withdrawers miss meetings. At other times, they are physically present but make no contribution to the discussion and refuse to take responsibility for doing any work. When a member has adopted this role, the group needs to find out why. When possible, the goals of the withdrawer need to be aligned with those of the group. For example, members of the Student Union's finance committee noticed that Marianne came late to meetings and never seemed to be prepared or to have anything to offer. The group finally confronted her and learned that she was late because of her job. She also indicated that she did not contribute because she usually missed so much of the early discussion that she was afraid of raising points that had already been dealt with. This group was able to change its meeting time, and Marianne became a fully participating member.

Monopolizers can be expected to talk all the time, giving the impression that they are well read, knowledgeable, and of value to the group. Monopolizers attempt to dominate the group, preventing others from contributing. They should be encouraged when their comments are helpful and reined in when they are talking too much or when their comments are not helpful.

OBSERVE & ANALYZE
Journal Activity

Analyzing Group Performance

Identify a group whose discussion you can observe. Prepare an analysis grid labelling each row to represent one of the member roles just discussed and each column to represent a member of the subject group. As you observe the group's interaction, put a check mark in the appropriate row and column each time you see a particular member demonstrate a behaviour associated with a specific role. For example, if one member responds to a teammate's comment by saying "good observation," place a check opposite his or her name in the supporter row. Review the data to identify all of the positive and negative roles adopted. What is the value of this kind of data collection and analysis to a person advising a group about its interactions?

TEST YOUR COMPETENCE

Reread the conversation at the beginning of this chapter. Identify the roles performed by Nubia, Dontonio, Frederick, Mikko, and Shawn.

IN BRIEF

Member Roles

A role is a specific pattern of behaviour that one group member adopts based on the expectations of the other members. Four common types of roles are

- *Task-related roles:* information or opinion giver, information or opinion seeker, analyzer
- *Maintenance roles:* supporter, tension reliever, harmonizer, interpreter
- *Procedural roles:* expediter, recorder, gatekeeper
- *Self-centred roles:* aggressor, joker, withdrawer, monopolizer.

Normal Distribution of Roles

What proportion of time in a *normal* group should be devoted to each of the various roles described in this section? According to Robert Bales (1971), one of the leading researchers in group interaction processes, 40 to 60 percent of discussion time is spent giving and asking for information and opinion; 8 to 15 percent of discussion time is spent on disagreement, tension, or unfriendliness; and 16 to 26 percent of discussion time is characterized by agreement or friendliness (positive maintenance functions). We can apply two norms as guidelines for effective group functioning:

1. approximately half of all discussion time should be devoted to information sharing
2. group agreement time should far outweigh group disagreement time.

Member Responsibilities in Group Meetings

In addition to adopting particular roles during discussion and problem solving, members of effective groups also assume responsibilities for making their meetings successful. Here are some guidelines prepared by a class of university students to help group members prepare, participate, and follow up in a manner that will increase the effectiveness of the meeting ("Guidelines," 1998).

Preparing

As this chapter's opening vignette illustrated, people too often think of group meetings as events that require attendance but no particular preparation. How many times have we observed people arriving at meetings with packets of material which they have spent little or no time studying. These people often then proceed to impose on their teammates by using valuable meeting time to read the briefing notes that they should have analyzed before arriving and to work out (often aloud) their positions with reference to that material. Meetings should not be treated as impromptu events but as structured activities during which well prepared people pool information and debate their positions. By taking the following steps *before* a meeting, a group member will be prepared to play a meaningful role *during* the meeting.

1. **Study the agenda.** We should consider the agenda as an outline for preparation. Understanding the purpose of the meeting reveals what we need to do to be prepared.
2. **Study the minutes.** If an upcoming meeting is one of a series, the minutes and our own notes from previous meetings will assist us in preparation by revealing what has been agreed upon, outstanding contentious issues and

major positions expressed, problems identified, and so on. Each meeting is not a separate event: what happened at one should provide the basis for preparation for the next.

3. **Prepare to contribute.** We should study briefing documents carefully and do as much research as necessary to become well informed about items on the agenda. If no documents have been circulated in advance, we should consider the kinds of information we will need to contribute to the discussion and find that information. We should then bring to the meeting any relevant materials that we have uncovered and be prepared to summarize the important content. If appropriate, we can also prepare by discussing the items on the agenda with others who may be affected by the group's decision making and solicit their input on issues to be discussed at the meeting.
4. **Prepare to play a major role.** Before every group meeting, we should consider which roles we have been assigned or are interested in playing in that particular group (people play different roles in different groups) and consider what preparation we need to be effective in those roles at this meeting.
5. **List questions.** If we are unable to satisfy our own information needs with reference to the items on the agenda, we should prepare a list of questions that we would like to have answered during the meeting.

Participating

We should go into every meeting with the expectation that we will be a full participant. If there are five people in the group, all five should be active throughout the meeting.

1. **Listen attentively.** By concentrating on what others are saying, we enable ourselves to use our own material to complement, supplement, or counter what they have presented. In this way our contributions will be timely and relevant, and the discussion will flow smoothly rather than lurching incoherently between unrelated topics.
2. **Stay focused.** Group discussion can easily become non-productive by breaking down into side conversations or by becoming disorganized or random. If all members restrict their comments to the specific agenda item under discussion, these problems will be avoided. If others stray off topic, we should do what we can to get everyone back on track.
3. **Ask questions.** Posing relevant questions helps to stimulate discussion and generate ideas.
4. **Take notes.** Even when one group member has been assigned responsibility for producing the official minutes, we should take notes of our own. These will later allow us to analyze lines of development and to recall what was said and by whom.

OBSERVE & ANALYZE
Journal Activity

Self-Monitoring

The next time you are part of a group meeting, make notes on your rate of participation. Do you talk less than other group members? Do you talk more? If you do either, develop a strategy for normalizing your rate of participation and apply it at the next meeting of the same group. Was your strategy effective? Why or why not? Do you feel that your overall contribution to the meeting was improved as a result of applying the strategy? Why or why not?

Effective meetings occur when well prepared participants choose to communicate in effective ways.

5. **Play devil's advocate.** When we think an idea has not been fully discussed or tested, especially when the idea is one that we believe has some merit, we should be willing to voice disagreement or encourage further discussion.

6. **Monitor contributions.** People who are well prepared sometimes have a tendency to dominate discussion, especially when other group members have not prepared adequately. We must be careful neither to dominate the discussion nor to abdicate our responsibility to share insights and opinions.

Following Up

When meetings end, group members too often leave and forget about what took place until the next meeting. As we have already seen, however, what happens in one meeting provides the basis for what happens in the next, so members should begin right away to prepare to move forward at the next meeting.

1. **Review and summarize notes.** We should try to perform this review as soon as possible after leaving the meeting, while ideas are still fresh in our minds. By elaborating our notes as necessary, we will ensure that they will be meaningful to us when the discussion is no longer fresh in our mind. We should make special note of what needs to be discussed at the next meeting so that we will know what to prepare.

2. **Evaluate performance.** One of the best ways to constantly improve our performance at group meetings is to evaluate our performance after every

THINKING ABOUT ...

Member Responsibilities

Consider your own behaviour when you are working as part of a group. Which of the preparation, participation, and follow-up guidelines do you need to work on to become a more valuable group member? Why?

meeting. We want to honestly assess our effectiveness at helping the group move toward achieving its goals. What were our strengths? What were our weaknesses? What should we do next time that we did not do during this meeting?

3. **Review decisions.** When decisions were being made during the meeting, what was our role? Did we do all that we could have done to affect the outcome?
4. **Communicate progress.** Often, information conveyed and decisions made at group meetings affect others outside the group. We should consider whether others need to be apprised of developments.
5. **Follow up.** If we received assignments during the meeting, we should be sure to complete them to the best of our ability and in a timely fashion.
6. **Review minutes.** When official minutes of the meeting are circulated, we should compare them to our own notes, and note any significant discrepancies. These should be raised at the next meeting, or sooner if we think they might affect ongoing work.

IN BRIEF

Member Responsibilities in Meetings

Group members have responsibilities before, during, and after meetings.

- *Prepare:* study the agenda and minutes and be ready to contribute and ask questions.
- *Participate:* stay focused, listen, contribute, ask questions, take notes, play devil's advocate.
- *Follow up:* review notes, decisions, and minutes, evaluate effectiveness, complete any assigned tasks.

Leadership

Performance of task, maintenance, and procedural roles assists groups to accomplish their goals, but good leadership is also necessary. Over the years, scholars have offered a great number of different definitions of leadership, but most definitions share the notion that **leadership** is the process of influencing group members to accomplish group goals (Shaw, 1981, p. 317). As you will recall from Chapter 1, influencing others is a basic communication function. We exert influence when we change the beliefs and actions of others. Leadership is more than just exerting influence, however. It is the use of influence to aid a group to reach its goals. Leadership involves motivating other group members to work toward common objectives. Leadership serves a group in a number of ways.

The Function of Leadership

Fisher and Ellis (1990) argue that leaders perform "vital functions" in the group. These functions include influencing the group's procedures and task accomplishment and maintaining satisfactory relationships between members.

Because the various member roles that we have already seen are designed to fulfill each of these functions, leadership can be shared by all group members. However, in most groups, some of the roles that are necessary for effective group functioning are not assumed by any members. Current thinking is that the leader's role is to step in and assume whatever roles the group needs filled

COMMUNICATE! Using InfoTrac College Edition

Using the Keyword Search, enter the name *Robert K. Greenleaf.* Scroll to "Reflections on Robert K. Greenleaf and Servant-leadership" by Larry Spears, December 1996. How well does Greenleaf's concept of a leader square with your own? Do you agree with Greenleaf's view that "True leadership emerges from those whose primary motivation is a deep desire to help others"? Can you identify any people in leadership roles who you think are motivated by other desires? What effect do these motives have on the quality of their leadership?

(those that are not being performed by other group members) at a particular time (Rothwell, 1998, p. 168).

Fisher (1985) believes that those filling the leadership role must be versatile and able to adapt their behaviour to the situation. Leaders are adept at listening to the group and becoming attuned to its needs. Based on their perceptions of the group's needs, leaders adapt their behaviour to the situation and influence group members to behave in ways that will lead to goal accomplishment.

Types of Leaders

As we mentioned above, groups can have more than one leader. In addition, leaders can obtain their position in different ways. We will look at two types of leader.

Many groups have a designated **formal leader,** an assigned leader who is given power to influence others. A formal leader is often appointed by some entity outside the group. For example, the director of a university's communication department might appoint a student to chair a student committee created to review the department's degree programs. In other settings, the group itself elects a formal leader. Instead of appointing a student to head the review committee, for example, the director of the communication department may request that the committee elect its own chair. In both cases, the person who assumes formal leadership will have gained legitimate power on which to base his or her attempts to influence the performance of the group. In the first case, the formal leader's authority comes from outside the group; in the second, it comes from within. Some groups may have more than one formal leader. For example, two students may act as co-chairs of the review committee, each assuming an equal authority to exercise influence.

Whether a group has no formal leader, one formal leader, or more than one, several people may play leadership roles. **Informal leaders** are members of the group whose authority to influence stems from the power they gain through their interactions within the group. Informal leaders do not have legitimate power; rather, their attempts to influence are based on their skills, knowledge, or expertise. For example, if members of the student review committee were feeling overwhelmed by data on the various programs offered by the department and the prerequisites and requirements of each one, a group member who had strong organizational skills might assume informal leadership because of his or her ability to help other group members understand how all of the data fit together. Similarly, a member with detailed knowledge of program requirements might emerge as informal leader if others were having difficulty understanding the structure of a particular program, and a member with strong analytical skills might assume informal leadership if the group was having difficulty agreeing on recommendations to modify an obsolete program. Formal leaders are more likely to be effective if they welcome and encourage the contributions of such informal leaders.

Gaining and Maintaining Informal Leadership

According to research by Bormann (1990), members who become informal leaders of a group are not really selected. Rather, they emerge through a two-step process of elimination.

During the first step, group members form crude impressions about one another based on early interactions. During this phase, members who do not demonstrate the commitment or skilfulness necessary to fulfill leadership roles are eliminated. Among those who are least likely to emerge as leaders are those who do not participate (either due to shyness or indifference), those who are overly strong in their opinions and positions and bossy toward others, those who are perceived as uninformed, less intelligent, or unskilled, and those with irritating interpersonal styles.

During the second step, those members who are acceptable leadership contenders may vie for power. Sometimes one contender will become an informal leader because the group faces a crisis that he or she recognizes and is best able to help the group remedy. At other times, a contender may become an informal leader because members of the group have come to trust him or her and openly support his or her attempts to influence.

In some groups, one of the contenders will eventually be recognized by most members of the group as the informal leader. In other groups, two or more contenders may comfortably share informal leadership by specializing and engaging in complementary behaviour. For example, one leader might be particularly attuned to group relationships and may use influence to keep conflict at healthy levels. The other leader may be skilled at keeping the group on track and moving through the agenda during meetings. In general, however, the members of the group will be more susceptible to the informal leadership of those contenders who provide appropriate combinations of task, maintenance, and procedural influences.

OBSERVE & ANALYZE
Journal Activity

Informal Leadership

Think of a group of at least five members to which you belong and in which informal leaders have emerged. Remembering that one member may perform more than one member role, identify the roles that each member of the group seems to play. Then, answer the following questions: Is there a formal leader? Who are the informal leaders? How did the informal leaders emerge? What does each informal leader do to lead you to believe that he or she is providing leadership? Why were each of the other members of the group eliminated from assuming informal leadership? If the goals of the group changed, how might leadership roles be affected?

Communicating to Achieve Leadership

We have identified a number of specific behaviours that can eliminate a group member from contention for leadership, but what behaviours are likely to cause a member to be selected? Because leadership is demonstrated through communication behaviours, following these recommendations can help us to gain influence in the groups to which we belong.

1. **Come to group meetings prepared.** Uninformed members rarely achieve leadership, whereas those who demonstrate expertise gain the power to influence others.

2. **Actively participate in discussions.** When members do not participate, others may view them as disinterested or uninformed. We indicate our interest in and commitment to the group by participating in group discussions.

3. **Actively listen to the ideas and opinions of others.** Because leadership requires analyzing what a group needs, a leader must understand the ideas

OBSERVE & ANALYZE
Journal Activity

Leadership Readiness

Identify a group (such as a student committee or social group) that you would like to lead. Assess your readiness for taking on leadership of the group. What qualifications do you have to show that you are knowledgeable about the group's work, that you are well prepared, that you have the skills needed to fill task-related, maintenance, and procedural roles, and that you can manage meaning?

and opinions of all members. When we actively listen, we also demonstrate our willingness to consider a point of view different from our own. Group members are more likely to be influenced by a person who they believe really understands them.

4. **Avoid stating overly strong opinions.** When group members perceive that someone is inflexible, they are less likely to accept that person as a leader.

5. **Actively manage meaning.** During problem solving, members can become confused about what is being said or unclear about what is happening. As a result, they experience uncertainty. If we have a mental map or framework that can help the group clarify and understand the issues it is facing, we can use it to influence the group. Gail T. Fairhurst has explored how leaders manage meaning in groups; she calls this process **framing.**

SPOTLIGHT ON SCHOLARS

Gail T. Fairhurst, University of Cincinnati

According to Gail T. Fairhurst, who has been studying organizational communication throughout her career, leadership is neither a trait possessed by only some people nor a simple set of behaviours that can be learned and then applied in any situation. Rather, Fairhurst's research has shown that leadership is the process of creating social reality by managing the meanings that are assigned to certain behaviours, activities, programs, and events. Further, she believes leadership is best understood as a relational process.

Fairhurst's work is now focused on how organizational leaders frame issues for their members. Framing is the process of managing meaning by selecting and highlighting some aspects of a subject while excluding others. When we communicate our frames to others, we manage meaning because we are asserting that our interpretation of the subject, and not others, should be taken as *real*. How leaders choose to verbally frame events at work is one way that they influence workers' and others' perceptions.

Framing is especially important when the organization experiences change. To reduce uncertainty during times of change, members of the organization seek to understand what the change means to them personally and to the way they work in the organization. Leaders are expected to help members understand what is happening and what it means. By framing the change, leaders select and highlight some features of the change while downplaying others, providing a lens through which organizational members can understand what the change means.

In *The Art of Framing* (with Robert A. Sarr), Fairhurst identifies five language forms or devices that leaders use to frame information: metaphors, jargon or catch phrases, contrast, spin, and stories. Suppose a company is to be substantially downsized. Here is how the company's leaders

(continued)

might use each of these devices to influence workers' perceptions of the change:

- Metaphors show how the change is similar to something that is already familiar. For instance, the leaders may frame downsizing with weight-loss and prizefighting metaphors, suggesting that the organization is "out of shape and in need of getting down to a better fighting trim so that it can compete effectively."
- Jargon or catch phrases are similar to metaphors. The user helps people understand a change by using language with which they are already familiar. For example, the leaders may frame their vision of the downsized company by using a catch phrase such as "lean and mean."
- Contrast frames help people understand what the change is by identifying what it is not. For example, the leaders would be using contrast frames if they suggest that the downsizing "is not an attempt to undermine the union; it is simply an attempt to remain competitive."
- Spin frames cast the change in either a positive or negative light. The leaders may use a positive spin frame by pointing out that there will be no forced layoffs, only early retirements and natural attrition to reduce the size of the workforce.
- Story frames make the change seem more real by serving as a model. For example, the leaders may recount the success of another well-known company that downsized in similar circumstances.

Fairhurst has also studied how the meaning of a change is continually reframed as members of the organization work out the specifics of how to implement it. She analyzed the transcripts of tape-recorded conversations between managers and their subordinates during times when a company was undergoing a significant change in the way it worked. Her analysis has revealed that employees' reactions to change are often framed as "predicaments" or "problems," showing that they are confused or unclear about the change. Sometimes employees feel that what they are being asked to do is in conflict with the goals of the change. In response, the leader might counter the employees' predicament by using one of several reframes; for example, personalization. Using personalization, a leader might point out the specific behaviours that an individual member needs to adopt to be in line with the change. Fairhurst suggests that such reframing techniques help members understand what to do next to bring about the change.

Fairhurst's experience in analyzing the real conversations of managers and subordinates indicates that many of those in organizational leadership roles are not very good at framing and, as a result, may need to be trained to develop mental models that they can draw on to be more effective in their day-to-day interactions with workers. For complete citations of many of Fairhurst's publications, see the references list at the end of this book.

Gender Differences in Emerging Leaders

A question that has generated considerable research is whether the gender of a leader has any effect on a group's acceptance of leadership. Some research suggests that gender does affect group acceptance, but not because women lack the necessary skills. A persistent research finding is that messages are evaluated differently depending on the source of the message (Aries, 1998, p. 65). Thus, the same behaviour may be perceived differently depending on whether it is performed by a woman or a man. For example, a group member says, "I think we are belabouring this point and should move on." If the speaker is a woman, the comment may well be perceived as bossy, dominating, or critical. If a man makes the same comment, he is more likely to be perceived as being insightful and task-oriented. One problem women face is that their efforts to show leadership may be differently interpreted.

Moreover, gender-role stereotypes can lead to devaluing co-operative and supportive behaviours that many women use quite skilfully. Yet, as Helgesen (1990) points out, many women are successful leaders because they respond to people and their problems with flexibility and because they are able to break down barriers between people at all levels of an organization.

Fortunately, changes in perception are occurring as the notion of *effective* leadership changes. Andrews (1992) supports this conclusion, noting that it is more important to consider the unique character of a group and the skills of the person serving as leader than the gender of the leader (p. 90). She goes on to show that a complex interplay of factors (including how much power the leader has) influences effectiveness more than gender does. Other research (Jurma & Wright, 1990) has shown that men and women are equally capable of leading task-oriented groups (p. 110).

Recent studies have shown that task-relevant communication is the only significant predictor of who will emerge as leaders, regardless of gender. Hawkins's (1995) study noted no significant gender differences in the production of task-relevant communication. Such communication, it seems, is the key to emergent leadership in task-oriented group interaction—for people of either gender.

IN BRIEF

Leadership

Leadership is the process of influencing group members to accomplish group goals.

- Leaders can be formal (appointed or elected) or informal.
- Informal leaders gain power through a two-step process of elimination.
- Leadership qualifications are demonstrated through effective communication behaviours.

Leading Group Meetings

How many times have we complained that a meeting we attended was a waste of time? Good group meetings do not just happen. Rather, they are intentionally planned, facilitated, and followed up. One of the principal duties that both formal and informal leaders perform is to plan and run effective group meetings. Here are some guidelines that can help leaders make meetings productive.

Before the Meeting

1. **Decide who should attend the meeting.** In most cases, all members of a group will attend all meetings. However, people outside the group may also be invited to attend all or part of some meetings
   - to provide expertise or advice (e.g., A land acquisition committee may require the advice of a solicitor).
   - to provide information (e.g., The campus discipline committee may want to hear eye-witness testimony).
   - to protect their own interests (e.g., Neighbours of a proposed university residence may be invited to hear deliberations of the site selection committee).

2. **Speak with each participant prior to the meeting.** It is important to give each group member an opportunity to have input into the planning of the meeting, and it is important that the leader understand members' positions and personal goals. Spending time pre-working issues helps the leader anticipate conflicts that are likely to arise and plan how to manage them so that the group makes effective decisions and maintains cohesiveness.

3. **Arrange an appropriate location and meeting time.** The location must be an appropriate size for the group, must be conveniently located, and must have all the equipment and supplies the group will need to work effectively. The leader may have to arrange for audiovisual equipment, computers, or other specialized equipment. Groups become less effective in long meetings, so ideally, a meeting should last no longer than 90 minutes. If a meeting must be planned for a longer period, scheduling hourly breaks will help prevent fatigue.

4. **Prepare the agenda.** An agenda is an organized outline of the items that need to be covered during a meeting. Items for the agenda come from reviewing the minutes of the last meeting to determine what the group agreed to take as next steps and from identifying new issues that have arisen since the last meeting. Effective leaders make sure that all group members have an opportunity to contribute to the agenda, and that the agenda is appropriate to the length of the meeting. Figure 11.1 shows an agenda for a meeting of a distance education committee assigned to decide which one of three courses to add to its on-line offerings in the coming year.

5. **Distribute the agenda.** The agenda should be in the hands of group members several days before the meeting. If they do not get the agenda well ahead of time, they will not be able to prepare for the meeting.

WWW

COMMUNICATE!
Using Technology

The larger and more complex a group becomes the greater the challenges faced by its leaders. Visit the Web site *House of Commons Canada: Précis of Procedure* at **www.parl.gc.ca/information/about/process/house/precis/titpg-e.htm**. Who is the formal leader(s) in the House of Commons? How closely do the responsibilities assigned to the leaders of the House compare with those that we have assigned to leaders during our discussion of leadership in this chapter? Can you suggest a reason for any differences you observe? Do House of Commons procedures allow for the emergence of informal leaders? Who might they be?

During the Meeting

1. **Review and modify the agenda.** The leader should begin the meeting by reviewing the agenda and modifying it based on suggestions from and agreeable to the group. Because circumstances can change between the time that an agenda is distributed and the time of the meeting, this review assures the group that all items on the agenda are still important and relevant. It also gives members some measure of control over the items to be discussed and the order in which they are discussed.

2. **Monitor member roles and play needed roles that are unfilled by others.** The role of the leader during a discussion is to provide whatever task or procedural direction and relationship management the group lacks. Leaders need to be aware of what specific roles are needed by the group at a specific time. When other group members assume the necessary roles, the leader need do nothing, but when no one assumes a needed role, the leader

should perform it. For example, if the leader notices that some people are talking too much and that no one else is trying to draw out quieter members, he or she should assume the gatekeeper role and ask reluctant members to contribute.

3. **Monitor the time so that the group stays on schedule.** It is easy for a group to get bogged down in a discussion. Although another group member may serve as expediter, it is the leader's responsibility to make sure the group stays on schedule.
4. **Monitor conflicts and intervene as needed.** A healthy level of conflict should be encouraged in the group so that issues are fully examined and debated. If the conflict level rises to the point that the group becomes dysfunctional, however, the leader may need to mediate so that member relationships are not unduly strained.

To: Distance Education Course Selection Committee Members
From: Adharma Kapoor, Chair
Date: August 1, 2004
Subject: Agenda for Meeting of August 8

The next meeting of the Distance Education Course Selection Committee will be held in Room 1234 of Patterson Hall on August 7, 2004, from 3:00 to 4:30 p.m.

Meeting Objectives:

- To familiarize ourselves with each of three courses that have been proposed for Internet-based delivery beginning in the January 2005 term
- To evaluate each course in terms of the established selection criteria for online distance courses (Policy Statement AD-133-2002)
- To arrive at a consensus decision on which of the three courses to offer

Agenda for Group Discussion:

1. Review of Philosophy 1401: Ancient Philosophies
   Report by Justin Greene on the Philosophy 1401 proposal
   Committee questions
   Evaluation of PHIL 1401 in terms of selection criteria
2. Review of Art History 1336: Prehistoric Times to Giotto
   Report by Marique Volpi on Art History 1336 proposal
   Committee questions
   Evaluation of ARTH 1336 in terms of selection criteria
3. Review of Communication 1235: Introduction to Interpersonal Communication
   Report by Kathryn Sinclair on Communication 1235
   Committee questions
   Evaluation of COMM 1235 in terms of selection criteria
4. Consensus building discussion and decision
   Which proposal best satisfies the established selection criteria?
   Are there non-criteria-related factors to consider?
   Which proposal is most acceptable to all members?
5. Discussion of next steps and task assignments
6. Date of next meeting.

Figure 11.1
Agenda for committee meeting

5. **Periodically check to see if the group is ready to make a decision.** The leader of the group should listen for agreement and move the group into its formal decision process when he or she senses that discussion is no longer adding new insights.
6. **Implement the group's decision rules.** The leader is responsible for ensuring that the decision-making process that the group has agreed to is used. If the group is deciding by consensus, the leader must make sure that all members feel that the chosen alternative is one that they can support. If the group is deciding by majority rule, the leader calls for the vote and tallies the results.
7. **Before ending the meeting, summarize decisions.** To bring closure to a meeting and to make sure that each member leaves with a clear understanding of what has been accomplished, the leader should summarize what has happened in the meeting, reiterate task responsibilities assigned to members, and review the next steps that have been planned.
8. **Ask the group to decide if and when another meeting is needed.** Ongoing groups should be careful not to meet just for the sake of meeting, but scheduling a needed meeting can be most easily accomplished when everyone is together in the same room. Scheduling the meeting at this time ensures that enough time is allowed for assigned tasks to be completed and also effectively creates a deadline for the completion of those tasks. The purpose of future meetings will dictate the agenda that will need to be prepared.

Michael Newman/PhotoEdit, Inc.

Leaders need to maintain awareness of the specific roles that are needed by the group at a specific time.

Meeting Follow-up

1. **Review the meeting outcomes and process.** A good leader learns how to be more effective by reflecting on and analyzing how well the previous meeting went. Leaders need to think about whether the meeting accomplished its goals and whether group cohesion was improved or damaged in the process. Perhaps most importantly, the leader should review and evaluate his or her own performance. A conscientious leader carefully considers the entire meeting, especially any problematic episodes, and asks, "What could I have done at that point to prevent that problem from arising or to resolve it more effectively?"
2. **Prepare and distribute a summary of meeting outcomes.** Although many groups have a member who serves as the recorder and distributes minutes (recording secretary), some groups rely on their leaders to perform this task. A written record of what was agreed to, accomplished, and next steps serves to remind group members of the work they have to do. If the group does have a recorder, the leader should check to make sure that minutes are distributed in a timely manner.
3. **Repair damaged relationships through informal conversations.** If the debate during the meeting has been heated, it is likely that some people have damaged their relationships with others or left the meeting feeling angry or hurt. Leaders can help repair relationships by seeking out these participants and talking with them. Through listening and empathizing (supporting and interpreting), leaders can soothe hurt feelings and spark a recommitment to the group.
4. **Follow up with members to see how they are progressing on items assigned to them.** When group members have been assigned responsibility for specific tasks, the leader should check with them to see if they have encountered any problems in completing them.

IN BRIEF

Leading Group Meetings

Group leaders have three sets of responsibilities in leading group meetings:

- planning before the meeting
- facilitating during the meeting
- following up after the meeting.

Other Leadership Functions

As we have seen, effective leadership is an essential component of successful group meetings, but guiding decision-making or problem-solving processes in organized meetings is not the only function of leaders. Anyone who has been a member of a sports team, a community group, or a work team knows that players, volunteers, and employees look to leaders for guidance of many sorts and in many settings. In addition, in our everyday lives, we frequently seek direction from people, such as teachers, parents, or mentors, whom we consider leaders in our ongoing journey toward our own personal development. Two particularly important leadership functions are coaching and counselling.

Coaching

Coaching "is a day-to-day, hands-on process of helping others recognize opportunities to improve their work performance" (Robbins & Hunsaker, 1996, p. 151). A good coach observes what group members are doing, points out individual members' problems or inefficiencies in their work methods, offers suggestions for improving those work methods, and helps the group member develop skill in using the method effectively. Of course, effective coaching requires a supportive climate and the use of the active listening skills of questioning, paraphrasing, and supporting.

1. **An effective coach is technically adept and a keen observer.** We cannot coach others effectively if we do not ourselves understand the correct or more efficient way to perform the subject task or skill. However, this technical expertise is of little value unless we can carefully watch others perform and clearly identify the deficiencies in their performance. Not every great performer is an effective coach, and an effective coach need not be an outstanding performer. Rather, the effective coach knows *exactly* how the task or skill should be performed and can critically analyze another's performance to see *exactly* where the performer is deficient. For example, Matthieu is chair of a Student Union committee delegated to recommend effective ways of promoting safe sex on campus. If Matthieu is a senior communication major who has studied how to give effective public presentations, has given many public presentations himself, and has volunteered at a local high school as a public speaking coach and judge, he would be in a good position to coach the other members of his team when they are rehearsing the presentation that they must give before an open meeting of the student government.

2. **An effective coach both analyzes the performance and provides specific suggestions for improvement.** Some people are capable of recognizing poor performance, but they are not able to tell the performer what he or she is doing wrong or what to do to improve. As a coach, we must be able to do both. For example, Jorge, a new sales clerk in an electronics shop, has extensive product knowledge but is weak on closing sales because he misses customers' verbal and nonverbal cues that they are ready to buy. Alicia, his sales manager, spots Jorge's problem—his failure to close—but also applies her expertise to help Jorge recognize the verbal and nonverbal cues that indicate the right time for moving into the close.

3. **An effective coach creates a supportive problem-solving environment.** Some people are excellent observers and know exactly what must be done to improve performance but are ineffective coaches because they antagonize the person they are trying to help by being too negative, aggressive, overbearing, or hostile. Effective coaches recognize that they and the people

THINKING ABOUT . . .

Effective Coaching

Think about two occasions when you were coached. Pick one occasion in which the coaching was effective and another in which it was not. What similarities and differences can you recall in the two coaches' approach?

TEST YOUR COMPETENCE

Coaching Skills

Working in groups of three, have each person think of a communication problem that he or she experiences. Have one group member describe or demonstrate his or her problem, while a second acts as a coach. The third person observes. When the first two have finished, the observer coaches the coach, by providing feedback on his or her coaching effectiveness. Change roles and repeat the exercise until everyone has had an opportunity to play each of the three roles.

they are coaching are on the same side, that by strengthening the performance of a team member, they strengthen the whole team. By employing active listening skills, responding empathically, and giving useful feedback (constructive criticism and praise), they create a supportive problem-solving environment which will help the person improve his or her performance.

An effective coach will often begin by acknowledging an area of strength, thereby recognizing the group member's undeveloped potential. For instance, Alicia may praise Jorge's product knowledge by saying, "Jorge, I've heard you talking to customers, and I am greatly impressed by your product knowledge. Your extensive computer background is a real asset to our sales team. I think you're going to do well at this job." She would then demonstrate further support for Jorge by offering to help him do better. "Would you like to know how you can increase our sales volume, and your commissions, by increasing your sales percentage?" This approach helps Jorge understand that he and Alicia have shared goals, and he will be more receptive to her instructions on how to recognize customers' verbal and nonverbal cues. Finally, when the person does succeed, the effective coach offers praise but also encourages the person to reflect on why he or she was successful: "A $3,500 sale! Good work, Jorge. What did you do differently this time to close such a big deal?"

Counselling

Where coaching deals primarily with work performance, helping others to improve their skills, counselling is usually directed to helping others deal with their personal problems. Specifically, **counselling** is the act of discussing a person's emotional problem in order to resolve the problem or to help the person to better cope with it (Robbins & Hunsaker, 1996, p. 153). Under the pressures of school, work, or, in some cases, just life in general, people experience a variety of problems that affect their personal lives and their academic or professional performance. Such problems could include, for example, the death of a loved one, a lingering physical or mental illness, the termination of a relationship, financial pressures, academic failure, peer pressure, substance abuse, weight control, or any combination of these or a host of other difficulties.

In a variety of group contexts, leaders are called upon to demonstrate their leadership to assist group members through counselling. Effective counsellors maintain confidentiality, listen empathically to the other person's expression of his or her feelings, and help the person determine what to do, including the possibility of seeking professional help.

1. **Effective counsellors assure others of confidentiality.** Personal problems are just that—personal. Under most circumstances effective counsellors do not tell anyone else about a person's problems. A person's desire for confidentiality does not, however, relieve us of the ethical responsibility to let him or her know the limits to which confidentiality will be maintained. For example, we would be morally wrong to keep confidential information that could endanger the safety or well-being of other people or even of the person himself or herself. Under such circumstances, we should first advise the person to disclose the information to an appropriate authority and, second, inform the person that we also are ethically bound to disclose.
2. **Effective counsellors are good listeners.** Good counselling begins with empathic listening. Empathic listening will lead us to clarifying questions, paraphrases to ensure understanding, and above all, to appropriate and comforting replies. Supportiveness and, at times, interpreting responses are key to effective counselling. When people are distraught, they need to talk about their feelings. Only after they have vented these powerful emotions can they begin the logical problem-solving process. Effective counsellors therefore must demonstrate caring and patience to allow people the time they need to deal with their emotions.
3. **Effective counsellors help people find help.** At times the best thing a good leader can do is to suggest that a person seek professional help to deal with his or her problem. Many of the problems that we encounter do not require professional treatment, but when we recognize that another's problem is long-term or severe, we are ethically bound to use our leadership—our influence—to help the person find appropriate professional guidance. By way of preparation, it is useful to be aware of the kinds of private and government-funded professional services available in our municipality and province and to know how such services can be accessed.

Leaders cannot be expected to and should not attempt to act as professional counsellors, but when they are faced with simple, short-term problems, they can use their influence to help others sort through and triumph over their personal difficulties.

THINKING ABOUT . . .

Counselling Guidelines

How can we know when another person needs more help than we are qualified to give? Develop a list of ten guidelines to help you recognize when peer counselling is not enough and when you should instead counsel the other person to seek professional help. Be prepared to share your guidelines with the class.

IN BRIEF

Coaching and Counselling

Coaching and counselling are two important functions that leaders are often called upon to perform.

- Effective coaches observe what people are doing, recognize the deficiencies in their performance, and assist them to correct their methods of performance to eliminate the deficiencies.
- Effective counsellors discuss a person's emotional problem with the goal of resolving the problem or helping the person to better cope with it.

Evaluating Group Effectiveness

"A camel is a horse built by a committee." The point of this old cliché is to suggest that groups are always less successful than individuals at accomplishing tasks. As we have just seen, this prejudice is unjustified, but if we are to avoid ending up with camels when we want horses, we need to understand how to assess our groups' effectiveness and how to improve group performance based on those evaluations. A group can be evaluated in terms of the quality of its overall performance, the quality of individual participation and role taking, and the quality of the leadership.

Overall Performance

The questionnaire in Figure 11.2 provides one method for evaluating the quality of a group's overall performance. It evaluates group performance in terms of three major criteria: the characteristics of the group, the relationship among the members, and the group's problem-solving ability.

Group Performance Evaluation Chart

Respond to each of the following questions using this scale:

1 = always 2 = often 3 = sometimes 4 = rarely 5 = never

Characteristics of the Group

1. Did the group have a clearly defined goal to which most members were committed? ____
2. Was the group an appropriate size to undertake the tasks required to meet its goals? ____
3. Was the group sufficiently diverse to ensure that all relevant viewpoints were expressed? ____
4. Did group cohesiveness aid in task accomplishment? ____
5. Did group norms help accomplish goals and maintain relationships? ____
6. Was the physical setting conducive to accomplishing the group's work? ____

Relationship Among Members

1. Did all group members feel valued and respected by others? ____
2. Were members comfortable interacting with others? ____
3. Did members balance speaking time so that all members participated? ____
4. Were conflicts viewed as growth opportunities and were they managed collaboratively? ____
5. Did members like each other and enjoy each other's company? ____

Problem-Solving Ability

1. Did the group take time to define and analyze its problem? ____
2. Was high-quality information presented to ensure understanding of the problem? ____
3. Did the group develop evaluation criteria before suggesting solutions? ____
4. Were the criteria discussed sufficiently and based on all of the information available? ____
5. Did the group use effective brainstorming techniques to develop a comprehensive list of possible solutions? ____
6. Did the group fairly apply each evaluation criterion to each possible solution? ____
7. Did the group follow its decision-making rules in choosing among possible solutions? ____
8. Did the group arrive at a decision that members agreed to support? ____

Figure 11.2
Checklist for evaluating overall group performance

That a group meets to discuss an issue does not necessarily mean that it will arrive at a decision. Indeed, some groups are so unproductive that, even after hours of discussion, they adjourn without having accomplished anything. On the other hand, some groups are dedicated to solving such serious and complex problems that a final decision cannot be made without several, sometimes many, meetings. In such cases, it is important that the group adjourn each meeting with a clear understanding of what part of the task has been accomplished and what the next step in the process will be. When a group *finishes* its work without having produced anything, the results are likely to be frustration and disillusionment.

Individual Performance Evaluation Chart

Name of Group Member: ____________________

Rate the participant named above on each of the following points using this scale:

1 = excellent 2 = good 3 = average 4 = passable 5 = poor

Contribution to Meetings

1. Was prepared and knowledgeable ____
2. Contributed ideas and opinions ____
3. Actively listened to the ideas of others ____
4. Politely voiced disagreement ____
5. Completed tasks assigned for between meeting periods ____

Performance of Task-Related Roles

1. Acted as an information or opinion giver ____
2. Acted as an information seeker ____
3. Acted as an analyzer ____

Performance of Maintenance Roles

1. Acted as a supporter ____
2. Acted as a tension reliever ____
3. Acted as a harmonizer ____
4. Acted as an interpreter ____

Performance of Procedural Roles

1. Acted as an expediter ____
2. Acted as a recorder ____
3. Acted as a gatekeeper ____

Avoidance of Self-Centred Roles

1. Avoided acting as aggressor ____
2. Avoided acting as joker ____
3. Avoided acting as withdrawer ____
4. Avoided acting as monopolizer ____

Qualitative Analysis

Based on the quantitative analysis above, write a two- to five-paragraph analysis of this group member's participation. Be sure to give specific examples of the person's behaviour to back up your conclusions.

Figure 11.3
Checklist for evaluating individual participation and role taking

IN BRIEF

Evaluating Group Effectiveness

Evaluation of group effectiveness is an important means of improving group performance. Groups should be evaluated in terms of

- overall performance
- individual participation and role taking
- leadership.

Individual Participation and Role Taking

Although a group will struggle without good leadership, it may not be able to function at all without members who are willing and able to meet the task, maintenance, and procedural needs of the group. The assessment form in Figure 11.3 provides a simple checklist that can be used for evaluating the individual performance of each group member.

Leadership

If a group has an appointed leader, the evaluation of leadership can focus on that person, unless an informal leader's contribution was more influential. If the group does not have an appointed leader, the evaluation should focus on the performance of the informal leader who emerged as most influential. Figure 11.4 contains a simple checklist for evaluating group leadership.

Leader Performance Evaluation Chart

Name of formal leader if any: ____________________

Name(s) of informal leaders: ____________________
____
____

Which of these leaders was most influential in helping the group meet its goals?

____

Rate this leader on each of the following points using this scale:
1 = always 2 = often 3 = sometimes 4 = rarely 5 = never

1. Demonstrated commitment to the group and its goals ___
2. Actively listened to ideas and opinions of others ___
3. Adapted his or her behaviour to the immediate needs of the group ___
4. Avoided stating overly strong opinions ___
5. Managed meaning for the group by framing issues and ideas ___
6. Was prepared for all meetings ___
7. Kept the group on task and on schedule ___
8. Made sure that conflicts were handled effectively ___
9. Implemented the group's decision rules effectively ___
10. Worked to repair damaged relationships ___
11. Followed up after meetings to see how members were progressing on assignments ___

Figure 11.4
Checklist for evaluating leadership

TEST YOUR COMPETENCE

Analyzing Participation

Divide into groups of four to six. Each group should be assigned or should select a problem that requires research to solve. Problems may relate to campus issues such as What should be done to improve parking (advising, registration) on campus? or community issues such as How can citizens be encouraged to recycle (vote in local elections, clear their sidewalks)?

After researching the problem, each group has about 30 to 40 minutes of class time to hold a problem-solving discussion. While group A is discussing, members of group B should observe and, after the discussion is completed, evaluate it. To practise using the three assessment forms, one-third of the observers should do an overall group performance analysis (Figure 11.2), one-third should do an individual performance analysis (Figure 11.3), and one-third should do a leadership analysis (Figure 11.4). After the discussions, the observers should share their observations with the group that they observed. In the next class period, group B holds their discussion, and group A observes and evaluates.

WHAT WOULD YOU DO?
A QUESTION OF ETHICS

"You know, Russell, as the executive of the Student Representative Council, we're going to be in deep trouble if the council doesn't support McGowan's resolution on dues reform and student activity fees. Being a money bill, it will count as a vote of confidence. If your treasurer's motion fails, we will have to resign."

"Well, we'll just have to see to it that all the arguments in favour of that resolution are heard, but in the end it's the council's decision."

"That's very democratic of you, Russell, but you know that if it doesn't pass, you're out on your tail."

"That may be, Sue, but I don't see what I can do about it."

"You don't want to see. Right now the council respects you, and a lot of the members owe you big time. Some of them never would have been elected without your support. If you would just apply a little pressure in a couple of places, you'd get what you want."

"What do you mean?"

"Look, this is a good cause. Without more money the council is going to have to start cutting student services. You've got something on just about every member. Take a couple of members aside and let them know that this is payoff time. I think you'll see that some key votes will swing your way."

Sue may well be right in thinking that Russell can manipulate the outcome of the student government's vote, but should he follow her advice? Why or why not?

Summary

When people interact in groups, they assume roles. A role is a specific pattern of behaviour that a member of a group performs based on the expectations of others.

There are four types of roles: task-related roles, maintenance roles, procedural roles, and self-centred roles. Members choose the roles they will play based on their personalities and the needs of the group. The leadership role is particularly important to effective performance of a group.

Leadership is the process of influencing group members to accomplish goals. Effective leaders perform whatever roles are needed by the group that are not being performed by other group members. Groups may have a single leader, but leadership is frequently shared among group members. Groups may have both formal and informal leaders. Formal leaders are given authority either by some entity outside the group or by the group members themselves. Informal leaders emerge through a two-stage selection process. Individuals who want to become recognized as informal leaders in a group should come to group meetings prepared, actively participate in discussions, actively listen to others, avoid appearing bossy or stating overly strong opinions, and manage meaning for other participants by framing.

Both members and leaders can improve the effectiveness of the meetings they attend by preparing before the meeting, participating during the meeting, and following up after the meeting.

Glossary

Review the following key terms:

aggressor (297) — a group member who seeks to enhance his or her own status by criticizing others' contributions, by blaming others for problems, and by deflating the ego or lessening the status of others.

analyzer (295) — a group member who is expected to probe the content of other members' contributions and the soundness of their reasoning during discussion.

coaching (311) — a day-to-day, hands-on process of helping others recognize opportunities to improve their work performance.

counselling (312) — the act of discussing a person's emotional problem in order to resolve the problem or to help the person to better cope with it.

expediter (296) — a group member who is expected to be mindful of what the group is trying to accomplish and to help move the group through the agenda of its meeting.

formal leader (302) — an assigned leader who is given legitimate power to influence other members of a group.

framing (304) — managing meaning in a group.

gatekeeper (296) — a group member who manages the flow of conversation so that all members of a group have an opportunity to participate in a discussion.

harmonizer (295) — a group member who intervenes in a discussion when conflict is threatening to harm group cohesiveness or the relationship between particular group members.

informal leader (302) — a member of a group whose authority to influence stems from the power he or she gains through interactions within the group.

information or opinion giver (294) — group members who provide content for discussion.

information or opinion seeker (294) — group members who probe others for their ideas and opinions on issues relevant to the group's discussion.

interpreter (295) — a group member who is familiar with the differences in the social, cultural, and gender orientations of the members of a group and uses this knowledge to help other group members understand each other.

joker (297) — a group member who attempts to draw attention to himself or herself by joking, clowning, and being generally disruptive.

leadership (301) — the process of influencing group members to accomplish group goals.

maintenance role (295) — a specific pattern of behaviour that helps a group to develop and maintain good member relationships and group cohesiveness, and to control conflict.

minutes (296) — a formal and official record of a group's deliberations and decisions.

monopolizer (297) — a group member who talks all the time to give the impression that he or she is well read, knowledgeable, and of value to the group.

procedural role (296) — a specific pattern of behaviour that helps a group to manage its problem-solving process.

recorder (296) — a group member who takes careful notes of what a group has decided and the evidence upon which its decisions are based.

role (294) — a specific pattern of behaviour that one group member performs based on the expectations of other members.

self-centred role (297) — a specific pattern of behaviour that focuses attention on group members' personal needs and goals at the expense of those of the group.

supporter (295) — a group member who encourages others in the group.

task-related role (294) — a specific pattern of behaviour that directly helps a group accomplish its goals.

tension reliever (295) — a group member who recognizes when others are stressed or tiring and intervenes in some way to relieve the stress or re-energize the group.

withdrawer (297) — a group member who meets his or her own goals at the expense of those of the group by missing meetings or by not participating in the discussion or the work of the group.

SELF-REVIEW

Group Communication from Chapters 10 and 11

How effective are you at working in problem-solving groups? The following checklist can help you evaluate your effectiveness in group settings. Use this scale to assess the frequency with which you display each behaviour:

1 = always 2 = often 3 = occasionally 4 = rarely 5 = never

1. I enjoy working with others to accomplish goals. (Ch. 10) ____
2. I actively listen and keep an open mind during problem-solving discussions. (Ch. 10) ____
3. I adapt my behaviour to the norms of the group. (Ch. 10) ____
4. I am comfortable with conflict. (Ch. 10) ____
5. I avoid performing self-centred roles in the group. (Ch. 11) ____
6. I am equally adept at performing task-oriented, procedural, and maintenance roles in the group. (Ch. 11) ____
7. I come to group meetings prepared. (Ch. 11) ____
8. During group meetings, I participate actively to contribute to goal accomplishment and maintain good relationships. (Ch. 11) ____
9. After meetings, I complete tasks I have been assigned and review meeting notes and minutes. (Ch. 11) ____

To verify your self-analysis, have a friend or fellow group member complete this review for you. Based on what you have learned from these two analyses, select the group communication behaviour you would most like to improve. To help you accomplish this goal, write a communication improvement plan similar to the one shown in the sample in Chapter 1 (page 26).

four

Developing public speaking skills is important. Why? Skill at public speaking is a form of empowerment. In a public forum, an effective speaker can stimulate interest in members of the audience, helping them to understand and remember. Good public speakers can also influence people's attitudes and behaviour.

In the workplace, effective public speaking skills are essential to advancement. From presenting oral reports and proposals to responding to questions or training workers, management-level employees spend much of their work day in activities that include public speaking.

Some people claim that great speakers are born, not made, but nothing could be further from the truth. Even Demosthenes—the great Athenian often cited as the prototype of the brilliant orator—was criticized as a poor speaker when he first entered public life. The time and effort he invested in improving his speaking skills stands as a testament to the value of hard work. The lesson to be learned? The ability to effectively address an audience is a *learned* skill.

In order to speak effectively in any situation, we need to have a clear strategy for achieving our goal and we must be thoroughly prepared. Effective preparation includes five essential steps that are explained in Chapters 12 through 14: (1) determine a specific speech goal that is adapted to the audience and occasion (Chapter 12); (2) gather and evaluate material for use in the speech (Chapter 12); (3) organize and develop the material in a way that is best suited to the audience and to achieving the speech goal (Chapter 13); (4) adapt the material to the needs of the specific audience for the speech (Chapter 14); and (5) practise the presentation of the speech (Chapter 14).

IV

PUBLIC SPEAKING

Steve Cole/PhotoDisc Green/Getty Images

OBJECTIVES

After you have read this chapter, you should be able to answer these questions:

- What is the difference between a subject area and a speech topic?
- How should a speaker select a topic?
- What is an audience analysis and how is it carried out?
- How do the setting and occasion affect the planning of a speech?
- What is the difference between a general speech goal and a specific speech goal?
- What is a specific goal statement and how is it developed?
- What are the key sources of information for speakers?
- What is the difference between a factual statement and an expert opinion?
- To what extent must speakers acknowledge their information sources?
- What is a thesis statement and how is it developed?

CHAPTER 12

Topic and Research

Talia Karabatsos is a marine biologist. She knows that her audience wants to hear her talk about marine biology, but she does not know which aspect of the subject will be of most interest.

Tim Brown is running for office. He has been invited to speak to a group of homeowners in the West End. His goal is to motivate these constituents to vote for him.

Yu Wong, a graduate student in pharmacology, has been invited to speak to students at his former high school. He has a lot to say to these students coming up behind him, but most of all, he wants them to understand the qualities they need to develop in order to do well in college.

Ayanna Cartland is taking a public speaking course, and her first speech to her class is scheduled for two weeks from tomorrow. So far, she has no idea what she is going to speak about.

Do any of these situations seem familiar? Talia has a general subject, but it is too broad for a single speech. Tim has identified a goal, but does not know what topic will help him to achieve it. Yu has isolated his most important message, but must now figure out how to present it to this audience. Then there is Ayanna. All she is sure of is that she must give a speech—soon.

Effective speech preparation will help solve all of these problems. This chapter considers the first and second steps: (1) determining a specific speech goal that is adapted to the audience and occasion, and (2) gathering and evaluating material for use in the speech.

Selecting a Topic from a Subject Area

Co-ordinators of conferences, symposia, and public meetings normally invite people who have expertise in a relevant subject to speak at their events, but selecting the actual topic of the speech is often left to the speaker. What is the difference between a subject and a topic? A **subject** is a broad area of knowledge, such as the stock market, baseball, conservation biology, or the history of the Middle East. A **topic** is a specific aspect of a subject. It is narrow and focused, allowing a speaker to state a main idea and thoroughly explain, support, or defend it in the space of a speech. A person could talk for days about the stock market. A speaker who chose this subject might focus his or her speech on any of a number of specific topics such as the Toronto Stock Exchange, investment strategies, or bull versus bear markets.

Identifying Subjects

An audience chooses to listen to a speaker because of his or her perceived expertise in a particular subject. When we are asked to give a speech, we should begin by identifying subjects (1) that we consider important and (2) that we know something about, and then select suitable topics from within those subjects.

Subjects that meet these criteria might include vocations (e.g., area of study, prospective profession, or present job), hobbies or leisure activities, and special interests (e.g., social, economic, scientific, artistic, educational, or political concerns). For example, law is Joshua's vocation, tennis his hobby, and illiteracy his special concern; these are subjects from which he could draw topics.

Even professional speakers can get in over their heads when they attempt to speak on subjects they know little about. It is especially important for inexperienced speakers to choose subjects in which they have already spent months or years developing expertise and insight. Figure 12.1 shows a sample of student subjects under the headings vocation, hobby, and special interest.

Vocation	Hobby	Special Interest
journalism	soccer	victimless crimes
marketing	guitar	governmental ethics
teaching	travel	air pollution
fashion design	photography	cloning
engineering	hockey	hunger relief
fire fighting	hiking	same-sex marriage
computer programming	magic	Trans-Canada Trail
medicine	sailing	censorship
banking	chess	national parks
agriculture	swimming	underwater wrecks

Figure 12.1
Lists of student subjects

Brainstorming for Topics

Once we have identified a subject area, a number of topics may spring to mind, but the chances of selecting a good topic are improved by identifying a number of possible topics before making a choice. Brainstorming, as we saw in Chapter 10, is a good method of generating ideas.

To brainstorm for topics, Gail, who is giving her first in-class speech, first divides a sheet of paper into three columns, which she heads vocations, hobbies, and special interests, as shown in Figure 12.1. She then lists as many subjects as possible under each of the three headings. Then she writes each subject that appeals to her on the top of a separate sheet of paper and brainstorms as many topics as she can for that subject, trying to list at least 20 topics for each subject before evaluating any. Finally, she marks the topics that she finds interesting and those that she thinks might interest her audience (her classmates). For example, if Gail listed magic under the hobby subject heading, she might then brainstorm some of the topics shown in Figure 12.2.

Brainstorming works because it is easier to select a topic from a list than it is to come up with a topic out of the blue. People who do use the out-of-the-blue approach to finding a topic often pick a poor one because they choose the first or second idea that comes to mind. By brainstorming, we give ourselves a broad range of choices.

OBSERVE & ANALYZE
Journal Activity

Brainstorming for Topics

Follow the method described here to brainstorm for speech topics.

1. Identify at least three subject areas (one vocational interest, one hobby, and one special issue of concern to you).
2. Brainstorm at least 20 topics for each subject.
3. Select the topic that appeals to you most.

Note: If, in assigning your first speech, your instructor has specified different subject areas than the ones listed in (1), use those instead.

Hobby: Magic		
tricks	Houdini	secrets
paraphernalia	Doug Henning	vanishing
staging	training	trap doors
sleight-of-hand	Magic Castle	staging
vocabulary	displacement	kids' shows
card tricks	animals	dexterity
dangers	rigging	rope tricks

Figure 12.2
Brainstorming

IN BRIEF

Selecting a Topic

To identify a good speech topic:

1. Identify subjects that you consider important and know something about.
2. Brainstorm for topics under each subject.
3. Select the topic that you find most compelling and that your audience will find most interesting.

Analyzing the Audience

No one can succeed as a speaker without understanding one critical fact: a public presentation is a communication interaction between a specific speaker and a specific audience. Just as an interpersonal communication event is changed if one or both of the participants are changed, a public communication event is changed if one or more of the participants are changed. To be effective as speakers, then, it is important that we conduct an audience analysis early in the planning stage so that we know whom we are communicating with. This information will have a significant effect on what topic we choose to speak about, what we choose to say about that topic, and how we choose to say it. An **audience analysis** is the study of the specific audience for a speech. It includes (1) gathering demographic information to determine what the majority of the audience members are like, and (2) predicting audience interest in, knowledge of, and attitude toward the speaker and the topic. The results of this analysis can guide us in selecting material, in organizing the material, and in presenting a speech that is adapted to our audience.

Methods of Gathering Audience Data

There are three main methods of gathering the data we need for an audience analysis.

1. **Observation:** If the members of the audience are people whom we know, such as classmates or partners in the work place, we can observe them. For instance, after just a couple of classes, we can determine the approximate average age of the class members, the ratio of men to women, and the general cultural makeup. As we listen to classmates talk, we learn about their knowledge of and interest in certain issues.
2. **Questioning:** When we are invited to make a speech, we can ask the contact person for audience information. We should particularly ask for audience data that is important to our topic. For example, someone planning to present a scientific speech would want to know the approximate level of the audience's scientific knowledge.
3. **Intelligent guesswork:** If information is unavailable in other ways, we can make informed guesses based on indirect data such as the general profile of people in a certain community or the kinds of people likely to attend a speech on our topic.

Kinds of Audience Data Needed

The first step in analyzing an audience is to gather demographic data to determine ways in which a majority of audience members are alike. Having the following information about the audience is helpful:

Jeff Greenberg/Photo Edit

What challenges would this audience pose to a candidate for city council?

- **Age:** Average age and age range?
- **Educational level:** High school, post-secondary, graduate school, or mixed?
- **Gender:** Predominantly male, predominantly female, or well-balanced?
- **Occupation:** Predominantly one occupation (e.g., nurse, police officer), several occupations, or many occupations?
- **Income:** Average income and income range?
- **Ethnicity:** Predominantly one ethnic group or mixed? (Which groups are represented?)
- **Religion:** Predominantly one religion or mixed? (Which religions are represented?)
- **Community:** Mostly from the same neighbourhood, city, and province, or mixed?
- **Group affiliation:** Mostly from the same social, academic, professional, or community group or mixed? (Which groups are represented?)

Using Data to Predict Audience Reactions

Once we have collected the data, the next step is to use it to predict the audience's interest in, knowledge of, and attitudes toward us and our topic. These predictions will play an important role in the development of our speech strategy, which we will consider in greater detail in the following two chapters.

OBSERVE & ANALYZE
Journal Activity

Audience Analysis

Follow the steps outlined in this section to conduct an analysis of the audience to which you must present your first speech:

1. State the topic on which you plan to speak.
2. Use one or more of the methods of gathering data to collect the kinds of audience data needed.
3. Use the data you collect to predict audience interest, understanding, attitude toward you, and attitude toward your topic. Justify your predictions.

Save the results of this exercise. You will use them later in adapting your presentation to your audience.

Audience interest First, we want to predict how interested our audience is likely to be in the topic. For instance, suppose Hedda is speaking on the dangers of a high-cholesterol diet to her classmates. She can predict that she will have to build audience interest. Why? Because most college or university students are not yet concerned about the link between cholesterol and heart disease. If she were speaking to her classmates' parents, on the other hand—people of prime heart-attack age—she could assume a higher level of interest.

Audience understanding Our second goal is to predict whether the audience has enough background to understand our information. For a speech on big band music, an older audience would be likely to have better background knowledge than a younger audience, but for a speech on rap music, a younger audience would probably be better prepared. If we determine that our listeners do not have the necessary background, we must then consider whether we have time to supply the background they need.

Audience attitude toward the speaker Our third goal is to predict our audience's attitude toward us. Our ability to succeed with an audience is likely to depend on whether the audience perceives us to be credible. **Credibility** is the power to inspire belief, and it is based on the audience's perception of the speaker's knowledge (having the necessary information), trustworthiness (appearing to be honest, dependable, and ethical), and amiability (showing enthusiasm, friendliness, warmth, and concern for members of the audience).

IN BRIEF

Analyzing the Audience

Success as a speaker requires understanding of the audience. Speakers use observation, questioning, and intelligent guesswork to gather information that will allow them to gauge

- audience interest
- audience understanding
- audience attitude toward the speaker
- audience attitude toward the topic.

Audience attitude toward the topic Our final goal is to predict our audience's attitude toward our topic. This prediction is especially important if our goal is to change beliefs or move the audience to action. Audience attitudes are usually revealed in opinions. Without conducting a poll, we cannot be sure of an audience's opinions, but we can make reasonably accurate estimates based on demographic knowledge. For instance, people attending a meeting of a Right-to-Life chapter will look at abortion differently than will people attending a local NAC (National Action Committee on the Status of Women) meeting. The more data we have about an audience, the better we will be at predicting audience attitudes.

Analyzing the Setting and the Occasion

The environment in which a speech is delivered, its **setting**, and the event or circumstances that give rise to its presentation, the **occasion**, can help us to determine audience expectations for the content and tone of a speech. Because public speaking classes generally meet at the same time and under the same conditions, consideration of the setting and occasion for an in-class speech is not much of a challenge. However, under other conditions, we must carefully consider the following questions:

1. **How large will the audience be?** If the audience is small (up to about 50), speakers can talk without a microphone and move about if they choose to do so. For larger audiences, they must remain fairly still to speak through a microphone.

2. **When will the speech be given?** A morning speech requires a different approach than an afternoon or evening speech. If a speech is to be given after a meal, the audience may be lethargic or sleepy, so the speaker will want to use more attention getters (examples, illustrations, and stories) to help counter lapses of attention.

3. **Where in the program will the speech occur?** Featured speakers have an advantage—they are the focal point of audience attention. In the classroom, however, or on other occasions when many people are speaking, a speaker's position in the program can affect the audience's reception. For example, a first speaker may need to warm up the listeners and be prepared to cope with people arriving late, while the last speaker may have to revive a weary audience.

4. **What is the time limit for the speech?** Any speech setting includes time limits, which affect the choice of the topic. For example, "Three Major Causes of Environmental Damage" could be presented as a 10-minute speech, but "A History of Humankind's Impact on the Environment" could not. Speakers who speak for more or less time than they have been invited to can seriously interfere with the program of an event and lose the respect of both their hosts and their audience.

OBSERVE & ANALYZE
Journal Activity

Analyzing the Setting and the Occasion

Respond to each of the seven questions in this section to analyze the setting and occasion of your first speech.

Save the results of this exercise. You will use them later in adapting your presentation to your audience.

© Tony Freeman/Photo Edit

In planning a speech, use the setting and the occasion as a guide in selecting the content and deciding on the tone.

5. **What are the expectations for the speech?** Every occasion provides expectations. At a graduation ceremony, for example, the speaker is expected to address the accomplishments of and opportunities for the graduates. A key expectation of a classroom speech is to satisfy the requirements of the assignment.

6. **Where will the speech be given?** Rooms vary in size, shape, lighting, and seating arrangements. Some are a single level, some have stages or platforms, and some have tiered seating. The space affects the speech. For example, in a long narrow room, we may have to speak loudly to be heard in the back row. The brightness of the room and the availability of shades may affect what kinds of visual aids we can use. We should always ask for detailed information about the room before planning a speech.

7. **What equipment will be needed to give the speech?** Some speeches require special equipment, for example, a microphone, a chalkboard, or a data projector and screen. Most speakers expect a podium or speaking stand, but it is wise not to count on having one. If the contact person has control over the setting, we should inform him or her of our needs; if not, we should ask whom to contact to make arrangements. Regardless of what arrangements have been made, however, things frequently go wrong, so experienced speakers are adaptable, always prepared with alternative plans.

IN BRIEF

Analyzing the Setting and Occasion

The setting and occasion affect the content and tone of a speech. In analyzing the setting and occasion, consider

- audience size
- time of day
- location of the speech in the program
- time limit
- audience expectations
- location
- equipment needs.

DIVERSE VOICES

March 21: A Day, A Memory, A Day of Reflection

by Remzi Cej

As Canadians, we are perhaps inclined to take some things, like our right to speak freely and openly, for granted because we have never had to worry about "a knock on the door." Remzi Cej, a native of Kosovo, is a student at Holy Heart High School in St. John's, Newfoundland.

In case you aren't familiar with the day, let me quickly summarize the origin of the International Day against Racial Discrimination. On the third week of March in 1960, an apartheid pass laws protest in South Africa was interrupted with casualties of 69 people killed by the government forces because they demanded justice and fair treatment. Years passed before the long-awaited 1966 came, when, in their General Assembly, the United Nations proclaimed March 21st as the International Day against Racial Discrimination. We in Canada have celebrated the day since 1989, when the Canadian Heritage begun its annual national promotion of the day.

Before I came to Canada, I didn't quite understand what racial discrimination meant. Perhaps I wasn't familiar with the phrase because I've grown up in a setting where my life was discrimination itself, and where my peers' actions were discrimination examples against me, my

(continued)

friends, my family, because we were different. Our differences weren't as clear as the race/colour, since living in Kosovo meant not seeing many coloured people. However, the neighbourhoods we lived in, stores we shopped in, schools we went to were clearly distinct, just because we were Muslim Albanians, and Serbs were Eastern Orthodox. I later on understood and comprehended that religion was one aspect politicians were successful in using to discriminate against an ethnicity. They succeeded in Kosovo. That is the reason my parents and I were forced to leave our home, among hundreds of thousands of others.

After coming to Canada, I was asked to help with a poster board on my country and a possible dance. I was so delighted to know that people are interested in knowing about my home and where I come from, and want to adopt my country's musical heritage. In the beginning, we had so many people join in the group that we had to split the group into two parts. I think those days were my best memories from my first couple of weeks in St. John's, Newfoundland, Canada. The best part came when we performed.

It was March 21st. I had butterflies in my stomach. I didn't know that March 21st is the day when most of the local and regional junior and high school students were coming to watch the joy of being in Canada, among other cultures. There were hundreds of students who came only on that day. The next day, another high number came. I was positively overwhelmed and filled with emotions when I gave my speech about my opinion on discrimination. It was incredible knowing that here, I wasn't going to have to pretend I speak perfect Serbian to get a bottle of Coke. Knowing that I could be free to tell people about my culture at that day made me love this city and this country. The eagerness of students wanting to learn whether or not Kosovo had snow in wintertime, their laughs when they tried to learn how to say "Hello" in Albanian, and giggling faces when I'd put my elliptical "plis" that opened my eyes to accepting others as they are. It made me think once again about how we are all the same, no matter what the differences are. As Michael Constantine said, in my favourite recent movie, *My Big Fat Greek Wedding,* "we're all different (kinds), but in the end, we're all fruit." It was an incredible beginning of life here, and an incredible microcosm of multicultural Canada.

As I took my lunch break, I took a walk around the booths set up by other people, to promote their countries. Nyake, from Sierra Leone, had traditional clothes on, showing the local students what the treasures of his home country were, as he pointed at pictures of vast warm beaches and tropical trees. I must say, I had to fantasize about the place itself, since St. John's had already had about 6 feet of snow by then, so Nyake's pictures made me imagine I was running on the beaches of West Africa. Just next to his booth was the setup that Eugena had made on Russia. She talked about Matrioshka (which I used to call Babushka before I found out), the traditional doll-like toy that keeps opening into smaller and smaller doll-like round boxes. I could sense a bit of nostalgia as she spoke about things that teenagers do for fun in her home country.

By the time my lunch break was over, a new group of students came in, and different concert performances started. Drum groups from South America, the Multicultural Choir of elementary-school students, poetry readings in native languages of the students and different songs were performed. Our dance group came out in the end. The choreography that I adopted from traditional Kosovar dances was being performed by my friends who were from all parts of the world. It was an indescribable feeling to come from a pessimistic life of having lost everything to a culture of acceptance and joy. My mom, who came to our evening performance, let out a tear as she watched dances of memories that were brought back.

I've been choreographing dances for my dance group since then, and it seems like there are more and more people joining every year. I am only grateful for being here, and being able to share my culture with others, without a fear of having police knock on my door, saying that I promote "illegal patriotism and separatism."

I am free, and March 21st is one of the many times I remember this. I hope this gives you a better idea of what March 21st means to me. Hopefully, it will have an effect on you.

Source: "March 21: A Day, a Memory, a Day of Reflection," by Remzi Cej. Reprinted with permission.

Determining the Speech Goal

Once we have chosen our topic and analyzed our audience and the setting and occasion of the speech, we can decide upon a general goal for the speech, and then a specific goal.

General Goal

The **general goal** is the intent of the speech. For most speeches, the general goal is to entertain, to inform, or to persuade. Though a persuasive speech may include some elements that are informative or entertaining, an informative speech some elements that are entertaining or persuasive, and so on, most speeches have a single overriding goal.

An **entertaining speech** is one that is intended to amuse or distract the audience. When sexual affairs correspondent Babe Bennett (Cathy Jones) presents a monologue on *This Hour Has 22 Minutes,* for example, her speech has a general goal of entertaining, as would a light-hearted presentation by the master of ceremonies at a wedding reception.

An **informative speech** is one that is intended to increase the audience's knowledge or understanding of something, or its appreciation for something. For example, presentations on the causes of lung cancer or on how to build an igloo would have informing as their general goal.

A **persuasive speech** is one that is intended to reinforce beliefs, change beliefs, or motivate listeners to act. For example, a presentation urging teenagers to practise safe sex or a speech in support of a Green Party candidate for member of parliament would have persuasion as its general goal.

Although some speakers give speeches solely for the purpose of entertaining, in this text, we focus on informative and persuasive speeches, the kinds of speeches given in most academic, professional, and political contexts.

Specific Goal

The **specific goal,** or specific purpose, of a speech is the exact response that a speaker wants from the audience. The **specific goal statement** is a single sentence that clearly specifies that response and reveals the focus of the speech.

A specific goal statement for an informative speech usually specifies whether the speaker wants the audience to learn about, understand, or appreciate the topic. "I would like my audience to understand the four major criteria for evaluating a diamond" is a goal statement for an informative speech. A specific goal statement for a persuasive speech specifies whether the speaker wants the audience to accept the belief that he or she is presenting: "I want my audience to believe that the militarization of space is wrong," or to act in a certain way: "I want my audience to donate to the United Way." Figure 12.3 gives further examples of specific goal statements that clearly state how each speaker wants the audience to react to his or her presentation.

To create an effective specific goal statement, we should follow these steps:

1. **Write a first draft of the speech goal statement, including an infinitive phrase that specifies the exact response that you want from the audience.** Suppose Julia writes her first draft on the topic of illiteracy as, "I want my audience to understand illiteracy." The infinitive phrase *to understand illiteracy* clearly shows that Julia recognizes that her goal is to have the audience understand something. Suppose she had written instead "I want to explain illiteracy." Although it seems to be a reasonable goal, this statement emphasizes the speaker rather than the audience. A specific goal statement *always* indicates the desired audience response.
2. **Revise the draft statement into a declarative sentence that specifies the focus of the presentation.** The draft, "I want my audience to understand illiteracy," was a good start, but it is an extremely broad statement. Just what is it about illiteracy that Julia wants the audience to understand? She narrows the statement to read, "I want my audience to understand three effects of illiteracy." This version is more specific than her first draft, but it still does not clearly capture her intention, so she revises it further to read, "I would like the audience to understand three effects of illiteracy in the workplace." Now the goal is limited not only by Julia's focus on a specific number of effects but also by her focus on a specific situation.
3. **Make sure that the goal statement contains only one idea.** Suppose Julia had written, "I want the audience to understand three effects of illiteracy in the workplace and to understand that illiteracy is detrimental to the affected person in his or her social life as well." This draft includes two distinct ideas; either one can be the focus of a speech, but not both. Julia must make a decision: "Do I want to focus on the effects of the problem in the workplace or on the effects of the problem on the person's social life?"
4. **Ensure that the infinitive phrase indicates the specific audience reaction desired.** If Julia is presenting factual information to her audience, her goal

OBSERVE & ANALYZE
Journal Activity

Speech Goal Statements

Follow the steps outlined in this section to write a speech goal statement for the topic you have selected for your first in-class speech.

Informative Goals
Increase understanding: I want my audience to understand the three basic forms of mystery story.
Increase knowledge: I want my audience to learn how to light a fire without a match.
Increase appreciation: I want my audience to appreciate the intricacy of the human hand.

Persuasive Goals
Reinforce belief: I want my audience to maintain its belief in drug-free sport.
Change belief: I want my audience to believe that SUV's are environmentally destructive.
Motivate to act: I want my audience to join Amnesty International.

Figure 12.3
Specific speech goals

SKILL BUILDERS Writing Specific Goal Statements

Skill	Use	Procedure	Example
Writing a single statement that specifies the exact response the speaker wants from the audience.	To give direction to the speech.	1. Write a first draft using an infinitive phrase to indicate the desired audience response. 2. Revise until you have a declarative sentence that specifies the focus of the presentation. 3. Make sure the goal statement contains only one idea. 4. Revise the infinitive phrase until it indicates the specific audience reaction desired. 5. Write at least three different versions.	Ken first writes, "I want my audience to know what to look for in buying a dog." As he revises, he writes, "I want my audience to understand four important considerations in buying the perfect dog." Once Ken has a goal with a single focus and a clearly specified desired audience reaction, he tests his first version by writing two differently worded versions.

IN BRIEF

Determining the Speech Goal

Speakers have two types of goals, general goals and specific goals.

- *General goals* identify the overall intent of the speech (to inform, to persuade).
- *Specific goals* identify the exact response the speaker wants from the audience.
- *Specific goal statements* are declarative sentences showing the focus of the speech and specifying the exact response that a speaker wants from an audience.

is primarily informative. The infinitive that expresses her desired reaction is *to know* or *to understand*. If, however, her presentation represents a statement of her beliefs or a call to action, her intent is persuasive and the desired reaction is *to believe* or *to act*. This distinction may appear to be trivial, but as we will see in Chapter 13, informative and persuasive speeches are differently constructed: to succeed, we must know what we are attempting to do.

5. **Write at least three different versions of the goal statement.** The clearer Julia's specific goal statement, the more purposeful and effective her speech will be. Even if she likes her initial statement, she should write several more versions. On a second or third try, she might write, "I would like the audience to understand three major effects of the problem of illiteracy in the industrial workplace." Changing "the workplace" to "the industrial workplace" gives the goal statement a different emphasis and a sharper focus. Julia may decide she likes it better.

Researching the Topic

Once we have identified the topic that we wish to speak about and our goal in speaking, we must determine the content of the speech. In order to perform this task, we frequently have to enhance our own knowledge of the topic. If we have

John A. Rizzo/PhotoDisc Green/Getty Images

Most on-line library catalogues allow you to do keyword searches, which are most likely to find material relevant to your topic.

chosen a topic that is important to us and one that we are knowledgeable about, we should already know a good deal about it, but that does not mean that we have all the information we need, or the right information, to allow us to develop a complete and coherent speech for our listeners. Similarly, having strong opinions on the topic does not mean that we have all of the data that we might need to support those opinions before a critical audience.

Researching a speech is no different from researching an essay, a report, or a research paper. We access the same types of sources of information and follow the same steps in collecting information from those sources. The same high standards that apply to using research material in an essay apply equally to using research material in a speech. In every case, we must ensure that the material is relevant to our topic and not distorted or misrepresented in its use; we must ensure that any quotations are exact and that paraphrases or summaries of research material are accurate; and we must ensure that all sources of borrowed material are given proper credit in the speech. We will briefly review the steps of the research process here, but if you have little research experience, you should consult a more detailed research manual.

Effective speakers develop a research strategy that starts with their own knowledge and experience, and moves on to **secondary research** sources—that is, information from relevant books, periodicals, and other published print or electronic sources. In researching some topics, they may also consider doing some **primary research**—that is, collecting information in the field by means of interviews, surveys, experiments, or observations, or by examining original artifacts, documents, or works of art.

Personal Knowledge, Experience, and Observation

We can draw on our own knowledge and use our own experiences as examples. Erin, a member of the varsity volleyball team, can draw on her own experience and that of her teammates in preparing her speech, "How to Spike a Volleyball."

Secondary Research

Most libraries store information about their holdings in electronic databases. Users retrieve the information on computer terminals. Students who have difficulty using library search tools should ask a librarian for help. Library holdings include the following sources of information:

- books
- periodicals (journals, magazines, newspapers, etc.) Most libraries provide electronic access to periodical articles.
- encyclopaedias (both general and specialized)
- statistical sources (demographic data, geographical data, national statistics, weather data, etc.)
- biographical sources (*Canadian Who's Who*, *International Who's Who*, etc.)
- books of quotations (*The Dictionary of Canadian Quotations and Phrases*, *The Oxford Dictionary of Quotations*, *Bartlett's Familiar Quotations*, etc.)
- government documents

More secondary research sources are available on the World Wide Web:

- on-line journals
- databases
- bulletin boards
- scholarly and professional electronic discussion groups
- library holdings at colleges and universities across Canada and abroad.

OBSERVE & ANALYZE
Journal Activity

Listing Sources

Working from your library's catalogue or from periodical indices, list at least six secondary sources of information relevant to the topic of your first speech.

Primary Research

Primary research should always be the option of last resort in satisfying our information needs because it is so much more labour intensive and time consuming than secondary research, and, in the professional world, much more costly. If we are sure, however, that the information we need has never been published anywhere, we can consider trying to obtain it through one of the following means:

- *Interviewing*: asking relevant questions to someone with expertise in our topic area.
- *Examining artifacts or original documents*: taking information from unpublished texts (anything from ancient manuscripts in company files) or objects.

Steve Mason/PhotoDisc Green/Getty Images

Interviews can be a good source of unpublished information.

- *Surveying*: gathering information directly from some group of people through the use of a questionnaire.
- *Observation, inspection, or testing*: visiting a location to watch people, things, or events or to examine conditions or to collect samples for analysis.
- *Experimenting*: designing and testing a hypothesis and analyzing the test data.

We will discuss interview techniques at greater length in Part Five. In order for the results of surveys, observations, and experiments to be meaningful and valid, correct procedures must be followed in designing and using these research instruments. A reliable research manual or a person with expertise in their design and use can provide help.

What Information to Look For

Whatever research methods we use, most of the information we collect will fall into one of two categories: factual statements and expert opinions.

Factual statements **Factual statements** are statements that can be verified. Canadian children (aged two to 11) average 14.2 hours per week watching television; The population of Fort Qu'Appelle, Saskatchewan is 2,210; and Johannes Gutenberg invented the first process for printing from movable type in the fifteenth century are all verifiable statements of fact.

COMMUNICATE!
Using Technology

On-line indices and databases available through both libraries and the World Wide Web can be used to find sources of supporting material for your speeches. Find out what indices and databases you can access through your library. For practice, access the Statistics Canada Web site at **www.statcan.ca**. Enter the keyword *crime* in the search window. Spend a few minutes acquainting yourself with the information available on this site. How might you use this information in a speech on youth crime?

We can verify that the facts we collect from one source are accurate by checking them against material presented in several other sources. When we discover conflicting *facts,* we must do additional research in reputable sources to discover which version is, in fact, not a fact. We should be especially careful of facts collected on line. Because much of the material presented on the Web is not edited or approved by anyone before it is published, erroneous information is commonly found there. By taking information only from reputable sites and verifying any information that we do take, we can prevent ourselves from being misled.

Expert opinions **Expert opinions** are interpretations and judgments made by authorities in a particular subject. Watching television for 14.2 hours per week contributes to childhood obesity; The population of Fort Qu'Appelle, Saskatchewan is maintained by the local resort industry; and Johannes Gutenberg's invention of the printing press marked the beginning of mass communication would be expert opinions if they were given, respectively, by an authority in child development, an expert in western Canadian regional development, and an expert in communication history. An expert is someone who is knowledgeable about a specific subject or topic and who is recognized for his or her expertise by others in that field. Citing an opinion by an expert who concurs in our view gives support to the opinion or analysis we are presenting.

Although they cannot take the place of documented facts, expert opinions can be used to interpret and give weight to facts that we have discovered. For example, in her speech on Canada–U.S. relations, Moira might say, "Pierre Elliott Trudeau once compared living next to the United States with sleeping with an elephant: 'No matter how friendly and even-tempered is the beast,' he said, 'one is affected by every twitch and grunt.' " Using a direct quotation from a recognized expert is an excellent way to reinforce a point, but we must be sure to always credit the source. To fail to do so is to commit **plagiarism,** an unethical act.

Forms of Research Information

Both factual information and expert opinions can take a number of different forms. Both can be or can be presented as examples, statistics, anecdotes or narratives, and comparisons or contrasts.

Examples **Examples** are specific instances that illustrate or demonstrate the truth of a factual statement. Blaine can use one or two short examples like the following to demonstrate the truth of his generalization that companies grow stronger through acquisitions:

> **One way a company increases its power is to buy out another company. In 1995, for example, Sobey's bought out The Oshawa Group, owners of IGA and Price Chopper, to become Canada's second largest grocery retailer.**

Examples should be clear and specific enough to present a clear picture for the audience, and they must not be misleading. To qualify as an example, the instance must reflect what is normally the case. If the instance is an unusual or one-time occurrence, then it does not *exemplify* anything, and presenting it as an example is dishonest and unethical.

Statistics **Statistics** are numerical facts. Statistical statements, such as "Only 63 percent of Canadians voted in the 2000 federal election, the lowest turnout since Confederation," or "The cost of living rose 0.6 percent in January of this year," enable a speaker to quickly provide impressive support for a point, but when they are poorly used in the speech, they may be boring and, in some instances, deceiving. Here are some guidelines for using statistics effectively.

- Use statistics from only the most reliable sources and double-check any startling statistics with another source.
- Use only verifiable statistics.
- Unless the topic of the speech is historical or a comparison of different points in time, use the most recent statistics available.
- Statistics are more meaningful when they are used comparatively. One number does not reveal much, but when compared with another number, it can show growth, decline, gain, loss, etc.
- Compare only statistics from the same period (for example, it would be misleading to compare population or sales figures from two different periods).
- Do not overuse statistics: even highly numerate people have difficulty listening to a long barrage of numbers presented orally.

Anecdotes and narratives **Anecdotes** are brief, often amusing stories; **narratives** are longer stories, including tales and accounts of personal experiences or observations. If they are relevant to the topic of a speech, such stories can help hold audience interest.

Comparisons and contrasts One of the best ways to give meaning to new ideas is through comparison or contrast. **Comparisons** illuminate a point by showing its similarities to something with which the audience is already familiar:

> **The walk from the lighthouse back up the hill to the parking lot is equal to walking up the stairs of a 30-storey building.**

Contrasts show differences, illuminating a point by showing its difference from something with which the audience is already familiar:

> **Though Halifax and Victoria are coastal cities of similar size, they have very different climates in winter. Victoria is mild and rainy, while Halifax has cold winters and frequently receives a lot of snow.**

Recording Information and Citing Sources

Whether the research material we find consists of factual statements, opinions, or both, we must record the information accurately and keep a careful account of the sources so that they can be cited appropriately.

Recording information How should we record the information we collect? Because we can never be sure of the final order in which it is used, it is best to record information on note cards.

Using the note-card method, each fact or expert opinion is recorded on a separate four-by-six-inch or larger index card. It may seem easier to record all of the information on sheets of paper, but sorting and arranging the material is much easier when each item is recorded on a separate card. On each card, we should note the information itself, and the publication data. Any part of the information that is quoted directly should be enclosed in quotation marks.

Publication data differ depending on the source. For a book, we require the name(s) of the author(s), the title, the place of publication, the publisher, the date of publication, and the pages on which the information was found. For an article from a periodical (journal, magazine, newspaper), the author names (if given), the title of the article, the name of the periodical, the date, and the page numbers. For on-line sources, the author names (if given), the name of the site (if given), the heading under which the information was presented, the date the site was last modified (if given), the date that we accessed the site, and the URL for the site.

It will save time later if we place each piece of information under an appropriate heading. For instance, for a speech on the threat posed by SARS, we might have note cards related to causes, symptoms, and means of transmission. The card in Figure 12.4 would be indexed under the heading Spread of the Disease.

The number of sources that we need for a speech depends in part on the type of speech. If we are speaking about a personal experience, we will probably be the main, if not the only, source. For reports and persuasive speeches, however, speakers ordinarily use several sources. Information should come from

COMMUNICATE! Using InfoTrac College Edition

Use InfoTrac College Edition to find information on the subject you have selected for your first speech. Click on *periodical references,* and look for articles that seem relevant to your topic. Whether you download the article or make note cards, make sure that you have all the data you will need to cite the source if you use it in your speech.

TEST YOUR COMPETENCE

Preparing Note Cards

Using information from the books, journals, magazines, newspapers, or on-line sources that you listed in the Observe & Analyze Journal Activity: Listing Sources on page 338 prepare six note cards noting factual statements and expert opinions (examples, statistics, anecdotes and narratives, comparisons or contrasts) that you can consider using for your first speech.

On your note cards, be sure to include the publication data required for each source (book, periodical, or on-line source) that you use.

Topic: SARS

Heading: Spread of the Disease

"SARS doesn't seem to be as deadly, nor spread as easily as, say, some highly infectious strains of influenza that have plagued the world."

Danylo Hawaleshka, "Killer Viruses: A Mysterious Disease Tests Our Ability to Deal with an Epidemic," Maclean's, March 31, 2003, pp. 50–51.

Figure 12.4
Sample note card

at least five different sources. One- or two- or three-source speeches are frequently plagiarized, the speaker simply reproducing someone else's argument or analysis, and do not contain sufficient breadth of material. Remember that the purpose of our research findings is to help us support and elaborate upon our own ideas. The use of several sources will enable us to seem authoritative while still developing an original approach to our topic.

Citing sources in speeches In our speeches, as in any communication in which we use ideas that are not our own, we must credit our sources. Including material from outside sources not only helps the audience to evaluate the content of a speech but also adds to our credibility—it shows that we have done our homework. Failure to cite sources, especially when presenting information that is meant to substantiate a controversial point, not only is unethical but also weakens our argument because we no longer have the support of the expert source.

In a written report, ideas taken from other sources are documented by parenthetical citations and a reference list; in a speech, attribution must be part of the text of the speech itself. Our citations need not include all of the bibliographical information we have collected, but they must make clear that we have taken the material from another source and who the source is. Figure 12.5 gives examples of several ways to cite sources in a speech.

IN BRIEF

Researching the Topic

Research enhances a speaker's knowledge of the topic and provides convincing support for the points made in the speech.

- Draw information from personal knowledge, secondary sources, and primary sources.
- Collect factual statements and expert opinions through secondary research.
- Record each item of information and the source data related to it on a note card.
- Cite the source as part of the text of the speech.

"According to an article about sweatshops in last month's *This Magazine* . . . "

"In a recent Environics poll cited in the February 10 issue of *Maclean's* . . . "

"But to get a complete picture, we have to look at the statistics. According to Human Resources Development Canada, the employment rate in Nova Scotia rose from . . . "

"In a speech on business ethics delivered to The Canadian Public Relations Society's annual conference in Québec City last June, national president Lisa Homer said . . . "

Figure 12.5
Sample source citations

SKILL BUILDERS Recording Data

Skill	Use	Procedure	Example
Making a written record of information drawn from a source with complete documentation.	To provide information and its source in a speech or to report the documentation to anyone who might question the accuracy of the information.	1. Label a note card by topic in the upper-left-hand corner. 2. Record each factual statement or expert opinion on a separate four-by-six-inch or larger index card. Direct quotes should be enclosed with quotation marks. 3. For a book, write the author's name, the title, the publisher, the date, and the page numbers. 4. For a periodical, write the author's name, if one is given, the title of the article, the name of the periodical, the date, and the page numbers. 5. For on-line sources, include the author names (if given), the name of the site (if given), the heading under which the information was presented, the date the site was last modified (if given), the date that you accessed the site, and the URL for the site.	While gathering material for a speech on environmental problems associated with fish farming, Gunther found an article with relevant information. In the upper-left-hand corner of one four-by-six-inch card, he wrote: Diseases. Then he wrote the data he had discovered: "Infectious salmon anaemia (ISA) is the most common, and deadly, disease affecting farmed salmon." Finally he wrote the publishing information: The David Suzuki Foundation, (n.d.) "Salmon Aquaculture," Retrieved March 15, 2004, from http://www.davidsuzuki.org/files/aquabrochure.pdf.

Developing a Thesis Statement

Once we have a satisfactory specific goal statement and have collected a body of research related to our topic, we should have a fairly clear idea of the main ideas that we want to develop and of what content our speech is going to include. At this point, we want to create a **thesis statement**—a single sentence which previews the form and major content of the speech and works with the rest of the introduction to orient listeners to what they are about to hear. As we will see in Chapter 13, the clearer our thesis statement, the easier it will be to organize our speech.

Subject, Topic, Goal, Thesis Statement

The thesis statement is related to and supports our specific goal statement but it does not merely duplicate the goal statement. The specific goal statement clarifies (for ourselves) our purpose in speaking. It essentially states what we wish *to do to* the audience. In contrast, the thesis statement identifies the main point that we are going to use to accomplish our purpose and helps listeners prepare to hear our message. It identifies the main things that we are going *to say to* the audience.

For example, for a speech on evaluating diamonds, Sandy wrote:

Specific goal statement: I want my audience to understand the major criteria for evaluating a diamond.

Thesis statement: Diamonds are evaluated on the basis of four major criteria: carat (weight), colour, clarity, and cutting.

Notice that the specific goal clearly states the response that Sandy wants from the audience (to understand the major criteria)—the effect, in other words, that her speech will have—but it does not *identify* the criteria for evaluating. The thesis statement, in contrast, identifies the information that Sandy will present to achieve the desired effect. Figure 12.6 illustrates the development of two speeches from subject and topic through goal statement and thesis statement.

Subject area: Career counselling

Topic: Networking

General speech goal: To inform

Specific goal statement: I want my audience to understand a procedure for networking in career development.

Thesis statement: You can use networking most advantageously if you make it a conscious priority, position yourself in places of opportunity, advertise yourself, and follow up on your contacts.

Subject area: Varsity sport

Topic: Athletic scholarships

General speech goal: To persuade

Specific goal statement: I want my audience to believe that athletic scholarships should not be permitted in Canada.

Thesis statement: Athletic scholarships should not be permitted in Canada because they have a negative effect on academic standards, they represent a financial strain for smaller universities, and they introduce an unwanted air of professionalism to varsity sport.

Figure 12.6
Relationship among subject, topic, general goal, specific goal, and thesis statement

OBSERVE & ANALYZE
Journal Activity

Writing a Thesis Statement

Following the procedure outlined in this section, develop a thesis statement for your first in-class speech.

Writing a Thesis Statement

To decide on a thesis statement, we must evaluate all of the information that we know about our topic and all of the information that we have collected through our research and decide which information, if presented to the audience, will help us to achieve our specific speech goal. For example, Emma's specific goal statement is, "I want my audience to understand the major criteria for choosing a credit card." By combining her own ideas with what she has learned through her research in several sources, Emma is able to compile a list of factors that affect choice of credit card:

- interest rates
- convenience
- discounts
- annual fees
- rebates
- institutional reputation
- frequent flier points

From this list, Emma must select *the major factors*. She reasons that because nearly every source mentioned interest rate and annual fee, these are major criteria. Only one of her sources mentioned institutional reputation, and through her research she has learned that all Canadian credit card providers are closely regulated, so she eliminates institutional reputation as a factor. She can find no evidence to support her idea that some cards are much more convenient than others, so she eliminates convenience as a factor. Finally, through her research, she has learned that different providers offer different incentives to prospective customers, but that they all offer them for the same reason, so she combines all individual incentives under a single heading: *perks*. At this stage, her list looks like this:

- interest rate
- ~~convenience~~
- discounts → perks
- annual fee
- rebates → perks
- ~~institutional reputation~~
- frequent flier points → perks

After sorting and analyzing her data in this way, Emma is able to write a tentative thesis statement: "Three major criteria for choosing the credit card that best meets your needs are the rate of interest charged on outstanding balances, the annual fee, and the value of the incentives offered by the credit card provider."

IN BRIEF

Developing a Thesis Statement

A thesis statement is a single sentence which previews the form and major content of the speech and works with the rest of the introduction to orient listeners to what they are about to hear. To write a thesis statement:

- list the elements that could become main points in the speech.
- select the elements that best reflect the speech goal and combine them in a complete sentence.

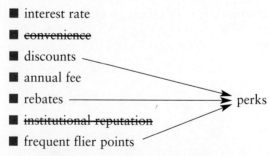

Skill Builders — Writing a Thesis Statement

Skill	Use	Procedure	Example
Developing a single sentence which previews the form and major content of a speech and works with the rest of the introduction to orient listeners to what they are about to hear.	To identify the main points of a speech and aid speech organization.	1. Based on your own knowledge and your research findings, list elements that could become main points in the speech. 2. After selecting the specific elements that best reflect your speech goal, combine them into a complete sentence.	Vanessa's specific goal statement is, "I want my audience to understand the major factors contributing to the increase in the levels of personal debt in Canada." She lists a number of possible factors: easy access to credit, low interest rates, the need for personal gratification, the high cost of imports, the low value of the dollar, etc. After analyzing and evaluating her list she writes the following thesis statement: "Increased personal debt loads being carried by Canadians today has resulted from easy access to credit and people's own need for instant gratification."

What Would You Do?
A Question of Ethics

After class, Laura and Amik were discussing what they intended to speak about for their first in-class speeches.

"I think I'm going to talk about the Mayan ruins," Amik said.

"That sounds interesting, Amik," Laura said, "but I didn't know that you were a history buff."

"I'm not. But Laura, the way I see it, Professor Mak will really be impressed with my speech because my topic will be so academic."

"That may be," Laura replied, "but didn't he stress that for the first speech we should talk about a topic that is important to us and that we know a lot about?"

"Right," Amik said sarcastically. "Like he wants to hear me talk about basketball. Not on your life. Trust me on this one, Laura—when I get the good mark, you'll know I was right."

1. Is Amik's proposed behaviour unethical? Why?
2. What should Laura say to challenge Amik's last statement?

Summary

The first step in preparing a speech is to determine the speech goal. We begin by selecting a subject that we know something about and are interested in, such as a vocation, a hobby, or an issue of special concern. To find a specific topic, we brainstorm a list of words that relate to the subject. When we have brainstormed 20 or so topics, we select from among them the most appealing one.

The next step is to analyze the audience and occasion. Audience analysis is the study of an audience's knowledge, interests, and attitudes. To perform an audience analysis, we gather specific data about the audience to determine how its members are alike and how they differ. We then use this information to predict audience interest in the topic, level of understanding, and attitude toward us and our topic. We also consider how the occasion of the speech and its setting will affect the speech plan.

After analyzing the audience, the occasion, and the setting, we are ready to write a speech goal statement. The general goal of a speech is to entertain, to inform, or to persuade. A specific goal statement is a complete sentence that specifies the exact response the speaker wants from the audience.

Next, we gather information for speech content by exploring our own knowledge, experience, and observations and performing secondary research. For some speeches we may also want to do some primary research. The two major types of supporting materials that are drawn from our research are factual statements and expert opinions. We must ensure all material collected is relevant to our topic and comes from a reliable source. Using note cards to record research findings makes the information easier to organize and work with. During the speech, we must be able to cite the sources of our information.

After completing our research, we are ready to write a thesis statement, a single sentence which previews the form and major content of the speech and works with the rest of the introduction to orient listeners to what they are about to hear.

Glossary

Review the following key terms:

anecdotes (341) — brief, often amusing stories.

audience analysis (328) — the study of an audience's knowledge, interests, and attitudes.

comparison (341) — illuminating a point by showing its similarity to something with which the audience is already familiar.

contrast (341) — illuminating a point by showing its difference from something with which the audience is already familiar.

credibility (330) — the power, based on an audience's perception of a speaker's knowledge, trustworthiness, and amiability, to inspire belief.

entertaining speech (334) — a speech which is intended to amuse or distract the audience.

examples (340) — specific instances that illustrate or demonstrate the truth of a general factual statement.

expert opinions (340) — interpretations and judgments made by authorities in a particular subject.

factual statements (339) — statements that can be verified.

general goal (334) — the intent of the speech (to entertain, to inform, or to persuade).

informative speech (334) — a speech which is intended to increase the audience's knowledge or understanding of something or its appreciation for something.

narratives (341) — longer stories, including tales and accounts of personal experiences or observations.

occasion (330) — the event or circumstances that give rise to the presentation of a speech.

persuasive speech (334) — a speech which is intended to reinforce listeners' beliefs, change their beliefs, or motivate them to act.

plagiarism (340) — the use of research material without crediting the source.

primary research (337) — collecting information in the field by means of interviews, surveys, experiments, or observations, or by examining original artifacts, documents, or works of art.

secondary research (337) — collecting information from published sources such as books, periodicals, and the World Wide Web.

setting (330) — the environment in which a speech is delivered.

specific goal (334) — the exact response that a speaker wants from an audience.

specific goal statement (334) — a single declarative sentence showing the focus of a speech and specifying the exact response that a speaker wants from an audience.

statistics (341) — numerical facts.

subject (326) — a broad area of knowledge.

thesis statement (344) — a single sentence which previews the form and major content of a speech and works with the rest of the introduction to orient listeners to what they are about to hear.

topic (326) — a specific aspect of a subject.

© Nancy Sheeham/Photo Edit

OBJECTIVES

After you have read this chapter, you should be able to answer these questions:

- How should a speaker determine the main points for a speech?
- How should an informative speech be organized?
- How should a persuasive speech be organized?
- What are the goals of introductions, transitions, and conclusions?
- What are effective approaches to introductions and conclusions?
- What are the major elements of a well-written speech outline?

CHAPTER 13

Organization

"Didn't you think that was a terrific speech, Vasily? I haven't heard so many good stories in a long time."

"You're right, Marte, the stories were interesting, but, you know, I had a hard time following the speech. I wasn't always clear on what he was trying to say."

"Well, he was talking about ways we can help save the environment, but, you're right, now that I think about it, I can remember only that one point about recycling. Let's see, what were his other key points?"

Vasily and Marte's experience is not unusual; even well-known speakers sometimes give speeches that are not as clearly organized as they should be, yet a well organized speech is far more likely to achieve its goal than a poorly organized one. In this chapter, we consider the third of the five essential steps to preparing an effective speech: organizing and developing the material in a way that is best suited to the audience and to achieving the speech goal. This step involves (1) outlining the body of the speech, (2) preparing the introduction, (3) preparing the conclusion, (4) listing sources, and (5) reviewing the outline. In this chapter, we also examine the difference between informative and persuasive speeches and consider how to best organize each.

We should think of an outline not as an entire speech written out but as a road map for the speaker and the audience to follow. An outline shows the structure of the presentation that a speaker is about to create in support of a thesis. Most of us have developed outlines for essays or other written compositions; a speech outline is very nearly the same.

An outline is a much more important document to a speaker than to a writer, however, because it is as near to a written *text* as most speakers ever get. As we will see in Chapter 14, most oral presentations are delivered extemporaneously. In delivering **extemporaneous speeches,** we carefully plan the points we are going to make and the order in which we are going to make them, but we never actually commit to a set of words. We select the words we use to make and explain our points as we speak. Having a good outline, then, is key to our success. We will use the outline in planning and practising the presentation of our speech, and our speaking notes will be derived from our outline.

Outlining the Body of a Speech

Because the introduction is the first part of the speech to be heard by the audience, many inexperienced speakers assume that they should begin by outlining the introduction. If we think about it, however, we will realize that it is difficult to work on an introduction before we are familiar with the body. Imagine having to introduce a stranger to a group of friends. It would be difficult because there is no basis for an introduction until we know something about the person we are trying to introduce. The same condition applies to speeches or any other type of text. Therefore, we should prepare the body of the speech first and work on the introduction after there is something to introduce.

Outlining the Main Points

Once we are satisfied with our thesis statement, we can begin outlining the body of the speech. A **main point** is a key idea, an assertion or argument, that supports the idea expressed in the thesis statement. Main points should be written as complete sentences. Recall from Chapter 12, for example, the thesis statement that Emma developed for her speech on credit cards: "Three major criteria for choosing the credit card that best meets your needs are the rate of interest charged on outstanding balances, the annual fee, and the value of the incentives offered by the credit card provider." Emma then wrote down these main points for her speech:

I. Examining the interest rate is one criterion to use when choosing a credit card that is suitable for where you are in life.

II. Another criterion you can use when choosing a credit card is the amount of the annual fee.

III. Which is the best credit card can also depend on weighing the perks that are available with it.

Because this is Emma's first draft, the sentences are still fairly rough, but they do identify the main divisions of the speech. Emma should now revise the sentences, by asking herself four questions:

1. **Are the main points clear?** Main points are clear when they are likely to be decoded the same way by all audience members, and the meaning decoded is the one that the speaker intended. In revision, Emma decides that her third point could be more clearly stated because the meaning of the phrase "weighing the perks" is unclear. She revises it as follows: "Which is the best credit card can also depend on the value of the perks, or incentives, offered with it."

2. **Are the main points parallel?** Main points are parallel when each one is expressed by way of the same grammatical structure. Parallel structure helps the audience recognize main points when they are stated. Emma's points are all differently worded.

   She might revise them as follows:

   I. One criterion for identifying the best credit card is the interest rate.

   II. A second criterion for identifying the best credit card is the annual fee.

   III. A third criterion for identifying the best credit card is the value of the perks, or incentives, that the credit card provider is offering.

3. **Are the main points meaningful?** Main points are meaningful when they provide significant information, information that the audience is likely to want to remember.

   Suppose that Emma had written her first main point this way:

   I. One criterion for identifying the best credit card is thinking about interest.

   This point is not meaningful because it seems to suggest that the thinking rather than the interest rate is the criterion.

4. **Are the main points limited in number?** Generally five or fewer is an acceptable number of points for an oral presentation. If we find ourselves with

Select material from your research that you believe is related to your main point.

more than five main points, our thesis is probably too broad, or perhaps we have strayed from our thesis by introducing points that do not actually support it. A third common problem is to confuse main points with supporting material. Emma would have been committing this error if she had listed discounts, rebates, and frequent flier points as main points. Since these are all kinds of perks, they should be listed as sub-points under main point III.

Selecting and Outlining Supporting Material

The main points of a speech outline show the overall structure of the speech. Whether the audience understands, believes, or appreciates what the speaker has to say, however, usually depends on how well those main points are explained and supported.

As we saw in Chapter 12, factual statements and expert opinions are the principal types of research information used in speeches. Once the main points are in place, we can select the most relevant research information and decide how to develop each main point.

Listing supporting material The first step in this procedure is to write out the main points, one on each of three sheets of paper, and under each one list all of the information that is relevant to it. We should not worry if ideas are out

I. One criterion for finding a suitable credit card is to examine the interest rate.
Most credit cards carry an average of 18 percent.
Some cards carry an average of as much as 21 percent.
~~Some cards offer a grace period.~~
~~Department store rates are often higher than bank rates.~~
Average rates are much higher than ordinary interest rates.
Variable rate means that the rate will change from month to month.
Fixed rate means that the rate will stay the same.
Many companies quote very low rates (6 percent to 8 percent) for specific periods.

Figure 13.1
Emma's supporting materials list and how she edited it

of order or do not seem to relate to one another. Our goal in this step is simply to make an inventory of what we have to work with. Figure 13.1 shows Emma's list of possible supporting material for her first main point. Emma's edits, showing which points she decided to use and how she decided to organize this material, are also shown.

Organizing supporting material Once we have listed the items of information that support our point, we must then look for relationships between and among them. We can draw lines to connect the information that fits together logically and cross out information that seems irrelevant or that does not really fit. We may also want to merge similar ideas that are stated in different words or obviously connected ideas.

Similar items can often be grouped under broader headings. For instance, Figure 13.1 shows how Emma identified four statements related to specific percentages and two statements related to types of interest rate. We are also likely to find information that we decide not to include in the outline; for example, Emma has crossed two items out.

Here is Emma's enhanced outline, showing support for her first main point. Under this main point, she has created two subheadings and then listed the supports for each sub-point. The outline follows a consistent form: main points are labelled with Roman numerals; sub-points with capital letters; and supporting points with Arabic numerals.

I. One criterion for finding a suitable credit card is to examine the interest rate.

- **A.** Interest rates are the fees, calculated as a percentage of your outstanding balance, that a company charges you to carry a balance on your card past the due date.

    - **1.** Credit card providers charge an average of 18 percent, which is much higher than ordinary interest rates on bank loans.

    - **2.** Some providers charge as much as 21 percent.

   3. Many companies quote very low rates (6 percent to 8 percent) for specific periods.

B. Interest rates can be variable or fixed.

   1. A variable rate changes from month to month.
   2. A fixed rate stays the same.

The outline lists supporting material; it does not include all of the development. For instance, in this speech, Emma might develop her points by describing personal experiences, giving examples or illustrations, telling anecdotes, presenting statistics, or quoting an expert. The outline needs to include only enough information to show how we intend to explain and clarify the point we are making. We can always add more supporting material later if we think we need it.

Outlining Section Transitions

Transitions are words, phrases, or sentences that show a relationship between other words, phrases, or sentences. **Section transitions** are complete sentences that link major sections of a speech. They may summarize what has gone before and show movement to the next main idea. These transitions function as guides leading the audience through the speech.

Section transitions work best when moving from one main point to another or from one sub-point to another. For example, suppose Kenneth has just finished the introduction of his speech on antiquing tables and is now ready to launch into his main points. Before stating his first main point he might say: "Antiquing a table is a process that has four steps—now let's consider the first of those four steps." When his listeners hear this transition, they are mentally prepared to listen to the wording of the first main point. When he finishes talking about the first main point, he might use another section transition: "Now that we have seen what is involved in cleaning the table, let's move on to the second step."

Section transitions are important for two reasons. Firstly, they help the audience follow the speech. If every member of the audience were able to pay 100 percent attention all the time, section transitions would not be needed, but as people's attentiveness rises and falls during a speech, they often find that they have lost track of what the speaker is talking about. Good transitions help readers in the same way, but they are even more important to listeners. If readers lose their concentration and think they have missed something, they can reread a paragraph or a page to get themselves back in the picture. Listeners cannot.

Secondly, section transitions are important in helping listeners retain information. We may well remember something that was said once in a speech, but our retention is likely to increase markedly if we hear something more than once. By using good transitions, speakers help listeners stay with them and remember more of the information. If, in a speech, we preview main points, then state each main point, and have transitions between each main point, audiences are more likely to follow and to remember the organization.

On a speech outline, section transitions are written in parentheses at the points where they will occur.

IN BRIEF

Outlining the Body of a Speech

An outline shows the structure of a speech that a speaker is about to make in support of a thesis. To make an outline, follow these steps:

1. Identify the main points that support the thesis.
2. List material that supports each main point.
3. Organize the supporting material.
4. Develop section transitions to help listeners follow and remember the speech.

The Structure of Informative Speeches

An informative speaker's primary rhetorical goals are to present information in a way that holds interest, facilitates understanding, and increases the likelihood of remembering.

The content of informative speeches can be organized in many different ways, but our objective in preparing any speech is to find or create a structure that will help the audience make the most sense of the information. We will begin by examining two basic and very adaptable informative structures that are useful for the beginning speaker to master. Then we will look at five methods of informing.

Two Basic Structures

Two of the most commonly used organizational patterns for informative speeches are topic order and chronological order.

Topic order A speech developed using **topic order** organizes the main points by categories or divisions of a topic. This pattern is extremely adaptable because nearly any subject can be subdivided in many different ways. The subtopics may be arranged from general to specific, specific to general, by order of importance (usually we want to open and close with important points and place less important ones in the middle of the speech), or in some other logical sequence. In this example, the topics are presented in the order that the speaker felt was most suitable for the audience and speech goal, with the most important point at the end:

Specific goal: I want the audience to understand three proven means of ridding our bodies of harmful toxins.

Thesis statement: Three proven means of ridding our bodies of harmful toxins are reducing our intake of animal foods, eating natural whole foods, and drinking plenty of water.

Main points:

I. One way to reduce the concentration of harmful toxins in the body is to lower our intake of animal products.

II. A second way to reduce the concentration of harmful toxins in the body is to eat more natural whole foods.

III. A third way to reduce the concentration of harmful toxins in the body is to drink plenty of water.

COMMUNICATE! Using InfoTrac College Edition

Under the subject *learning* in InfoTrac College Edition, click on *learning, psychology of.* To gather additional information that is relevant to informative speaking, look for articles that discuss *how people learn* and *how people think.* Read one or more articles that you think will help you better understand how to prepare to deliver an informative speech.

Emma's speech on three major criteria for choosing the best credit card is another example of a speech using topic order.

Chronological order A speech using **chronological order** presents information according to a time-based sequence of events, stages, or steps; it focuses on what comes first, second, third, and so on. When we select a chronological arrangement of main points, the audience understands that there is a particular importance to the sequence of those points. Chronological order is most appropriate when we are explaining how to do something, how to make something, how something works, or how something happened. Kenneth's speech on the steps in antiquing a table is one example of the use of chronological order: he presents the steps in order, from first to last. In the following example, notice how the order of main points is as important to the logic of the speech as the wording:

Specific goal: I want my audience to understand four steps to preparing an effective résumé.

Thesis statement: The steps to preparing an effective résumé are identifying and collecting the relevant information, creating an attractive and readable design, organizing the content, and editing and proofreading the document.

Main points:

I. The first step is to identify and collect the relevant information.

II. The second step is to create an attractive and readable design.

III. The third step is to organize the content.

IV. The fourth step is to edit and proofread the document.

Although the designations first, second, and so forth are not necessary to this pattern, their inclusion helps the audience to follow the presentation and to understand that the sequence is important.

Methods of Informing

We will now examine five methods of informing: narrating, describing, defining, explaining processes or demonstrating, and exposition. Which method we use to inform our audience has a major impact on the structure of the speech. At times, we may use more than one method in a single speech, usually by using one method to give shape to the overall speech and others to develop specific sections or points; at other times, we may base an entire informative speech on only one method of informing.

Narration In Chapter 12, we defined narratives as stories, including tales and accounts of personal experiences or observations. Narratives are chronologically organized, and whether they are humorous or serious, they have a point. A joke has a punch line; a fable has a moral; other narratives build to a climax that gives the story meaning. Thus, the primary goal of a narrative is to make a point in such a unique or interesting way that the audience will remember it. For example, in a speech about the costs of faulty listening, Jake decides to demonstrate his point by narrating his experience of working very hard for several days and nights to complete a midterm paper, only to discover upon turning it in that he was a week early.

Being aware of three major elements of narration can assist Jake to increase the power of his narrative:

1. **Narratives are built with supporting details.** For instance, in narrating his experience with his midterm paper, Jake could introduce details such as how he got up at 6 a.m. for two days and did not sleep at all on the last night, how he had to turn down an invitation to a party being held by a woman whom he had been trying to meet for weeks, and how he had been unable to play for his house in the first game of the intramural hockey finals.
2. **Narratives usually maintain suspense.** The power of a narrative can be increased by delaying the climax. By creating suspense, we hold the audience's attention. If Jake does not reveal the outcome of his story until the end, the audience will listen carefully to find out how it is going to unfold.
3. **Narratives can include dialogue.** Jake could just say what happened, but notice how his story improves with this bit of dialogue at the climax:

As I arrived at Professor MacMillan's office with my paper in my hand, the deadline was less than a minute away.

"Here's my midterm paper, Professor MacMillan," I said, panting for breath, "right on the dot!"

"Why, Jake," she replied, "this assignment isn't due until next Thursday."

OBSERVE & ANALYZE
Journal Activity

Narration

Think of an incident which you witnessed or in which you participated that you think could be used to effectively make a point. What would the important details of the story be? How could you maintain suspense? Can you recall any passages of dialogue that you could use to improve the narrative?

Description Informative speeches can be made more vivid through **description**, sharing sensory data about someone or something: the look, the sound, the feel, the smell, or the taste. Most descriptions focus on physical characteristics such as size, shape, weight, colour, composition, age, and condition and are organized spatially, from top to bottom, bottom to top, left to right, right to left, east to west, inside to outside, and so on. Relatively few speeches are completely descriptive, but descriptive sections can be valuable in all kinds of speeches.

To describe effectively, we must describe clearly. We must precisely and accurately observe revealing characteristics of the people or things we wish to refer to and then find vivid, concrete language through which to communicate those characteristics to our audience.

- In showing size and weight, we can compare things to other things with which the audience is familiar: "The book is the same length and width as your text, but about twice as thick." "The suitcase weighed 35 kg, about twice the weight of a normally packed suitcase."

- Simple shapes are easily described by words such as round, triangular, oblong, spherical, conical, cylindrical, and rectangular, but complex objects are best described as a series of simple shapes.
- Although most people can visualize black, white, the primary colours (red, yellow, and blue), and their complements (green, purple, and orange), very few objects are exactly these colours. One way to describe colours clearly is to couple them with common referents; for instance, *lemon yellow* or *brick red.*
- What is the object made of? What is its age or condition? Objects are often discussed in terms of condition. Well-read books become tattered, older buildings become dilapidated, land becomes eroded. Age and condition together often prove valuable in developing informative descriptions.
- How do the parts of an object fit together? If the object is complex, its parts must be fitted into their proper relationship before a mental picture emerges.

Descriptions are improved through careful revision. For most people, vivid description does not come easily—we are not used to describing vividly in ordinary conversation. In a speech, we have the opportunity to work on the language, revising general and bland statements to make them more concrete and vivid. Consider this sentence:

Several pencils were on Jamal's desk.

This statement of fact tells us that pencils were on a desk, but it gives no real description. Revising this description begins by asking questions that relate to the essentials of description we have discussed. By asking, How many pencils? What colour were they? specific descriptive details come to mind. This revision answers those questions:

Five yellow pencils decorated Jamal's desk.

Five is more descriptive than *several* because it is more specific; *yellow* begins to reveal their appearance, and *decorated* is more concrete than *were on.*

Now we ask the questions What condition were the pencils in? and How were they arranged? In the following two sentences, we get completely different images based on the answers to these questions:

Five finely sharpened yellow pencils lined the side of Jamal's desk, side by side, in perfect order from longest to shortest.

Five stubby, well-chewed yellow pencils, all badly in need of sharpening, were scattered about Jamal's desk.

These examples begin to show the different pictures that we can create depending on how well we observe and use the observed details.

Definition **Defining**, explaining what a word means, is essential for effective communication because it helps audiences understand and relate to key concepts (Weaver, 1970, p. 212). Short definitions occur in many speeches; extended definitions can constitute entire speeches.

Short definitions are used to clarify concepts in as few words as possible. Effective speakers learn to define by synonym and antonym, classification and differentiation, use or function, and etymological reference.

- *Synonyms and antonyms:* Using a synonym or an antonym is the quickest way to define a word. Defining by **synonym** is defining by comparison. Defining by **antonym** is defining by contrast. In both cases, we explain an unfamiliar word by pairing it with a familiar one. Synonyms for *prolix* include *wordy* and *verbose.* Its antonyms are *short* and *concise.* Synonyms are not duplicates for the word being defined, but they do give a good idea of what the word means.
- *Classification and differentiation:* When we define by classification, we identify first the class or category to which the thing identified by the particular word belongs and then the features that differentiate it from other members of that class or category. Most dictionaries take this approach to definition. For instance, a dog may be defined as a domesticated mammal of the family *Canidae. Mammal of the family Canidae* identifies the class, one which includes dogs, jackals, foxes, and wolves. *Domesticated* differentiates dogs from the other members of the class.
- *Use or function:* A third way to briefly define a word is by explaining the use or function of the object represented by it. Thus, when we say, "A *plane* is a hand-powered tool used to smooth the edges of boards," we are defining the word by indicating the tool's use. Because the use or function of an object may be more important than its classification, this is often an excellent method of definition.
- *Etymology:* A word's **etymology** is its derivation or history. Because meanings of words change over time, a word's origin may reveal very little about its modern meaning. In some instances, however, the history of a word lends additional insight that will help the audience not only better remember the meaning but also bring the meaning to life. For instance, a *censor* originally was one of two Roman magistrates appointed to take the census and, later, to supervise public morals. The best source of word derivations is the *Oxford English Dictionary.*

Regardless of which type of short definition we use, many definitions, especially of abstract words, need to be supplemented with examples, comparisons, or both to make them understandable. Consider Richard's definition of the word *just* in the following sentence: "You are being just in your dealings with another when you deal honourably and fairly." Although he has defined *just* by synonym, his listeners still may be unsure of its meaning. If he adds, "If Paul

OBSERVE & ANALYZE
Journal Activity

Definition

Think of six technical terms related to your field of study. Choose terms that would not be easily understood by people outside your field. Use several methods of defining to create a short definition for each term. Consider which method of defining works best for each term. Why?

and Mary do the same amount of work, and we reward them by giving them an equal amount of money, our dealings are just, but if we give Paul more money because he's a man, our dealings are unjust." In this case, the definition is clarified with both an example and a comparison. Sometimes, a single example or comparison will be enough, but for some words and certain audiences, we may need to use several.

An extended definition can serve as an entire main point in a speech or, at times, an entire speech. For example, we could build a speech out of an extended definition of *equality, glycolysis, impressionistic painting,* or *good will.* Extended definitions often begin with a single-sentence definition; for example, the *Nelson Canadian Dictionary* defines rock'n'roll as "a form of popular music arising from and incorporating a variety of musical styles, especially rhythm and blues, country music, and gospel." This definition suggests three natural divisions that could form the basis of an informative speech organized in topic order. The key to the effectiveness of the speech would be to explain each musical influence well by using examples, illustrations, comparisons, personal experiences, and observations.

OBSERVE & ANALYZE
Journal Activity

Instruction

Identify something that you know how to do. Plan an instructional speech which would allow you to share that skill with others. Would you use a demonstration? Would it be a complete or modified demonstration? What steps would you have to prepare in advance? What types of visual aids do you think would be effective in this speech?

Instruction or process explanation Many informative speeches involve **instruction**, telling how to do or make something, or **process explanations**, telling how something works or how something came about, or how something is done. Both types of speech involve identifying and detailing a series of steps, and both are organized chronologically (first step, second step, etc.) The difference between the two is that speakers expect their listeners to attempt to duplicate the process outlined in a set of instructions (how to build a bird bath, or how to get a book published) but not to attempt to duplicate the steps of a process explanation (how the fur trade evolved in the eighteenth century, how nuclear fission works).

To give instructions and explain processes clearly, speakers need to delineate and explain each step. Perhaps more than in any other kind of informative speech, carefully prepared visual material may be essential to listeners' understanding of an instruction or process explanation.

Instruction frequently (and process explanation occasionally) involves **demonstration,** performing the steps in the process that the speaker is explaining. For example, as Tabitha goes through her speech on how to deliver an accurate wrist shot, she might perform each step in the sequence to show how it should be done. When, like Tabitha, we are presenting a relatively simple process, we can use a *complete demonstration,* going through the entire process in front of the audience. For a relatively complicated process, such as how to make a lasagne, we may want to consider using a *modified demonstration,* in which we complete some parts of the process before the speech and do only the remaining parts in front of the audience. Modified demonstrations are commonly used in cooking, craft, and home improvement programs on television.

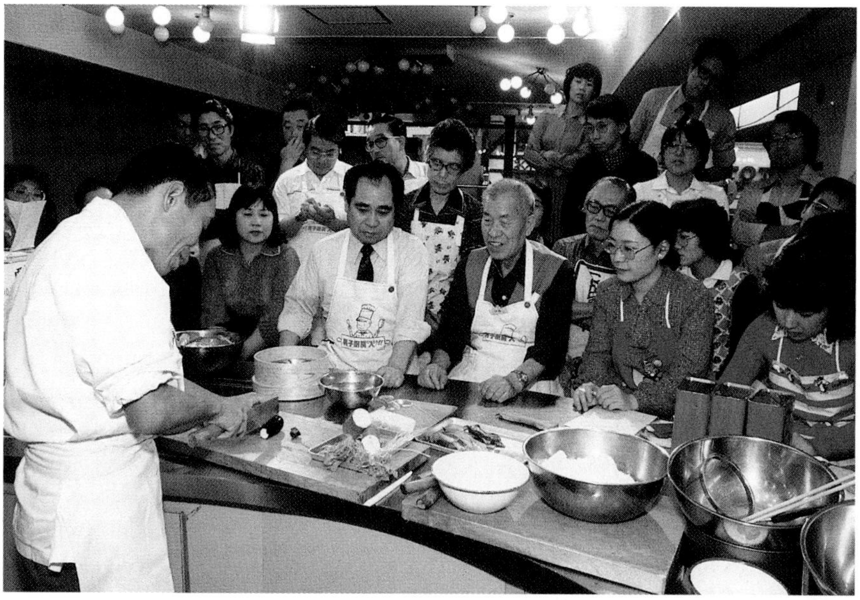

J.P. Laffont/Corbis Sygma/Magma

Demonstrations must be carefully prepared and organized if audiences are to retain the information.

Exposition An **expository speech** is one that is focused on causing the audience to understand an idea. Such speeches normally require researched material to give them depth. For example, we could give an expository speech on the causes of teen violence, the tenets of the Islamic religion, the origin and classifications of nursery rhymes, or the principles of probability theory.

To succeed as an expository speaker, it is important that we establish and maintain our credibility as a spokesperson on the subject, that we stimulate the audience intellectually by presenting new and relevant information, that we present our information in an interesting and creative manner, and that we emphasize the information that is key to the audience's understanding of the idea we are presenting.

IN BRIEF

The Structure of Informative Speeches

Informative speeches should be organized to help the audience make the most sense of the information. Two basic and very adaptable informative structures are

- topic order
- chronological order.

Five common methods of informing have a major impact on the structure of the speech:

- narration
- description
- definition
- instruction or process explanation
- exposition.

The Structure of Persuasive Speeches

As we have seen, a persuasive speaker's primary rhetorical goal is to reinforce a belief that audience members share, to change a belief that audience members hold, or to move audience members to action. In a persuasive speech, the thesis statement becomes essentially a proposition that the speaker is attempting to cause the audience to accept. For example,

Specific goal statement: I want my audience to donate money to the United Way.

Thesis statement (proposition): Donating to the United Way is an effective way of making the most of your charitable donations because your one donation contributes to many charities, because you can stipulate specific

Hostile	Opposed	Mildly opposed	Neither in favour nor opposed	Mildly in favour	In favour	Highly in favour

Figure 13.2
Opinion continuum

charities which you wish to support, and because a high percentage of your donation actually gets to the charities.

How we should organize the content of a persuasive speech, the support for our proposition, depends largely on what our audience analysis has told us about our audience's attitude toward us and our speech goal. As shown in Figure 13.2, audience attitudes can vary widely, from strongly supportive at one extreme to openly hostile at the other. Frequently, of course, audience attitudes will be mixed, but we should try to ascertain the majority view before outlining the speech.

We will begin by examining several characteristics of reasons, the building blocks of persuasive speeches, and then look at several patterns into which our reasons can be organized, each pattern adapted to a certain perceived audience attitude.

Giving Good Reasons and Evidence

Human beings take pride in being rational; we seldom do anything without some real or imagined reason. Since the 1980's, persuasive speech theory has focused sharply on persuasion as a cognitive activity; that is, people form cognitive structures to create meaning for experiences (Deaux, Dane, & Wrightsman, 1993, p. 19). To meet this audience need, the main points of a persuasive speech are usually stated as **reasons**—statements that tell why a proposition is justified (Woodward & Denton, 2000, p. 100).

Reasons are statements that answer why we should believe or do something. If Mujahid is an exercise buff and he "wants his audience to walk five kilometres at least three times a week," he knows that three good reasons for walking are (1) to control weight, (2) to strengthen the cardiovascular system, and (3) to increase stamina. For most of our persuasive speeches, however, we will want to do research to verify or discover reasons.

Characteristics of good reasons How will we recognize good reasons when we see them? Suppose we were planning a speech with the goal statement "I want my audience to believe that the welfare system should be overhauled." Here are some guidelines for evaluating reasons:

1. **Good reasons can be supported.** Some reasons that sound impressive cannot be supported with facts. For example, "The welfare system has been grossly abused" is a good reason only if we can find data to show undeserving people receiving benefits. Many reasons mentioned in various sources have to be dropped from consideration for a speech because they cannot be well supported.

2. **Good reasons are relevant to the proposition.** Sometimes statements look like reasons, but they do not supply proof. For instance, "The welfare system is supported by socialists" may sound like a reason for overhauling it to people who dislike socialism, but it does not offer any proof of a problem with the system.

3. **Good reasons will have an impact on the intended audience.** Suppose we find a great deal of factual evidence to support the idea that the welfare system discourages recipients from seeking work. Even though it is a well-supported reason, it would be an ineffective reason in a speech to an audience that did not accept effect on recipients seeking work as a legitimate criterion for evaluating the welfare system. For instance, some audiences would be more concerned with evaluating the system in terms of its effects on eliminating illness, child poverty, illiteracy, and other social ills.

Finding evidence to support reasons By themselves, reasons are only unsupported statements. Although some reasons are self-explanatory and occasionally have a persuasive effect without further support, most listeners look for factual statements and expert opinion to support reasons before they will either accept or act on them. Thus, if Hilary gives the reason "Diabetes is a major contributor to health care costs" in a speech designed to motivate people to donate research money to the Canadian Diabetes Association, the statement "According to Health Canada, approximately 2 million Canadians now have diabetes" is factual support. Whether our evidence is a factual statement or an expert opinion, we will want to ask at least three questions to assure ourselves that it is good evidence:

1. **What is the source of the evidence?** This question involves both the people who offered the opinions or compiled the facts and the publication in which they were reported. Some sources are more reliable than others.

2. **Is the evidence recent?** For some topics, evidence must be recent. We must ask when the evidence was true. Five-year-old evidence may no longer be valid.

3. **Is the evidence relevant?** Regardless of whether the evidence touches on our topic, if it does not support our reasons it is not relevant.

Testing reasoning To test the validity of our reasoning completely, we must look at the relationship between the reasons and the evidence given in support. When we do that, we are testing the logic of our reasoning. Several kinds of links can be established between reasons and their evidence or between reasons, evidence, and the thesis statement:

1. **Generalization from example:** We are **reasoning by generalization from example** when we argue that what is true in some instances (evidence) is true in all instances (conclusion). For example, Cecilia might say to Ken,

"Tom, Jin, and Tajo studied hard for Prof. Smythe's midterm and got A's. If you study hard, you will get an A too." The reasoning link can be stated, What is true in these representative instances will be true in all instances. To test this kind of argument, we should ask, Were enough instances (examples) cited? Were the instances typical? Are negative instances accounted for? If the answer to any of these questions is no, the reasoning is not sound.

2. **Causation:** We are **reasoning by causation** when our conclusion is presented as the effect of a single circumstance or a set of circumstances. Causation links are among the most prevalent types of arguments. For example, Abel might say, "We've had a very dry spring" (evidence); "The wheat yield will be lower than usual" (conclusion). The reasoning link can be stated, The lack of sufficient rain causes a poor crop. To test this kind of argument, we should ask, Are the conditions (evidence) alone able to bring about the particular conclusion? If we eliminate these conditions, would we eliminate the effect? If the answer to one of these questions is no, the reasoning is not sound.

3. **Analogy:** We are **reasoning by analogy** when our conclusion is the result of a comparison of one set of circumstances with another similar set. Although reasoning by analogy is very popular, it is the weakest form of reasoning. The analogy link is often stated, What is true or will work in one set of circumstances is true or will work in a comparable set of circumstances. For example, Abena might argue, "Since New Zealand has a parliamentary system of government like Canada's and a system of proportional representation was successfully introduced there, such a system would work in Canada too." To test this kind of argument, we should ask, Are the situations really comparable? Are the subjects being compared similar in all important ways? If the answer to these questions is no, the reasoning is not sound.

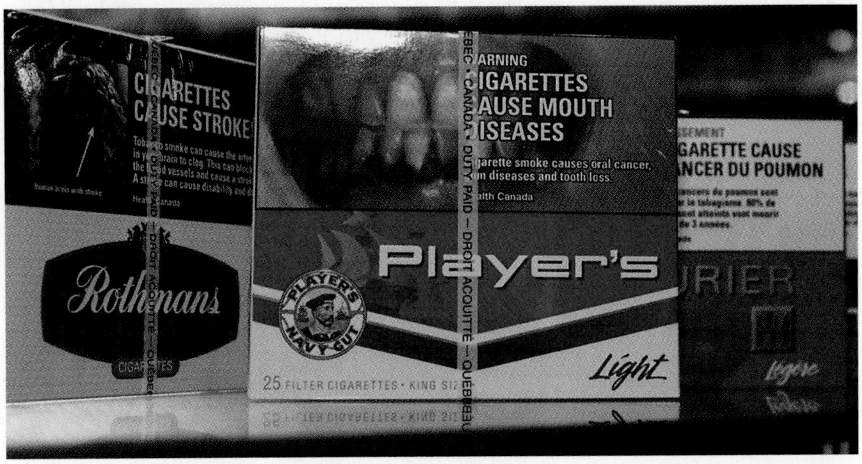

When the government makes manufacturers place warning labels on products, it is trying to influence consumers through reasoning by causation.

Jacques Boissinot/CP Picture Archive

4. **Sign.** We are **reasoning by sign** when our conclusion is based on the presence of observable data that usually or always accompany other unobserved variables. If, for example, Alexander sees longer lines at the downtown soup kitchen, he may reason that the presence of that condition (longer lines) is usually or always an indicator of something else (increased poverty) and predict the existence of this unobserved variable. Signs are often confused with causes, but they are indicators or sometimes effects, never causes. Longer lines at soup kitchens are a sign of increased poverty. The longer lines may be seen as an effect of poverty, but they do not cause the poverty. To test this kind of argument, we should ask, Do the data cited always or usually justify the conclusion drawn? Are sufficient signs present? If not, the reasoning is not sound.

OBSERVE & ANALYZE
Journal Activity

Selecting Reasons

Write a specific goal statement for a persuasive speech.

1. Write at least six reasons that support your specific goal.
2. Place stars next to the three or four reasons you decide to use. Which type of reasoning does each one exemplify? Briefly explain why you think they are the best.

Avoiding fallacies In Chapter 5, we defined an inference as a claim or assertion, which may or may not be true, based on observations of fact. A **fallacy** is a statement or argument based on a false or invalid inference. When we think that we have finished constructing the reasons for a persuasive speech, we should take an extra few minutes to make sure that, in framing them, we have not committed any of the four most common fallacies:

1. **Hasty generalization:** When we generalize, the number of instances upon which the generalization is based should represent most to all possibilities: enough must be cited to satisfy the listeners that the instances are not isolated or hand-picked. If Aarne interviewed two women in his residence and found that both opposed abortion, he would be guilty of the very common fallacy of **hasty generalization** if he stated, "Most young women today oppose abortion."
2. **False cause:** A **false cause argument** occurs when the alleged cause is unrelated to, or does not produce, the effect. Just because one thing happened before another does not make the first event a cause of the second. We recognize most superstitious beliefs (e.g., I had the accident because I walked under a ladder) as examples of the false cause fallacy.
3. **Appeal to authority:** Basing an argument on expert opinion is valid only so long as the expert is an expert in the subject being discussed. **Appeal to authority fallacy** arises when the so-called authority cited does not have expertise in the subject being discussed. The suggestion that we should buy a particular brand of car because a famous hockey player says so exemplifies this fallacy.
4. ***Ad hominem* argument:** An ***ad hominem* argument** is an attack on a person rather than on the views or arguments expressed by that person. Literally, *ad hominem* means "to the man." For instance, if Senator Sharon Carstairs gave a speech in which she spoke of the valuable environmental protection work done by the senate, the response, "Great, another member of the

THINKING ABOUT . . .

Fallacies

For the next day, pay attention to what your friends, relatives, and acquaintances say to support their arguments. Did you hear people committing any of these four fallacies? Why do you think people do so?

politician's retirement club justifying her own existence" would be an example of an *ad hominem* argument. Such a personal attack often is made as a smokescreen to cover the lack of a good counterargument. *Ad hominem* arguments are often used in political campaigns, and though they are at times highly successful, they are almost always fallacious.

Organizing Reasons in Response to Audience Attitudes

As we mentioned above, the anticipated audience reaction to us and to our topic are important factors in determining how we organize a persuasive speech. We are more likely to persuade an audience when we organize our reasons according to the response we anticipate. We will describe five organizational patterns, discuss the audience attitudes for which each is most suited, and describe the logic of each pattern. To contrast the patterns and better demonstrate their use, we will use the same thesis statement (proposition) and the same (or similar) reasons to illustrate each one.

Statement-of-logical-reasons pattern The statement-of-logical-reasons pattern is a straightforward organization which calls for the best-supported reasons we can find to be presented in the following order: second-strongest first, strongest last, and others in between. Its use is appropriate when we judge that our listeners have no opinion on the subject, are apathetic, or are perhaps only mildly in favour or opposed.

Specific goal statement: I want my audience to support increased funding of school boards by the provincial government.

Thesis statement (proposition): The provincial government should increase funding to school boards by 15 percent in each of the next three years.

- **I.** Increased income will enable the boards to restore valuable programs that have been cut in recent years. (second strongest)
- **II.** Increased income will enable the boards to give teachers the raises they have been denied for several years, putting the boards in a better position to attract new teachers.
- **III.** The actual cost to each member of the community, in increased taxes, will be less than $20 per year. (strongest)

In a speech using the statement-of-logical-reasons pattern, the logic of the organization may be stated as follows: When good reasons and evidence are presented supporting a proposal, the proposal should be adopted.

Problem–solution pattern The problem–solution pattern provides a framework for clarifying the nature of a problem and for illustrating why a given solution is the best one. A speech in this pattern is often organized around three general statements: (1) there is a problem that needs to be solved, (2) this proposal will solve the problem, and (3) the proposal is the best solution to the problem because it will provide positive consequences. This pattern is also straightforward, so it again would be appropriate for an audience that has no opinion or is mildly for or against the proposition, but it is likely to work best for an audience that is unaware that a problem exists. A problem–solution organization for the school funding proposition might look like this:

Specific goal statement: I want my audience to support increased funding of school boards by the provincial government.

Thesis statement (proposition): To address a serious problem in our public schools, the provincial government should increase funding to school boards by 15 percent in each of the next three years.

I. The present shortage of money is resulting in serious problems for public education. (statement of problem)

II. The proposed funding increase is large enough to solve those problems. (solution)

III. For now, increasing school board budgets is the best method of solving the schools' problems. (consequences)

In a speech using the problem–solution pattern, the logic of the organization may be stated as follows: When a problem is presented that is not or cannot be solved with current measures, and the proposal can solve the problem practically and beneficially, then the proposal should be adopted.

Comparative-advantages pattern The comparative-advantages pattern enables the speaker to place all of the emphasis on the superiority of the proposed course of action. Rather than presenting the proposition as a solution to a grave problem, it presents the proposition as one that ought to be adopted solely on the basis of the advantages of that proposition over what is now being done. Although this pattern can respond to any audience attitude, it works best when the audience agrees either that there is a problem that must be solved or that the proposition is superior to its competitors when no particular problem is at issue. For example, when people elect to go out to eat, they have a variety of choices, so a speech advocating La bonne gueule would emphasize its advantages over the competition. A comparative-advantages approach to the school funding proposition would look like this:

Specific goal statement: I want my audience to support increased funding of school boards by the provincial government.

Thesis statement (proposition): Our public schools would be greatly improved if the provincial government increased funding to school boards by 15 percent in each of the next three years.

I. Increased funding of the boards will enable schools to raise the standards of their programs. (advantage 1)

II. Increased funding of the boards will enable them to attract better teachers. (advantage 2)

WWW

COMMUNICATE! Using Technology

Who better to demonstrate persuasive speaking skills than a lawyer? Select a movie or an episode of a television series that depicts a trial. Evaluate the way the barristers try to persuade the jury to accept their point of view. What do they do to build their credibility? How do they incorporate emotional appeal in their remarks? How do they reason with juries? What do they do that makes them particularly effective or ineffective in their speeches?

III. Increased funding of the boards will enable schools to better the educational environment. (advantage 3)

In a speech using the comparative-advantages pattern, the logic of the organization may be stated as follows: When reasons are presented that show a proposal offers a significant improvement over what is being done, then the proposal should be adopted.

Criteria-satisfaction pattern The criteria-satisfaction pattern is an indirect pattern that seeks to gain audience agreement on criteria that should be considered when evaluating a particular proposition and then shows how the proposed course of action satisfies those criteria. When we encounter listeners that are opposed to a proposition, we need a pattern of organization that will not aggravate their hostility. The criteria-satisfaction pattern is likely to work because it focuses on developing a *yes* response to each criterion before introducing the proposition and reasons. A criteria-satisfaction organization for the school funding proposition might look like this:

Specific goal statement: I want my audience to support increased funding of school boards by the provincial government.

Thesis statement (proposition): We owe it to our children to do all that we can do to provide them with the best possible education.

I. We all want good schools. (a community value)
- **A.** Good schools offer programs that prepare our children to succeed as citizens and in reaching their own goals. (one criterion for evaluating good schools)
- **B.** Good schools are those with the best teachers available. (a second criterion for evaluating good schools)

II.
- **A.** Increased provincial government funding of the school boards will enable us to increase the quality of programs offered to our children. (satisfaction of criterion one)
- **B.** Increased provincial government funding of the school boards will enable us to hire and keep the best teachers. (satisfaction of criterion two)

In a speech using the criteria-satisfaction pattern, the logic of the organization may be stated as follows: When a proposal satisfies a set of agreed upon criteria, it should be adopted.

Motivational pattern The motivational pattern combines problem solving and motivation. It follows a problem–solution pattern but includes steps designed to heighten the motivational effect of the organization. Motivational patterns usually include a five-step, unified sequence that replaces the normal introduction, body, conclusion model: (1) an attention step, (2) a need step that fully explains the nature of the problem, (3) a satisfaction step that explains how the proposal solves the problem in a satisfactory manner, (4) a

OBSERVE & ANALYZE
Journal Activity

Outlining the Speech Body

Outline the body of an informative or persuasive speech that you must present in class.

1. Write your speech goal statement at the top of the page.
2. Write your thesis statement next.
3. Write main points that will support the thesis.
   Revise the wording of the main points so that each is written in a complete sentence that is clear, parallel, and meaningful.
   Based on your material and your audience, determine the best organizational pattern for the main points. If need be, rewrite the main points in this order.
4. List the factual statements, expert opinions, and other information you have found to develop and support each main point.
   Group the points of information that relate to each other.
   Subordinate material so that each sub-point contains only one idea.
5. Write section transitions that summarize the previous main point or forecast the next main point.

visualization step that provides audience members with a heightened sense of the benefits to be derived from accepting the proposal, and (5) an action appeal step that emphasizes the specific actions that listeners should take to make the proposal a reality. A motivational pattern for the school tax levy proposition would look like this:

Specific goal statement: I want my audience to support increased funding of school boards by the provincial government.

I. Comparisons of worldwide test scores in math and science have refocused our attention on education. (attention)

II. The shortage of money being experienced by school boards is resulting in cost-saving measures that compromise our ability to teach basic academic subjects well. (need, statement of problem)

III. A 15-percent per year increase in funding over each of the next three years would allow the boards to solve those problems by placing more emphasis on academic need areas. (satisfaction, how the proposal solves the problem)

IV. Think of the contribution you will be making not only to the education of your future children but also to returning our educational system to the world-leading status it once enjoyed. (visualization of future benefits)

V. Here are forms that you can fill in and send to your MLA to show that you are willing to support this much-needed funding increase. (action appeal showing specific action required)

Because motivational patterns are variations of problem–solution patterns, the logic of the organization is much the same: When the existing approaches are not solving the problem, a new solution that does solve the problem should be adopted.

Listing Sources

When we have completed outlining the body of a speech, we will know which of the expert opinions and facts that we collected during research have actually found their way into the speech. This is a good point to create a reference list of the sources that we have used. By following the rules of a particular bibliographic style, such as APA style or MLA style, we can be sure that we have all of the necessary information about each source.

Outlining the Introduction and Conclusion

As we said earlier, it makes sense to prepare the introduction and conclusion of a speech *after* we have outlined the body. That way, we have a good understanding of the content to be introduced and wrapped up. Because the introduction establishes the relationship between the speaker and the audience, and the

OBSERVE & ANALYZE
Journal Activity

Selecting an Organizational Pattern

Select a pattern of organization for a persuasive speech that you have to give. Discuss why you are planning to use this organizational pattern. Why do you think it fits in well with what you believe will be your audience's reaction to your proposition?

IN BRIEF

The Structure of Persuasive Speeches

Persuasive speeches should be organized to reinforce a belief that audience members share, to change a belief that audience members hold, or to move audience members to action. Each of five persuasive speech patterns is designed to respond to differing audience attitudes to a proposition:

- *Statement-of-logical-reasons pattern:* when listeners have no opinion or are mildly for or against
- *Problem–solution pattern:* when listeners are unaware of the problem
- *Comparative-advantages pattern:* when the audience agrees
- *Criteria-satisfaction pattern:* when the audience is hostile
- *Motivational pattern:* when the audience requires motivation.

conclusion is the speaker's last opportunity to reinforce his or her message, it is worth investing some time in preparing and trying different openings and closings; then we can pick the one that we think will work best for our specific audience and speech goal.

Most introductions range from 5 to 10 percent of the speech and conclusions are typically less than 5 percent. Thus, for a five-minute speech (approximately 750 words), an introduction of 35 to 75 words and a conclusion of 35 to 40 words is appropriate. Ideally, the introduction and conclusion should somehow resonate with the same tone. We should try to identify some theme or detail in the introduction that we can pick up in the conclusion; for example, we might ask a question or pose a problem in the introduction that we answer or resolve in the conclusion, or we might use an image in the introduction that we return to in the conclusion. By referring to some element of the introduction in the conclusion, we give the speech a satisfying sense of completeness.

Goals of the Introduction

A good introduction must get attention and lead into the content of the speech. It may also establish the speaker's credibility, set the tone for the speech, and create a bond of good will between the speaker and the audience.

Getting attention The physical presence of our audience members does not guarantee that they will listen to our speech. Therefore, our first goal is always to create an opening that will draw the listeners' attention. We can arouse their interest by providing them with a reason they need to know the information we will be presenting.

Leading into content Audience members want to know what the speech is going to be about and how it is going to proceed, so it is important to forecast our content and organization in the introduction. For instance, in a speech on campaigning, after his attention-getter, Byron says, "In this speech, I'll explain the four stages of a political campaign." Such a clear forecast of the main points is appropriate unless we have some special reason for not revealing the organization. Having this information helps the audience members to listen by giving them a sense of direction.

Establishing credibility Audience members need to know why they should pay attention to what *we* have to say. Although credibility is built and maintained throughout the speech, it is a good idea to indicate right away why we have the right to talk on this topic. For instance, during Erin's speech on the volleyball spike, her audience is likely to feel more comfortable with her as an authority if she mentions during her introduction that she is a member of the women's varsity volleyball team.

Setting a tone A humorous opening will signal a light-hearted tone; a serious opening signals a more thoughtful tone. A speaker who starts with a rib-tickling ribald story is putting the audience in a light-hearted, devil-may-care mood. If that speaker then says, "Now let's turn to the subject of abortion [or nuclear war or drug abuse]," the audience will be confused and the speech may be doomed.

Creating a bond of good will Within the first few words, we often determine how an audience will feel about us as a person. If we are enthusiastic, warm, and friendly and give a sense that the message we are about to deliver is in the audience's best interest, the audience will be more willing to listen.

Types of Introductions

Ways to begin a speech are limited only by our imaginations. In very short speeches—the kind usually given in class—we want to focus especially on getting attention and leading into the content of the speech. The following six types of openings allow us to achieve these goals:

Startling statement One excellent way to grab listeners' attention and focus on the topic quickly is to open with a startling statement that will override the various competing thoughts in our listeners' minds. This example illustrates the attention-getting effect of a startling statement:

> **If I pointed a pistol at you, you would be justifiably scared, but at least you would know the danger to your life. Every day we let people *fire away at us* with high-speed steel projectiles weighing several tonnes, and we get no warning at all. I'm talking about reckless drivers. Today, I want to look at how we can go about getting reckless drivers off the roads.**

In just 68 words—about 27 seconds—this introduction grabs attention and leads into the speech.

Rhetorical question Asking a **rhetorical question**, a question seeking a mental rather than a vocal response, is another appropriate opening for a short speech. Here a student begins her speech on counterfeiting with three short questions:

> **What would you do with this $20 bill if I gave it to you? Take your friend to a movie? Treat yourself to a pizza and drinks? Well, if you did either of those things, you would get into big trouble, because this bill is counterfeit.**
>
> **Today, I want to talk to you about the counterfeiting of Canadian currency and what our government is doing to curb it.**

Again, a short opening (68 words) gets attention and leads into the speech.

Story A good story that gets an audience's attention and is *really* related to the goal of the speech makes an unbeatable opening. Because many good stories are rather long, this type of introduction is more often suited to speeches over 10 minutes long, but we will occasionally find a story that we can abbreviate:

> **One weekend last fall, my family was watching *Sports Saturday* on CBC. At the beginning of the show, a collage of photos showed the stars, including Vince Carter, Mario Lemieux, and Christine Sinclair, who would be featured on the show that day.**
>
> **Suddenly, my 10-year-old sister piped up and asked, "Dad, who are those guys with Christine?"**
>
> **My optimistic belief is that women athletes are finally getting the recognition they deserve, and that role models like Christine Sinclair are setting the stage for a new world view.**

This 87-word introduction would work well for a five- to seven-minute speech.

Personal reference Although any good opening should engage the audience, a personal reference to members of the audience is directed solely to that end. In addition to getting attention, a personal reference can be especially effective at engaging listeners as active participants in a speech:

> **Were you panting when you got to the top of those four flights of stairs this morning? I'll bet there were a few of you who vowed you would never take a class on the top floor of this building again. But did you ever stop to think that maybe the problem isn't that this class is on the top floor?**
>
> **Today I want to talk with you about how you can build an exercise program that will get you and keep you in shape yet only cost you three hours a week and not one red cent.**

Quotation A particularly vivid or thought-provoking quotation makes an excellent introduction, but only if the quotation *really* relates to the topic:

> **"If I can be proscribed today, for defending myself and my friends in the newspapers, another Nova Scotian may be rejected tomorrow because the Governor likes not the colour of his hair." So said Joseph Howe in defending freedom of the press in 1844. Must we fight those ancient battles again? It seems we may have to because, in this post-9/11 world, the right to free speech seems conditional upon what we have to say.**

Suspense If we can start a speech in a way that gets members of the audience to ask, "What is he or she leading up to?" we may well get them hooked for the entire speech. The suspense opening is especially valuable when the topic is one that the audience ordinarily might not be willing to hear about. Consider the attention-getting value of this introduction:

It costs the Canadian economy more than $18.5 billion per year. It has caused the loss of more jobs than a recession. It accounts for more than 19,000 deaths a year, including 920 suicides. It is involved in more than 50 percent of violent crimes. I'm not talking about the abuse of narcotics—the problem is alcoholism. Today I want to show you how you can protect yourself from the grip of this inhumane killer.

Notice that by putting the problem, alcoholism, at the end, the speaker encourages the audience to try to anticipate the answer. And because the audience may well be thinking *narcotics,* the revelation that the answer is alcoholism is likely to be that much more effective.

OBSERVE & ANALYZE
Journal Activity

Writing Speech Introductions

Prepare three separate introductions that you believe would effectively introduce the speech body that you outlined in the previous Observe & Analyze Journal Activity and present them aloud. Which do you believe is most effective? Why?

Goals of the Conclusion

Shakespeare said, "All's well that ends well," and nothing could be truer of a good speech. A conclusion has three major goals: (1) to wrap up the speech, (2) to review what we have said, and (3) to hit home so that the audience will remember our words or think about our appeal.

Types of Conclusions

We should select the conclusion for a speech on the basis of our speech goal and its likely appeal to the audience. As with the introduction, trying out two or three types of conclusions and choosing the one that best reinforces our thesis is the best approach. Here are four basic types of conclusion:

Summary conclusion By far the easiest way to end a speech is to summarize the main points that we have made. Thus, the shortest appropriate ending for a speech on the warning signs of cancer might be,

So remember, if you experience a sudden weight loss, lack of energy, or blood in your urine or bowels, you should see a doctor immediately.

Such an ending restates the key ideas the speaker wants the audience to remember. Summaries are appropriate for either informative or persuasive speeches.

Summaries easily achieve the first two goals of a conclusion—wrapping up the speech, and reviewing what we have said, but effective speakers are likely to supplement their summaries with material designed to achieve the third goal—hitting home so that the audience will remember their words or consider their appeal. The other types of conclusions presented here can be used to supplement or replace the summary.

Appeal-to-action conclusions The appeal to action is a common way to end a persuasive speech. The appeal describes the behaviour that we want our listeners to follow.

Romilly Lockyer/The Image Bank

An effective conclusion will wrap up your speech and hit home in a way that will help the audience remember your message.

So I want you to reconsider whether you are doing your bit for the environment. If your household is generating more than one bag of garbage per person per month, you can do better. Each time you go to toss something in the garbage this week, I want you to think: *reduce, reuse, recycle*. If we all do our share, we can leave our children something more than a garbage dump.

By their nature, appeals are most relevant for persuasive speeches, especially when the goal is to motivate an audience to act.

Emotional-impact conclusions No conclusion is more impressive than one that drives home the most important points with real emotional impact. This conclusion to a speech by Prime Minister Pierre Elliott Trudeau at the proclamation of Canada's patriated constitution on April 17, 1982, is a good example:

It must however be recognized that no Constitution, no Charter of Rights and Freedoms, no sharing of powers can be a substitute for the willingness to share the risks and grandeur of the Canadian adventure. Without that collective act of the will, our Constitution would be a dead letter, and our country would wither away. It is true that our will to live together has sometimes appeared to be in deep hibernation; but it is there nevertheless, alive and tenacious, in the hearts of Canadians of every province and territory. I wish simply that the bringing home of our Constitution marks the end of a long winter, the breaking up of the ice-jams and the beginning of a new spring. For what we are celebrating today is not so much the completion of our task, but the renewal of our hope—not so much an ending, but a fresh beginning. Let us celebrate the renewal and patriation of our Constitution; but let us put our faith, first and foremost, in the people of Canada who will breathe life into it.

OBSERVE & ANALYZE
Journal Activity

Writing Speech Conclusions

Prepare three separate conclusions that you believe would be appropriate for the body of the speech you outlined in the second last Observe & Analyze Journal Activity and present each aloud. Which one works best? Why?

Like the appeal, the emotional conclusion is likely to be used for a persuasive speech where the goal is to reinforce belief, change belief, or motivate an audience to act.

Story conclusions Stories or anecdotes that reinforce the message of the speech work just as well for conclusions as for introductions. This story conclusion also offers some emotional impact and includes an appeal for action:

> **It's been over 10 years now since a speeding drunkard put me in this wheelchair. For months after this so-called *accident,* I was alone. I was alone in the midst of caring doctors, nurses, and therapists; alone though I was surrounded by a loving family and devoted friends. I was alone because I could see only myself and my own suffering. It was only when I tried to help someone else that I rediscovered a sense of community, and the satisfaction that I've got from working with Wheelchair Kids is greater than from anything else I've ever done. So I urge you to find someone to reach out to. Volunteer. The winner could be you.**

Story conclusions work for either informative or persuasive speeches.

Reviewing the Outline

Now that we have all the parts of a speech outline completed, it is time to put everything together and to review the document to ensure that the parts fit together as we would like. By following this checklist, we can be sure that we have an outline that will be useful to us as we move into adaptation and rehearsal.

1. **Have I used a standard set of symbols to indicate structure?** Main points usually are indicated by Roman numerals, major subdivisions by capital letters, minor subheadings by Arabic numerals, and further subdivisions by lowercase letters.
2. **Have I written main points and major subdivisions as complete sentences?** Complete sentences help us to see (1) whether each main point actually develops our speech goal and (2) whether the wording makes our intended point. Unless the key ideas are written out in full, it will be difficult to follow the next guidelines.
3. **Do main points and major subdivisions contain a single idea?** This guideline ensures that the development of each part of the speech will be relevant to the point. Thus, rather than

   I. The park is beautiful and easy to get to.

   divide the sentence so that each point is presented separately:

   I. The park is beautiful.

   II. The park is easy to get to.

IN BRIEF

Outlining the Introduction and Conclusion

Introductions and conclusions are short but important parts of any speech. The introduction should:

- get attention
- lead into the speech content
- establish the speaker's credibility on the subject
- set the tone for the speech
- create a bond of good will with the audience.

The conclusion should:

- wrap up the speech
- review the main points
- hit home so that the audience will remember.

OBSERVE & ANALYZE
Journal Activity

Reviewing the Speech Outline

Assemble the sentence outline of your speech from the parts that you created in the earlier Observe & Analyze Journal Activities. Review your outline using the checklist presented here. Make sure you have included a speech goal statement, a thesis statement, an introduction, clearly written main points, support for the main points, transitions between main points, a conclusion, and a list of sources.

The speaker will then be sure to obtain supporting material for each point.

4. **Does each subdivision relate to or support its major point?** This principle is called *subordination*. Consider the following example:
   - **I.** Proper equipment is necessary for successful play.
     - **A.** Good gym shoes are needed for manoeuvrability.
     - **B.** Padded gloves will help protect your hands.
     - **C.** A lively ball provides sufficient bounce.
     - **D.** And a good attitude doesn't hurt.

   Notice that the main point deals with equipment; A, B, and C (shoes, gloves, and ball) relate to the main point, but D, attitude, is not equipment and should appear somewhere else in the speech, if at all.

5. **Is the number of words in the outline one-third or less the number of words in the anticipated speech?** An outline is only a skeleton of the speech, not a manuscript with letters and numbers. The outline should be short enough to allow us to experiment with methods of development during practice periods and to adapt to audience needs during the speech itself. Approximate figures are all we need. If we assume a speaking rate of about 160 words per minute, a three- to five-minute speech would contain roughly 480 to 800 words, so the outline should be 160 to 300 words in length. An eight- to ten-minute speech, roughly 1,280 to 1,600 words, should have an outline of approximately 426 to 533 words.

Figure 13.3 shows a completed outline for an informative speech. The analysis in the outside columns shows how the outline satisfies the guidelines that we have considered throughout this chapter.

IN BRIEF

Reviewing the Outline

When the outline of the speech is completed, it should be reviewed to ensure

- correct outline structure
- main points and major subdivisions as complete sentences
- a single idea in each point
- correct subordination of subpoints
- length is no more than one-third that of the speech.

WHAT WOULD YOU DO?
A QUESTION OF ETHICS

As Marna and Gloria were eating lunch together, Marna happened to ask Gloria, "How are you doing in Woodward's speech class?"

"Not bad," Gloria replied. "I'm working on this speech about product development. I think it will be really informative, but I'm having a little trouble with the opening. I just can't seem to get a good idea for getting started."

"Why not start with a story—that always worked for me in public speaking class."

"Thanks, Marna, I'll think about it."

The next day when Marna ran into Gloria again, she asked, "How's that introduction going?"

"Great. I've prepared a great story about Tim Horton—you know, the doughnut guy? I'm going to tell about how he was terrible in school and no one thought he'd amount to anything. But he loved dabbling with dough so much that he decided to start his own business—and the rest is history."

(continued)

"That's a great story. I really like that part about his being terrible in school. Was he really that bad? I thought he was a hockey player."

"I really don't know—the material I read didn't really give much biographical information. But I thought that angle would get people listening right away. And after all, I did it that way because you suggested starting with a story."

"Yes, but . . ."

"Listen, he did start the business. So what if the story isn't quite right? It makes the point I want to make—if people are creative and have a strong work ethic, they can make it big."

1. What are the ethical issues here?
2. Is anyone really hurt by Marna's opening the speech with this story?
3. What are the speaker's ethical responsibilities?

Summary

A speech must have an introduction, a body, and a conclusion.

The body of the speech is organized first, starting with a thesis statement based on the speech goal statement. Then main points are selected to support the thesis. Main points are written as complete sentences that are specific, vivid, and parallel.

A speech can be organized in many different ways depending on the type of speech and the nature of the material. Two of the most common organizational patterns for informative speeches are topic order and chronological order. These patterns can be varied, depending on whether the speaker uses narration, description, definition, instruction or process explanation, or exposition as the primary method of informing. Persuasive speeches are based on reasons. Depending on the attitude of the audience to the speaker and topic, a number of patterns are available: statement-of-logical-reasons pattern, problem–solution pattern, comparative-advantages pattern, criteria-satisfaction pattern, and motivational pattern.

Main points are embellished with supporting material. A useful process is to begin by listing the potential material, then subordinating the material in a way that clarifies the relationship between and among sub-points and main points. Transitions must be used to link major sections of a speech.

After the body is finished, the introduction and conclusion are outlined. The introduction should gain attention, lead into the body of the speech, establish credibility, set the tone for the speech, and create good will. Typical speech introductions include startling statements, rhetorical questions, stories, personal references, quotations, or suspense. The conclusion wraps up the speech, reminds the audience of the main points, and hits home so that the audience will remember. Typical conclusions include summaries, appeals to action, emotional impact statements, and stories.

ANALYSIS	OUTLINE
Write your specific goal statement at the top of the page. Refer to the goal to test whether everything in the outline is relevant.	*Specific speech goal statement:* I want my audience to understand the major criteria for choosing a credit card.
The heading *Introduction* sets the section apart as a separate unit. Whether or not every goal of speech is shown in the wording of the thesis statement, the introduction attempts to (1) get attention, (2) lead into the body, (3) establish credibility, (4) set a tone, and (5) gain good will.	**Introduction** I. How many of you have been hounded by credit card vendors outside the Student Union Building? II. They make a credit card sound like the answer to all of your dreams, don't they? III. Today I want to share with you three criteria you need to consider carefully before deciding on a particular credit card.
The thesis statement states the main idea of the speech and forecasts the main points.	*Thesis statement:* Three major criteria for choosing the credit card that best meets your needs are the rate of interest charged on outstanding balances, the annual fee, and the value of the incentives offered by the credit card provider.
The heading *Body* sets this section apart as a separate unit. In this example, main point I begins a topic order organizational pattern. It is stated as a complete, meaningful sentence. The two major subdivisions of I, designated by A and B, indicate the equal weight of these points. The second-level subdivisions designated by 1, 2, and 3 for the major sub-point A and 1 and 2 for the major sub-point B give the necessary information for understanding the sub-points. The number of major and second-level sub-points is at the discretion of the speaker. After the first two stages of subordination, words and phrases may be used in place of complete sentences in further subdivisions.	**Body** I. One criterion for identifying the best credit card is the interest rate. A. An interest rate is the percentage fee that a provider charges you to carry a balance on your card past the due date. 1. Credit card providers charge an average of 18 percent. 2. Some providers charge as much as 21 percent. 3. Many companies quote very low rates (6 to 8 percent) for specific periods. B. Interest rates can be variable or fixed. 1. Variable rates change from month to month 2. Fixed rates stay the same.
This transition reminds listeners of the first main point and forecasts the second.	(Now that we have considered rates, let's look at the next criterion.)
Main point II, continuing the topic-order pattern, is a complete, meaningful statement paralleling the wording of main point I. Notice that each main point considers only one major idea.	II. A second criterion for identifying the best credit card is the annual fee. A. The provider charges an annual fee in return for extending you credit. B. The charges vary widely. 1. Some cards advertise no annual fee. 2. Most providers charge fees of about $25 per year.

OUTLINE

(After you have considered the interest rate and the annual fee, you can evaluate the other benefits that each provider promises you.)

III. A third criterion for identifying the best credit card is the value of the perks, or incentives, that the credit card provider is offering.
   A. Perks are extras that you get for using a particular card.
      1. Some companies offer rebates.
      2. Some companies offer frequent flier miles.
      3. Some companies offer discounts on a wide variety of items.
   B. The value of the perks never outweigh the costs associated with having a card (interest and annual fee).

Conclusion

I. So, getting the credit card that's right for you may be the answer to your dreams.
II. But only if you exercise care in examining interest rates, annual fee, and perks.

References

Lee, J., & Hogarth, J. M. (2000, Winter). Relationships among information search activities when shopping for a credit card. *Journal of Consumer Affairs, 34,* 330. Retrieved January 22, 2004, from InfoTrac College Edition database.

Orman, S. (1998, February). Minding your money. *Self,* 98.

Rose, S. (1998, September). Prepping for college credit. *Money,* 156–57.

Royal, L. E. (2000, November) Smart credit card use. *Black Enterprise, 31,* 193. Retrieved January 24, 2004, from InfoTrac College Edition database.

The Ultimate Credit Card Guide. (2002.) Retrieved January 22, 2004, from http://www.creditcardguide.org/.

ANALYSIS

This transition summarizes the first two criteria and forecasts the third.

Main point III, continuing the topic-order pattern, is a complete, meaningful statement paralleling the wording of main points I and II.

Throughout the outline, notice that main points and sub-points are factual statements. The speaker adds examples, experiences, and other developmental material during practice sessions.

The heading *Conclusion* sets this section apart as a separate unit. The content of the conclusion is intended to summarize the main ideas and leave the speech on a high note.

A list of sources should always be a part of the speech outline. The sources should show where the factual material of the speech came from. The list of sources is not a total of all available sources, only those that were used directly or indirectly in the speech. Each of the sources is shown here in APA style.

Figure 13.3
Sample speech outline with annotation

Finally, the outline should be reviewed to ensure use of a standard set of symbols, use of complete sentences for main points and major subdivisions, placement of a single idea in each point, relevance of supporting points to major points, and that the outline is no more than one-third the length of the planned speech.

Glossary

Review the following key terms:

***ad hominem* argument** (367) — a fallacy which occurs when a speaker attacks a person rather than the views or arguments expressed by that person.

antonyms (361) — words that have opposite meanings.

appeal to authority fallacy (367) — the use of "expert" testimony from a person who is not an authority on the subject being discussed.

chronological order (358) — an informative speech pattern that presents information according to a time-based sequence of events, stages, or steps.

definition (361) — an explanation of the meaning of a word.

demonstration (362) — a speaker's performance of the steps in an instruction or process explanation.

description (359) — a presentation of sensory data about someone or something: the look, the sound, the feel, the smell, or the taste.

etymology (361) — the derivation or history of a word.

expository speech (363) — speech that emphasizes understanding of an idea and that usually requires outside source material.

extemporaneous speech (352) — a presentation given by a speaker who has carefully planned the points to be made and the order in which they are to be made, but who selects the words to make and explain the points as he or she speaks.

fallacy (367) — a statement or argument based on a false or invalid inference.

false cause arguments (367) — a fallacy that occurs when the alleged cause is unrelated to, or does not produce, the effect.

hasty generalization (367) — a fallacy that occurs when someone generalizes from too few examples.

instruction (362) — telling how to do or make something.

main point (352) — a key idea, an assertion or argument, that supports the idea expressed in the thesis statement of a speech.

process explanations (362) — telling how something works or how something came about, or how something is done.

reasoning by analogy (366) — drawing a conclusion as the result of a comparison of one set of circumstances with another similar set.

reasoning by causation (366) — presenting a conclusion as the effect of a single circumstance or set of circumstances.

reasoning by generalization from example (365) — arguing that what is true in some instances is true in all instances.

reasoning by sign (367) — drawing conclusions based on observable data that usually or always accompany other unobserved variables.

reasons (364) — statements that tell why a proposition is justified.

rhetorical question (373) — a question that calls for a mental rather than a spoken response.

section transitions (356) — complete sentences that link sections of a speech.

synonyms (361) — words that have the same or nearly the same meaning.

topic order (357) — an informative speech pattern that organizes the main points by categories or divisions of a topic.

transitions (356) — words, phrases, or sentences that show a relationship between other words, phrases, or sentences in a speech.

Dave Schaefer/Jeroboam

OBJECTIVES

After you have read this chapter, you should be able to answer these questions:

- What steps can we take to adapt a speech for a particular audience?
- What criteria should we apply in selecting and constructing visual aids?
- What is extemporaneous speaking?
- What elements of language are most relevant to public speaking?
- How can we develop a conversational style of speaking?
- What is an effective method of speech practice?
- How can we control nervousness in a public speaking situation?
- By what criteria are the effectiveness of a speech measured?

CHAPTER 14

Adaptation and Delivery

Jeremy asked his friend Gloria to listen to one of his speech rehearsals. After he had finished the final sentence of the speech, "So, violence does affect people in several ways—it not only desensitizes them, it also contributes to making them behave more aggressively," he asked Gloria, "So, what do you think?"

"You're giving the speech to the Kinsmen Club, right?"

"Yeah."

"Well, you had a lot of good material, but I didn't hear anything that showed that you had your fellow members in mind—you could have been giving the speech to any audience!"

Jeremy had failed to consider an essential fact of public speaking: that a speech is intended for a specific audience. You will recall that effective speech preparation includes five steps. In this chapter, we will consider the final two steps: (4) develop a strategy for adapting material to your specific speech audience, and (5) practise the presentation of your speech.

Audience adaptation is the process of verbally and visually relating material directly to the specific audience. Good delivery is also an essential characteristic of effective speaking. Why? Delivery is the source of the audience's contact with the mind of the speaker, and though delivery cannot improve the ideas in a speech, it can help the speaker make the most of those ideas. The wording of a speech should be clear, vivid, and emphatic, and our delivery should be in a conversational style characterized by enthusiasm, vocal expressiveness, spontaneity, fluency, and eye contact. Integrating those qualities into our performance takes practice. Even those who are not naturally gifted speakers can improve their delivery immensely if they are willing to practise.

Adapting to the Audience

The process of **audience adaptation** involves developing common ground, building and maintaining audience interest, relating to the audience's level of understanding, and reinforcing or changing audience attitudes toward the speaker or topic.

Developing Common Ground

Common ground is the feelings, ideas, opinions, or experiences shared by a speaker and audience. We can develop common ground with an audience by applying four strategies:

1. **Use personal pronouns.** Pronouns that refer directly to ourselves, audience members, or the people that we are speaking about (I, we, you, us, our) suggest to listeners that we are talking directly to them.

   To personalize his speech on the effects of television violence, Jeremy could say, "When *you* think about violence on TV, *you* may wonder how it is affecting your children" instead of "When people think about violence on TV, they may wonder how it affects their children."

2. **Ask rhetorical questions. Rhetorical questions** are questions phrased to stimulate a mental response rather than an actual spoken response. For instance, in his speech on television violence, Jeremy could make one more simple change to increase his audience's sense of participation: "When you watch a particularly violent TV program, have you ever asked yourself, "I wonder whether watching such violent programs is negatively affecting my children?" Sincerely voiced rhetorical questions generate audience participation.

Ryan Remiorz/CP Picture Archive

When you develop common ground with your audience, they will relate better to what you are saying.

3. **Share common experiences.** By selecting and presenting personal experiences, examples, and illustrations that *show* what we and the audience have in common, we build common ground. For instance, Jeremy might ask, "Have your children ever run over to you for a hug during a particularly scary moment in a violent TV program?"

4. **Use familiar points of comparison.** We make unknown information easier to understand by relating it to information already known to audience members. If Florence wanted to share geographical data about France with a Canadian audience, she might say "The area of France is 547,030 sq km. That's about 20 percent smaller than Saskatchewan."

Reworking information to create common ground will take time, but the effort pays big dividends. People are more likely to listen to and accept information or ideas from speakers with whom they feel they have something in common.

Creating and Maintaining Audience Interest

Listeners' interest depends on whether they believe the information affects them personally: "What does this have to do with me?" We can apply four principles to build and maintain audience interest: timeliness, proximity, seriousness, and vividness.

1. **Timeliness:** Listeners are more likely to be interested in information they perceive as timely—that is, information they can use *now*. Suppose that Sandy determines that her speech on the criteria for evaluating diamonds is

not likely to kindle much immediate audience interest. Here is an introduction that may help motivate her listeners to regard knowledge of diamonds as timely: "In thinking about a gift for your significant other, you may have thought briefly about purchasing diamond jewellery, but you shied away because you really don't know much about diamonds, and you thought you might be taken advantage of. Well, today I'd like to help you out by explaining the major criteria for evaluating the quality of diamonds."

2. **Proximity:** Listeners are more likely to be interested in information that has proximity, a relationship to their personal space. Psychologically, we pay more attention to information that affects our *territory* than to information that we perceive as remote from our lives. Speakers who say, "Let me bring this closer to home by explaining how these toxins are affecting our lake," are developing proximity.

3. **Seriousness:** Listeners are more likely to be interested in information that is serious, that has a physical, economic, or psychological impact on them. To build or maintain interest during a speech on toxic waste, Frances could show serious *physical* impact by saying "Toxic waste affects the health of all of us"; she could show serious *economic* impact by saying "Toxic waste cleanup and disposal are expensive—they increase our taxes"; or she could show serious *psychological* impact by saying "Toxic waste diminishes the quality of our lives and the lives of our children."

4. **Vividness:** Listeners are more likely to be interested in anecdotes, examples, and illustrations that are vivid—that stimulate the senses. For instance, in the middle of her speech on toxic waste, Frances may see attention flagging as she presents technical information. Instead of waiting until she has lost the audience, she might choose this time to say, "Let me share with you a story that illustrates the gravity of toxic waste in our fresh water lakes."

   Just because we have a great number of attention-getting stories, examples, and illustrations does not mean that we have to use all of them. The effective speaker is sensitive to audience reaction at all times. When the audience is really with us, there is no need to break the rhythm, but when we sense the audience is not following along, that is the time to introduce material that will pique attention. We must bear in mind, however, that such information must pertain directly to the point that we are making.

Adapting to the Audience's Level of Understanding

If we predict that our listeners do not have the necessary background to understand the information we will be presenting, we will need to orient them. If, however, we predict that our audience has sufficient background, we will need to present our information in a way that will ensure continuous understanding.

1. **Orient listeners.** Because listeners are likely to stop paying attention if they are lost at the start of a speech, a good rule of thumb is to err on the side of expecting too little knowledge rather than on that of expecting too much. If it seems likely that some people may not have necessary background knowledge, take time to review it. For instance, if Gavin is giving a speech about changes in political and economic conditions in the Middle East, he can be reasonably sure that all members of his audience are aware of the American invasion of Iraq. However, they may not all remember the names of specific cities that have been conquered or the geography of the country, so before launching into details of life in the country today, he should remind his listeners of the names of the places that he is going to refer to.

   Because some of Gavin's listeners will be knowledgable, a good way to present the information without insulting their intelligence is to give the impression that he is reviewing information. For example, he could begin by saying "As you will recall . . ."

2. **Present new information.** Even when we predict that our audience has the necessary background information, we still need to consider ways of presenting new information to ensure understanding. We can use devices such as defining, describing, exemplifying, and comparing to help clarify information that may be difficult for some audience members. A speaker must keep in mind that an audience is made up of individuals with different comprehension styles. Considering these questions can ensure that we leave no one out:

   a. *Have you defined all key terms carefully?* For instance, if Gail's specific goal statement is, "I want my audience to understand four major problems faced by those who are functionally illiterate," she might include this definition in her introduction:

      "By functionally illiterate, I mean people who have trouble performing tasks that require reading and writing."

   b. *Have you supported every generalization with at least one specific example?* For instance, suppose that Gail made the statement, "Many Canadians who are functionally illiterate cannot read well enough to understand simple directions."

      She could then add the example, "For instance, they might not be able to understand a label that says, 'take three times a day after meals.' "

   c. *Have you compared or contrasted new information to information your audience already understands?* For instance, if Gail wanted the audience to sense what it feels like to be functionally illiterate, she might compare it to trying to function in a foreign country which uses a different language.

d. *Have you used more than one means of development for significant points you want the audience to remember?* This final bit of advice is based on a sound psychological principle: the more different kinds of explanations a speaker gives, the more listeners will understand. To return to Gail's statement: "Large numbers of Canadians who are functionally illiterate cannot read well enough to understand simple directions."

To this statement she added an example: "For instance, a person who is functionally illiterate might not be able to read or understand a label that says 'take three times a day after eating,'" but she could build that statement even further: "A significant number of Canadians are functionally illiterate. That is, about 9.7 percent of the adult population, or around 2.9 million people, have serious difficulties with common reading tasks. They cannot read well enough to understand simple cooking instructions, directions for an appliance, or rules to play a game. For instance, a person who is functionally illiterate might not be able to read or understand a label that says 'take three times a day after eating.'" In short speeches we cannot fully develop every item of information; we can, however, identify our highest priority concepts and build them fully using two or three different approaches to development.

Building a Positive Attitude toward the Speaker

If we predict that the audience will have a positive attitude toward us, then we need only maintain that attitude. If, however, we predict that the audience has no opinion or, for some reason, has a negative attitude toward us, then we will want to develop our credibility—our power, based on the audience's perception of our knowledge, trustworthiness, and amiability, to inspire belief. There are several ways to do this.

1. **Build audience perception of your knowledge and expertise.** The first step in building a perception of knowledge and expertise is to go into the speech fully prepared. Audiences have an almost instinctive knowledge of when a speaker is *winging it,* and most audiences lose respect for a speaker who has not thought enough of them to be well prepared. The next step is to show that we have a wealth of high-quality examples, illustrations, and personal experiences. For example, students generally perceive a professor who has a good supply of supporting information more favourably than one who seems to have only the bare facts. The third step is to show any direct involvement we have had in the area about which we are speaking. In addition to increasing the audience's perception of our depth of knowledge, personal involvement increases the audience's perception of our practical understanding of the issues and our personal concern about the subject. For example, if, in her speech on toxic waste, Frances shares her personal experiences in local and national environmental action groups, her credibility will increase.

2. **Build audience perception of your trustworthiness.** The more listeners see us as one of them, the easier it is for us to establish our trustworthiness. The more our listeners see us as different, the more difficult it will be. Part of building credibility depends on our ability to bridge gaps between us and our audience.

   Listeners will make value judgments about us, so we should consider what we can do to demonstrate that we are honest, industrious, dependable, and ethical. Listeners will also judge our motives, so it is important to show, early in the speech, why they need to know our information. Then, throughout the speech, we can emphasize our sincere interest in their well-being. For her speech on toxic waste, for example, Frances could explain *how* a local dumpsite adversely affects the community.

3. **Build audience perception of your personality.** Audience perceptions of a speaker's personality are likely to be based on first impressions. Therefore, we should dress appropriately, groom ourselves carefully, and carry ourselves with poise. In addition, audiences react favourably to speakers who are friendly. A smile and a pleasant tone of voice go a long way in showing warmth and will increase listeners' comfort with us and our ideas.

We will discuss three additional features of building a positive relationship with an audience (enthusiasm, vocal expressiveness, and eye contact) later when we turn our attention to speech presentation.

Adapting to the Audience's Attitude toward Your Speech Goal

This adaptation is especially important for persuasive speeches, but it can be important for informative speeches as well. An audience **attitude** is a predisposition for or against people, places, or things, and it usually is expressed as an opinion. At the outset, we should try to predict whether listeners will view our topic positively, negatively, or in a neutral manner. If Kenneth thinks that listeners will view antiquing furniture as difficult or unimportant, he will need to take time early in the speech to change their opinion.

Speakers from different cultures can have special problems adapting to an audience's attitude because they are less familiar with the dominant Canadian culture. Two specific problems commonly faced by people with different backgrounds are difficulty with the English language and the lack of a common set of experiences to draw upon. Difficulty with the language includes both difficulty with pronunciation and difficulty with vocabulary and idiomatic speech. Both of these could make a speaker feel self-conscious. However, the lack of a common set of experiences to draw upon is more significant. Much of our information is gained through comparison and examples, and the lack of common experiences may make drawing comparisons and finding appropriate examples difficult.

IN BRIEF

Adapting to the Audience

Speakers must adapt themselves and their material to their specific audiences by

- finding and developing common ground with the audience
- creating and maintaining audience interest in the speech topic
- adapting speech content to the audience's level of understanding
- building a positive attitude toward themselves as speaker
- adapting their material and presentation to the audience's attitude toward the speech goal.

Difficulty with pronunciation might require a speaker to speak more slowly and to make a special effort to articulate as clearly as possible. It also helps to be comfortable with the topic, and it is useful to practise at least once with a native speaker of English who can help make sure that the language in the speech is appropriate, and the examples and comparisons meaningful. Most listeners are much more tolerant of mistakes made by people who are speaking in a second language.

Creating Visual Aids

At this point in the speech preparation, we are ready to consider whether and how we should present speech content visually. **Visual aids** can clarify verbal information by enabling members of the audience to see as well as hear information. People are likely to learn considerably more when ideas appeal to both eye and ear than when they appeal to the ear alone (Tversky, 1997, p. 258). People are also likely to remember information shown on visual aids longer (Patterson, Danscreau, & Newbern, 1992, pp. 453–461).

It is important to remember that visual aids are *always* an aid to the audience, never to the speaker, so we should decide on how many and which visual aids we need based only on what we consider to be the audience's need for assistance. We will consider common types of visual aids, presentation media for showing visual aids, and design issues.

Types of Visual Aids

The number of types of visual aids is really limited only by a speaker's imagination, but the following types are among the most commonly used.

The speaker On occasion, *we* can be our own best visual aid. For instance, through descriptive gestures, we could show the height of a tennis net; through posture and movement we could show the motions involved in swimming the butterfly stroke; and through our attire we could illustrate the native dress of a co-culture or foreign culture to which we belong.

Objects A cell phone, a basketball, or a braided rug are examples of objects we could present to an audience. Objects make good visual aids if (1) they are large enough to be seen (consider how far away people will be sitting) and (2) they are small enough to carry. For instance, Erin used a volleyball throughout much of her speech to show the audience how to spike.

Models When an object is too large to bring to the speech site or too small to be seen, a three-dimensional model may be an acceptable substitute. If we were talking about a turbine engine, a suspension bridge, an Egyptian pyramid, or the structure of an atom, a model might well be the best visual aid. Working models can be especially eye-catching.

Photographs Photos are useful visual aids when we need an exact reproduction. To be effective, they must be large enough to be seen from the back of the room and simple enough to make the point at a glance.

Films Although films can be brought to an audience, they are seldom appropriate for speeches—mostly because they so dominate the situation that the speaker loses control. Occasionally, during a longer speech, we may want to use short clips of a minute or two each. Still, because projecting film usually requires darkening the room for a portion of the time, using film in a speech is often disruptive. DVD players and data projectors have made it much easier to project film than was possible with film projectors, but they still must be used with caution. A film can very easily overwhelm a speaker.

Still images (slides) The advantage of still images over film is that the speaker can control when each image will be shown. The remote-control device enables us to pace the projection of the slides and to talk about each one as long as necessary. As with using film, projecting slides can require darkening the room, and novice speakers may lose control of their audience.

Mary Stangolis/Thomson Nelson

Still images get and hold attention and can be seen by the entire audience.

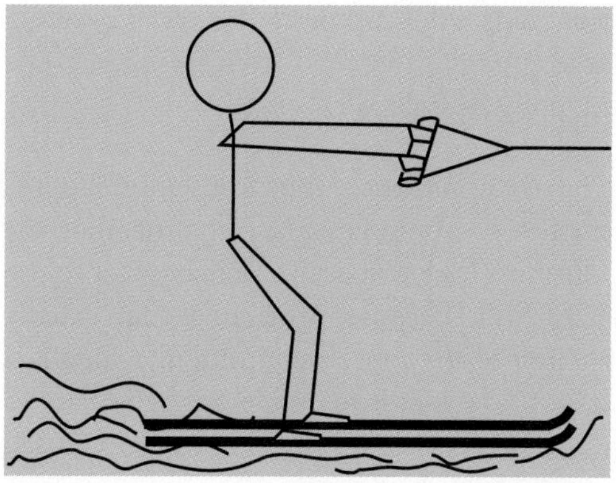

Figure 14.1
Sample drawing

Drawings Simple drawings are easy to prepare. Anyone who can use a compass, a straight edge, and a measure can draw well enough for most speech purposes. For instance, if we wanted to make the point that water skiers must hold their arms and back straight and their knees slightly bent, a stick figure such as the one shown in Figure 14.1 would illustrate the point. Stick figures may not be as aesthetically pleasing as professional drawings, but they work just as well. In fact, elaborate, detailed drawings may obscure the point we wish to make.

Maps Like drawings, maps are relatively easy to prepare. Simple maps enable viewers to focus on landmarks (mountains, rivers, and lakes), countries, provinces, cities, land routes, or weather systems. Figure 14.2 is a good example of a map that focuses on weather systems.

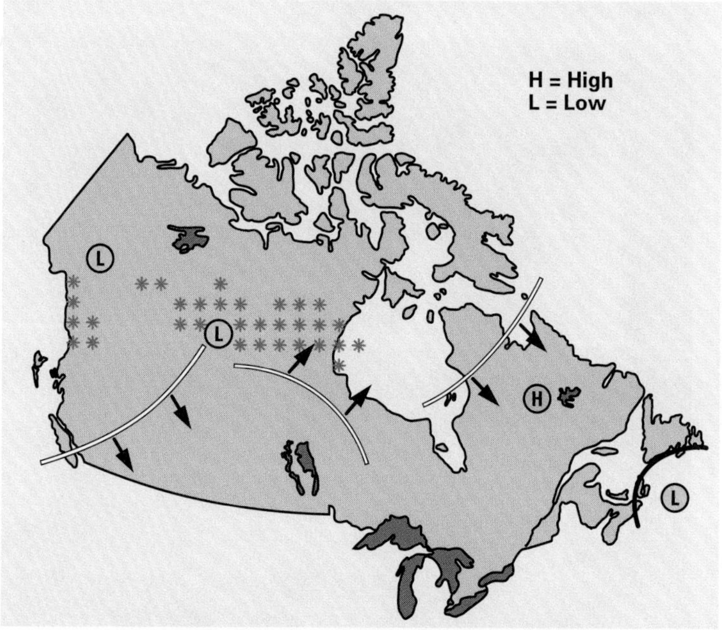

Figure 14.2
Sample map

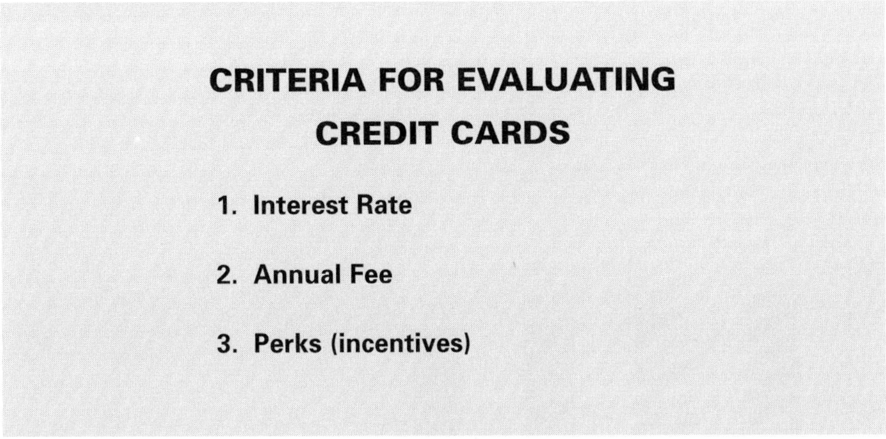

Figure 14.3
Sample word chart

Charts A **chart** is a graphic representation that distils a lot of information and presents it to an audience in an easily interpreted format. Word charts and organizational charts are the most common. **Word charts** are often used to preview material that will be covered in a speech, to summarize material, and to remind an audience of speech content. For her speech on credit cards, Emma might make a word chart that lists key topics such as the one shown in Figure 14.3. A brief outline can be considered a word chart. **Organizational charts** use symbols and connecting lines to diagram step-by-step progressions through a complicated procedure or system. The chart in Figure 14.4 illustrates the organization of a student union board.

Graphs A **graph** is a diagram that presents numerical or statistical data visually. Graphs can have many uses; for example, to make comparisons, show trends, or present results. **Bar graphs**, used to compare data represented by vertical or horizontal bars, can show relationships between two or more variables at the same time or at various times on one or more dimensions. For instance, the bar graph in Figure 14.5 shows a drop in Canada's GDP (gross domestic

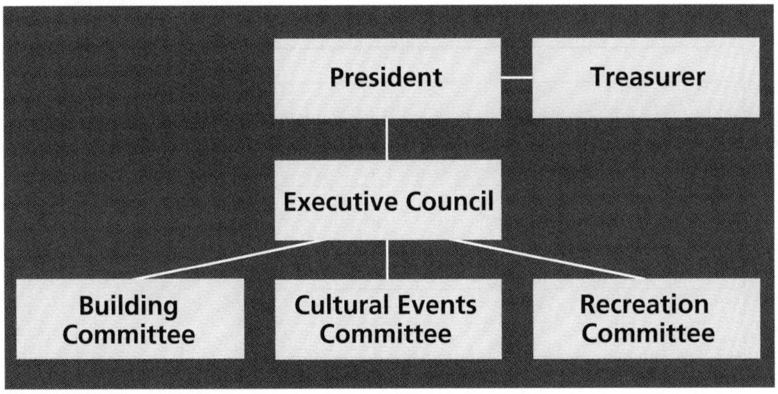

Figure 14.4
Sample organizational chart

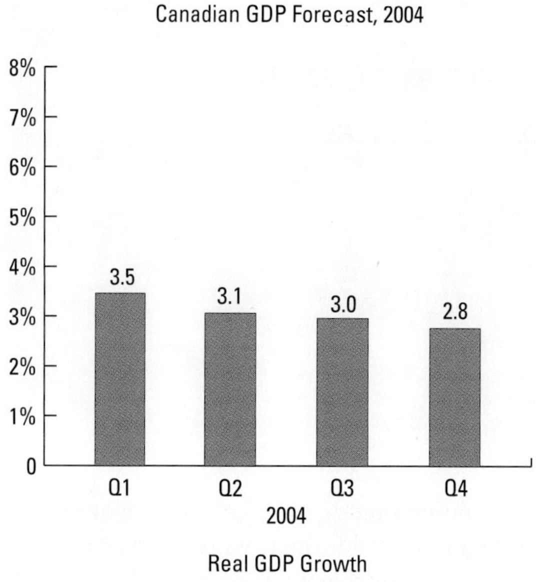

Figure 14.5
Sample bar graph

product) between the end of the first and fourth quarters in 2004. **Line graphs** are diagrams that indicate changes in one or more variables over time. In a speech on the population of Canada, for example, the line graph in Figure 14.6 shows the population increase, in millions, from 1851 to 2001. **Pie graphs** are diagrams that show relationships among parts of a single unit. In a speech on the effect of tax cuts, a pie graph such as the one in Figure 14.7 could be used to show public opinion.

Media for Showing Visual Aids

Though computer-mediated visual aids are becoming increasingly dominant today, a number of other media may work just as well or better, depending on the setting and the occasion.

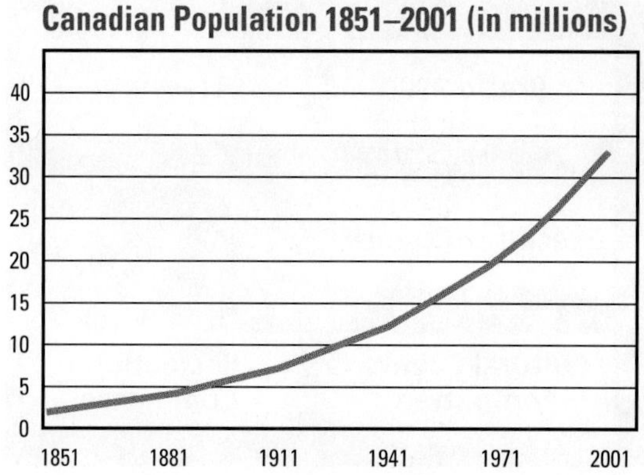

Figure 14.6
Sample line graph

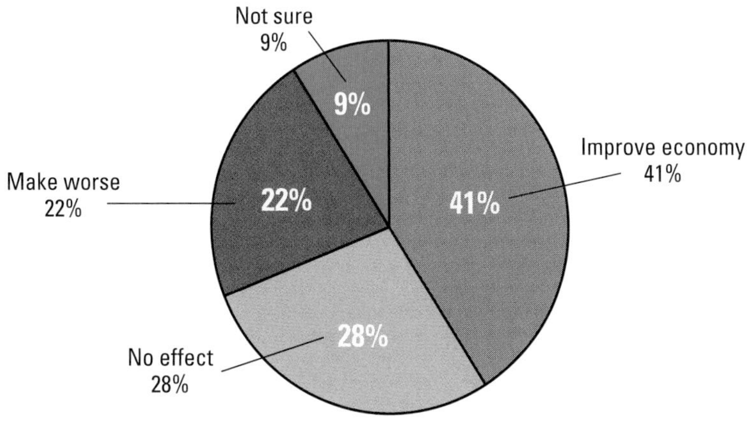

Figure 14.7
Sample pie graph

Source: *Time*, February 19, 2001, p. 30.

Handouts On the plus side, we can prepare handouts (material printed or drawn on sheets of paper) quickly, and all the people in the audience can have their own professional-quality material to refer to and take with them from the speech. On the minus side are the distractions of distributing handouts and the potential for losing the audience's attention. Before deciding on handouts, we should consider each of the following means of showing visual aids. Handouts should be distributed at the end of the speech.

Chalkboard/whiteboard As a means of displaying simple information, the chalkboard or whiteboard, still a staple in many college and university classrooms, is unbeatable. Unfortunately, it is also easy to misuse and to overuse. Moreover, it is unlikely that the chalkboard would be our first choice for any major analysis of a process or procedure because of its limitations in displaying complex material. One common error in using the chalkboard is to write too much material while talking, an error that often results in displays that are either illegible or partly obscured by the speaker's body as he or she writes. A second common error is to spend too much time talking to the board instead of to the audience. Right-handed people should stand to the right of what they are writing, left-handed people to the left, and both should try to face at least part of the audience while they work.

Overhead transparencies Another old standby was to project visual aids onto a screen via an overhead projector. Though they have been largely replaced by computerized data projectors today, overheads still offer several advantages: they do not require dimming of the lights in the room; the speaker can write, trace, or draw on the transparency while talking; and the speaker need not turn away from the audience to write or point to a visual aid.

Computer-mediated visual aids Today, most of the graphics used as visual aids are rendered by computer and projected using computerized data projectors. If the hardware and software is in place, these systems allow speakers to produce professional-quality visual aids at very low cost. Except for complex multimedia presentations, computer graphics are not so much a new type of visual aid as a new way of producing and projecting visual aids. Speakers should familiarize themselves with one of the many computer graphics systems (such as Microsoft PowerPoint, Apple Keynote, or Lotus Freelance Graphics) to prepare visual material for speeches.

Designing Visual Aids

The visual aids that people are most likely to use in their presentations are computer-generated slides, drawings, and overheads. Observing the following design principles will result in effective visual aids.

1. **Use a typeface that is pleasing to the eye.** Modern software packages come with a variety of typefaces. Figure 14.8 shows Helvetica (a sans-serif font) and Times (a serif font). Sans-serif characters do not have cross strokes at the ends of the lines, while serif characters do. In print, sans-serif fonts are used for headings and serif fonts for text type. However, many people claim that sans-serif type is easier to read on computer screens. Be sure the typeface you choose is easy to read. Many typefaces that look especially pretty or dramatic are not.

2. **Use words or images that can be seen easily by the entire audience.** We can check an image or lettering for size by moving as far away from the visual aid as the most distant audience member. If words and details are not legible from that distance, they should be enlarged. Because projection will increase the size of lettering, 36-point type for major headings, 24-point for subheadings, and 18-point for text usually are large enough. Figure 14.9 illustrates how these look on paper. Use a sans-serif font for type that is going to be electronically projected.

3. **Use upper- and lowercase type.** The combination of upper- and lowercase is easier to read. Some people think that printing in all capital letters adds emphasis, but it is more difficult to read—even when the phrases are short.

Helvetica	Selecting Typefaces **Selecting Typefaces**
Times	Selecting Typefaces **Selecting Typefaces**

Figure 14.8
Typefaces in 18-point regular and boldface

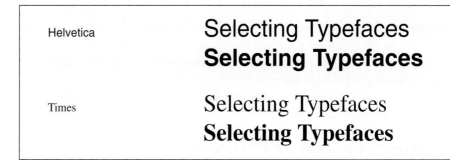

Points	Use
36	Major Headings
24	Subheads
18	Text material

Figure 14.9
Visual-aid print sizes

4. **Put no more than six lines of type on a visual aid.** We do not want the audience to have to spend a long time reading our visual aids. We want them to listen to us. Write points as phrases rather than as complete sentences.
5. **Focus on information that will be emphasized in the speech.** We often get ideas for visual aids from other sources, and the tendency is to include all the material that was in the original, but for speech purposes, we should keep the aid as simple as possible, focusing on key information and eliminating anything that distracts or takes emphasis away from the point we want to make. Consider the two graphs in Figure 14.10. The graph on the left shows all 11 categories mentioned; the graph on the right simplifies this information by combining age ranges with small percentages. The graph on the right is not only easier to read but also emphasizes the highest percentage classifications.
6. **Make sure information is laid out in a way that is aesthetically pleasing.** Layout involves ensuring white space around the whole message, indenting subordinate ideas, and using different sized type as well as different typographic features, such as bolding and underlining.

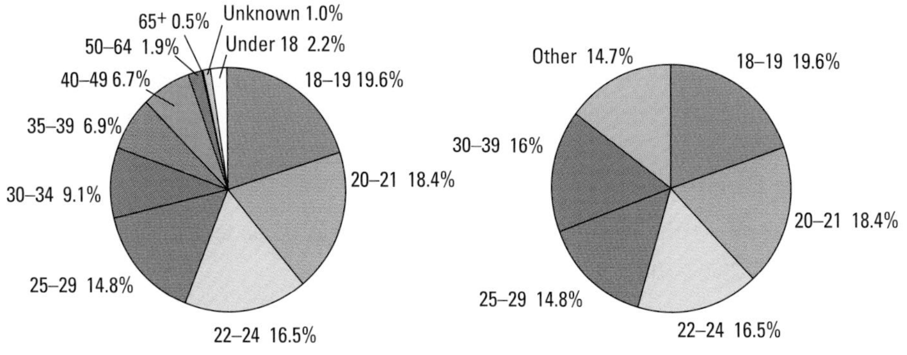

Figure 14.10
Comparative graphs

Source: *Chronicle of Higher Education,* Almanac Issue, August 28, 1998, p. 18.

I WANT YOU TO REMEMBER THE THREE R'S OF RECYCLING

Reduce the amount of waste people produce like overpacking or using material that won't recycle.

Reuse by relying on cloth towels rather than paper towels, earthenware dishes rather than paper or plastic plates, and glass bottles rather than aluminum cans.

Recycle by collecting recyclable products, sorting them appropriately, and getting them to the appropriate recycling agency.

Figure 14.11
A cluttered and cumbersome visual aid

7. **Add clip art where appropriate.** When working with computer graphics, adding clip art can make language-based slides look both more professional and more dramatic. Most computer graphics packages have a wide variety of clip art to choose from and much more is available on the Internet. Clip art can be overdone, however, so we should be careful not to let our message be overpowered.

8. **Strive to get beyond language-based visual aids.** If we remember that the purpose of visual aids is to help audience members understand information that we are presenting in words, we should recognize that visuals filled with words are likely to be less helpful than those that present the information in a different way. We should try to find creative ways to present difficult information *visually*.

Now let's see if we can put all of this advice to work. Figure 14.11 contains a lot of important information, but notice how unpleasant this visual aid is to the eye. It violates all the rules for effective presentation. However, with some thoughtful simplification, this speaker could produce the visual aid shown in Figure 14.12, which sharpens the focus by emphasizing the key words (reduce, re-use, recycle), highlighting the major details, and adding clip art for a professional touch.

Making Choices

Here are some of the key questions that we should consider to make the best choices with visual aids.

1. **What are the most important ideas to help me achieve my speech goal?** Visual aids and the material on them are likely to be remembered. We should use them only to reinforce important ideas.

Figure 14.12
A simple but effective visual aid

2. **How large is the audience?** The kind of visual aid that will work for a group of 20 or fewer is far different from the kind that will work for an audience of 100 or more. For instance, for a small audience, we can show relatively small objects and small models—everyone will be able to see them. For very large audiences, we will need projections that can be seen from 30 to 60 metres away.
3. **Is the necessary equipment readily available?** There will be times when we will be speaking in an environment that does not have all of the equipment or the same equipment that we would like. We should make sure that any electronic projection equipment at the speech site is compatible with the equipment that we use to produce the visual aids. In any situation, equipment can fail, so experienced speakers always have a (usually low-tech) backup set of visual aids.
4. **Is the time involved in making or getting the visual aid or equipment cost-effective?** Visual aids are supplements. We use them to accent what we are doing verbally. If a particular visual aid will help us to better achieve a goal, then the time spent is well worth it, but spending a large amount of time preparing visual aids to illustrate minor points is seldom cost-effective.

OBSERVE & ANALYZE
Journal Activity

Selecting Visual Aids

1. Carefully study the verbal information you are planning to use in your speech. Indicate where you believe visual aids would be effective in creating audience interest, facilitating understanding, or increasing retention. Limit your choices to four or five spots at most, since your time limits for an in-class speech are likely to be four to six minutes.
2. Then indicate which kinds of visual aids would be most effective in each of the places you have identified: Yourself? Objects? Models? Charts? Pictorial representations? Projections? Chalkboard? Handouts? Computer graphics?
3. Finally, indicate specifics for the visual aids themselves. For instance, if you have elected to use a chart for one place, what are you likely to put on it?

IN BRIEF

Creating Visual Aids

Visual aids will attract audience members' attention, help them understand complex ideas, and aid their recall. Create visual aids

- with the audience, occasion, and setting in mind
- that are simple and easy to read
- that emphasize major points in the speech.

5. **How many visual aids should I consider?** Except in the case of a slide show, in which the total focus of the speech is on visual images, the number of visual aids to use is likely to be relatively few. For the most part, we want the focus of the audience on us, the speaker. For a five-minute speech, three visual aids used at crucial times will get attention, exemplify, and stimulate recall far better than six or eight.

Speech Components that Require Practice

Although speeches may be presented impromptu (on the spur of the moment without prior preparation), by manuscript (completely written out and then read aloud), or by memory (completely written out and then memorized), the material you have been reading is designed to help you present your speeches extemporaneously. As pointed out in Chapter 12, *extemporaneous speeches* are carefully prepared and practised, but the exact wording is determined at the time of utterance. Now that our outline and visual aids are prepared, it is time to practise. As we practise, we will be analyzing the verbal and nonverbal components of our presentation.

Verbal Components

Listeners cannot re-read what a speaker has said. To be an effective speaker, it is important to use specific, concrete, and precise words (as discussed in Chapter 3), but we will also want to work to make our wording vivid and emphatic.

Vivid language Vivid words are descriptive, full of life, vigorous, bright, and intense. For example, a play-by-play commentator might say, "Jackson made a great save," but a more vivid account would be, "Jackson dived and made a scintillating one-handed grab just as he was sent sprawling to the ice." The words *dived*, *one-handed grab*, and *was sent sprawling* paint an intense verbal picture of the action. Vivid speech begins with vivid thought. We are much more likely to *express* ourselves vividly if our listeners can *sense* the meanings that we are trying to convey. Similes and metaphors can add vividness to a speech, but it is wise to stay away from trite clichés. We should try to express our ideas in original ways.

Emphatic language **Emphasis** gives force or intensity to words or ideas. In our speeches, we should try to emphasize through proportion, repetition, and use of transitions. **Emphasis by proportion** means spending more time on one idea than on another, resulting in listeners' *perceiving* that point as more important.

Emphasis by repetition means saying important words or ideas more than once. We can either repeat the exact words, "A ring-shaped coral island almost or completely surrounding a lagoon is called an *atoll*—the word is atoll," or we can restate the idea in different language, "The test will comprise about four essay questions; that is, all the questions on the test will be the kind that require you to discuss material in some detail." **Emphasizing through transitions** means using words that show and emphasize idea relationships. In Chapter 14, we talked about section transitions that summarize, clarify, and forecast. Word transitions can be used to serve some additional functions:

- To add material: also, and, likewise, again, in addition, moreover, similarly, further.
- To sum up, summarize, or show results: therefore, and so, so, finally, all in all, on the whole, in short, thus, as a result.
- To indicate changes in direction or contrasts: but, however, yet, on the other hand, still, although, while, no doubt.
- To indicate reasons: because, for.
- To show causal or time relationships: then, since, as.
- To explain, exemplify, or limit: in other words, in fact, for example, that is to say, more specifically.

Finally, whether we are trying to be specific, precise, vivid, or emphatic, we should make sure that we use words that are understood by all our listeners. Sometimes speakers believe they will be more impressive if they use big words, but big words often seem pompous, affected, or stilted. When you have a choice, select the simplest, most familiar word that expresses your precise meaning.

Nonverbal Components

As we saw in Chapter 4, the nonverbal components of speech presentation are voice, articulation, and bodily action.

Voice **Voice** includes pitch (highness and lowness on a scale), volume (loudness), rate (speed of speech), and quality (tone, timbre, or sound of voice). We strive to ensure that our listeners perceive our voice as pleasant: neither too high nor too low; neither too loud nor too soft; neither too fast nor too slow.

Pronunciation and articulation **Articulation** is shaping speech sounds into recognizable oral symbols that combine to produce a word. Articulation is often confused with **pronunciation**, the form and accent of various syllables of a word. In the word *statistics*, for instance, articulation refers to shaping the ten sounds (s-t-a-t-i-s-t-i-k-s); pronunciation refers to grouping and accenting the sounds (sta-tis*-tiks). Whenever we are unsure of how to pronounce a word in a speech, we should consult a dictionary for the proper pronunciation.

"LADIES AND GENTLEMEN... IS THAT MY VOICE?.. I NEVER HEARD IT AMPLIFIED BEFORE. IT SOUNDS SO WEIRD. HELLO. HELLO. I CAN'T BELIEVE IT'S ME. WHAT A STRANGE SENSATION. ONE, TWO, THREE... HELLO. WOW..."

We want to avoid adding a sound where none appears (ath*a*lete for athlete), leaving out a sound where one occurs (libary for lib*r*ary), transposing sounds (re*va*lent for re*le*vant), or distorting sounds (tru*f* for tru*th*). Although some of us have consistent articulation problems that require speech therapy (such as substituting *th* for *s* consistently in speech), most of us are guilty of carelessness that can be corrected through more careful attention and practice.

Two of the most common articulation faults are slurring sounds (running sounds and words together) or leaving off word endings. Spoken English always will contain some running together of sounds. For instance, most people are likely to say "tha-table" for "that table"—it is simply too difficult to make two "t" sounds in a row—but many of us slur sounds and drop word endings to excess. "Who ya gonna see?" for "Who are you going to see?" illustrates both of these errors. A mild case of *sluritis,* caused by not taking the time to form sounds clearly, can be overcome by taking 10 to 15 minutes three days a week to read passages aloud, trying to over-accentuate each sound. Some teachers advocate *chewing* the words—that is, making sure that lips, jaw, and tongue move carefully to voice each sound. As with most other problems of delivery, speakers must work conscientiously several days a week for months to improve significantly.

Figure 14.13 lists many common problem words that people are likely to mispronounce or misarticulate.

THINKING ABOUT . . .

Voice and Articulation Problems

Indicate what you regard as your major problem of voice and articulation (such as speaking in a monotone or slurring words). Outline a plan for working on the problem.

Word	Correct	Incorrect
arctic	arc*-tic	ar*-tic
athlete	ath*lete	ath*a-lete
family	fam*-a-ly	fam*-ly
February	Feb*-ru-ary	Feb*-yu-ary
get	get	git
larynx	ler*-inks	lar*-nix
library	ly*brer-y	ly*-ber-y
particular	par-tik*-yu-ler	par-tik*-ler
picture	pic*-ture	pitch*-er
recognize	rek*-ig-nize	rek*-a-nize
relevant	rel*-e-vant	rev*-e-lant
theatre	thee*-a-ter	thee-ay*-ter
truth	truth	truf
with	with	wit or wid

Figure 14.13
Problem words

A major concern of speakers from different cultures and different parts of the country is their *accent:* the inflection, tone, and speech habits typical of the natives of a country, region, or even a province or city. When should we work to lessen or eliminate any accent we may have? If an accent is so heavy or different from people's expectations that the speaker has difficulty communicating effectively, or if he or she expects to go into teaching, broadcasting, or another profession where an accent may have an adverse effect on performance, he or she should make an effort to lessen or eliminate the accent.

Bodily action **Bodily action** includes facial expression, gestures, posture, and movement. We discussed bodily actions in Chapter 4, and in this section, we want to focus on aspects of those nonverbal behaviours that affect public speaking.

We should try to make sure that our **facial expressions** (eye and mouth movements) are appropriate to what we are saying. Audiences respond negatively to deadpan expressions or perpetual grins or scowls. Audiences respond positively to honest and sincere expressions that reflect our thoughts and feelings. If we think actively about what we are saying, our faces will respond appropriately.

Gestures are the movements of our hands, arms, and fingers that describe and emphasize. Gesturing does not come easily to some people; for them, it is probably best not to force themselves. To encourage gestures, we should keep our hands free at all times to help us do what comes naturally. If we clasp our hands behind our back, grip the sides of the speaker's stand, or put our hands into our pockets, we will not be able to gesture naturally even if we want to.

Posture is the position or bearing of the body. In speeches, an upright stance and squared shoulders communicate a sense of poise to an audience. Speakers who slouch may give an unfavourable impression of themselves, including the

IN BRIEF

Components to Practise in a Speech

In practising a speech, we should focus on two sets of components:

1. Verbal components
   - vividness
   - emphasis.
2. Nonverbal components
   - voice
   - articulation and pronunciation
   - bodily action
   - poise.

impression of limited self-confidence or an uncaring attitude. If we find ourselves in some peculiar posture during a speech, we should return to the upright position with our weight equally distributed on both feet.

Movement refers to the motion of the entire body. Ideally, movement should help focus on transitions, emphasize ideas, or call attention to a particular aspect of the speech. We should try to avoid such unmotivated movement as bobbing and weaving, shifting from foot to foot, or pacing from one side of the room to the other. Standing up straight on both feet at the beginning of the speech will help.

Poise **Poise** refers to assurance of manner. A poised speaker is able to avoid mannerisms that distract the audience such as taking off or putting on glasses, smacking the tongue, licking the lips, or scratching the nose, hand, or arm. As a general rule, anything that calls attention to itself is negative, and anything that helps reinforce an important idea is positive. Likewise, a poised speaker is able to control speech nervousness, a topic we will discuss later in this chapter.

Achieving a Conversational Quality

In our speech practice, as well as in the speech itself, the final measure of our presentation is how well we use our vocal and nonverbal components to develop a **conversational quality,** a style of presentation that *sounds* like conversation to our listeners. Five components of conversational quality are enthusiasm, vocal expressiveness, spontaneity, fluency, and eye contact.

Enthusiasm

Enthusiasm is excitement or passion about the topic of a speech. If sounding enthusiastic does not come naturally to us, we should make sure that we have a topic that really excites us. Even normally enthusiastic people can have trouble

TEST YOUR COMPETENCE

Monitoring Voice and Bodily Action

Use one of these methods to monitor your nonverbal behaviour.

1. Practise a portion of your speech in front of a mirror to see how you look to others when you speak. (Although some speakers swear by this method, others find it a traumatic experience.)
2. Videotape your speech, and replay it for analysis.
3. Have a friend listen to a practice. Give your friend some directions, such as "Raise your hand every time I begin to rock back and forth." By getting specific feedback when the behaviour occurs, you can learn to become aware of it and make immediate adjustments.

Skill Builders Enthusiasm

Skill	Use	Procedure	Example
Using your voice and bodily action to show the audience that you are excited about the topic and your opportunity to talk with them about it.	To ensure audience perception of the importance and relevance of the information to them.	1. Make sure you are truly excited about your topic. 2. As you speak, re-create your original feelings of excitement. 3. Focus on sharing that feeling of excitement with the audience.	As Trisha was practising her speech on her trip to Alberta, she refocused on her feelings of awe as she first saw mountain peak after mountain peak. She also reminded herself of how much she wanted her audience to actually feel what she had experienced.

sounding enthusiastic when they choose an uninspiring topic. Then, we should focus on how the audience will benefit from the speech. If we are convinced that we have something worthwhile to communicate, we are likely to feel and show more enthusiasm. A speaker who looks and sounds enthusiastic will be listened to, and that speaker's ideas will be remembered (Williams & Ware, 1976, p. 50).

Vocal Expressiveness

The greatest indication of enthusiasm is **vocal expressiveness,** the vocal contrasts in pitch, volume, rate, and quality that affect the meaning audiences get from the sentences a speaker presents. A total lack of vocal expressiveness produces a **monotone,** a voice in which the pitch, volume, and rate remain constant, with no word, idea, or sentence differing significantly from any other. Although few people speak in a true monotone, many severely limit themselves by using only two or three pitch levels and relatively unchanging volume and rate. An actual or near monotone not only lulls an audience to sleep, but more importantly, diminishes the chances of audience understanding.

For instance, if the sentence *We need to prosecute abusers* is presented in a monotone, listeners would be uncertain of the message the speaker wanted to communicate. To illustrate how vocal expressiveness affects meaning, read this sentence aloud four times, each time emphasizing the italicized word:

- *We* need to prosecute abusers.
- We *need* to prosecute abusers.
- We need to *prosecute* abusers.
- We need to prosecute *abusers.*

When we emphasize *We,* the sentence answers the question "Who will do it?" When we emphasize *need,* it answers the question "How important is it?" When we emphasize *prosecute,* it answers the question "What are we going to

SKILL BUILDERS Vocal Expressiveness

Skill	Use	Procedure	Example
Using contrasts in pitch, volume, rate, and quality.	To express the meanings you want audiences to get from the sentences you present.	1. Identify the words you want to stress to best express your intended meaning. 2. Raise your pitch or increase your volume on key words.	As Margaret thought about what she wanted to emphasize, she said, "You need to put your *left hand* at the *bottom* of the bat."

do?" When we emphasize *abusers,* it answers the question "Who will be prosecuted?" To ensure audience understanding, a voice must be expressive enough to delineate shades of meaning.

Spontaneity

Speakers who are enthusiastic and vocally expressive are also likely to present their speeches so that they sound spontaneous. **Spontaneity** means being so responsive to our ideas that the speech seems as fresh as a lively conversation, even though it has been well practised. How can we make our outlined and practised speech sound spontaneous? By learning the *ideas* of the speech—not *memorizing the words.* Suppose someone asks us about the route we take to drive to school. Because we are familiar with the route, we need not have it written out or memorized—we can present it spontaneously because we *know* it. We develop spontaneity in our speeches by getting to know the ideas in them as well.

SKILL BUILDERS Spontaneity

Skill	Use	Procedure	Example
Being responsive to the ideas of your speech.	To ensure that your audience perceives your speech as a lively and fresh interaction even though it has been well practised.	1. Learn the ideas of your speech. 2. In each practice session, express the idea and its development in slightly different language.	As Connie was talking about day care, she allowed herself to report a personal experience that she had not planned on using in the speech.

Fluency

Effective presentation is also **fluent,** devoid of hesitations and such vocal interferences as *eh, ah, uh, er, well, okay, you know,* and *like* (see Chapter 4). Fluency can be developed through awareness and practice. We can train ourselves to hear our own interferences by getting a friend to listen to practice sessions and call attention to them. As we learn to hear them, we will find that we can start to eliminate them from our speech practices and eventually from the speech itself.

Eye Contact

In public speaking, **eye contact** involves looking at various groups of people in *all parts* of an audience throughout a speech. As long as we are looking at people and not at our notes or the ceiling, floor, or window, everyone in the audience will perceive us as having good eye contact.

One way of ensuring eye contact is to think of the audience as a collection of groups sitting in various places around the room. Then, at random, we can talk for four to six seconds with each group perhaps starting with a Z pattern, talking with the group in the back left for a few seconds, then glancing at people in the far right for a few seconds, and then moving to a group in the middle, a group in the front left, and then a group in the front right. Then perhaps reverse the order, starting in the back right. Eventually we will find ourselves going in a random pattern and looking at all groups over a period of a few minutes. Such a pattern ensures that we do not spend a disproportionate amount of time talking with those in the front or the centre of the room.

Maintaining eye contact improves a speech in several ways.

1. **Maintaining eye contact helps the audience concentrate on the speech.** If we do not look at the members of the audience, they are unlikely to maintain eye contact with us. This break in mutual eye contact often decreases concentration on the speaker's message.
2. **Maintaining eye contact increases the audience's confidence in the speaker.** Just as we are likely to be skeptical of people who do not look us in the eye as they converse, so too audiences will be skeptical of speakers who do not look at them. Eye contact is perceived as a sign of sincerity. Speakers who fail to maintain eye contact with audiences are perceived almost always as ill at ease and often as insincere or dishonest (Burgoon, Coker, & Coker, 1986).
3. **Maintaining eye contact helps speakers gain insight into audiences' reaction to the speech.** Audiences that pay attention are likely to look at us with varying amounts of intensity. Listeners who do not pay attention are likely to yawn, look out the window, and slouch in their chairs. By monitoring our audience's behaviour, we can determine what adjustments, additions, and deletions we should make in our plans. As we gain greater skill, we can make more and better use of the information we get about listeners through eye contact with them.

IN BRIEF

Achieving a Conversational Quality

The final test of a speech is in how well the speaker uses his or her vocal and nonverbal skills to develop a conversational quality. A conversational speech has five qualities:

- enthusiasm
- vocal expressiveness
- spontaneity
- fluency
- eye contact.

Skill Builders Eye Contact

Skill	Use	Procedure	Example
Looking directly at listeners while you are talking with them.	To strengthen the sense of interaction.	1. Consciously look at the faces of groups of people in your audience while you are talking. 2. If your eyes drift away, try to bring them back.	As Bertha was talking about how people can sign up to tutor other students, she was talking to people near the back of the room. When she looked down at her notes to make sure she had included all of her information on the point, she found herself continuing to look at her note card rather than at the audience. As she moved to the next point of her speech, she forced herself to look at people sitting in the front right of the room.

Spotlight on Scholars

Jill Tomasson Goodwin, University of Waterloo

Known for developing the first university-degree granting program in speech communication in Canada, Jill Tomasson Goodwin researches how people present themselves and others in public. Since her graduate studies at the University of Toronto, she has been fascinated with the everyday use of language and especially with its ability to construct identity.

One of her projects promotes Canadian public address. Her "Canadian Great Speeches" project involves collecting and preserving important political speeches, from Mackenzie King's farewell address to the Liberal Party in 1948 through Pierre Trudeau's 1970 FLQ Crisis speech and Jean Chrétien's 1995 Québec Referendum address. "Working on this ongoing project is exciting for me in two different ways," says Tomasson Goodwin. "Firstly, I'm an ardent nationalist, so helping to show others that we have accomplished Canadian speakers is satisfying in itself. Secondly, studying how these speakers accomplish their speaking goals is rewarding. For example, Trudeau's use of a

(continued)

formal speaking tone, combined with a systematic, almost legal, layout of the *facts* against the FLQ members explains why, from a persuasive speech perspective, so many Canadians so easily accepted the implementation of the War Measures Act—84 percent of us supported suspending our own civil rights. It's fascinating to look at what strategically constructed language can *do* in the public sphere." So far, Tomasson Goodwin has edited two videotape volumes of "Canadian Great Speeches."

Tomasson Goodwin's research also explores legal persuasion. Why law? "Because," she says, "how lawyers use language to characterize people and events shapes our judgment, and in the law, our personal judgments have legal and binding consequences on other people." She has examined the language strategies used in lawyers' opening statements and closing arguments in court, in the psycho-legal reports of psychologists who work for lawyers, and in trial training manuals for law students.

In each of these studies, she shows how lawyers' and legal experts' descriptions and narrations are inherently persuasive and, therefore, how language *constructs* reality in the courtroom. "I start with the *ethos*—that is, the credibility—of the speaker. How important is he or she? How respected? From that, I try to gauge the potential impact of his or her message on the audience, and particularly to identify the strategies used in creating the message. Here, I can apply many analytic tools, from basic grammar and stylistic tagging to theories of narrative coherence, classification, and attribution.

"I quite often start with something someone's said or written that puzzles or shocks me. One of my favourites is from a trial training manual in which the author advised his students, 'You will always approach the female witness as if she were a wild animal ready to tear you apart if she could get near enough.' Out of shock, I wrote about how female witnesses were classified and characterized in advocacy handbooks," says Tomasson Goodwin.

Most recently, she has expanded her interest in credibility and characterization to examine how image is created, maintained, and defended. How well did Mike Harris respond to the Walkerton tainted water crisis? Paul Martin to charges of the Chrétien Liberal government's fiscal mismanagement? Janet Jackson to the Super Bowl bodice ripping?

Tomasson Goodwin is also extending her research into presentations in the digital realm. As a member of the research team at the Canadian Centre of Arts and Technology, housed at the University of Waterloo, she is working on the differences between how we public speak face-to-face and how we speak on line.

For more information about Jill Tomasson Goodwin and her research activities, log on to www.speechcommunication.uwaterloo.ca.

Rehearsal

At this stage of preparation, we are ready to begin **rehearsing,** practising the presentation of our speech aloud. In this section, we consider a timetable for preparation and practice, use of notes, use of visual aids, and guidelines for effective rehearsals.

Timetable for Preparation and Practice

Inexperienced speakers often believe they are ready to present the speech once they have finished their outline. But a speech that is not practised is likely to be far less effective than it would have been had the speaker given himself or

7 days (or more) before	Select topic; begin research.
6 days before	Continue research.
5 days before	Outline body of speech.
4 days before	Work on introduction and conclusion.
3 days before	Finish outline; find additional material if needed; have all visual aids completed.
2 days before	First rehearsal session.
1 day before	Second rehearsal session.
Due date	Give speech.

Figure 14.14
Timetable for preparing a speech

herself sufficient practice time. In general, experienced speakers should try to complete the outline at least two days before the speaking date so that they have sufficient practice time to revise, evaluate, and mull over all aspects of the speech. Figure 14.14 provides a useful timetable for preparing a classroom speech.

Is there really a relationship between practice time and speech effectiveness? A study by Menzel and Carrel (1994) offers tentative confirmation for the general hypothesis that more preparation time leads to better speech performance. They concluded that "the significance of rehearsing out loud probably reflects the fact that verbalization clarifies thought. As a result, oral rehearsal helps lead to success in the actual delivery of a speech" (p. 23).

Using Notes in a Speech

Speech notes consist of a word or phrase outline of the speech, plus hard-to-remember information such as quotations and statistics. Appropriate notes are composed of key words or phrases that help trigger the speaker's memory. Notes will be most useful when they consist of the fewest words possible written in lettering large enough to be seen instantly at a distance. Many speakers condense their written preparatory outline into a brief word or phrase outline.

For a speech in the three- to five-minute range, one or two three-by-five-inch note cards are enough. For a speech in the five- to ten-minute range, two to four three-by-five note cards should be enough: one card for introduction, one or two cards for the body, and one card for the conclusion. If a speech contains a particularly good quotation or a complicated set of statistics, we may want to write them in detail on separate three-by-five cards. Two typical sets of notes made from the body of the preparatory outline illustrated in Chapter 13 are shown in Figure 14.15.

During practice sessions, we should use the notes as we would in the speech. Set the notes on the speaker's stand and refer to them only when needed. Speakers often find that the act of making a note card is so effective in helping cement ideas in the mind that during practice, or later during the speech itself, they do not need to use the notes at all.

Phrase Note Cards	**Brief Word Note Cards**
How many hounded by vendors?	Hounded?
Three criteria: IR, Fee, Perk	3C's
1st C: examine IR's	IR's
IR's are % charged	percents
• average of 18%	18 avg
• as much as 21%	21 high
• start low 6 to 8% but restrictions	6–8
IR's variable or fixed	variable fixed
• variable change	change
• fixed stay same	stay same
T considered IR's: next C	T
2d C: examine annual fee	Ann Fee
AF cost company charges	charges
vary	vary
• some no annual	from no
• most average $25	avg $25
T IR's, fees, weigh bens	T
3d C: weigh perks—extras	Perks—extras
• rebates	rebates
• freq flier miles	freq flier
• discounts	discounts
P's not outweigh factors	not outweigh
So, 3 C's IR, Fee, Perk	So, 3 C's

Figure 14.15
Two examples of note cards for credit card criteria speech

Using Visual Aids in a Speech

Many speakers think that once they have prepared good visual aids, they will have no trouble using them in the speech. However, many speeches with good visual aids are ruined because the speaker failed to practise with the visual aids. Here are several guidelines for preparing to use visual aids effectively in a speech.

1. **Carefully plan when to use visual aids.** We should indicate on our outline (and on our speech notes) exactly when we will reveal the visual aid and when we will remove it and then work on statements for introducing the visual aids, and practise different ways of showing the visual aids until we are satisfied that everyone in the audience will be able to see them.

2. **Consider audience needs carefully.** If a visual aid does not contribute directly to the audience's attention to, understanding of, or retention of information in the speech, then eliminate it.

3. **Show visual aids only when talking about them.** Because visual aids will draw audience attention away from a speaker, we should show them only

Mary Stangolis/Thomson Nelson

Visual aids can add dramatic interest to your speech.

when they are relevant and remove them from sight when they are no longer the focus of attention. Often a single visual aid contains several bits of information. To keep audience attention where we want it, we can prepare the visual aid with cover ups. Then, as we move from one portion of the visual aid to another, we can remove covers to expose the portion that we are discussing.

4. **Talk about the visual aid while showing it.** We know what we want our listeners to see in the visual aid, so we should tell them what to look for, explain the various parts, and interpret figures, symbols, and percentages.
5. **Display visual aids so that everyone in the audience can see them.** If holding the visual aid, we should position it away from our body and point it toward the various parts of the audience. If we place the visual aid on a chalkboard or easel or mount it in some way, we should stand to one side and point with the arm nearest the visual aid. If it is necessary to roll or fold the visual aid, we should bring some transparent tape to mount it to the chalkboard or wall so that it does not roll or wrinkle.
6. **Talk to the audience, not to the visual aid.** We may need to look at the visual aid occasionally, but it is important to maintain eye contact with the audience as much as possible, in part so that we can gauge how it is reacting to our visual material. When speakers become too engrossed in their visual aids, they tend to lose contact with the audience entirely.

7. **Pass objects around the audience with caution.** People look at, read, handle, and think about whatever they hold in their hands. While they are so occupied, they may not be listening to the speaker. We can maintain control of people's attention by revealing visual aids only when appropriate to the content of our speech and placing them out of sight when they are no longer relevant.

Guidelines for Effective Rehearsal

A good rehearsal period involves practising the speech, analyzing it, and practising it again. The following sets of instructions offer a step-by-step guide to each phase of rehearsal.

First practice

1. Plan to audiotape the practice session. If you do not own a recorder, try to borrow one. You may also want to have a friend sit in on the practice.
2. Read through the outline once or twice before you begin to refresh ideas in your mind. Then put the outline out of sight. Use the note cards you are planning to use in your speech.
3. Make the practice as similar to the speech situation as possible, including using any visual aids you have prepared. Stand up and face your imaginary audience. Pretend that the chairs, lamps, books, and other objects in your practice room are people.
4. Write down the time that you begin.
5. Begin speaking. Keep going until you have presented your entire speech.
6. Write down the time you finish. Compute the length of the speech for this first practice.

Analysis Replay the tape. Look at your outline again. Did you leave out any key ideas? Did you talk too long on any one point and not long enough on another? Did you clarify each of your points? Did you try to adapt to your anticipated audience? (If you had a friend or relative listen to your practices, have him or her help with your analysis.) Were your note cards effective? Make any necessary changes before your second practice.

Second practice Go through the six steps outlined for the first practice. By practising a second time right after your analysis, you are more likely to make the kind of adjustments that begin to improve the speech.

After you have completed one full rehearsal consisting of two sessions of practices and analysis, put the speech away for several hours or until the next day. Although you may need to go through the speech one or several more times, there is no value in cramming all the practices into one long rehearsal

OBSERVE & ANALYZE
Journal Activity

Rehearsal Log

Keep a separate log for each time you practised your speech aloud while standing up as if facing your audience. For your first practice, indicate how long you spoke. Then write two or three sentences focusing on what went well and what you need to improve. For each additional practice, indicate where in the speech you made changes to build interest, clarify points, and build a positive attitude toward you and your topic. Also, indicate where you made changes to improve language, delivery, and use of visual aids. How many times did you practise aloud for this speech? When did you feel you had mastery of the ideas of the speech?

COMMUNICATE!
Using Technology

Arrange to videotape yourself rehearsing your speech. As you review the videotape, focus on your enthusiasm, vocal expressiveness, fluency, spontaneity, and eye contact. Identify the sections where your delivery was particularly effective and the sections where you need to improve. Then, practise the sections that you believe need the most work. After a few run-throughs, re-record those sections of the speech. Are you pleased with the improvement?

IN BRIEF

Rehearsal

A speaker must practise a speech aloud to become skilled at delivery:

1. make a practice timetable
2. make note cards from outline
3. have all visual aids ready
4. practise until fluent, but do not memorize.

time. You may find that an individual practice right before you go to bed will be very helpful; while you are sleeping, your subconscious will continue to work on the speech. As a result, you are likely to find significant improvement in your mastery of the speech when you practise again the next day.

How many times you practise depends on many variables, including your experience, your familiarity with the subject, and the length of your speech.

Ensuring spontaneity When practising, try to learn the speech, not memorize it. Recall that memorizing the speech involves saying the speech the same way each time until you can give it word for word without notes. **Learning the speech** involves understanding the ideas of the speech but having the freedom to word the ideas differently during each practice.

Coping with Nervousness

By far, the most commonly asked question about speaking is What can I do to control nervousness? It is important to realize that nearly everyone reports nervousness about speaking, and we can all learn to cope with it. Although we may feel some degree of nervousness in any situation, many people notice it most in public speaking. Some of this nervousness is cognitive—that is, we think about how nervous we are likely to be. Much of it is behavioural—that is, we physically display characteristics (stomach cramps, sweaty palms, dry mouth, vocal interference). At times, the behaviour is avoiding speaking in public or speaking for the shortest period of time possible when required to speak. Nervousness is a *matter of degree.* Most of us are somewhere between the two extremes of no nervousness and total fear. The point is, nervousness about speaking in public is *normal.*

Many of us would like to be totally free from nervousness, but according to Phillips (1977), "learning proceeds best when the organism is in a state of tension" (p. 37). In fact, it helps to be a little nervous to do your best. If you are lackadaisical about giving a speech, you probably will not do a good job. Because at least some tension is constructive, our goal is to learn how to cope with our nervousness. Phillips cites results of studies that showed that, at the end, nearly all students with nervousness still experienced tension, but almost all of them had learned to cope with it. "Apparently they had learned to manage the tension; they no longer saw it as an impairment, and they went ahead with what they had to do" (p. 37).

Now let's look at some reassuring information about nervousness.

1. **Despite nervousness, you can make it through your speech.** Very few people are so bothered that they are unable to function. We may not enjoy the *flutters,* but we can still deliver an effective speech.

2. **Listeners are not as likely to recognize your fear as you might think.** The thought that audiences will notice an inexperienced speaker's fear often increases that fear. But the fact is that members of an audience, even speech instructors, greatly underrate the amount of stage fright they believe a person has (Clevenger, 1959, p. 136).

3. **The better prepared you are, the better you will cope with nervousness.** Many people show extreme nervousness because either they are not well prepared or they think they are not well prepared. As Gerald Phillips has said, a positive approach to coping with nervousness is "(1) learn how to try, (2) try, and (3) have some success" (1991, p. 6). As we learn to recognize when we are truly prepared, we will find ourselves paying less attention to our nervousness. A study by Kathleen Ellis (1995) reinforces previous research "that indicates that students' self-perceived public speaking competency is indeed an important predictor of their public speaking anxiety" (p. 73).

4. **The more experience you get in speaking, the better you can cope with nervousness.** Beginners experience some fear because they do not have experience speaking in public. As we give speeches—and see improvement in those speeches—we gain confidence and worry less about any nervousness. As a recent study of the impact of basic courses on communication apprehension indicated, experience in a public-speaking course was enough to reduce students' communication apprehension scores (Rose, Rancer, & Crannell, 1993, p. 58).

5. **Experienced speakers learn to channel their nervousness.** The nervousness we feel is, in controlled amounts, good for us. A certain amount of nervousness helps us to do our best. What we want is for our nervousness to dissipate once we begin to speak. Just as athletes are likely to report that the nervousness disappears once they engage in play, so too should speakers find nervousness disappearing once they get a reaction to the first few sentences of their introduction.

THINKING ABOUT . . .

Nervousness

Are you nervous at the thought of giving a speech? What thoughts and behaviours show your nervousness?

Specific Behaviours

Now let's consider specific behaviours that are likely to help control nervousness.

1. **Pick a topic you are comfortable with.** Having an unsatisfactory topic lays the groundwork for a psychological mind-set that almost guarantees nervousness at the time of the speech. Having a topic we know about and that is important to us lays the groundwork for a satisfying speech experience.

2. **Take time to prepare fully.** If we back ourselves into a corner and must find material, organize it, write an outline, and practise the speech all in an hour

or two, we almost guarantee failure and reduced confidence. However, if we do a little work each day for a week before the assignment, we will experience considerably less pressure and increased confidence.

3. **Try to schedule your speech at a time that is psychologically best for you.** When speeches are being scheduled, we may be able to choose the time. Some people prefer getting it over with. They can volunteer to go first. Others feel better if they listen to others first, and they can seek a late point in the schedule.

4. **Control your food and beverages.** We should not eat a big meal right before speaking and avoid stimulants like caffeine and sugar as they can get us too revved up. Milk and milk products are also to be avoided as they can produce a mucous that can affect the voice negatively. The best thing to drink before a speech is water. Speakers who experience dry mouth can try sucking on a mint.

5. **Visualize successful speaking experiences. Visualization** is a technique for controlling nervousness that involves developing a mental strategy and picturing oneself implementing that strategy successfully. Ayres and Hopf (1990) have found that if people can visualize themselves going through an entire process, they have a much better chance of succeeding when they are in the situation (p. 77).

   Visualization has been used as a major means of improving sports skills. One example is a study of players trying to improve their foul-shooting percentages. Players were divided into three groups. One group never practised, one group practised, and one group visualized practising. As any of us would expect, those who practised improved far more than those who did not. What seemed amazing was that those who only visualized practising improved almost as much as those who actually did (Scott, 1997, p. 99). Imagine what happens when you visualize *and* practise.

   By visualizing speechmaking, people seem not only to be able to lower general apprehension but also to report fewer negative thoughts when they actually speak (Ayres, Hopf, & Ayres, 1994, p. 256). Successful visualization begins during practice periods: We picture ourselves as calm and smiling as we approach the podium. We remind ourselves that we have good ideas, that we are well prepared, and that our audience wants to hear what we have to say. We see the audience nodding approvingly as we speak. We see them applauding as we finish.

6. **Give yourself positive affirmations before you approach the stand.** For instance, we might say to ourselves, "I'm excited about having the opportunity to share this information with the class," "I've done my best to get ready, and now I am ready to speak." Such statements help put us in a positive frame of mind. Although these statements are not magic, they get us thinking on the right track.

COMMUNICATE! Using InfoTrac College Edition

Visualization

Visualization has been recognized as a means of improving performance in many areas, most specifically in athletics. Open PowerTrac and type the keyword *visualization.* You will find many recent sources covering many different areas. Look for "Do Try This at Home," in *Women's Sports and Fitness,* May 1997, and "The Mind of a Champion," *Natural Health,* Jan.–Feb. 1997. Look specifically for suggested procedures for using visualization.

OBSERVE & ANALYZE Journal Activity

Controlling Nervousness

Interview one or two people who give frequent speeches (a minister, a politician, a lawyer, a businessperson, a teacher). Ask about what is likely to make them more or less nervous about giving the speech. Find out how they cope with their nervousness. Summarize the results of your interviews. Then write which behaviours you believe might work for you.

ActionPress/CP Picture Archive

Speakers can use the secrets of winning athletes: Realize that your initial nervousness can prime you for the speech ahead and will decline once you start speaking, and visualize success before you start.

If we find ourselves doing negative self-talk instead, we must counter our negative statements with positive ones. For instance, if Jill finds herself saying, "I'm scared," she can intervene and say, "No, I'm excited." If she finds herself saying, "Oh, I'm going to forget," she can say, "I've got note cards. If I forget, I'll pause, look at my notes, and go on." If she finds herself saying, "I'm a lousy speaker, what am I doing here?" she can say, "I'm doing the best I can do for today—and that's okay."

7. **Pause for a few seconds before you begin.** On reaching the stand, we should pause for a few seconds before we start to speak. Taking a deep breath while making eye contact with the audience may help get our breathing in order, and moving about a little during the first few sentences can help too; sometimes a few gestures or a step one way or another is enough to break some of the tension.

IN BRIEF

Coping with Nervousness

Some degree of nervousness before public speaking is normal and can give us an edge. To help ourselves cope with nervousness, we can:

- pick a topic we are comfortable with
- prepare well
- schedule the speech at a time that is good for us
- avoid food and beverages other than water
- visualize success
- practise positive self-talk
- pause briefly before we begin.

Criteria for Evaluating Speeches

In addition to learning to prepare and present speeches, we are learning to critically analyze the speeches we hear. From a learning standpoint, critical analysis of others' speeches not only provides us with an analysis of where the speech went right and where it went wrong but also gives us insight into the methods that we may want to use or avoid in presenting our own speeches.

IN BRIEF

Evaluating Speeches

Speeches are evaluated in terms of the quality of their
- content
- organization
- presentation.

Classroom speeches are usually evaluated on the basis of how well the speaker has met specific criteria of effective speaking. In Chapters 12 through 14, we have examined not only steps of speech preparation but also the criteria by which speeches are measured. The critical assumption is that if a speech has good content, is well organized, and is well presented it is likely to achieve its goal. Thus, the critical apparatus for evaluating any speech comprises questions that relate to the basics of content, organization, and presentation. Figure 14.16 is a diagnostic speech checklist. Use this series of questions to analyze your own speeches and those of your classmates.

Thinking Critically about Speeches

Check all items that were accomplished effectively.

Content

1. Was the goal of the speech clear? ____
2. Did the speaker have high-quality information? ____
3. Did the speaker use a variety of kinds of developmental material? ____
4. Were visual aids appropriate and well used? ____
5. Did the speaker establish common ground and adapt the content to the audience's interests, knowledge, and attitudes? ____

Organization

6. Did the introduction gain attention, gain good will for the speaker, and lead into the speech? ____
7. Were the main points clear, parallel, and in meaningful complete sentences? ____
8. Did transitions lead smoothly from one point to another? ____
9. Did the conclusion tie the speech together? ____

Presentation

10. Was the language clear? ____
11. Was the language vivid and emphatic? ____
12. Did the speaker sound enthusiastic? ____
13. Did the speaker show sufficient vocal expressiveness? ____
14. Was the presentation spontaneous? ____
15. Was the presentation fluent? ____
16. Did the speaker make eye contact with the audience? ____
17. Were the pronunciation and articulation acceptable? ____
18. Did the speaker have good posture? ____
19. Was the speaker's movement appropriate? ____
20. Did the speaker have sufficient poise? ____

Based on these criteria, evaluate the speech as (check one):

Excellent ____ Good ____ Satisfactory ____ Fair ____ Poor ____

Figure 14.16
Speech critique checklist

TEST YOUR COMPETENCE

Presenting Your First Speech

1. Prepare a five-minute informative or persuasive speech. An outline is required.
2. As an addendum to the outline, you may wish to write a specific plan for adapting the speech that discusses strategies for (1) getting and maintaining attention, (2) facilitating understanding, (3) and building a positive attitude toward you and your speech.
3. Criteria for evaluation include the essentials of topic and purpose, content, organization, and presentation. Use the speech critique checklist to evaluate the speech. As you practise your speech, use the checklist to ensure that you are meeting the basic criteria in your speech.

WHAT WOULD YOU DO?
A QUESTION OF ETHICS

"Kendra, I heard you telling Jim about the speech you're giving tomorrow. You think it's a winner, huh?"

"You got that right, Omar. I'm going to have Bardston eating out of the palm of my hand."

"You sound confident."

"This time I have reason to be. See, Professor Bardston's been talking about the importance of audience adaptation. These last two weeks that's all we've heard—adaptation, adaptation."

"What does she mean?"

"Talking about something in a way that really relates to people personally."

"Okay—so how are you going to do that?"

"Well, you see, I'm giving this speech on abortion. Now here's the kick. Bardston let it slip that she's a supporter of Right to Life. So what I'm going to do is give this informative speech on the Right to Life movement. But I'm going to discuss the major beliefs of the movement in a way that'll get her to think that I'm a supporter. I'm going to mention aspects of the movement that I know she'll like."

"But I've heard you talk about how you're pro-choice."

"I am—all the way. But by keeping the information positive, she'll think I'm a supporter. It isn't as if I'm going to be telling any lies or anything."

1. In a speech, is it ethical to adapt in a way that resonates with your audience but is not in keeping with what you really believe?
2. Could Kendra have achieved her goal using a different method? How?

Summary

Speakers adapt to their audiences by speaking directly to them and by planning strategies that create or build audience interest, adapt to audience levels of understanding, and adapt to the audience's attitude toward the speaker and toward the speech goal.

Direct audience adaptation includes using personal pronouns, rhetorical questions, common experiences, and personalizing information.

Strategies for maintaining or increasing interest include stressing the timeliness of the information, the impact on the audience's personal space, and the seriousness of the personal impact. Strategies for adapting to the audience's understanding of the information depend on the audience's existing knowledge level, filling in background and information where the audience lacks knowledge. Strategies for building credibility include going into the speech fully prepared and showing a sincere interest in the audience's well-being. To adapt to audience attitudes toward the speech goal, a speaker should focus on showing why the audience needs to know about the topic.

Visual aids include the speaker, objects, charts, pictorial representations, projections, chalkboard, handouts, and computer graphics. Visual aids have the greatest impact if they are used in ways that best reinforce the points of the speech. Visual aids should be large enough, pleasing to the eye, and focus on items of information that are relevant to the speech.

Although speeches may be presented impromptu, by manuscript, or by memory, most professional speeches are presented extemporaneously—that is, carefully prepared and practised but with the exact wording determined at the time of utterance.

The verbal components of effective presentation are clarity, vividness, and emphasis. The nonverbal elements of presentation include voice, articulation, and bodily action.

Effective speaking uses verbal and nonverbal components to achieve a conversational quality that includes enthusiasm, vocal expressiveness, spontaneity, fluency, and eye contact.

To rehearse an extemporaneous speech, a speaker should complete the outline at least two days in advance, make note cards, have visual aids ready, and practise the speech several times, weighing what he or she did and how well after each practice.

All speakers feel nervous as they approach their first speech. Some nervousness is cognitive (in the mind) and some is behavioural (physically displayed). Rather than being an either–or matter, nervousness is a matter of degree.

Because at least some tension is constructive, the goal is not to get rid of nervousness but to learn how to cope with it. Nervousness is normal, and speakers can use several specific behaviours to help control excessive nervousness. Being well prepared is the best defence against nervousness.

Speeches are evaluated on how well they meet the guidelines for effective content, organization, and delivery.

Glossary

Review the following key terms:

articulation (403) — shaping speech sounds into recognizable oral symbols that combine to form words.

attitude (391) — a predisposition for or against people, places, or things that is usually expressed as an opinion.

audience adaptation (386) — the process of verbally and visually relating speech material directly to a specific audience.

bar graph (395) — a diagram that compares information using vertical or horizontal bars to show relationships between two or more variables.

bodily action (405) — facial expression, gesture, posture, and movement.

chart (395) — a graphic representation that presents information in an easily interpreted format.

common ground (386) — feelings, ideas, opinions, or experiences shared by a speaker and audience.

conversational quality (406) — a style of presentation that sounds like conversation to listeners.

emphasis (402) — giving force or intensity to words or ideas.

emphasis by proportion (402) — spending more time on ideas that you want to be perceived as more important.

emphasis by repetition (403) — saying important ideas several times.

emphasis by transitions (403) — using words that show relationships between ideas.

enthusiasm (406) — excitement or passion about a speech topic.

eye contact (409) — looking at various people in all parts of an audience throughout a speech.

facial expression (405) — eye and mouth movement.

fluency (409) — devoid of hesitations and vocal interferences.

gesture (405) — movements of hands, arms, and fingers.

graph (395) — a diagram that presents numerical or statistical data visually. Graphs have many uses; for example, to make comparisons, show trends, show divisions, or present results.

learning a speech (416) — understanding the ideas but using different wording during each practice.

line graph (396) — a diagram that indicates changes in one or more variables over time.

monotone (407) — a voice in which the pitch, volume, and rate remain constant.

movement (406) — motion of the entire body.

organizational chart (395) — a diagram of a complicated system or procedure using symbols and connecting lines.

pie graph (396) — a diagram that shows relationships among parts of a single unit.

poise (406) — assurance of manner.

posture (405) — the position or bearing of the body.

pronunciation (403) — the form of and accent on the various syllables of a word.

rehearsal (411) — practising aloud the presentation of a speech.

rhetorical question (386) — a question that calls for a mental rather than a spoken response.

speech notes (412) — a word or phrase outline of a speech plus hard to remember information.

spontaneity (408) — a quality that exists in a speech when a speaker is so responsive to his or her ideas that the speech sounds fresh and lively, even though it has been well practised.

visual aid (392) — an object or image that helps to clarify verbal information by allowing the listener to see as well as hear it.

visualization (418) — a method of coping with nervousness that involves picturing oneself doing something successfully.

vocal expressiveness (407) — vocal contrasts in pitch, volume, rate, and quality that affect the meaning audiences receive from a speaker.

voice (403) — the pitch, volume, rate, and sound quality of a person's speech.

word chart (395) — a visual aid used to preview material that will be covered in a speech, to summarize material, or to remind an audience of speech content.

SELF-REVIEW

Public Speaking from Chapters 12 to 14

What kind of a public speaker are you? The following analysis looks at 11 specifics that are basic to a public-speaking profile. On the line provided for each statement, indicate the response that best captures your behaviour:

1 = almost always   2 = often   3 = occasionally   4 = rarely   5 = never

1. When I am asked to speak, I am able to select a topic and determine a speech goal with confidence. (Ch. 12) ____
2. When I speak, I use material from a variety of sources. (Ch. 12) ____
3. In my preparation, I construct clear main points and organize them to follow some consistent pattern. (Ch. 13) ____
4. When I organize informative speeches, I consider which method of informing will best meet my audience's information needs. (Ch. 13) ____
5. When I organize persuasive speeches, I organize reasons to meet audience attitudes. (Ch. 13) ____
6. In my preparation, I am careful to be sure that I have developed ideas to meet audience needs. (Ch. 14) ____
7. When I speak, I sense that my audience perceives my language as clear and vivid. (Ch. 14) ____
8. I look directly at members of my audience when I speak. (Ch. 14) ____
9. My public-speaking voice shows variation in pitch, speed, and loudness. (Ch. 14) ____
10. When I speak, my bodily actions help supplement or reinforce my ideas; I feel and look involved. (Ch. 14) ____
11. I have confidence in my ability to speak in public. (Ch. 14) ____

Based on your responses, select the public-speaking behaviour you would most like to change. Write a communication improvement plan similar to the sample in Chapter 1 (page 26). If you would like verification of your self-analysis before you write your plan, have a friend or a co-worker complete this same analysis for you.

five

Regardless of what type of professional career we plan to follow, most of our professional lives will be devoted to communication: communicating with employers and job supervisors, communicating with co-workers, communicating with clients or customers, perhaps even communicating with the public on behalf of the organization we represent. As we have mentioned throughout this text, it is through communication that we will forge and maintain professional relationships, give and receive positive and negative feedback in the workplace, collaborate with other professionals, and manage any workplace conflicts that arise. In other words, all of the approaches to communication that we have examined so far play as important a role in professional contexts as they do in personal contexts. Professional interactions can also give rise to challenges not found in most personal contexts, however, and in this final section of *Communicate!* we will examine some of those. First we will look specifically at the communication challenges inherent in finding a job; then, we will review some features of the professional communication context itself—what to expect once we have secured that job.

V

WORKPLACE COMMUNICATION

Josef Fankhauser/The Image Bank/Getty Images

OBJECTIVES

After you have read this chapter, you should be able to answer these questions:

- What are the steps in an effective job search?
- What are the components of a personal inventory?
- What are some effective methods of identifying prospective employers?
- How should a résumé be designed?
- What information should a résumé contain?
- How should a letter of application be designed?
- What information should a letter of application contain?
- How do electronically transmitted application materials differ from traditional ones?
- How should a job applicant prepare for an interview?
- What types of questions are employment interviewers likely to ask?
- What form is an employment interview likely to take?

CHAPTER 15

The Job Search

Wyn strode confidently over to the True North Industries booth at his university's annual job fair. The fair provided graduating students with an opportunity to meet recruiters representing employers from across Canada and to submit applications for entry-level positions. When Wyn told the receptionist who greeted him that he would like to apply for a job, she led him into a cubicle at the rear of the booth and introduced him to Ms. Melissa Beddington, from True North's personnel department.

"Please sit down," Ms. Beddington said. "How did you become interested in True North Industries?"

"One of the counsellors at our student placement office said you hired a lot of graduates and that your company was a good place to work," Wyn replied.

"And what kind of a position do you think you would be most suited for?"

"One where I could use my skills."

"What skills do you have to offer our company that would make you a good hire for us?"

"Well, I'm a hard worker."

"Are you familiar with our major products?"

"Not really. I haven't had time yet to look you up."

"I see. Well, how do you know that you could be helpful to us?"

"Well, because I work really hard."

"What kinds of experience have you had in business?"

"Um, let's see. Well, I have fundraising experience: I canvassed local businesses to raise money for our senior prom, and I've worked part-time for my sister-in-law, who owns her own outdoor recreation business."

"Okay, what do you see as some of your major skills?"

"Well, as I said, I can work really hard."

"Well, Wyn, we are certainly impressed by hard workers. We're talking to many other applicants, of course. Please leave a copy of your résumé at our reception desk. We'll be contacting applicants whom we want to formally interview over the next month."

When Wyn got home, his sister Branwen asked, "How did the job fair go?"

"Great," Wyn replied, "Ms. Beddington at True North was impressed by the fact that I'm a hard worker. I should be hearing from her sometime this month."

How likely is Wyn to receive a follow-up call from True North? How could he have improved his chances?

Attempting to secure a job is often a challenge, especially for recent graduates who have little professional experience to offer employers. A person who lands that first job is rarely fixed for life, however, as statistics show that the average Canadian employee remains in a job for a little less than eight years (Kapica, 2002). Being able to conduct a job search and successfully market one's talents to prospective employers is therefore an essential skill that modern professionals can expect to employ repeatedly during the course of a career.

Job fairs provide graduating students with opportunities to meet recruiters and to submit applications for entry-level positions.

Christina Strong/CP Picture Archive

Whether the goal is a part-time job to help pay school costs, an internship, a first career job, a promotion within a field, or a career change, we must recognize that finding the right job is a complex process that can take time and effort. It is a process that must be approached methodically. People who conduct haphazard searches and expect quick results are likely to be disappointed, either by not finding a job at all or by ending up in an unsatisfying job. A properly conducted job search can be divided into five discrete steps: (1) taking an inventory of one's career goals and marketable skills, (2) identifying prospective employers, (3) creating a résumé, (4) drafting a letter of application, and (5) participating in an interview.

Conducting a Personal Inventory

When we set out to secure employment, we are essentially offering for sale our time, talents, knowledge, and skills, and as any effective salesperson knows, to succeed at marketing a product, we must know the product. In other words, we must have a clear understanding of what we have to offer that someone else is likely to be willing to pay for. In addition, to draw satisfaction from any job we take, we must have a clear idea of what we want do with our lives. We all have a general understanding of our abilities and our goals, but to be successful in a job search, we must develop and sharpen that understanding by conducting a **personal inventory**, a thorough and methodical assessment of our career goals and marketable skills.

Clarifying Career Goals

To some extent, our career path is shaped by our education and training. Gordon's decision to major in history, for example, probably rules out a career in chemical engineering. However, regardless of our specific academic or professional background, many career paths are likely to be open to us. Figure 15.1 shows some of the career options available to communication studies majors. Clearly not all of these options would appeal to the same person, and because job performance is closely related to job satisfaction, we should endeavour to identify the types of positions within our field that we will find enjoyable and personally fulfilling. Answering the following questions will help in narrowing the number of career choices that we will actively consider:

1. **What things have I done that I most enjoyed?** Identifying leisure, school, or work activities that have brought us pleasure provides information about the types of things we like to do.
2. **What would I do with my time if I did not have to work?** Most people's primary motivation for working is to support themselves and their family. Considering how we would occupy ourselves if we were independently wealthy helps identify activities that would bring us a sense of fulfillment.

Careers in Field of Communication

Careers in communication education include language arts co-ordinator, high school composition/speech/drama teacher, forensics/debate coach, drama director, college or university professor, and communication department administrator.

Careers in writing/journalism include reporter, editor, author, copywriter, scriptwriter, publisher, news service researcher, technical writer, and acquisitions editor.

Careers in electronic media/radio-television/broadcasting include broadcasting station manager, director of broadcasting, film/tape librarian, community relations director, unit manager, film editor, news director, news writer, transmitter engineer, technical director, advertising sales coordinator, traffic/continuity specialist, media buyer, market researcher, actor, announcer, disc jockey, newscaster, news anchor, media interviewer, talk show host, public relations manager, comedy writer, casting director, producer, researcher, account executive, and floor manager.

Careers in advertising include advertising or marketing specialist, copywriter, account executive, sales manager, media planner, media buyer, creative director, media sales representative, and public opinion researcher.

Careers in public relations include publicity manager, advertising manager, marketing specialist, press agent, lobbyist, corporate public affairs specialist, account executive, development officer, fundraiser, membership recruiter, sales manager, media analyst, media planner, creative director, audience analyst, and public opinion researcher.

Careers in theatre/performing arts/dramatic arts include performing artist, script writer, producer, director, arts administrator, performing arts educator, costume designer, scenic designer, lighting designer, theatre critic, makeup artist, stage manager, model, theatre professor, and casting director.

Careers in Fields Related to Communication

Careers in business and communication include sales representative, executive manager, personnel manager, public information officer, industrial and labour relations representative, negotiator, director of corporate communication, customer service representative, newsletter editor, communication trainer, human resources manager, mediator, and buyer.

Careers in communication and education include teacher (elementary and secondary), school counsellor, educational researcher, audiovisual specialist, educational administrator, school/university information specialist, director of college news, director of a collegiate information centre, educational tester, development officer, educational fundraiser, alumni officer, college placement officer, college admissions director, and college recruiter.

Communication and government/politics-related careers include public information officer, speech writer, legislative assistant, campaign director, research specialist, program co-ordinator, negotiator, lobbyist, press secretary, and elected official.

Careers in technology and communication include trainer for communication technologies, closed circuit television producer/director, systems analyst, technical copywriter, language specialist, speech synthesizer, cognition researcher, audio and visual computer display specialist, and performance assessor.

Careers in health and communication include health educator, school health care administrator, medical grants writer, hospital director of communication, clinic public relations director, health communication analyst, research analyst, medical training supervisor, communications manager for federal health agencies, health personnel educator, medical centre publications editor, hospice manager, drug rehabilitation counsellor, health care counsellor, activities director, and health facility fundraiser.

Careers in international relations/negotiations and communication include on-air international broadcasting talent, corporate representative, translator, student tour co-ordinator, diplomat, foreign relations officer, host/hostess for foreign dignitaries, and foreign correspondent.

Careers in law and communication include legal aid lawyer, corporate lawyer, Crown attorney, public interest lawyer, private practice lawyer, legal researcher, mediation and negotiation specialist, paralegal researcher, legal secretary, legal reporter, and legal educator.

Careers in social and human services and communication include public administrator, social worker, recreational supervisor, human rights officer, community affairs liaison, park service public relations specialist, philanthropic representative, religious leader, and mental health counsellor.

Source: Reprinted by permission of National Communication Association.

Figure 15.1
Career options for communication studies majors

3. **Do I prefer working with people, data, or things?** Each of these preferences will rule out some types of work while recommending others.
4. **What are my major accomplishments?** Looking back, what achievements stand out? Considering academic work, leisure activities, personal interactions, and any paid or volunteer work, with what types of tasks have we most often succeeded, and for what types of accomplishments have we most often received praise or recognition from others?
5. **How important to me is recognition or prestige?** Some people like to be on the front line, while others are uncomfortable with attention and prefer to work anonymously in the background.
6. **How strong are my control needs?** People with very strong control needs will probably prefer management roles or perhaps being their own boss, while those with low control needs may prefer a directed role.
7. **Am I a team player?** People who enjoy teamwork and function well as part of a team may enjoy being part of large or small organizations; those who do not would probably prefer a career that offered them the chance to work independently.
8. **How much money do I need to be happy?** In choosing a career path, we make a decision that will affect many aspects of our lives and limit or enlarge the number of other choices that may be available to us.
9. **Do I want to live in a specific place?** People who are strongly attached to one geographic location would not be happy in jobs that require frequent relocation.
10. **What type of environment do I enjoy?** Outdoor people would be unhappy working in a high-rise office tower. People who dislike cold weather would be dissatisfied with a position in the North. People who need the hustle of an urban environment would be unhappy in a rural area.

OBSERVE & ANALYZE
Journal Activity

Clarifying Career Goals

Use the list of questions presented in this section to help clarify your career goals. Based on your answers to the questions, what types of careers do you think would be least satisfying to you? Which do you think would be most satisfying?

Recognizing Abilities

The list of skills, abilities, knowledge, competencies, and personal characteristics that we compiled in the self-perception and others' perceptions exercises in Chapter 2 offer an excellent starting point for recognizing the abilities that we have to offer to an employer, but we want to eliminate from those lists characteristics that do not relate to the field of employment that we wish to enter (singing ability would become irrelevant, for example, if one wanted to become an accountant, as would mathematical skill if one wanted to become an addictions counsellor). We may also want to add to our list some employment-related characteristics that we did not include in assessing our self-perceptions because, being outside of the career context in which they would be relevant, we did not consider them an important factor in determining our self-image. In other words, we want to focus this new assessment on **marketable skills,** those skills for which there is a demand in the labour market.

The Conference Board of Canada in conjunction with its private and public-sector partners in the Employability Skills Forum and the Business and Education Forum on Science, Technology, and Mathematics has developed *Employability Skills 2000+*, a framework for assessing and developing marketable skills. The Conference Board (2000) groups marketable skills into three categories, as follows:

Fundamental skills **Fundamental skills** form the basis for developing other more specialized skills:

1. **Communication:** the ability to read and understand information presented in a variety of forms (e.g., words, graphs, charts, diagrams); to write and speak so others pay attention and understand; to listen and ask questions to understand and appreciate the points of view of others; to share information using a range of information and communications technologies (e.g., voice, e-mail, computers); to use relevant scientific, technological, and mathematical knowledge and skills to explain or clarify ideas
2. **Information management:** the ability to locate, gather, and organize information using appropriate technology and information systems and to access, analyze, and apply knowledge and skills from various disciplines (e.g., the arts, languages, science, technology, mathematics, social sciences, and the humanities)
3. **Numeracy:** the ability to decide what needs to be measured or calculated; to observe and record data using appropriate methods, tools, and technology; and to make estimates and verify calculations
4. **Thinking and problem solving:** the ability to assess situations and identify problems; to seek different points of view and evaluate them based on facts; to recognize the human, interpersonal, technical, scientific, and mathematical dimensions of a problem; to identify the root cause of a problem; to be creative and innovative in exploring possible solutions; to readily use science, technology, and mathematics as ways to think, gain, and share knowledge, solve problems, and make decisions; to evaluate solutions; to make recommendations or decisions to implement solutions; to check to see if a solution works; and to act on opportunities for improvement.

Teamwork skills **Teamwork skills** and attributes are needed to contribute productively in a work group:

1. **Working with others:** the ability to understand and work within the dynamics of a group; to ensure that a team's purpose and objectives are clear; to be flexible, respecting, being open to, and being supportive of the thoughts, opinions, and contributions of others; to recognize and respect people's diversity, individual differences, and perspectives; to accept and

provide feedback in a constructive and considerate manner; to contribute to a team by sharing information and expertise; to lead or support when appropriate, motivating a group for high performance; to understand the role of conflict in reaching group decisions; and to manage and resolve conflict when appropriate

2. **Participation in projects and tasks:** the ability to plan, design, or carry out a project or task from start to finish with well-defined objectives and outcomes; to develop a plan, seek feedback, test, revise, and implement; to work to agreed quality standards and specifications; to select and use appropriate tools and technology for a task or project; to adapt to changing requirements and information; and to continuously monitor the success of a project or task for the purpose of identifying ways to improve.

Personal management skills **Personal management skills**, attitudes, and behaviours drive a person's potential for growth.

1. **Demonstration of positive attitudes and behaviours:** the ability to feel good about ourselves and be confident; to deal with people, problems, and situations with honesty, integrity, and personal ethics; to recognize our own and other people's good efforts; to take care of our personal health; and to show interest, initiative, and effort
2. **Responsibility:** the ability to set goals and priorities balancing work and personal life; to plan and manage time, money, and other resources in order to achieve goals; to assess, weigh, and manage risk; to be accountable for our actions and the actions of our group; and to be socially responsible and contribute to our community
3. **Adaptability:** the ability to work independently or as a part of a team; to carry out multiple tasks or projects; to be innovative and resourceful, identifying and suggesting alternative ways to achieve goals and get the job done; to be open and respond constructively to change; to learn from our mistakes and accept feedback; and to cope with uncertainty
4. **Continuous learning:** the ability to be willing to continuously learn and grow; to assess personal strengths and areas for development; to set our own learning goals; to identify and access learning sources and opportunities; and to plan for and achieve our learning goals
5. **Workplace safety:** the ability to be aware of personal and group health and safety practices and procedures, and to act in accordance with them.

By turning each entry on this long checklist into a question (e.g., Do I have the ability to read and understand information presented in a variety of forms?), we can make it an excellent assessment tool for evaluating our marketable skills.

OBSERVE & ANALYZE
Journal Activity

Recognizing Abilities

Turn each entry in the Conference Board of Canada's framework into a question to identify your marketable skills. Which of your skill sets do you think are strongest? Which are weakest? How well do your skills match the skills needed to pursue the career path you identified in the previous section?

IN BRIEF

Conducting a Personal Inventory

The first step in the job application process is to take an inventory of one's career goals and marketable skills. We determine:

- which career paths are appealing and likely to lead to job satisfaction
- which specific abilities we have to *sell* to prospective employers.

Identifying Prospective Employers

Many jobs, as many as 95 percent according to some estimates, are never advertised, so if we limit our search to those that are, we greatly reduce our chances of finding a job with which we will be satisfied. Once we have identified the type of work we want and are qualified to do, therefore, our next task is to identify organizations that hire people to do that type of work. Once again, it is important to approach the task methodically using a variety of approaches. The following are some of the main methods of discovering job vacancies:

1. **Personal contacts:** As we go through college or university, we have many opportunities to meet people who are important in our field of study, beginning with our instructors but also including researchers, guest speakers, work term supervisors, and so on. Many of these people will have a variety of contacts in the field, including people who hire. Recruiters at many companies rely on trustworthy people within universities and colleges to lead them to outstanding graduates. Developing such personal contacts and letting them know when we are searching for work can therefore be very advantageous.

2. **Professional associations:** Serious students should join as many scholarly associations or professional societies as are available in their field. Membership fees for students are generally very reasonable, and such societies provide a wealth of opportunities for networking. By reading print or on-line newsletters and journals and attending conferences, students become familiar with many of the leading people in their field and have opportunities to meet or correspond with some of them. Recruiters frequently attend conferences, conducting interviews on the spot, and newsletters published by such societies are often the best source of advertisements for positions in the field.

OBSERVE & ANALYZE
Journal Activity

Identifying Prospective Employers

Use three or more of the methods listed here to identify 10 jobs for which you are qualified and in which you are interested.

3. **Career and job fairs:** Placement centres at many colleges and universities, especially large urban ones, organize annual fairs that attract recruiters from companies from across the country. Because these recruiters are specifically looking for entry-level employees, such fairs are a rich source of information for students. We need not restrict ourselves to fairs offered by our own school—we should find out where the biggest and best for people in our field occur and plan to attend.

4. **Campus placement centres:** Whether our school's placement centre sponsors a job fair or not, it certainly will be hosting recruiters from specific organizations and posting hiring announcements from many others. By checking the centre's bulletin boards or Web site regularly and discussing our career goals with placement centre staff, we are sure to find out when a position of interest to us arises.

5. **Human Resources Development Canada employment offices:** HRDC offices are available across Canada, and all job notices are available through the Job Bank on the Web at www.jobbank.gc.ca/Search_en.asp. The Job Bank lists job vacancies across the country by location and job category.

6. **Employment agencies:** Privately operated employment agencies can be helpful for some job seekers in some fields, though employers do not always seek their help to fill entry-level positions. They are most useful to people with well-defined goals and directly relevant education and experience. To find the best agency for us, we can ask people in our field to recommend one, consult the agencies' Yellow Pages ads, or study newspaper ads to see which agencies are advertising jobs of interest to us. Before getting involved with a private employment agency, we should ensure that all of the agency's fees will be paid by the employer, not by us.

7. **Organizations themselves:** By using professional directories, society membership lists, even the Yellow Pages, we can identify organizations that hire people with our skills and career goals. Even if an organization has not advertised a vacancy, we can send an application, indicating the type of work we are interested in doing.

8. **The World Wide Web:** There are literally thousands of job sites available on the Web today, some of them very narrow in their focus (e.g., offering only jobs for ESL teachers in Japan), others very general, promoting jobs of all kinds worldwide. The best sites are secure and reliable, of course, but also designed for efficiency, allowing searches by specific job type and location. If the design of a site forces us to spend hours scrolling through announcements for jobs that are not suitable for us, we can probably make better use of our time.

9. **Classified ads:** Though not as important as they once were, employment sections in newspapers can still be a useful source of information. Local newspapers are best for entry-level positions, and many such papers are available on line. Because of the high cost of advertising in national newspapers, ads found in them are usually for senior or very specialized positions. A list of Web sites for newspapers all over the world is available at www.onlinenewspapers.com/.

To conduct a successful job search, we will almost certainly want to use several of these methods of identifying employers and jobs.

In conducting our search, it is very important to keep accurate records. We will waste valuable time if we end up going through the same databases or publications more than once and perhaps even risk the embarrassment of applying more than once for the same job. We should keep a record of all the sources searched, noting information such as newspaper dates, dates that Web sites were last visited, and so on.

COMMUNICATE!
Using Technology

The Canada Career Consortium is a national organization made up of government and private-sector partners that initiates, develops, and coordinates career and labour market information for the purpose of enabling Canadians to make transitions. Among other activities they sponsor Canada Career Week on college and university campuses each fall. Visit their Web site at **www.careerccc.org/ccc/nav.cfm**. For additional assistance with career planning, follow some of the links to career services and exercises.

IN BRIEF

Identifying Prospective Employers

In identifying and applying for jobs, we should use a variety of search methods and sources and keep careful records of our activity. Major sources of information are

- personal and professional contacts
- employment offices (HRDC, campus, and private)
- job fairs
- employers themselves
- print and electronic publications.

We should maintain this same methodical approach throughout the steps in the application process to follow. Many job opportunities are lost by applicants who come across to the employer as sloppy or disorganized. As a minimum, we should file the following information for each application that we make:

- a copy of the job ad or announcement
- the date and method (e.g., e-mail, regular mail, employment office) of application
- the version of our résumé that was sent
- a copy of our letter of application
- a list of the referees that we provided
- any correspondence (print or electronic) that we receive from the employer and notes of any phone conversations
- notes from an interview
- copies of follow-up correspondence after an interview.

Mary Stangolis/Thomson Nelson

Use a variety of search methods and sources to identify prospective jobs.

Creating a Résumé

The purpose of a résumé and letter of application is to win the applicant an invitation to an interview. Many people confuse a résumé with an autobiography. An autobiography is a narrative through which an author strives to tell the story of his or her life, emphasizing the events and experiences that had a formative influence on him or her. The goal is to be thorough, if not exhaustive, in showing how the subject turned out as he or she did. A **résumé,** in contrast, is a short list, normally one or two pages long, of a person's qualifications and experience relative to a *specific* job opening. It strives to do only one thing: show that the subject is qualified for the job in question. It becomes, in effect, our "silent sales representative" (Stewart & Cash, 2000, p. 274) in pitching our qualifications for the job.

We can distinguish between two types of résumés: **solicited résumés** and **unsolicited résumés.** A solicited résumé is sent in response to an advertisement or announcement of a job vacancy. An unsolicited résumé is a prospecting document sent to an organization that has not advertised a vacancy. Unsolicited résumés are most often sent by graduates seeking a first career job or, especially in times of high unemployment, by employees who have lost their positions and seek re-entry to their career field.

Solicited résumés are much easier to write. In the job advertisement, the employer normally states the qualifications and experience that are required to take on the vacant position. The task of the résumé writer therefore becomes simply to demonstrate that he or she has those qualifications. Typically, employers specify four to six major qualifications and perhaps several minor ones, qualities which, though not essential, are desirable. Candidates who lack one or two qualifications might apply on the chance that no fully qualified applicants are available. A person who lacks a majority of the major qualifications, however, is wasting everyone's time by applying.

Unsolicited résumés are more difficult to compose because applicants do not have the employer's list of qualifications to serve as a guide. Instead, they must identify what they consider the important qualifications for a position like the one they wish to have and demonstrate that they have those qualifications. The uncertainty arises from the fact that not all organizations value the same qualifications for workers in similar positions. In comparing a half dozen job ads from different organizations for the same type of position, it is common to see a broad range of required qualifications.

To create an effective résumé, an applicant must address two important characteristics: design (or format) and content.

Résumé Format

A résumé should be designed for quick reading. Employers typically receive many more applications than they can process, and a standard procedure has become to use the résumé as a first screening tool. If, for example, 200 applications have been received in response to an advertisement, the recruiter's goal might be to eliminate 90 percent, or 180 of the applications, in this initial screening. He or she would scan the résumés, devoting perhaps 10 to 15 seconds to each one, looking for evidence of essential qualifications (the ones that the employer specified as essential). At the same time, the recruiter would be alert to reasons to reject an application—a misspelling, an unprofessional presentation, sloppy design. Any of these would suggest a lack of care or attention, and, of course, employers do not wish to hire careless or inattentive people.

The following design features will allow the document to be read quickly while still ensuring that important information stands out (refer to Figure 15.3 on pages 444–445 for a sample résumé).

1. **Present the information in vertical columns.** Remember that a résumé is a list. People who scan a document run their eyes down the page rather than across it. A résumé should therefore include no full sentences, just short phrases that can be quickly decoded by recruiters as they cast their eyes down the page.

2. **Ensure that all components are clearly aligned.** Think of the résumé as a table. A table would be very difficult to read if the cells on one row or column were differently aligned than those on another. Once the reader starts scanning a column, his or her gaze should be able to follow it to the bottom without changing focus.

3. **Include lots of white space.** The most common mistake that students make in designing résumés is to crowd too much information on to the page. The thinking seems to be that the more information they can get into the résumé, the more convincing it will be. In fact, just the opposite is true. Cluttered documents are very difficult to scan, so by putting more information in, the designer actually ensures that less stands out. By placing white space around important points (evidence of major qualifications), we ensure that the recruiter recognizes them.

4. **Use a clean, easy-to-read font.** Always use serif fonts (e.g., Times, Bookman) for text. The serifs (the cross strokes on the lines of each letter) make the type easier to read. Sans-serif type (e.g., Helvetica, Arial) may be used for headings and subheadings.

5. **Make intelligent use of typographic features to make important information stand out.** Boldface type, italics, underlining, and so on can be used to emphasize important points, but we should always remember that to emphasize everything is to emphasize nothing; therefore, we want to be

selective in what we emphasize and also conservative in the number of different typographic features we employ. A document that is too tarted up looks unprofessional.

6. **Be consistent (parallel) in the use of design features.** Every part of the document should be designed in the same way. Therefore, spacing, alignment, typography, and so on in one section or page of the résumé must match that of all other sections or pages.
7. **Proofread the résumé until it is flawless.** Any mistake, no matter how seemingly insignificant, sends a message that does the applicant no good. Perfect design and execution of the document tells the recruiter that the applicant is sufficiently interested in the job to exercise a high standard of care.

Résumé Content

Good format may get the résumé read, but good content is required to secure the invitation to an interview. Good content is relevant content. The only criterion for deciding whether to include a particular item of information is its ability to show qualification for the job. Remember that a résumé is not an autobiography. Even someone who had led a completely sheltered life could not hope to tell the story of his or her life in one or two pages. Rather, it is a *selection* of achievements and experiences that *show* qualification for a particular job in terms of the expressed needs of the employer.

Because a résumé refers to a specific job, it follows that to apply for two jobs would require creating two different résumés. We should make each résumé that we submit as reflective of the employer's specified needs as honesty will permit. It does not matter that we consider something to be our most important achievement; if it does not reflect the employer's stated needs, it does not belong in the résumé we use to apply for that particular job.

Creating every résumé from scratch can be extremely time consuming, especially when we are applying for a number of jobs. A way to eliminate this problem is simply to draft and design one exhaustive résumé, including all of the qualifications that we have identified through our personal inventory. Though it is unlikely that we would ever send this document to an employer, we can copy and paste from it to quickly create many different, more specific résumés geared to particular job applications.

Nathan is graduating from university this year and seeking an entry-level position as a news reporter. In the course of his job search, he comes across the advertisement presented in Figure 15.2. As the employer asks for a résumé, he must develop one which responds to the employer's stated needs.

Nathan decides to create a **chronological résumé,** the most widely used and simplest type of résumé. In a chronological résumé, the applicant's qualifications and experience are categorized and presented in reverse chronological order within each category. The categories included in a résumé will vary

JUNIOR REPORTER Join the staff of the *Estevan Mercury,* one of Saskatchewan's oldest and most respected weekly newspapers. The ideal candidate will have • a university degree in journalism or equivalent education • experience covering local government • the ability to write engaging feature stories • knowledge of photography • copy-editing and rewrite skills This is a great opportunity to work with an experienced editor on an award-winning weekly newspaper and experience the best that community journalism has to offer. We offer a competitive salary and excellent benefits. Send letter of application, résumé, and samples of your writing to Mr. Peter Ng, Publisher *The Estevan Mercury* 68 Souris Avenue North Estevan, SK S4A 2A6

Figure 15.2
Job advertisement

depending on the job the applicant is applying for and the manner in which his or her qualifications were acquired. The most commonly included categories are listed below. Nathan's résumé is shown in Figure 15.3.

1. **Contact information:** name, complete mailing address, phone number(s), e-mail address, and fax number (if available)

   Nathan makes it as easy as possible for the employer to contact him.

2. **Objective (optional):** a single clear sentence, stating the applicant's goal

   An objective is unnecessary in solicited résumés (obviously, the objective is to secure the advertised position), but this goal statement can be very useful in acquainting the readers of unsolicited applications, especially in large organizations that employ people with many different types of skills, with the kind of position that the applicant is seeking. If Nathan were sending out unsolicited applications to newspapers across Canada he would state his objective; for example:

   Objective: an entry-level news reporting position that offers opportunity for advancement.

3. **Education:** degree or certificate expected or received, dates of study, school, city and province, GPA if it is strong, and any academic highlights that show job qualifications (relevant courses, research projects, prizes, scholarships)

Notice that in each case, Nathan highlights the degree that he received (and his major), not the name of the school that he attended. The degree title reveals most about him and his qualifications.

In applying for his first career job, Nathan puts his education first because, as he is applying for a job in the field in which he has trained, it represents his major qualification. On the other hand, if he were applying for a summer job as a lifeguard, he would start with his employment history as it shows stronger qualification for that type of work. Later, in applying for more advanced jobs in journalism—once he has acquired some professional experience—he will again place his work experience first. In other words, we want to lead with our strongest qualification.

4. **Employment history:** position title, dates worked, name of the organization, the city and province, and any relevant experience gained through the job

   Nathan lists his most recent summer jobs, not elaborating on his duties because they show no qualification for the job he is seeking. Notice that in each case, he highlights the job title, not the name of the employer. The job title reveals most about him and his qualifications.

5. **Honours and awards (optional):** name of award, purpose if not widely known, granting agency, city and province, and date

   Academic awards, athletic awards, community service awards, and so on are normally given in recognition of outstanding performance. Nathan selects awards that reveal skills and characteristics relevant to the job he is applying for: knowledge of politics, consistent high achievement, and photographic skill. His goal here, as with all parts of the résumé, is to show qualification for the position, not to demonstrate what a wonderful person he is.

6. **Special skills or training (optional):** skill or course, training centre, certification or proficiency level, dates (as apply)

   Many jobs require applicants to have computer skills, language skills, special driving permits, lifesaving or first aid training, coaching or counselling certifications, and so on. A variety of such skills can be grouped together under a general heading like Special Skills or Special Training, or particularly important skills can be highlighted in separate categories; for example, Language Skills or Computer Training.

7. **Volunteer work (optional):** position title, dates worked, name of the organization, the city and province, and any relevant experience gained through the job

   Volunteer positions can show the same qualifications as paid work of the same type. However, the two should never be mixed together.

OBSERVE & ANALYZE
Journal Activity

Résumés

Follow the guidelines in this section to create a résumé, not more than two pages long, to show your qualifications for one of the jobs that you identified in the previous Observe & Analyze journal activity.

Nathan R. O'Reilly

6109 Jubilee Road, Apt. 5
Halifax, NS
B3H 2E6

Phone (902) 422-9644
Fax (902) 422-1193
E-mail nathan.oreilly@ns.sympatico.ca

Education

Sept. 2003–present	**Bachelor of Journalism** (Expected May 2004) University of King's College Halifax, NS G.P.A. 3.65/4 Relevant Course Work • Advanced Newspaper Workshop • Newspaper Workshop • Journalism Research Internship Halifax *Chronicle Herald* (City Desk)
May 2003	**Bachelor of Arts (Political Science)** University of Victoria Victoria, BC G.P.A. 8.4/9 Relevant Course Work • Issues in Canadian Politics • Canadian Government • Canadian Public Policy • Constitutional Law and Politics in Canada

Work Experience

Summers 2002–03	**Head Lifeguard** Red Deer Recreation Centre Red Deer, AB
Summers 2000–01	**Counsellor and Swimming Instructor** Pine Lake Camp Red Deer, AB

Résumé of Nathan R. O'Reilly 2

Honours and Awards

May 2003	**Hiram P. Macintosh Memorial Prize** For highest achievement by a graduate in political science University of Victoria
1998–2003	**Dean's List Member** University of Victoria
August 2002	**Best Action Photograph** Picture Alberta Competition Alberta Professional Photographers Association

Extra-curricular Activities

May 2002–May 2003	**Editor in Chief** *The Martlett* University of Victoria • edited weekly student newspaper • wrote editorials • reported on student government • supervised editorial staff • assigned and edited news and feature stories

Hobbies and Interests

Reading, photography, swimming, wilderness camping

References

Dr. Girish B. Anand
Department of Political Science, University of Victoria
3800 Finnerty Road, Victoria BC V8P 5C2
Phone: (250) 721-7211 Fax: (250) 721-7212

Prof. Elaine MacDonald
School of Journalism, University of King's College
6350 Coburg Road, Halifax, NS B3H 2A1
Phone: (902) 422-1271 Fax: (902) 425-8183

Mr. Robert Valerio, Aquatics Director
Red Deer Recreation Centre
P.O. Box 5008, Red Deer AB T4N 3T4
Phone: (403) 309-8411 Fax: (403) 342-6073

Figure 15.3
Sample résumé

THINKING ABOUT . . .

Real vs. Ideal Résumés

Review the *content* of the résumé that you prepared in response to the preceding Observe & Analyze exercise. Think about where you want to be upon graduation from college or university. How must your résumé change to allow you to become what you want to be? What specific actions must you take now to ensure that your future résumé looks as it must to allow you to accomplish your goals?

IN BRIEF

Creating a Résumé

The purpose of a résumé (with the letter of application) is to win the applicant an invitation to an employment interview. A successful résumé is judged in terms of its

- *Design:* tabular (information presented in vertical columns; all parts aligned and parallel throughout) incorporating plenty of white space, clear type, intelligent use of typographic features, and no errors
- *Content:* relevant; all content shows qualification for the job in terms of employer's specified needs.

8. **Extra-curricular activities (optional):** activity, organization, dates, special achievements

   Involvement in extra-curricular activities can often be as valuable as paid work experience, especially to students with little relevant work experience. Nathan's experience with his varsity newspaper, for example, reveals relevant qualifications.

9. **Hobbies and interests (optional):** a list of activities, noting special achievements if any

   Nathan uses this entry to reveal different relevant aspects of his character: physical, intellectual, artistic. A list of five team sports, in contrast, would suggest that the applicant was rather one-dimensional.

10. **Memberships (optional):** name of organization, dates, offices held, or activities

    Membership in relevant academic or professional associations demonstrates a serious interest in a student's field of study.

11. **References:** titles (Dr., Ms., Sgt., etc.), names, positions, organizations, and complete workplace contact information for three persons

    Nathan chooses referees who know his work well and can speak knowledgeably and accurately about his strengths and skills. Many students make the mistake of going for the high-profile referee (the head of the department, or vice president of the university), when that person knows them only in passing and cannot give the detailed reference that an employer would want. The references are always presented last in the résumé.

    When sending unsolicited résumés, applicants frequently replace the names and contact information with the phrase *Available on request.* When the employer calls for references, they then know that they are being actively considered for a position.

It is highly unlikely that all of these categories would occur in a single résumé, as applicants are likely to draw on different parts of their experience to show their qualifications for different jobs. In every case, deciding whether an element should be included or not depends entirely on its ability to show qualification for the job.

Once we believe that the design and content of our résumé is perfect, we should laser print it on high quality, white or off-white, letter size stationery, and then proofread it carefully to ensure that no small flaws have been overlooked.

Writing a Letter of Application

Occasionally employers will ask applicants to drop off or send only a résumé, but most often a **letter of application** (sometimes called a cover letter) should accompany the résumé. A letter of application is largely an interpretative document. It draws connections between the employer's needs as outlined in the job ad and the applicant's qualifications as detailed in the résumé. Ideally, the letter of application shows that the applicant's qualifications satisfy the employer's needs.

Letter Design

Where the résumé is tabular and fragmentary, the letter of application should be reflective of our best writing skills: clear and grammatically correct sentences in unified and coherent paragraphs.

Only a few letter designs are widely used today; the simplest and most commonly used is full block style. In a **full block style** letter, all lines begin at the left margin (there are no tabs). The letter is single spaced and divisions are indicated by a double space left between letter parts or paragraphs. Again, we should use a clear and easy-to-read serif font in a reasonable size (12 point for most fonts).

A block style letter has the following parts with a double space between all parts except the complimentary close and the name, where three blank lines are left for the writer's signature. (If the body of the letter is short, additional spaces can be inserted before and after the date to balance the letter vertically on the page.)

1. **Return address:** the writer's complete mailing address, including postal code, usually on three or four lines

   The writer's name should *never* be included as part of the return address; it goes at the bottom of the letter.

2. **Date:** the date on which the letter was written: e.g., March 15, 2004

3. **Inside address:** on four or five lines, the title (Mr., Dr.), full name, position, organizational name, and complete mailing address, including postal code, for the person to whom the letter is addressed

   If the person's name is not included in a job ad, we can easily find it by visiting the company's Web site or calling its switchboard and asking for the name of the personnel director.

4. **Salutation:** Dear Mr. Brown: or Dear Ms. Smith:

   Note that the salutation is followed by a colon.

5. **Body:** typically three to five paragraphs

   Letters of application rarely exceed a page in length.

6. **Complimentary close:** e.g., Yours truly, or Sincerely,

   Note that the complimentary close is followed by a comma and that only the first word is capitalized.

7. **Name:** The full name of the writer

8. **Enclosure** Note: Encl.: résumé

If the letter should extend beyond a page, place a page header in the top left corner of each subsequent page with the following information on three lines: the reader's full name, the date, and the page number; for example,

Mr. John Smith
March 15, 2004
Page 2

After printing the letter, the writer signs his or her full name between the complimentary close and the name. Figure 15.4 shows Nathan's letter of application for the reporter position, presented in full block style.

The Content of the Letter of Application

A letter of application is essentially a sales letter, a type of persuasive text. As a writer of a letter of application, our goal is to sell our services to the employer. It is therefore necessary that we focus on the employer's needs. This point is crucial. A great many applicants destroy their chances of being invited to an interview by focusing on their own needs, saying essentially: hire me because I need money to pay for my education; hire me because I need work experience; or hire me because I want to have a career in your industry. This approach is comparable to a business advertising with the slogan "Buy here because we want your money." Employers are not charities; they hire to serve their own needs, not those of the applicant. To succeed, applicants must focus on the benefits the company will derive from hiring them.

An effective letter of application is divided into three parts and performs three functions: catches the reader's favourable attention, demonstrates that the applicant is qualified for consideration, and requests an interview. We must remember that winning an interview is the goal of the résumé and letter of application.

COMMUNICATE! Using InfoTrac College Edition

Under the subject *cover letter,* see "The Intelligent Standout Résumé and Cover Letter" by Linda Bates Parker (1998) and "Great Letters and Why They Work" by Dean Rieck (1998). Compare the two authors' recommendations. Note at least two recommendations on preparing résumés and cover letters that you would want to follow.

Part 1—The introduction: (usually a single paragraph of three or four sentences). We identify the specific job (position title, competition number) or the employment area (in the case of an unsolicited résumé) that we are applying for;

6109 Jubilee Road, Apt. 5
Halifax, NS
B3H 2E6

April 25, 2004

Mr. Peter Ng, Publisher
The Estevan Mercury
68 Souris Avenue North
Estevan, SK S4A 2A6

Dear Mr. Ng:

I am very interested in the Junior Reporter position that you advertised in the April 22, 2004, issue of the *Edmonton Journal*. I am knowledgeable about Canadian politics and government, experienced in photography, and in just a few weeks, will receive a Bachelor of Journalism degree with a specialization in newspaper reporting.

My education has prepared me very well for the position that you are offering. I majored in political science at the University of Victoria, and my studies included several courses in Canadian government. In addition, my concentration in print journalism at the University of King's College, including an internship on the City Desk of the Halifax *Chronicle Herald*, has provided me with well rounded reporting skills. I believe my achievements in both of these academic programs speak for themselves and that this combination of education will enable me to provide excellent local government coverage for the readers of the *Estevan Mercury*.

As you will see from the enclosed résumé, my extra-curricular activities have also prepared me for a position on your staff. I am an avid photographer (portraits and action photography), and I develop and print my own work. Two years ago, I won first prize for action photography in an Alberta-wide competition. In addition, my involvement in the student press has given me much more newspaper experience than most recent journalism graduates. As editor-in-chief of *The Martlett* at the University of Victoria, I not only covered weekly meetings of the Students' Society but also wrote editorials on student political issues. During my four years on staff, I edited copy, worked on the rewrite desk, and wrote news, feature, and entertainment stories.

I am confident, Mr. Ng, that I am well qualified to serve on your staff and would welcome an opportunity to discuss my qualifications with you personally. Please call me at (902) 422-9644 to schedule an interview at a time convenient to you.

Sincerely,

Nathan O'Reilly

Encl.: Résumé
Writing samples

Figure 15.4
Letter of application

identify our source of information about the vacancy (newspaper ad, agency, contact, etc.); and briefly summarize our ability to satisfy the primary qualifications (especially education and work experience) required by the employer.

Part 2—The body: (usually two to four paragraphs). We expand on our qualifications, keeping like information together. There are two effective ways of organizing the body of the letter of application: (1) in terms of the employer's requirements as specified in the job ad or (2) in terms of the applicant's qualifications as specified in the résumé. In drafting his letter of application, for example, Nathan could organize his letter in terms of the employer's stated needs:

Paragraph 1: education

Paragraph 2: reporting and feature writing experience

Paragraph 3: associated skills: photography and copy editing

In each paragraph, he would draw from different parts of his experience to show that he could satisfy the employer's need with regard to one of the hiring criteria. Alternatively, he could organize it in terms of the categories in his résumé:

Paragraph 1: my education and training

Paragraph 2: my extra-curricular activities

In each paragraph, he would attempt to show how the particular aspect of his qualifications satisfied the employer's needs. (In most cases, a third paragraph would be devoted to the applicant's work experience, but Nathan's work experience is not relevant to the job he is seeking.) Regardless of which pattern he used, he would want to highlight experience that was most relevant to the job, show how the experience is relevant when it is not obvious (particularly with non-work experience), and refer the reader to his résumé for more details.

OBSERVE & ANALYZE
Journal Activity

Letter of Application

Draft a letter of application to accompany the résumé that you created in response to the earlier Observe & Analyze exercise.

Part 3—The close: (usually one short paragraph). We ask for an interview, stating where we can be contacted to make arrangements and when we are available. Some weak closings to avoid are thanking the reader in advance for considering the application (this is presumptuous; we should thank him or her after the fact when we receive an invitation to an interview), or ending with a plea or a cliché (e.g., I look forward to hearing from you soon).

Electronically Submitted Letters of Application and Résumés

Electronically submitted application packages have become popular with many employers and job seekers. For example, from 1995 to 1999 the percentage of résumés received electronically by Microsoft increased from 5 to 50 percent (Criscito, 2000, p. 2). Employers like electronic résumés because they can very quickly scan large numbers looking for particular qualifications or characteristics. Candidates like them because they save time and money.

Although electronically transmitted letters of application and résumés contain the same content, they may differ in several ways (Schmidt & Conaway, 1999, pp. 98–99). Many of the differences derive from the fact that they will be scanned electronically. Thus, it may be necessary to avoid formatting (using tabs) and typographic features such as boldface type, italics, and bullets because they will "only confuse computerized word searches or interfere with the scanning process" (p. 98).

There are three kinds of electronically transmitted application documents: attachments of print-formatted documents; ASCII texts (a generic computer file) that can be transmitted in the body of an e-mail message; and HTML documents presented as Internet Web pages (Criscito, 2000, p. 2). The first of these three is easiest to create and transmit and has become increasingly popular as computer software has become more standardized. A résumé or letter that has been prepared, saved, and sent as a generic ASCII text file has the advantage of being readable by anyone regardless of the word processing software he or she is using (Criscito, 2000, p. 3). Such a document can be sent as a file to company recruiters or posted to the Web site of a company, a job bank, or a newsgroup. Finally, when we post our résumé on a Web site, we increase the likelihood that someone who is seeking employees with our qualifications will find us.

More detailed information on electronically transmitted résumés and letters of application is widely available on the Web. For example, the *Advanced Résumé Concepts* site at www.reslady.com/electronic.html gives instructions on how to create ASCII and HTML résumés.

IN BRIEF

Letters of Application

A letter of application is an interpretative document which draws connections between the employer's needs as outlined in the job ad and the applicant's qualifications as detailed in the résumé. A successful letter of application should

- be correctly formatted in a recognized business letter style such as full block style
- function as a sales letter by persuading the employer that his or her needs will be satisfied by hiring the applicant.

WWW

Employment Interviews

The job interview is a special type of interpersonal situation with specific demands. We will consider some of the procedures and methods used by an interviewer in conducting an employment interview as well as those that an interviewee can use to prepare for and take part in an employment interview.

Interviews are an important part of the process of seeking employment. Even for part-time and temporary jobs, we benefit by approaching the interview process seriously and systematically. Although being interviewed for a job can be a traumatic experience, especially for those who are going through it for the first time, applicants for nearly every position in nearly any field will go through at least one interview and possibly several.

At its worst, an interview can be a waste of time for everyone; at its best, it can reveal vital information about an applicant as well as enable the applicant to judge the suitability of the position, the company, and the tasks to be performed. Skilful interviewers can gauge an applicant's specific abilities, ambitions, energy, knowledge, intelligence, and integrity. More importantly, they can help the interviewee show his or her strengths in these same areas.

Interview Methods

An interviewer represents a link between a job applicant and the organization. Much of the applicant's impression of the company will depend on his or her impression of the interviewer, so he or she will want to be able to provide answers to questions that the applicant may have about the organization. In addition to the obvious desire for salary information, an applicant may seek information about opportunities for advancement, the influence of personal initiatives on company policy, company attitudes toward personal life and lifestyle, working conditions, and so forth. Moreover, the interviewer is primarily responsible for determining whether an applicant will be considered for the position available or for possible future employment with the company.

Interview structure An **interview** is a structured conversation, a type of pragmatic problem-consideration conversation (see Chapter 6), with the goal of exchanging information that is needed for decision making. A well-planned interview comprises a list of questions designed to get the needed information. Interviews, like speeches and essays, have an appropriate opening, body, and conclusion.

1. **Opening:** The interviewer opens the interview by stating its purpose and introducing himself or herself to the interviewee if they have not previously met. Sometimes interviewers begin with warm-up or easy questions to help establish a rapport. A good interviewer senses the nature of the situation and tries to use a method that is most likely to encourage the other person to talk and provide adequate answers. Although warm-up questions may be helpful, most participants are ready to get down to business immediately, in which case warm-up questions may be counterproductive (Cogger, 1982).
2. **The body:** The body of the interview consists of the questions to which the interviewer needs answers. The quality of information depends on how the questions are phrased. We can classify questions into one or more of six categories: open or closed, neutral or leading, primary or secondary (Stewart & Cash, 2000, p. 80).

   Open questions are broad-based questions that ask the interviewee to respond with whatever information he or she wishes. Open questions range from those with virtually no restrictions, such as "What can you tell me about yourself?" to those that give some direction, such as "What accomplishment has best prepared you for this job?" Interviewers ask open questions to encourage the other person to talk, providing the interviewer with an opportunity to listen and to observe. Open questions take time to answer, however, and give respondents more control, which means that interviewers can lose sight of their original purpose if they are not careful (Tengler & Jablin, 1983).

In contrast, **closed questions** are narrowly focused and require very brief answers. Closed questions range from those that can be answered with yes or no, such as "Have you had a course in marketing?" to those that require only a short answer, such as "How many restaurants have you worked in?" By asking closed questions, interviewers can both control the interview and obtain large amounts of information in a short time. Closed questions seldom enable the interviewer to know why a person gave a certain response, nor are they likely to yield much voluntary information; therefore, a mix of open and closed questions are used in employment interviews.

Open and closed questions may be either neutral or leading. **Neutral questions** allow a person to give an answer without direction from the interviewer. "How do you like your present job?" is an example. The neutral question avoids giving the respondent any indication of what the interviewer thinks about the issue or how the question should be answered. In contrast, **leading questions** are phrased in a way that suggests the interviewer has a preferred answer; for example, "You don't like your present job very much, do you?" In most employment interviews, neutral questions are preferred.

Primary questions are those open or closed questions that the interviewer plans ahead of time. They serve as the main points on the interview outline. **Secondary** or **follow-up questions** may be planned or spontaneous, but they are designed to pursue the answers given to primary questions. Some follow-up questions encourage the person to continue ("And then?" "Is there more?"); some probe into what the person has said ("What does *frequently* mean here?" "What were you thinking at the time?"); and some probe the feelings of the person ("How did it feel to get the prize?" "Were you worried when you didn't find her?"). The major purpose of follow-up questions is to motivate the interviewee to enlarge on incomplete or vague answers or answers that were less detailed than the interviewer expected.

3. **The close:** Toward the end of the interview, interviewers should always explain to the interviewee what will happen next and how the information that they have gathered will be used. They should also explain the procedures for making decisions based on the information and let the interviewee know whether and how he or she will receive feedback on the decision. Interviewers then close the interview in a courteous, neutral manner, thanking the interviewee for his or her time and interest.

Interview procedure The most satisfactory employment interviews are probably highly to moderately structured. In an unstructured interview, the interviewer tends to talk more and to make decisions based less on valid data than in the structured interview (Stewart & Cash, 2000, p. 238). Especially when screening a large number of applicants, interviewers are likely to make

OBSERVE & ANALYZE
Journal Activity

What Interviewers Look For

Call a large local company and make an appointment to interview a person in the human resources department whose job is to interview candidates for employment. Develop a set of interview questions and follow-ups. Focus your interview on obtaining information about the person's experiences that will help you to prepare for interviews. For example, you might ask, "What are the characteristics you like to see an interviewee demonstrate?" or "How do you decide whom to interview?" Write out the questions you plan to ask, leaving space between each question. During the interview take notes on the answers to each of the questions and any follow-up questions you may have used. After you have conducted the interview, be prepared to discuss your findings in class.

sure that all have been asked the same questions and that the questions cover subjects that will be most revealing of the kind of information they will need to make a reasonable decision.

Before the time scheduled for the interview, the interviewer will become familiar with all the available data about the applicant by studying the applicant's résumé, letter of application, letters of recommendation, transcripts, and test scores, if available. These written data will help determine some of the questions he or she will want to ask.

DIVERSE VOICES

Our Sister's Keeper

by Sheema Khan

Interviewers, like others, rely on their perceptions in making their judgments of others. Sheema Khan, chair of the Council on American-Islamic Relations, Canada, reveals what can happen when those perceptions are distorted by stereotypes or prejudice.

"Do you have to wear that thing on your head?"

This was the final question during my job interview for a research position at a Canadian university. Apparently, my Ph.D. in chemical physics from Harvard, research publications and postdoctoral research at MIT weren't enough to convince my interviewer that I qualified for the job. It came down to "that thing" on my head, the hijab—the Islamic headscarf that forms part of my faith.

While at Harvard, I had undergone personal changes that reflected spiritual evolution, including a renewed commitment to Islam. For me, prayer, modesty and gratefulness filled a void. Wearing the hijab as stipulated in the *Koran* is an act of worship—not unlike the head-covering worn by an Orthodox Jew or observant Sikh.

Trying to control my anger, I replied that the way I chose to dress was irrelevant to my ability to do scientific research. If the interviewer felt I could do the job based on my track record, then he should hire me. If not, then we should stop wasting each other's time. I also knew that, if I were turned down, my next step would be to go to the provincial Human Rights Commission.

Then the interviewer confided that he had no problem but feared that others would. How ironic, I thought: Scientists claim to be rational but think so illogically about an individual's potential. (I got the job, and my employer and I developed a good working relationship.)

But many Muslim women, who choose to abide by the hijab, aren't so lucky in Canada's most multicultural city. According to a government-funded study, "No Hijab Is Permitted Here," visible Muslim women faced clear discrimination when applying for jobs at fast-food outlets, retail stores, and factories in Toronto. Some were even told to remove their hijab as a prerequisite. The study's authors made 23 recommendations, including educating Muslim women on their rights, and advising employers that wearing the hijab has no impact on a woman's ability to carry out her job.

Some have minimized this study by saying the sample size was too small. Yet, imagine tossing a coin 16 times and coming up with 10 heads, two tails and four indeterminate outcomes. One would reasonably conclude that the coin was tailored toward *heads*. In the study, a pair of equally qualified women—one with hijab, one without—inquired at 16 job sites. The result: at 10 sites, the woman without hijab was asked to fill out applications immediately, while only two sites asked the woman with hijab to do the same. Would tossing the coin more times give very different results?

For all their self-righteous efforts to "save" Muslim women in other countries from oppressive cultural practices—such as the denial of education and employment, female genital mutilation, and honour killing—Canadian women's groups and prominent feminists have been conspicuously silent on the denial of job opportunities to Muslim women right here at home.

Our sisters are not asked to agree with the hijab—only to stand by the principle that no woman should be denied the right to choose her religious practices or to work at a job for which she's qualified because of her appearance. Some excuse the prejudice of employers, citing the Western perception of hijab as a symbol of oppression. Yet, isn't it oppressive to tell a Muslim woman in Canada that she cannot work because of her choice of dress?

In 1994, Québec schools expelled female Muslim students for wearing the hijab. The rest of Canada seemed to feel that such overt racism only existed in Québec. Suffice it to say that racism, a human weakness, exists across Canada.

Our multicultural paradigm has actively promoted inclusiveness, and provided means of redress to those denied opportunities to rightfully participate. These are values that Canadians hold dear. But the events of 9/11 have increased mistrust of Muslims; our mosaic strains under the weight of fear.

Education and legislation are key to the fight against racism. Leaders in government, community relations, academia and business must denounce it. Employers must know they are breaking the law when they discriminate, and Muslim women must know they have recourse to justice.

Finally: Please don't feel sorry for us. Given the post-9/11 climate, a Muslim woman who chooses to wear her hijab and participate fully in society has courage. Despite prevalent negative attitudes, she is secure in the knowledge that God strengthens those who seek divine help. And isn't a confident woman an excellent asset for our society?

Source: "Our Sister's Keeper" by Sheema Khan. Reprinted by permission of the author.

Preparing for and Participating in Interviews

Interviews are used by the company to decide whom to hire. During the interview, the interviewer assesses candidates to determine whether they have the skills and abilities needed for the job and make judgments about their personality and motivation. Following these guidelines will help us prepare for and function well in the interview.

1. **Research the organization.** We must learn about the organization's services, products, ownership, and financial health. Knowing about a company shows that we are interested in that company. Moreover, it will put us in a better position to discuss how we can contribute to the company's mission.

2. **Rehearse the interview.** For most of us, job interviews are at least somewhat stressful. To help ourselves perform at our best, it is a good idea to practise the interview by anticipating some of the questions we will be asked and crafting thoughtful answers. We might even try writing out or saying answers aloud. Being able to answer questions on subjects such as our salary expectations, our possible contributions to the company, and our special skills requires careful thought. Figure 15.5 presents some frequently asked interview questions.

3. **Dress appropriately.** When we are invited to an employment interview, we must remember that we are there to sell ourselves and our qualifications. Recall from our discussion of self-presentation in Chapter 4 how much our nonverbal behaviour contributes to the impression we make. To show ourselves in the best possible light, we must take care with our appearance; if we want a particular job, we must dress in a way that is acceptable to the person or organization that may hire us. Men should wear a collared shirt, dress pants, a jacket, and a tie. Women should wear a conservative dress or a suit. A survey of 153 companies showed that the factor that is first in leading to rejection is poor personal appearance (Schmidt & Conaway, 1999, p. 110).

Mary Stangolis/Thomson Nelson

Listen carefully and give yourself time to think before answering an important question.

4. **Be punctual.** The interview is the employer's first exposure to our work behaviour. If we are late for such an important event, the interviewer will conclude that we are likely to be late for work. We should plan to arrive 15 or 20 minutes before the appointment and to allow ourselves extra travel time in case of traffic problems.
5. **Be alert, look at the interviewer, and listen actively.** Again our nonverbal communication tells a lot about us. Company representatives are likely to consider eye contact and posture as indicators of our level of self-confidence.
6. **Take time to think before answering a question.** If the interviewer asks a question that we have not anticipated, we should take time to think before answering. It is better to pause and appear thoughtful than to give a hasty answer that may cost us the job. When we do not understand a question, we should paraphrase it before attempting to answer.
7. **Ask questions about the type of work expected.** The interview is our chance to find out if we would enjoy working for this company. We might ask the interviewer to describe a typical workday for the person who will get the job. If the interview is conducted at the company offices, we could ask to see where we would be working. In this way, we prepare ourselves to know how we will respond to a job offer.
8. **Show enthusiasm for the job.** If we are not enthusiastic during an interview, the interviewer is likely to reason that we are not the person for the job. Employers look for and expect applicants to look and sound interested.
9. **Do not engage in long discussions of salary.** The time to discuss salary is when the job is offered. If the company representative tries to pin us down, we could ask, "What do you normally pay someone with my experience and education for a position at this level?" Such a question enables us to get an idea of what the salary will be without committing ourselves to a figure first.
10. **Do not harp on benefits.** Again, detailed discussions about benefits are more appropriate after the company has made us an offer.

THINKING ABOUT . . .

Perceptions of an Interview

Think of a recent interview that you participated in. Consider the person who interviewed you. How did your reaction to the interviewer influence your desire to work for the organization? Try to remember what he or she said or did that affected your opinion.

IN BRIEF

Employment Interviews

A job interview is a structured conversation with the goal of exchanging information that is needed for deciding who is the best candidate for a job. An interview has three parts:

- *Opening:* statement of purpose
- *Body:* questions designed to collect needed information
- *Close:* explanation of next steps followed by courteous leave taking.

Applicants attending job interviews should be well prepared, appropriately dressed, punctual, alert, attentive, thoughtful, and enthusiastic.

TEST YOUR COMPETENCE

Interviewing

Work with a classmate to perform a mock interview. Assume that you are going to be interviewed for the job that you have applied for. Have your partner interview you using some of the questions from Figure 15.5. After completing the interview, discuss how you performed. Which questions did you handle well? Which were hard for you?

Questions about School:

- How did you select the college or university you attended?
- How did you decide on your major?
- Did you change your major during college or university?
- If you were starting your post-secondary education over again, what major would you choose?
- In which extra-curricular activities did you participate? Why? Which did you most enjoy? Do you think they were worth the time you invested in them? Why?
- In what ways does your transcript reflect your ability?
- How were you able to help with your college or university expenses?
- Which courses did you like most? Least? Why?
- Which of your years in school was most difficult?
- What do you know about opportunities in the field in which you are trained?

Personal Questions:

- What are your hobbies? How did you become interested in them?
- Give an example of how you work under pressure.
- What jobs have you held? How were they obtained and why did you leave?
- At what age did you begin supporting yourself?
- What causes you to lose your temper?
- What are your major strengths? Weaknesses?
- Give an example of when you were a leader and what happened.
- Do you prefer working by yourself or with others?
- What do you do to stay in good physical condition?
- What was the last non–school-assigned book that you read? Tell me about it.
- Who has had the greatest influence on your life?
- What have you done to show your creativity?
- What kind of boss do you prefer?
- Can you take correction without becoming upset?

Questions about the Position:

- What type of position are you most interested in?
- What are your future vocational plans?
- What personal characteristics are most important for success in your chosen field?
- What do you know about the company?
- Under what conditions would you be willing to relocate?
- Why do you think you would like to work for us?
- What do you hope to accomplish?
- How long do you expect to work?
- What do you think determines a person's progress in a good company?
- Why do you feel that your qualifications would make you beneficial to us?
- How do you feel about travelling?
- What part of the country would you like to settle in?
- What kind of people do you enjoy interacting with?
- What do you regard as an equitable salary for a person with your qualifications?
- What new skills would you like to learn?
- What are your career goals?
- How would you proceed if you were in charge of hiring?
- What are your most important criteria for determining whether you will accept a position?

Figure 15.5

Frequently asked interview questions

What Would You Do?
A Question of Ethics

After three years of working at as a counter clerk in the classified advertising department of a city newspaper, Mark had decided to look for another job. As he thought about preparing a résumé, he was struck by how little experience he had for the kind of job he wanted.

When he discussed his problem with his friend Bernardo, Bernardo said, "Exactly what have you been doing at *The Gleaner*?"

"Well, for the most part I've simply been serving customers—you know, selling ads and processing them. Sometimes, I've done a bit of editing when we were short-handed."

"Hm," Bernardo thought for a while. "Why not retitle your job as Editorial Assistant—it's more descriptive."

"But my official title is Clerk."

"Sure, but it doesn't really describe what you do. This way you can show major editorial experience. Don't worry, everybody makes these kinds of changes—you're not really lying."

"Yeah, I see what you mean. Good idea."

1. Is it ethical for Mark to follow Bernardo's advice? Why?
2. How should we deal with statements like "Everybody does it"?

Summary

Finding a job is a complex process that takes time and effort and must be approached methodically. A properly conducted job search can be divided into five discrete steps: (1) taking an inventory of one's career goals and marketable skills, (2) identifying prospective employers, (3) creating a résumé, (4) drafting a letter of application, and (5) participating in an interview.

A personal inventory requires a thorough assessment of our career goals and our marketable skills, to determine what type of job we would find satisfying and what abilities we have, including fundamental skills, teamwork skills, and personal management skills, to offer prospective employers.

Because only a small percentage of jobs are advertised, we should use a variety of search methods to identify prospective employers. Valuable sources of information are personal and professional contacts; job fairs; government, university, and private-sector employment offices; employers themselves; and print and electronic publications that carry job advertisements.

The purpose of a résumé and letter of application is to win the applicant a job interview. So that it can be read quickly, a résumé is designed as a table with vertical columns, aligned elements, plenty of white space, clear easy-to-read type, and intelligent use of typographic features to make important information stand out. The only criterion for evaluating the content of the résumé is its ability to show qualification for the job in terms of the employer's stated needs. A letter of application is an interpretative document that draws connections between the employer's needs and the applicant's qualifications. A successful letter is correctly formatted and functions as a sales letter to interest the employer in the applicant. Electronically submitted résumés and letters of application are becoming increasingly popular.

An interview is a structured conversation with the goal of exchanging information that is needed for decision making. Job interviews are structured to elicit the maximum quantity of information about the candidate. Before the interview, the interviewer will review the applicant's résumé, letter of application, letters of recommendation, and test scores, if available. During the interview, the interviewer will ask primary and secondary, open and closed, and neutrally worded questions, avoid leading questions, and give the applicant an opportunity to ask questions. At the end of the interview, he or she will explain what will happen next in the process.

Before attending a job interview, applicants should learn about the company and rehearse answers to likely questions. At the interview itself, they should be punctual, be alert and look directly at the interviewer, give themselves time to think before answering difficult questions, ask intelligent questions about the company and the job, and show enthusiasm for the position.

Glossary

Review the following key terms:

chronological résumé (441) — a résumé document in which the applicant's qualifications and experience are categorized and presented in reverse chronological order within each category.

closed questions (453) — narrowly focused questions that require very brief answers.

full block style (447) — a full business letter design in which all lines of type begin at the left margin.

fundamental skills (434) — the skills that form the basis for developing other more specialized skills.

interview (452) — a structured conversation with the goal of exchanging information that is needed for decision making.

leading questions (453) — questions phrased in a way that suggests the interviewer has a preferred answer.

letter of application (cover letter) (447) — an interpretative document which draws connections between an employer's needs as outlined in the job ad and an applicant's qualifications as detailed in the résumé.

marketable skills (433) — those skills for which there is a demand in the labour market.

neutral questions (453) — questions that allow a person to give an answer without direction from the interviewer.

open questions (452) — broad-based questions that ask the interviewee to respond with whatever information he or she wishes.

personal inventory (431) — a thorough and methodical assessment of one's career goals and marketable skills.

personal management skills (435) — personal skills, attitudes, and behaviours that drive a person's potential for growth.

primary questions (453) — open or closed questions that the interviewer plans ahead of time.

résumé (439) — a short list, normally one or two pages long, of a person's qualifications and experience relative to a *specific* job opening.

secondary or **follow-up questions** (453) — planned or spontaneous questions that are designed to pursue the answers given to primary questions.

solicited résumé (439) — a résumé sent in response to an advertisement or announcement of a job vacancy.

teamwork skills (434) — the skills and attributes needed to contribute productively to a work group.

unsolicited résumé (439) — a prospecting document sent to an organization which has not advertised a vacancy.

Chris Wattie/CP Picture Archive

OBJECTIVES

After you have read this chapter, you should be able to answer these questions:

- What is an organization?
- What is organizational communication?
- What is the difference between internal and external communication?
- What is the difference between formal and informal communication?
- What are upward, downward, and lateral communication?
- What is an organizational culture?
- What are the common barriers to effective organizational communication?
- How can barriers to effective organizational communication be overcome?

CHAPTER 16

Communication in Organizations

"Hi, Jane, I'm glad I ran into you."

"Oh, hi, Halima, good to see you too."

"Sorry to talk shop over lunch, but can you tell me how you are processing payroll requisitions for part-time staff? I'm completely confused about what to do."

"Really, what's the problem, Halima?"

"Well, Johnston in accounting says that I should be including part-time workers' hours along with all other staff hours in my regular weekly report, but Ms. Reiter, my division manager, says she wants to see a separate requisition for part-time hours so she can keep an eye on weekly costs. Then, this morning, I searched the operations manual for some guidance on this problem and found a two-year-old memo from the personnel director stating that part-time hours from all divisions should be processed through Mr. Scott in her department. No matter what I do, it seems I'm going to end up catching flak from someone!"

Halima's dilemma is not uncommon to people working in large organizations. When messages must be delivered to receivers through complex organizational channels, there are many more opportunities for noise to arise and misunderstanding to occur. In this chapter, we will define organizations and organizational communication, examine types of communication carried on inside organizations and between organizations and other people or organizations, examine organizational cultures, identify some common barriers to organizational communication, and suggest ways to overcome those barriers.

Organizations and Communication

All of us begin organizing at an early age—as children, we organized with friends in order to play tag or catch or jump rope—and we participate in formal organizations of various kinds throughout our lives: for example, minor sports teams, youth groups, religious organizations, schools, and service clubs. **Organizations** have been defined as "goal directed, boundary maintaining, and socially constructed systems of human activity" (Aldrich, 1999, p. 2). A **system** is a group of interdependent elements forming a complex whole. Thus, the elements that make up organizations are humans and their actions. Organizations are **goal directed** in that the members come together to accomplish goals that are beyond the ability of the individual; **boundary maintaining** in that they are identifiable from the outside world; and **socially constructed** in that cultural norms, including a range of environmental, political, and behavioural factors, affect how societies view and classify them.

THINKING ABOUT . . .

Organizations

How many organizations are you a part of? What is the goal of each organization? What are the boundaries of each one? How does each one relate to the larger society?

Kevin Frayer/CP Picture Archive

It is through communication that the relationships between members of an organization are created.

If we consider a familiar organization, a hockey team, we can see how each of these defining characteristics comes into play. A hockey team exists to achieve the goal of playing the game of hockey (perhaps also to win trophies, make money, etc.), something the members could not do individually. We recognize the boundaries that define the team: persons and things either belong to the team or do not. The team is socially constructed in that our society recognizes the division *hockey team,* whereas, for example, a sixteenth-century society or a contemporary society in which hockey is unknown would not; we are able to acknowledge this organization because hockey is part of our culture.

No organization could exist without communication. Communication is the primary driving process in organizations because it is through communication that the relationships between members of an organization or between a representative of the organization and someone outside the organization are created. We can thus picture any organization as a network of human elements joined by communication. The network can be simple or complex, depending on the organization's size, structure, and purpose, but regardless of its degree of complexity, the connection between every pair of human elements in the network is formed and maintained through communication. By referring back to our definition of communication in Chapter 1, then, we can define **organizational communication** as the process of creating or sharing meaning through interaction with other human beings within a system of human activity.

IN BRIEF

Organizations and Communication

- Organizations are goal directed, boundary maintaining, and socially constructed systems of human activity.
- Organizational communication is the process of creating or sharing meaning through interaction with other human beings within such a system of human activity.

Patterns of Organizational Communication

Communication events participated in by members of an organization can be classified in several ways, depending on the relationship between the sender and receiver, the direction of information flow, and the degree of formality which characterizes the interaction.

External and Internal Communication

External communication is communication between one or more members of an organization and individuals or groups outside the organization. External communication can take many forms, from a telephone call, e-mail message, or business letter to a client, customer, or supporter of an organization to a multimillion dollar advertising campaign directed to prospective customers. If Don and Mallory staff a booth in a shopping mall to provide members of the public with information about the local teen crisis centre, they are engaging in external communication on behalf of the centre. When executives representing the RJR-Macdonald Tobacco Company appear before a parliamentary committee to challenge proposed advertising restrictions on the company's products, they also are engaged in external communication.

Internal communication occurs when one or more members of an organization direct a message to another member or other members of the same organization. Like members communicating externally, members communicating internally generally have a range of channels to choose from in sending internal messages. If Brent, captain of Howe Hall's intramural volleyball team, schedules a team meeting after practice to inform team members of the game schedule for the next month, he is engaging in internal communication. Likewise, a principal who circulates a policy directive to teachers on her staff is also communicating internally.

Formal and Informal Communication

Formal communication occurs through prescribed channels and in compliance with specific rules. Like group norms, the rules governing the use of the formal communication system within or between some organizations may be explicitly stated in a manual or other document, while in other situations, they may be implicit, but either way, members of the organizations involved will know the rules and comply with them or face sanctions if they do not. **Informal communication**, which occurs outside these prescribed channels and rules, is often referred to as the *grapevine*. Messages that are exchanged in casual social conversations between members of an organization or members and non-members would be classed as informal.

Formal external communication The rules governing formal external communication are most likely to be determined by convention, protocol, or agreement between leaders of the organizations involved, but sometimes they are specified by law or regulation. For example, convention dictates that a business executive who wishes to communicate in writing on a business matter with an executive in another firm should write a business letter. International protocol requires leaders of one government to channel certain types of messages to leaders of another nation through that country's ambassador or consul. Manufacturers of toys, however, are restricted by Advertising Standards Canada regulations in the types of messages they can send to children.

Formal internal communication Rules governing formal internal communication are generally prescribed by leaders or managers of particular organizations. Figure 16.1 shows the management structure of a typical commercial organization. At all levels of the organizational hierarchy, members would be aware of *whether* and *how* they are expected to communicate with members at other levels as well as with various types of external audiences. Formal internal messages can be conveyed in writing as memos, reports, or proposals; electronically as e-mail or instant messages; and orally through interpersonal exchanges, group interactions, public presentations, telephone conversations, or voice mail messages. We can distinguish three types of formal internal communication,

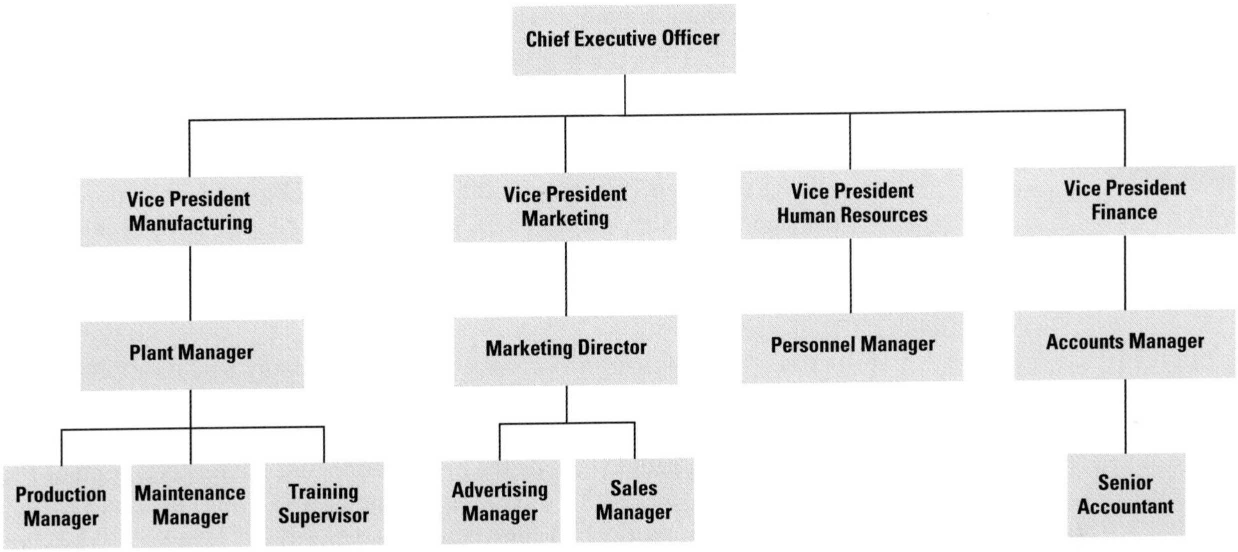

Figure 16.1
Management structure of a commercial organization

depending on the relationship that exists between the persons involved in the interaction. Generally, the greater the distance on the organizational hierarchy between the two people communicating, the more formal the communication is likely to be.

1. **Downward communication:** Messages that flow from decision makers such as managers, or supervisors to their subordinates represent **downward communication.** These messages can include instructions, explanations, policy statements, plans, rules, and other informative messages; persuasive messages such as motivational appeals or ideological messages that encourage support for the organization's values and goals; and positive and negative feedback (Katz & Kahn, 1978). A sales manager circulating a memo to his staff informing them of sales quotas for the coming month exemplifies downward communication.
2. **Upward communication:** Messages that flow upward from subordinates to managers or supervisors represent **upward communication.** These messages can provide management with insights into subordinates' performance, achievements, and progress; information about problems in the organization that must be addressed; subordinates' suggestions for improvements in their departments or the organization as a whole; and feedback on subordinates' feelings about and level of satisfaction with their positions, their peers, their leaders, and the organization (Planty & Machaver, 1977). An assembly line worker who informs her shift supervisor of an equipment malfunction would be engaging in upward communication.

OBSERVE & ANALYZE
Journal Activity

Patterns of Communcation

Consider your communication activity in one organization of which you are a part (e.g., your college or university, your workplace, a sports organization, a student group). Keep a log of all of the exchanges you participate in during one day. How would you classify each exchange: internal or external, formal or informal? If internal, was the exchange upward, downward, or lateral? Make a graph to show the volume of each type of message. Into which category did most of your communication activity fall?

3. **Lateral communication**: Messages that flow across an organization between people of the same status, rank, or position represent **lateral communication**, one of the most important types of communication in modern organizations. Lateral communication can occur at any level of the organization. These messages are important for sharing information, co-ordinating tasks, solving problems, resolving conflicts, and boosting morale. A production manager and sales manager who meet to co-ordinate their activities with regard to the introduction of a new product would be engaged in lateral communication.

Informal external communication Although many organizations try to carefully manage messages that are conveyed to the outside world, informal communication can play an important role in shaping members' professional relationships with people outside the organization and public perception of the organization as a whole. This type of communication typically arises out of social or professional relationships that an organization's members have with people outside the organization. For example, an executive might discuss work-related matters with her husband or children, friends, service people, associates in other organizations, or even with strangers encountered in travel. All of these exchanges have the potential to benefit or harm the organization, for example, by enhancing or damaging its public image, by generating or losing good will, and by establishing or severing valuable contacts.

Informal internal communication As consequential as informal external communication can be, informal internal communication is likely to have a much greater impact on an organization's operations. In any organization, a great deal of information is exchanged informally through the grapevine: for example, water cooler or electronic chat and casual social conversations between members who develop personal or professional relationships. Much of the information exchanged through these informal channels is personal gossip, but the grapevine can also be an important source of work-related information, often taking over when formal channels fail: "Formal communication networks allow people to handle predictable, routine situations, but they are inefficient means of meeting unanticipated communication needs, for managing crises, for dealing with complex or detailed problems, sharing personal information, or exchanging information rapidly" (Conrad & Poole, 1998, p. 91).

Hellweg (1983) suggests that the grapevine actually carries a great deal of an organization's messages and operates in conjunction with, not in opposition to, the formal communication system. Her research further found that the grapevine is fast, and that information is usually more accurate than inaccurate, though it is often incomplete; that it involves members from all levels of an organization, including both men and women, and usually grows in importance as an organization grows in size; and that it is a primarily oral phenomenon, running in all directions in an organization.

IN BRIEF

Patterns of Organizational Communication

Depending on the relationship between the sender and receiver, the direction of information flow, and the degree of formality in the interaction, organizational communication can be classified as

- internal or external
- formal or informal
- upward, downward, or lateral.

Organizational Culture

In Chapter 9, we defined *culture* as a group's shared collective meaning system through which its values, attitudes, beliefs, customs, and thoughts are understood, and we further pointed out that in any society, a dominant culture reflects the values, attitudes, beliefs, customs, and thoughts of the majority and that any number of co-cultures may exist within that dominant culture. What was true of societies is also true of organizations.

Like social cultures, **organizational cultures** develop over time, becoming codified as norms and rules that members are expected to follow. Many organizations, from the Boy Scouts of Canada to the Canadian Armed Forces to Wal-Mart Canada, devote a great deal of effort and resources to influencing their members to adopt a shared meaning system and to associating that meaning system with the organization in the public mind. The extent to which members do adopt this meaning system may determine the extent to which they feel a part of the dominant organizational culture and, thus, the level of comfort they feel in being part of the organization. In many organizations, several separate cultures compete for the members' allegiance.

Official Organizational Culture

An **official organizational culture** is the system of meaning that the leaders of an organization attempt to project as the *true* culture of the organization. Values associated with an organization's official culture are generally expressed through its mission statement and its stated organizational goals. These values are usually given prominent display in any advertising or promotional material associated with the organization and in its efforts to recruit new members. An environmental group, for example, might in its internal and external communication highlight values such as its belief in co-operative approaches to solving environmental problems, its non-profit status, its belief in non-violence, and its dedication to finding creative and sustainable ways for human beings to inhabit the earth as the hallmarks of its organizational culture.

Unofficial Organizational Culture

Over time, the members of the organization may, through carrying out their day-to-day activities, through interaction with one another or people outside the organization, and through making sense of their function and role in the organization, develop a culture that is markedly different from and sometimes even opposite to the organization's official culture. The rank and file members of our environmental group, for example, may develop a sense of competitiveness with other environmental agencies, gradually lose sight of the group's non-profit goals as opportunities for personal enrichment present themselves, or grow bitter or cynical in the face of lost opportunities for sustainable development projects.

COMMUNICATE!
Using Technology

Visit the Web sites of five major organizations. Choose a broad range of public and private, national and international organizations (e.g., The World Health Organization, The Vancouver Canucks, The National Action Committee on the Status of Women, Honda Motor Corporation, and The Fraser Institute). What does the Web site tell you about the official culture of each organization?

OBSERVE & ANALYZE
Journal Activity

Organizational Culture

Think about an organization of which you are a member (e.g., your school, your workplace, or a volunteer group). Can you identify official, unofficial, and co-cultures within the group? Which one do you participate in? If the culture in which you participate is not the dominant culture, how does it differ for the dominant culture? If it is the dominant culture, which values are most important to your participation?

DIVERSE VOICES

Good Cop, Bad Cop

by Stephen Kimber

Sometimes the dominant organizational culture punishes dissent. The RCMP once considered Calvin Lawrence a model officer. Later, he was passed over for promotions and struggled in career limbo. Was it because he complained about racism? Stephen Kimber teaches journalism at the University of King's College in Halifax, NS.

You'd think that in this post-9/11, us-versus-them, axis-of-evil world, a person like Corporal Calvin Lawrence would be much in demand. After all, he has more than 30 years of relevant policing experience. He served in a special Mountie unit charged with protecting Canada's prime ministers. He headed up the bodyguard team for prime minister Brian Mulroney at the 1988 Economic Summit in Toronto. He did the same for U.S. President Bill Clinton at the 1995 Summit in Halifax. He has taught hundreds of high-level training courses in bodyguarding, site security, route surveying, terrorist tactics, and officer survival. And his RCMP file is stuffed to overflowing with thank-yous and commendations ("exceptionally professional," "probably the best instructor I have been exposed to") by everyone from former students to the U.S. Secret Service to the prime minister himself.

You'd think he could get work easily.

Well, think again. Lawrence, a onetime Halifax city policeman who joined the RCMP in 1978, can't buy a meaningful Mountie posting in Ottawa these days. Holds a non-position. Last summer, after diddling, umming, and awing, the Mounties finally transferred him from exile in Regina back to Ottawa. But instead of giving him a job fitting his credentials, the RCMP powers-that-like-to-be shuffled him off to the oblivion of an STE—"surplus to establishment"—non-position in human resources. He's now on stress leave and in limbo.

Why?

Could it be because Lawrence, a seventh generation black Nova Scotian, filed a very public complaint with the federal Human Rights Commission back in 1994 claiming racial discrimination after he was denied permanent promotion from constable to corporal? Though the commission eventually dismissed his complaint, the Mounties settled with him anyway. The details of that settlement are confidential, but it's probably not coincidental that soon after it was negotiated, he was promoted to corporal. Or that that settlement turned out to be only the beginning of what Lawrence believes is ongoing retaliation harassment by Mountie higher ups.

In 1997, he transferred to Regina to get away from what he called a poisonous Ottawa workplace. But after four years as a training instructor in Regina, he began applying for positions back in Ottawa, where his family is based.

No one in authority in 2003, of course, will be as blunt as Mountie memo writers were back in 1941. The officer who then ran the RCMP's Sydney subdivision wrote his superiors in Halifax to warn them "two coloured men" wanted to join the force. He was instructed to let them take the educational test "with the hope that we shall find that they have not successfully passed." He was instructed to send the test results to headquarters for the commissioner to deal with, "unless they are so bad they could not be considered when, naturally, they may be so advised."

But has the message really changed?

(continued)

These days, says Lawrence, no one mentions race. Those in charge "will simply not answer e-mails, phone calls, neglect to give me positions and limit official documentation on my abilities, accomplishments and knowledge."

Still, the hints in e-mails among Mountie brass that Lawrence has obtained under access-to-information certainly raise questions about whether race or the fact he'd already filed a human rights complaint are factors in his treatment.

One message, from a staffing officer in A Division, which handles diplomatic protection, to his opposite number at Headquarters, who was supposed to be Lawrence's "career manager," warned that Lawrence "has a bit of a history . . . he may not be what we are looking for." Another wrote that HQ managers were very "demanding (and) they usually get what they need and want. Cal is not what they need and want."

One manager who initially appeared positive about having Lawrence in his unit changed his mind after "lengthy discussion and deliberation" with colleagues.

Lawrence is convinced the RCMP has engaged in "the covert and deliberate destruction" of his career. And he's filed yet another federal human rights complaint.

"If you're a black police officer," he told me when he filed his first complaint seven years ago, "you come to a crossroads. You either have to stand up and be counted, or you can lie down and be counted out."

Calvin Lawrence will stand up and be counted. Again.

Source: "Good Cop, Bad Cop" by Stephen Kimber. Reprinted by permission of The Daily News *Halifax.*

Organizational Co-cultures

As with other groups, co-cultures may arise or develop within the dominant culture of the organization, regardless of whether that dominant culture is the official or unofficial one. As we saw in Chapter 9, co-cultures draw some or all of their cultural identity from membership in other groups. These other groups may be ones which are separate from the organization (e.g., ethnic, religious, or gender groups) or they may be smaller groups that arise within the organization among members of particular departments, divisions, or teams. Thus co-cultures could exist in our environmental group if members separated along ethnic or gender lines or if the cultural bonds unifying members of one department became stronger than those drawing the members of that department to the organization.

IN BRIEF

Organizational Culture

Organizational culture is an organization's shared collective meaning system through which its values, attitudes, beliefs, customs, and thoughts are understood. Three levels of culture may compete for the allegiance of an organization's members:

- official culture
- unofficial culture
- co-cultures.

Barriers to Organizational Communication

Throughout this text, we have identified a number of barriers to effective communication, problems that prevent the successful transfer of meanings from a sender to other individuals, groups, or audiences. These have included barriers attributable to problems arising from factors including:

perception	cultural differences
language	group characteristics
nonverbal communication	group problem-solving methods

conversational skill
listening
responding
self-disclosure
feedback (praise and criticism)
assertiveness
conflict management
gender differences
group roles
leadership
speech goals or content
speech structure (organization)
speech adaptation
speech presentation
anxiety
ethics

Since these barriers can block interpersonal, group, and public communication, their effects will be as great in organizational contexts as in others, because organizations are made up of persons and groups and frequently communicate publicly to internal or external audiences. The following types of barriers to communication, though not limited to organizational contexts, are particularly apt to arise there.

Structural Barriers

Structural barriers to organizational communication arise because of the way in which an organization or the communication channels within the organization are designed.

Vertical organizational structure Organizations which are strongly hierarchical, particularly those with many levels of upper management, are likely to experience difficulty with upward and downward communication. Messages travelling down the hierarchy are likely to be distorted, delayed, or lost in reaching their destination, resulting in miscommunication. In addition, members at the bottom of the organizational hierarchy are likely to feel intimidated at the thought of sending messages upward when they have to pass through many people before they can be acted upon. As a result, management loses valuable input from subordinates in the organization.

Inadequate downward communication Particularly in traditional, top-heavy organizations, a culture of secrecy often limits the flow of downward communication. As a result of being kept in the dark about organizational goals or plans, members at the middle or lower ranks of the organization have a poor sense of the organization's direction, do not know what is expected of them, and experience a sense of uselessness or inadequacy and, frequently, low morale. In such an environment, upward communication is also likely to suffer because members of the lower ranks will feel insecure about initiating communication with those above them.

Filtering **Filtering,** the process of abridging, adding to, combining, or otherwise modifying the content of messages as they are passed from one person to the next (Pace & Boren, 1973), occurs in both oral and written messages that are conveyed through long networks. As a result of filtering, Hamilton (1990) points out, messages are

- levelled: details are left out
- condensed: contents are simplified
- sharpened: some details are selectively highlighted
- assimilated: confusing information is interpreted and clarified
- embellished: details are added.

The greater the distance between the source of a message and its destination, the more likely filtering is to represent a barrier to communication.

OBSERVE & ANALYZE
Journal Activity

Filtering

Form a human chain of 20 to 30 people. The person at the left end of the chain formulates a message of five to 10 sentences and writes it on a piece of paper. He or she then whispers the message, exactly as worded on the paper, to the person to his or her right, ensuring that no one else can hear. That person then whispers the message to the person on his or her right, and so on until it has been passed secretly to every person in the chain. The last person in the chain writes the message on a piece of paper. Compare the two written messages. Can you see evidence of filtering? What types of filtering occurred?

Overcoming Structural Barriers

The most effective solution to the three structural barriers to organizational communication described here is modification of the organization's structure. These problems most commonly occur in organizations with tall structures—that is, organizations with many layers in their organizational hierarchies. Tall structures are associated with large organizations and those with a traditional top-down chain of command. However, communication in flat organizations is more direct, and messages are less likely to be distorted because they pass through fewer people. Figure 16.2 contrasts the structure of a tall and a flat organization.

Flat organizational structures also encourage upward and downward communication in the organization. Because upper-level managers are not insulated by several levels of middle management from lower-level producers, they are more likely to communicate directly with producers, and their subordinates are less likely to feel intimidated about communicating with them. As a result, members of the organization at both the upper and lower levels are more likely to get accurate information and feedback more quickly, and lower-level members are likely to feel much more influential in and valuable to the organization; therefore, their satisfaction levels and morale are likely to be much higher (Carzo & Yanouzas, 1969).

Social Barriers

Social barriers to organizational communication result from behaviours of members of the organization.

Competitiveness In many organizations members compete for advancement, honours, and material rewards. Because information can frequently be used to further a member's career, enhance his or her status in the organization, or put money in the bank, members who have information may be reluctant to share it with others because they do not want to risk losing an opportunity to a competitor.

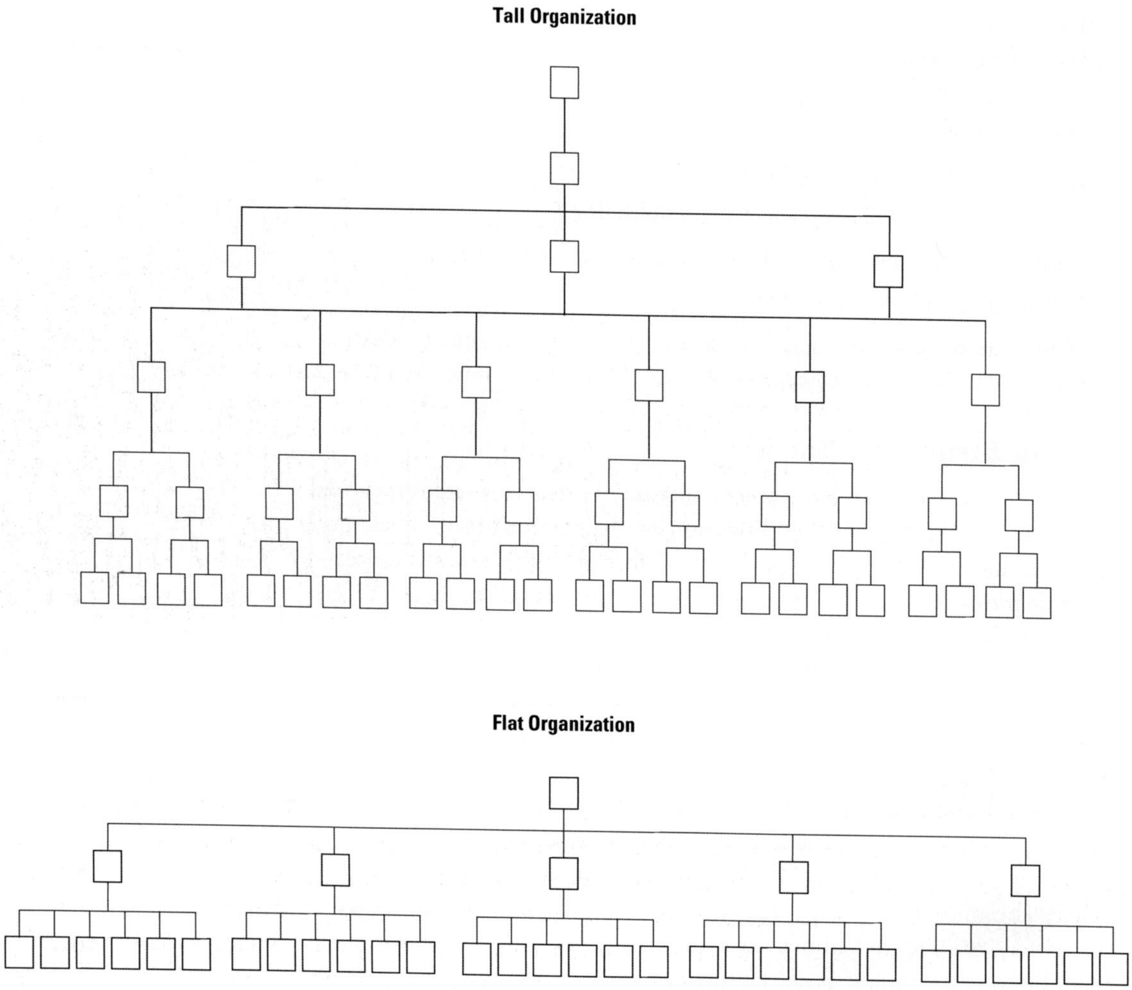

Figure 16.2
Tall and flat organizational structures

Distrust Members of organizations are not likely to communicate openly with peers or supervisors whom they feel they cannot trust. Members are likely to distrust people whom they compete against, particularly in highly competitive organizations, and they may mistrust their supervisors if they feel that they are manipulative, cold, or overly critical. If a member feels that he or she has been treated unfairly by a supervisor (e.g., unfairly denied a promotion, overtime pay, or vacation time), communication between the two is often reduced to observing the formalities.

Unequal distribution of power Because some members of an organization exercise some degree of control over others, and the members with the control wish to appear to be in control, people at different levels of an organization frequently do not communicate openly with one another. For example, a supervisor

SPOTLIGHT ON SCHOLARS

James R. Taylor, Université de Montréal

Jim Taylor is unquestionably the "dean" of organizational communication studies in Canada. But although he has been a leader in pioneering a new approach to organizational communication—an approach that emphasizes the role of discourse—his career has not followed the usual academic trajectory. Returning from doctoral studies in English Literature at the University of London, England, in the 1950's, he farmed for four years in his home province of New Brunswick. He then joined the Canadian Broadcasting Corporation as a producer in the Department of Public Affairs, the agency that was responsible for all current affairs and political broadcasts in both radio and television in Canada at that time. In 1965 he left his position as Regional Supervisor of Public Affairs Programming, Ottawa, to join the Royal Commission on Bilingualism and Biculturalism. As a member of that commission, he worked closely with the co-presidents, André Laurendeau and Davidson Dunton. In 1966, he enrolled in the doctoral program in Communication Studies at the University of Pennsylvania's Annenberg School.

Ten years of experience in a professional broadcasting organization proved to have a determining influence on Taylor's subsequent research. On the one hand, as a radio and television producer, as well as teacher at the Annenberg School, he had become fascinated by the role of media in communicating models of social interaction to the audience and in framing our perception of society. On the other hand, working for the CBC at a time of rapid expansion and considerable internal turmoil and conflict left him with a permanent curiosity about how organization works.

The experience of graduate school, at a time when positivism was running at its fullest tide, left Taylor feeling deeply dissatisfied with the conventional models of both broadcasting and organization to which he was exposed. His research can thus be seen as a long struggle to free himself from the shackles of traditional ways of thinking in the social sciences. It has led him to follow two paths: on the one hand, empirical research into the interface of new information and communication technologies and the organizational contexts in which they are implemented; on the other hand, the development of an original theory of organizational communication. In both of these areas, his work has been recognized for its originality, eclecticism, and theoretical sophistication. The distinguished American management theorist Karl Weick has described his book with E.J. Van Every, *The Emergent Organization*, as "one of the most important books about organization to be published in the past 20 years."

In 1970, the Université de Montréal invited Taylor to assume responsibility for launching a new program of studies in communication, and he has been there since. In 1982, he was loaned by the university to work as policy adviser to the federal Department of Communication. He continued to collaborate with that ministry on a part-time basis until it was disbanded at the end of the 1980's, serving among other roles as scientific adviser to its newly founded *Canadian Workplace Automation Research Centre* in Laval, Québec, from 1985 to 1987. Later he was part of the organizing secretariat of the federal

(continued)

Roundtable on the Information Society, a forum of senior government officials re-examining the role and practice of government in an information and communication environment characterized by rapid technological change.

Taylor has twice served as Chair of his department at the Université de Montréal, and was accorded the status of Emeritus in 1999. Since retirement he has taught at universities in places as widely separated as New Zealand and the Netherlands, and has lectured in some 12 countries. Since 1988 he has authored or co-authored five books, with two more now in preparation, as well as some 45 articles. He has been awarded numerous distinctions, including several "top papers" at the National Communication Association and the International Communication Association. He was invited to give the George Gerbner Lecture at the University of Pennsylvania, as well as the Southam Lecture at the Canadian Communication Association. This last year he had the privilege of delivering the inaugural Kurt Baschwitz Lecture at the University of Amsterdam.

The accomplishment of which Taylor is proudest, however, is the development of the field of organizational communication in Canada, led by his former students, François Cooren, Carole Groleau, Lorna Heaton, Daniel Robichaud, Hélène Giroux, and Joël Mulamba Katambwe. Collectively, they are establishing in Canada one of the premier research centres focused on organizational communication anywhere in the world.

PhotoDisc Collection/Getty Images

Some members of organizations may be reluctant to share information for professional or personal reasons.

may not wish to appear ignorant or unprepared in front of her subordinates, so she will pretend to have information that she lacks, even though she could satisfy her needs by asking for information. Similarly, subordinates may not ask for information because they worry that they will make themselves look bad in front of the boss, or they may conceal information about problems or failures to avoid receiving blame.

Sexual harassment One particular result of inequalities of power is sexual harassment. Sexual harassment occurs when one person receives unwelcome sexual contact, including unwanted touching or verbal or nonverbal messages, from another. Though sexual harassment can occur between any two people, members of organizations are particularly susceptible to this form of victimization because other people in the organization have control over their livelihood and future. Frequently, people are offered positive or negative inducements for sexual favours.

Overcoming Social Barriers

Social barriers to organizational communication can be overcome through promoting an organizational culture that is open and receptive to upward, downward, and lateral communication. Openness counters competitiveness and distrust by taking away the advantages to be gained through secrecy. If all members of an organization feel free to express themselves on any topic and to anyone, people will no longer feel that their security is threatened by communicating. Such an organizational culture also reduces opportunities for abuses of individual power because the exercise of power is open for all to see.

IN BRIEF

Barriers to Organizational Communication

Two types of barriers to communication that arise out of the organizational context are

- *Structural barriers:* vertical organizational structure, inadequate downward communication, and filtering
- *Social barriers:* competitiveness, distrust, unequal distribution of power, and sexual harassment.

Structural barriers are reduced by flattening the organizational structure. Social barriers are reduced by promoting an organizational culture which encourages openness through upward, downward, and lateral communication.

WHAT WOULD YOU DO?
A QUESTION OF ETHICS

"Georgia, would you sign a few of these claim forms, please? I want to get the expense claim for our trip to Edmonton last week in the system so we will get reimbursed before my credit card bills come due."

"Sure, Hans. What am I signing?"

"Oh, just claims for meals, tips, and local transportation. You know we're allowed to claim $200 per day each."

"Well, I guess so, but we hardly left the hotel during the whole conference, and all of our meals were provided by our hosts. We certainly didn't spend $200 a day in tips."

"Now, Georgia, don't be a Goody-Two-Shoes. No one cares if we claim the full allowance, and I've already filled mine out for that amount, so you'll make me look dishonest if you don't claim the same. Here, sign up."

"Okay, Hans. You're the boss, but I don't like doing this."

1. What ethical issues arise from this case?
2. What responsibility does Hans bear for the unethical conduct shown here? Georgia?

COMMUNICATE! Using InfoTrac College Edition

Using the keyword search enter the words *communication skills* and *workplace*. Select the article "A Managerial Perspective: Oral Communication Competency Is Most Important for Business Students in the Workplace" (1997) by Jeanne D. Maes, Teresa G. Weldy, and Marjorie L. Icenogle. Consider which skills the authors found to be important to employers. Having completed this course, do you feel you possess those skills? Are you ready for the workplace? If not, decide which skills you need to improve and how you will improve them.

Summary

Organizations are goal directed, boundary maintaining, and socially constructed systems of human activity. Organizational communication is the process of creating or sharing meaning through interaction with other human beings within such a system of human activity.

Depending on the relationship between the sender and receiver, the direction of information flow, and the degree of formality in the interaction, organizational communication can be classified as internal or external and formal or informal. Formal internal communication can be further categorized as upward, downward, or lateral.

Organizational culture is an organization's shared collective meaning system through which its values, attitudes, beliefs, customs, and thoughts are understood. Three levels of culture may compete for the allegiance of an organization's members: official culture, unofficial culture, and co-cultures.

Two types of communication barrier to arise out of the organizational context are structural barriers, including vertical organizational structure, inadequate downward communication, and filtering, and social barriers, including competitiveness, distrust, unequal distribution of power, and sexual harassment. Structural barriers are reduced by flattening the organizational structure. Social barriers are reduced by promoting an organizational culture that encourages openness through upward, downward, and lateral communication.

Glossary

Review the following key terms:

boundary maintaining (464) — a characteristic of organizations; they are identifiable from the outside world.

downward communication (467) — the transfer of messages from leaders, managers, or supervisors to their subordinates in an organization.

external communication (465) — communication between one or more members of an organization and individuals or groups outside the organization.

filtering (472) — the process of abridging, adding to, combining, or otherwise modifying the content of messages as they are passed from one person to the next.

formal communication (466) — communication that occurs through prescribed channels and in compliance with specific rules.

goal directed (464) — a characteristic of organizations; they are organized for the purpose of accomplishing goals.

informal communication (466) — communication that occurs outside the prescribed channels and rules.

internal communication (466) — communication between or among members of an organization.

lateral communication (468) — the transfer of messages across an organization to people of the same status, rank, or position.

official organizational culture (469) — the system of meaning that the leaders of an organization attempt to project as the *true* culture of the organization.

organization (464) — goal directed, boundary maintaining, and socially constructed systems of human activity.

organizational communication (465) — the process of creating or sharing meaning through interaction with other human beings within a system of human activity.

organizational culture (469) — an organization's shared collective meaning system through which its values, attitudes, beliefs, customs, and thoughts are understood.

social barriers to organizational communication (473) — barriers which result from behaviours of members of the organization.

socially constructed (464) — a characteristic of organizations; they have an identity that is affected by cultural differences, including a range of environmental, political, and behavioural factors.

structural barriers to organizational communication (472) — barriers which arise because of the way in which an organization or the communication channels within the organization are structured.

system (464) — a group of interdependent elements, forming a complex whole.

upward communication (467) — the transfer of messages from subordinates in an organization to their leaders, managers, or supervisors.

SELF-REVIEW

Workplace Communication from Chapters 15 and 16

How prepared are you for workplace communication? The following checklist can help you evaluate your effectiveness in communicating for the world of work. Use this scale to assess your competence:

1 = always   2 = often   3 = sometimes   4 = rarely   5 = never

1. I prepare to make an application by making an inventory of my abilities and marketable skills. (Ch. 15) ____
2. I prepare a specific résumé for each job application, focusing on demonstrating my qualifications to satisfy the employer's needs as described in the job ad. (Ch. 15) ____
3. I use my letter of application to match my skills as listed in my résumé to the employer's needs as listed in the job ad. (Ch. 15) ____
4. I prepare for an interview by researching the company, listing likely questions, and practising my answers. (Ch. 15) ____
5. I pay attention to the culture of the organizations of which I am a member. (Ch. 16) ____
6. I endeavour to be open in communicating with all members of organizations. (Ch. 16) ____

To verify your self-analysis, have a friend or fellow group member complete this review for you. Based on what you have learned from these two analyses, select the workplace communication behaviour you would most like to improve. To help you accomplish this goal, write a communication improvement plan similar to the one shown in the sample in Chapter 1 (page 26).

References

Adamopoulos, J. (1999). The emergence of cultural patterns of interpersonal behavior. In J. Adamopoulos & Y. Kashima (Eds.), *Social psychology and cultural context* (pp. 63–76). Thousand Oaks, CA: Sage.

Adler, R. B. (1977). *Confidence in communication: A guide to assertive and social skills.* New York: Holt, Rinehart & Winston.

Affifi, W. A., & Guerrero, L. K. (2000). Motivations underlying topic avoidance in close relationships. In S. Petronio (Ed.), *Balancing the secrets of private disclosures* (pp. 165–180). Mahwah, NJ: Erlbaum.

Alberti, R. E., & Emmons, M. L. (1995). *Your perfect right: A guide to assertive living* (7th ed.). San Luis Obispo, CA: Impact.

Aldrich, H. E. (1999). *Organizations evolving.* Thousand Oaks, CA: Sage.

Anderson, J. (1988). Communication competency in the small group. In R. Cathcart & L. Samovar (Eds.), *Small group communication, A reader.* Dubuque, IA: Wm. Brown.

Andrews, P. H. (1992). Sex and gender differences in group communication: Impact on the facilitation process. *Small Group Research, 23,* 90.

Aries, E. (1998). Gender differences in interaction: A reexamination. In D. J. Canary & K. Dindia (Eds.), *Sex differences and similarities in communication: Critical essays and empirical investigations of sex and gender in interaction* (pp. 65–81). Mahwah, NJ: Erlbaum.

Asante, M. K. (1998). *The Afrocentric idea.* Philadelphia, PA: Temple University Press.

Axtell, R. E. (1999). Gestures: *The do's and taboos of body language around the world* (rev. ed). New York: Wiley.

Ayres, J., & Hopf, T. S. (1990, January). The long-term effect of visualization in the classroom: A brief research report. *Communication Education, 39,* 75–78.

Ayres, J., Hopf, T. S., & Ayres, D. M. (1994, July). An examination of whether imaging ability enhances the effectiveness of an intervention designed to reduce speech anxiety. *Communication Education, 43,* 252–258.

Bach, K., & Harnish, R. M. (1979). *Linguistic communication and speech acts.* Cambridge, MA: MIT Press.

Bales, R. F. (1971). *Personality and interpersonal behavior.* New York: Holt, Rinehart & Winston.

Balgopal, P. R., Ephross, P. H., & Vassil, T. V. (1986). Self help groups and professional helpers. *Small Group Research, 17,* 123–137.

Banks, M. A. (1997). *Web psychos, stalkers and pranksters.* Scottsdale, AZ: Coriolis Group.

Barnett, G. A., & Lee, M. (2001). Issues in intercultural research. In W. B. Gudykunst & B. Mody (Eds.), *Handbook of international and intercultural communication* (2nd ed., pp. 275–290). Thousand Oaks, CA: Sage.

Baron, R. A., & Byrne, D. (2000). *Social psychology* (9th ed.). Boston: Allyn & Bacon.

Barsky, A. E. (2000). *Conflict resolution for the helping professions.* Belmont, CA: Brooks/Cole.

Beebe, M. B., Anthony, T., Salas, E., & Driskell, J. E. (1994). Group cohesiveness and quality of decision making. *Small Group Research, 25,* 189–204.

Berger, C. R. (1979). Beyond initial interactions. In H. Giles & R. Sinclair (Eds.), *Language and social psychology* (pp. 122–144). Oxford: Basil Blackwell.

———. (1994). Power, dominance, and social interaction. In M. L. Knapp & G. R. Miller (Eds.), *Handbook of interpersonal communication* (2nd ed., pp. 450–507). Thousand Oaks, CA: Sage.

Berger, C. R., & Bradac, J. J. (1982). *Language and social knowledge: Uncertainty in interpersonal relations.* London: Arnold.

Bern, S. (1993). *The lens of gender.* New Haven, CT: Yale University Press.

Bigelow, J. D. (1999). The Web as an organizational behavior learning medium. *Journal of Management Education, 23,* 635–650.

Bormann, E. (1990). *Small group communication: Theory and practice.* New York: Harper & Row.

Bosmajian, H. A. (1983). *The language of oppression.* Lanham, MD: University Press of America.

Bostrom, R. (1970). Patterns of communicative interaction in small groups. *Speech Monographs, 37,* 257–263.

Brown, P., & Levinson, S. (1987). *Politeness: Some universals in language usage.* Cambridge, U.K.: Cambridge University Press.

Burgoon, J. K. (1994). Nonverbal signals. In M. L. Knapp & G. R. Miller (Eds.), *Handbook of interpersonal communication* (2nd ed., pp. 229–285). Thousand Oaks, CA: Sage.

Burgoon, J. K., Coker, D. A., & Coker, R. A. (1986). Communicative effects of gaze behavior: A test of two contrasting explanations, *Human Communication Research, 12,* 495–524.

Burleson, B. R. (1994). Comforting messages: Significance, approaches and effects. In B. R. Burleson, T. L. Albrecht, & I. G. Sarason (Eds.), *Communication of social support: Messages, interactions, relationships, and community* (pp. 3–28). Thousand Oaks, CA: Sage.

Burleson, B. R., & Samter, W. (1990). Effects of cognitive complexity on the perceived importance of communication skills in friends. *Communication Research, 17,* 165–182.

Cahn, D. D. (1990). Intimates in conflict: A research review. In D. D. Cahn (Ed.), *Intimates in conflict: A communication perspective* (pp. 1–24). Hillsdale, NJ: Erlbaum.

Canary, D. J., & Hause, K. (1993). Is there any reason to research sex differences in communication? *Communication Quarterly, 41,* 129–144.

Canary, D. J., Cupach, W. R., & Messman, S. J. (1995). *Relationship conflict: Conflict in parent–child, friendship, and romantic relationships.* Thousand Oaks, CA: Sage.

Carzo, R. Jr., & Yanouzas, J. N. (1969). Effects of flat and tall organization structures. *Administration Science Quarterly, 14,* 178–191.

Cegala, D. J., & Sillars, A. L. (1989). Further examination of nonverbal manifestations of interaction involvement. *Communication Reports, 2,* 45.

Clark, N. (1994). *Teambuilding: A practical guide for trainers.* New York: McGraw-Hill.

Clark, R. A., Pierce, A. J., Finn, K., Hsu, K., Toosley, A., & Williams, L. (1998, Fall). The impact of alternative approaches to comforting, closeness of relationship, and gender on multiple measures of effectiveness. *Communication Studies, 49,* 224–239.

Clark, W. (1998, Autumn). Religious observance: Marriage and family. *Canadian Social Trends.* Retrieved from http://www.statcan.ca/english/ads/11-008-XPE/religion.pdf.

Clevenger, T. Jr. (1959, April). A synthesis of experimental research in stage fright. *Quarterly Journal of Speech, 45,* 134–145.

Cloven, D. H., & Roloff, M. E. (1991). Sense-making activities and interpersonal conflict: Communicative cures for the mulling blues. *Western Journal of Speech Communication, 55,* 134–158.

Cogger, J. W. (1982). Are you a skilled interviewer? *Personnel Journal, 61,* 842–843.

The Conference Board of Canada. (2000). *Employability Skills 2000+* [Brochure].

Conrad, C., & Poole, M. S. (1998). *Strategic organizational communication: Into the twenty-first century* (4th ed.). Fort Worth, TX: Harcourt Brace.

Criscito, P. (2000). *Résumés in cyberspace* (2nd ed.). Hauppauge, NY: Barron's Educational Series, Inc.

Crumlish, C. (1997). *The Internet for busy people* (2nd ed.). Berkeley, CA: Osborne/McGraw-Hill.

Cupach, W. R., & Canary, D. J. (1997). *Competence in interpersonal conflict.* New York: McGraw-Hill.

Dale, P. (1999). *"Did you say something, Susan?" How any woman can gain confidence with assertive communication.* Secaucus, NJ: Carol.

Deaux, K., Dane, F. D., & Wrightsman, L. S. (1993). *Social psychology* (6th ed.). Belmont, CA: Wadsworth.

DeKlerk, V. (1991). "Expletives: Men only?" *Communication Monographs, 58,* 156–169.

Demo, D. H. (1987). Family relations and the self-esteem of adolescents and their parents. *Journal of Marriage and the Family, 49,* 705–715.

Dennis, A. R. (1996). Information exchange and use in small group decision making. *Small Group Research, 27,* 532–550.

Derlega, V. J., Barbee, A. P., & Winstead, B. A. (1994). Friendship, gender, and social support: Laboratory studies of supportive interactions. In B. R. Burleson, T. L. Albrecht, & I. G. Sarason (Eds.), *Communicating of social support: Messages, interactions, relationships, and community* (pp. 136–151). Thousand Oaks, CA: Sage.

Derlega, V. J., Metts, S., Petronio, S., & Margulis, S. T. (1993). *Self- disclosure.* Newbury Park, CA: Sage.

Dewey, J. (1922). *How we think.* Boston: D.C. Heath.

Dindia, K. (2000a). Relational maintenance. In C. Hendrick & S. S. Hendrick (Eds.), *Close relationships: A sourcebook* (pp. 287–300). Thousand Oaks, CA: Sage.

———. (2000b). Sex differences in self-disclosure, reciprocity of self-disclosure, and self-disclosure and liking: Three meta-analyses reviewed. In S. Petronio (Ed.), *Balancing the secrets of private disclosures* (pp. 21–36). Mahwah, NJ: Erlbaum.

Dindia, K., Fitzpatrick, M. A., & Kenny, D. A. (1997, March). Self-disclosure in spouse and stranger interaction: A social relations analysis. *Human Communication Research, 23,* 388–412.

Duck, S. (1987). How to lose friends without influencing people. In M. E. Roloff & G. R. Miller (Eds.), *Interpersonal processes: New directions in communication research* (pp. 278–298). Beverly Hills, CA: Sage.

———. (1998). *Human relationships* (3rd ed.). Thousand Oaks, CA: Sage.

Eggins, S., & Slade, D. (1997). *Analyzing casual conversation.* Washington, DC: Cassell.

Ekman, P., & Friesen, W. V. (1969). The repertoire of nonverbal behavior: Categories, origins, usage, and coding. *Semiotica, 1,* 49–98.

———. (1975). *Unmasking the face.* Englewood Cliffs, NJ: Prentice-Hall.

Ellis, K. (1995, January). Apprehension, self-perceived competency, and teacher immediacy in the

laboratory-supported public speaking course: Trends and relationships. *Communication Education, 44,* 64–78.
Estes, W. K. (1989). Learning theory. In A. Lesgold & R. Glaser (Eds.), *Foundations for a psychology of education* (pp. 1–49). Hillsdale, NJ: Erlbaum.
Evans, C., & Dion, K. (1991). Group cohesion and performance: A meta-analysis. *Small Group Research, 22,* 175–186.
Fairhurst, G. T. (1993). Echoes of the vision: When the rest of the organization talks total quality. *Management Communication Quarterly, 6,* 331–371.
———. (2001). Dualism in leadership. In F. M. Jablin & L. L. Putnam (Eds.), *The new handbook of organizational communication* (pp. 379–439). Thousand Oaks, CA: Sage.
Fairhurst, G. T., & Sarr, R. A. (1996). *The art of framing.* San Francisco: Jossey-Bass.
Fehr, B. (1996). *Friendship processes.* Thousand Oaks, CA: Sage.
Filley, A. C. (1975). *Interpersonal conflict resolution.* Glenview, IL: Scott, Foresman.
Fisher, B. A. (1985). Leadership as medium: Treating complexity in group communication research. *Small Group Research, 16,* 167–196.
Fisher, B. A. & Ellis, D. G. (1990). *Small group decision making: Communication and the group process* (3rd ed.). New York: McGraw-Hill.
Flaherty, L. M., Pearce, K. J., & Rubin, R. B. (1998, Summer). Internet and face-to-face communication: Not functional alternatives. *Communication Quarterly, 46,* 250–268.
Floyd, K., & Morman, M. T. (1998, Spring). The measurement of affectionate communication. *Communication Quarterly, 46,* 144–162.
Forgas, J. P. (1991). Affect and person perception. In J. P. Forgas (Ed.), *Emotion and social judgments* (pp. 263–291). New York: Pergamon Press.
———. (2000). Feeling and thinking: Summary and integration. In J. P. Forgas (Ed.), *Feeling and thinking: The role of affect in social cognition* (pp. 387–406). New York: Cambridge Press.
Freedman, J. L., Klevansky, S., & Ehrich, P. R. (1971). The effect of crowding on human task performance. *Journal of Applied Psychology, 1*(1), 7–25.
Gardenswartz, L., & Rowe, A. (1998). *Managing diversity: A complete desk reference and planning guide* (rev. ed.). New York: McGraw-Hill.
Gentry, G. (1980). Group size and attitudes towards the simulation experience. *Simulation and Games, 11,* 451–460.
Gmelch, S. B. (1998). *Gender on campus: Issues for college women.* New Brunswick, NJ: Rutgers University Press.
Goldberg, B. (1999). *Overcoming high-tech anxiety: Thriving in a wired world.* San Francisco, CA: Jossey-Bass.
Goleman, D. (1998). *Working with emotional intelligence.* New York: Bantam Books.
Gordon, T. (1970). *Parent effectiveness training.* New York: Peter H. Wyden.
———. (1971). *The basic modules of the instructor outline for effectiveness training courses.* Pasadena, CA: Effectiveness Training Associates.
Gouran, D. S., & Hirokawa, R. Y. (1996). Functional theory and communication in decision-making groups: An expanded view. In R. Y. Hirokawa & M. S. Poole (Eds.), *Communication and group decision making* (2nd ed., pp. 55–80). Thousand Oaks, CA: Sage.
Grice, H. P. (1975). Logic and conversation. In P. Cole & J. L. Morgan (Eds.), *Syntax and semantics. Vol. 3. Speech acts* (pp. 41–58). New York: Academic Press.
Griffiths, M. (1998). Internet addiction: Does it really exist? In J. Gackenbach (Ed.), *Psychology and the Internet: Intrapersonal, interpersonal, and transpersonal implications* (pp. 61–76). San Diego, CA: Academic Press.
Gruzuk, Michael (Producer). (2002, October 15). Everquest [Television series episode]. In Leslie Peck (Executive Producer) *Marketplace.* Toronto: The Canadian Broadcasting Corporation.
Gudykunst, W. B., & Kim, Y. Y. (1997). *Communicating with strangers: An approach to intercultural communication* (3rd ed.). Boston: Allyn & Bacon.
Gudykunst, W. B., & Matsumoto, Y. (1996). Cross-cultural variability of communication in personal relationships. In W. B. Gudykunst, S. Ting-Toomey, & T. Nishida (Eds.), *Communication in personal relationships across cultures* (pp. 19–56). Thousand Oaks, CA: Sage.
Gudykunst, W. B., & Mody, B. (Eds.). (2001). *Handbook of international and intercultural communication* (2nd ed.). Thousand Oaks, CA: Sage.
Guerrero, L. K., & Andersen, P. A. (2000). Emotion in close relationships. In C. Hendrick & S. S. Hendrick (Eds.), *Close relationships: A sourcebook* (pp. 171–184). Thousand Oaks, CA: Sage.
Guidelines for meeting participants. (1998, Fall). Unpublished manuscript developed by students in BAD 305, Understanding behavior in organizations. Northern Kentucky University.
Hall, E. T. (1959). *The silent language.* Greenwich, CT: Fawcett.
———. (1969). *The hidden dimension.* Garden City, NY: Doubleday.
Hall, J. A. (1998). How big are nonverbal sex differences? The case of smiling and sensitivity to nonverbal cues. In D. J. Canary & K. Dindia (Eds.), *Sex differences and similarities in communication: Critical essays and empirical investigations of sex and gender in interaction* (pp. 155–178). Mahwah, NJ: Erlbaum.

Hamilton, C. (with Parker, C). (1990). *Communication for results*. Belmont, CA: Wadsworth.
Hattie, J. (1992). *Self-concept*. Hillsdale, NJ: Erlbaum.
Hawkins, K. W. (1995). Effects of gender and communication content on leadership emergence in small, task-oriented groups. *Small Group Research, 26,* 234–249.
Helgesen, S. (1990). *The female advantage: Women's ways of leadership*. New York: Doubleday.
Hellweg, S. (1987). Organizational grapevines: A state of the art review. In B. Dervin & M. Voight (Eds.) *Progress in the communication sciences*: *Vol. 8* (pp. 213–230). Norwood, NJ: Ablex.
Hirokawa, R. Y. (1987). Why informed groups make faulty decisions. *Small Group Behavior, 18,* 3–29.
———. (1988). Group communication and decision-making performance: A continued test of the functional perspective. *Human Communication Research, 14,* 487–515.
Hofstede, G. (1979). Value systems in forty countries. In. L. Eckensberger, W. Lonner, & Y. Poortinga (Eds.), *Cross-cultural contributions to psychology* (pp. 389–407). Amsterdam: Swets & Zeitlinger.
———. (1980). *Cultures consequences: International differences in work-related values*. Beverly Hills, CA: Sage.
———. (1997). *Cultures and organizations: Software of the mind* (rev. ed.). New York: McGraw-Hill.
Hofstede, G., & Bond, M. (1984). Hofstede's culture dimensions. *Journal of Cross-Cultural Psychology, 15,* 417–433.
Hollman, T. D. (1972). Employment interviewers' errors in processing positive and negative information. *Journal of Psychology, 56,* 130–134.
Hotz, R. L. (1995, April 15). Official racial definitions have shifted sharply and often. *Los Angeles Times,* p. A14.
Human Resources Development Canada. (2002). *Growing up in Canada: A detailed portrait of children and young people*. Retrieved February 10, 2004, from http://www.hrdc-drhc.gc.ca/sp-ps/arb-dgra/publications/books/class90/growingup.shtml.
Hurley, M. C. (2003). Sexual orientation and legal rights. *Library of Parliament: Parliamentary Research Branch*. Retrieved February 2, 2004, from http://www.parl.gc.ca/information/library/PRBpubs/921-e.htm#adiscrimtxt.
Infante, D. A., Rancer, A. S., & Jordan, F. F. (1996). Affirming and nonaffirming style, dyad sex, and perception of argumentation and verbal aggression in an interpersonal dispute. *Human Communication Research, 22,* 315–334.
Janis, I. L. (1982). *Groupthink: Psychological studies of policy decisions and fiascoes*. Boston: Houghton Mifflin.
———. (1989). *Crucial decisions: Leadership in policy making and crisis management*. New York: Free Press.
Jedwab, J. (2003). What is most important to our identity? Retrieved from http://www.acs-aec.ca/Polls/Poll30.pdf.
Jensen, A. D., & Chilberg, J. C. (1991). *Small group communication: Theory and application*. Belmont, CA: Wadsworth.
Johnson, D., & Johnson, F. (2000). *Joining together: Group theory and group skills* (7th ed.). Boston: Allyn & Bacon.
Jones, E. E. (1990). *Interpersonal perception*. New York: W. H. Freeman.
Jordan, J. V. (1991). The relational self: A new perspective for understanding women's development. In J. Strauss & G. R. Goethals (Eds.), *The self: Interdisciplinary approaches* (pp. 136–149). New York: Springer-Verlag.
Jurma, W. E., & Wright, B. C. (1990). Follower reactions to male and female leaders who maintain or lose reward power. *Small Group Research, 21,* 110.
Jussim, L. J., McCauley, C. R., & Lee, Y.-T. (1995). Why study stereotype accuracy and inaccuracy? In Y. T. Lee, L. J. Jussim, & C. R. McCauley (Eds.), *Stereotype accuracy: Toward appreciating group differences* (pp. 3–28). Washington, DC: American Psychological Association.
Kapica, J. (2002, September 4). Survey reveals motivation behind IT job hoppers. *Globeandmail.com*. Retrieved March 1, 2004, from http://www.theglobeandmail.com/servlet/story/RTGAM.20020904.gtsurv/ BNPrint/Front/.
Katz, D., & Kahn, R. L. (1978). *The social psychology of organizations* (2nd ed.). New York: John Wiley & Sons.
Kellerman, K. (1992). Communication: Inherently strategic and primarily automatic. *Communication Monographs, 59,* 288–300.
Kennedy, C. W., & Camden, C. T. (1983). A new look at interruptions. *Western Journal of Speech Communication, 47,* 55.
Keyton, J. (1993). Group termination: Completing the study of group development. *Small Group Research, 24,* 84–100.
Kim, M. S., & Wilson, S. (1994). A cross-cultural comparison of implicit theories of requesting. *Communication Monographs, 61,* 210–235.
Knapp, M. L., & Hall, J. A. (1992). *Nonverbal communication in human interaction* (3rd ed.). New York: Holt, Rinehart & Winston.
Kramer, J., & Kramarae, C. (1997). Gendered ethics on the Internet. In J. M. Makau & R. C. Arnett (Eds.), *Communication ethics in the age of diversity* (pp. 226–244). Chicago: University of Illinois Press.

Kunkel, A., & Burleson, B. (1999). Assessing explanations for sex differences in emotional support. *Human Communication Research, 25,* 307–340.

LaFollette, H. (1996). *Personal relationships: Love, identity, and morality.* Cambridge, MA: Blackwell.

Leathers, D. (1997). *Successful nonverbal communication: Principles and applications* (3rd ed.). Boston, Allyn & Bacon.

Lenden, Darlene. (1995, April). *French-Canadian business philosophies in corporate America: A cross-cultural approach.* Paper presented at the fourteenth annual conference of Languages and Communication for World Business and the Professions, Ypsilanti, MI.

Littlejohn, S. W. (1999). *Theories of human communication* (6th ed.). Belmont, CA: Wadsworth.

Luft, J. (1970). *Group processes: An introduction to group dynamics.* Mountain View, CA: Mayfield.

Lulofs, R. S., & Cahn, D. D. (2000). *Conflict: From theory to action* (2nd ed.). Boston: Allyn & Bacon.

Markham, A. N. (1998). *Life online: Researching real experience in virtual space.* Walnut Creek, CA: AltaMira.

Markus, H. R., & Kitayama, S. (1991). Cultural variation in the self-concept. In J. Strauss & G. R. Goethals (Eds.), *The self: Interdisciplinary approaches* (pp. 18–48). New York: Springer-Verlag.

Martin, J. N., & Nakayama, T. K. (1997). *Intercultural communication contexts.* Mountain View, CA: Mayfield.

Martin, M. M., Anderson, C. M., & Horvath, C. L. (1996). Feelings about verbal aggression: Justifications for sending and hurt from receiving verbally aggressive messages. *Communication Research Reports, 13*(1), 19–26.

McCrae, C. N., Milne, A. B., & Bodenhausen, G. V. (1994). Stereotypes as energy-saving devices: A peek inside the cognitive toolbox. *Journal of Personality and Social Psychology, 66,* 37–47.

McLuhan, E. (1996). The source of the term "global village." *McLuhan Studies 2.* Retrieved February 4, 2004, from http://www.chass.utoronto.ca/mcluhanstudies/v1iss2/12index.htm.

McLuhan, M. (1962). *The Gutenberg galaxy.* Toronto: University of Toronto Press.

Meadahl, M. (2000, April 6). Violence against gays continues, study finds. *Simon Fraser News, 17*(7). Retrieved from http://www.sfu.ca/mediapr/sfnews/2000/April6/janoff.html.

Media Awareness Network. (2001). *Young Canadians in a wired world: The students' view: Final report.* Retrieved October 20, 2003, from http://www.mediaawareness.ca/english/resources/special initiatives/surveyresources/studentssurvey/loader.cfm?url=/commonspot/security/getfile.cfm&PageID=31571.

Menzel, K. E., & Carrell, L. J. (1994). The relationship between preparation and performance in public speaking. *Communication Education, 43,* 17–26.

Michener, H. A., & DeLamater, J. D. (1999). *Social psychology* (4th ed.). Orlando, FL: Harcourt Brace.

Miller, M. (1999). *The Lycos personal Internet guide.* Indianapolis, IN: Que Corporation.

Morreale, S., & Peltak, J. (2004). Pathways to careers in communication. National Communication Association Web site. Retrieved March 2, 2004, from http://www.natcom.org/Instruction/Pathways/5thEd.htm.

Mruk, C. (1999). *Self-esteem: Research, theory, and practice* (2nd ed.). New York: Springer.

Mulac, A. (1998). The gender-linked language effect: Do language differences really make a difference? In D. J. Canary & K. Dindia (Eds.), *Sex differences and similarities in communication: Critical essays and empirical investigations of sex and gender in interaction* (pp. 127–154). Mahwah, NJ: Erlbaum.

Nieto, S. (2000). *Affirming diversity: The sociological context of multicultural education* (3rd ed.). New York: Longman.

Ogden, C. K., & Richards, I. A. (1923). *The meaning of meaning.* London: Kegan, Paul, Trench, Trubner.

Okrent, D. (1999, May 10). Raising kids online: What can parents do? *Time,* 38–43.

Pace, R. W., & Boren, R. R. (1973). *The human transaction: Facets, functions, and forms of interpersonal communication.* Glenview, IL: Scott, Foresman.

Parks, M. R., & Floyd, K. (1996). Making friends in cyberspace. *Journal of Communication, 46,* 80–97.

Patterson, B. R., Bettini, L., & Nussbaum, J. F. (1993). The meaning of friendship across the life-span: Two studies. *Communication Quarterly, 41,* 145.

Patterson, M. E., Danscreau, D. F., & Newbern, D. (1992). Effects of communication aids on cooperative teaching. *Journal of Educational Psychology, 84,* 453–461.

Pearson, J. C., West, R. L., & Turner, L. H. (1995). *Gender & communication* (3rd ed.). Dubuque, IA: Brown & Benchmark.

Phillips, G. (1977). Rhetoritherapy versus the medical model: Dealing with reticence. *Communication Education, 26,* 34–43.

———. (1991). *Communication incompetencies: A theory of training oral performance behavior.* Carbondale, IL: Southern Illinois University Press.

Planty, E., & Machaver, W. (1977). Upward communication: A project in executive development. In R. C. Huseman, C. M. Logue, & D. L. Freshley (Eds.), *Readings in interpersonal and organizational communication* (3rd ed., pp. 159–178). Boston: Holbrook Press.

Preece, J. (2000). *Online communities.* New York: Wiley.

Reardon, K. K. (1987). *Interpersonal communication: Where minds meet.* Belmont, CA: Wadsworth.

Reis, H. T. (1998). Gender differences in intimacy and related behaviors: Context and process. In D. J. Canary & K. Dindia (Eds.), *Sex differences and similarities in communication: Critical essays and empirical investigations of sex and gender in interaction* (pp. 203–232). Mahwah, NJ: Erlbaum.

Renz, M. A., & Greg, J. B. (2000). *Effective small group communication in theory and practice.* Boston: Allyn & Bacon.

Richards, I. A. (1965). *The philosophy of rhetoric.* New York: Oxford University Press.

Richmond, V. P., & McCroskey, J. C. (1995). *Communication: Apprehension, avoidance, and effectiveness* (4th ed.). Scottsdale, AZ: Gorsuch Scarisbrick.

Robbins, S. P., & Hunsaker, P. I. (1996). *Training in interpersonal skills: Tips for managing people at work.* Upper Saddle River, NJ: Prentice-Hall.

Rose, H. M., Rancer, A. S., & Crannell, K. C. (1993, Winter). The impact of basic courses in oral interpretation and public speaking on communication apprehension. *Communication Reports, 6,* 54–60.

Rosenfeld, L. B. (2000). Overview of the ways privacy, secrecy, and disclosure are balanced in today's society. In S. Petronio (Ed.), *Balancing the secrets of private disclosures* (pp. 3–18). Mahwah, NJ: Erlbaum.

Rothwell, J. D. (1998). *In mixed company* (3rd ed.). Fort Worth, TX: Harcourt Brace.

Samovar, L. A., & Porter, R. E. (2000). Understanding intercultural communication: An introduction and overview. In L. A. Samovar & R. E. Porter (Eds.), *Intercultural communication: A reader* (9th ed., pp. 5–16). Belmont, CA: Wadsworth.

———. (2003). *Communication between cultures* (5th ed.). Belmont, CA: Wadsworth.

Samovar, L. A., Porter, R. E., & Stefani, L. A. (1998). *Communication between cultures* (3rd ed.). Belmont, CA: Wadsworth.

Sampson, E. E. (1999). *Dealing with differences: An introduction to the social psychology of prejudice.* Fort Worth, TX: Harcourt Brace.

Samter, W., Burleson, B. R., & Murphy, L. B. (1987). Comforting conversations: The effects of strategy type evaluations of messages and message producers. *Southern Communication Journal, 52,* 263–284.

Schippers, T. K. (2001, Winter). Cultural identity: Search for a definition. *International Scope Review 3*(6). Retrieved February 9, 2004, from http://www.internationalscope.com/journal/volume%202001/issue%206/p df/2Schippers.pdf.

Schmidt, W. V., & Conaway, R. N. (1999). *Results-oriented interviewing: Principles, practices, and procedures.* Boston: Allyn & Bacon.

Schutz, W. (1966). *The interpersonal underworld.* Palo Alto, CA: Science & Behavior Books.

Scott, P. (1997, January–February). Mind of a champion. *Natural Health, 27,* 99.

Semic, B. A., & Canary, D. J. (1997, Fall). Trait argumentativeness, verbal aggressiveness, and minimally rational argument: An observational analysis of friendship discussions. *Communication Quarterly,* 355–378.

Shaw, M. E. (1981). *Group dynamics: The psychology of small group behavior* (3rd ed.). New York: McGraw-Hill.

Sherman, R. A. (1999). *Mr. Modem's Internet guide for seniors.* San Francisco, CA: Sybex.

Shimanoff, M. (1992). Group interaction and communication rules. In R. Cathcart & L. Samovar (Eds.), *Small group communication: A reader.* Dubuque, IA: Wm. Brown.

Shimanoff, S. B. (1980). *Communication rules: Theory and research.* Beverly Hills, CA: Sage.

Snell, N. (1998). *Teach yourself the Internet in 24 hours* (2nd ed.). Indianapolis: Sams.Net.

Sorrentino, R., & Short, J. (1986). Uncertainty orientation, motivation, and cognition. In R. Sorrentino & E. Higgens (Eds.), *Handbook of motivation and cognition* (pp. 379–403). New York: Guilford.

Spitzberg, B. H. (1997). Violence in intimate relationships. In W. R. Cupach & D. J. Canary (Eds.), *Competence in interpersonal conflict* (pp. 174–201). New York: McGraw-Hill.

———. (2000). A model of intercultural communication competence. In L. A. Samovar & R. E. Porter (Eds.), *Intercultural communication: A reader* (9th ed., pp. 375–387). Belmont, CA: Wadsworth.

Spitzberg, B. H., & Cupach, W. R. (Eds.). (1998). *The dark side of close relationships.* Hillsdale, NJ: Lawrence Erlbaum Associates.

Spitzberg, B. H., & Duran, R. L. (1995). Toward the development and validation of a measure of cognitive communication competence. *Communication Quarterly, 43,* 259–274.

Stafford, L., & Canary, D. J. (1991). Maintenance strategies and romantic relationship type, gender, and relational characteristics. *Journal of Social and Personal Relationships, 8,* 217–242.

Statistics Canada. (2003). *2001 census: Canada's ethnocultural portrait: The changing mosaic.* Retrieved July 13, 2003, from http://www12.statcan.ca.

Stewart, C. J., & Cash, W. B. Jr. (2000). *Interviewing: Principles and practices*. Boston: McGraw-Hill.

Stewart, L. P., Cooper, P. J., Stewart, A. D., & Friedley, S. A. (1998). *Communication and gender* (3rd ed.). Boston, MA: Allyn & Bacon.

Stiff, J. B., Dillard, J. P., Somera, L., Kim, H., & Sleight, C. (1988). Empathy, communication and prosocial behavior. *Communication Monographs, 55*, 198–213.

Sundstrom, E., DeMeuse, K. P., & Futrell, D. (1990, February). Work teams: Applications and effectiveness. *American Psychologist*, 120–133.

Svennevig, J. (1999). *Getting acquainted in conversation: A study of initial interactions*. Philadelphia: John Benjamins.

Tajfel, H., & Turner, J. C. (1986). The social identity theory of intergroup relations. In S. Worchel & W. Austin (Eds.), *The social psychology of intergroup relations* (pp. 33–47). Monterey, CA: Brooks/Cole.

Tannen, D. (1990). *You just don't understand*. New York: Morrow.

Taylor, D. A., & Altman, I. (1987). Communication in interpersonal relationships: Social penetration theory. In M. E. Roloff & G. R. Miller (Eds.), *Interpersonal processes: New directions in communication research* (pp. 257–277). Beverly Hills, CA: Sage.

Tengler, C. D., & Jablin, F. M. (1983). Effects of question type, orientation, and sequencing in the employment screening interview. *Communication Monographs, 50*, 261.

Terkel, S. N., & Duval, R. S. (Eds.). (1999). *Encyclopedia of ethics*. New York: Facts on File.

Thibaut, J. W., & Kelley, H. H. (1986). *The social psychology of groups* (2nd ed.). New Brunswick, NJ: Transaction Books.

Ting-Toomey, S., Yee-Jung, K., Shapiro, R., Garcia, W., Wright, T., & Oetzel, J. G. (2000). Cultural/ethnic identity salience and conflict styles. *International Journal of Intercultural Relations, 23*, 47–81.

Tomlinson, A. (2002). Bay Street's dressing up again. *Canadian HR Reporter, 15*(17), 2.

Trenholm, S. (1991). *Human communication theory* (2nd ed.). Englewood Cliffs, NJ: Prentice-Hall.

Triandis, H. C. (1988). Collectiveness vs. individualism: A reconceptualization of a basic concept in cross-cultural psychology. In G. Verma & C. Bagley (Eds.), *Cross-cultural studies of personality, attitudes and cognition* (pp. 60–95). London: MacMillan.

Tuckman, B. (1965). Developmental sequence in small groups. *Psychological Bulletin, 63*, 384–399.

Turk, D. R., & Monahan, J. L. (1999, Spring). "Here I go again": An examination of repetitive behaviors during interpersonal conflicts. *Southern Communication Journal, 64*, 232–244.

Tversky, B. (1997). Memory for pictures, maps, environments, and graphs. In D. G. Payne & F. G. Conrad (Eds.), *Intersections in basic and applied memory research* (pp. 257–277). Mahwah, NJ: Erlbaum.

Valacich, J. S., George, J. F., Nonamaker, J. F. Jr., & Vogel, D. R. (1994). Idea generation in computer based groups: A new ending to an old story. *Small Group Reseach, 25*, 83–104.

Vanaja, D. (2000). People of colour and national identity in Canada. *Journal of Canadian Studies, 35*(2), 166–175.

Watzlawick, P., Beavin, J. H., & Jackson, D. D. (1967). *Pragmatics of human communication*. New York: Norton.

Weaver, J. B. III, & Kirtley, M. B. (1995). Listening styles and empathy. *Southern Communication Journal, 60*, 131–140.

Weaver, R. (1970). Language is sermonic. In R. L. Johanannesen, R. Strickland, & R. T. Eubanks (Eds.), *Language is sermonic* (pp. 201–226). Baton Rouge: Louisiana State University Press.

Weiten, W. (1998). *Psychology: Themes and variations* (4th ed.). Pacific Grove, CA: Brooks/Cole.

Weston, D. (1999). *Psychology: Mind, brain, and culture* (2nd ed.). New York: Wiley & Sons.

Wheelen, S. A., & Hochberger, J. M. (1996). Validation studies of the group development questionnaire. *Small Group Research, 27*(1), 143–170.

Whetten, D. A., & Cameron, K. S. (1998). *Developing management skills* (4th ed.). New York: HarperCollins.

Widmer, W. N., & Williams, J. M. (1991). Predicting cohesion in a coacting sport. *Small Group Research, 22*, 548–570.

Williams, R. G., & Ware, J. E. Jr. (1976, February). Validity of student ratings of instruction under different incentive conditions: A further study of the Dr. Fox effect. *Journal of Educational Psychology, 68*, 48–56.

Winstead, B. A., Derlega, V. J., & Rose, S. (1997). *Gender and close relationships*. Thousand Oaks, CA: Sage.

Wolvin A., & Coakley, C. G. (1996). *Listening* (5th ed.). Dubuque, IA: Brown & Benchmark.

Wood, J. T. (1997). *Gendered lives: Communication, gender, and culture* (2nd ed.). Belmont, CA: Wadsworth.

Wood, J. T., & Dindia, K. (1998). What's the difference? A dialogue about differences and similarities between women and men. In D. J. Canary & K. Dindia (Eds.), *Sex differences and similarities in communication: Critical essays and empirical investigations of sex and gender in interaction* (pp. 19–40). Mahwah, NJ: Erlbaum.

Woodward, G. C., & Denton, R. E. Jr. (2000). *Persuasion and influence in American life* (4th ed.). Prospect Heights, IL: Waveland.

Young, K. S., Wood, J. T., Phillips, G. M., & Pederson, D. J. (2000). *Group discussion: A practical guide to participation and leadership* (3rd ed.). Prospect Heights, IL: Waveland.

Zebrowitz, L. A. (1990). *Social perception.* Pacific Grove, CA: Brooks/Cole.

Zillmann, D. (1991). Empathy: Affect from bearing witness to the emotions of others. In J. Bryant & D. Zillmann (Eds.), *Responding to the screen: Reception and reaction processes* (pp. 135–167). Hillsdale, NJ: Erlbaum.

Index